YOUR CALIFORNIA BUSINESS

What you should know to start and run a business in California today

JOHN F. HULPKE

Gulf Publishing Company
Houston, London, Paris, Zurich, Tokyo

While this book will be very helpful to anyone in, or looking into, the small business arena, it is sold with the express understanding that neither the publisher nor the authors are engaged in either legal or accounting services. This book does talk about various legal and tax possibilities, but every situation is unique. We suggest you use this book to help you formulate the right questions. Then, make final decisions after consulting with legal and accounting advisers.

We would also like to let you know that Gulf Publishing Company and the authors strongly endorse the following statement, from a declaration of principles jointly adopted by a committee of the American Bar Association and a committee of publishers:

"This publication is designed to provide accurate and authoritative information in regard to the subject matter covered. It is sold with the understanding that the publisher is not engaged in rendering legal, accounting, or other professional service. If legal advice or other expert assistance is required, the services of a competent professional person should be sought."

Your California Business

Based on the book *Your Texas Business* by Richard Alderman and Tom Oldham.

Gulf Publishing Company
Book Division
P.O. Box 2608 □ Houston, Texas 77252-2608

10 9 8 7 6 5 4 3 2 1

Printed in the United States of America.

Library of Congress Cataloging-in-Publication Data

Hulpke, John F.
Your California business : what you should know to start and run a business in California today / John F. Hulpke.
p. cm.
Based on the text of: Your Texas business / by Richard Alderman and Tom Oldham. 2nd ed. c1992.
Includes index.
ISBN 0-88415-052-6
1. Business enterprises—California. 2. Business law—California. I. Alderman, Richard M. Your Texas business. II. Title.
KFC337.Z9H85 1994
346.794′065—dc20
[347.940665] 93-8718
CIP

Contents

Chapter 4

Forming a Limited Partnership, 25

Chapter 5

The Corporation: Best of Both Worlds? 33

Chapter 6

Hiring and Firing: At-Will Employment Is California Law, But . . . 45

Chapter 7

Miscellaneous Taxes, Fees, and Statutes: Keep Your Eyes Open! 52

Chapter 8

Consumer Protection in California: Let the Seller Beware, 60

Chapter 9

Warranties: Watch What You Say! 64

Chapter 10

Credit Sales: Tempting But Risky, 72

Chapter 11

Getting Paid: Eyes on the Bottom Line, 79

Chapter 12

You and Your Lawyer: Things to Keep in Mind, 87

Appendix A

Statutory Supplement, 93

Appendix B

Forms and Sample Agreements, 179

Appendix C

Immigration Law Supplement, 253

Appendix D

Free Help, 273

Index, 286

Acknowledgments

I sincerely hope you enjoy, and benefit from, this book. If you do, a great part of the thanks should go to others, the folks whose ideas and tips helped bring life into this text. The many entrepreneurs across the Golden State who told me their successes and horror stories deserve appreciation. Thanks also for the ideas and feedback from students at Long Beach City College, California State University, Westmont College, University of California, Irvine, Golden Gate University, Laney College, College of Marin, Bakersfield College . . . actually, students at so many colleges and universities, taking small business, legal environment of business, or business law courses, have helped shaped this book, that it is impossible to name them all. Please accept my heartfelt thanks.

Special thanks also to those providing case materials. Bob Hawkes at Bakersfield College; Katherine Xin at University of California, Irvine; Laurie Meamber, previously at University of California, Riverside; Tony Ortega at California State University, Bakersfield; Dewey Johnson, California State University, Fresno; and Ron Jones of Laney College were especially helpful. Rudolfo "Rudy" Aros, Sacramento attorney, helped bring us up to date on the legal minefield out there. Reviewers also made useful suggestions. Oliver Galbraith III of San Diego State University, Brian G. Wilson of College of Marin, and Jim Dowell of American River College all commented on earlier versions of this book, and their suggestions led to substantial changes. However, as usual, any errors or omissions are my oversight, not theirs.

California has a strong network of small business assistance providers. This includes our own secretary of state office, right down to the business license section of the local city halls. Many of these people provided tips to improve this book. Melissa Warren, in the office of Secretary of State March Fong-Eu; Jeff Johnson, Colleen Love, Debbie Orr-Carpenter, and their colleagues affiliated with Small Business Development Centers (SBDCs); Manuel Lerma and associates of NEDA; Howard Toole, Don Harvey, and many others with Small Business Institutes (SBIs); Ed Young and others across the state with SCORE—all have the appreciation of the small business community of the state.

This book could not have been written without Richard Alderman and Tom Oldham, who conceived and wrote *Your Texas Business,* the book upon which this one is based. The people at Gulf Publishing Company also deserve a note of thanks. Katie Daily did more than should be expected of an executive assistant. Elizabeth Raven McQuinn, my editor, helped whip the draft into final, publishable form. Thanks to all these people.

Special thanks to Katherine, back on the home front, who pushed, and helped make this happen.

Finally, my best wishes to you, the present-day California entrepreneur, and also to the students—the California entrepreneurs of the 21st century.

Foreword

Office of the Secretary of State
March Fong Eu

Executive Office
1230 J Street
Sacramento, California 95814

(916) 445-6371

Congratulations! Simply by reading books such as Your California Business you are helping ensure that as California looks to the twenty-first century the opportunities will be limitless. What you do will be important not only to you, but to the overall economy, since by far the most jobs in California are in small businesses. The ideas and new products that will be the keys to important industries in the future start here, with people like you. But the future will belong to those who do their homework! That is why I am pleased you are studying business formation and management.

Study this and other materials. Take advantage of free help, from agencies such as the small business development centers and the small business institutes listed in Appendix D of this book. Contact my office, or the other state offices listed in various chapters and in Appendix A. Then, use professional help. Bear in mind that no book can give you up-to-date advice on accounting or legal matters.

But the key is the attitude that says, "Let's do it!" Reading this book is an important first step toward success -- go for it!

March Fong Eu

MARCH FONG EU
Secretary of State
Sacramento, California

Introduction

A California businessperson must answer vital legal questions every day. Having the right information is essential if you are going to start or operate a business. It is not smart business to make decisions without considering the legal implications.

This book will help you understand these implications by explaining important issues, helping you recognize potential problems, and showing you how to avoid or solve them. In many cases a slight change in how you say or do things can save you thousands of dollars in liability. For example, if you tell a customer "the bolts will be delivered on Tuesday," and fail to deliver, you could be responsible for three times your customer's damages. But if you say, "I will do my best to see that the bolts get there on Tuesday," no liability will exist.

In this book we discuss the most common questions that arise when you start or operate a business. We have also provided forms and models to help you prepare certain documents yourself. One of the most common questions businesspeople ask is, "can I do it myself, or do I need a lawyer?" We have adopted a compromise position. Whenever possible we have provided you with the forms and information necessary to complete basic legal tasks, such as forming a partnership or incorporating. But we do this with a **big warning:** Doing it yourself can be dangerous, it is easy to make mistakes, and every situation is just a little different. So the compromise approach we suggest is that you use this book to help you prepare your own documents and tentatively make important legal decisions, and then let an attorney review what you have done. This way you get the best of both worlds. You save substantial legal fees by preparing documents yourself, and you have the protection of an attorney's review before an important decision is made. Of course, if you are comfortable with the documents you have prepared, you may consider using them without an attorney's review. But remember that it can be difficult, even with the help of this book, for a nonlawyer to make legal decisions without the help of a lawyer. You might not realize that something about your particular situation makes some general statement inapplicable to you. If you are making a significant decision regarding your business, or completing an important transaction, we encourage you to discuss it with a lawyer.

We should also point out that although we have done everything we could to make sure that all the important information you need is in this book, law is not unchanging. The information in this book is believed accurate as of the time of publication. But keep in mind that laws, and their interpretation by the courts, continually change. This is another reason why an attorney or appropriate government office should be consulted before an important decision is made.

Finally, a quick review of the Table of Contents will show that some of the chapters apply to everyone, while some apply to only those persons starting a business. We suggest that anyone who is thinking about starting a business, or who has just started one, should review the entire book, paying particular attention to Chapters 1 through 5. If you are already operating an established business, and are comfortable with the form of the business you have chosen, you may want to skip Chapters 1 through 4. You should still read Chapter 5, however, to make sure that you do not wish to consider another form of operation. We also encourage you to read Chapter 12 at your leisure. While there may not be an immediate need for an attorney, it is helpful to be prepared if the need arises.

Of course, if you are reading this book as a part of a college or university business course, we suggest you read whatever your instructor assigns. But be prepared, she or he will probably assign the whole thing. With this in mind, we've tried to keep this book breezy, informal, and easy to follow. The content is solid enough—we checked numerous sources to bring you the right information. But the style—that was developed with you, the reader, in mind.

John F. Hulpke

1

Starting a Business in California: Preliminary Considerations

Chances are good that someone close to you is involved in running a California business today. This is no doubt true whether you picked up this book in a bookstore, or an instructor assigned it to you. And, you may seriously be thinking of starting your own California business. But before taking the plunge, we strongly recommend that you seriously consider your decision to start a business and talk to some people who have done it. It is a terrific amount of work, and many new businesses fail. Do not underestimate the commitment you will be making if you start a business.

We do not mean to scare you away from starting a new business. Many people find it one of the most satisfying things they have ever done. Still, you should choose to do it "with your eyes open." Starting a business is a major financial and personal commitment, and you must consider all of the ramifications. For example, do you have the financial resources you will need, the expertise, the time, and the necessary drive? Have you considered the effect the time commitment will have on your family and your social life? These are just some of the things you should consider, and talk over with friends, family, and experts.

If you do decide to open a business, some of your first decisions will be among the most important. In this chapter, we discuss some of the things you should consider when making these decisions. These are not just legal points, but practical economic factors as well. And by the way, if you have already started a business you should still read this chapter.

Choosing Partners vs. "Going It Alone"

One of the most important decisions you will make when starting a business is your choice of who, if anyone, will be involved in the business with you. Many new businesses are sad stories of people with good intentions, who did not get along. Before you decide to involve someone in the venture, have a long talk with him or her. Do you have the same goals? How much time and money do each of you want to devote to the venture? Do you enjoy working together, or is it at least tolerable? Can you trust each other? How will decisions be made, particularly if you disagree? Remember, just because you are friends doesn't mean you can be business associates.

Or you may decide to "go it alone." This has certain obvious advantages. You get to make all the decisions, and the business will "make it or break it" based upon them. Also, you will receive all the profits. But starting a business by yourself can cause other problems. There is no other source of funds, and no other owner is available to supervise the business if you need to do something else. Sometimes you may want to share the responsibilities a new business imposes.

As you can see, there is no right or wrong decision regarding whether you should include one or more additional partners in your venture. If you do decide to include other owners, however, be very careful about the people you choose.

Build, Buy, or Franchise a Business?

There is another decision to be made early on. Whether you decide to go the route of the sole proprietorship, partnership, or corporation, you still face the choice of starting all on your own, or buying an existing business. Or, you could buy a franchise from anyone from McDonald's to Best Western Motels.

Many small business owners we know got into business simply because they heard of such-and-such business for sale. "We learned from our neighbor that The Olde Yogurte Shoppe was secretly for sale, and we got it for less than the cost of equipment alone!" Of course, if the business is losing money every single month of operation, and the buyers also bought some unpaid liabilities, they may soon wish dearly that they had not stumbled onto (or into) such a bargain! But this should not cloud the fact that thousands of small businesses are sold, and bought, here in California monthly.

Frequently, this is the easiest way to get into business. Most likely, whatever business you have in mind, one is available for sale today. For example, we recently heard of an opportunity to buy "existing ATT (900) numbers, 25 to 250 calls per day, $10/$15 per call, 30-day payout, $2,500 fee." Anything and everything is for sale, somewhere. A recent *Los Angeles Times* had 528 "business opportunities" classified ads in one Sunday edition, and many of those ads listed more than one business for sale. For example, one ad listed 15 laundromats for sale and another ad offered 6 pizza parlors for sale (by a bankruptcy trustee!). Our experience is that for every business LISTED for sale, there are ten others available to the person who looks around. The caveat here is, you must know what you are getting into! Before you start your own business from scratch, check the business opportunities section of the want ads of any local newspaper. Bigger newspapers have more such ads, but the best deals where YOU want to live may be in your tiny neighborhood paper.

Talk to your local Board of Realtors, too, and ask who does business brokerage. Or check your Yellow Pages for "Business Brokers." If "Business Brokers" draws a blank, look under "Real Estate Brokers—Commercial" or other such titles. A business broker is a licensed real estate agent, but specializes in the sale of businesses. These folks do not get their commissions unless deals close, so they are GLAD to talk to you. Once you establish rapport with a good one, you are onto a wealth of information. Remember, however, that the broker will get her or his commission from the seller, and that the commission will be higher if the selling price is higher. But, you can at least talk to a broker or two.

The seller is hoping for a high price too, but with careful negotiation on your part, buying through a broker can still be a good way to go. And, as always, ask around. Someone you know may know someone trying to sell just the business you have in mind.

So, one way to go would be to buy an existing business. On the other hand, every time you buy the assets of a going business, you also buy the liabilities. Here we are not only talking about those liabilities you see on the balance sheet: you will be assuming the bad reputation, the buried hazardous wastes behind the shop, the potential lawsuit from last year's disgruntled customer, the unfunded pension liabilities or benefits to former employees, or who knows what else. You may decide your best bet is to strike out on your own instead of buying a dubious bargain.

But you also have the option of starting your own business without doing everything blindly: you could buy a franchise. There is a new franchise opening about every 17 minutes across America, and California gets the lion's share of those. Just one issue of the *San Francisco Examiner* listed franchise possibilities in more than 30 separate fields, ranging from accounting franchises to yogurt shops. All the opportunities you would expect are available: carpet cleaning, fast food, janitorial, mail boxes, smog checking, and tune up or lube shops. Some you might not think of are also ready to take the entrepreneur's cash: fashion photography, food delivery (not tied to any one restaurant), maid service, computer schools, and indoor golf. You name it, it is available by franchise somewhere in California. A good franchise organization will really help you succeed, with training, marketing plans and help, and even assistance in financing. Unfortunately, many franchise sellers are selling little more than half-baked ideas, so here again, take your time. Check it out carefully before jumping off the deep end.

If you are sure that YOU alone have the framework for your dream business in mind, then you probably do not want to buy an existing business or pay somebody for a franchise. Buying an existing business *can* be an excellent way to get started: those few who really do their homework may enjoy the benefits of someone who did all the tough start-up chores.

All these different approaches have advantages. All have disadvantages. Be sure to think it through, and read whatever you can on the topics. A good place to start would be the "For More Information" section at the end of this chapter.

Obtaining Seed Money

When you decide to start a business, the first problem is obtaining enough seed money for the business. This really presents three different problems. First, how much money is needed? Second, when will it be needed? Third, who will pay it?

How Much Money Is Needed?

When a business is started, "seed money" is needed. All businesses require some outlay of cash before the business opens its doors. For example, inventory might have to be purchased, rent might have to be prepaid, telephones and other equipment are needed, some salary probably must be paid, accountant's and lawyer's fees may be necessary, and some advertising is normally necessary. Some or all of these expenditures may require cash; it is quite difficult for a new business to obtain a significant amount of credit.

Also, after the business is started, it probably initially will be unprofitable. Normally a business is not profitable until a significant number of people realize that the business exists, and a substantial group of repeat customers has been established. Think about how long it takes you to discover that a new business has been opened in your area. Anyone starting a new business must make a financial plan so that the business can weather this initial period of financial losses.

For example, assume you start a flower shop with some friends. Each person contributes $5,000 seed money. Much of this is used to buy plants and decorate the store that has

BUYING A BAKERY IN BAKERSFIELD

The first night of class, Cathy wrote about her dream business: owning a bakery. Probably, she put down on the student profile sheet, she would try to do this in about five years. Meanwhile, she got some satisfaction from visiting the local bakery near her home. Her greatest dream was that someday, she too could own a place just like this one.

A few weeks later, while still in my "Starting a Small Business" class, Cathy stumbled across an eye-opening ad in the local paper. A bakery was for sale. Due to an illness in the owner's family, the bakery would be let go at far below actual value, the ad said. While not really in the market for a bakery just yet, something still made Cathy pick up the phone and inquire. To her amazement, it was her *dream* store, right in her neighborhood! Truly this must be a sign!

Maybe it was lucky, or maybe it was unlucky, but Cathy was still taking my class, so she asked me to go along with her to talk with the sellers. Since Cathy, like any buyer, was about to dump a great portion of her life savings into this deal, I had to set some tough ground rules. Rule 1 was that the seller had to answer *every* question that the buyer asked. Rule 2 was that if asked the seller then had to provide documentation to back up these answers.

The questions seemed harmless. "Have you made good money from the business for the last five years?" The answer was a resounding "My God, yes! It has paid for itself many times over, and provided us with enough to retire in Montana, where we are moving in order to preserve our health." That "going to Montana for health" answer should have been enough to suggest problems. People go to forty degrees below zero because you can live there cheap, NOT because it's healthy. But, no matter. They answered the question. Now, according to Rule 2, we could ask for documentation. Cathy might have been too shy to ask, but I certainly wasn't.

"We'll need the tax returns for the past five years, of course, so we can get a clearer idea of just how much you made. We'll need the whole thing, not just the front page and the Schedule C describing the profit and loss of the business. We'll get the returns back to you within a week, so this shouldn't pose any problems."

About this time, the sellers started to have a fit. "What business is it of yours what our personal finances are like? This is an invasion of privacy." We answered, "Fine, but that was the rule. Best wishes in finding another buyer," and then we left!

A couple of weeks later, the sellers called Cathy again. After discussing the idea, they agreed to show us the tax returns. And do you know what? There was little profit shown in one year, and losses in the other four. "But this is a cash business," they said, "and of course, we don't actually report everything we bring in." Now we have established beyond dispute that the sellers are liars. The only question is, are they lying to the IRS, or are they lying to us? It seemed they were lying to us. But even if this had not been the case, something else was fishy.

There were very high deductions on Schedule A for interest on a personal loan, which was in the form of a second mortgage against their home. This loan would not have showed up on the bakery's balance sheet at all, but a close analysis showed they had poured this personal money, obtained from their home mortgage, into the bakery to keep the business afloat.

The morals of this story are several. For one thing, ASK. Ask for federal tax returns and state sales tax records, if appropriate, and *always* get a credit report, either from TRW, Equifax, or a similar credit agency. If the seller objects, the deal is off: Rule 2 stands or no deal. The main point is to keep control of the negotiation process. Sticking to Rule 1 and Rule 2 is a good way to start—*never* make an exception. Once you do, the *seller,* not you, has control of the negotiations. The seller already has a thousand times as much information as you do, so if you give away the one thing you have—control of the negotiation process—the game is over.

Cathy never forgave me. She thought that I ruined her dream, just because I asked so many questions. But one thing was certain: once she knew the truth, there was no way she was going to put her hard-earned money into THAT bakery. I heard she did eventually find an available bakery with an honest seller, so her dream did come true in due course. And that's how it happened, right here in Bakersfield.

—Thanks to Bob Hawkes, with the Weill Institute Small Business Development Center, Bakersfield College, for this insight.

been rented. No plan is made for obtaining additional money. If the business is not successful immediately, how will you pay the rent or the salaries of your employees? What if only one of you has additional capital? Can you force each person to contribute more, or do you just close up shop? If you need credit in a hurry, it will probably be hard to get, and the terms will probably be terrible.

Few businesses have sufficient capital when they are started, in large part because people don't plan ahead and prepare. And not having enough money puts a great deal of strain on the business right away. People starting a business have a tendency to make financial plans based upon a very rosy picture of the initial success of the business. Be realistic when you estimate your budget. Be prepared if the business is not an immediate cash machine. Few new businesses are. Talk to others who are familiar with the type of business you are planning to start. Find out how long it takes for this type of business to become profitable. What initial capital expenditures are required? Can some expenditures be postponed? Can some things be rented, rather than purchased? How much inventory will be needed initially? Can some things be obtained on credit?

One way to help protect against early financial problems is to estimate a proposed budget for the business. Prepare a "worst case" budget. Could the business lose money? If so, for how long? How will these losses be financed? You may want to speak with an accountant to get some professional help in estimating your expenses. Remember, underestimating the costs of your new business could mean a business failure.

When Will the Money Be Needed?

Not only is it necessary to determine how much money you will need, but you also need to determine when certain funds will be needed. This frequently will be the period immediately after the business starts, but in some instances a significant payment may be necessary at some later point. You must consider if such funds may be necessary and how they will be raised if they are.

For example, assume Juanita and Elvia start a restaurant. Initially they rent a small restaurant, but they had always planned to move to a larger space. The restaurant is successful, and they decide to move but now suddenly find they don't have the money, or any plans for raising it. Early planning might have eliminated this dilemma. An agreed-upon line of credit with a bank, for example, would have given them the flexibility to expand when they wanted to.

Who Will Contribute the Seed Money?

Once you determine how much money you need, and when you will need it, you must decide how to obtain the money. Basically there are three choices: you, a bank, or other investors. Obviously the simplest solution is for you to contribute the money. This is not, however, always the most desirable, or feasible, solution. Many entrepreneurs do not have a significant amount of cash to contribute to a new business. And even if you have the cash, you may not want to risk it in the venture. For these reasons, many entrepreneurs attempt to obtain seed money from other sources. Ideally this money will be provided in a manner such that the other party, not you, assumes the risk of failure.

When most people think of money they think of banks, and a bank is a second possible source of funds. This funding approach has advantages and disadvantages. On one hand, the bank probably will not want to be involved in the operation of the business, nor would it want a percentage of the profits of the business. A bank will usually let you, the entrepreneur, retain all rights to the profits of the business if it is successful, and it won't interfere in the day-to-day operations of the business. But the bank isn't going to just "give" a new business money. It will probably want collateral or a "personal guarantee" from the business owner—you. This way if the loan isn't paid the bank can then either take the collateral or sue the business owner and attach his or her personal assets, in addition to the assets of the business, to collect the loan amount unpaid. Some owners do not want to take such a risk with their personal assets. As a practical matter, however, it is very difficult to borrow money on any other terms for a new business. Be prepared to run a personal financial risk if you start a business.

But banks sometimes do give unsecured loans to a corporate business without obtaining a personal guarantee from the owner. If this kind of loan is obtained, and the business is unsuccessful, the owner's personal assets are not at risk. However, banks will generally only do this for a good customer who had started successful companies in the past. Of course, if the banker has to make a judgment call, it seems likely that the entrepreneur who personally knows the banker will have an advantage. This is one reason why common advice is to have TWO banks, and to figure out some excuse to get to know your bankers BEFORE you need help! More on this later. (See appendix D, Free Help.)

In any event, you also should shop around for the best financial package. New businesses frequently fail. Because of this risk, a bank might try to charge a high interest rate. The banking business is very competitive, and you may find different rates at different banks. Additionally, if you agree to do all your banking with one lender or allow the bank to do your payroll, the bank might be willing to make concessions on the interest rate. Further, the more money you have in non-interest-bearing, or low-interest-bearing accounts, the more likely a bank is to make concessions in loan transactions.

Private investors are another source of money, especially seed money. Investors normally do not make loans to the business. Instead, they contribute funds to the new business in exchange for a percentage of the profits of the business. So, if the business is unsuccessful, they receive nothing; if the business is successful, they receive a portion of the profits of the business. This funding source, therefore, can reduce the owner's share of the profits of the business. Carefully weigh whether this form of funding is worth the financial risk it eliminates.

Not all investors are strangers. Some new business owners ask their friends to become involved in a new venture. This should be done only after much reflection. Friends and business partners relate quite differently. After a friend invests in your business, you may find that the friendship has been ruined. This is particularly likely if the business is not successful.

The Bottom Line

Almost all new businesses need "seed money." This money is needed to establish the business and cover any initial losses of the business. If you are starting a new business, you must realistically determine how much seed money is necessary. If, after deciding how much seed money will be needed, you do not have that amount of money or for some other reason do not want to contribute your money, another source of the seed money must be found. Banks sometimes will loan money to new companies, but usually want a personal guarantee and charge high interest rates. Alternatively, investors might be sought. Personal liability can be avoided by doing this, but you will lose some of the profits, and possibly control, of the business.

Liability Concerns

When you start a new business, you will and should be concerned about what will happen if the business is unsuccessful or is the subject of a lawsuit. Many people have assets that they do not want to risk losing on a new business. Even if you do not have assets, now it is possible to jeopardize your future assets due to a business failure now. This can happen if a creditor gets a judgment against you that can be used to attach assets acquired in the future. Some business risks can, and should, be insured against, but others may not be covered by insurance. For these reasons, you understandably want to organize your business in such a way that your personal assets will be safe, no matter what happens to the business.

There are a number of ways insurance concerns can be met. As before, personal relationships may make a difference. Just as it is a good idea to be on good terms with an accountant, an attorney, and a banker or two, *know your insurance agent.* Talk to several, in general terms, to learn what you can about what your business would need. Then, select the agent who seems to be giving you the most informed answers. Rates are important, but you probably should not choose insurance strictly on the basis of rates. If the cheaper "coverage" doesn't "cover" you, the wrong choice of agent can cost you your business.

The Structure of the Business

A new business can be structured in a number of forms. Almost all new businesses can be established either as a proprietorship, partnership, or corporation. The particular form chosen depends upon the needs and tax concerns of the owner, rather than any characteristic of the business. For example, think of the businesses you frequent. Do you have any idea whether the business is a proprietorship, partnership, or corporation? Generally this is not very clear to the public, and the public normally does not care. The particular business form chosen depends solely upon the concerns of the owner. It usually doesn't affect the day-to-day operations of the business.

You should remember to try to keep you and your business separate once you have begun operations. When a business is started, many documents must be signed. What they say and how they are signed will affect your personal liability. Remember that there is no such thing as a "form" anything! Do not sign anything until you have reviewed it carefully, thought about it, and determined that it is fair and consistent with your understanding. If you are uncomfortable or unsure, consult with an attorney. Anything you sign can make you personally liable, sometimes for a significant amount of money. Take your time. Every time you put your signature on a piece of paper, it is important.

What follows is a very brief discussion of common forms of business. A more detailed discussion of each can be found in later chapters.

The Proprietorship

The simplest form of doing business is the proprietorship. No filing with any governmental body is required to form a proprietorship. The business is owned by one person, and that person makes all the decisions regarding the business. No rules specify how those decisions are to be made. This is the simplest form of business.

But a proprietorship is not necessarily the best form for all businesses. For example, if there is more than one owner, it cannot be a sole proprietorship. Also, it cannot exist separately from its owner. This means that a creditor of a proprietorship can attach the personal assets of the owner if the proprietorship does not pay the claim. You may not want to jeopardize personal assets when you start a business. Tax concerns will also affect your decision. Proprietorship income is taxed at the marginal tax rate of the owner. If you have significant other income, you may want to see if the corporate tax rate would be lower. (Proprietorships are discussed further in Chapter 2.)

Partnerships

A partnership is similar to a sole proprietorship in many ways. Both are easy to get into, and neither requires much start-up capital or operating paperwork. No formal agreement or filing is required to form a partnership. It's possible to have established one and not realize it. Consider this:

> Frank and Tom buy a four-plex apartment building, taking title jointly. Both collect rents, show apartments to prospective tenants, and sign leases. Frank and Tom have agreed to share all profits or losses generated by the building. They are partners, regardless of whether or not they think they are.

There are certain disadvantages to partnerships. For example, all partners can manage the business of the partnership. But this can complicate things if the partners do not agree. Also, each partner's personal assets can be attached, for the total amount due by the partnership, if the partnership does not pay something it owes. Finally, the income of the partnership is taxed according to the marginal personal tax rate of each individual partner.

Some of the problems of a partnership can be solved by forming a limited partnership. In order to form a limited partnership, a filing must be made with the California secretary of state. Only "general" partners can manage a limited partnership; "limited" partners are passive investors. The personal assets of limited partners cannot be attached to collect partnership debts, however, the personal assets of any general partners can be attached. (Partnerships and limited partnerships are discussed further in Chapters 3 and 4.)

Corporations

Many times the best way to do business is to form a corporation. A corporation is formed by filing a certificate of incorporation with the secretary of state. Corporations have certain advantages, the most important of which is limited personal liability. Only the assets of the corporation can be attached to collect claims against the business. Even if these assets are not sufficient to pay all creditors of the business, creditors cannot attach the personal assets of the owners. Also, a corporation is managed by the president and the board of directors of the business. Lines of authority are clear.

Tax consequences are also different for a corporation. Normal "C" corporations pay tax at corporate tax rates, regardless of the incomes of the shareholder-owners. This can be good or bad, depending upon the marginal tax rates of the owners. If the company decides to distribute money to the owners as a dividend, the owners must pay income tax on that distribution.

Sometimes owners want their corporation to be treated for tax purposes as if it were a partnership. If this is desired, an "S" corporation election is possible. Such a corporation is treated for liability purposes as a corporation, and for tax purposes as a partnership. There are also other types of corporations, such as non-profit corporations and professional corporations, all with special attributes. (Corporations are discussed in more detail in Chapter 5.)

Choosing the Right Form for Your Business

There are many factors that will affect your decision whether to operate your business as a proprietorship, general partnership, limited partnership, or corporation. No one can give you an absolute rule regarding when one form is better than the others. We encourage you to read Chapters 2 through 5, where we discuss in detail the different characteristics of each business form. Following is a summary of the types of businesses that may help you decide:

A **sole proprietorship** is a good choice when:

1. The business has one owner.
2. The type of business has little risk of liability.
3. The owner is not concerned about any tax savings that might result from forming a corporation.

A **general partnership** is a good choice when:

1. The business has more than one owner.
2. All partners wish to manage the business.
3. All partners know one another and have some degree of trust in one another.
4. Any tax savings that could result from a corporation are not desired.
5. The business has little risk of liability.

A **limited partnership** is desirable when:

1. Businesses have more than one investor and some want to manage the business while others do not.
2. Some investors want limited liability.
3. Tax savings that could result from a corporation are not desired.

A business should **incorporate** when:

1. There is a significant risk of liability.
2. Clear delegation of management authority is desired.
3. Corporate tax benefits are desired.

4. The business is expected to continue even if the principals should withdraw or die.

The Bottom Line

Your choice of a business form is very important and must be based on an analysis of your particular needs and the law. You should carefully read Chapters 2–5 before making a decision on how you will set up your business.

Summary

Finally, if you are considering starting a business, it may be very helpful to retain a lawyer and an accountant. The accountant can, among other things, help ensure that the seed money estimates and budgets are reasonable, help you set up decent records, and assist with tax preparation. The attorney can talk to you about the best organizational form for the business, and can tell you what actions should be taken before the business is begun. A lawyer can also review important documents before you sign them. It does not cost much money to consult a lawyer and an accountant before starting a business, and significant problems can be avoided by doing so up front.

As mentioned, there are other professionals you will want to get to know as well. You do not need to "retain" insurance agents or bankers, but you will surely learn to depend on their advice too. A bit more information on related topics is found in "Hiring a Lawyer," which is discussed in Chapter 12, and in "Free Help," Appendix D.

FOR MORE INFORMATION

"Annual Franchise 500." *Entrepreneur.* Published annually, usually in the January issue of this magazine. The annual franchise issue always contains a wealth of information on how to evaluate, select, and, if appropriate, get into the hottest franchises going.

Author unknown. "Financing Options for Small Business," and "How to Prepare a Loan Package." In *Small Business Success.* This undated publication was published about 1990 with joint cooperation between the U.S. Small Business Administration and Pacific Bell, 101 Spear Street, Communications Department CWS-4, San Francisco, CA 94105.

Apilado, Vincent, and J. Kent Millington. "Restrictive Loan Covenants and Risk Adjustment in Small Business Lending." *Journal of Small Business Management,* January 1992, pages 38–48.

Burstiner, Irving. *The Small Business Handbook,* Revised Edition. New York: Prentice Hall Press, 1989. See especially Chapters 1 and 4.

Dunn, Paul, Leo R. Cheatham, and Carole Cheatham. "Small Business Person, What Your Banker Does Not Know Can Hurt You!" *Journal of Business and Entrepreneurship,* March 1991, pages 105–113.

Fleury, Robert E. *The Small Business Survival Guide.* Naperville, IL: Sourcebooks Trade, 1991. See "Sources of Cash," Chapter 13.

Hyatt, Joshua. "Should You Start a Business?" *Inc.,* February 1992, pages 48–58.

Jones, Constance. *The 220 Best Franchises to Buy.* New York: Bantam Books, 1987.

Khandekar, Rajendra, and John E. Young. "Selecting a Legal Structure: A Strategic Decision." *Journal of Small Business Management,* January 1985, pages 47–55.

Posner, Bruce G. "How to Finance Anything." *Inc.,* April 1992, pages 50–62.

Ramakrishnan, Kumoli, Alan M. Weatherford, and Walter W. Perlick. "Financing Small Business: Collateral Requirements From The Lender's Perspective." *Proceedings of the Western Decision Sciences Institute 21st Annual Meeting.* Reno, Nevada, March, 1992, pages 825–827.

Stanworth, John, and Brian Smith. *The Barclay's Guide to Franchising for the Small Business.* Oxford, UK, and Cambridge, MA: Basil Blackwell, Ltd. 1991. See especially Chapter 7, on deciding if a franchise makes sense for you.

Tate, Curtis. *Small Business Management and Entrepreneurship.* Boston: PWS-Kent Publishing Co., 1992. See Chapter 10.

Tuller, Lawrence W. *Financing the Small Business.* New York: Prentice Hall, 1991. Chapter 2, on understanding bankers, and Chapter 7, on financing franchises, are particularly pertinent.

U.S. Small Business Administration. *Selecting the Legal Structure for Your Firm.* (Pamphlet MP25). 1991.

POINTS TO PONDER

1. Sometimes an entrepreneur decides that the business form originally chosen may not have been the best. How easy would it be to change from corporate form to partnership or sole proprietorship? How easy would it be to change from partnership to sole proprietorship? Corporation? How easy would it be to change from sole proprietorship to another form? Consider paperwork issues and people issues as you think through your answers.
2. Why is it that the only folks that seem to be able to borrow money are those who don't need it? And, given the near impossibility of borrowing start-up funds, what other sources exist?

3. In your personal opinion, what are the two most important advantages, and the two most important disadvantages, of sole proprietorships? Of partnerships? Of corporations?
4. In your personal opinion, what are the two most important advantages, and the two most important disadvantages, of buying an existing business? Of buying a franchise? Of starting from scratch?
5. We have talked about how to get into a sole proprietorship, partnership, and corporation. How easy would it be to get out of each? What steps would be involved?

DON'T JUST SIT THERE, DO SOMETHING!

1. In the next several days, take a little informal survey. In ten businesses that you have occasion to visit, see if you can find out HOW the present owners came about getting into this particular business. Did they purchase an existing business? Did they buy a franchise? Or, did they start out on their own from scratch? Write a short paragraph summarizing your findings. Also, discuss briefly how easy (or how difficult) it was to get people to tell you whether they bought, started from scratch, or bought a franchise. Typically, an employee other than the owners will not have a clue.
2. In the next two or three days, take another informal survey. In ten businesses that you have occasion to visit, see if you can find out the form of ownership and organization. How many are sole proprietorships? How many are partnerships? How many are corporations? Write a short paragraph summarizing your findings. You may notice some trends. For example, are the larger businesses more likely to have a corporate form?

2

The Sole Proprietorship: California's Number One Choice

The simplest business structure to select, if there is only one owner, is the sole proprietorship. No documents must be filed with any governmental office and no other agreement of any kind is needed to form one or keep the business in good standing. This minimizes organizational costs of starting the business.

A proprietorship is created every time one person starts a business. Any name can be chosen as the name of the business, and the name does not have to include the word proprietorship. But you should be sure that no one else has previously started a business by the same name. If they have, you may not have the right to use that name. While you probably won't get into any trouble if you innocently use someone else's name, you can be forced to stop using it and this can cost you money when you have to start all over again with printing and advertising costs. At a minimum, you ought to contact the secretary of state's office in Sacramento and the county clerk's office in the county where you are doing business to see if someone else has registered the name. You may also want to consider hiring a name-search company to protect you if you are going to make a big investment in advertising or promotional materials. Name-search companies will check whether anyone else is using your proposed business name.

One of the best things about doing business as a proprietorship is that decisions can be informally made. No board of directors meetings or other formal authorizations or record-keeping is needed. You simply act as the business. This reduces the expense and increases the ease of operating a business.

But sole proprietorships do have certain disadvantages. Certain tax advantages available to a corporation, such as deductible medical insurance plans, disability insurance plans, and life insurance plans, are not available to an owner of a sole proprietorship. These tax advantages of a corporation are discussed in Chapter 5.

In a proprietorship, there is only one owner. This can create a problem if you get sick, want to take a vacation, or need to be out of town. There may be no other responsible person you would trust to run the business when you cannot.

And even more importantly, a creditor of a sole proprietorship can attach the personal assets of the owner, if the proprietorship does not pay the claim. This "unlimited liability" feature of the sole proprietorship can be quite scary to a person starting a new business. Consider what happened to poor Mary:

> Mary recently started a small dry cleaning business by the name of Mary's Cleaners. She signed a two-year lease when she started the business. Things went fine, until business dropped off after six months and Mary could no longer make a profit. She closed up, but now the landlord is demanding the remaining 18 months rent. Because she operated the business as a sole proprietorship, Mary is individually liable for the remainder of the lease term.

It would be an oversimplification to say that one should avoid sole proprietorships because of the unlimited liability. This is one of the biggest disadvantages of the sole proprietorship, but even if you've formed a partnership or a corporation, a lender may well require you to pledge personal assets as collateral anyway. Furthermore, owners of corporations, supposedly shielded from liability by the corporate form, can be sued and are being sued as individuals on issues as diverse as malfeasance and sexual harassment. You could lose it all anyhow! So, while the liability issue is greatest in sole proprietorships, there is really no way to totally shield yourself, or your assets, from liability. But don't forget, you could get hit by a falling meteor, too. The excitement and potential opportunity of owning your OWN business entails some financial risk, no matter how you go about it.

This chapter details some of the things you should consider before starting a sole proprietorship.

TAX CONCERNS

Before deciding to operate a business as a sole proprietor, you need to understand the income-tax effects of this choice. The sole proprietorship is not considered a separate entity for tax purposes. The income (or loss) is treated as personal income of the owner. So, if in any given year the owner and his spouse have other income of $50,000, and net income from the proprietorship business of $30,000, the couple would pay income tax, based upon individual tax rates, on both the $50,000 other income and the $30,000 business income. Unless they had any deductions, the total income for the year would be $80,000. In a proprietorship business, the marginal tax rate for this couple on the business income would be 28%; the tax due on the $30,000 income would be $8,400.

But if the couple in the example above operated the business as a corporation, the tax effect would be very different. The tax rate on the $30,000 business income would be 15%, or $4,500. On the surface, this is much better than the $8,400 proprietorship tax due. But there are disadvantages to this corporate savings as well.

In a proprietorship, income is only taxed once. The income is taxed when the proprietorship makes it. The money can then be used by the owner, and no tax is due on such a withdrawal. In a corporation, however, the business first pays tax on its income according to corporate tax rates. If you wish to take money out of the corporation and use it, however, this withdrawal is called a "dividend" and, is considered income to you, and you must pay taxes again, at personal tax rates. This is commonly referred to as the corporate "double tax." Of course, the double tax does not have to be paid if you plan to keep profits in the business for some reason, such as for capital improvements or to buy inventory. In most cases, however, owners do want profits paid out, so the double tax is a problem.

If your business makes money, a proprietorship can also be desirable, from a tax standpoint, for reasons other than the double tax. Personal tax rates are graduated. In a typical recent year the lowest rate was 15% and the highest rate was 31%. The profits of a proprietorship business are taxed based upon these rates (plus all other income you earn). All other income of the owner (and the owner's spouse) for the tax year is added to compute the owner's total taxable income for the year. If the owner will not have significant other income, and the business is not going to make much money, it might be easier to pay taxes based upon the personal tax rates.

Therefore, tax treatment of a proprietorship may be advantageous for some successful businesses and not for others. If your business will lose money initially, the proprietorship is normally a better business form than a corporation, from a tax standpoint. Losses from the proprietorship business can offset other personal income. If you plan to lose money initially (and many new businesses do), this characteristic of the proprietorship can be helpful. In contrast, in Chapter 5 you will discover that if a corporation loses money during any one year this loss generally cannot be used by a shareholder to offset other income. The loss can only be carried over to offset future business income. While this shouldn't be your only concern, the ability to write off losses may be a big plus for a sole proprietorship.

Running the Business

A proprietorship can sign agreements just like any business organization. For example, the proprietorship can sign a lease, purchase inventory, or borrow money. You simply sign the name of the business.

More complicated arrangements are also possible. If you want to motivate employees or a manager, you might want to compensate the employee at least partially in terms of the profitability of the business. This can be in an employment agreement between the employee and the proprietorship. Some sample employment agreements are set forth in Appendix B, Forms 9 and 10.

But you should remember that agreements involving a proprietorship business really are agreements obligating you as the owner, since proprietorships do not have limited liability. Any agreements involving the business should clarify this. For example:

> Assume Janie Alt is running a florist shop by the name of "The Green Thumb" as a proprietorship. If she signs a lease for space, the lease should be between the landlord and Janie Alt, d/b/a (doing business as) The Green Thumb.

In this example, the signature line on the lease could look like this:

____
Janie Alt, d/b/a The Green Thumb

But the bottom line is that, from a financial point of view, it is not important how you sign agreements for a proprietorship, because in a proprietorship business *you* are personally liable for the obligations set forth in the contract.

LIABILITY AND BANKRUPTCY

We have said that an owner of a proprietorship business is personally liable for all claims against a business. This means that a creditor of the business can attach any property owned by you that is not exempt under California law, regardless whether the property was used in the business. (Exemptions are discussed in Chapter 11.) If you don't have any property the creditor can attach, or if you

EXTRA SERVICE MAKES THE DIFFERENCE

What kind of business will typically be a sole proprietorship? Wedding photographers are likely candidates. Are they all the same? Not on your life! In this or any other business, you may find out that it is not the form of business organization that counts so much, as the way you conduct business! Lisa and James Hirsch found this out the hard way. Checking around, they found out that too many businesses don't care much about what the customers want!

"Our disappointment was their indifference to us, their lack of acknowledgement that this was our big day. To them, it was just another paycheck, bills signed in triplicate." But finally, James and Lisa found some "wondrous entrepreneurs who demonstrated how to succeed in the marriage market. Personal service, enthusiasm and a soothing voice make all the difference."

Luckily, photographer Larry Alan Rauschenbach had all this and more. And when its your special day, the fact that he was expensive was irrelevant. This vendor who made the extra effort got the business.

Does it take a big corporation to succeed? To James and Lisa, it was just the opposite: It's the entrepreneur who can keep the human element that will win the day.

—Thanks to Dewey Johnson, California State University, Fresno, for this insight. See Hirsch, James. "This Should Get Their Picture on the Studio Wall." *Wall Street Journal,* June 16, 1991, page A12.

don't have enough property to fully satisfy the creditor's claim, the creditor can get a court judgment against you for the claim. If this happens, the creditor can attach any property you acquire in the future.

For these reasons, the unlimited liability of a proprietorship can have terrible consequences. If you start a proprietorship business, try to minimize the likelihood you will lose your personal assets. For example, consider obtaining insurance regarding foreseeable possible claims. For instance, will anyone operate a car or truck on behalf of the business? If so, be sure there is adequate auto liability insurance. Similarly, are you selling or making a product that could hurt someone if it malfunctions or is defective? If so, consider product liability insurance.

Unfortunately, there is no way to obtain insurance that your business will be successful. If a business is unsuccessful, there can be a significant number of unpaid creditors. And in many cases, bankruptcy is the only way to deal with all of the money the business owes.

Under federal bankruptcy law, any legal entity may file a petition and generally be released, or discharged, from most debts it owes. For example, a corporation can go out of business, file bankruptcy, and basically leave its shareholders suffering only the loss of their investment. But as we have pointed out, a sole proprietorship is not a separate legal entity. The law treats it as one and the same as its owner. Even if it is the business that has run up debts the owner must file personal bankruptcy. For example:

> Sam recently started a small fix-it shop in his backyard workshop. Business got better and soon he had a store in a local mall. Within a few years he was making a nice profit and gave up his other job. Then things started getting worse. Business went down, he owed thousands of dollars in bills, and he was sued by a customer after a stove he fixed exploded. Unfortunately he didn't have insurance, and when the customer won a lawsuit for $150,000, Sam couldn't pay it. The only choice was to go out of business, and file bankruptcy. But because Sam was operating the business as a sole proprietorship, he will have to file personal bankruptcy, and in all likelihood his wife will have to file as well. Sam won't owe any money anymore, and he probably will get to keep his house, and most of his property, but he will lose his savings, his IRA, and the stocks and bonds he has saved for his kids' education.

We are not trying to scare you, but a business failure can mean personal financial ruin. The best way to avoid this is to have proper insurance coverage, and if you want to fully protect your personal assets, consider incorporating. Incidentally, someone else's bankruptcy may cause you serious problems. See Chapter 11 for a horror story.

Fictitious Name Statement

Most proprietorship businesses have a name that is different from the owner's name. For example, Harold might start a tailoring business under the name of Arnold's Tailoring, or The Alteration Shop. In either case Harold should file a fictitious name statement, since he would be doing business under a name different from his own name. The manner in which a fictitious name statement is filed is set forth in Chapter 7.

Miscellaneous Taxes and Fees

Although forming and operating a proprietorship is relatively simple, proprietorship businesses must comply with tax withholding rules and other regulations applicable to all businesses, such as worker's compensation and social security. These state and federal requirements are discussed in Chapter 7.

The Bottom Line

Sole proprietorships are easy to form and easy to run, but remember, you and the business are one and the same.

ADVANTAGES AND DISADVANTAGES OF THE PROPRIETORSHIP

A proprietorship is very simple to form and operate. You as owner can make all the decisions and you can do it informally. Also, you can keep all the profits of the business. But there may be a high price for this independence. You as the owner are personally liable for all claims against the business. In addition, there may be no one else you would trust to help run the business if you get sick or need to be away.

FOR MORE INFORMATION

California Chamber of Commerce. *Business Startup Kit For Sole Proprietors and Partnerships.* Sacramento: California Chamber of Commerce, 1991.

Coleman, Bob. *The New Small Business Survival Guide.* New York: W. W. Norton, 1991. See especially Chapter 3, Choosing a Business Structure.

Hopson, James F., and Patricia D. Hopson. "Helping Clients Choose The Legal Form For A Small Business." *The Practical Accountant,* October 1990, pages 67–84.

Norwood, John M. "Personal Liability of Officers Who Sign Corporate Checks." *Journal of Small Business Management,* October, 1984, pages 49–52.

Sexton, Donald L. and Nancy Bowman-Upton. *Entrepreneurship: Creativity and Growth.* New York: Macmillan Publishing Co., 1991. See especially Chapter 1.

Winter, Ralph E., and Thomas F. O'Boyle. "Bankruptcy-law Filings by Firms Spurt." *Wall Street Journal,* April 6, 1990, page A2.

POINTS TO PONDER

1. Assume you started a sole proprietorship, and that you had to tap just about every source of funds you could think of to get enough to survive the critical first six-months. Then assume that at the end of that six-month period, it was clear you would have to quit forever, unless you could somehow get another $14,000 to carry you another month. What would you do?
2. The chapter mentions the problems a sole proprietor may have if the owner gets sick, or simply wants a vacation. How might these problems be minimized?

DON'T JUST SIT THERE, DO SOMETHING!

1. Find a business near you that has failed recently. What factors contributed to the failure?
2. Find a fairly new business near you that is doing well. What key factors are contributing to its success?
3. Check a local newspaper classified ads section for "legal notices." Any evidence of firms that are in financial trouble? Write a short paragraph explaining what one could learn from looking at such legal notices.

3

The General Partnership: So Easy You May Fall Into It

In Chapter 2 we discussed the sole proprietorship, the simplest form of business. As we told you, a sole proprietorship is run and owned by one person. This form is not appropriate for some businesses, however, because many businesses are started by more than one person. If there is more than one owner of a business, another organizational structure is necessary. A general partnership, limited partnership, or a corporation would probably be the best choice in this situation.

A general partnership is a business form wherein all the owners are *general partners*. In other words, all the partners run the business equally and have full responsibility. This may sound like a good idea and it may be what you want, but before you make the decision to form a general partnership you should consider all the benefits and drawbacks.

No Limited Liability

In Chapters 4 and 5 we will discuss the idea of *limited liability* for an owner. If a business form has limited liability, the investor is assured that, at worst, the investor will lose only the capital invested. (Of course, as we said in Chapter 2 and will say again later, even an individual investor can be sued if that individual also plays an active role in running the firm, and an individual who sets up a business as a corporation may find that it is necessary to pledge personal assets to get financing.) Many people starting a business are not particularly concerned about the extent of their potential liability. The euphoria of the moment blinds them to the possibility that the business might be unsuccessful. Business founders, however, must remain aware that many new businesses are not successful; the risk relating to each possible business form should be carefully considered before the business form is selected. For example:

> Frank and Bob want to start a discotheque. They need to borrow a significant amount of money to decorate the club. A bank loans money to the business for these expenses. If the business is unsuccessful, Frank and Bob would not be personally liable for the bank loan if the business was a corporation, or if they were limited partners.

But in a general partnership, the partners *do not have* limited liability. This means that a creditor of the partnership can attach the assets of any partner to collect a debt of the partnership. It doesn't even matter whether a partner is a "silent" partner. Compare this example with the one you just considered:

> Steve and Lynn recently formed a general partnership. Steve runs the day-to-day operations and Lynn put up most of the cash. An employee of the partnership ran over a woman with a car while doing something for the partnership, and the injured person sued the partnership and Steve and Lynn. If the injured person wins, she could attach the individual assets of the partners if the partnership does not have adequate assets. Additionally, either Steve or Lynn could owe the full amount if the other couldn't pay.

The result would be the same if the debt stemmed from a business failure, instead of an accident. For example:

> Joe and Dan's business is unsuccessful and is closed six months after it was opened. If the business signed a lease for two years on the property used for the business, the lessor can sue Joe and Dan individually for all amounts due under the partnership's lease.

The importance of the unlimited liability that arises from a general partnership depends upon the circumstances of the individual partners. For example, if one or more partners have significant personal assets, this aspect of partnership law could scare them a great deal. Even if the partners do not have assets now, they may accumulate assets later that could be made liable for claims against the partnership. Before the general partnership form is chosen, the problem of unlimited liability must be considered.

If you are considering forming a general partnership, think about the type of business you plan to open and what types of claims could be made against that type of business. For example, will any employees of the business have to drive a car to make sales or deliver items? If so, you need to consider possible personal injury claims that could stem from the driver's negligence. Some types of specific liability, such as an accident, can be insured against. Also, "umbrella" liability coverage to protect you against excessive loss is available. But although adequate insurance is one way of minimizing some of the risks involved in a general partnership, many risks, such as a business failure, cannot be insured against and you will be personally responsible.

The Bottom Line

In a general partnership, each partner has unlimited liability for the debts of the partnership. If you do form a partnership you must consider this and, at a minimum, make sure you have sufficient insurance.

Making Decisions

In a general partnership, all partners normally participate in the management of the business. This management arrangement may or may not be what the owners desire. If you do not want to share all management decisions, you should have an agreement saying so. For example, the partners might agree that one partner should be the "managing partner," and that others should only be consulted for big decisions. If the partnership manages a shopping center, here's an example of how such an agreement might look:

> **Managing Partner's Authority.** The Managing Partner shall have the full, exclusive, and complete authority of management and control of the affairs of the Partnership consistent with the provisions hereof; he shall make all decisions affecting the Partnership affairs and shall have full power and authority to negotiate the terms of and to execute such documents and instruments relating to the Partnership affairs as may in his opinion be appropriate, necessary, or advisable in the conduct of the Partnership business, including, without limitation, leases, tenancy agreement, and subordination agreements, provided such document or instrument covers or relates to the Property and business of the Partnership; provided, however, the Managing Partner shall not be authorized to sell or encumber any portion of the Property, to borrow any funds on behalf of the Partnership, or enter into any contracts with any related person or entity of the Managing Partner without the written consent of the Investing Partner.
>
> **Investing Partner's Authority.** Except as otherwise provided in this Agreement, the Investing Partner shall not take an active part in the management of the Partnership business or transact any business for the Partnership, and shall have no power to sign for or to bind the Partnership.
>
> **Managing Partner's Obligations.** Upon the decision of the Partnership to proceed with any development, the Managing Partner shall do all things as may be necessary or appropriate to complete such development substantially in accordance with the plans and specifications. To such end, the Managing Partner shall obtain all necessary architectural, engineering, surveying, and other assistance necessary to develop such shopping center, shall engage a contractor or contractors to construct such shopping center, and shall oversee and manage the entire development process. The Managing Partner shall manage the Partnership and its affairs in a prudent, businesslike manner in accordance with good practices in the industry. The Managing Partner shall prepare an annual rental budget (pursuant to paragraph 8.05(k) below) and shall use its best efforts to consummate leases with tenants for occupancy of any development. The Partnership may engage to develop the Property, but any such engagement shall be invalid unless contained in a written contract executed by the Investing Partner on behalf of the Partnership.
>
> **Financing.** The Managing Partner shall use its best efforts to obtain interim construction financing and permanent financing for any development of the Partnership, but all costs and expenses involved in obtaining such financing shall be borne by the Partnership.
>
> **Prohibited Transactions.** Notwithstanding any language contained herein to the contrary, the Managing Partner shall not, without the written consent or ratification of the specific act by the Investing Partner, have the power or authority to do any of the following:
>
> (a) Do any act in contravention of this Agreement.
> (b) Do any act which would make it impossible to carry on the ordinary business of the Partnership.
> (c) Confess a judgment against the Partnership.
> (d) Possess Partnership property, or assign such Partner's rights in the Partnership property for other than Partnership purposes.
> (e) Admit a person as a partner.
> (f) Execute or deliver any assignment for the benefit of the creditors of the Partnership.
> (g) Lend to any persons any of the funds of the Partnership.
> (h) Mortgage, encumber, pledge or otherwise hypothecate any of the assets of the Partnership or extend, renew, replace, or substantially modify such financing.
> (i) Sell any portion of the Property or improvements thereon.
> (j) Develop or lease any portion of the Property not used for construction of a shopping center.
> (k) Lease on behalf of the Partnership (as lessor) any portion of the shopping center at a rate (taking into account all free rent) less than that approved by the Investing Partner based on a budget prepared by the Managing Partner. Such budget shall include (i) a minimum rent below which no leases shall be made without Investing Partner's consent, (ii) a budgeted average rent, and (iii) a percentage of the total

rentable square feet which shall be the maximum number of square feet which may be leased at a rent below the budgeted average rent (but not below the minimum rent) without Investing Partner's consent.

The Bottom Line

Unless partners agree otherwise, all partners can manage the business. If some other arrangement is desired, an agreement is necessary.

Liability for Partner's Acts

A general partnership is liable for all wrongs done by any partner in connection with its business. For this reason it is very important that you know and trust all partners. For example:

> Smith and Jones form a law partnership. In connection with a real estate transaction for a client, Jones is given some funds from the client to hold in escrow until the sale closes. If Jones steals the money, Smith probably would be liable to the client for the money stolen, if Jones disappeared or spent the stolen money.

Of course, partners are not liable for everything done by another partner. A partner is not liable for an act of another partner if the act is unrelated to the business. For example, if Barb and Sue run a shoe store in Oakland, and Sue has a car accident in Bakersfield while doing something unrelated to the shoe store's business, Barb is not liable for this.

The Bottom Line

Partners are personally liable for negligent acts of a partner done in connection with the partnership's business. If you are thinking about becoming a partner in a general partnership, be sure that you trust your partners and believe they are all responsible.

Taxes

General partners pay individual income taxes (or get individual deductions) based upon the results of the business of the partnership. There is no separate "partnership tax." For example:

> Smith and Jones, a general partnership, makes a profit of $50,000 for the calendar year. Smith and Jones are equal partners. Both Smith and Jones must report personal income of $25,000 for that year. The partnership pays no tax (although an "information return" must be filed with the IRS).

or:

> Smith and Jones, a general partnership, loses $50,000 for the calendar year. Smith and Jones are equal partners. Smith and Jones can each deduct $25,000 on their personal tax returns for that year, as long as they both actively manage the business.

These examples assume that the partners are 50-50 partners. Of course, partners can share profits and losses differently, such as 40-60, or 30-70. Also, there can be more than two partners. And remember, unless you provide otherwise in your agreement, the law presumes you are equal partners.

The taxable income or loss of each partner is determined by the income or loss of the partnership. It does not matter whether money was actually transferred from the partnership to the partner, or from the partner to the partnership.

The Bottom Line

There is no separate partnership tax. Partners pay personal income tax on their respective share of the partnership's profits.

Forming A Partnership

No formal action need be taken to form a general partnership. No written agreement is normally required, and nothing normally must be filed with any state or local office, unless the partnership owns realty. Also, nothing must be done or filed with any state office to keep the partnership in good standing, other than the miscellaneous taxes and fees discussed in Chapter 7. For example, partnerships still must withhold federal income tax and social security for employees, and worker's compensation payments must be made. We do strongly recommend, however, that partners sign a written partnership agreement. What follows are some suggested important subjects that should be addressed in your agreement.

But first we should emphasize that partners need not consider themselves "partners" to establish a partnership. A partnership can be defined as "an association of two or more persons to carry on as co-owners a business for profit." If owners agree to share profits, and both owners participate in the management of the venture, they probably will be considered partners, unless it can be established that some other arrangement was agreed upon. This can sometimes come as quite a surprise. For example:

> Smith and Jones agree that Smith will contribute $10,000 to purchase timber, and Jones will supervise the milling of the timber. They agree to split the profits. If the enterprise is unprofitable, it is likely that they would be considered partners, and would share any losses. Also, each would be personally liable for the losses.

If Smith and Jones had signed a written agreement that clarified that Jones was an employee of the business, not a partner, and that his compensation was one-half of the profits of the business, Jones would not be a partner, and would not be liable for the losses. Smith would be liable for all losses. Written agreements can clarify the relationship between people who are doing business, as well as their respective rights and duties. This is one of the many reasons why we recommend written agreements.

The Bottom Line

No formal action is needed to form a partnership. If you are sharing profits with someone and both of you exercise management power in the business, you will probably be considered partners. If this is not desired, clarify this in a written agreement.

THE PARTNERSHIP AGREEMENT

As we have pointed out, a general partnership can be established without an agreement. California, like most states, has enacted laws based on the Uniform Partnership Act (the "UPA"), which create an agreement for the partners if the partners do not negotiate one between themselves. This statute, reproduced in Appendix A, contains some controversial provisions that many business owners would not accept if they considered them. Some of these provisions will be discussed below. If partners want to change these provisions, an agreement is necessary. Also, a written agreement is always a good idea, so the parties can remember the terms of the deal.

The Partnership Name

The name of a partnership is obviously important to identify the business. It also normally is a partnership asset. If this is not the intention of the parties, the understanding should be clarified. For example, after the business is no longer operated by the partners, who will have the rights to use the name? Consider this:

> Jim and Bob start a night club named "Fast and Cool." This club becomes quite popular. People in other towns want to buy the rights to use the name. Who should receive this money, Bob, Jim, or the partnership? A provision in the partnership agreement could clarify that the name "Fast and Cool" is a partnership asset.

For example, one clause could be:

> **Partnership Name.** All rights in and to the partnership name, "Fast and Cool," shall belong to the partnership, and not to any individual partner.

Authority of Partners

A partnership can only do business through the partners or their agents, and you should be concerned with the right of each partner to bind the partnership. For example, suppose your partner goes out and buys some new lavish furniture for the business for $20,000, when all you told him to spend was $2,500. The partnership, and in turn you as a partner, probably would be responsible for this debt even though it was not what you expected. Unless you say otherwise, every partner has the right to bind the partnership for matters "in the ordinary course of business." If you wish to limit this right, by giving only one partner the right to make decisions for the partnership, for example, you must do so by agreement.

If your agreement provided that only you had the right to make purchasing decisions, and your partner, without your authority, bought expensive furniture, the partnership might not be responsible for the bill. We say "might" because even though you had an agreement giving you the sole right to make purchasing decisions, your partner could still be viewed as the partnership's agent, and would by law have authority to bind the partnership.

Let's say that in the past your partner has always purchased furniture for the business, and the partnership had always paid the bills for expenses he incurred in the name of the partnership. Under the law, he now has what is called *apparent authority* to bind the partnerships. Even though your agreement provides otherwise, the law gives him the right to make decisions binding the partnership, if the person dealing with him does not know of any restriction upon his authority. This is designed to protect people who in good faith rely on the appearance of authority that you have allowed to exist.

Remember, the partnership agreement may limit a partner's authority to bind the partnership, but the law may still impose liability when innocent people deal with the unauthorized partner. The best way to protect yourself from this happening is to closely supervise all transactions between the partnership and others.

The Bottom Line

Unless your agreement says otherwise, each partner has the right to enter into contracts and bind the partnership. If you are not happy with that result, make sure you have a partnership agreement. And remember, even with an agreement, repeatedly allowing anyone to act on behalf of the business may result in liability to you, even for unauthorized acts.

Making Decisions

Under the law, unless you say otherwise, a majority of partners must approve important decisions. This can cause strange results if some partners have a large interest in the venture, and some partners have a small interest. For example:

> Smith, Jones, and Hernandez form a general partnership. Hernandez has a right to 60% of the profits, and Smith and Jones each have a right to 20% of the profits. Unless the parties had agreed to another arrangement, Smith and Jones could make important decisions over the objections of Hernandez.

To many people, this does not seem fair. Hernandez should have more control than Smith and Jones. For this reason many partners agree that voting should be based upon a majority in interest, not a majority of the partners. For example, here is a clause Hernandez may want included in the agreement:

> **Management Decisions.** Management decisions shall be decided by a majority vote. In such a vote, partners shall have different voting power, based upon their respective interests in the partnership. So, for example, if the interests of the three partners are 25%, 20%, and 55%, respectively, the voting power of each partner shall be based upon these relative interests.

The Bottom Line

Unless you have another agreement, important decisions will be made by a majority of the partners, regardless of their ownership percentages. If you want another arrangement, this needs to be included in an agreement.

Compensation for Services

General partners are *not* entitled to any salary from the partnership, unless there is an express agreement approving it. Consider the problem of Smith and Jones:

> Smith and Jones form a general partnership. Smith and Jones both contribute seed money, and Jones manages the business. They agree to share profits. Jones will not be entitled to any salary, unless there is an agreement providing for compensation. Both would simply split the profits equally.

Many times one partner will render more services than another partner. In this situation, it may seem fair to compensate the partner for these services. But unless there is an agreement about being paid, the partner will not have a claim against the partnership. For this reason, if one partner will be rendering services and others will not, the compensation issue should be considered and provided for in the agreement. Here is how such a clause might look:

> **Compensation of Manager.** ____________ will manage the business of the partnership. He or she will devote a reasonable amount of time to the partnership's business. In consideration of these management services, he or she will be paid a monthly management fee of $____.

Also, if a partner is going to do anything else on behalf of the partnership and wants to receive payment for any of these other services rendered on behalf of the partnership, such as a real estate commission, or a legal or accounting fee, this should be specified and approved by all the partners in the agreement.

The Bottom Line

If you think you, or your partner, should be paid for the services contributed to the partnership, you had better say so in the agreement. If you don't, you will simply share the profits equally, regardless of any services performed.

Dividing Profits and Losses

Under California law, profits and losses are divided equally after each partner's capital contribution has been returned. The results can be surprising if partners have contributed varying amounts to the partnership.

> Smith and Jones form a general partnership. Smith contributed $5,000, and Jones contributed $15,000. Assume the business makes a profit of $120,000 during the first year. Unless there is some agreement, Smith will receive his $5,000 contribution and Jones will receive his $15,000. Then the remaining $100,000 of the profits will be divided equally. In other words, Smith will receive $55,000 and Jones $65,000. This may not be what they intended.

Smith and Jones could have agreed to share profits according to their respective contributions. If the partnership agreement contained a provision such as this, the profits would have been split differently:

> **Profit Share.** After capital contributions of all partners have been returned to the partners from the partnership, any additional profits shall be divided among the partners based upon the relative amounts of their respective capital contributions.

The Bottom Line

Profits of a partnership are split equally, unless there is an agreement to the contrary. If you want a different arrangement, you need an agreement.

Capital Contributions

New businesses almost always need seed money. Owners must decide the relative initial capital contributions to be made. Some owners might want to make their initial contribution in installments, rather than in a lump sum. If so, the owners should decide whether the company's budget can accommodate such an installment arrangement.

Owners also may want to contribute property instead of cash. If property that has appreciated in value is to be contributed, the contributing partner might have to pay tax on the increased value. For example, assume one partner had purchased a building for $10,000 in 1970. If the building is now worth $50,000, and the partner wants to contribute the building to the partnership, there could be a tax due. A tax counselor should be consulted if this is a concern.

Once the partners have decided the capital contributions to be made, each partner's share of profits should be clarified. Are profits to be divided based upon capital contributions, or on some other basis?

Some partners might want to contribute services rather than cash or property. If this is to be done, the amount and type of services should be clarified, as well as the profit percentage the "service" partner will obtain and whether the partner will receive any compensation other than the profit percentage. For example, what type of service is contemplated, and approximately how many hours per week will be needed? What happens if the partner ends up working much more or less than initially predicted? Also, will there be any limit upon the "service" partner's right to receive profits (for example, such as a maximum annual payment), or will the service partner be treated like all other partners? For example:

> Assume one partner will manage the partnership's restaurant, and one contributes capital. The basic arrangement is that the partners will split the profits. If the restaurant is very successful, would some other profit split be fairer?

California law provides that partners do not receive any interest from the partnership on capital contributions, unless the partners agree otherwise. This question should be discussed by the partners. Here is how a clause would look that gives a partner interest on capital contributions:

> **Interest on Capital Contributions.** In addition to the profit share of each partner, each partner shall be entitled to an annual interest payment from the partnership, each year on December 1, until the partner has had his initial capital contribution repaid in full by the partnership. The interest payment shall be ____% of the amount of capital contribution not repaid as of December 1 of that year.

Additional Capital

When a business is started, owners normally try to estimate the amount of seed capital that business will need. This, of course, is only an estimate and can be very wrong. Many new businesses find that they need more money after the business has been started. There can be many reasons for this need for additional capital. For example, the business might be less profitable initially than planned, or more money might be needed for expansion, advertising, or inventory.

This need for additional capital can cause problems. For example, assume that Tom and Becky have started a video store, and that each contributed $10,000. They have agreed to share profits equally. What if they discover three months after the business has opened that the business needs more money? Assume Becky has some money and Tom doesn't. If Becky contributes more money, will this change her profit percentage? If so, how will it change it?

The agreement should address what happens if this occurs. First, who decides whether the business needs more capital? After it is decided that more money is needed, who must contribute, and how much? Should each partner have to contribute the portion of the additional capital based upon the partner's percentage of profits? What if one partner does not have any more funds, or does not want to contribute any more funds?

The Bottom Line

Owners of a new business need to consider what will happen if the initial "seed money" is inadequate and additional capital is needed. If you don't do this, it will be unclear to the partners what each partner's obligations are, if the business needs more money.

Partnership Draws

Simply saying partners share profits doesn't mean much. More importantly, when do you get whatever money you are entitled to? Partners need to decide when payments will be made to partners, in addition to any salary payments agreed to. New businesses need seed capital, and most are initially unprofitable. It frequently is unwise to drain the business of its capital via payments to partners. Many agreements provide the procedure for approving partnership draws. For example, the agreement could provide that two-thirds of the partners must approve a payment arrangement before the partners could receive a payment from the partnership. Alternatively, the agreement could state that, except for partners receiving a salary from the partnership, no payment would be made until the business is profitable for a three-month period.

The Bottom Line

The amount and timing of partnership draws can be quite controversial in a partnership. Partners should discuss how the partnership will determine when draws are appropriate.

Bank Accounts and Signing Checks

Businesses need bank accounts. An important management decision for the partnership is who should be able to make withdrawals from the account. This may be determined by the mechanics of the business. For example, if one partner is running the business, he probably will be the one authorized to make withdrawals.

The decision regarding banking for the business highlights an issue of trust among the owners. If one person has the right to make withdrawals, that person could steal money from the business. This does sometimes occur. As a safeguard, many businesses require two people to authorize withdrawals from a business account.

After you and your partners have decided upon the best arrangement for withdrawals, this can be worked out with your bank for the business. When the account for the business is opened, one important provision of the account agreement is who is authorized to make withdrawals. Partners should go to the bank and clarify with the bank officer the arrangement desired, and this arrangement should be set forth in the new account agreement.

The Bottom Line

Control of the bank account means control of the funds of the partnership. Be sure to work with your bank to ensure that funds are not misappropriated.

Partnership Property

A partnership is considered a separate entity that can own property. Partners can also let the partnership use property owned by a partner. If the agreement does not clarify the status of property, it can be unclear whether a partner has given the partnership certain property, thereby making property partnership property, or whether the partner has merely let the partnership use property. To the extent possible, it is always a good idea to clarify what property is being given to the partnership, and what property is merely being used by the partnership. For example:

> Richard and Janie start an athletic equipment store. Richard owns some typewriters and computers and lets the store use them. When the business ends and the assets of the partnership are being divided, this equipment may be divided up as a partnership asset.

If a partner is contributing property to the partnership, he should receive credit for contributing the full value of the property, less any liens on the property. If the partner is letting the partnership use property, he should be given credit for the rental value of the property. This clarifies that the property is not partnership property.

The Bottom Line

Make sure it is always clear whether property belongs to the partnership or an individual partner.

The Partnership Business

Partners obviously should clarify the type of business the partnership will carry on. For example, it could be quite a shock if a partner contributed money to a partnership he thought would be operating a restaurant, and then the other partners decided that they would sell flowers instead. To solve this problem, the agreement should set forth the type of business of the partnership, and all the approval of all partners should be necessary to make any change in that provision. For example, a clause could look like this:

> **Partnership Business.** The purpose of the Partnership shall be to develop, lease, or sell approximately 100 acres of real property located at 400 Wildcrest, Chico, California, which real property is more fully described on Exhibit "A"attached hereto. Such real property and any improvement thereon shall be hereinafter referred to as the "Property." The purposes of the Partnership shall include the acquisition, ownership, holding for investment purposes, development, encumbering, leasing (as lessor), maintaining, operating, and disposing of all or part of such Property.

The Bottom Line

Silly as it may sound, be sure to decide what type of business your partnership will be in before you agree to it. Remember, you may be personally liable for the losses of the business.

Opening a Competing Business

Fortunately most partners can get along well. However, some find that they cannot work together, and one or more decide to leave. Before this happens to you, you must consider whether any departing partner should have the right to open a business that competes with the partnership. If you decide that this shouldn't be allowed, you must consider what a reasonable noncompetition period and area would be. Then a noncompetition provision must be added to the partnership agreement.

Also, even without an express agreement, partners cannot operate a business that competes with the partnership, or is similar to the partnership business, as long as the partner is still a partner, unless the partnership agreement permits this. This surprises many partners. For example, assume Bob and Ray agree to be partners in an oil and gas venture regarding one location. If Bob found another promising oil and gas location, he would have to offer Ray an opportunity to participate in this other venture. This may not be what Bob expected. Bob and Ray might want to be partners as to the one parcel, but don't want to have to offer each other any other parcels discovered. If so, this should be set forth in the agreement. A sample provision might look like this:

> **Partner's Activities.** The Managing Partner shall devote to the Partnership business such time as, in his sole discretion, he deems reasonably necessary. Any Partner or person with any interest in such Partner may engage in or possess an interest in other business ventures of any nature or description, independently or with others, even if such ventures are in direct competition with the Partnership, which ventures may include, but are not limited to, the real estate business in all its phases which shall include, without limitation, ownership, operation, management, syndication and development of real property, and neither the Partnership nor any partner shall have any rights in or to such independent ventures or income or profits derived therefrom; provided, however, neither the Managing Partner, nor any of his affiliates shall, without the written consent of the Investing Partner, directly or indirectly participate in any way in the development, ownership, leasing or operation of any type of shopping center within ____ miles of the Property at any time while the Partnership, the Investing Partner or the shareholders of the Investing Partner have any ownership interest in the Property.

Some partners also might have ownership interests in businesses that are similar to that contemplated by the partnership. If so, this should be disclosed to the partners. The agreement should set forth the approval by the other partners of the competing business, and what activities the partner will be permitted to do without violating any of his rights to the partnership. If such a provision is not added, the partner with the competing business interest could be considered in violation of his duties to the partnership.

The Bottom Line

Under the law a partnership is a serious commitment and it prohibits you from going out on your own in similar ventures. If this isn't what you want, say so in your agreement.

Adding New Partners

No matter how carefully you plan at first, you may find that you want to add a new partner after the business is started. For example, additional money might be needed, or the new partner might have expertise that would be useful for the business. Similarly, you might want to add new partners in connection with an expansion of the business, or to give an employee more of a stake in the business. This is a topic that should be covered in your partnership agreement. For example, partners should consider whether a partner should be admitted by a majority vote, or whether all partners must approve a new member.

Also, if a new partner is to be added, how much will he have to contribute, and what will he get for the contribution? Sometimes the specifics of the arrangement are left to be decided by the partners when the new partner is to be admitted.

When a new partner is added, the partnership should clarify the interest the new partner holds. For example, for what period does the partner's profit percentage apply? Similarly, what debts and liabilities is the new partner responsible for? The UPA provides that the new partner is personally liable for debts that arise after the new partner becomes a partner, but is not personally liable for prior debts. If another arrangement is desired, this should be clarified.

The Term of the Partnership

When you start a business, it is important to consider the term of your commitment. Is the business to be operated indefinitely, or should some end point be set forth? For example:

> Harold and Carolyn invest in an apartment, and will manage it. When should the apartment be sold? What if one partner wants to sell, or leaves California, and the other doesn't want to sell?

A possible answer to the problem of Harold and Carolyn would be a clause like this:

Sale of Partnership Property. The Partnership property shall be sold, and the proceeds divided, when any partner desires to sell the property and wind up the business of the partnership.

Ending a Partnership

A partnership is perceived as a special relationship, and according to the law, it only continues to exist as long as all the initial partners remain. If one dies, desires to sell his interest, or is thrown out, the relationship is disturbed. This "break" in the relationship is called *dissolution.*

You might say, so what? Well, the effects of a dissolution can be significant. Unless partners agree otherwise, at dissolution any partner normally can force the partnership business to be broken up and sold. Once a business has developed significant goodwill, this can be a terrible result. For example:

Bill, Bob and Tom start a restaurant in San Diego called "George's" which becomes quite successful. Bill wants to withdraw from the partnership and start a restaurant in Los Angeles. If the partners had no agreement, Bill could force the partnership to liquidate, even though the business is successful.

When one partner quits or dies, the remaining partners normally want to carry on the business of the partnership. If the agreement deals with this and sets forth that the remaining partners can continue the business, this is effective. Most agreements therefore contain fairly long provisions about these problems. For example, a portion of such a clause might look like this:

In the event of the withdrawal of a partner, for whatever reason, the partnership shall not be dissolved, but the partnership business may be continued uninterrupted by the remaining partners.

The Bottom Line

Unless you say otherwise, a partnership lasts only so long as all the partners are alive and want it to continue. Any partner can end it at any time. If you don't want this result you'd better have a clause in your agreement.

Buyout Arrangements

Any business needs to plan for what happens if one owner dies, or for some other reason needs to withdraw. As we have just told you, if a partner wants out he can force the sale of the partnership. Two basic questions are presented when planning for this problem. **First,** how is the interest to be valued? **Second,** once a value is determined, who will buy the interest?

There are a number of formulas that can be used to value businesses. For example, the net value of the assets of the business could be used. This is what the law will do if you don't say otherwise. This might not be a bad way to value the worth of a very new business. However, this does not incorporate a factor for the "goodwill" of the business, the value of the business as an ongoing concern. For example, common sense tells us that a successful business is worth more than the value of its assets; a successful business is also an income stream, and this has value.

The goodwill component can be satisfied in a few ways. For example, a formula could be set forth to quantify the value. One formula commonly used is a specified multiple of the earnings of the business. Alternatively, the partners could agree to set a value each year for the business; if any partner needed to sell that year, the value of the interest would be a pro rata percentage of the agreed value. Another common method used is to obtain an appraisal (or three) of the value of the business from specified appraisers.

A partnership does not have to have one valuation method for all purposes. For example, one valuation method, such as the book value method, could be used if the partner has only been a partner for a short period, while another method could be used if the person has been a partner for a long period. Similarly, one method could be used to value the interest if the partner dies, but another method could be used if the partner merely wants to leave the business.

As you can see, it is important that the agreement establish the value of a buyout. But in addition to value you should consider the terms of the sale. For example, does the buyout have to be in cash, or can some or all of the payment be made over time? If it can be made over time, what amount of interest should be paid? Sometimes the interest rate is tied in some way to the prime rate, as it changes. For example, the former partner could receive interest payments for each year based upon that year's average prime rate plus 2% on all monies until paid.

Once the value of the interest is established, the identity of the payor must be set forth. All of the partners might wish to buy out the partner. On the other hand, only some might want to, or none might want to. Some buyout agreements give the business the right to buy the interest first; this does not change the relative ownership interests of the other partners. If the business does not buy it, some mechanism must be established for determining which partner (or partners) can buy the share.

An important issue is whether the partners *must* buy the interest, or whether they only have the option to buy the interest. Many partners do not want to make it possible for the interest to be sold to a third party, since they do not want to have a new partner whom they might not trust or enjoy working with.

HOW NOT TO END A PARTNERSHIP

Even a clause saying that the partnership would carry on in event of a partner's death might not have helped Jim Mitchell. You see, the circumstances of his partner's death got Jim into trouble with the law.

As the newspapers described it, the business was successful enough. At one time the partners had as many as 11 theaters, and the holdings at the time the partnership dissolved were estimated at around $50 million. But, all was not well. And, for one reason or another, in the middle of the night of February 27, 1991, Jim Mitchell kicked in the door of the home of his partner and brother, Artie Mitchell. Moments later Artie Mitchell was dead, and one of America's most successful porn partnerships died with it. Producers of the early porn movie hit "Behind the Green Door," which helped turn Marilyn Chambers into a sex star and managed to gross more than $25 million, the brothers also ran the O'Farrell Theatre in San Francisco and numerous related ventures.

Jim maintained that he busted into Artie's house to force Artie to enter an alcohol rehab program, and that was why he broke in carrying both a rifle and a pistol. The eight shots he fired were more or less accidental, including the three that hit and killed his brother, Jim said. Minutes later Jim was unable to explain to police why he was walking down the street with a rifle stuffed down his pants, and was arrested and charged with the death. As the prosecuting attorney saw it, Jim "wanted to be rid of his younger brother and business partner."

Fortunately, not all partnerships end this way (!), and indeed many family partnerships are extremely rewarding to all concerned. Family businesses have always been an important part of the economy and, by most accounts, their importance is growing. In addition, their recognition is growing. Does this mean all family businesses run smoothly? Not on your life. Watch what happens to Harry and Sally's Flower Shop when Sally asks for a divorce. Or, remember the story of the Mitchell brothers. Don't count on automatic peace and harmony. The Mitchell Brothers prove just how bad it can get.

—Thanks to Katherine Xin, Graduate School of Management, University of California, Irvine, for this insight. For additional information see: Paddock, Richard C. "Porn King Jim Mitchell Guilty in Slaying." *Los Angeles Times,* February 29, 1992, page A-3.

The Bottom Line

Many complications can arise if a partner dies, wants to withdraw, or wants to sell his interest and the partnership agreement does not address this. If this is not planned for, it is unclear how the partnership would value and purchase the interest of a departing partner. It is a good idea to include a detailed provision in your partnership agreement, regarding the manner in which a withdrawing partner's share will be valued and paid.

Selling an Interest

Your partnership agreement should deal with what happens if a partner wants to sell his interest. Does the partner have the right to sell to a third party? Any third party? Must the interest be offered to the partnership or the other partners first? What valuation method will be used to value the interest? To solve these questions you need a specific clause in your agreement. For example, a clause could look like this:

Right of First Refusal. If any Partner desires to sell its interest in the Partnership (the "Selling Partner"), he or she must first give notice of same to all of the nonselling Partners (the "Remaining Partners") including the name of the proposed purchaser and the net price and terms of the proposed sale. In such event, the Remaining Partners shall be entitled, during a period of ninety (90) days from the date of receipt of such notice, to participate in the purchase of the Selling Partner's interest at the same net price and terms. In the event more than one Remaining Partner desires to purchase a portion of the Selling Partner's interest at such price and terms, such interest shall be divided among them as they may agree, or if they fail to agree within such ninety (90) day period, in proportion to their respective Capital Interests in the Partnership. The purchase price of such Selling Partner's interest shall be allocated among the purchasing Partners in proportion to the respective portion of the interest purchased by each of them.

Sale to Third Parties. If the Remaining Partners do not exercise their right of first refusal above within a ninety (90) day period, the Selling Partner may sell his interest to a third party provided such sale is (a) to the purchaser specified and at the price and terms specified in the notice to the Remaining Partners, and (b) such sale is consummated within sixty (60) days of the termination of the right of first refusal. Notwithstanding any provision of this Agreement to the contrary, except for transfers due to death or incapacity, the Managing Partner shall not, without the written consent of the Investing Partner, (i) sell or transfer a portion of his Capital Interest to more than one person or entity other than his immediate family, or (ii) sell or transfer during any Development Stage any portion of the

Partnership Interest which would result in its remaining Capital Interest being less than twenty-five percent (25%).

You also should know that the law permits a partner to sell his right to profits from the partnership, and this does not dissolve the partnership. The person buying the rights to profits does not become a "partner" and cannot exercise management power or participate in decisions. Is this arrangement desired? If not, the agreed upon terms should be set forth.

The sale of an interest in a partnership can create tax liabilities. A tax counselor should be consulted before such a sale is effected to be sure that there is no excess tax liability incurred in connection with the transaction.

Expelling a Partner

Sometimes a partnership might want to expel a partner. This obviously is a drastic step, and should be undertaken only rarely when no other solution seems workable. The grounds and procedure for expulsion should be set forth in the agreement.

If a provision regarding expulsion is included, other terms need to be addressed, such as how the expelled partner's interest is to be valued and paid. Presumably the partner's interest in the partnership's profits would stop when he is expelled, but this should also be clarified.

Bankruptcy of a Partner

Under the UPA the bankruptcy of a partner dissolves the partnership. Many partners do not want this arrangement. If so, the agreement should provide that the bankruptcy of one partner does not dissolve the partnership. One common approach is to expel a partner if he becomes bankrupt; the remaining partners would buy out the bankrupt partner and continue the business of the partnership, if the agreement states that the remaining partners have this power.

Death of a Partner

If a partner dies, this presents both dissolution and buyout issues. Under the UPA, the death of partner dissolves the partnership. If this is not desired, this should be set forth.

The buyout procedure should be set forth. For example, how is the interest to be valued? Who purchases the interest? What are the terms of the sale?

Other Partnership Agreement Issues

Some common partnership agreement subjects are mentioned above. Still, every new business is unique. Think about your business. Imagine various scenarios for the business. Consider what the business will be like if it becomes successful. Does the agreement deal with the significant matters that would arise? Similarly, imagine what would happen if the business is not successful. Does the agreement cover all significant matters that would arise? If you are planning to prepare the partnership agreement yourself, we do encourage you to have a lawyer review the agreement. The lawyer can then tell you whether anything needs to be changed or added.

Miscellaneous Partnership Information

A general partnership can have any number of partners, as long as there are at least two. All partners of a general partnership are general partners.

A *joint venture* is a partnership for a specific limited purpose, and in many ways is treated as a general partnership.

ADVANTAGES AND DISADVANTAGES OF A GENERAL PARTNERSHIP

There are a number of desirable features of a general partnership. It is quite simple to form and operate, no special filing with any state office normally is required, and no minutes of meetings of any kind must be maintained. This simplicity can save owners time and legal fees. Also, there is no partnership tax; owners of a general partnership only pay taxes individually.

Other features of a general partnership can cause problems. General partners have no limited liability; their personal assets can be attached to collect claims against the partnership. Also, management of a general partnership is not centralized; the law presumes that all general partners have the right to make normal management decisions and obligate the partnership. If owners want to centralize management of the business in one owner, the general partnership format does not work well.

FOR MORE INFORMATION

California State Chamber of Commerce. *Business Start-Up Kit for Sole Proprietors/Partnerships.* Sacramento: Chamber of Commerce. Valuable resource. Well worth the price. Numerous sample letters and forms included. This kit is updated annually.

Coleman, David. "How to Achieve a Productive Partnership." *Journal of Accountancy,* May 1992, pages 113–114.

Handler, Wendy C. "Key Interpersonal Relationships of Next-Generation Family Members in Family Firms." *Journal of Small Business Management,* July 1991, pages 21–32.

Resnik, Paul. *The Small Business Bible.* New York: John Wiley and Sons, 1988. Chapter 2, "No Room for Illusions," contains a "Partnership Problems" checklist. Useful paperback book.

Sitarz, Daniel. *The Complete Book of Small Business Forms.* Carbondale, IL: Nova Publishing Company, 1991. The sample partnership agreements in the Sitarz book are simpler in appearance than those we include in this book, and might be of interest to the very small start-up partnership.

"Seeking Shelter: Partnership Structures Called into Question as Liability Risk Rises." *Wall Street Journal,* June 10, 1992, page A1.

Ward, John L., and Craig E. Aronoff. "Sibling Partnerships," *Nation's Business,* January 1992, pages 52–53.

POINTS TO PONDER

1. Which of your own family members would probably be good candidates for your partnership? Why?
2. Which of your own family members would probably be poor candidates for your partnership? Why? You might think about in-laws, who are a frequent source of both capital and headaches.
3. Who else might you consider going into partnership with? Why?

DON'T JUST SIT THERE, DO SOMETHING!

1. Check locally for professional partnerships (doctors, attorneys, CPAs, etc.). Make a list of ten. Then double check the form of business organization. Did some of the folks you thought were partnerships turn out to be corporations? Were they partnerships in the past that changed form into corporations? If so, why the change?
2. What other local businesses can you identify that are partnerships? Nonlocal businesses? Make a list of at least five, not included above. Comment on trends, patterns, characteristics.

4

The Limited Partnership: Not For Everybody

In Chapter 3, the characteristics of a general partnership were discussed. The general partnership has certain advantages, but for many new businesses it has significant drawbacks. The general partnership presumes that all partners want to manage the business, and that they are all willing to assume unlimited liability for the debts of the business. However, in many instances, one partner is the manager, and all others wish only to be passive investors. Also, many investors want some limit to their liability; they do not want to be personally liable for all claims against the business. In such situations a "limited" partnership has significant advantages over a general partnership.

There are some significant differences between a general partnership and a limited partnership. For example, a limited partnership has two types of partners: general partners and limited partners. General partners manage the business and have the unlimited liability normally associated with general partners. Limited partners are essentially investors who do not manage the business and who have limited liability. They can lose, at most, the amount they invest in the business; creditors of the business cannot attach the other assets of a limited partner. This new class of "limited partner" is the significant difference between a limited partnership and a general partnership. The liability of a limited partner resembles that of a shareholder in a corporation.

The limited partnership can be useful if some owners are concerned about the unlimited liability that results from a general partnership, and these owners do not want to manage the business of the partnership. These owners can be limited partners, and their liability is limited to the investment in the partnership. Those partners who manage the business would be the general partners, and they would not have limited liability.

There must be at least one general partner and at least one limited partner to create a limited partnership. Of course, there can be many partners of both types, if this is desired.

Limited partnerships and general partnerships are similar in many ways. For example, they are taxed in the same way. There is no limited partnership tax, so partners pay only individual tax, according to their respective profit percentage. Also, many issues that should be resolved in a general partnership agreement need to be included in a limited partnership agreement. These issues will be discussed below.

Forming a Limited Partnership

Unlike a general partnership, something must be filed with the California secretary of state to form a limited partnership. If this limited partnership "certificate" is not filed, the business normally will be considered a general partnership, and all partners can be considered general partners, even those who believed they were limited partners. This can create quite a problem, since limited partners generally do not want unlimited liability. To avoid this problem, if you want to form a limited partnership, be sure to file a certificate that satisfies all the requirements of California law. Specifically, you must meet the requirements of the Revised Limited Partnership Act enacted in 1984.

The information that must be included in a limited partnership certificate is set forth in the Revised Limited Partnership Act (see Appendix A-2 for pertinent provisions of this act, which is found in sections 15611-15723 of California Corporations Code). The certificate, called form LP-1, must include the name of the partnership, the location of the principal place of business, the name, mailing address, and street address of the business or residence of each general partner, the address of the registered office, and the name and address of the agent for service of process. A filing fee must be paid to the secretary of state when the certificate is filed. The fee was $70 in a recent year but is subject to change. The certificate should be sent to the California secretary of state, P.O. Box 704, Sacramento, CA 95803. For information about this filing process, call the secretary of state at (916) 324-6769. The certificate should be amended if the identity of the partners change, or some other term in the agreement is changed.

Also, keep in mind that limited partnerships in California pay an annual franchise tax equivalent to the minimum corporation franchise tax. In the year this material was collected, that minimum fee was $800.

The Bottom Line

To form a limited partnership, a certificate must be filed with the California secretary of state. If you decide to form a limited partnership, be sure you file a certificate that satisfies California law.

Partnership Name

The certificate should set forth the name of the partnership business. The partnership agreement should also clarify whether the rights to this name will be a partnership asset.

Before a name is selected, it is important to determine whether anyone else has used the name before. If someone has, you may not have the right to use the name. You may check to see if your proposed name is available by calling the secretary of state's office, Limited Partnership Division, (916) 324-6769. If your name is still available, you can lock it in for $10 (subject to change) by sending a "Name Reservation Fee." This will hold your name temporarily while you complete other requirements.

The name of a limited partnership must include "limited partnership," or "L.P." The surname of a limited partner should not be included in the name of a limited partnership. If this is done, the limited partner can be treated as a general partner. There is a fear that if the surname of a limited partner is included in the name of the business, creditors could rely upon the credit of such a limited partner when extending credit to a limited partnership. In order to clarify the limited liability status of limited partners, no surname of a limited partner should be included in the name of the business.

Powers of Limited Partners

Limited partners cannot take an active role in the management of the limited partnership. If they do, they can be considered general partners, and they lose their limited liability as a limited partner. It is vital for limited partners to be aware of this when a limited partnership business is doing poorly. In this situation, a limited partner can be tempted to become more involved in the business to try to salvage his investment. The partner must be aware that too active a role can lead to his being considered a general partner. If this occurs, the limited partner might not lose just his initial investment, but his other personal assets.

Limited partners can participate in important decisions, however, without losing limited liability. The statute sets forth certain things a limited partner can do. For example, a limited partner can advise the general partner about the operation of the business, guarantee partnership debts and provide collateral for partnership loans, be employed by the partnership, and act as an officer. In addition, the limited partners can be given the right to approve certain important things, such as a plan to dissolve the partnership, an amendment to the limited partnership certificate, and a sale of all the assets of the partnership. If the limited partners want any of these powers, the agreement should specify this.

The Bottom Line

Limited partners cannot exercise normal management powers. They can be given the power to approve important decisions, if the agreement provides for this.

Tax Treatment of Limited Partners

A limited partnership normally is taxed as a partnership, not a corporation. So, the partnership profits are allocated among the partners, and these partners pay individual income tax on the profits. However, if a limited partnership looks too much like a corporation to the Internal Revenue Service, the IRS can take the position that the limited partnership really is a corporation and should be taxed as one. This can be quite a costly result, since corporations have to pay a corporate income tax on the profits of the business, and then shareholders have to pay a tax on money distributed to them. (This is discussed in detail in Chapter 5.) Technical rules have evolved to determine whether a limited partnership will be taxed as a partnership or a corporation. If you want to form a limited partnership, and it is important to you whether the business will be treated as a corporation or a partnership for tax purposes, consult a tax advisor to verify that the business will be taxed as a partnership.

Securities Regulation

Limited partnership interests are considered "securities." Because of this, rules regarding the sale of securities should be followed when forming a limited partnership. If these rules are not followed, a limited partner has the right to have his investment refunded to him by the general partner. In an extreme case, the general partner could also be fined and possibly even jailed if the securities laws are not followed. Securities laws will be discussed in Chapter 5.

Interstate Business

If the partnership wants to do business in other states, it's likely that the business will have to "qualify" to do business there. In order to "qualify" to do business in another state, some filing must be made with the appropriate state office. This filing normally requires a filing fee, and the part-

MOTHER-DAUGHTER TEAMS SUCCEED WHERE MOM-AND-POP LEFT OFF

Father and son businesses? old hat. Nowadays, it's mother and daughter teams, and the increasing numbers are significant. Do they work well? It depends. It's either feast or famine: they can be really great or really awful, like any other family-owned businesses.

But business after business shows how great it can be when it does work. Shirley Pepys has been running NoJo, Inc. in Orange County, making children's clothing, for more than 20 years. Now, Shirley has invited her grown daughter to join the business. Even though both mother and daughter are strong-willed, it works. In fact, this keeps the partnership from getting too one-sided.

Does success mean always agreeing? No way! In fact, disagreement helps clarify issues. One key is communication: sitting down to talk things over makes all the difference. And, women-owned businesses make a difference in the economy as well. According to one study, the Fortune 500 companies employed some 12 million employees in 1990, but were cutting jobs at the rate of 200,000 to 300,000 a year. Soon the 5.4 million U.S. small businesses will employ more people than the Fortune 500. When that happens, it will be hard to ignore the truth: mother-daughter businesses are not mere Mom-and-Pop operations anymore!

—Thanks to Edward Poll, UCLA Extension Programs, and Anne Michaud, for these insights. For more information, see "Women Entrepreneurs: A Pretty Big Game," in *Nation's Business,* August 1992, page 53, and "Mother-Daughter Teams," by Anne Michaud, *Los Angeles Times,* May 10, 1992, page D1.

nership must agree to appear in court in that state if there is a dispute involving business transacted in that state. The partnership must also designate an agent for service of process in connection with any such dispute. This filing in each state should be made before the partnership transacts any business in that state.

Fictitious Name Statement

If the business plans to do business under a name other than the name of the partnership, a fictitious name statement must be filed. This is discussed in Chapter 7.

The Limited Partnership Agreement

The limited partnership agreement should set forth the terms of the understanding between the parties. If the partners have no express agreement, California law provides an agreement for the partners. This is the California Revised Limited Partnership Act (RLPA).

However, partners frequently want to change the RLPA terms in some ways. Some important issues that frequently are dealt with in a limited partnership agreement will be mentioned below.

Contributions by the Partners

The agreement should specify how much each partner must contribute, as well as when the amount should be contributed. Such a provision could look like this:

General Partner's Initial Capital Contribution. The General Partner has previously contributed to the Partnership as his Initial Capital Contribution (i) the sum of Fifty and No/100 Dollars ($50.00) upon the formation of the Partnership, and (ii) his entire interest in the Tract and all contracts therefor, plans and specifications, construction contracts, financing commitments, and other items involved in the purchase of the Tract and construction of Improvements.

Limited Partners' Capital Contributions. By the execution and delivery of this Agreement, each Limited Partner agrees to opposite such Limited Partner's name on the signature pages hereof. The total of the Limited Partner's Capital Contributions shall be Two Million Three Hundred Thousand and No/100 Dollars ($2,300,000.00), comprised of Ninety-Two (92) Units of Twenty-Five Thousand and No/100 Dollars ($25,000.00) each. Each Limited Partner's Initial Capital Contribution shall be the sum of Four Thousand and No/100 Dollars ($4,000.00) for each Unit purchased by such Limited Partner. Each Limited Partner's Additional Capital Contribution shall be the sum of Twenty-One Thousand and No/100 Dollars ($21,000.00) for each Unit purchased by such Limited Partner, to be paid to the Partnership over a five year period plus interest at a per annum interest rate equal to One Percent (1%) over the prime commercial lending rate charged from time to time by ____________ Bank, N.A., Fresno, California to its most creditworthy customers, in accordance with the following schedule: $7,500.00 per Unit plus accrued interest on or before February 15, 1994; $6,500.00 per Unit plus accrued interest on or before February 15, 1995; $4,000.00 per Unit plus accrued interest on or before February 15, 1996; and $3,000.00 per Unit plus accrued interest on or before February 15, 1997. Each such Additional Capital Contribution shall be evidenced by a Promissory Note to be executed and delivered upon the admission to the Partnership of such Limited Partner. The proceeds of such Capital Contributions, including the Promissory Notes evidencing a portion of same, may be used by the General Partner for any proper Partnership purpose, including securing any Partnership borrowings. Each Promissory Note is to be secured by the delivery by the respective Limited Partner of a certificate of deposit, letter of credit or other security acceptable to the General Partner in the amount of Twenty-one Thousand and No/100 Dollars ($21,000.00) per Unit represented by such Limited Partner's Promissory Note, such Security Instrument to continue in force until the Promissory Note is paid in full.

General Partner's Additional Capital Contributions. In the event the Partnership requires additional operating funds, the General Partner shall be obligated to contribute such funds to the Partnership as an Additional Capital Contribution.

Permissible Partnership Contributions

A limited partner cannot acquire an interest in a limited partnership in exchange for future services. A partner can contribute cash, other property, the value of past services rendered, or a promissory note in exchange for a partnership interest.

Additional Contributions

If any additional contributions are to be required, the respective amounts and dates of these contributions should be specified. For example, should each partner have to contribute a pro rata amount, based upon each partner's interest in the partnership? If so, many agreements set forth what will occur if a partner defaults on his obligation to make an additional contribution. This is one such provision:

Advances by Other Partners. In the event a Partner fails to make a Capital Contribution to the Partnership at any time when required to do so, and such default continues for a period of ten (10) days from receipt of written notice of such default from the General Partner (or any other Partner if the General Partner is in default), the General Partner (provided he is not the Partner in default) shall be entitled to elect to advance to the Partnership any such amount which the defaulting Partner has failed to contribute. In the event the General Partner does not elect to advance or cause to be advanced any amount which a Partner failed to contribute within thirty (30) days of the original notice to the defaulting Partner, then the General Partner (or any other Partner if the General Partner is in default) shall send written notice of such default to all other Partners, and all nondefaulting Partners shall be entitled, during the period that such defaulting Partner continues to be in default, to elect to participate in the making of any such advance. The advances by the nondefaulting Partners electing to so advance funds shall be apportioned among them as they may agree, or if they fail to agree, such advances shall be made in proportion to the respective Capital Interests of the nondefaulting Partners electing to make such advances. Any advances pursuant to this paragraph shall be deemed to be a loan by each Partner making such an advance to the defaulting Partner, and any such Advancing Partner shall earn interest on such advance at the maximum rate of interest allowed by law, but if no such maximum rate then exists, at Twenty-Four Percent (24%) per annum. Any and all distributions which otherwise would be distributed to the defaulting Partner in accordance with terms hereof shall instead be distributed to the Advancing Partners in partial repayment of any interest accrued on such advances, and then in repayment of any advances made in accordance with this paragraph, until such advances plus accrued interest have been fully repaid, such repayments to be allocated among the Advancing Partners in proportion to their respective advances on behalf of such defaulting Partner or in addition to there being an Advancing Partner the defaulting Partner additionally owes funds to the Partnership.

The Bottom Line

Partners need to plan for what will occur if the business needs more capital. The agreement should deal with who will have the obligation to provide this additional capital, and what benefits will result from making such an additional contribution.

Profit Percentage

The respective profit percentages of each partner obviously should be set forth. The California Revised Limited Partnership Act provides that all partners share profits in proportion to their respective capital contributions. For example:

Assume three limited partners contribute $5,000, $10,000, and $20,000 to a venture, respectively, and the general partner contributes $15,000. Assume the business makes a profit of $150,000. Unless the partners made another agreement, after the capital contributions are returned to the partners the remaining $100,000 of profit would be divided in a proportion to the amount contributed.

Profit division provisions can be simple or quite complicated. For example, limited partners might be given a fixed profit percentage regardless of the extent of the profits of the business. On the other hand, the general partners might want the profit percentage of the limited partners to be limited after the partners receive a certain return on their investment.

The Bottom Line

Profits are normally shared based upon each partner's capital contribution. If a different arrangement is desired, an agreement is necessary.

Dividing Losses

Losses normally are shared in the same manner as profits. A different arrangement can be made, if the partners all agree.

Compensation of General Partner

The general partner normally manages the business of the limited partnership. Unless there is another agreement, a partner is not compensated for services rendered in the partnership business. The agreement should set forth the compensation, if any, to be received by the general partner for any work. For example, the partner might receive a salary; most would agree that a partner should at least receive reimbursement for expenses. This is an example of one such provision:

> **Compensation of General Partner.** The General Partner shall receive no compensation for his services as General Partner. If the General Partner, however, renders services to the Partnership other than as required hereunder, the General Partner shall be entitled to reasonable compensation for such services. The General Partner shall be entitled to be reimbursed by the Partnership out of Partnership funds for any and all direct costs and expenses incurred by it in relation to the formation of the Partnership and the operation of the Partnership affairs.

The Bottom Line

Partners are not entitled to be compensated for services rendered to the partnership, unless the agreement so provides.

Obligation to Repay Contributions of Limited Partners

If a limited partnership is unsuccessful, the limited partners normally lose their investment. In some instances the general partner will guarantee the return of the contributions made by the limited partners. If this is the partners' understanding, the agreement should include this guarantee.

Partnership Business

The agreement should set forth the types of business to be conducted by the partnership. This gives the limited partners some protection. If this is done, the general partner cannot change the character of the business without obtaining the consent of the limited partners. This is an example of one such provision:

> The purposes of the Partnership are to (i) acquire, own and hold the Tract containing approximately 10.7522 acres out of the ____________ Survey, San Anselmo, Marin County, California, (ii) construct the Improvements on the Tract, (iii) manage, operate and lease (as lessor) apartments in the Project, (iv) encumber and obtain financing for the Project, and (v) sell, transfer, convey, and exchange the Project. The Partnership shall have the power to do everything necessary, advisable, proper or convenient for the accomplishment of the purposes specified above; provided, however, nothing contained in this Article 3 or elsewhere in this Partnership Agreement shall obligate the General Partner to take any action on behalf of the Partnership if he deems such action inappropriate or not necessary to accomplish the Partnership purposes.

Partnership Property

If partners plan to let the partnership use property owned by a partner, the agreement should clarify what property will be owned by the partnership, and what property will be considered still owned by a partner. Alternatively, partners can contribute property to the partnership instead of cash. If this is done, the agreement should clarify that such property will be owned by the partnership.

Term of the Partnership

If the partners plan to do business only for a known period of time, this should be set forth in the agreement. In contrast, if partners do not know when the business will end, some provision should be made for how this decision will be made. This is one such provision:

> **Partnership Term.** The term of the Partnership commenced November 22, 1994, and shall continue until December 31, 2024, unless sooner terminated in accordance with the provisions of this Partnership Agreement.

Competing Businesses

Limited and general partners have a fiduciary duty to each other regarding the business. Because of these duties, unless the agreement provides otherwise partners must refer to the partnership all business related to the partnership's business. This can be a significant problem, since many business people have more than one investment in the same type of business. For example:

> Humboldt Properties, Ltd., is a limited partnership. Smith is the general partner. The business of the partnership is real estate development. Unless the agreement provides otherwise, Smith

must do all his real estate development transactions through Humboldt Properties, Ltd.

Many general partners do not want this arrangement, since they may be the general partner of a number of real estate developments, or may want to develop some property in their individual capacity. If this is desired, the scope of the partnership business should be carefully described, and the agreement should outline the types of activities the general partner can be involved in as an individual. This is an example of one such provision:

General Partner's Activities. The General Partner shall devote to the Partnership business such time as he reasonably shall deem necessary to manage the business and affairs of the Partnership. The General Partner may engage in or possess an interest in other business ventures of any nature or description, independently or with others, even if such ventures are in direct competition with the Partnership, which ventures may include, but are not limited to, the real estate business in all its phases including ownership, operation, management, syndication and development of apartment complexes and other real property, and neither the Partnership nor any Partner shall have any rights in or to such independent ventures or income or profits derived therefrom.

The Bottom Line

A partner cannot carry on any other business that is at all competitive with the partnership. If a partner wants to do this, all partners must approve.

Adding New Partners

The limited partnership agreement should deal with how new partners will be added. It normally is not very important how limited partners are added. Since they are passive investors in many respects, the only significant issue is the cost of the profit percentage for the new partner.

The addition or replacement of a general partner is much more significant. The agreement should address this process in much more detail.

Buyout Arrangement

Limited partnership interests normally are not very marketable. For this reason, some arrangement must be provided for the sale of shares. These provisions can apply if a limited partner dies, becomes bankrupt, or for some other reason wants to sell. If a partner dies or becomes bankrupt, some means for establishing the value of the partnership interest should be established. Various means of doing this were discussed in Chapter 3. Also, the identity of the purchaser (that is, the partnership or the limited partners) should be clarified, as well as the terms of the purchase (that is, all cash, or in installments).

Different issues are presented if a limited partner wants to sell his interest. Sometimes partners want a "right of first refusal" if this occurs. This is an example of one such provision:

12.02 Right of First Refusal. If any Partner desires to sell his Partnership Interest (the "Selling Partner"), he must first give written notice of same to the General Partner, including the name of the proposed purchaser and the net price and terms of the proposed sale. In such event, the General Partner shall be entitled, during a period of ten (10) days from the date of receipt of such notice, to elect to purchase the Selling Partner's Partnership Interest at the same net price and terms. In the event the General Partner does not elect to purchase the Selling Partner's Partnership Interest as provided above, the General Partner shall distribute the Selling Partner's notice to all other Partners, and the Partners other than the Selling Partner shall be entitled, during a period of twenty (20) days from the date of the Selling Partner's original notice, to elect to participate in the purchase of the Selling Partner's Partnership Interest at the same net price and terms as contained in such notice. In the event more than one Partner elects to purchase a portion of the Selling Partner's Partnership Interest, such Partnership Interest shall be divided among them as they may agree, or if they fail to agree within such twenty (20) day period, in proportion to their respective Capital Interests. The purchase price of a Selling Partner's Partnership Interest under this Paragraph 12.02 shall be allocated among the purchasing partners in proportion to the respective portion of the Partnership Interest purchased by each of them. Any purchase under this Paragraph 12.02 shall be closed within thirty (30) days of the above-referenced election to purchase.

12.03 Sale to Third Parties. If the General Partner and the Remaining Partners do not exercise their right of first refusal as provided in paragraph 12.02 above within the twenty (20) day period provided therein, or any such purchase is not closed within the thirty (30) day period provided therein, the Selling Partner may sell his interest to a third party provided such sale is (i) to the purchaser specified and at the price and terms specified in the notice to the General Partner, and (ii) such sale is consummated within forty-five (45) days of the termination of the right of first refusal provided for in paragraph 12.02.

The Bottom Line

California law does not provide clear rules regarding how a partner's interest should be valued and paid for if he dies or withdraws. Partners should specify how a partnership interest will be valued in that event. Also, the partners should consider what should occur if a partner wants to sell his interest to a third party.

Firing the General Partner

Limited partners sometimes grow disenchanted with the general partner. Unless the agreement addresses this subject, the limited partners have no right to "fire" the general partner. Some limited partners want to have this right, if at least 50% or 67% of the limited partners want to remove the general partner. Such a provision should set forth the grounds for which the general partner can be removed; if no reason is needed, this should be set forth. The effect of such a removal upon the profit percentage of the removed general partner also should be specified.

Distributions to the Limited Partners

Someone must decide when the limited partner will receive distributions from the partnership. Normally this decision is made by the general partner. If the limited partners want to limit the discretion of the general partner, this should be set forth. This is an example of one provision regarding distributions:

> **6.02 Current Distributions.** The General Partner shall distribute to the Partners, not less often than quarterly, the Distributable Funds of the Partnership (if any), being all cash generated from the operation of the Project, after the retention of adequate working capital and the establishment of a reasonable reserve for current, future, and contingent liabilities, as reasonably determined by the General Partner. All such distributions shall be made to the Partners in the proportion of their respective Capital Interests.

Reports to the Limited Partners

Limited partners desire financial information about the partnership. The agreement should state how often reports will be sent to the partners, and what kind of reports will be prepared. This is an example of one kind of provision:

> **7.05 Monthly Statements.** The General Partner shall prepare or cause to be prepared monthly statements showing the income and expenses of the Partnership and the assets and liabilities thereof as of the end of each calendar month. Such monthly statements shall be distributed to the Partners within thirty (30) days after the end of each calendar month.

Making Important Decisions

Under California law, a general partner has general management power. Limited partners frequently want to participate in important management decisions affecting the business of the partnership, as long as the powers do not subject them to personal liability for exercising control, as mentioned above. Decisions requiring the approval of the limited partners should be clarified. This is an example of one such provision:

> **9.02 Approval Rights.** Anything to the contrary contained in this Partnership Agreement notwithstanding, without the written consent of Limited Partners owning three-quarters (¾) of the Capital Interests owned by Limited Partners, the General Partner shall not:
>
> (a) Do any act in contravention of this Partnership Agreement.
> (b) Except for a permitted dissolution of the Partnership or sale of the project, do not act which would make it impossible to carry on the ordinary business of the Partnership.
> (c) Confess a judgment against the Partnership.
> (d) Possess Partnership property or assign their rights in specific Partnership property, for other than a Partnership purpose.
> (e) Admit a person as a general partner.
> (f) Except to the extent otherwise permitted in this Partnership Agreement, admit a person as a limited partner.
> (g) Refinance and replace any Permanent Loan with another loan secured by a lien against the Project, but nothing contained herein shall require the consent of any Limited Partners to the initial Permanent Loan or other proper Partnership borrowings which are not secured by an interest in the Project.
> (h) Sell or exchange any real property interest in the Project.

Death or Bankruptcy of a Partner

The agreement should set forth whether the business of the partnership can be carried on after the death or bankruptcy of a limited or general partner. Also, as mentioned above, a means for valuing the partner's interest should be set forth.

The agreement should specify whether the business can be continued if a limited or general partner dies, retires, is declared bankrupt, or sells his interest. Most businesses want to have such a right. If the business is to be continued after the general partner dies or retires, a means for selecting a substitute general partner should be set forth.

Other Limited Partnership Agreement Issues

This chapter has discussed some common partnership agreement subjects. Still, every new business is unique. Imagine various scenarios for your business. Consider what will happen if it becomes successful; does the agreement deal with the significant matters that would arise? Similarly, imagine what would happen if the business is not successful. Does the agreement cover all significant matters that would arise? If you are planning to prepare the partnership agreement yourself, we do encourage you to have a lawyer review the agreement. The lawyer can tell you whether anything needs to be changed or added.

ADVANTAGES AND DISADVANTAGES OF A LIMITED PARTNERSHIP

The limited partnership form has a number of advantages. Limited partners have limited liability. This enables the partnership to attract investors who are willing to invest a certain amount of money in the venture, but only if their liability is limited. Also, management of the business is centralized in the general partner. This can be desirable, since in many instances not all investors want to manage the business. Frequently there is a tax advantage to the limited partnership form. Also, if the business loses money it may be possible for the limited partners to use these losses to shelter personal income from other sources.

There are a few disadvantages. To form a limited partnership, a filing must be made with the California secretary of state. Also, securities law requirements must be obeyed. Limited partners cannot control the general partner or manage the business. This can be a problem if the general partner is doing a poor job. Certain tax benefits available to a corporation, such as preferred treatment of life insurance, health insurance, and disability insurance, cannot be obtained in a limited partnership.

FOR MORE INFORMATION

Berle, Gustav. *The Small Business Information Handbook.* New York: John Wiley and Sons, 1990. See "Partnerships."

Dedon, John. "Protecting Personal Assets (With Trusts and Limited Partnership in Case of Professional Liability Suits)." *Journal of Accountancy,* July 1991, pages 60–62.

De Young, John E. *Cases in Small Business Management.* New York: Merrill/Macmillan Publishing Company, 1991. See especially cases 2 and 3.

Longenecker, Justin G., and Carlos W. Moore. *Small Business Management,* 8th edition. Cincinnati: South-Western Publishing Co., 1991. See chapter 10.

Thomas, Stephen G. "Why Partnerships Break Up." *Inc. Magazine's Guide to Small Business Successes,* Boston, MA, 1991.

Thorne, Paul. "Taken on Trust (Partnership)." *International Management (European edition),* November 1991, page 96.

Williams, Terry. "New Fund for Minority Biz" (J. Price's Limited Partnership to Help Minority Enterprise Small Business Investment Corporations). *Black Enterprise,* September 1991, page 18.

POINTS TO PONDER

1. Assume you wanted to contact an attorney to advise you on setting up a limited partnership. What are some of the ways you might locate an appropriate attorney?
2. Has anyone you know been involved in a limited partnership? What was the business? Were all parties served well by the limited partnership form of organization?

DON'T JUST SIT THERE, DO SOMETHING!

1. Check the *Wall Street Journal* or the business section of a local newspaper. Any limited partnerships discussed? Advertised?
2. Look through recent publications such as *Entrepreneur, Inc., Nation's Business,* or the *Wall Street Journal.* Find something involving a partnership. Comment on the advantages or disadvantages of the partnership form for the business in question.

5

The Corporation: Best of Both Worlds?

Whenever they think of "doing business," many people immediately think "corporation." To a beginning entrepreneur, forming a corporation is the American dream. But although many people think that an essential requirement of starting a business is to incorporate, that just isn't true. As we have shown you in Chapters 2, 3, and 4, there are several other forms of doing business, and in many cases one of them may be the best way. The corporation, however, does have one attribute different from all the other forms of businesses: it is a legal entity separate from its individual investors. Perhaps that is why California has more than 10 times as many corporations as limited partnerships. As you will see, the reason that so many corporations are formed and exist is in large part due to this distinction.

The Separate Entity

As we have pointed out, one aspect of a corporation makes it very different from the types of business forms discussed in the earlier chapters. A corporation is considered an entity separate from the individual owners. This *separate entity concept* has a number of effects. For example, the corporation normally pays a corporate tax on its profits, and then the individual owners also pay a tax when money is distributed to them from the corporation. (This is not true of an S corporation, which will be discussed shortly.)

The separate entity idea also affects the liability of the owners of the business. A corporation has *limited liability.* Limited liability means that creditors of the corporation can only reach assets of the corporation; the assets of the owners cannot be reached. As mentioned in Chapters 2 and 3, this limitation on liability is not absolute, but when compared to sole proprietorships or partnerships, this corporate form does still have a liability advantage. In these respects the corporation is quite different from the sole proprietor and the general partnership, as described in Chapters 2 and 3. Neither the sole proprietor nor the general partnership pays an additional tax on the profits of the business, and neither the proprietor nor any general partner has limited liability. The limited partnership also does not pay a separate tax on its profits. Limited partners do have limited liability, while a general partner in a limited partnership does not. But remember, a limited partner pays a high price for this protection: he cannot manage the partnership's business.

Continuity and Marketability

A second major difference between a corporation and the other forms of business is that the corporation, as a separate legal entity, exists independently of its owners or managers and ownership interests can be transferred simply through the sale of its stock. For example, a partnership generally is automatically dissolved when one of its partners dies. A corporation, on the other hand, usually continues to exist even if its major shareholder or its president dies. Unless a corporation is organized in a manner that provides for its dissolution upon the happening of a certain event, the business will continue to exist, and have the legal authority to do business, regardless of what happens to the individuals who control it.

And because the corporation is independent of its owners and managers, the sale of a corporation usually may be effectuated much easier than the sale of a partnership or sole proprietorship. Ownership of a corporation is based on the amount of stock in the corporation that a person owns, and this stock may often be sold and transferred with ease. Of course we don't expect that shares in your beginning corporation will be as easy to sell as shares in General Motors, but they will most likely be easier to sell than a partial interest in a partnership or sole proprietorship.

If you are thinking about establishing a business that will endure beyond your lifetime, or one that you can easily sell or transfer to another, you should consider incorporating.

Identity of the Manager

In a corporation, it is clear who will manage the business. A corporation is managed by its "officers." The chief officer is the "president." Regardless of how many different owners there are, the president operates the business. Corporations also must have an officer called a "secretary," who is responsible for maintaining corporate records. In a small business, it is common for the same person to be both the president and the secretary. A corporation can also choose to have other officers, such as vice presidents, executive vice presidents, a treasurer, and assistant treasurers and assistant secretaries. An officer can be a shareholder or a member of the board of directors, but does not have to be.

Corporate officers are selected by the "board of directors." The board of directors approves significant business decisions. The board may be comprised of only one person, or the owners may choose to have a much larger board. The size of the board of directors is set forth in the articles of incorporation, which will be discussed below.

The members of the board are normally selected by the owners of the business, who are called the *shareholders.* Board members are elected by a majority vote of the shareholders, whose relative voting power stems from the number of shares owned. The initial members of the board are set forth in the articles of incorporation. A member of the board can also be a shareholder, but does not have to be.

Issuing Shares

The shareholders are issued shares in proportion to their percentage interest in the business. So, for example, if there are two owners, and owner A has a 40% interest and owner B has a 60% interest, if there are 100 shares total, owner A would receive 40 shares and owner B would receive 60 shares.

Authority of Shareholders

The shareholders do not participate in most management decisions; these are made by the board of directors and the officers. However, the shareholders do select the board of directors, and can remove the board of directors at any time, if the internal rules of the business provide for it. In such situations the shareholders do effectively control decisions of the board.

In small business it is quite common for a shareholder to be an officer and a member of the board of directors. There can be one shareholder or many shareholders.

Do not be overwhelmed by all these technicalities. It's not normally that complicated. For example, in many small businesses the same person is the president and secretary, the sole director, and the only shareholder. In this situation, the owner for all practical purposes operates the business himself, even though there is a corporation.

FORMATION OF A CORPORATION

Where to Incorporate

You may have noticed that many large corporations are "incorporated" in unlikely places, such as Delaware and Nevada. This is possible because a corporation can be "formed" anywhere; it doesn't matter where the corporation will actually do business. A corporation is "formed" by filling articles of incorporation with the appropriate governmental office in the chosen state.

A large corporation might choose Delaware due to certain complex transactions the company plans to complete. The law of Delaware might facilitate these transactions more than the law of other states. Also, the law of Delaware makes it more difficult for shareholders to sue the officers for bad decisions, so corporate management might prefer it.

It is possible for California residents to form a corporation in a state other than California, even if the business of the corporation will be conducted only in California. However, for the normal small business it is cheaper and simpler to form a California corporation. Even if the corporation is formed in another state, if the corporation does business in California the business will have to "qualify" to do business in California. In order to qualify to do business, a filing must be made with the California secretary of state, and the filing fees and franchise tax due are $1,165 (subject to change). This qualification fee is more expensive than the fee for forming a California corporation. For this reason, it is best for most small California businesses to incorporate in California. The discussion below summarizes the procedure for forming a corporation in California.

Once the decision has been made to incorporate in California, as opposed to Delaware for example, there is still another decision facing the entrepreneur. Is the business going to be engaged in a professional field, such as accounting, marriage counseling, or law? If so, California law requires that (most) professionals incorporate as a special "professional corporation." If not engaged in a profession, there are still several ways to go. The "close corporation" is similar to a limited partnership but with some of the attributes, including liability limitations, of a corporation. You must file special articles of incorporation in order to qualify for this quasicorporate status. This "close corporation" is not for the do-it-yourself incorporator. It is best to check with your attorney if you are considering this route.

Then, you still have a couple of options left, after deciding the close corporation doesn't suite your style and the professional corporation doesn't apply because you are not an acupuncturist or shorthand reporter or whatever. The remaining choices are a full-blown California corporation, if you are thinking big time and want to issue securities, or the privately held California corporation. Chances are good that the privately held corporation is the one most small business owners want. Also, if you plan to raise funds from friends and family only, you may well qualify for the limited offering stock issuance exemption. More on this below.

Creating a Corporation

To form a corporation, articles of incorporation must be filed with the California secretary of state. In order to be sure that the corporation is properly formed, it is important that you obey the rules regarding the contents of the articles, and the proper procedure for filing them.

Choosing a Name

The secretary of state frequently does not accept articles of incorporation because the name of the proposed corporation is identical or too similar to the name of an existing California corporation. In order to avoid this result, you can "reserve" the name you want. Before the secretary of state will let you reserve the name, the availability of the name will be checked. The best way to check the availability of a corporate name is by attempting to reserve the name with the secretary of state. A sample letter to reserve a name is set forth here.

Application for Reservation of Corporate Name

Secretary of State
1230 J Street, Room 100
Sacramento, CA 95814
Attn: Name Availability Unit

Dear Secretary of State:
I would like to reserve the name "California Software Inc." for 60 days. Enclosed is my check payable to your office in the amount of $10.

Dated: December 1, 1994.
Signed by:________________________
Albert Einstein

5000 Montrose Blvd.
Suite 200
Arcadia, CA 91234

You may request that up to four names be reserved in one letter. In any case, be sure to enclose $10 for each name requested. (Fees are, of course, subject to change.)

This name reservation letter should be sent by someone who plans to sign the articles of incorporation.

If the secretary of state discovers that the name requested is not available, she will tell you this, and your $10 check will be returned. If the secretary of state determines that the name is available, you will be permitted to reserve the name. This "reservation" is good for 60 days, and the cost is only $10.

As we said above, if you have enough time to go through this process with the secretary of state, the written name reservation request is the best way to clarify whether the name you desire is available. If you do not have time to reserve the name before the articles are filed, telephone the secretary of state at (916) 322-2387 to determine if the name is available. An employee of the secretary of state will tell you whether the name is available. This is only an unofficial check of name availability, and the secretary of state may later determine that the name is not available. Still, it is better than nothing. Up to two names can be checked per call.

The name of a corporation must include the word *corporation, company,* or *incorporated,* or some abbreviation of any of these words (*corp., co.,* or *inc.*). The name can include arabic numerals, as well as other symbols commonly found on a typewriter, such as " !, ″, $, %, -′, ( ), *, ?, =, @, , /, +, &, and –."

Even if the secretary of state accepts the articles of incorporation, or allows you to reserve the name, this does not mean you have the right to use the chosen name in the state of California. The secretary of state only searches names of corporations in California. Another corporation could have established an interest in the name by using the name in another state before you started your business, or a sole proprietorship or partnership could have used the name in California. A more thorough name search must be made if you want to be sure that you have the sole right to use the name in California.

Where to Send the Articles

Articles of incorporation must be signed by at least one person, and all signatures must be notarized. People who sign articles of incorporation are called *incorporators.* Articles of incorporation signed by all incorporators, plus two copies, should be sent to the secretary of state, Corporate Filing Division, 1230 J Street, Sacramento, CA 95814. The filing fee for the articles is $900; this includes a prepayment of $800 for franchise tax. The check should be made out to the California secretary of state.

Contents of the Articles

The California Corporations Code lists the information that must be included in the articles of incorporation. Sections of this law are included in Appendix A. For example, the articles must include the name of the business, the general type of business to be carried on, the total number of shares of stock, and the different classes of shares, that the corporation is authorized to issue, the street address of its office and the registered agent (agent for service of process) for the business. Directors are not required on articles of incorporation. If they are included, you must then include the names and addresses of the persons who will be initial members of the board, and each board member must sign and acknowledge the articles of incorporation. A basic form for articles of incorporation is included in Appendix B, Form 5a. This gives wording that meets current legal requirements.

The description of the articles of incorporation above sounds complicated. However, in many instances a standard form articles of incorporation is fine. For example, Figure 5-1 (page 39) is a sample articles of incorporation for California Software, Inc. Assume that Albert Einstein has already reserved the name, and that he intends to be the sole shareholder and director of the company.

Although articles of incorporation can be quite simple, depending upon your situation it may be a good idea to make some changes in the basic sample set forth above. For example, the corporation might want to eliminate "preemptive rights" of the shareholders, create different classes of stock, or elect to be a "close corporation." In order to do any of these things, the simple form of article shown in Figure 5-1 cannot be used. For this reason it is a good idea to have a lawyer review your articles of incorporation to be sure that the articles best suit your needs.

Corporations normally are formed by mail. This process can take a few weeks. It normally is a good idea to tell the secretary of state to form the business as of the date the secretary of state received the articles of incorporation. They will do this, if you ask. Otherwise, the articles can sit on someone's desk, and the corporation's existence would begin weeks later. This could be a problem if the corporation is doing business or signing contracts in the interim.

If you go to the office of the secretary of state in Sacramento, or to satellite offices in Los Angeles, San Diego, or San Francisco, incorporation can be completed while you wait. There is an added fee for this "over-the-counter" service ($15 as of our publication date, but subject to change). This expedited service can be a good idea if you plan to do business right away. This facilitated incorporation service verifies that the articles were accepted, the name is available, and the corporation is in existence when the business is begun. If business is conducted before the corporation is formed, this can create personal liability for the owners. We strongly encourage you not to do this. *Wait until the corporation is formed before you conduct business or sign agreements.*

If the articles in the form filed satisfy California law, the name is available, and the appropriate filing fee is enclosed, the secretary of state will file the articles of incorporation. The incorporator will be notified of this when the secretary returns articles of incorporation, copies duly certified. Once the articles are so certified, the corporation exists, and no owner normally is personally liable for claims against the business that arise after this date.

After the corporation is formed, you should order a book of stock certificates, a corporate seal, and a minute book. These three items are normally sold as a corporate kit. A number of companies sell these corporate kits. The kits generally cost less than $100. The stock certificates are used as the stock in the corporation. Each shareholder receives a certificate; the certificate states how many shares the certificate represents. The corporate seal is sometimes useful to authorize action on behalf of the corporation. The minute book is used to hold records of corporate actions.

Incorporating an Ongoing Business

It is possible to incorporate an ongoing business. Some or all of the assets of the business can be transferred to the corporation (after the corporation is formed) in exchange for stock in the corporation. The tax consequences of the transaction are important, so talk to an accountant or lawyer about this before you do it.

The incorporation of an ongoing business may also need to comply with the "Bulk Transfer Act." Consult your lawyer regarding whether this is required in your case. Usually, such an incorporation is "exempt."

When you are incorporating an ongoing business, be sure to notify your creditors in writing that you are doing this.

Issuing the Shares of Stock

After the articles of incorporation are filed and the secretary of state certifies the articles, the corporation is in existence. The board of directors then needs to authorize the issuance of shares to the investor-owners. There can be only one shareholder or many shareholders, depending upon what is desired. The board needs to decide both the price of each share to be issued, as well as the identity of the shareholders. The price of each share should be determined after it is decided how much capital the corporation needs, and each investor decides how much money he wants to invest. The price of the shares obviously depends upon how many shares are to be issued. For example, if it is decided that capitalization of $1,000 is adequate for the business, if there are going to be two equal owners, each will contribute $500. If only one share is to be issued to each shareholder, the stock will cost $500 per share. If 500 shares are to be issued to each shareholder, each share would cost $1. Stock should be sold for at least the "par value" of the shares, if the shares have a par value.

In many small businesses, the identities of the shareholders normally are known before the articles are filed. The investors normally know one another, decide to form the business, and choose the corporate form. The investors frequently are also directors. After the issuance of the shares is authorized by the board, shares can be issued to each shareholder, when the shareholder presents a check to the corporation for the agreed value of the shares to be purchased. In most instances stock is issued in exchange for a check, but stock can also be issued in exchange for property or past services. Stock cannot be issued for a promissory note or a promise of future services. Shares are "issued" by a corporate officer filling out a share certificate for each shareholder, signing the certificate, affixing the corporate seal, and noting on the certificate how many shares of the company the shareholder purchased. After this is done, the corporation will then have some initial capital, and shareholders will exist.

How much should shareholders contribute? In some circumstances shareholders can lose their limited liability if it is determined that the corporation was grossly undercapitalized by the founders, in light of the probable needs of the business. So, before the amount to be contributed is determined, the owners must prepare a projected budget and estimate how much initial capital the business will need, and how much insurance the company will maintain. When deciding upon the initial capitalization of the company, it is a good idea to discuss this with an accountant. A corporation should have adequate capital and insurance to satisfy foreseeable claims.

Shares of a corporation are "securities." The sale of securities in a corporation therefore must satisfy state and federal rules governing the issuance of securities. These rules are discussed on pages 38–39.

The First Board Meeting

After the corporation is formed, it is a good idea to have the board of directors adopt resolutions so that the corporation will be ready to function. For example, it was mentioned above that the board should authorize the issuance of shares, so the company will then have stockholders. A number of other things should be done by the board as soon as possible after the corporation is formed.

These resolutions can be adopted by the board at a meeting of the board of directors, or the board can adopt these resolutions by written consent, if all directors approve. Many small businesses find board meetings a stupid legal formality, and adopt simple resolutions by written consent. This is particularly useful if there is only one director.

At the first meeting of the directors the board should elect the officers of the corporation. Each California corporation should have a president, a secretary, and a treasurer. One person can hold more than one of these offices; for that matter, one person can hold all the offices. It is a good idea to have more than one officer, though, so that if one person is out of town there is someone who can act for the corporation.

The board of directors normally does a number of things in its first meeting, in addition to authorizing the issuance of shares and the election of officers. Significant agreements to be signed by the corporation should be approved at this first meeting of the board. For example, if the business is signing a lease, the board should approve the terms of the lease, and authorize an officer to signing the lease on behalf of the corporation. Any other significant agreements, such as employment agreements, shareholder agreements, or purchase contracts should be approved at this time, if the corporation is to be a party. The board also normally authorizes an officer to open a bank account at a certain bank, and the authorized signatories are specified. The form of the corporate stock certificate and the corporate seal are approved. An example of resolutions adopted by directors at a first meeting is included in Appendix B, Form 7.

At the first meeting of the board, the board approves the *bylaws* for the company. The bylaws essentially are the rules that will govern the operation of the business. For example, the different officers of the corporation are specified, such as the president, vice president, secretary and treasurer, and the functions and authority of the various officers are set forth. Also, the procedure for the election of directors is established. The frequency of shareholder and board meetings is also established, as is the manner in which notice of additional meetings is to be sent. An example of corporate bylaws is included in Appendix B, Form 6.

A number of other matters might be considered at the first meeting of the board. For example, the business sometimes selects a fiscal year. Also, it is a good idea to formally choose the address of the principal executive office or location of the business. The S corporation election and Section 1244 stock will be discussed later. If either of these elections are desired, the board must approve the necessary filings. Also, if the corporation is going to conduct business under a name other than its corporate name, a fictitious name certificate must be filed with the secretary of state, and the board must approve this.

After the articles are filed, shares are issued, and the first meeting of the board of directors has occurred, the corporation is prepared to begin doing business. The corporate entity exists, and the corporation has shareholders, officers, and a board of directors. Before the corporation commences business, however, the corporation should also comply with all federal, state, and local rules regarding tax withholding, social security, worker's compensation, and other matters. These matters are discussed in Chapter 7.

The Shareholders' Agreement

Owners of a new corporate business should consider whether they need a shareholders' agreement. When people agree to start a business together, they normally do it because of a special relationship between the owners. If the business is successful and continues for a significant period, it is likely that one owner will die or for some other reason want to sell his shares. This can create a number of problems, if a procedure for transferring shares has not been arranged. First, the other owners may not want a stranger to be an owner. The stranger might not have the particular talent that attracted them to the person who is selling the shares. Also, there probably will not be much of a market for the shares of a small business. It would violate the securities law to advertise that the shares were available, so not many people will know the shares are for sale. In addition, few people might want to get involved in the small business.

So, most people try to work out an arrangement so that the other shareholders, or the company, will buy back the shares from a shareholder if a shareholder dies or for some other reason wants to sell. If this arrangement is chosen, some procedure must be set forth for valuing the shares. These various valuation methods were discussed in Chapter 3 in connection with general partnerships. The agreement should address whether the shares will be purchased pursuant to some specific valuation procedure, or whether the company (or the shareholders) need only to match any offer to buy the shares made by a third party. The agreement should also specify whether each shareholder must buy his pro rata share of the seller's shares, or whether each other shareholder merely has the right to buy them, but doesn't have to.

If shareholders choose to have an agreement regarding these matters, the shareholders need to consider what situations will create the buyout right for the other shareholders. For example, what if one shareholder divorces, and the divorce court grants the spouse some shares? What happens if a shareholder goes bankrupt?

If there are two equal shareholders, it is a good idea to try to plan for what would happen if the shareholders disagree regarding fundamental business matters. If there is a "deadlock" in such a situation, the business can become paralyzed.

A copy of one shareholders' agreement is in Appendix B, Form 8.

The Bottom Line

Formation of a corporation is not very difficult. For many small businesses simple forms can be used, and it normally is not complicated. Still, some businesses might have special needs not addressed by the simple forms. If you do plan to incorporate, it is a good idea at least to have a lawyer review your incorporation papers.

SELLING SECURITIES

If you are receiving an interest in a limited partnership or a corporation, you are receiving a "security." Sales of securities are regulated by both federal and California law. Many people have been defrauded in connection with sales of securities, and laws have been enacted to try to prevent this.

As a general rule, securities can only be sold, in California, after a "registration statement" has been filed with the U.S. Securities & Exchange Commission (the SEC), and after the sale has been "qualified" by the California Commissioner of Corporations. This process is very expensive, however. Detailed disclosure documents must be prepared about the company, and many hours must be spent dealing with the state and federal securities offices. Most small businesses want to be able to issue securities without spending this much time and money. Federal law and California law do permit this, but only if the exemptions set forth below are satisfied.

Federal Law

Under federal law, securities can be sold without a registration statement if the sale is one "not involving any public offering." Unfortunately, it is not clear what constitutes such an exempt private offering. If one person or a husband and wife are forming a corporation, and there will be no other stockholders, this clearly would be an exempt offering. Such an offering requires no filing with any government office. If shares will be sold to more than one person, whether the sale would constitute an exempt private offering would depend upon a number of things, such as the wealth and business experience of the investors, and whether the investors had a prior business or social relationship before the securities were sold. If you are planning to sell shares in your corporation to others, it is not clear whether the sale would be an exempt private offering; it therefore would be best to rely upon a more definite exemption to be sure that the sale complies with the law. One useful exemption for small businesses is promulgated by "Regulation D." Under Regulation D, a small business can raise funds if certain rules are satisfied. No advertising or public solicitation can be made regarding the stock, resale of the shares must be restricted (this will be discussed), and a form must be filed with the SEC (see Appendix B, Form 22). If Regulation D is complied with, the company does not have to file a registration statement with the SEC.

ARTICLES OF INCORPORATION OF CALIFORNIA SOFTWARE, INC.

Article One:

The name of the corporation is California Software, Inc.

Article Two:

The purpose of this corporation is to engage in any lawful act or activity for which a corporation may be organized under the General Corporation Law of California other than the banking business, the trust company business, or the practice of a profession permitted to be incorporated by the California Corporations Code.

Article Three:

The name and street address in the State of California of this corporation initial agent for service of process is:

Name: ______________________________

Street Address: ______________________________

City ______________________________, California

Zip: ______________

Article Four:

This corporation is authorized to issue only one class of shares of stock; and the total number of shares which this corporation is authorized to issue is ___________.

Figure 5-1. An example of articles of incorporation.

California Law

Although Regulation D applies to the federal level, California has a similar policy. California allows certain corporations to sell securities without facing the voluminous paperwork required in a larger stock issue. In many cases, a small business can issue stock without having to deal with the federal SEC and without requiring your stock issue be prequalified by California's Commissioner of Corporations.

The stock sale would be exempt if it meets certain complicated federal and state laws, which would be impossible to thoroughly cover in this small book. However, here are some of the broad issues on which the California exemption is based.

To be exempt, the sale would have to:

1. Result in 35 or fewer noninsider (for example, nonfamily) shareholders. Ideally, all live in California, or the exemption may be on shaky ground.
2. Involve no advertising at all. Even an indirect public relations campaign, if geared to raising interest and thus facilitating the sale of stock, could invalidate the exemption.
3. Involve sale of stock only to owners, as opposed to speculators. Put another way, the stock is not for "resale." (The law is more complex than this but this conveys the idea.)
4. Sell only to "sophisticated" shareholders, or at least shareholders relying on professional investment advice, when going outside the "close family-friends-business associates" circle.

These rules cover pages and pages in California's Corporation Code and Administrative Code. But if this quick introduction makes it look like you may qualify for the exemption, check into it. "Exempt" is the way to go if you qualify. You may, however, read the entire corporation code and still not be certain. For example, even though your prospective investors are university educated, and have substantial assets, will they qualify as "sophisticated investors?" Unfortunately, case law gives a variety of answers. This may be one of those times when it would be a good idea to consult that attorney you chose after reading Chapter 1 of this book!

Resales of Shares

Shares sold pursuant to a private offering exemption are "restricted" shares. The shares cannot be resold to another, unless that sale complies with the securities laws.

OPERATING THE CORPORATION

In many respects a corporate business is operated just like any other business. If you are the sole owner and the president of the corporation, you will make all the decisions regarding the business. If there are other owners, they will want to be consulted regarding important decisions, as would any owner. However, if you operate your business as a corporation you need to satisfy a few additional requirements.

Corporate Funds

You should keep corporate funds separate from your individual funds. This is very important. If you mix your funds with the funds of the business, it is quite likely that a court later would hold all your assets liable to creditors of the business.

Signing Contracts

Similarly, contracts and promissory notes regarding the business should be signed in the name of the corporation, not in your name alone. This is vital if you want limited liability.

Example 1. John Smith is making a contract for himself as an individual. The contract says that he is a party to the contract, and the signature line looks like this:

____

John Smith

John Smith is a party to this contract, and is personally responsible for performing it.

Example 2. John Smith is president of California Software, Inc. John is making a contract for the company. The contract says that California Software is the party responsible for satisfying the terms of the contract, and the signature line on the contract looks like this:

California Software, Inc.

____

BY John Smith, as its president

California Software is a party to this contract; John Smith is not. If there is a breach of this contract, the other party can sue California Software and attach its assets, but not John Smith's assets.

If the procedure set forth above is not followed, it is quite possible that John Smith could find himself personally liable for the debts of the corporation.

Example 3. John Smith is president of California Software, Inc., and is making a contract for the company. Assume the signature line of the contract looks like this:

California Software, Inc.

____

John Smith

John Smith is probably personally liable if he signs this contract. When signing a contract or a promissory note on behalf of a business, it is very important to make it clear in what capacity you are signing.

If you are signing something on behalf of a corporation, make sure the signature line states that you are signing for that entity, states your relationship to the entity (e.g., its president), and be sure the entity is correctly referred to. If you don't do this, there is a good chance you will be personally liable for the contract or note you have signed. Since most business people do not want this result, they should read contracts very carefully before they sign.

For example, a recent case involved a situation where a corporation (E.D. Jones Co.) was doing business under another name (Industrial Telephone Systems). The president of the company signed a contract under its trade name, Industrial Telephone Systems. The contract did not state that Industrial Telephone Systems was the fictitious business name of E.D. Jones Co. The other party to the contract was able to sue the president of the company *individually* because the correct identity of the corporation was not disclosed when the contract was made.

People signing things on behalf of a business should have the authority to do what they are doing. It is common for the board of directors to approve important transactions involving the business. The board then authorizes a certain officer to do what was approved, such as sign an agreement or a promissory note. This clarifies that the person has the authority to bind the business.

Corporate Formalities

Even in a small business, it is a good idea each year for the shareholders to elect directors, and for the directors to elect officers. This makes sure that there are people authorized to act on behalf of the corporation. Also, the directors should approve important transactions involving the corporation.

These corporate formalities clarify whether the company has properly approved a certain transaction, and keeps a current list of officers able to act on behalf of the company.

These "corporate formalities" also serve another purpose. If the limited liability of the shareholders is ever an issue, many courts consider it important whether the corporation complied with these procedures. In small businesses, particularly when the same person is the president and the sole director and sole shareholder, it does seem silly to have to go through with the formality of director approval of important decisions. Still, it can be important.

California Taxes

When operating your corporate business, you should comply with the various licensing requirements and pay all taxes and fees due for the business and the employees. Some of these are discussed in Chapter 7. It is particularly important that all California franchise taxes are paid. If you do not do this, the secretary of state can suspend the corporation, and the officers and directors of the corporation can be personally liable for debts created after that happens.

The Bottom Line

You can operate a corporate business much like any other business. Still, there are a few things to remember. Keep your personal funds separate from corporate funds. Try to keep good records of directors' meetings and shareholder meetings. Also, when signing contracts on behalf of the business, be sure that it is clear that you are signing these contracts on behalf of a corporation, and that the name of the corporation is correctly set forth.

Corporations and Federal Taxes

In the 1970s, a business operated as a corporation enjoyed a number of tax advantages, as compared to the tax treatment of partnerships and sole proprietorships. One big advantage was that a corporation could deduct from its income much larger pension contributions for employees than could sole proprietors or partnerships. A number of these advantages have been eliminated by recent amendments to the Internal Revenue Code. For example, rules regarding pension contributions are now essentially the same for all business forms.

Corporations do still offer some tax advantages. The main advantage is the fringe benefits that a corporation can provide for employees. The benefits are valuable, but are not taxed as income to the employee. Even though the benefits are not taxed as income to the employee, the corporation is able to deduct the expense of the benefit from its income.

For example, by the date of publication of this book, an individual can only deduct medical expenses to the extent that the expenses exceed 7.5% of the individual's adjusted gross income. Most people do not deduct any medical expenses, since their medical expenses never reach that portion of their income. In contrast, a corporation is permitted to adopt a medical and dental expense reimbursement plan for its employees and their dependents. All amounts paid to the employees under the plan as expense reimbursements are deductible by the corporation (if the corporation chooses to purchase health insurance, then the price of the premiums is deductible), and the employee does not have to pay tax on the amount received.

Similar benefits are available for disability insurance and life insurance. The corporation can purchase specified amounts of life insurance for an employee, and the expense is deductible by the corporation but is not counted as income to the employee. Also, disability insurance can be purchased for an employee, and the cost of this insurance is deductible by the corporation and is not income to the employee.

In many small businesses there is only one employee of the business: the owner. In this instance, if the owner establishes insurance protection for himself through the company, there will be significant tax savings.

The discussion above mentions that various expenditures are "deductible" by the corporation. This is a significant concern for corporations, since normal "C" corporations pay a tax on income. This is the *corporate tax.* Shareholders pay additional personal income tax when funds are distributed to them as a dividend, and dividends are not deductible by the corporation. Because of this system, it is said that corporations are subject to a "double tax." First corporate income tax is paid by the corporation, and then personal income tax is paid by the shareholders on dividends.

In light of this double tax, why would anyone ever choose to do business as a corporation? The tax penalty, or advantage, depends upon the particular business. For example, if the tax rate for the first $50,000 of corporate income is 15%, which it has been in typical recent years, this is significantly lower than the marginal personal tax rate of most Americans. If the business plans to retain its profits (for example, to buy inventory or equipment) and not pay out profits to its shareholders, it might be a good idea for tax purposes to incorporate. If the business does plan to pay its profits to its shareholders, however, there may be a tax penalty due to the corporate status.

Many small businesses pay their owners' salaries for working for the business. "Salaries" are deductible; "dividends" are not. The IRS frequently wages war with small business owners over whether certain payments really were salary payments or dividends. In any event, after the payment of salaries, many small businesses have little taxable income, so the corporate double tax is not too important. As a practical matter, some small firms use a flexible approach when setting the salaries of principals. When times are tight, salaries shrink or disappear. When times are good, salaries of principals may be increased. If things are planned carefully, the increase in salaries may reduce corporate profits, thus corporate tax. Of course, then the principals pay an increased individual tax.

If you want to operate your business as a corporation but are concerned about the double tax, there is an alternative that many find useful. An "S" corporation is a corporation that is taxed like a partnership. In order to be an S corporation, the corporation must have 35 or fewer shareholders. Also, there must be only one class of stock, all shareholders must be individuals, and no shareholder may be a nonresident alien. In order to be an S corporation, the corporation and all shareholders must sign an election form and file it with the IRS. This election is then valid until the corporation revokes it.

S corporations are taxed as a partnership, so there is no double tax. Shareholders merely report as income their share of the income of the company S corporations do have limited liability, but they lose many of the tax benefits of a corporation that were discussed above. For example, an S corporation cannot deduct the cost of insurance for employees, if the employees are shareholders.

The tax effects of incorporating and the S corporation election can be quite significant. It is a good idea to discuss these tax consequences with your accountant or your lawyer before you incorporate or make an S corporation election.

If a regular "C" corporation has a loss for any tax year, the company can carry this loss over to the next year to offset it against any future income, but the shareholders cannot offset the loss against personal income they have from other sources. Before the 1986 tax reform law, shareholders of an S corporation could offset losses of the business against income from most other sources. After the 1986 law, if the loss is a "passive" loss under the new rules, the shareholder can only use the loss to offset other "passive" income.

This is another area to watch. A number of firms have decided that the subchapter S corporation no longer holds the advantages it once did. And, new changes are being considered. Stay tuned!

The Bottom Line

Corporations still offer certain tax advantages. An owner of a small business can have the business provide him with various fringe benefits, such as family medical and dental insurance, disability insurance, and life insurance. The cost of this insurance is not taxable to the employee-owner, and the business can deduct the cost.

Also, due to the separate tax rate for corporate income, a business might pay less tax as a corporation than the personal tax the owner would have to pay if the business was a partnership or proprietorship. If the corporation plans to accumulate profits in the business, and the owner's marginal tax rate is high, a corporation can offer tax savings. In contrast, if the corporation plans to distribute its profits to its owners, there may be a tax disadvantage to the normal "C" corporation.

Miscellaneous Issues

If a corporation is unsuccessful, and the business goes bankrupt, under normal circumstances the investment loss by the shareholders is considered a *capital loss.* There is a limit upon the amount of capital losses that can be used to shelter income from other sources; only $3,000 per year can be used. If the corporation issues shares under Internal Revenue Code Sec. 1244, a shareholder can deduct all losses up to $50,000 ($100,000 for a husband and wife filing jointly) if the business is unsuccessful. In order to qualify for 1244 treatment, the capitalization for the corporation must be less than $1 million, and the corporation must earn less than 50% of its revenue from passive sources like royalties, dividends, interest, and rents. When issuing corporate shares, discuss with your lawyer or accountant whether the 1244 election would be desirable.

If you want a California corporation to do business in another state, the corporation should "qualify" to do business there before any business is conducted in the state. Each state's qualification procedure is different, but all generally want the corporation to agree to be sued in the state regarding disputes arising from business transacted in the state, and a certain filing fee will be due. Contact the secretary of state or department of corporations of each state in which you want to do business, and see what needs to be done to qualify.

ADVANTAGES AND DISADVANTAGES OF FORMING A CORPORATION

The corporation offers some advantages for the owner of a small business. The owners enjoy limited liability; they are not personally liable for claims against the business. Also, management power is easily centralized in the president. This is desirable if one owner wants to run the business, and the others do not. Ownership interests are relatively easy to transfer, and the business clearly continues even if one owner retires or dies.

The "C" corporation can provide tax savings. Owner-employees can receive tax advantaged fringe benefits. Also, money can be accumulated in the corporation at lower corporate tax rates, compared to the personal marginal tax rate of most Americans.

The corporation has some disadvantages, however. It is somewhat expensive to form, since expenditures for both lawyer's fees and filing fees will be required. Also, it is cumbersome to operate, since shareholders' meetings and board meetings are necessary.

CORPORATION FORMATION CHECKLIST

These are the basic documents you need to prepare to form a California corporation:

- Name reservation letter
- Articles of incorporation
- Minutes of board of directors meeting
- Bylaws

WHERE DO I GO FROM HERE?

Richard Howell could not sleep. He was unsure what strategic course of action he should take. He was just about ready to dissolve his law firm and become an independent tax consultant. This seemed almost inevitable given recent events: Within the last four months, his firm of six had become a one-person operation. Howell was unsure what caused this rapid turnover, but was beginning to accept that his management style might be at the core. Even if he chose to continue his practice, he was uncertain that he could retain any staff. Howell faced a sleepless weekend before deciding a course of action by Monday morning.

The Issues

Richard Howell has only the weekend to make his decision on the future of the law firm. With no staff and inconsistent service in the past, the firm is close to losing many clients. His goal is to reduce staff turnover, improve service to retain existing clients, and gain/attract new clients for the firm's economic survival. Howell certainly cannot handle all of the current clients adequately on his own. He does not have the up-to-date training he needs in legal procedures—for example, he has not drafted a trust or will or done any corporation documentation in more than five years. He is also computer illiterate, despite repeated attempts to teach him how to run the client database or how to locate documents and boilerplates on disk. He has no idea how to retrieve data or work on any client documents.

Strategic Options

Continue as an Independent Law Firm

Howell could conceivably maintain the practice as a sole proprietorship, incorporated as a California professional corporation. This has the advantage of requiring no action on his part. However, it seems likely that this choice would solve none of the very serious existing problems.

Merge with Another Law Firm

Another alternative is for Howell to merge his operations with those of Howard Perry's. This would be a partnership arrangement. His role would be as head of the tax-law department. Howell is well acquainted with the firm. By merging, Mr. Howell will have immediate access to trained legal staff, who will take over billing and other computer operations. On the down side, Howell will only be one in a firm of partners, losing his independence. He also runs the risk of this relationship eventually failing, given his past record. If the relationship ends, he will incur huge restarting costs if he decides to continue his practice, having given up his lease, sold off his furniture, etc.

Dissolve the Firm; Become a Tax Consultant

Howell's other choice is to dissolve his firm and become an independent tax consultant. This is the form of law he enjoys—being creative in tax-shelter creation. As mentioned, he is out of practice in several other areas of law. Eighty percent of his existing clients do not have tax problems, but own corporations or need updates on wills or trusts. This choice would leave him with almost no existing client base from which to build, and would cause animosity between himself and his clients, who would then have to seek legal advice elsewhere. But, making this choice would solve immediate and future staff problems, as he would not need to work with subordinates.

The Decision

It is now 2 a.m. on Saturday. Howell has less than 48 hours in which to make the most crucial decision of his career. He has no trained staff, and he needs to send out the bills for June this next week, besides completing the firm's regular legal work. He knows he cannot cope by himself, but he feels he might jeopardize his negotiating strength by admitting to Howard Perry his dire situation. Yet he is determined to practice law. He will not fall asleep easily, if at all, until he reaches a decision.

—Thanks to Laurie A. Meamber
Written while pursuing graduate study at University of California-Riverside.

- Stock certificates
- Bank account card for company account

You should also consider whether these documents would be advisable:

- Shareholders' agreement
- S Corporation election
- Section 1244 plan election for stock issuance
- Securities filings with the SEC and the California Securities Board

There are several companies that sell what are called "corporate kits," which contain most of the documents necessary to complete the formation of your corporation once the articles of incorporation have been filed. Contact the California State Chamber of Commerce for the current price of their "Business Start-up Kit for California Corporations." The Chamber is located at P.O. Box 1736, Sacramento, CA 95812, (800) 331-8877.

FOR MORE INFORMATION

Branton, Tom. *How to Incorporate Your Texas Business,* 2nd Edition. Houston, TX: Gulf Publishing Company, 1990. About 90% of this great little book would apply anywhere: should you incorporate, purchasing or selling a corporation, personal legal matters, etc. Besides, when you're done you could send it to a friend in Texas to use the other 10%!

California State Chamber of Commerce. *Business Start-up Kit for California Corporations.* Sacramento: Chamber of Commerce, 1993. This entire volume is well worth the price. Numerous tear-out forms are included.

Mancuso, Anthony. *The California Professional Corporation,* 4th Edition. Berkeley, CA: The Nolo Press, 1989.

Mancuso, Anthony. *How to Form Your Own California Corporation, 7th Edition.* Berkeley, CA: Nolo Press, 1988.

Pipkin, Ashmead P. "Shareholder Liability." *Wall Street Journal,* July 29, 1992, page A15.

Royalty, Kent, Robert Calhoun, Radie Bunn, and Wayne Wells. "The Impact of Tax Reform on the Choice of Small Business Legal Form." *Journal of Small Business Management,* January 1988, pages 9–17.

POINTS TO PONDER

1. Would an optometrist want to form a corporation? How would this incorporation differ from the incorporation of a transmission business?
2. Since sample forms and model letters are readily available in books similar to this one, why would a small firm consult an attorney to take care of the incorporation process?

DON'T JUST SIT THERE, DO SOMETHING!

1. Call the offices of three attorneys, chosen based on their ads in the Yellow Pages. Describe very briefly a business venture in which you might one day be involved. See if you can get an estimated price for the handling of the paperwork of incorporation. Write a one-page summary of your findings.
2. Do a survey of five of your friends (choose those who are not already involved in a corporation). Ask them what they think about the steps involved in setting up a corporation, and their estimates of costs involved. Write one page summarizing the accuracy or inaccuracy of their views.

6

Hiring and Firing: At-Will Employment Is California Law, But . . .

When you start a business, one of the first things you have to do is hire employees. When hiring people, you need to comply with the various rules applicable to withholding for taxes, social security, workers' compensation, and so on, as we discuss in Chapter 7. But you also need to be aware of other kinds of legal problems that relate to hiring employees. In particular you should know that your personal beliefs about people of a different age, sex, race, or religion are not a legal basis upon which to decide whom you will employ.

Federal law says that if you have 15 or more employees, you may not discriminate based on color, sex, religion, national origin, or age, with respect to:

- Job advertisements
- Recruitment
- Testing
- Hiring and firing
- Compensation, assignment, or classification
- Transfer, promotion, layoff, or recall
- Use of company facilities
- Training and apprenticeship programs
- Fringe benefits such as life and health insurance
- Pay, retirement plans, and disability leave
- Causing or attempting to cause a union to discriminate
- Other terms and conditions of employment

California laws are almost identical, except employers may not discriminate if they have five or more employees. Investigations and dispute resolutions are handled by your local Department of Fair Employment and Housing (DFEH), rather than the EEOC.

Age Discrimination

Consider this:

> Susan and Cindy have formed a catering business. Wilma, a woman 57 years old, interviewed for a job with the company. Susan and Cindy decided that they wanted to hire a younger person who would tire less easily, and they did hire a younger person for the job. Wilma probably can sue the business for age discrimination in hiring. In addition to the wages Wilma lost by not getting the job, Wilma could also possibly recover damages for pain and suffering.

Under federal law, it is illegal to discriminate in employment on the basis of age against anyone over the age of 39, unless the employer can establish that, for the particular task involved, age is a "bona fide occupational qualification." This exception is very hard to establish.

So, as a practical matter, what does this mean you should do when interviewing prospective employees? First, *never* advertise that you are looking for a "young" person for a job. Every qualified applicant should be considered for a job. But even if you follow this policy, you can still be sued for unlawful discrimination. The best way to protect yourself from such suits is to keep a record of all interviews. Note on the interview record the reason the interviewee was not hired. For example, was the interviewee late, poorly dressed, or did the references provided state something negative? If the employment decision is ever challenged, it is quite useful to have a record of the thoughts of the interviewer. A good idea is to have printed interview forms to ensure that you question, and evaluate, each applicant the same way.

Racial Discrimination

Race discrimination in hiring is illegal, even if it seems "logical" to you. Consider the following:

> Bob and Jim start a business selling golf equipment to golf pro shops. They need to hire salespeople to contact golf pro shops and talk to the golf professionals at various golf courses. Bob and Jim perceive that a white person could relate better to the golf pros than a black person could, so Bob and Jim do not hire an otherwise qualified black applicant. The applicant could sue the business for racial discrimination.

Civil rights laws prohibit racial discrimination in hiring. It does not matter whether in fact you, as an employer, are correct in your belief that a person of one race might incur more problems trying to deal with the customers of the business in question. Hiring must be done on the basis of ability to perform the job. Your perception that a white, black, or brown may do better, or worse, is not a sufficient basis upon which to discriminate. Make a decision based on race and you invite a lawsuit. Again, keeping good records of each interview, and asking the same questions of each applicant, can help prevent lawsuits.

Sex Discrimination

Like age and race discrimination, sex discrimination in employment is prohibited.

> Diego and Juan have formed a business to sell tires to gas stations. Diego and Juan believe that a man would be better able to do this job than a woman. If Diego and Juan did not hire a qualified woman based on this belief, the woman could sue the business for sex discrimination.

It is illegal to discriminate on the basis of sex in hiring decisions, unless sex is a "bona fide occupational qualification." This exception is construed quite narrowly by the courts. Your personal belief that a man could do the job better is probably not sufficient justification for discriminating against a woman.

Sexual Harassment

Another sensitive issue that courts have constituted as illegal discrimination is sexual harassment. Both males and females can be victims of sexual harassment of, although most cases involve the harassment of women. Sexual harassment is not limited to obvious lewd comments and behavior. Consider the following:

> Amy works as an accountant at Barker and Associates. Doug, a co-worker of Amy's, comments that he wishes her new dress was a few inches shorter. Amy files a sexual harassment complaint.

Does an incident such as this constitute sexual harassment? If Doug's comments made Amy feel uncomfortable or affected her work performance, chances are the answer would be yes. Sexual harassment involves unwelcome sexual advances, requests for sexual favors, and other conduct of a sexual nature that affects a person's employment or work performance. To avoid sexual harassment from occurring in the workplace, employers should take a firm stance by clearly defining sexual harassment, producing a list of possible penalties for violators, and ensuring victims that they will be protected if they make harassment charges.

There's another requirement also. Since January 1, 1993, every California employer, regardless of size, must give every new person hired and every current employee information about harassment in the work place. And, you must display an informational poster. California is serious about this. Don't allow sexual harassment to exist in your company.

Hiring the Disabled

The purposes of the Americans with Disabilities Act (ADA) are as noble as any found in any law: Those with disabilities must be allowed to compete for any job which they are able to accomplish. The problem, if there is any, is that it may take years of court cases to define exactly what employers can and cannot do. One jokester in the *Wall Street Journal* even called the law, which took effect in 1992, "the lawyer's bill of full employment." But in spite of the complaints of "more and more government regulation," this law makes sense to a lot of people, including employers. The law sets different standards for different sized businesses, but all businesses with 25 or more employees are subject to fines for violation of the law.

What does this mean to you? Whether or not you have more than 25 employees, you might as well get with the program. Make sure you do not discriminate against any job seeker because of a disability, unless that disability prevents the applicant from being able to perform necessary job tasks. Even if it looks like the applicant may not be qualified, check into the possibility of modifying the worksite, or the job tasks themselves. If the tasks are necessary, and the applicant cannot be reasonably accommodated, only then should you give up the attempt to provide a job.

In addition to physical disabilities such as paraplegia, the law also covers a host of other conditions, from asthma to emotional disturbances to retardation to drug addiction. And, while some businesses worry about the law, others are doing their best to adopt the law in letter and in spirit. After all, the disabled have a lot to offer, and it just makes sense to put talent to work. Or, at least to give it your best shot.

Other Prohibited Discrimination

In addition to the rules outlined above, federal law prohibits discriminating in hiring on the basis of religion, national origin, or handicap. Remember that "handicap" can be broadly construed. For example, there is now a dispute over whether AIDS victims are "handicapped," and it appears that the courts will say they are. This means that if that is your only reason for not hiring a qualified applicant, you may be illegally discriminating.

The Bottom Line

When you interview applicants for a job, be sure you interview all qualified people who apply. When you decide not to hire someone, keep a record of the reason or reasons you didn't hire that person. Be particularly careful about keeping such a record when the person rejected is a racial minority, a woman, a person over the age of 39, or a handicapped person. You do not have to hire such a person; however, the employment decision must be based upon some rational factor. If you need more information about employment discrimination, call 1-800-669-3362. In addition, the California Department of Fair Employment and Housing, with offices in many California cities, has numerous free pamphlets. Drop by or give them a call.

Immigration Law

As most of you already know, Congress recently enacted immigration laws, making it illegal to hire an alien knowing that the alien is not a lawful permanent resident of this country or does not have legal permission to be employed. It is a criminal offense to do this. The Act does not require, however, that you verify employees who were working for you prior to the effective date of the Act. In other words, the new law basically says that **if you hire someone, you must verify that they are working here legally.**

To comply with the Act you should examine certain documents to determine if the person is working here legally and is who they say they are. You are not required to establish the validity of the document, but you must see if it reasonably appears to be valid. Here is a list of documents that you can use:

1. The individual's United States passport.
2. The individual's Certificate of United States Citizenship.
3. The individual's Certificate of Naturalization.
4. The individual's unexpired foreign passport if such passport has a notation of an unexpired endorsement from the INS authorizing the individual's employment in the United States.
5. The individual's resident alien card or "green card," or any other form of alien registration card if it contains a photograph of the individual or any other personal identifying information relating to that individual and is evidence of authorization of employment in the United States.

Any of these documents will be sufficient to establish the person's identity and employment authorization, as required by the law. You may also use separate documents to establish each of these prerequisites. For example, you may verify identity with either of the following:

1. The individual's driver's license or similar document issued for purposes of identification by a state, provided that it contains a photograph of the individual or such other personal identifying information relating to that individual as required by regulations.
2. When the individual is under 16 years of age or is in a state that does not provide an identification card or document other than a driver's license, production of documentation of personal identity as deemed acceptable for identification purposes under INS regulations.

As this book went to press, the U.S. Department of Justice, Immigration and Naturalization Service published *The Employment Eligibility Verification Form* and *Handbook for Employers.* These documents may be found in Appendix C.

Authorization to work may be proven by:

1. The individual's social security card, provided such card does not state on its face that it does not authorize employment in the United States, or contain similar language.
2. The individual's certificate of birth in the United States, or an authorized certificate establishing U.S. nationality at birth.
3. Any other documentation evidencing employment authorization in the United States granted by the INS.

The new immigration laws can be very tough on employers. Before you hire someone, take steps to ensure that they are who they say they are and that they have the legal right to work here. You also should contact your attorney, the Department of Labor, or the Department of Immigration to find out exactly what the law requires.

The Bottom Line

The new immigration law places a burden on employers to make sure that their workers are here legally. If you violate this law you may suffer stiff criminal penalties. Make sure that you understand this law before you hire anyone. For more information about this law, contact the local office of the Immigration and Naturalization Service.

Employment Contracts

In most instances, employees are "hired" by the boss simply telling the applicant he or she has a job. No written contract is signed, and no definite term of employment is specified. This creates what a lawyer would call "at-will" employment. So, the employer or the employee can terminate the relationship at any time. As long as the employee works, however, the employer is bound by this oral contract to pay the employee at the agreed-upon salary rate.

Even though you do not have any sort of a formal contract, you and your employee are bound to perform in a certain manner. Suppose you hire a new employee to work at your store. Nothing much is said except that the salary will be $5.00 per hour, and she should start next Monday. Do you have a contract? Yes, you do. The terms of your contract are everything said, basically just $5.00 an hour, start on Monday, and everything that one would normally imply in such an agreement. For example, your employee would be expected to work an eight-hour day, with a reasonable time for lunch and a break similar to every other employee. If you have given your employees vacation pay in the past, your agreement with the new employee would probably incorporate similar items. In other words, the law implies an agreement based on what a reasonable employee and employer would expect in similar circumstance. If you acted differently, for example, by refusing to give the new employee vacation time as you did the others, you could be found to have breached your employment contract. In theory, because this is still an employment-at-will contract you have the right to fire the employee at any time. (Turn to pages 49–50 for more on this point.)

But at-will employment with no formal contract is not always a good idea for an employer. For example, you may be training the employee at significant expense. Do you care whether the employee quits immediately after training, and takes the knowledge to a competitor? If you do, you need to have an employment agreement that states what happens if the employee does this. We have included some model agreements in Appendix B, Forms 9a and b, but you probably should have your lawyer help you with this contract because each one is slightly different.

You also should know that if you want to hire an employee for a term of more than one year, the contract with the employee must be in writing. Other kinds of contracts don't have to be in writing. However, a written agreement is usually a good idea, so that at a later date parties can refer back to what was agreed to. For example, it might be a good idea to set forth what kind of fringe benefits or expense account will be provided the employee. Also, when will the employee be considered for a raise or promotion? Will the employer pay any moving expenses? What will be the employee's duties and responsibilities?

If you decide to enter into a written contract with your employees, you should probably try to cover the major terms of your agreement. It isn't necessary that every little detail be covered, but you can avoid problems by setting out each party's duties and responsibilities. For example, here are some of the things you may want to include:

- Amount and method of payment
- Length of employment period, if it is known
- Description of job to be performed
- Vacation terms
- Termination terms
- Dispute resolution terms
- Liability and indemnification terms
- Any other terms special to your situation

Additionally, you may want to consider protecting your investment by limiting the rights of your employees to compete with you. For example:

> Melanie and Joyce start a company that sells tires to gas stations. They hire Shirley as a salesperson to call on the stations. Shirley gradually builds up a relationship with the customers. If Melanie and Joyce have no agreement with Shirley, she can quit at any time and start a new company that would sell tires to her old customers.

People like Melanie and Joyce frequently do not want Shirley to be able to do this. To stop Shirley from doing this, Melanie and Joyce should have Shirley sign a "covenant not to compete" with their business. Historically, courts have enforced such covenants if they were bargained for by the parties, the geographical area covered by the covenant is reasonable, and the length of time she could not compete is also reasonable.

A recent Texas case makes it somewhat unclear whether such covenants not to compete will be enforced. In that case, the Texas Supreme Court held that such covenants will only be enforced if these four factors are present: the covenant is necessary to protect the employer; the covenant is not oppressive to the employee; the covenant is not injurious to the public; and there was separate consideration for the covenant. It is unclear how California courts will interpret this Texas case. If a covenant not to compete is important to you, as an employer, we suggest that you offer an employee additional money if he or she agrees to the covenant. For example, offer an annual salary of $20,000 without the covenant, and $25,000 with the covenant. This will increase the likelihood a court will enforce the covenant.

You also may want to protect the ideas that your employees come up with.

> Jim and Bob start a medical research business. Part of their business is a research laboratory where employees of the business do experiments regarding new medical equipment and drugs. Deborah is a research chemist for the company. Assume Deborah gets a great idea and wants to quit her job and start a new company to sell her new product.

Employers normally own research created by employees while on the job. Still, it is a good idea in such situations to clarify in the employment agreement that any patents will be in the name of the employer and the employee will not be compensated for assigning the patent rights to the employer. Also, the agreement should clarify that the employee cannot divulge to anyone any confidential information regarding any company projects, even after the employee quits or is fired. For an example of such an agreement, see Appendix B, Forms 10 and 11.

Independent Contractors

As we said before, if you hire anyone as an employee you are responsible for complying with state and federal laws regarding employees, and probably are responsible for the acts of your employees while on the job. If you use an independent contractor, however, you may avoid some of the legal hassle and liability.

> Ace Construction builds small homes. They employ about twenty people and do almost all the work themselves. They do not, however, have a person who can build brick chimneys. Instead of hiring a new employee, the president decides to hire an outside contractor to do the occasional jobs they need done. The contractor would not be considered an employee, withholding would not have to be taken out, social security would not have to be paid, and he would not be covered under workers compensation.

If you hire an independent contractor, your obligations toward that person are much less than if he or she is an employee. To be an independent contractor you usually must show that the person you hire meets these criteria:

1. Has his or her own place of business at a definite location.
2. Doesn't perform all of his services at your place of business.
3. Holds himself out as being independent.
4. Uses his or her own tools.
5. Is responsible for the final result.
6. Is not controlled by you (for example, sets own schedule).

These are not absolute tests, but usually they must be met to qualify the person as an independent contractor.

Remember that the law doesn't allow you to hire an employee and call him an independent contractor just to avoid compliance with employer-employee laws. As an employer, you need to be careful about whether someone is treated by you as an independent contractor and not an employee. For example, if you do treat someone as an independent contractor and do not withhold taxes from compensation, if the IRS later establishes that the person was an employee, significant penalties can be imposed.

The Bottom Line

Employment contracts may be as formal or informal as you wish. But to protect yourself, and to make sure that there are no misunderstandings, a written contract is usually helpful.

Terminating Employment*

As of this writing, the law regarding your right to fire someone in California is: If you don't have a contract, the agreement is "at will" and you can fire without cause, without notice. If you have a contract, or union agreement, you can only fire that employee in accordance with that agreement. The major exceptions to this are those enforced by the discrimination laws. For example, you may not fire a person based on race, religion, sex, or because they are handicapped. Also, courts in many states (including California) have ruled that you may not fire an employee because he has refused to perform an illegal act. As it is sometimes stated, employment-at-will allows you to fire someone for a good reason, or even for no reason at all. But, you cannot fire for a bad reason. You cannot fire on a discriminatory basis, nor can you fire an employee who called OSHA to report a safety issue.

Also, consider the following:

> Juanita recently hired a new employee to work in her secretarial pool. She had 20 other employees, and for the past few years she had followed a policy of giving each employee one week of vacation, and two weeks of severance pay to anyone who was fired. The new employee started and then business got slow so Juanita fired her. Juanita didn't pay any severance pay, and didn't give the employee any notice. Juanita believed that under the employment-at-will doctrine she could fire at any time without notice. She didn't have a written contract with the employee that said anything differently.

Juanita may be wrong. The employment-at-will doctrine says you can fire without cause, without notice, but if there is a contract, the terms of the contract control. Even though Juanita didn't have a written contract, Juanita has an implied agreement with the employee, basically saying that she will treat her the way she treats other employees. In this case, Juanita had established a policy of giving two weeks of severance pay and that policy probably became part of her agreement with the new employee. Just because nothing is said doesn't mean you don't have an agreement. Past action can establish a policy that becomes part of your contractual agreement with your employees.

*This is a rapidly changing area of law with much litigation. Before relying on the information in this section, you may want to make sure that the "employment-at-will doctrine" has not been further changed.

There is a substantial body of California law based on court decisions suggesting that even in the absence of a formal written employment agreement, an employment agreement may be implied. This may provide the employee with grounds to demand that the employer show "just cause" for termination. Letting employees go is not as simple as it once was, and new court decisions are adding to the burden on the employer. In any event, treating ALL employees fairly is a good starting point.

One final point on firing employees. If your employees are unionized, you must follow the terms of your agreement with the Union. Firing is one of the terms that is subject to bargaining and will be covered in the collective bargaining agreement. Make sure you don't violate it.

The Bottom Line

California law is changing on the matter of terminations. In the past, California followed the "employment-at-will" doctrine. Under this doctrine, employers could usually fire anyone, whenever they wanted to, provided no laws were broken. Things are more complex now. Be sure you do not fire anyone for any kind of a discriminatory reason, because they filed a discrimination or harassment charge, or contrary to your written or implied employment contract. Even in a small business, it is smart business to follow the letter, and the spirit, of the employment laws described in this chapter.

Hiring Temporaries

If employment presents so many pitfalls, and even using "contract labor" has potential problems, what can a poor entrepreneur do? One answer is in the explosion of temporary help agencies. Look in any issue of *HRMagazine,* or a big city newspaper. You will find ads for Kelly Services, Manpower, AppleOne, Volt Temporary Services, and so on. You call them, explain what you need, and they hire.

Is this for you? It will cost more, but it is worth considering especially if your need is clearly temporary. But, as one *Wall Street Journal* article put it, the trend towards temporaries is starting to look permanent. Why the increasing popularity of temporaries? A review of the section above, describing the difficulties in terminating workers, gives a clue. Also, temporaries can be easier. Consider the time and effort required to recruit and screen applicants, the time required to set up employment procedures, etc. Temporary help may be just the ticket. At least, it will be worth your while to check it out.

Drug Testing

As of the writing of this book, a private employer in California has the right to require his or her employees to submit to drug testing, and can fire them if they refuse. This is in line with the employment-at-will doctrine, so court

RUN THAT BY ME ONE MORE TIME

A small printing company was in financial distress and sought help. "Can you come out to talk to us about our poor cash flow?" they asked. As a small business consultant, I could not refuse such a request. The business manager explained the problems. They were: 1. No measurable cash flow, 2. No payroll procedure for paying employees, 3. No clue as to the current status of business tax payments, 4. No idea of the worth of the business, and 5. No vision for the future. "Should we sell the business?" "No," I said. "Where is the value in what you intend to sell? Let's get the business to perform and then decide." The owners agreed to pay for assistance in developing business procedures and a strategic business plan.

Work began immediately to create a simple bookkeeping system that was effective in tracking business performance. Simple business procedures were implemented. A list of questions was developed for the accountant who handled the company's business affairs. A strategic plan was outlined and meetings were held to complete it. The accountant remarked that no one had asked for any information before. The owners and business manager began to see improvement in business operations.

Later, during a business meeting I remarked that it was surprising that these procedures had not been developed. Weren't they aware of the need? "Oh, yes," the business manager replied. We did hire a consultant some years ago." After a file search, the managers handed me the consultant's report. It was 10 years old and contained the same advice I had given them in the past month. "Gosh, this report looks good to me," I said. "Why didn't you follow this advice?" "Oh," the business manager said, "this consultant was from the business school of the local university and didn't charge us. We didn't understand what he was trying to tell us."

—Thanks to Tony Ortega, Associate Professor of Management, California State University, Bakersfield, for this insight.

decisions in this area may change. Similarly, if you have a union agreement or employment contract, that will determine your rights to test your employees. This is a fast-changing area of law. Before requiring testing, check with your lawyer to make sure that the law has not changed.

FOR MORE INFORMATION

Bernstein, Aaron. "Tell It to the Arbitrator." *Business Week,* November 1991, page 109.

California State Department of Fair Employment and Housing. *Discrimination Is Against the Law.* Sacramento: Department of Fair Employment and Housing, 1992.

Fosberg, Barry. "Blind Entrepreneurship: An Analysis of the Randolph-Sheppard Program in the State of Louisiana." *Journal of Business and Entrepreneurship,* March 1991, pages 23–33.

Holley, William H., Jr., and Roger S. Wolters. "Employment at Will: An Emerging Issue." *Journal of Small Business Management,* October 1987, pages 1–8.

Raisner, Jack. "How to Survive the New ADA Litigation." *HRMagazine,* June 1992, pages 78–83.

Rutsohn, Philip, and Donald Law. "Acquired Immune Deficiency Syndrome: A Small Business Dilemma." *Journal of Small Business Management,* January 1991, pages 62-71.

Schellhardt, Timothy D. "Temporary-Help Rebound May Prove to Be Permanent." *Wall Street Journal,* July 28, 1992, page B3.

Slonaker, William M., and Ann C. Wendt. "Profile of Employment Discrimination in Micro-Business." *Journal of Business and Entrepreneurship,* October 1991, pages 33–46.

Spraggins, Ellen E. "How to Fire." *Inc.,* May 1992, pages 66–72. See also page 146, same issue.

Teves, John C. "Helping: Disabilities Act Both Cheers, Worries." *Bakersfield Californian,* July 25, 1992, page 1.

Ward, Edward A. "Employee Drug Testing: Aalberts and Walker Revisited." *Journal of Small Business Management,* January 1991, pages 77–87. See also the rejoinder by Aalberts in the same issue.

Whitman, D., and Gergacz, J. W. *Legal Environment of Business, 3rd Edition.* New York: McGraw Hill Publishing Company, 1990. See especially Chapter 22.

POINTS TO PONDER

1. Why do you think the idea of "employment-at-will" is losing power?
2. Do the laws on equal employment opportunity require you to hire someone just because of minority status? Discuss.
3. Why is it in the employer's best interest to carefully follow guidelines on ensuring legal status of all employees?

DON'T JUST SIT THERE, DO SOMETHING!

1. In local newspapers or magazines, find an example of an employer who got into hot water about some employment-related law. Write a short report suggesting how you would minimize such problems.
2. Is California really an "employment-at-will" state? Can you think of any court cases that help support your point?
3. Get a copy of the pamphlet "Discrimination Is Against the Law." Copies are available in State of California offices in various California cities, in college or university libraries, as well as many local government offices. Check the telephone directory under California State Government or local governments for a listing near you. Write a short commentary on how easy (or difficult) it was to obtain. Do you think most employers have access to this pamphlet? How about a poor, non-English speaking job seeker?

7

Miscellaneous Taxes, Fees, and Statutes: Keep Your Eyes Open!

TAXES

Taxes are a fact of life for your business. As was discussed in Chapter 1, federal income tax normally will be imposed on the profits of your business, regardless of whether you operate your business as a sole proprietorship, a partnership, or a corporation. California has corporate income taxes and a personal income tax. A business in California is also subject to municipal taxes, state taxes, and other federal taxes. These will be discussed later in the chapter.

To help you keep track of your business income and make it easier for you to compute your taxes, it is a good idea to hire an accountant who can help you get started on a bookkeeping system that is suitable for your business. He or she can tell you what taxes you will have to pay, when you will have to pay them, and what filings need to be made. An accountant can also make you aware of all the deductions that you can take, and how to properly document them. But even more importantly, the accountant can help you establish an effective recordkeeping system, vital to the success of your business. A good recordkeeping system will not only help you manage your business more efficiently, it will help you comply with the tax laws. Your records should clearly indicate the source of your receipts, keep track of your deductible expenses, allow you to figure your depreciation deductions, and maintain a record of all amounts withheld from employees' wages.

Federal Taxes

The federal tax laws and regulations are very complicated. For example, employers have the obligation to withhold from employees' wages amounts for social security (FICA) and personal income tax, and employers must make contributions for social security and unemployment compensation. The IRS has published a helpful guide entitled "Employer's Tax Guide" (Circular E). We encourage all business owners to read this.

Tax Identification Number

When you file your individual federal tax return you can use your social security number as your taxpayer identification number. It may be necessary, however, for you to have an employer identification number (EIN) as well, once you are in business. Every partnership and corporation (including S Corporations) must have an EIN to use as a taxpayer identification number. A sole proprietor must also have an EIN if either of the following is true:

1. It pays wages to one or more employees.
2. It is required to file any excise tax returns, including those for alcohol, tobacco, or firearms.

To apply for an EIN, use Form SS-4, Application for Employer Identification Number. This form is available from the Internal Revenue Service, or the Social Security Administration, and if you have any questions they will be glad to help you—at no cost.

Withholding For Uncle Sam

As an employer, you have certain tax responsibilities for your employees. In general, you must withhold income tax from an employee's taxable wages based on the employee's wage level, marital status, and number of withholding allowances claimed. Each employee is required to file with you a Form W-4 which will provide the employee's social security number and all information you need regarding the employee's withholding allowances. The IRS "Employer's Tax Guide" contains tables from which you can determine how much to withhold.

You will also be required to withhold amounts from employee's wages for contributions to FICA (social security). Currently 7.65% of the employee's wages must be paid by the employee; however, in 1993 if an employee earned more than $57,600 annually, any wages above this amount were not subject to FICA. However, in a typical recent year individuals earning over $54,300 paid a 1.4% medicare supplement tax on the income between $54,300 and $125,000. These numbers change each year, so be sure to check the current social security situation. An employer must match the FICA contribution made by its employees. So, if $50 is withheld from an employee's wages for FICA during a pay period, the employer must pay an equal amount.

Amounts withheld from employee's pay must be deposited within a reasonable time with the Federal Reserve Bank in your area, or with a financial institution authorized to accept these deposits. Check with the Federal Reserve Bank in your area to learn what institutions can accept these deposits.

IRS employees have informed us that the frequency of the deposits depends upon the amount of the taxes owed. For example, if you owe less than $500 at the end of any quarter, you don't have to deposit the money. You can merely send it to the IRS, with a Form 941. If you owe more than $500 for the quarter, a deposit will have to be made. The deposits should be made with a Form 8109 federal deposit coupon. Copies of these coupons will be sent to you by the IRS after you apply for a federal employer identification number. Instructions for using this coupon are included in the coupon book. Until you have received your coupon book, you can use the blank Form 8109-B, available from the IRS. If you owe less than $500 in taxes for any one month, you do not have to make a deposit; you can wait until the next month. If you owe more than $500, but less than $3,000 at the end of any month, the amount owed must be deposited within 15 days after the end of the month. If your monthly tax bill significantly exceeds $3,000, it may be necessary to make more than one deposit per month. Additional copies of the Form 8109 can be obtained from the IRS by using the reorder form included in the coupon book. If you are a large enough company to pay more than $3,000 monthly in withholding, you are large enough to have an accountant. Be sure to check with your accountant and the IRS about when and where you should make these deposits. There are penalties for late payments, and the later you are, the bigger the penalties.

Remember that the IRS considers an employer, as well as other "responsible individuals," as trustees for amounts withheld from employees' wages. If amounts withheld are not paid to the IRS, the employer and all responsible persons will be liable for all such taxes, plus a 100% penalty. Criminal sanctions are also possible. There is also the famous "padlock-the-door" policy. If you don't want the IRS to shut you down, follow the laws. Your fellow business owners do it and so can you.

A Form 941 must be filed quarterly with the IRS regarding withheld income tax and social security tax. These quarterly returns must be filed within 30 days after the end of each calendar quarter. The return should be sent to the address listed on the form. It will go either to Ogden, Utah, or Fresno, California, depending on what part of California you live in.

You must fill out a Form W-2 Wage and Tax Statement for each employee, and the employee must receive it by January 31 for the prior calendar year. The W-2 should include all wages the employee received, as well as "other compensation." This includes certain payments considered taxable income that are not subject to withholding, such as reimbursement of moving expenses. Copy A of all W-2 Forms prepared for each employee should be filed annually with the Social Security Administration with the Form W-3.

A Form W-3, Transmittal of Income and Tax Statements, must be filed by the end of February with the Social Security Administration, Salinas Data Operations Center, Salinas, California 93911.

If you are self-employed, you have to pay a self-employment tax. This is essentially a social security payment. Schedule SE (Form 1040) is used to compute the amount owed.

Federal Unemployment Tax Act (FUTA)

The federal unemployment tax system, together with the state systems, provides for payments of unemployment compensation to workers who have lost their jobs. If you pay wages of at least $1,500, or if you employ at least one person for some period during 20 different weeks during a calendar year, you are subject to this tax. Although subject to change, in a typical recent year this tax was 6.2% of the first $7,000 earned by each employee for each calendar year. However, if you are an employer subject to the California Unemployment Insurance Tax, which is discussed below under California Taxes, a credit will be given for contributions to the California fund. This credit can be as much as 5.4% of the first $7,000 of wages, which may very significantly reduce the amount you will pay under this federal tax. Form 940 is used to report and pay the aggregate federal unemployment compensation tax due. FUTA payments should be made with Form 8109 deposit coupons relating to other federal taxes due. If additional FUTA payments are due at the end of the year, this payment should accompany the Form 940. This Form 940 must be filed by January 31, to the IRS office serving your part of California. This will either be Ogden, Utah, or Fresno, California, as directed on Form 940 (or 940EZ) instructions. This is not a tax that you withhold from your employees' wages; the employer pays this tax.

To order any forms or information booklets relevant to federal taxes, write to: Internal Revenue Service, Western Area Distribution Center, Rancho Cordova, California 95743-0001. You can use the order form in Appendix B,

Form 20. Some of the publications that might be of particular interest to you are:

- Publication 583—Information for Business Taxpayers
- Publication 334—Tax Guide for Small Business
- Publication 589—Tax Information on S Corporations
- Publication 541—Tax Information on Partnerships
- Publication 542—Tax Information on Corporations
- Publication 552—Recordkeeping for Individuals and a List of Tax Publications
- Publication 539—Employment Taxes
- Publication 533—Self-Employment Taxes
- Publication 535—Business Expenses
- Publication 15—Circular E-Employer's Tax Guide
- Form W-2—Wage and Tax Statement
- Form W-3—Transmittal of Income and Tax Statements
- Form W-4—Employee's Withholding Allowing Certificate
- Form 940—Employer's Quarterly
- Form 941—Employer's Quarterly Federal Tax Return
- Form 1120—U.S. Corporation Income Tax Return
- Form 1120S—U.S. Income Tax Return for an S Corporation
- Form 1120-W—Corporation Estimated Tax
- Form 1040—Schedule SE-Social Security Self-Employment Tax
- Form 2553—Election by a Small Business Corporation
- Form SS-4—Application for Employer Identification Number

California Taxes

Withholding for State Income Tax

Since California has followed Uncle Sam's lead and adopted an income tax too, employers have to withhold for Sacramento as well as for Washington, D.C.

The California Employment Development Department (EDD) publishes a helpful "Employer's Guide" each year to give the latest information on state personal income tax withholding, as well as other pertinent tax data. This booklet is available at EDD offices across the state.

At the federal level, firms send in deposits of withheld taxes to the IRS on varying time schedules, from 8 times a month to quarterly, using the Form 8109 federal deposit coupon. The same employers will deposit California income taxes withheld at approximately the same varying time schedule, typically using a state form DE-88 (Form 10).

At the federal level, the employer balances things out and submits withheld taxes (social security and federal income tax) on a quarterly basis using IRS Form 941. Roughly the same thing is accomplished at the state level using a Form DE3 (which comes in several versions, depending on the size of the firm, etc.). Any employment development department tax office can help you with these forms, but be sure to start with the EDD "Employer's Guide." Check the phone book under California State Government, Taxes: Employment Development Department.

Sales Taxes

In general, retail sales of products sold in California are subject to sales tax. The State Board of Equalization sets the rules for collection of this tax, but who does the actual collection? The businesses here in California. This is where you come in. Because if you do business in California and sell "tangible personal property that is ordinarily subject to sales tax," then you must apply for a "seller's permit."

What is included in the "tangible personal property" category? Furniture, giftware, toys, antiques, clothing, photographs, artwork—you name it. Pure labor, such as a charge to clean a room or wash a car, is not taxable. Although this distinction sounds pretty simple, it wouldn't hurt to check with the Board of Equalization if you have any questions. The Board has more than 50 offices, so it shouldn't be too tough to get into contact with someone who can help you.

Unless your business is *not* involved in selling, you must obtain a California seller's permit. This is true whether you are a sole proprietorship, partnership, or corporation. Even if you only plan to be involved in the business of selling for a short time, such as the Christmas season, you need your seller's permit.

Now the surprising part: the seller's permit is *free,* and remains valid for as long as your business remains active. If you have more than one location, you will need a permit for each location.

There are two ways to obtain a seller's permit. You could write the California State Board of Equalization, P.O. Box 942879, Sacramento, California 94279-0001, and ask them to mail you an application. The more common way to obtain a seller's permit would be to visit or phone your nearest Board of Equalization office and request an application.

After providing background information on you and your business, the Board will issue you a permit. And, while there is no permit fee, you may well be required to post a security deposit to insure that you don't go out of business leaving taxes unpaid.

Once you open your doors and start selling, you are obligated to pay sales tax. Since as a *customer* all your life you thought you were paying sales tax, it may come as a surprise to you that the law says that the seller is actually obligated to pay the tax, whether or not the customer pays it. In fact, if the seller does not pay the correct tax to the Board of Equalization, penalties and interest will apply.

In actual practice, 99.9% of all sellers follow the hint in the law that says although it is the *seller* who is required to pay taxes to the Board, the seller may be reimbursed for those taxes by the customer. This explains why you, as a customer, pay sales tax. Technically, you are reimbursing the seller, who in turn pays the tax. Not to worry: one way or another, the state gets its share.

The actual percentage of that share varies over time, and by location. There is a basic statewide rate, typically around 6 to 6.5%. Then, local transit districts add another ½% or so in areas covering about two-thirds of the state's businesses. So, the specific rate for your business depends on where you do business, and the rates at that moment in time. Your nearest Board of Equalization office will be glad to help you with these issues. If you are buying an existing business, you should be careful to note if the business has an outstanding sales tax liability. If you purchase the business, it is strongly advised that you withhold from the purchase price an amount sufficient to pay any sales taxes that the firm may still owe the state. By purchasing the firm, you may become liable for any sales tax owed by the firm, up to the amount of the purchase price. California's Bulk Transfer Law, affecting business sales, should help you in this regard.

You are required by law to collect sales tax and to file tax returns and pay the tax to the Board. Once you get your seller's permit, you will be told to file tax returns monthly, quarterly, or annually, depending on sales volume. Your return is filed on preprinted forms that will be sent to you by the Board at the appropriate intervals.

Sales taxes are not imposed if an item is purchased for resale. However, you do need a seller's permit even if you only purchase goods for resale. If your business is buying goods for resale, give the seller a resale certificate. A copy of a sample resale certificate is in Appendix B, Form 26. A copy of it should be shown to the supplier. Use the resale certificate each time tangible personal property is purchased for resale. This will exempt you from the state and local sales and use taxes. An item is purchased for resale if you intend to sell, lease, or rent the item within the United States in the regular course of your business. Forms for resale certificates are also available from many office supply or stationery stores.

For more information on sales taxes, contact the nearest Board office. They have numerous pamphlets available, and are generally very helpful. If you do run into the one totally uncooperative employee, call the Board's "Taxpayer Advocate" at (916) 324-2798. The Advocate is on *your* side.

Unemployment Insurance

If, in addition to selling products, you employ people, you are subject to a whole new set of taxes and requirements. In the next few pages we will discuss the more "popular" of these responsibilities. Keep in mind that laws and procedures change. By the time your business is up and running, specific figures used here will most likely have changed, and the laws themselves will most likely have been modified. That is why we always advise you to *ask questions.* Ask your Board of Equalization, ask the Employee Development Department, or check the "Free Help" section in this book. If your question seems tricky or significant, be sure to check with the pro—your attorney or your accountant.

With these caveats in mind, let's take a look at Unemployment Insurance. The bottom line is that you as an employer will pay a tax, at a rate which may be about 3.4% of the first $7,000 of wages, for each employee. From here on the issue gets a bit more complicated, but keep this basic principle in mind. This tax is Unemployment *Insurance* (UI), which is in some cases boosted a bit higher by a mandatory Employment Training Tax. If everyone is employed, and no one needs training, the taxes you pay for insurance won't be needed. Thus, the basic philosophy is, reward those employers whose employees do not become unemployed, and who therefore do not require retraining. With this goal in mind, the State of California set up a sliding scale for Unemployment Insurance. You will probably start out paying 3.4% of the first $7,000—subject to change, of course. If no one you hire ever leaves, you may find your UI tax rate down to almost nothing in a few years. If a high percentage of your hires later file for unemployment benefits, you may find your firm paying about 5½%, which would include both Unemployment Insurance and the Employment Training Tax. It is worth watching, as the cost differences can be significant.

There are numerous fine points in the law, including a provision for employers in good standing to pay extra amounts into the "reserve account" for their business. This can impact the tax rates. Whether or not this makes sense in your case will involve some calculation. The booklet "Employer's Guide," published annually by the California Employment Development Department, will help you analyze your situation.

The process begins when you file the Form DE-1, registering you as a California employer. You must register within 15 days from becoming an employer. A business is considered an employer if it pays $100 or more in wages in any calendar quarter. The $100 figure may include wages, salary, commissions, bonuses, or other compensation, and may be with one or more employees. Basically, unless you do it all yourself, you are an employer, and are subject to the Unemployment Insurance laws.

In many cases, you will not actually file the Form DE-1 to register. Why? in a brilliant move, the authorities realized that the average business needs to register both as a *seller* and as an *employer.* With this in mind, the "Application for Seller's Permit" provided by the Board of Equalization (called the BT-100 Form, as of the time of publication of this book) doubles as an employer registration form for the Employment Development Department. Your business will still have to work with both agencies, but at least at registration time, you can start things with just one form.

Be sure to obtain an up-to-date "Employer's Guide" from the nearest Employment Development Department office. Although not all 50-plus pages will apply to you, it is in your best interest to at least look at each page. Then, carefully follow the sections that do fit your situation.

Workers' Compensation

Workers' Compensation Insurance protects an employer from lawsuits arising out of the death or personal injury sustained by his employees in the course of their employment. Workers' compensation insurance is required in California, and can save you a lot of money and prevent large lawsuits against you by your employees. If you are unsure about workers' compensation you should talk with your attorney. You can purchase workers' compensation through the State Compensation Insurance Fund or through any insurance company authorized to sell liability or accident insurance in California. To get further information about workers' compensation insurance, contact any business insurance broker, or the nearest office of the State Compensation Insurance Fund. This is an important area, and an area where you can control your costs to some extent. If you control the worker environment, and your employees have no accidents (and no claims), your costs theoretically will be kept at a minimal level. Unfortunately, costs statewide do seem to be rising, partly due to "stress" claims, and partly due to plain old fraud. Keep alert.

FEDERAL REGULATION OF SAFETY AND HEALTH

Occupational Safety and Health Act (OSHA)

Under a federal law called the Occupational Safety and Health Act of 1970, every employer has the "general duty" to provide a workplace that is safe and healthful, free from recognized hazards. The Occupational Safety and Health Administration, which is part of the U.S. Department of Labor, has put into effect specific standards and regulations that employers must follow that are relevant to occupational safety and health. Not to be outdone, California then passed a law of its own, the California Occupational Safety and Health Act of 1973. For a period of time in the 1980s, CAL-OSHA was dormant, and the federal OSHA called the shots in California. Now, CAL-OSHA is back, and will enforce the federal OSHA laws plus additional California-only requirements. As an employer, you had better know both. These standards vary in accordance with the kind of workplace you have. An employer is "any person engaged in a business affecting commerce who has employees." Self-employed persons and farms at which only the immediate members of the farm employer's family are employed are not covered under this Act.

OSHA standards fall into four major categories: General Industry, Maritime, Construction, and Agriculture. As an employer, it is your responsibility to become familiar with the standards applicable to your particular establishment and to be sure that your employees have, and use, personal protective gear and equipment when required for safety. As it is not possible to include the specific standards that may apply to your establishment in the scope of this chapter, please use the order form in Appendix B, Form 19, to obtain some publications containing the applicable standards.

The law also requires that you must display the official "CAL-OSHA poster," which describes rights and responsibilities under the CAL-OSHA law, in a prominent place so that your employees can readily see it. In general, your employees have a right to know which OSHA standards apply to your workplace. To get the poster, order "Job Safety and Health Protection on the Job" from the nearest CAL-OSHA office. We think posting this information is an excellent idea. For one thing, it tells your employees their rights to a safe workplace, and tells them how to file complaints if necessary. Second, putting up the poster in a prominent place is a good idea because Section 6431 of the California Labor Code requires posting this information, and provides for a penalty of up to $1,000 for each violation of the posting requirement. CAL-OSHA also requires employers to post emergency telephone numbers (ambulance, fire, police, etc.). Again, this is not only a good idea, but Title 8, Section 1512(e) requires it. Ask you local OSHA office for a blank poster S-500, and be sure to fill in the right numbers before posting.

If you employ 11 or more employees, you must maintain records of occupational injuries and illnesses as they occur. Most OSHA recordkeeping is not required for employers with no more than 10 full- or part-time employees at any one time in the previous calendar year. Also exempt from the recordkeeping requirements are all employers in retail trade, finance, insurance, and real estate. Service industries are exempt, except for building materials and garden supplies, general merchandise and food stores, hotels and other lodging places, repair services, amusement and recreational services, and health services.

If you are not exempt from the recordkeeping obligation, record each injury on OSHA Form No. 200, which is called the Log and Summary. Not every injury or illness occurring in the workplace is recordable. Definitions on the back of OSHA Form No. 200 explain which cases must be recorded. Then, prepare a supplementary record of occupational injuries and illnesses for recordable cases either on OSHA Form No. 101 or on a worker's compensation report giving the same information. Every year, prepare the annual summary, which is also OSHA Form No. 200, and post it no later than February 1. It should be kept posted until March 1. The form itself will explain in detail how and when to post it. A good place to post it would be near the official OSHA poster. You need to retain these records for at least five years. You can use Form 19 in Appendix B to order these forms.

Reporting of Fatalities or Multiple Hospitalization Accidents

You must report every accident that results in one or more deaths or in the hospitalization of five or more employees. This is necessary even if you are exempt from the routine recordkeeping described above. The report must be made within 48 hours after the occurrence of the accident. You can report either in writing or orally to the OSHA area director. (Please see Appendix B, Form 20 for the addresses of the district and area offices.)

SB 198 Reporting

It is hoped that you will never have to report any accident involving death or even serious injury. We all want safe workplaces. In order to help in this regard, your business should have a program to prevent work-related injuries or

BETWEEN A MOVING ROCK AND A HARD PLACE

California is earthquake country. Californians must be sensitive to the risks that earthquakes pose to daily life. The state of California has identified unreinforced masonry buildings as being seismically unsafe and, therefore, a serious threat to public safety. The state has passed a law directing property owners to make their unreinforced masonry buildings safe for public use.

An owner of a building constructed of unreinforced masonry finds himself in an uncomfortable legal position. If the owner does nothing and an earthquake causes property damage or loss of life, he could be held liable for the loss. If he retrofits the building to improve its seismic resistance, it will cost a lot of money without improving the building's use, other than now being seismically resistant.

In 1952, Bakersfield and Kern County experienced the second most powerful earthquake in California in this century. Only the 1906 San Francisco earthquake was greater in magnitude. Forty years later, Bakersfield businessmen are still trying to reconcile the cost of making buildings seismically safe with the cost of doing business. Finding a reasonable middle ground is difficult.

On the one hand, no building can ever be made completely earthquake proof. On the other hand, taking precautions in modifying building construction can significantly reduce loss in an earthquake. What is a prudent and reasonable course of action? The stakes are high for Bakersfield and other communities.

There are four stakeholders in this situation: the state, local government, the public, and the property owners. Bakersfield property owners have formed an organization for mutual support, coordination with state and local government, and the exchange of information. Open meetings are announced and held to inform the public.

Clear and practicable criteria are needed to determine whether a building is worth saving. If it is, then a program is needed to modify these buildings to revitalize the downtown. If it isn't, then a program is needed to tear these buildings down and then revitalize the downtown. In either case, a prudent course of action can be uniformly applied to all unreinforced masonry buildings.

—Thanks to Tony Ortega, Associate Professor, California State University, Bakersfield, for this insight. For additional information see Gay, Dean. "Owners Are Taking a Risk." *The Bakersfield Californian,* July 5, 1992, B5; Keith, Bruce, "Earthquake Safety is Downtown Concern." *The Bakersfield Californian,* July 5, 1992, B5; and McCarthy, Robert. "1952 Quake Impact Felt." *The Bakersfield Californian,* July 5, 1992, B5.

illnesses. Not only does this kind of prevention program make sense, it is required by California Law SB 198.

SB 198 requires you as an employer (even if you have only one employee, and no matter what type of business you have) to have a *written,* formal, illness and injury prevention program. You must have, in writing, your plan to provide a safe and healthy workplace, and your plan must show how you will convey this safety plan to your employees. Your plan must list, by name, the person responsible for carrying out your injury and illness prevention program.

Some of the SB 198 requirements apply primarily to firms of 10 or more employees, but the bottom line is the same in every case: California means business when it says you should work hard to prevent workplace hazards. For you, this means having a good program, but it also means *documenting* that you have a good program.

It may be a good idea for you to attend a seminar about CAL-OSHA, and the SB 198 program. Most larger communities will have several such seminars in any year. For more information, you could call any of the agencies listed in the "Free Help" sections of the Appendix. Also, feel free to contact the California State Chamber of Commerce, (800) 331-8877. They have publications, some of which are listed at the back of this chapter, and seminars as well. It's worth looking into.

Proposition 65 Compliance

We live in a world made better by chemicals. However, sometimes we have paid too little attention to the possible side effects of the things we use. With this in mind, the people of California voted into law "Proposition 65," which mandates specific requirements that impact almost every California business.

Officially known as the Safe Drinking Water and Toxics Enforcement Act, Proposition 65 gives special attention to firms with 10 or more employees. You will be required to check your business for hazardous chemicals, which may include everything from pesticides to cleaning agents to the white-out we used to use to correct typos before we had computers. Then, after identifying hazardous chemicals in your place of work, you will need to develop a plan to ensure safety for potentially exposed workers, especially for "significant" situations.

Even if you do not have 10 employees, Proposition 65 may impact you in another way. Are your *customers* potentially exposed to hazardous materials at your place of business? If so, be sure to post the "Proposition 65 Warning" poster or card. Fortunately, any office supply store can provide you with warning posters.

Proposition 65 is another example to prove that "little things can mean a lot" in running a successful business. If you spend a little time ensuring that you are in compliance, no problem. However, if you fail to comply, the potential impact on your business is substantial. With terms like "up to $2,500 per day" fines and "up to one year in prison" sprinkled throughout the law, it would seem worth complying. The good thing is, our state will be safer because of it. The "paperwork" aspects of the law do seem burdensome, but the bottom line is clear. We insist on compliance with environmental laws. Call your nearest CAL-EPA office for more information.

Licenses and Permits

One of your start-up business requirements will be to secure the licenses and permits that may be required by the county or city in which you plan to operate. The kinds of permits and licenses necessary will vary in accordance with the type of business you plan to operate. For instance, the permits necessary for the operation of a restaurant may differ from those required for an automobile repair shop.

If you are picking a new site for your business, it is advisable to visit the county clerk's office to obtain any information about deed or zoning restrictions that may apply. Restrictions may impose additional requirements, such as: setbacks, height and size, architectural specifications, signs, maintenance, parking, refuse storage and collection, noise, odors, smoke, and others. Any applicable zoning rules should also be complied with.

Your city or county may require that you get some of the following permits or approvals for your business. Check with your city or county offices about:

- Certificate of occupancy
- Building permit approval
- Development plat approval
- Wastewater capacity reservation
- Sign administration
- Fire marshall
- Finance and administration
- Health department; consumer health services
- Public works department; industrial waste
- California Alcoholic Beverage Control Department (if alcoholic beverages are to be served)
- Bureau of Alcohol, Tobacco, and Firearms
- Additional permits—occupational permits

Fictitious Name Statement

If your firm will be doing business under an assumed name—any name other than that of the owners—you need to file a "fictitious business name statement" with the county clerk's office in the county where your business will operate. The fictitious business name statement is a relatively simple form. A small filing fee normally is due.

Contact the office in your county to determine the exact form needed and the filing fee.

If you are doing business as a corporation, and you plan to use a name other than the exact corporate name given in your Articles of Incorporation, you must file a fictitious business name statement with the secretary of state of California as well as with the county clerk of the county where the principal office of your business is located. If you plan to use more than one assumed name, you will have to file a certificate for each one. The fictitious business name statement is valid for five years and may be renewed. A sample of the Fictitious Business Name Statement for an Incorporated Business is in Appendix B, Form 17. Once you file your fictitious business name statement with your county clerk, you will no doubt be given a list of "Newspapers of General Circulation" in your county. This is to help you comply with another facet of the law, which is publication of the statement in a newspaper. Typically, the "Newspaper of General Circulation" chosen will be a newspaper with *minimal* circulation. That is because it will be cheaper to publish the information there, and as long as the county clerk is happy, you should be too. Sound complex? It's not. Your county clerk's office will be glad to help.

FOR MORE INFORMATION

CAL-OSHA Handbook. Sacramento: California Chamber of Commerce, 1992, about $40. Or, consider the Chamber's loose-leaf 3-ring binder, *CAL-OSHA: Beyond the Basics,* about $50, with an update service available for $120 per year.

Driscoll, Lisa. "Compensating for Workers' Comp Costs." *Business Week,* February 3, 1992, page 72.

Groves, Martha. "23% Increase in Workers' Comp Rates Requested." *Los Angeles Times,* April 14, 1992, page D1.

Hollman, Kenneth W., and Saeed Mohammad-Zadeh. "Risk Management in Small Business." *Journal of Small Business Management,* January, 1984, pages 47–55.

Proposition 65 Compliance. Sacramento: California Chamber of Commerce, 1993. If you deal in anything chemical, this may be well worth the price ($40).

Royalty, Kent, Robert Calhoun, Radie Bunn, and Wayne Wells. "The Impact of Tax Reform on the Choice of Small Business Legal Form." *Journal of Small Business Management,* January, 1988, pages 9–23.

Starman, Kurt J., Editor. *California License Handbook,* 2nd Edition. Sacramento: California Department of Commerce, Office of Small Business, 1988. Although a bit old, where else can you look up information on the Division of Inspection Services, Egg Quality Control Branch of the State Department of Food and Agriculture? More information than you want on everything from "Accountancy, Board of," to "Vocational Nurse and Psychiatric Technician Examiners, Board of."

Survival Guide to Workers' Compensation. Sacramento: California Chamber of Commerce, 1993, ($35 in 1993). Check how much you will be paying in workers' comp before you decide not to buy. Incidentally, your local library may have a copy.

Thompson, Roger. "Workers' Comp Costs: Out of Control." *National Business,* July 1992, pages 22–26. California's tendency to grant workers' compensation even to fired workers is strongly criticized.

U.S. Internal Revenue Service. *Employers Tax Guide* (Publication 15, Circular E). Available at any IRS office, or write to IRS Forms Distribution Center, Rancho Cordoba, California 95743-0001.

U.S. Internal Revenue Service. *Tax Guide for Small Business* (Publication 334). Available at any IRS office, or write to IRS Forms Distribution Center, Rancho Cordoba, California 95743-0001.

POINTS TO PONDER

1. With so many laws and taxes, why is it that California is still the location of choice for so many people, and so many businesses? To what extent do people come here because of the "protect the public" atmosphere?
2. Should your community or, for that matter, your state, actively recruit new businesses to locate here? Should tax incentives be used to attract businesses?

DON'T JUST SIT THERE, DO SOMETHING!

1. Do some manipulation of figures to demonstrate the importance of keeping mandatory insurance rates low. For example, consider the difference in cost for a firm with $120,000 in annual wages paying 6% unemployment insurance and the same size firm paying 1%. Discuss the significance of your findings.
2. Name a specific type of business. What special requirements, not covered in this chapter, would apply? Write a short essay describing your analysis of this situation.

8

Consumer Protection in California: Let the Seller Beware

Dealing with Customers

The typical business person believes that legal questions concerning the business arise, and are answered, before the business is opened. When a business person thinks of "legal questions," he or she may think of decisions regarding the form of the venture, the arranging of financing, and the satisfaction of state and federal employment and tax requirements. These issues are resolved when a business starts. From that point on, the business usually operates under the old maxim *caveat emptor,* let the buyer beware. So long as you do not intentionally defraud or mislead your customers and business contacts, you assume that you have no liability.

Unfortunately, a number of legal problems can arise after the business is started. Consider the following:

> Joe recently opened a car dealership. He took in trade a late-model car and was told by the customer "I have had no problems. It is good as new." An independent mechanic verifies that there is nothing wrong. Joe sells the car and tells the customer "The car is good as new." Due to a hidden defect, the car breaks down the day after the sale. **Joe may be liable for the buyer's damages and attorney's fees.**

Or what about this:

> Sally's travel agency recently received a beautiful brochure from the Sea Isle Hotel. The picture shows a beautiful hotel with a large pool. Sally tells the customer "The Sea Isle has a beautiful pool." The customer takes the trip and the hotel has filled in the pool to make room for more tennis courts. **Sally may be liable to the customer for the traveler's damages and attorney's fees.**

And finally:

> Melanie opens a small "bed-and-breakfast," since her big old house is right on State Highway 178 near Lake Isabella. In order to let people know she is now a business, and not just Melanie anymore, she posts a sign saying "Stay at Melanie's! Only $49 and up!"

Already, she appears to be in violation of the Business and Professions Code that says it is unlawful for a hotel or inn to post a price rate sign unless "the sign shall have posted thereon the rates charged for ALL rooms." The same law specifically states that "signs bearing the legend 'and up' do *not* comply with the law" (section 17564). Perhaps Melanie can think about this when she is enjoying "imprisonment of not less than 10 days nor more than six months, or by both fine and imprisonment" (17568). Actually, time in prison will not happen, right? But that is what the law says, so if you were Melanie. . . .

These are just a few examples of how laws dictate the way business should operate in this state. Under California law the maxim *caveat emptor* has been replaced with a new credo, *caveat vendor.*

California law doesn't require intent, doesn't require knowledge, and doesn't allow you to escape liability by claiming that it was only a good-faith mistake. You can't contractually avoid the law and, if you violate it, you may be responsible for damages plus all court costs and attorney's fees. Not to mention possible fines! And don't think that this law doesn't apply to you. California may be the land of opportunity but it is also the land of laws. It sometimes seems that we have a law for everyone and for every purpose.

Laws, Laws, and More Laws

One problem facing the prospective small business owner is that California has so many laws that it seems almost impossible to be aware of all of them. How could poor Melanie have known that signs saying "and up" violate the law? Apparently no one else in California knows about that law either since you can see such signs almost everywhere. And the fact that some laws are strictly enforced and others seem to be regularly ignored makes it even more of a jungle out there.

The Bottom Line

Watch your step!

Unfair Practices Act

To start with, you had better be aware that many things you thought were common practice violate one law or another. And, just because somebody else does it doesn't mean YOU can get away with it. Case in point:

Monster Tee Shirt Company notices that Junior Tees is creeping into their college-and university-logo shirt market. Monster decides to drop prices so low for a year that Junior will be forced out of the college shirt market. This may sound familiar to you, but Monster had better not try it. The California Unfair Practices Act says, among other things, that it is unlawful to sell below cost or even to give products away if the purpose is to injure competitors. So, Monster decides instead to bring in new customers by selling one line at prices so low that customers will come charging in. Wrong again. The same law says "it is unlawful for any person engaged in business within this State to sell . . . any product as a 'loss leader.'. . ."

In truth, if it was only the Unfair Practices Act that you had to worry about, things wouldn't be all that tricky. But this law is only the beginning.

Warranties: Whether You Said So or Not

If you sell something in California, the basic assumption is that it will work. You do not have to put a sign on it saying "Warranty: this Gizmo is working, and will do the job for which you purchased it." Even without the sign, if you sell it, you are in effect giving a warranty. To put it in legalese, when "the buyer is relying on the skill and judgment of the seller to select and furnish suitable goods, then there is an implied warranty that the goods shall be fit for such purpose. . . ."

Any consumer who feels damaged by violation of this implied warranty can sue. The best bet here is a phrase that we will repeat later: if you say it, it *had better* be the truth.

Much more will be said about warranties in the next chapter. Unfortunately for the small business person, this is not the last law we should mention. There are laws on debt collection practices, discussed in Chapter 11. There are laws on interest rates, briefed in Chapter 10. When you deal with the California consumer, you should basically be willing to walk the path of righteousness and cut square corners. It is as if the consumers of the state are saying, "Be fair or take your business elsewhere!" When you think about it, this is not a bad way to go. After all, we are all consumers. With this in mind, let's take a look at a couple of other topics of importance to the small business operator in California.

False Advertising

The basic rule in California is that it is illegal to make any untrue or misleading statement in order to make a sale. The laws on advertising are more than 60 pages long and cannot be easily summarized. One easy-to-remember part says that, in addition to other penalties such as fines, a consumer wronged by a willful violation of the law is entitled to damages of *two* times the sale price. The same law sets a minimum "damages" amount of $250, so even if you sell a $1 product using misleading ads, you could be subject to penalties of $250 per sale.

Using the telephone in a fraudulent way is a subject of great interest in the law. Very detailed rules apply, and fines up to $10,000 are possible for one "who directly or indirectly employs any device, scheme, or artifice to deceive . . ." by telephone sales. In the case of telephone sales, buyers can sue for *treble* damages, so the $10,000 civil penalty is not the only reason to tell the truth. Honest dealings make sense for all.

Special Attention to Special Areas

Laws sometimes focus on specific topics. As of this writing, California has detailed laws on vending machines, barbers and cosmetology—virtually all the professions from audiology to veterinarians, pest control, tanning facilities, check-cashing operations, water treatment devices, and even the newly competitive business of selling telephone directory advertising. You name it, and we probably have a law for it. All in all, these laws exert a powerful influence on the business person. Simply put, if you say something, make sure it's true.

All of these legal provisions may come as a shock to anyone schooled under the rules of *caveat emptor.* Under today's law it is no longer lawful to just sit back and say nothing. If you know the product has a defect, or is going to be discontinued, or is going on sale, and you know that the buyer wouldn't buy the product at the price you asked if he or she knew these facts, you may have an obligation to disclose this information. If you don't, you could find yourself on the wrong side of a substantial lawsuit. Consider again the warranty issue:

Rid-a-Bug Exterminator agrees to exterminate a house. The employee is careless, and improperly applies the chemicals, damaging the property and not getting rid of the bugs. Under the law, the company impliedly warranted that they would perform in a workmanlike manner, and the failure to do so could result in liability.

Tiny Store sells a new toaster that causes fire damage to the customer's house. The company that manufactured the toaster has filed bankruptcy. The store, which has warranted the toaster to be merchantable, may be liable for damages.

MY FAVORITE MARKETING SUCCESS STORY

A local grocer was struggling to develop his business and increase his market awareness. He tried all of the advertising and promotional tactics he could afford and seemed to be stalled.

One day he heard that the local "Farmer's Market" needed a location from which to operate on Saturdays. The Farmer's Market is a co-op of local growers who sell fresh produce twice a week at two locations in town. The 20 or so farmers needed a new spot for the busy Saturday sales day.

The grocer suggested that they could use his parking lot. Everyone said, "Are you crazy? Why give your competition prime space right next to your front door? They sell the same produce that you are trying to sell." He donated the parking lot in spite of advice he received. Here's what happened.

1. The free publicity brought hundreds of new customers to his store every week.
2. Sales of meat and grocery items increased fourfold on Saturday.
3. Produce sales doubled. He stocked a complete line of produce, not just the limited variety in season at any one time locally.
4. Overall sales increased 22%, in response, he feels, to the increased market exposure.
5. His store became a focal point for the community.

—Thanks to Bob Hawkes, Bakersfield College, for this insight.

It is very important that you read and understand Chapter 9 on warranties. As you will see in Chapter 9, there are ways to limit liability under warranty law, and this will help to protect you.

It should be obvious that laws enacted since about 1970 have altered what were the previously generally accepted norms of doing business. No longer can you drive the best bargain at any cost to the consumer; no longer can you take advantage of your superior knowledge about the product or service you sell; and no longer can you make representations concerning the goods or services without standing behind them. Penalties for violations of various consumer laws can be extreme, and remember, if you lose you will also have to pay the consumer's attorney's fees, an amount often in excess of the consumer's damages.

The Bottom Line

California laws affect everything you, as a business person, do. Carefully read the next section and find out how some minor changes in the way you do business can help you avoid problems.

Avoiding Liability

The first thing is that basically the only way to avoid liability is to not act in a way that violates the law. Once a violation has occurred there is little in the way of a legal defense. As stated, your good-faith or honest mistake will not get you off. And don't think that you can put up a sign, or have the customer sign a release, to avoid liability. Under many laws, customer rights may not be waived or disclaimed. In other words, once you have violated its provisions you should probably seriously consider settling the matter with the consumer.

But there are some things you can do to prevent violations. First, and foremost, don't say anything about your goods or services unless you are willing to stand behind the statement 100%. For example, if you tell a client that the computer program you designed will serve his needs for one year and it doesn't, you are responsible under this law. You are responsible even if the reason that the program doesn't work is because *his* business increased tenfold, a totally unexpected condition. To avoid liability you must state precisely what you are willing to guarantee. Tell the consumer, "As far as *I can tell,* this will last you for the next year." Now you will have no liability if the product doesn't last because it was just an opinion, an opinion based on the present facts. Here are some other helpful hints to help prevent problems:

1. Never make absolute representations of facts. Whenever possible, qualify your statements to present conditions. Say, "Based on your present conditions, it should last a year," not "It will last a year."
2. Whenever you rely on another source, say so. "This resort has a beautiful pool," may result in liability if it doesn't. "According to their brochure they have a beautiful pool," is the proper way to say it.

3. Always state your opinions as such. "As far as I am concerned it is good as new," not "It is good as new."
4. Be honest. Don't try to hide anything. Remember, under the law you can be liable if you try to induce a person into something by not disclosing everything you know.

Finally, there is one very important idea that can save you a lot of money. Once you become aware of a complaint, you can offer a written settlement of the matter. If you offer to settle in full, the consumer usually cannot collect damages or attorney's fees. In fact, if you offer to settle in full and the consumer still goes to court, you may be entitled to *your* attorney's fees. Even if you do not offer to settle in full, a partial settlement can still help you.

The Bottom Line

Whenever you feel that you may ultimately bear some responsibility, propose a settlement. As a practical matter, many settlement offers are accepted—even if it is not accepted, it may save you a lot of money if the matter proceeds to a trial.

Your Worst Enemy, Your Best Friend

California's consumer laws could be considered the business person's worst enemy, but that is not the only way to look at it. This is the law that your customers will use when you make an error or sell a defective product. But the same laws protect you when you are the consumer and, one time or another, we are all consumers.

The Bottom Line

Consumer protection laws place an obligation on sellers of goods or services to live up to their customers' obligations. This law is your best friend when you are the purchaser.

FOR MORE INFORMATION

Hodgetts, Richard M., and Donald F. Kuratko. *Effective Small Business Management,* 4th Edition. New York: Dryden Press, 1992. See especially Chapter 15, "Pricing, Advertising, and Selling."

Huneycutt, Archer W., and Elizabeth A. Wibker. "Liability Crisis: Small Businesses at Risk." *Journal of Small Business Management,* January 1988, pages 25–30.

Lyons, James. "Seller Beware." *Forbes,* May 27, 1991, pages 184–185.

Morrison, Alan. "The Role of Litigation in Consumer Protection." *Journal of Consumer Affairs,* Winter 1991, pages 209–220.

Scarborough, Norman M., and Thomas W. Zimmerer. *Effective Small Business Management,* 3rd Edition. Columbus, OH: Merrill Publishing Company, 1991. See especially Chapter 26 on governmental responses to consumer issues.

Schwartz, Evan I. "The Rush to Keep Mum: Pressure for Consumers Has Companies Tightening Privacy Protections." *Business Week,* June 8, 1992, pages 36–38.

Tate, Curtis E., Jr., et al. *Small Business Management & Entrepreneurship.* Boston: PWS-Kent Publishing Company, 1992. See Chapter 18, "Satisfying Your Customers."

POINTS TO PONDER

1. Describe a case you know about in which a customer was treated unfairly by a business. Did the business break the law?
2. Describe a situation in which a customer filed a formal complaint against a business. What happened? What can be learned from this example?

DON'T JUST SIT THERE, DO SOMETHING!

1. Visit merchants in your area. What methods do they use to encourage customer feedback (and presumably complaints)? Hint: A number of restaurants have forms requesting comments; some use the back of the bill for this purpose. Write a short commentary on how easy or how difficult it is for customers to let management know what they think.
2. Contact the Better Business Bureau nearest you, or the nearest office of the State of California Department of Consumer Affairs. How easy (or how difficult) would it be to file a complaint? Write a short report on your findings.

9

Warranties: Watch What You Say!

Most people think of a warranty as something on a little tag that comes attached to a product, telling you what the manufacturer might do if a product doesn't work. If you are a businessperson you don't pay much attention to warranties because they are the manufacturer's, not yours.

Well, we have some news for you. This is not what warranty law is all about. In fact, every time you sell something or perform a service you probably give a warranty to your customer. And if you breach that warranty, by not doing what you said, or selling goods that are defective, you are in big trouble. In California, a breach of warranty is just about automatically a violation of California's Song-Beverly Consumer Warranty Act, and a seller can easily find himself or herself liable for damages *and* attorney's fees. You may even be liable for *twice* the damages. Here's an example of how warranty law could affect you:

> Fred and Sara recently opened a small appliance store. They sell stoves, refrigerators, toasters, and microwaves. The other day a customer came in the store and asked if a certain microwave would work in her apartment complex. The customer explained that the complex had special wiring and that there was less power than usual coming through the lines. Fred had just read that the Expo model 890 worked on lower power and told the customer "The Expo 890 is just what you need, it will work in your apartment." Unfortunately for Fred he was wrong. The microwave did not work; in fact, it exploded and set off a small fire, causing $500 in damage. The Expo, which cost $300, was also destroyed. When the customer came back and told Fred the story Fred said he would check with Expo to see what they would do. As you might expect with a product like this, Expo had gone out of business. Fred told the customer he was sorry, there was nothing he could do.

If the customer sued Fred she could recover $800 in damages plus the attorney's fees, which could amount to several thousand dollars more. By saying the Expo would work Fred had made an express warranty to the customer, and by selling a product to do a specific job he made an implied warranty that the product was fit. Both of these warranties were breached when the microwave did not work. The customer is therefore entitled to her damages ($500 for the fire, $300 for the microwave). If the courts determine that Fred actually knew the Expo 890 wouldn't work in the customer's apartment complex, but gambled that the landlord would fix the wiring, or somehow the customer would not come back, then "willful" failure to comply comes into play. The courts may award double damages, plus attorney's fees. **If you are going into business in this state, you had better know warranty law.**

What is a Warranty?

Basically a warranty is a promise that a product or a service will do a certain thing in a certain way. Warranties may be made in two ways: expressly, by your words or conduct; or impliedly, arising as a matter of law simply by virtue of the fact that a sale occurred. These two types of warranties are generally called *express warranties* and *implied warranties.*

Express Warranties

An express warranty is any promise about a good or a service. One may arise out of the contract between you and your customer, from the statement made by you or your salesperson to the customer, from your conduct, or even from the statements of the customer to you. For example, if the customer describes the goods she wants to buy, and then you supply them, the customer's description becomes your express warranty.

The most common examples of express warranties are those made by manufacturers, in writing, whenever a product is sold. Whenever the product sold is a consumer good, and this includes most things you will sell, the warranty is subject to a federal law called the Magnuson-Moss Warranty Act. Similarly, if you sell consumer goods in California, you are definitely subject to the Song-Beverly Consumer Warranty Act. These laws impose certain obligations on the warrantor.

If You Write Your Own Warranties

The Magnuson-Moss warranty law was passed by congress in response to the many problems that existed in state warranty law. Basically this law requires that any written warranty be in simple and readily understandable language. It also requires that all written warranties must be labeled *full* or *limited.* Under the law any warranty that is not a full warranty must be clearly labeled *limited* and the only warranties that can be labeled *full* are those that meet the following requirements:

1. The warrantor (the person making the warranty) must repair or replace the product, or give the consumer a refund within a reasonable time and at no charge if the product does not conform with the warranty.
2. The warrantor may not impose any limitation on the duration of any implied warranty (those warranties that arise by operation of law and are discussed on pages 68–69).
3. The warrantor may not exclude or limit consequential damages (those caused by the defective product) unless the exclusion is conspicuously written on the face of the warranty.
4. If the product can't be repaired after a reasonable number of attempts, the consumer must be permitted to elect to receive a refund or a replacement.
5. The warranty is good for anyone who owns the product during the warranty period.

As we said, under the law, a warranty can be labeled *full* only if it meets *all* of these requirements.

Magnuson-Moss also places restrictions on the content of written warranties. By law, your written warranty must include certain basic information about:

1. What parts of the product or what types of problems the warranty covers (and, if necessary for clarity, what parts or problems it does not cover).
2. What the period of coverage is.
3. What you will do to correct problems (and, if necessary for clarity, what you will not do).
4. How the customer can get warranty service.
5. How state law may affect certain provisions of the warranty.

In addition, if there are limitations or conditions on the warranty coverage you provide, you must include a statement of them in your warranty. You may want to consider what conditions and limitations you really need and eliminate those that are unnecessary.

If your warranty contains certain particular conditions or restrictions, you must include additional information. Check the FTC's Rule on Disclosure of Written Consumer Product Warranty Terms and Conditions, included in Appendix A-9, to determine what you must disclose in your warranty.

Finally, the law requires that your warranty include a title that indicates whether it is *full* or *limited.* What these terms mean and how to use them in titling your warranty are explained in detail in this manual.

Of course, you should consult your lawyer to ensure that your warranty meets all the requirements of both federal and state warranty law.

There are also some things you want to make sure are not included in your warranty. For example, promotional statements, instructions to service agents, and other extraneous material in a warranty may confuse customers about the purpose of the document. Include only necessary information in your warranty. A concise, straightforward warranty will promote your product better than a crowded document full of praise for your product.

If you feel that it is necessary to include promotional material about your product with your written warranty, keep it separate from the warranty. If possible, put it in a separate brochure. If you put promotional statements on the same page as your warranty, clearly set apart your warranty, for example, by placing a border around it. The customer should be able to separate at a glance the warranty from the promotional material.

One way to make sure that your warranty covers all the necessary material, and does so in a clear concise manner, is to use the basic elements required by law as headings for your warranty. The Federal Trade Commission, which enforces federal warranty law, recommends that you use the following headings:

- What the Warranty Covers (and, if necessary for clarity, What it Does *not* Cover)
- What the Period of Coverage Is
- What We (the Company) Will Do to Correct Problems (and, if necessary for clarity, What the Company Will *Not* Do)
- How You (the Customer) Can Get Service
- How State Law Relates to the Warranty

You may need to use additional headings in your warranty if all of the conditions and limitations cannot be dealt with adequately using only the recommended headings.

Regardless of which headings you use to organize your warranty, be sure the headings are specific and informative. You may, for example, want to use questions as headings because they reflect what consumers ask about warranty coverage. We do not recommend headings that consist of a single noun or a string of nouns. These are usually vague and general and do not give readers enough information to let them know what follows in the text. For example, the following headings, all of which come from one warranty, are not very useful or informative:

Full Two Year Warranty On The Black Star 2001 Clothes Washer

What is Covered:	For How Long:	What Black Star Will Do:
Any defect in your 2001 Clothes Washer.	Two years after the date you bought your 2001 Clothes Washer.	Repair, or if repair is not possible, either replace your 2001 Clothes Washer, or refund the purchase price, whichever you prefer.

Limited Warranty on Parts for the Third Through Fifth Years

What is Covered:	For How Long:	What Black Star Will Do:
Any defect in your 2001 Clothes Washer.	From the start of the third year after you bought your 2001 Clothes Washer until the end of the fifth year after you bought it.	Provide free new or rebuilt replacement parts, but not labor to install the parts. Any servicer you choose can do service during this period.

How to Get Service: Contact any Black Star Dealer or any Authorized Black Star Service Center. See the Yellow Pages under "Appliance Repair" for the name of a Black Star Servicer near you, or call 800-111-1111.

Your Rights Under State Law: This warranty gives you specific legal rights, and you may also have other rights which vary from state to state.

Figure 9-1. A "full' and "limited" warranty.

- Parts Warranty
- Extended Porcelain Finish Warranty
- Warranty Service
- Extended Warranty Service Labor Allowance
- Ownership
- Warranty Conditions
- Federal Regulatory Provisions
- Purchaser's Responsibility
- Purchase Registration
- Model and Serial Numbers
- Factory Assistance

A warranty does not have to be just "full" or "limited." Different parts may be covered by different warranties, or the warranty may change after a period of time. For exam-

Polarity Corporation Limited Warranty

What is Covered?

This warranty covers all defects in workmanship or materials in your Polarity Automobile Battery.

How Long is the Coverage Period?

The warranty coverage runs for 36 months from the date you buy your Polarity Automobile Battery.

What Will Polarity Corporation Do?

If your Polarity Auto Battery fails during:	Polarity will provide you with a credit of:
The 1st through the 9th month	100%
The 10th through the 18th month	75%
The 19th through the 27th month	50%
The 28th through the 36th month	25%

The credit will be a percentage of the original price you paid for the battery. The credit will be good only toward purchase of a new Polarity Auto Battery of the same or equivalent model.

How Can You Get Service?

Bring the battery and proof of date and amount of purchase to any retailer that carries Polarity products. Check the Yellow Pages under "Auto Parts" for the name and address of a Polarity dealer near you.

How Does State Law Apply?

This warranty gives you specific legal rights, and you may also have other rights which vary from state to state.

Figure 9-2. A limited warranty with pro-rata coverage.

ple, Figure 9-1 shows (page 66) a "full" and "limited" warranty.

Figure 9-2 gives an example of a limited warranty, with pro-rata coverage.

Warranties are a very important part of any sale. For this reason they are regulated by federal and state law. If you are going to give your customers a written warranty you should be careful to comply with the law. If you would like more, free, information about written warranties, you can write the Federal Trade Commission, 6th & Pennsylvania Ave. N.W., Washington, D.C. 20580, and ask for their booklet "Writing Readable Warranties."

The Bottom Line

Written express warranties are strictly regulated by federal law. If you give your customers a written warranty be sure that it complies with Magnuson-Moss and is labeled *full* or *limited.*

Oral Express Warranties

Express warranties do not have to be written. In fact, few small businesses make written express warranties, relying instead on the warranties made by the manufacturer. But oral representations about the quality of the goods can also turn out to be legally binding as a warranty.

Under the law, any representation about the goods, or a promise relating to them, constitutes a warranty. For example, if you tell a customer that the product is finished with "100% oil base enamel" it better be, because you just warranted it. And don't say that the table is "stain resistant" unless you know for a fact it is because the buyer could sue for breach of warranty and recover damages. Be careful about what you or your salespeople say about a product. Any affirmation of fact about a product, or a description of its qualities or benefits can become an express warranty. The only major exceptions to this are statements of your opinion. A mere statement of opinion, salesperson "puffing" does not constitute a warranty. So if you say that the spark plug is the "best made" it may not constitute a warranty. But be careful, most courts to have considered whether a statement is "puffing" or a warranty generally favor the consumer and find that it is a warranty. To protect yourself be sure to say "in my opinion," or "as far as I am concerned." This will let the buyer know that it is just your opinion and not a warranty.

The Bottom Line

Representations about a product, whether oral or written, can easily become warranties if they enter into the bargain. Be careful about what you and your employees say. To fully protect yourself you may also want to consider limiting your warranty liability contractually. This alternative is discussed on pages 69–70.

Implied Warranties

Many people think that a warranty is something that arises only if a seller makes a promise, or guarantee, to a buyer about a product. Many sellers think that as long as they don't make any promises they don't have to worry about warranty law. Well think again. **Under the law any time you sell something the law implies certain warranties.** These implied warranties arise simply by virtue of the sale; you do not have to do or say anything special. For example, consider this:

> Janie and her friend Bess recently opened a small shop to sell wool and knitting supplies. Both had a lot of experience with knitting but little with business. They were doing pretty well, however, and even made a small profit. Generally, they made their money from the sale of wool, and offered their advice as part of their customer service program. All of the wool they sold was provided by a local wholesaler. The wool was marked with a written guarantee by the manufacturer against defects in workmanship.
>
> About four weeks ago a customer came in and bought $75 worth of wool for a sweater. The customer didn't know much about wool and told Janie she needed a heavy-duty wool that would be good for a ski sweater. Janie gave her the wool she would use. Needless to say, the wool was defective and after the sweater was finished, while she was on a ski vacation, the sweater came apart, and the customer got frostbitten as a result.

Even though Janie never "guaranteed" the wool, or said anything about its quality, she has violated the implied warranty of merchantability and the implied warranty of fitness for a particular purpose. If the customer were to sue, she would be entitled to the cost of the wool and her damages from the frostbite under the Song-Beverly Act. Of course Janie could sue the wool company, but if they have gone out of business, Janie still owes her customer.

Basically, the law imposes a warranty upon a seller guaranteeing that the goods sold are what they are supposed to be. This is called the "implied warranty of merchantability," and the law reads like this:

> (1) Unless excluded or modified, a warranty that the goods shall be merchantable is implied in a contract for their sale if the seller is a merchant with respect to goods of that kind. Under this section the serving for value of food or drink to be consumed either on the premises or elsewhere is a sale.
>
> (2) Goods to be merchantable must be at least such as:
>
> (a) pass without objection in the trade under the contract description; and
>
> (b) in the case of fungible goods, are of fair average quality within the description; and
>
> (c) are fit for the ordinary purposes for which such goods are used; and
>
> (d) run, within the variations permitted by the agreement, of even kind, quality and quantity within each unit and among all units involved; and
>
> (e) are adequately contained, packaged, and labeled as the agreement may require; and
>
> (f) conform to the promises or affirmation of fact made on the container or label if any.

Without boring you with all the details, this law basically means that whenever a merchant sells something he guarantees the buyer that the buyer is getting a product that will do what it is supposed to do, in the way in which it is supposed to, for the amount of time it usually does.

And there is one other implied warranty that arises when you sell goods, called *the implied warranty of "Fitness for a Particular Purpose."* This law is as follows:

> "Where the seller at the time of contracting has reason to know any particular purpose for which the goods are required and that the buyer is relying on the seller's skill or judgment to select or furnish suitable goods, there is unless excluded or modified under the next section an implied warranty that the goods shall be fit for such purpose."

In our example above, Janie made this warranty because her customer needed wool for a "particular purpose," a ski sweater, and the buyer relied on Janie's judgment. Because the wool was not fit for any purpose, Janie would have breached both the warranty of merchantability and the warranty of fitness for a particular purpose. **If you are in a business where your customers rely on your skill and judgment to choose products for them, remember that you are probably warranting that what you sell will do what the customer asked for.**

Implied warranties, however, are not absolute. They can be disclaimed and may not arise in the sale of used goods. Implied warranties are considered part of the contract, and as such they can be disclaimed by a seller. For example, if you sell something "as is" there are no implied warranties. Also, many California courts have held that there are no implied warranties when you sell used goods. But there is one big exception to your right to get out of liability under this warranty. Under the Magnuson-Moss Warranty Act, a seller who makes any written express warranties may not disclaim implied warranties. The Song-Beverly Act says about the same thing: a "retailer . . . transacting a sale in which express warranties are given, may not limit, modify, or disclaim the implied warranties" guaranteed by the act. For example, if you give your customer a 30-day written guarantee on parts, you may not disclaim the implied warranties that go along with the sale.

The Bottom Line

Remember, anytime you sell something an implied warranty probably arises. Be sure to either take steps to disclaim this warranty, or make sure that you have sufficient insurance to protect yourself.

Limiting Warranty Liability

Warranty is a creature of contract, and because it is you may contractually limit, or disclaim, your warranty liability. Consider this:

> Bob, a car dealer, recently sold a used car to Mr. and Mrs. Jones. Before they signed the contract Bob said "This car is a real gem. It has been completely overhauled." Unfortunately for the Jones', that was not true. But the contract the parties signed said "Seller has made no representations about the quality of the car. There are no warranties except those contained in this written contract. Seller disclaims all other warranties express and implied including the warranty of merchantability. Buyer accepts the car 'as is.'" Even though the contract is probably sufficient to limit Bob's liability for breach of warranty, he could still be liable under the California laws on false advertising.

Under the laws on false or misleading advertising, liability may not be contractually limited or disclaimed. Even though you may be able to insulate yourself from warranty liability for oral promises, you can't do so under laws on deceptive advertising. **In California if you say it you had better be willing to stand behind it 100%.**

Keeping in mind the limited effect of disclaiming warranty liability, there are ways that you can do so. First, oral promises, even if they are sufficient to give rise to a warranty, are usually not enforceable if the written contract states that it is your complete agreement and that there are no other promises. For example, language such as this would probably be sufficient to eliminate warranty liability based on an oral statement:

> This contract is the full and complete expression of the parties' warranty liability. The entire agreement of the parties regarding warranties is contained herein and no evidence of any prior or contemporaneous agreement, whether agreement, representation, understanding, or the like, may be used to add to, subtract from, or modify the content of the warranties here set forth. **There are no warranties that extend beyond the description of the goods contained in this contract and only such warranties are given as we expressly set out herein.**

If the contract your customer signed contained this statement you probably would not be responsible for any express warranties that arose out of your conversations, or those of your salesperson, with the customer before the contract was signed. Of course, even this is subject to legal interpretation. Any business law textbook will tell you that to be valid, a contract must have an offer, acceptance, consideration (usually, some money must change hands), capacity (not a minor), and legality (no contract to murder a competitor could be legal). But, what do all these terms mean? A crash course in contract law might help. But the truth is, your case might still not fit any other case. Do the best you can, and when in doubt, seek professional advice.

A second way to limit your express warranty liability is to limit the buyer's remedy. For example, the following clause could be used in a written contract to limit the buyer to repair of the goods or a refund of the purchase price, and limit damages.

> **Buyer's exclusive remedy.** In the event of a breach of this contract by seller, the Buyer's exclusive remedy shall be to return the goods or any part thereof which may be defective or nonconforming and receive repayment by the Seller of all, or in the case of a partial breach, a pro-rata share of the purchase price that has been paid by the buyer at the time of the breach. Repayment of the purchase price shall discharge the Seller from all obligations under this contract. Buyer shall in no event recover consequential damages.

Here is an example of how these two clauses would work:

> Frank recently opened a small auto parts store. Recently he sold a fuel pump to California Super Truckers, a long-distance hauling company. His salesperson told the buyer the pump "would last at least a year." The fuel pump cost $189.00 and the trucking company and its mechanic installed it.

As it turns out the pump only lasted six months, an otherwise reasonable length of time. It broke down during a long haul of refrigerated vegetables and caused the loss of the entire load. California Trucker had insurance to cover the loss, but not the income they would have made. They now want to sue Frank for $189.00 plus the $750 profit they would have made on the hauling.

If Frank did not have a written agreement with the trucker he probably will have to settle because if he goes to court he is going to lose. The salesperson's statement probably constituted an express warranty about the pump.

On the other hand, if Frank's invoice or contract of sale contained the two above clauses he would have only limited contract liability for breach of warranty. The first clause would prevent the buyer from using the oral statement as a warranty and the second clause would probably be sufficient, even if liability arose, to limit his damages to return of the purchase price. **Remember, unless you act to limit damages you will be responsible for all foreseeable damages that result from your breach of warranty.** For example, if the buyer didn't have insurance, Frank might have been liable for the cost of the damaged vegetables as well.

Finally, there is one more way to eliminate most of your warranty problems: sell the good "as is." If the contract is clearly indicated to be on an "as-is" basis you probably have no warranty liability, unless the buyer can establish that you made an express warranty. To eliminate even this problem use a contract that contains the clause excluding oral warranties with your "as-is" clause. But again remember that even a contract "as-is" does not automatically insure you against every possible liability. For example, if your salesperson tells the buyer the car is in great condition, and then you sell it "as-is," you would be responsible if what the salesman said wasn't true. You wouldn't have any warranty liability because of the "as-is" but you could have liability because of the misrepresentation about the goods.

The Bottom Line

It is possible to contractually limit or eliminate warranty liability and you should consider doing so. But remember, California law, and California courts, favor buyers. Best advice . . . don't say it unless you will stand behind it.

FOR MORE INFORMATION

"Accounting for Extended Warranty Contracts." *Journal of Accountancy,* August 1990, pages 101–102.

Blackburn, John D., Elliot I. Klayman, and Martin H. Malin. *The Legal Environment of Business,* 4th Edition. Homewood, IL: Irwin Publishing Company, 1991. See especially Chapter 8.

Freeman, Laurie. "Service Contracts: Warranties Impact Bottom Line." *Stores,* January 1992, page 122.

Kelley, Craig A., and Jeffrey S. Conant. "Extended Warranties: Consumer and Manufacturer Perceptions." *Journal of Consumer Affairs,* Summer 1991, pages 68–83.

Ryan, J.D., et al. *Small Business: An Entrepreneur's Plan,* 2nd Edition. New York: Harcourt Brace Jovanovich, 1990. See Chapter 3 on marketing, keeping in mind the possible pitfalls.

Tate, Curtis E., Jr., et al. *Small Business Management & Entrepreneurship.* Boston: PWS-Kent Publishing Company, 1992. Chapter 23 helps show how to ensure quality products and service, which can be keys to satisfied customers.

POINTS TO PONDER

1. Since California law gives the customer an "implied warranty" on just about everything anyhow, why and when would you want to use a written warranty?

2. Describe a case where a product (perhaps an automobile) was "recalled" for product modification. What were the circumstances surrounding this recall? Was the final result customer satisfaction?

DON'T JUST SIT THERE, DO SOMETHING!

1. Find examples of warranties in ads in newspapers. Make a photocopy of your example. How do these warranties protect the customer? The seller? Write a short description of your analysis of the warranty or warranties you found.
2. Find examples of warranties on products for sale in your area. For example, check the back of a cereal box. How do these warranties protect the customer? The seller? If possible, photocopy your example or examples. Discuss briefly.

10

Credit Sales: Tempting But Risky

CASH

It goes without saying that the best way to do business is to have your customers pay you in cash, at or before delivery. But unfortunately most people don't pay in cash; a check or some form of credit is the more usual method of payment. And even though you probably consider a check and cash to be one and the same, because no extension of credit is involved, there are some subtle differences you should be aware of.

First, remember that a check is nothing more than a person's order to his or her bank to pay you money. If the money isn't there the bank has no liability to pay you. In other words, taking a check means relying on the honesty of the person that gave it to you. But there are some ways you can decrease the risks inherent in taking a check. First, make sure that you have proper identification from the person writing the check. If it is a forgery you will be out of luck. A drivers license or other picture ID card at a minimum should be required. Second, there are several check verification services you can subscribe to that you can call and have the check guaranteed. These services charge a small fee for each check but it will be worth it if one of the checks bounces. Finally, you should know that if a customer gives you a check without having money in the bank to cover it this is a criminal offense and you can have the person arrested. To find out more about this law read pages 79–85, which discuss collection.

As you can see, there are risks involved in accepting a check but if you require proper identification the risks may be minimal, and the threat of criminal prosecution is a big help in collecting on a bad check. Whenever in doubt about an individual's honesty or ability to pay, however, demand cash, or a cashier's or certified check. You have the legal right to do so.

CREDIT

Credit has become an essential part of any business. If you purchase goods or supplies you may want to buy them on credit, and if you sell goods or services your customers may want to pay on credit. Even though we all know that the easiest way to do business is to do it on a cash-only basis, a commercial reality is that to exist and compete in today's marketplace you will probably have to give your customers an alternative way to pay. No one wants to lose a sale because the customer went somewhere else where he could pay it off on time.

So what are your alternatives to selling things only for cash? Well first, as we just pointed out, taking a check is not really an alternative. The law treats checks as cash, and you and your customers should also. Payment by a check obligates the person who wrote the check to have money on hand in the bank to cover it, and may allow you to use the criminal courts to collect if the check bounces. In other words, it is not an extension of credit. The only real alternative to cash is some form of credit, and here you have two choices: you may extend the credit yourself; or you can rely on third-party credit grantors.

Third-Party Credit

Credit, by definition, involves a risk; the risk that the debtor will not pay and the creditor will suffer a loss. The best way to ensure that you will not suffer this loss is to arrange for someone else to extend the credit. This is what we are talking about when we use the term *third-party credit.* Perhaps the most common example of this arrangement is the credit card. For example, suppose you sell $900 worth of goods to a customer who needs several months to pay off the bill. The customer gives you a credit card to pay the $900. You then collect from the credit card company, and the credit card company extends credit to your customer. If the customer doesn't pay, the credit card company, not you, bears the loss. Additionally, all of the terms of the credit agreement, the problems of compliance with federal disclosure laws and state usury laws, and the process of collection are handled by the credit card company. **Accepting credit cards is the simplest, safest way of**

extending credit. But as you might expect, this simplicity and safety does not come free.

Credit card companies make their money two ways. First, they charge the customer a fee for the card and interest on any money borrowed. Second, they charge a fee to you when you accept the card. How much you pay the credit card company will depend on how many credit card transactions you process and the amount each transaction is for. Generally you can expect to pay the credit card company anywhere from 1–5% of the transaction amount as a commission for their services. For example, in the case above, the customer would sign a credit card draft in the amount of $900. You would deposit this in your bank and be credited with $900 minus the credit card commission. If it was 5% you would receive $855. As you can tell, credit card commissions can add up—but remember, you have taken no risk if the customer doesn't pay, and you have your money relatively quickly. **Each credit card company, and many of the banks that issue credit cards, have their own commission and payment terms. Shop around for the best buy. You can decide how many, if any, credit cards you will accept.** Be sure to find out:

- How much do I have to pay for the use of the card?
- Will this amount increase or decrease depending upon the number or dollar amount of my transactions?
- How soon will I receive the funds for the charge?

Once you do enter into an agreement with a credit card company or bank, be sure to read the agreement carefully and make sure you comply with its terms. For example, in many cases the credit card company will hold you responsible if you forget to get a transaction approved, and the customer doesn't pay.

Another way of using third-party credit, which is feasible only if you deal in large transaction amounts, is to refer the customer to a lending institution to get the cash to pay you. For example, if your business is home repair, you can have your customers go to their bank and arrange for a home improvement loan to pay you cash at the time you do the work. Before you do this very often, however, there are several things to keep in mind.

First, if the customer is going to borrow money against their home to pay you for your work, make sure the loan is approved by the bank and the bank has arranged for payment *before* you do any work. Ask to see a written commitment from the bank for the loan, and have the checks issued in either your name, your name *and* the customer's name, or a third party, such as a general contractor, whom you trust. Talk with the bank before you do anything.

A second problem you may face if you use this type of third-party credit is compliance with federal disclosure laws. Under federal law you can be treated as a creditor and subject to various penalties, if you are what the law calls an "arranger of credit." An arranger of credit is someone who regularly arranges for the extension of credit more than 25 times a year. For example, if you sold cars, and each of your customers was referred by you to a finance company for his or her loan, you would, under this law, be treated as a creditor if you did this more than 25 times in a calendar year period. Without going into a lot of detail about just what this means, suffice it to say that if the bank or creditor messed up, you could be responsible. Only use this type of third party credit occasionally. If you are going to regularly refer your customers to another for financing, you must take steps to ensure that the creditor has complied with all the federal disclosure laws. You or your attorney should examine the creditor's forms, and ask to see a copy of the completed contract before delivering the goods or performing the services.

The Bottom Line

Third-party credit is simple. Letting someone else be the creditor avoids all of the risk and most of the hassle of extending credit yourself. But, this protection does cost money, and if you regularly refer your customers to another for credit, you may end up being treated as a creditor yourself.

Special Credit Card Rules

If you accept credit cards you should know about the special federal laws that protect consumers who use them. Although these laws actually deal with the consumers' rights against the credit card company, and not you, as you will see, whenever the credit card company has to give back these consumers' money, the company in turn will debit your account.

Let's start with an example:

> Your business has been booming and you discover a new, untapped, market—mail order. After you place several ads in local papers you begin to receive orders, which you promptly fill and send back to the customers. Because your product is not very large or heavy you use the U.S. mail to send it. You also allow your customers to pay by credit card and most have chosen to do so. Each of your devices sells for $69.95, and you include an extra $4.00 for postage and handling. Everything is fine until you suddenly receive a memo from your bank that the credit card company has debited your account for over $700. It turns out that ten customers have written the credit card company to dispute their bill because they did not receive your product. Your records show that they were shipped, but you have no other proof.

Under federal laws you are probably out of luck. The law states that a consumer may dispute his bill, and refuse to pay, whenever there is a "billing error." Most billing errors are between the credit card company and the consumer; however, a charge for goods that were not received is considered a billing error. If your product never arrived, and you will have to prove it did, the consumer doesn't have to pay the credit card company. The credit card company, in turn, has the right to debit your account.

If you ship goods and accept credit cards as payment, be sure to use a method of shipment that allows you to prove that the goods have been received and accepted. For example, although goods mailed through the U.S. mails do not have a receipt, goods shipped by United Parcel Service must be signed for and you would have proof of receipt. But even if the goods are shipped and accepted you may still not get your money. Consider this:

> Your business is still flourishing. You have resolved your problem of undelivered goods by using UPS and profits are rolling in. One day you receive a large order over the phone. You get all the information and call the order in to be approved, which it is. You then ship the 10 items. A few days later you get a call from the consumer that all of the items were broken when they arrived. You don't believe you have any responsibility for the shipping company so you tell the consumer to take it up with them. A few weeks later you find out that the credit card company has debited your account because the consumer refused to pay his bill, saying that the goods were defective and that he doesn't owe you the money.

Under the same federal law that protects buyers when goods do not arrive, a consumer doesn't have to pay his credit card bill if he has a dispute with the merchant. In most cases when the customer disputes the bill the credit card company will debit your account and ask for your side of the story. Only if you can show that the customer's dispute is invalid will they give you back your money. In most other cases the credit card company will tell you to resolve the problem yourself with the customer. Don't think that when you take a credit card your rights against the customer are secured. **Under federal law the customer may raise his claims against you, against the credit card company, any time the following three requirements are met:**

1. The cardholder has made a good faith attempt to settle the matter with the merchant.
2. The goods or services cost over $50.
3. The transaction took place within the cardholder's home state, or within 100 miles of his home.

Whenever you take a credit card, and a dispute arises with a customer, be sure to try and resolve it. Don't take the attitude that you have the money and the customer has to try and get it back. Under federal law it is very easy for the customer to turn the tables on you by simply disputing the charge.

The Bottom Line

Taking credit cards is convenient, but federal law offers the customer special protection against the credit card company if the goods don't arrive, or are defective. These laws are important to you because if the credit card company has to pay the cardholder, they will simply debit your account to get their money back.

Extending Credit

Let's begin with a warning: **Extending credit is very risky, both financially and legally.** You are aware of the financial risks when you extend credit; you may not get paid back. You may not, however, be aware of the legal risks. Credit laws are very specific and failure to comply with any of the many federal and state laws could be very costly. Consider this:

> Susan recently opened a new catering service. After just a few weeks in business she was contacted by one of the city's best known and wealthiest families. They wanted her to cater a large party for more than 500 people. The total cost of the affair would be nearly $10,000. Susan was elated. This would be bigger than all her previous jobs combined, and it also would establish her as one of the "in" caterers in the city. Everything was perfect until they discussed payment. When the client asked for 60 days to pay, the "usual" in the catering business, Susan didn't know what to do. She had often given people the right to pay off their bill in four or five installments with a small interest charge but she had never dealt with this much money. When she told the client she would have to charge him interest, he said, "O.K., just pick a fair amount." Susan suggested 10% and he approved. She then drew up a quick agreement on a piece of paper, saying that the client agreed to pay 10% interest, or $1,000, for the right to pay the bill in 60 days. Susan then told him that as far as she was concerned, their handwritten agreement was all they needed and it was a legally valid contract.

Even though Susan has acted in complete innocence, she could be in real trouble. Susan has probably violated California usury laws and may owe the client three times the interest, or $3,000. She has probably violated federal credit laws and owes him another $1,000. In other words, Susan's little mistake, of charging too much interest and telling the client that everything was legal, could cost her $4,000 plus whatever court cost and attorney's fees were involved. **If you ever decide to extend credit, be careful! Credit laws have high penalties for those who fail to follow them.**

ANNUAL PERCENTAGE RATE The cost of your credit as a yearly rate.	FINANCE CHARGE The dollar amount the credit will cost you.	Amount Financed The amount of credit provided to you or on your behalf.	Total of Payments The amount you will have paid after you have made all payments as scheduled.	Total Sale Price The total cost of your purchase on credit, including your downpayment of $ __________.
%	$	$	$	$

You have the right to receive at this time an itemization of the Amount Financed.

☐ I want an itemization. ☐ I do not want an itemization.

Your payment schedule will be:

Number of Payments	Amount of Payments	When Payments Are Due

Insurance

Credit life insurance and credit disability insurance are not required to obtain credit, and will not be provided unless you sign and agree to pay the additional cost.

Type	Premium	Signature
Credit Life		I want credit life insurance. ________ Signature
Credit Disability		I want credit disability insurance. ________ Signature
Credit Life and Disability		I want credit life and disability insurance. ________ Signature

You may obtain property insurance from anyone you want that is acceptable to (creditor). If you get the insurance from (creditor), you will pay $__________.

Security: You are giving a security interest in:

☐ the goods or property being purchased.

☐ (brief description of other property).

Filing fees $ ________ **Non-filing insurance** $ ________

Late Charge: If a payment is late, you will be charged $________/________% of the payment.

Prepayment: If you pay off early, you

☐ may ☐ will not have to pay a penalty.

☐ may ☐ will not be entitled to a refund of part of the finance charge.

See your contract documents for any additional information about nonpayment, default, any required repayment in full before the scheduled date, and prepayment refunds and penalties.

e means an estimate

Figure 10-1. Credit sale model form.

So what are the credit laws you should be aware of? First, California, like every other state, has usury statutes that regulate how much interest you can charge. In fact, we have a usury law written into our state constitution! **Usury laws are very complicated.** There is no one amount that you can always use as a ceiling to be safe. The amount of legally permissible interest depends upon the nature of the transaction, the nature of the parties, and the rate the Federal Reserve Board in San Francisco charges member banks. The best advice we can give you is before you agree on a rate of interest, check with your attorney or accountant to find out the maximum legal rate you can charge. **If you charge an amount in excess of the legal rate, you may be responsible for a penalty in the amount of three times the interest you charged.** You also may find yourself subject to additional penalties under laws regulating false advertising, if you represent to your customer that the law allows you to charge the amount you have, when in fact usury law prohibited it. Under this law you are liable for up to three times the customer's damages. It is worth noting that California usury laws are specific, detailed, and downright scary. Remember Susan and the "10%" interest (which was actually closer to a 60% annual percentage rate)? Well, any person who "directly or indirectly" charges and receives interest in excess of that allowed by law "is guilty of loan-sharking, a felony." But not to worry, the maximum sentence (in addition to treble damages) is only five years in state prison. What should Susan remember from

Big Wheel Auto Alice Green

ANNUAL PERCENTAGE RATE The cost of your credit as a yearly rate.	FINANCE CHARGE The dollar amount the credit will cost you.	Amount Financed The amount of credit provided to you or on your behalf.	Total of Payments The amount you will have paid after you have made all payments as scheduled.	Total Sale Price The total cost of your purchase on credit, including your downpayment of $ 1500 –
14.84 %	$1496.80	$6107.50	$7604.30	$9129.30

You have the right to receive at this time an itemization of the Amount Financed.
☐ I want an itemization. ☒ I do not want an itemization.

Your payment schedule will be:

Number of Payments	Amount of Payments	When Payments Are Due
36	$211.23	Monthly beginning 6-1-91

Insurance
Credit life insurance and credit disability insurance are not required to obtain credit, and will not be provided unless you sign and agree to pay the additional cost.

Type	Premium	Signature	
Credit Life	$120 –	I want credit life insurance.	Alice Green Signature
Credit Disability		I want credit disability insurance.	Signature
Credit Life and Disability		I want credit life and disability insurance.	Signature

Security: You are giving a security interest in:
☒ the goods being purchased.
☐ ____________________.

Filing fees $ 12.50 **Non-filing insurance** $ ________

Late Charge: If a payment is late, you will be charged $10.

Prepayment: If you pay off early, you
☐ may ☐ will not have to pay a penalty.
☒ may ☐ will not be entitled to a refund of part of the finance charge.

See your contract documents for any additional information about nonpayment, default, any required repayment in full before the scheduled date, and prepayment refunds and penalties.

I have received a copy of this statement.

Alice Green 5-1-91
Signature Date

e means an estimate

Figure 10-2. Example of completed credit sale form.

all this? Check with someone before you decide how much to charge for interest.

And once you have determined the proper amount of interest, you must be very careful how you disclose it and what your loan agreement looks like. If you begin to regularly extend credit, that is, 25 times or more a year, you are subject to Truth-in-Lending, a federal law that regulates how the terms of a credit transaction are disclosed.* For example, Figure 10-1 (page 75) shows a credit sale model form a creditor subject to Truth-in-Lending should use.

Here is an example of how the Federal Reserve Board recommends you complete this form. Suppose that you sold a car for a cash price of $7,500 with a down payment of $1,500. You charge interest at an 8% add-on rate (under the law, interest must be disclosed at an Annual Percentage * Rate) and the term is three years, with 36 equal payments. The credit life insurance premium and filing fees are also financed by you. There is a $25 credit-report fee paid by the buyer before the sale. The form when complete should look like the example in Figure 10-2.

As you can tell, some of the terms used in this form appear to have special meaning under the law. Federal law requires the use of certain terms in every credit contract. For example, the finance charge is defined as follows:

This law also prohibits discrimination. See Appendix A-4 for a copy of the federal rules regarding credit discrimination.

(a) *Definition.* The finance charge is the cost of consumer credit as a dollar amount. It includes any charge payable directly or indirectly by the consumer and imposed directly or indirectly by the creditor as an incident to or a condition of the extension of credit. It does not include any charge of a type payable in a comparable cash transaction.

You may have assumed that the interest you charged was part of the finance charge, but did you know that all of the following are also included in the legal definition of that term:

(1) Interest, time price differential, and any amount payable under an add-on or discount system of additional charges.
(2) Service, transaction, activity, and carrying charges, including any charge imposed on a checking or other transaction account to the extent that the charge exceeds the charge for a similar account without a credit feature.
(3) Points, loan fees, assumption fees, finder's fees, and similar charges.
(4) Appraisal, investigation, and credit report fees.
(5) Premiums or other charges for any guarantee or insurance protecting the creditor against the consumer's default or other credit loss.
(6) Charges imposed on a creditor by another person for purchasing or accepting a consumer's obligation, if the consumer is required to pay the charges in cash, as an addition to the obligation, or as a deduction from the proceeds of the obligation.
(7) Premiums or other charges for credit life, accident, health, or loss-of-income insurance, written in connection with a credit transaction.
(8) Premiums or other charges for insurance against loss of or damage to property, or against liability arising out of the ownership or use of property, written in connection with a credit transaction.
(9) Discounts for the purpose of inducing payment by a means other than the use of credit.

This may appear to be a lot of legal gobbledygook, but it is the law! Don't think that you can just say to someone "that will be 10% a year interest." Under the Truth-in-Lending law, there is no such thing as interest, there is a "finance charge." And this finance charge must be disclosed as an "annual percentage rate," another defined term that involves a very complicated formula. The easiest way to determine the annual percentage rate is to use charts prepared by the Federal Reserve Board. **If you don't want to bother with these charts, ask your accountant.** There are also special provisions dealing with disclosure of pay, net amounts and dates, insurance, late fees, prepayment penalties, and the taking of any security for the loan.

The Bottom Line

Compliance with federal credit laws is very complicated; a mistake can be very costly. Before you begin regularly extending credit yourself, ask your attorney to approve all of your forms and advise you on how they should be filled out. For the occasional loan, however, the promissory notes in Appendix B, Forms 12a and 12b, should be sufficient.

If you find yourself extending credit very often, you should write the Federal Reserve Board, Washington D.C., and ask for a free copy of Regulation Z-Truth-in-Lending.

FOR MORE INFORMATION

Bakersville, Dawn M. "The Big Comeback" *Black Enterprise,* January 1992, pages 61–63.

Burstiner, Irving. *The Small Business Handbook.* New York: Prentice Hall, 1989. See especially Chapters 17 and 18, "Managing the Company's Finances."

Carlson, Eugene. "Collecting Overdue Bills Involves Walking Delicate Line." *Wall Street Journal,* October 10, 1990, page B-2.

Longenecker, Justin G., and Carlos W. Moore. *Small Business Management.* Cincinnati: Southwestern Publishing Company, 1991. See Chapter 12, "Pricing and Credit Policy."

Maynard, Roberta. "Smart Ways to Manage Cash." *Nation's Business,* August 1992, pages 43–44.

U.S. Small Business Administration. *Business Basics: Credit and Collections: Policy and Procedures.* Washington, D.C.: U.S. Government Printing Office, 1981. This booklet, "Self Instructional Booklet 1014," is out of date and apparently out of print. But, it may be in your local library, and it contains excellent sample letters for extracting cash from folks who owe you money.

Woodyard, Chris. "TRW to Offer Free Credit Reports Next Week." *Los Angeles Times,* April 25, 1992, page D-5. Describes how individuals can now get a copy of their own credit information. For more information write to TRW Consumer Assistance, P.O. Box 2350, Chatsworth, California 91313-2350.

POINTS TO PONDER

1. Why do so many small businesses extend free credit?
2. Usually this free credit is not available to everybody, but just to some customers. Why?

DON'T JUST SIT THERE, DO SOMETHING!

1. Talk to someone about having Visa and Mastercard accounts for your proposed business. Talk to the offices of both of these cards by phone and see what information you can have mailed to you. Write a short description of your findings.

2. Try the same with other credit cards, such as American Express or Discover. Any differences in the way your request is received?
3. Why do so many small businesses extend free credit? Find at least three examples of businesses offering free credit, ranging from local neighborhood bookstores to perhaps a lawnmower shop. ("90 days same as cash" or "payment due when we bill you—no interest if paid within 30 days"). Discuss briefly whether or not this is actually free credit, and discuss whether you think the policy makes good business sense.

11

Getting Paid: Eyes on the Bottom Line

Whether you are selling goods or providing a service the bottom line is always the same: if you are not paid for what you do, you will soon be out of business. And as you will see, in California getting your money from a recalcitrant debtor can be difficult. So the best advice is: **Whenever possible, make sure you are paid either before or at the same time you perform.** In other words, try not to deliver goods on credit and try to get paid in advance for the services you perform. Here is an example of what can happen if you don't:

> Joe is a plumber who recently went into business on his own. He thought he was lucky when a large apartment complex hired him to do all its repairs. For several months things went well, then he wasn't paid for the past month's work. When he asked about it he was told, "Don't worry, we will get you a check next week." After working for six weeks, Joe was finally given a check. Relieved, he put the check in the bank and paid his bills. Unfortunately the check bounced, the company filed bankruptcy, and all of Joe's checks to his creditors bounced.

This story points out two things about getting paid. First, you must always remember a check isn't exactly the same as cash. Until the bank pays the check you have only the promise of the person who gave you the check to rely on. **Don't assume that once you have a check you have been paid . . . wait until it clears the bank.** Second, if someone who owes you money files bankruptcy, you will probably never be paid. Even though you are allowed to file a claim in bankruptcy court to get your share of what the person owed, there usually is very little money left to pay the average creditor.

So what can you do to prevent this from happening to you? First, don't wait long periods of time between payments from an unknown creditor. Arrange a payment plan whereby you will be paid every week, instead of every month. Next, if you are going to take a check, ask for a cashier's check, a bank draft, or a certified check. Without going into all the legal reasons why, these checks almost assure that you will get your money because the bank stands behind them. Finally, if possible get partial payment in advance, something like the security deposit landlords have tenants pay. And if you extend credit, which you often must, get a credit report to make sure you are not dealing with a person with a bad credit history.

But no matter how diligent you are, there will be times that you have to extend credit, and then try to collect. When this happens you should know that there are laws that regulate what you do in your role as debt collector, and violating them can be costly.

Debt Collection

Whenever you try to collect money you are owed, you are subject to the debt collection laws. Under these laws, wrongful and abusive debt collection may result in civil liability. Additionally, if the debt involves a consumer, you are subject to the Fair Debt Collection Practices Act. This Act prohibits most harassing and deceptive practices, and a violation could result in civil and criminal penalties. Here is what the law says you may not do:

> Threats; Unlawful Conduct
>
> No debt collector shall collect or attempt to collect a consumer debt by means of the following conduct:
>
> (a) The use, or threat of use, of physical force or violence or any criminal means to cause harm to the person, or the reputation, or the property of any person;
> (b) The threat that the failure to pay a consumer debt will result in an accusation that the debtor has committed a crime where such accusation, if made, would be false;
> (c) The communication of, or threat to communicate to any person the fact that a debtor has engaged in conduct, other than the failure to pay a consumer debt, which the debt collector knows or has reason to believe will defame the debtor;
> (d) The threat to the debtor to sell or assign to another person the obligation of the debtor to pay a consumer debt, with an accompanying false representation that the result of such sale or assignment would be that the debtor would lose any defense to the consumer debt;

(e) The threat to any person that nonpayment of the consumer debt may result in the arrest of the debtor or the seizure, garnishment, attachment or sale of any property or the garnishment or attachment of wages of the debtor, unless such action is in fact contemplated by the debt collector and permitted by the law; or
(f) The threat to take any action against the debtor which is prohibited by this title.

Obscene or Profane Language; Use of Telephones; Unlawful Practices

No debt collector shall collect or attempt to collect a consumer debt by means of the following practices:

(a) Using obscene or profane language;
(b) Placing telephone calls without disclosure of the caller's identity, provided that an employee of a licensed collection agency may identify himself by using his registered alias name as long as he correctly identifies the agency he represents;
(c) Causing expense to any person for long distance telephone calls, telegram fees, or charges for other similar communications, by misrepresenting to such person the purpose of such telephone call, telegram, or similar communication;
(d) Causing a telephone to ring repeatedly or continuously to annoy the person called; or
(e) Communicating, by telephone or in person, with the debtor with such frequency as to be unreasonable and to constitute an harassment to the debtor under the circumstances.

Communications with Third Parties; Unlawful Practices

No debt collector shall collect or attempt to collect a consumer debt by means of the following practices:

(a) Communicating with the debtor's employer regarding the debtor's consumer debt unless such a communication is necessary to the collection of the debt, or unless the debtor or his attorney has consented in writing to such communication. A communication is necessary to the collection of the debt only if it is made for the purposes of verifying the debtor's employment, locating the debtor, or effecting garnishment, after judgment, of the debtor's wages, or in the case of a medical debt for the purpose of discovering the existence of medial insurance. Any such communication, other than a communication in the case of a medical debt by a health care provider or its agent for the purpose of discovering the existence of medical insurance, shall be in writing unless such written communication receives no response within 15 days and shall be made only as many times as is necessary to the collection of the debt. Communications to a debtor's employer regarding a debt shall not contain language that would be improper if the communication were made to the debtor. One communication solely for the purpose of verifying the debtor's employment may be oral without prior written contact;
(b) Communicating information regarding a consumer debt to any member of the debtor's family, other than the debtor's spouse or the parents or guardians of the debtor who is either a minor or who resides in the same household with such parent or guardian, prior to obtaining a judgment against the debtor, except where the purpose of the communication is to locate the debtor, or where the debtor or his attorney has consented in writing to such communication;
(c) Communicating to any person any list of debtors which discloses the nature of existence of a consumer debt, commonly known as "deadbeat lists," or advertising any consumer debt for sale, by naming the debtor; or
(d) Communicating with the debtor by means of a written communication that displays or conveys any information about the consumer debt or the debtor other than the name, address and telephone number of the debtor and the debt collector and which is intended both to be seen by any other person and also to embarrass the debtor.
(e) Notwithstanding the foregoing provisions of this section, the disclosure, publication or communication of a debt collector of information relating to a consumer debt or the debtor to a consumer reporting agency or to any other person reasonably believed to have a legitimate business need for such information shall not be deemed to violate this title.

Misrepresentations in Communications; Unlawful Practices

No debt collector shall collect or attempt to collect a consumer debt by means of the following practices:

(a) Any communication with the debtor other than in the name either of the debt collector or the person on whose behalf the debt collector is acting;
(b) Any false representation that any person is an attorney or counselor at law;
(c) Any communication with a debtor in the name of an attorney or counselor at law or upon stationery or like written instruments bearing the name of the attorney or counselor at law, unless such communication is by an attorney or counselor at law or shall have been approved or authorized by such attorney or counselor at law;
(d) The representation that any debt collector is vouched for, bonded by, affiliated with, or is an instrumentality, agent or official or any federal, state, or local government or any agency of federal, state, or local government, unless the collector is actually employed by the particular governmental agency in question and is acting on behalf of such agency in the debt collection matter;
(e) The false representation that the consumer debt may be increased by the addition of attorney's fees, investigation fees, service fees, finance charges, or other charges if, in fact, such fees or charges may not legally be added to the existing obligation;
(f) The false representation that information concerning a debtor's failure or alleged failure to pay a consumer debt has been or is about to be referred to a consumer reporting agency;

(g) The false representation that a debt collector is a consumer reporting agency;
(h) The false representation that collection letters, notices, or other printed forms are being sent by or on behalf of a claim, credit, audit, or legal department;
(i) The false representation of the true nature of the business or services being rendered by the debt collector;
(j) The false representation that a legal proceeding has been, is about to be, or will be instituted unless payment of a consumer debt is made;
(k) The false representation that a consumer debt has been, is about to be, or will be sold, assigned, or referred to a debt collector for collection; or
(l) Any communication by a licensed collection agency to a debtor demanding money unless the claim is actually assigned to the collection agency.

Affirmation from Bankrupt; Collection of Collector's Fee and Expenses from Debtor; Communication with Debtor Instead of Debtor's Attorney; Unlawful Practices

No debt collector shall or attempt to collect a consumer debt by means of the following practices:

(a) Obtaining an affirmation from a debtor who has been adjudicated a bankruptcy, of a consumer debt which has been discharged in such bankruptcy, without clearly and conspicuously disclosing to the debtor, in writing, at the time such affirmation is sought, the fact that the debtor is not legally obligated to make such affirmation;
(b) Collecting or attempting to collect from the debtor the whole or any part of the debt collector's fee or charge for services rendered, or other expense incurred by the debt collector in the collection of the consumer debt, except as permitted by law; or
(c) Initiating communications, other than statements of account, with the debtor with regard to the consumer debt, when the debt collector has been previously notified in writing by the debtor's attorney that the debtor is represented by such attorney with respect to the consumer debt and such notice includes the attorney's name and address and a request by such attorney that all communications regarding the consumer debt be addressed to such attorney, unless the attorney fails to answer correspondence, return telephone calls, or discuss the obligation in question. This subdivision shall not apply where prior approval has been obtained from the debtor's attorney, or where the communication is a response in the ordinary course of business to a debtor's inquiry.

And don't think because this law uses "their debt collector" it doesn't apply to you. Anyone who collects debts, including their own, is a debt collector under this law.

So how should you go about collecting a debt? First, after you have read the law very carefully, make reasonable phone calls and send a reasonable letter letting the person who owes you money know that you expect to be paid and if you are not, you will take all available steps to try and collect through the courts. Sometimes the threat of a lawsuit, which usually increases the amount owed through the addition of court costs and attorney's fees, is enough to get your money. You also should consider trying to work out a payment plan with the debtor, or even taking less than 100 cents on a dollar. Remember, a bird in the hand is worth two in the bush. As we told you before, it is very difficult, and sometimes impossible, to make someone pay who just refuses to do so.

If after sending your letters and making your phone calls you still don't have your money, you now have three options:

1. Give up, and take a loss (learning a lesson and knowing never to deal with that person again).
2. Give the account to a collection agency. (The collection agency may charge you a small amount up front but usually takes its money from the amount it ultimately collects).
3. Sue (either in small claims court or with an attorney).

The decision of what to do at this point depends on what you think the likelihood of getting your money through continued efforts is. Remember, everything you do from this point on will cost you in terms of time and money. If the amount is small, or recovery unlikely (read the rest of this chapter to determine if you will be able to collect) you may be better off to just chalk this one up as a lesson of doing business. On the other hand, if there is a good chance you will get your money, you may want to sue; and contrary to what you may think, you can do this without a lawyer whenever the amount is less than $5,000.

When You Have to Sue

Now that you have made the decision that you are owed enough money that it is worth your time and effort to sue, you must next decide whether to do it yourself or with an attorney. If the amount you are owed is less than $5,000 you can sue in small claims court without the assistance of an attorney. Small claims court is easy and efficient and usually gets you the money you are owed, but there are some reasons why you might want to consider hiring an attorney to file your suit in District Court:

1. Small claims court is limited to $2,500, but for up to 2 cases a year you can file up to $5,000. If your claim is for more than that you must file in District or County Court.

2. Your claim is legally or factually complicated. An attorney may be better able to successfully resolve the problem.
3. The person you are suing is going to fight the claim. If you win in small claims court, the person you sue has a right to file an appeal and start the whole thing all over again. While this is not the usual case, if the person you are suing makes it clear that this fight is "going all the way to the Supreme Court," it may be better to get an attorney and start in District or County Court. Appeal from this court is not absolute and only issues of law can be appealed.
4. You are uncomfortable representing yourself. Don't be embarrassed to admit that going to court to represent yourself scares you. You are not alone. There is an old saying that the person who represents him or herself has a fool for a client. Sometimes this applies to us all.
5. Finally, the use of an attorney may let the other party know you are serious and result in an early settlement. Even though you have written letters telling the other person you are going to sue, they may still not take you seriously until they receive a letter from a real attorney.

Remember, in most cases when you sue for money owed you for payment you will be entitled to attorney's fees from the other side if you win. Therefore, hiring an attorney may not really cost too much if you do recover a judgment. Once you decide to hire an attorney, read Chapter 12, and by all means make sure you find out how much he or she is going to charge, and how and when the fee will be collected, before you hire an attorney.

Going To Small Claims Court

Suing in small claims court is easy. You can sue anyone who is actually in California, or who has a permanent home in California, or who is doing business in California. To sue a sole proprietorship, the proprietor must be in California; to sue a partnership, the partners must be in California; and to sue a corporation, it must do business in the state. For more information on each of these forms of business reread Chapters 1–5.

There are many small claims courts, so after you decide to go to court you must find the proper location for your complaint.

Generally you must sue in the court that covers the area where the person you are suing lives or where your business operates or where the transaction took place. For example, suppose you repair a garage in a rental unit for a landlord who lives in another part of town. You could sue either where the rental property is located or where the landlord responsible lives. If you sue anywhere else, he or she has the right to have it moved back to one of those courts.

Small claims courts are part of the Municipal Courts, so look in the phone book under County Governments. If you are not sure which court covers the location where your claim arises, call any of the clerks and ask for their help. Small claims clerks are generally very helpful.

After you find the right court, go down to the clerk's office and fill in what is called a *petition.* This is the document that starts the lawsuit. Make sure that you have the correct name and address of the person you are suing. If you do not, the court will be unable to serve them with your papers and the suit will never be brought to court. If you are suing a corporation, call the secretary of state in Sacramento and ask for the name of the "agent for service." This is the person who is designated to accept legal papers for the corporation.

You, the person suing, are called the *plaintiff.* After you file the petition and pay your filing fee (which is as low as $18), the court will have the marshall or sheriff serve the *defendant,* the person or business being sued, with the papers. The court can also mail the papers to the defendant, which will be cheaper than the service fee charged by the sheriff. Or, you can pay a "process server" to do the service. Most court clerks who deal with small claims can provide a list of process servers, or check the Yellow Pages. This process service will vary in price, so check carefully. The defendant will then have a short period of time to answer your complaint; that is, state the other side of the story and say why you should not win. If the defendants think **you owe them money,** they can counterclaim and ask the court to award a judgment against you. If the defendant does nothing, he or she is considered to be in default, and you will win so long as you can convince the judge that you are entitled to the money. Make sure that you ask for the cost of your lawsuit in your petition so the judgment will cover your damages plus the costs incurred.

If the defendant answers, a date will be set for trial. Most small claims court hearings are very informal. Both sides have a chance to tell their story to a judge or commissioner and then the judge may ask some questions. There will not be any attorneys, for either side, in small claims court. Be sure to be prepared. If you have any evidence such as invoices, receipts, pictures, etc., bring them with you. The better prepared party usually wins. Also, if you have any witnesses, for example, the worker who completed the work, bring them along.

The judge will make sure that you are treated fairly and have a fair chance to tell your side of the story. This isn't television; the judge won't allow the other side to jump up and object to everything you say.

After both sides have had their chance to talk, the judge will make a ruling. Usually the judge acts as soon as you are through but he or she may wait a brief period of time to think about it. In most cases once a ruling is made that is the end. If you win you are usually paid promptly, and if you lose you know that you had a fair day in court. But two problems can arise. First, as we said before, either side can appeal this judgment and start the whole thing over again. You will have to wait to see if the defendant is going to appeal. If you lose and want to appeal you will probably need an attorney to help you and you will have to post a bond. Remember, you have 30 days to appeal so act promptly. The more serious problem that can arise, however, is getting your money once you win if the defendant does not voluntarily pay. As you will see, California is a debtor's paradise.

The Bottom Line

Small claims court really is a "people's court"; don't be afraid to use it. It is fast, simple, and very often just filing suit gets you the money you are owed.

Collecting a Judgment

After you go to court and win, whether it is small claims court or district court, the judge will award you a judgment. Basically this is an official pronouncement that you are right and the defendant owes you the money you said he did. The problem is that simply getting a judgment does not put any money in your pocket. As we said before, most people will voluntarily pay a judgment once they lose, but you should know what your legal rights are if they don't; and as you will see, in California it can be very difficult to get your money after you win in court.

Once you have a judgment, the next step is to use the available legal proceedings to enforce that judgment, and force the debtor to pay. For example, let's say that you recently sold a $350 washing machine to someone who never paid you. You went to small claims court and won. Now what do you do with this judgment? Well, basically you go back to the court to have the court *execute* on your judgment. In other words, you ask the court to have the sheriff go out and take some of the debtor's property, sell it, and give you the money you are owed. And there are two ways the court can do this. First, they can issue what is called an *abstract of judgment.* This is a piece of paper that you file in the county courthouse to get a lien on the debtor's real estate. If the person you sue owns real estate, you have the right to force its sale to get your money. As a more practical matter the abstract will tie up any purchase or sale of real estate by the debtor and will appear on his or her credit report. This usually is enough to get you your money.

The second method of forcing payment is called a *writ of execution.* This is a court order to the sheriff telling him to take the debtor's non-exempt personal property such as a boat, or a valuable painting, and sell it to pay you the money you are owed. Similar to this device is a *writ of garnishment,* which allows you to get money or property of the debtor that another person is holding. For example, if you know the debtor has money in the bank, or an IRA, or stocks and bonds, you can get a writ of garnishment to have these funds seized and sold to pay you off. If you have any questions about getting your money after you have won in court, don't be afraid to ask the clerk for help.

Homesteads and Bankruptcy

Now that you have just finished reading how to sue someone, and what devices there are to get your money, it is time to fill you in on the truth about California law. **California is a debtor's state. If the person you sue doesn't want to pay you, it is very hard to force them to do so.** This is because of the California homestead laws and bankruptcy laws. As we said before, you can theoretically ask the sheriff to force the sale of your debtor's property so you can finally get paid. But, chances are, the person who did not pay you does not own property. Even if they do, that property may be exempt from sale (up to limits varying from $30,000 to $75,000 of equity) if the person filed a free "Declaration of Homestead." But that is not the most likely problem you will face. If the person does have a home and a car and is employed, but still can't find the money to pay you, he or she may well have overextended themselves and owes lots of folks, not just you. If you file suit, what may he or she do? Respond to the ads on TV, on benches at bus stops, everywhere, and "File Bankruptcy Now." As one recent Yellow Pages ad put it, "New law, everyone qualifies! Keep everything! Pay back nothing! Keep: house, cars, furniture, appliances, and almost everything you own, even $1,500 cash and pay back nothing, 97% of the time!" As another ad says, "Stop garnishments, lawsuits, repossessions!" With all this going for your deadbeat debtor, what chance do you have? Not much!

As you can see, if the person declares bankruptcy, there is very little for you to collect against. If you are thinking of suing someone, you should find out whether they have any non-exempt property. If they do not, and you do not think an adverse credit report will be enough to compel payment, you may be better off just writing off the debt. A lawsuit could be throwing good money after bad.

Incidentally, someone else's bankruptcy may end up throwing you for a loop, too. What if you are just barely surviving in your small business, and then someone who owes you $22,000 declares bankruptcy? You may get a percentage of the $22,000, depending on how much the person or firm filing bankruptcy had left, and depending on who else is demanding to be paid. Or, you may lose it all. If you do lose it all, this may throw you into bankruptcy as well. This will then impact those to whom you owe money, creating a chain reaction of misfortune. So, for the sake of the California economy, we should hope that neither you nor your creditors nor your suppliers are forced to declare bankruptcy. Whether you are organized as a sole proprietorship, corporation, or partnership, the actions of others can easily put you into hot water.

The Bottom Line

Small claims court is easy to use, and you are ensured your day in court. But winning a judgment in court doesn't guarantee you will be paid. Try to find out if your debtor has any assets before you throw good money after bad.

Ways to Protect Against Nonpayment

As you have seen from reading this chapter, collecting money that people owe you can often be difficult, or impossible. To protect yourself from this happening there are basically two things you can do. You can demand payment in cash, cashier's check, or certified check, in advance; or you can take steps to ensure that if you are not paid you have some of the debtor's property to go after. Taking a personal check is also fairly safe. Even though a check may bounce, you are still substantially protected. Giving someone a check that bounces, in exchange for goods or services, is criminal. **You can criminally prosecute someone who gives you a bad check.**

So, if you take cash or a check you are usually protected, but many customers will not want to pay in advance, or will need time to pay off a large sum. In these cases you should protect yourself by taking a *lien* on some of their property. Even though you may not have thought about it, you are probably already familiar with how this works. For example, when you bought your car you probably gave the bank a lien on the car to ensure that you would pay the note. **A lien gives the creditor the right to take a specific piece of property, and sell it, in the event the debt is not paid.** In the case of your car, if you don't pay the bank or finance company, they have the right to take your car, sell it, and apply the proceeds to your debt. Basically there are two types of liens you should know about: the security interest and the mechanic's or materialman's lien.

A security interest is a voluntary agreement, between you and your customer, where your customer agrees to let you have the property back if he doesn't pay you. Your interest in the property is called a "security interest" and you file a form, called a financing statement, with either the county clerk or the secretary of state to make your interest superior to everyone else's. (A copy of a security agreement may be found in Appendix B, Form 16.) Once you have a security interest, the law lets you take the property back yourself, sell it, and apply the proceeds to the amount you are owed. The only major restriction on your rights is that you must take the property back peacefully; that is, without any action that results in, or is likely to result in, violence. Here is an example of how you might take advantage of this legal device:

> Marvin sells appliances. Most of his sales are on credit and the average price for an appliance is $500. Recently he sold a washing machine to Mary. Mary paid $100 down and agreed to pay the rest in monthly installments of $25. Marvin had Mary sign a promissory note, gave all the proper disclosures (read Chapter

HOW ABOUT A HORROR STORY?

An experienced backhoe operator with entrepreneurial designs heard about a backhoe service for sale. He contacted the owner and, after brief negotiations, agreed to purchase a backhoe, trailer, and a customer list for $20,000 cash. The buyer checked out the equipment and after confirming that all was well, consummated the deal.

One month later he got a phone call from the note department of a large bank. They wanted back payments or the equipment. "But I don't have a loan with you," he protested. Then he learned about a little form called a UCC-1. This is a financing statement that the bank had filed with the secretary of state in Sacramento. It placed a lien on the equipment. It seems that the seller had borrowed $10,000 and had used the equipment as collateral. The UCC-1 gave the bank title or legal ownership of the equipment until the debt was paid. The seller had flown the coop. The buyer had to pay off someone else's loan or lose everything.

The Moral: Never purchase equipment, separately or as a part of a package, without conducting a UCC search. Obtain a UCC-2 form, have the seller sign, and request a search of the state's files for UCC-1's filed under the business *and* owner's name(s). If one is on file, make sure it is paid and removed before you buy!

—Thanks to Bob Hawkes, with the Weill Institute Small Business Development Center, Bakersfield College, for this insight.

10 carefully), and took a security interest in the machine. After a few months Mary came upon hard times and stopped paying.

If Marvin didn't take a security interest his only right would be to try and collect the $350 Mary still owes by sending letters, and taking her to court if necessary. And, as we just explained, even if he wins in court he may not get anything. On the other hand, because he has a security interest he has the right to go to her home and ask for the return of the machine. If he gets it he can sell it and keep the money he gets. If she refuses he can go to court and in a relatively simple proceeding have the court order her to give him the machine. Of course he would be entitled to collect whatever costs he incurred.

It should be obvious that a security interest gives you a much greater chance of getting paid in full. But it does take additional time and cost a few extra dollars to create one. If you think this device is what your business needs, speak with your attorney. For a small fee he or she should be able to provide you with all the forms you need and tell you just what to do to protect yourself. You should not have to pay much for this information. Be sure to shop around for an attorney you can afford.

A second way to achieve a result similar to a security interest is by taking what is generally called a mechanic's or materialman's lien. This lien is similar to the security interest in that it gives you rights against a debtor's property without the need to sue and get a judgment and in spite of exemption laws. The basic difference is that this lien can arise automatically; that is, there is not always the need for the debtor to sign an agreement before the work is done. For example:

Sylvia is a mechanic who specializes in expensive German cars. Recently she repaired a car for a customer, who didn't have the money to pay and asked for credit. Sylvia learned long ago not to extend credit, so she said no, when you pay you can have the car. The customer told her it was his car and he wanted it back.

Under the law Sylvia has a mechanic's lien on the car for the value of the repairs she has done. This means that she can keep the car until she is paid, and if she is not paid she can sell the car, take the money she is owed, and give the rest, if any, back to her customer. We also should point out that if the customer were to give Sylvia a bad check to get the car back, Sylvia would have the right to re-take the car when the check bounced. Similar rules help the person who repairs or supplies materials for the repair of a home.

L and L Construction recently agreed to remodel Fred's house. The contract price was $15,000 with periodic payments as the work progressed. The final payment of 20% was to be made after completion. Everything went fine until the work was complete and Fred refused to pay. L and L knew that filing a lawsuit was expensive and often useless, but fortunately they had taken the proper steps to create a mechanic's lien on Fred's homestead. They now have the right to file their lien and if he still doesn't pay they can sell his home to get their money.

Whenever a person repairs or improves the property of another they are entitled to a mechanic's lien on the property. Also, when you supply the materials for such work you can get a lien for the value of the materials. **But there are certain legal prerequisites that must be met before such a lien is valid.** If you do not follow these rules, you may not have a lien, and trying to assert a lien when you don't have one can get you in lots of trouble. For example, to get a lien on a homestead, you must:

1. Have a written contract before any work is done.
2. If the owner is married, both spouses must sign.
3. The lien must be filed with the county clerk.

For example, if you began work before the contract was signed you would not have a lien. **These liens are not very complicated, but you should talk to your attorney to find out exactly what you should do and how and when you should do it.** Once your attorney gives you the basic instructions, you can do it yourself from then on.

One last point for those of you who do home repair. Under the law an owner is required to withhold 10% of the contract price owed a contractor for 30 days after the work is completed. An owner who does this is usually relieved of any obligations to unpaid subcontractors or suppliers. This means that if you have a claim against the owner based on the fact that you were not paid by a general contractor, you had better assert it within 30 days after completion. If you don't, you may lose your lien.

The Bottom Line

There are ways to protect yourself when it comes to being paid. First, try and insist on cash or a cashier's or certified check. Second, when you must extend credit have your attorney help you prepare the papers necessary for you to get a lien on your customer's property.

FOR MORE INFORMATION

Bleakley, Fred R. "Bad Hangover: Many Firms Find Debt They Plied On in 1980s Is a Cruel Taskmaster." *Wall Street Journal,* October 9, 1990, pages A-1, A-15.

Harper, Lucinda. "Debt Collector's Aggressive Tactics Bring Mounting Protests From Irate Consumers." *Wall Street Journal,* December 3, 1991, pages B-1, B-7.

Longenecker, Justin G., and Carlos W. Moore. *Small Business Management.* Cincinnati: Southwestern Publishing Company, 1991. See Chapter 21, "Working Capital and

Capital Budgeting," for information on the importance of managing accounts receivables carefully.

Maness, Terry. *Small Business Management Using Lotus 1-2-3,* 2nd Edition. Cincinnati: Southwestern Publishing Company, 1991. Chapter 8 tells how to analyze and manage accounts receivables using your personal computer.

Milling, Bryan E. "Find Hidden Profits in Your Receivables." *Small Business Reports (Monterey, California),* February 1991, pages 47–50.

Pekar, Sheila. "Managing Receivables: Both Yours and Your Clients (Accounts)." *The CPA Journal,* June 1991, pages 71–74.

Swearingen, James G., Floyd A. Wilkes, and Sandra L. Swearingen. "Confirmation Response Differences Between Business, Clerks and Consumers (Accounts Receivable)." *The CPA Journal,* May 1991, pages 58–60.

Winter, Ralph E., and Thomas F. O'Boyle. "Bankruptcy-Law Filings by Firms Spurt." *Wall Street Journal,* April 6, 1990, page A-2. Contains interesting information on overdue bill payments.

POINTS TO PONDER

1. When should you give up on a past due account?
2. Is the bankruptcy law too lenient, or does the law correctly allow for a fresh start? On the other hand, does bankruptcy actually give a fresh start?

DON'T JUST SIT THERE, DO SOMETHING!

1. Can a business use Small Claims Courts? Find out when Small Claims Court will be in session near you, and visit for an hour or so. Write a short report on your findings. The visit will be well worthwhile!
2. In your community, what businesses will help you collect past due accounts? What do they charge? Newspapers or the Yellow Pages may give clues. Write a short report on the situation.
3. What agencies in your areas will BUY your accounts receivables? At what sort of rates? Summarize your findings in a page or less.

12

You and Your Lawyer: Things to Keep in Mind

Let's face facts. No matter how many self-help books you buy, no matter how much you learn about the law, and no matter how hard you try to avoid legal hassles, nearly every businessperson finds that, sooner or later, he or she needs a lawyer. And unfortunately, some who use a lawyer discover that they sometimes have problems dealing with lawyers. Studies have shown that many people avoid lawyers because they do not trust them. We can't emphasize enough that this approach is wrong. If you feel that the advice of a lawyer is necessary, by all means get it! But protect yourself by taking steps to ensure that you choose a lawyer who is right for you, and that you know your rights if a problem arises.

Finding a Lawyer Who's Right for You

We would like to be able to tell you that now that you own this book you will never need the assistance of a lawyer, but unfortunately that isn't so. No matter how much law you learn from reading this book there will still be times when the advice and assistance of a professional is necessary; either because the problem is too complex to resolve yourself, or because the amount involved is so large and the risk so great, that you want to make sure things are done properly. When this happens you should know how to locate lawyers, what questions to ask to make sure that the one you choose is the best one for you, and how to deal with a lawyer once he or she has been hired. One thing you should always keep in mind: **The lawyer you hire works for you, and with you. It is essential that you find someone you trust, whom you can communicate with, and who will treat you fairly.**

Shop Around and Compare

The first thing to remember when you are looking for a lawyer is that there are probably many lawyers in your area who can competently help you, and you should shop around before you make the decision of who to hire. For example, one of the authors did a television report recently and called more than twenty lawyers asking what they would charge for a basic will. They were all given the same information and asked for a price. Their prices ranged from $45 to more than $600. A reporter went and got the $45 will and showed it to an expert who stated that it was a perfectly fine will and did everything that was requested. Perhaps the lawyer who charged $600 would have done more, but that is not the point. All that was asked for was a simple will, and paying for things you don't need is a waste of money. As this points out, a few simple phone calls can save you a lot of money, especially on standard legal services such as incorporation, partnership agreements, bills of sale, leases, promissory notes, and security agreements.

So how do you decide whom to call? Well, do the same thing you would do if you needed a doctor or mechanic or a plumber. (Lawyers love to be compared to plumbers and mechanics.) Ask your friends. See if they have dealt with a lawyer lately and what they thought of him or her. Next, try the Yellow Pages and other advertising. Lawyer advertising is still relatively new, and more and more lawyers are starting to use it. Granted, some lawyer advertising is sleazy, but that doesn't mean you should not consider calling the lawyer who has a tasteful ad in the Yellow Pages. Review lawyer advertising the same way you would any other ads. The advertising is a good reflection of the lawyer's character. If you still haven't come up with enough names, the legal community itself has organizations to help you. Local and state bar associations maintain lawyer referral services that list attorneys who specialize in certain areas, and who have agreed to talk with you for a very small fee. Call these organizations and tell them what type of a lawyer you need. They will give you several names of people in your area for you to call.

Once you get several names you should arrange to speak with several before choosing one. It may even be a good idea to get a lawyer before you have problems. Once you think about starting your business, find yourself an attorney who will represent you if you have any problems or have to make big decisions. View the attorney as the family doctor, someone you call in an emergency. The probabilities are that some time in the future you will need an attorney. Find one before a crisis arises.

The Bottom Line

Find a lawyer you trust and whose judgment you respect. Contact the lawyer before you sign an agreement or complete a significant transaction. At this point the lawyer can help you structure the transaction to protect you and your business.

Talking With Your Lawyer

So what should you ask the lawyer when you first meet with him or her? Well first, talk about what you are interested in and get a feel for what kind of person the lawyer is. For example, if you think you will need someone that you can call every couple of days and ask questions, let the attorney know. Ask how he or she would feel about that. Are they in their office a lot or do they do mostly trial work? How many other clients do they have with problems like you will have? How long have they been in practice? Where did they get their college degrees? And finally, but most importantly, how are they going to charge you and how much are they going to charge you? Remember, many lawyers charge differently, and things that sound similar can be quite different.

Some lawyers charge an hourly fee, so your fee will depend upon how many hours the lawyer spends on the matter. Other lawyers will agree to a set fee, regardless of how much time is spent. If you are asking a lawyer to sue someone, some lawyers will accept as their fee a percentage of whatever they recover for you. With this type of fee arrangement, you only pay a fee if the lawyer recovers something. However, most lawyers would want you to pay the costs of the lawsuit, such as court filing fees, no matter what happens in the case.

Make sure you understand how any given situation will be billed. Let's say that you want a lawyer to incorporate you. One tells you that it will cost $500 and another says $1,250. The first one is cheaper, right? Not necessarily. If the filing fees charged by the State of California are included in the second one, and they are not included in the first, then the second attorney would actually be charging you less. Always ask what the total fee will be and how it will be computed.

Also, be sure to ask if the attorney uses paralegals, non-lawyer personnel who help and are billed at a different rate, and how phone calls are billed. Most lawyers have minimum billing units. You may be surprised to find that you were charged for a quarter of an hour every time you called to see how your case was going. This could happen if the lawyer's minimum billing unit was a quarter of an hour.

Ask if the lawyer will handle your case personally or if it will be given to another person in the firm to handle. It doesn't do you any good to be impressed with one person only to find that you have hired another.

And finally, one piece of advice on how to deal with the lawyer who doesn't want to be bothered with all these questions and tells you, "I don't have to answer all these questions. I have been practicing law for a long time and if you don't trust me find another lawyer." Take his or her advice—find another lawyer.

The Bottom Line

Talk with the attorney before you hire him or her. If you are uncomfortable, talk some more, or talk to someone else. Until you find a lawyer you trust and are comfortable with, keep looking.

Problems With Your Attorney

It is unfortunate, but many people have disputes with their lawyer. In most cases these disputes could have been avoided through better communication and more complete understanding of exactly what the attorney was going to do, how long it would take, and what it would cost. As we have emphasized, it is extremely important to talk with prospective lawyers and feel comfortable before you choose one. By doing this, it is much less likely that a dispute will arise. But it is still no guarantee, and if you have a problem with your attorney you should know what rights you have if it can't be resolved.

But before you even consider pursuing your rights against your lawyer, talk with him/her. Many disputes are simply misunderstandings and can be resolved through better communication. If after talking with your lawyer you are still dissatisfied, there are two alternatives: you can sue your lawyer; or you can file a complaint with the California State Bar Association. Unlike most professions, lawyers depend upon a license issued by the state to practice their trade. And the organization that issues that license, the California State Bar, also regulates the profession and maintains a grievance committee to hear complaints about lawyers and to discipline them, if that is warranted. Although many argue that self-regulation is too easy on lawyers, each year some lawyers are either suspended from the practice of law for a period of time, or disbarred and prohibited from practicing in this state.

Filing a Grievance

So what types of problems should you consider filing a grievance about? Lawyers are governed by what is called a "Code of Ethics," and if they violate that Code they are subject to discipline. Without going into all of the details, there are certain things that lawyers may not do, and if they do any of them they will be considered to be acting unethically, and subject to being suspended, or removed, from the practice of law. For example, lawyers may not:

- Take a client's property.
- Abandon a client's case.
- Lie to a client.
- Refuse to talk with a client.
- Represent a client if there is a conflict of interest that has not been disclosed.
- Fail to perform for a client.
- Act incompetently.

As you read this list, you probably have noted one thing that is missing: disputes about fees. In most cases disputes about fees are not reviewable by the grievance committees. If the fee is grossly excessive, however, it could constitute unethical conduct on the part of the lawyer and could therefore be reviewed by the grievance committee.

But don't panic yet. Perhaps there is a middle ground. The California State Bar Association has set standards for lawyer-client fee arbitration programs, which are run by local county bar associations.

If your lawyer engages in any of the above-listed acts, it would be appropriate to file a grievance. The Bar will then investigate, and if it feels it is appropriate, the Bar will hold a hearing. To get more information about filing a complaint against a lawyer you should call the Bar Association's toll free number, 1-800-843-9053. They will be glad to send you a form to get the complaint process started.

For information on the fee arbitration program, call your county Bar Association. If they do not have the program in operation, the State Bar can help you. Call the California State Bar Association in San Francisco at (415) 241-2000 or Los Angeles at (213) 580-5000.

Remember, filing a complaint against a lawyer is a very serious matter. The lawyer may lose the right to practice if you are successful. If you are not sure about your complaint, talk with your lawyer and ask him or her to explain what is going on. You may be surprised to find out that there was a reasonable explanation for what you believed was unethical conduct. On the other hand, if you truly believe your lawyer has acted in an unethical manner, you should not hesitate to file a complaint with the Bar.

Suing Your Attorney

It shouldn't come as a surprise that lawyers, like anyone else, can be sued when they mess up. Just like doctors, a lawyer who acts negligently, or who lies, can be sued for malpractice. And if you can prove that your lawyer deceived you or didn't live up to the standards of other lawyers in your area, you may be able to recover damages. We say maybe because you must show more than just the fact that your lawyer messed up; you probably must also show that if he or she hadn't, you would have won your suit.

So what should you do if you believe your lawyer has acted negligently? Simple, see another lawyer. Although some lawyers have been reluctant to take cases against other lawyers, many now will, and will tell you if you have a case. You also should know that lawyers are subject to the law just like anyone else. If you can show that your lawyer violated the law, by either charging a grossly excessive fee or deceiving you, you can recover your damages plus your court costs. It is not necessary that you show your lawyer acted negligently, only that he or she misrepresented what they were going to do for you, or took advantage of you, or charged you a grossly excessive price. Make sure that you discuss the possibility of suing for malpractice under California Malpractice Laws when you talk about suing your lawyer.

The Bottom Line

Lawyers are not above the law, and, in fact, law is one of the most regulated professions. If you believe your lawyer has misled, deceived, or not properly represented you, consider filing a grievance with the State Bar or suing for malpractice.

Problems With Your Accountant . . .

Roughly the same information discussed regarding attorneys can relate to your accountant too. If a question arises, discuss it. Chances are you can resolve the issue by good communication. If this doesn't seem to work, however, it's the same as it is with your lawyer. You have recourse. If worse comes to worse, you can talk to your lawyer (your *new* lawyer?) about filing a malpractice suit against your accountant!

Hopefully, things won't get that far. First, talk. Then, if there are no results, or if you feel there is an issue of dishonesty, fraud, or gross negligence, call the California Board of Accountancy, at (916) 574-2155. They will send you a consumer complaint form with instructions.

Or, if you prefer, simply send a letter describing your complaint. Mail it to: California Board of Accountancy, 2135 Butano Drive, Suite 112, Sacramento, CA 95825.

FOR MORE INFORMATION

Burstiner, Irving. *The Small Business Handbook.* New York: Prentice Hall, 1989. See especially Chapters 4 and 20.

Gobelli, David H., and Mary Alice Seville. "The Small Business-CPA Interface." *Journal of Small Business Management,* October 1989, pages 8–16.

James, David L. "A Shopper's Guide to the New Legal Profession." *Across the Board,* April 1989, pages 9–12.

Millar, David. "Criteria for Selecting an Attorney for Small

Businesses." *National Underwriter* (Life & Health/Financial Services Edition), March 5, 1990, page 24.

Resnik, Paul. *The Small Business Bible.* New York: John Wiley and Sons, 1988. Chapter 7 has a sample CPA engagement letter you may find useful.

Richardson, Clinton. " Dealing With Lawyers: Hope Behind the Horror Stories." *Venture,* July 1988, page 18.

Sheehy, John J. "Control the Risks of High-Stakes Litigation (Dealing with Litigation Crisis)." *Journal of Business Strategy,* June 7, 1991, pages 37–40.

Stolze, William J. *Startup: An Entrepreneur's Guide to Launching and Managing a New Venture.* Rochester, New York: Rock Beach Press, 1990. Chapter 26, "Care and Feeding of Public Accountants, Bankers, and Lawyers" will be especially helpful.

POINTS TO PONDER

1. Do you want a lawyer who puts fairness and justice first, or one who puts clients first? (Or, how could you find one striving for BOTH fairness and client interest? Is this possible?)
2. What advantages might there be to having your lawyer and your accountant know each other? Why might you not want to choose an accountant who is close friends with your attorney?

DON'T JUST SIT THERE, DO SOMETHING!

1. Name a specific business that you might start in the future. At what stage would you talk to an attorney? An accountant? A banker? Insurance agent? Discuss briefly.
2. Look in the Yellow Pages. Based on what you see, which attorneys would you be LEAST likely to want to do business with? Why? Discuss.
3. Again, look in the Yellow Pages. Based on what you see, which accountants would you be LEAST likely to want to do business with? Why? Discuss.

CLOUD NINE ART BAR RESTAURANT

On July 1, 1994, Club Bar, dba Cloud Nine Art Bar Restaurant, a California Subchapter S corporation located in San Francisco, was started by Peter Housely, majority shareholder and sole manager, along with seven other shareholders.

The Cloud Nine Art Bar Restaurant's concept was to be a trendy, pop-art gallery/entertainment nightclub/restaurant, with lunch and dinner seating for 60, and nightclub seating capacity for 650. Cloud Nine employed eight full-time employees, including three full-time bartenders, five club/restaurant employees, and 10 part-time employees. The seven shareholders were investors, not involved in the day-to-day operations of the business.

As a pop-art gallery, Cloud Nine displayed about 80 pictures throughout the club and restaurant areas. As a nightclub, Cloud Nine offered live rock and new wave music with well-known established Bay Area artists on Wednesdays and Saturday evenings, an amateur band night on Mondays, and a jam session on Tuesday nights.

Mr. Housely's goal was to develop, refine and market this new pop-art gallery/restaurant/nightclub concept, so that Cloud Nine would be a successful trendsetting enterprise from both a business and art point of view.

The location of the club was in an up-and-coming redeveloped warehouse area of the city. In prior years, the area had been dominated by warehouses and supply firms, but because of the expansion in the area, new business, such as restaurants and nightclubs, had begun to spring up. There were several successful clubs already in the area.

Cloud Nine Performance: Fiscal Period July 1994 to June 1995

The first year proved to be successful, with gross sales of $765,487.53 and average monthly gross sales of $63,790.63. The bulk of the gross sales for this period resulted from the following: liquor/beer/wine sales (approximately 52%) and door entrance fees (approximately 42%).

The sale of food from the restaurant provided only 6% of the total income, an unexpected disappointment. The first-quarter food sales of $15,308 and second-quarter food sales of $18,786.43 (a total of $34,094.43) were the highest total food sales ever. From the third quarter to the fourth quarter, the sales from the restaurant dropped dramatically to $15,133.34. The cost of running the restaurant proved to be very expensive.

Expenses, including maintenance/repairs, remodeling, subcontracting, employee wages, and food production (4% of the total costs) resulted in a gross profit of

2% before operating expenses. Overall, Cloud Nine's loss for the fiscal year was $36,712.40 before depreciation.

The first year should be considered a successful year for Cloud Nine in terms of gross sales, especially since it was a new business; however, it proved to not be profitable due to loans, restaurant, and remodeling costs.

A management consultant was hired to assess the problems and provide recommendations for the following reasons:

1. The firm was experiencing high cash-flow shortages, which could not be explained, considering the firm's gross sales of approximately $60,000 per month.
2. The firm's recordkeeping system was several months in the arrears, and the investors/shareholders and suppliers were constantly requesting a current up-to-date financial statement.

Some of the unique problems that existed for Cloud Nine during the first fiscal year were:

1. The high cost of running the restaurant.
2. The high cost of remodeling.
3. The high cost of labor due to employee turnover, keeping the bar staffed five days a week, and maintaining a restaurant crew.
4. Inadequate management of the day-to-day business.
5. Inadequate communication between management and employees.
6. Lack of proper job descriptions for key employees.
7. Lack of budget planning for the restaurant and bar.
8. Slow, ineffective bookkeeping procedures.

Club Performance: July 1995 to October 1995

In the first four months of the next fiscal year, Cloud Nine grossed $254,351.43. 49.7% of gross sales was from door sales. Restaurant sales were again very low due to inadequate demand and overall sales had decreased in the last two months of this fiscal quarter.

Some of the same problems that existed during the previous fiscal year were present during the first four months of the new fiscal year and new problems had arisen. The problems were:

1. The high cost of running the restaurant (now run on a limited basis).
2. The high employee turnover rate.
3. Embezzlement by the new bookkeeper.
4. Inadequate management of the day-to-day operations.
5. Lack of proper job descriptions for employees.
6. Inadequate communication between management and employees.
7. Lack of budget planning in the restaurant and bar.

Discussion Questions

1. List and discuss the problems in the Cloud Nine Art Bar Restaurant case.
2. What advice should the management consultant give Mr. Housely?

—Thanks to Ronald Wendell Jones, Ph. D., CMC, Laney College.

Appendix A

Statutory Supplement

1. California Uniform Partnership Act

ARTICLE 1. PRELIMINARY PROVISIONS

§ 15001. Title of chapter

This chapter may be cited as "Uniform Partnership Act." *(Added by Stats.1949, c. 383, § 1.)*

§ 15002. Definitions

In this act, "court" includes every court and judge having jurisdiction in the case.

"Business" includes every trade, occupation, or profession.

"Person" includes individuals, partnerships, corporations, and other associations.

"Bankrupt" includes a debtor under Chapter 7 of the federal bankruptcy law or an insolvent under any state insolvent act.

"Conveyance" includes every assignment, lease, mortgage, or encumbrance.

"Real property" includes land and any interest or estate in land. *(Added by Stats.1949, c. 383, § 1. Amended by Stats.1980, c. 501, § 8.)*

§ 15003. Knowledge and notice defined

(1) A person has "knowledge" of a fact within the meaning of this act not only when he has actual knowledge thereof, but also when he has knowledge of such other facts as in the circumstances shows bad faith.

(2) A person has "notice" of a fact within the meaning of this act when the person who claims the benefit of the notice

(a) States the fact to such person, or

(b) Delivers through the mail, or by other means of communication, a written statement of the fact to such person or to a proper person at his place of business or residence. *(Added by Stats.1949, c. 383, § 1.)*

§ 15004. Interpretation and construction

(1) The rule that statutes in derogation of the common law are to be strictly construed shall have no application to this act.

(2) The law of estoppel shall apply under this act.

(3) The law of agency shall apply under this act.

(4) This act shall be so interpreted and construed as to effect its general purpose to make uniform the law of those states which enact it.

(5) This act shall not be construed so as to impair the obligations of any contract existing when the act goes into effect, nor to affect any action or proceedings begun or right accrued before this act takes effect. *(Added by Stats.1949, c. 383, § 1.)*

ARTICLE 2. NATURE OF PARTNERSHIP

§ 15006. Partnership defined; application to prior associations; limited, special, and mining partnerships

(1) A partnership is an association of two or more persons to carry on as co-owners a business for profit.

(2) But any association formed under any other statute of this State, or any statute adopted by authority, other than the authority of this State, is not a partnership under this act, unless such association would have been a partnership in this State prior to the adoption of this act; but this act shall apply to limited, special, and mining partnerships except insofar as the statutes relating to such partnerships are inconsistent herewith. *(Added by Stats.1949, c. 383, § 1.)*

§ 15006.1. Repealed by Stats.1977, c. 579, § 38

§ 15007. Rules for determining existence of partnership

In determining whether a partnership exists, these rules shall apply:

(1) Except as provided by Section 15016 persons who are not partners as to each other are not partners as to third persons.

(2) Joint tenancy, tenancy in common, tenancy by the entireties, joint property, common property, or part ownership does not of itself establish a partnership, whether such co-owners do or do not share any profits made by the use of the property.

(3) The sharing of gross returns does not of itself establish a partnership, whether or not the persons sharing them have a joint or common right or interest in any property from which the returns are derived.

(4) The receipt by a person of a share of the profits of a business is prima facie evidence that he is a partner in the business, but no such inference shall be drawn if such profits were received in payment:

(a) As a debt by installments or otherwise.

(b) As wages of an employee or rent to a landlord.

(c) As an annuity to a surviving spouse or representative of a deceased partner.

(d) As interest on a loan, though the amount of payment vary with the profits of the business.

(e) As the consideration for the sale of a good will of a business or other property by installments or otherwise. *(Added by Stats.1949, c. 383, § 1. Amended by Stats. 1976, c. 1171, § 6.)*

§ 15008. Partnership property; conveyance of realty

(1) All property originally brought into the partnership stock or subsequently acquired by purchase or otherwise, on account of the partnership, is partnership property.

(2) Unless the contrary intention appears, property acquired with partnership funds is partnership property.

(3) Any estate in real property may be acquired in the partnership name. Title so acquired can be conveyed only in the partnership name.

(4) A conveyance to a partnership in the partnership name, though without words of inheritance, passes the entire estate of the grantor unless a contrary intent appears. *(Added by Stats.1949, c. 383, § 1.)*

ARTICLE 3. RELATIONS OF PARTNERS TO PERSONS DEALING WITH THE PARTNERSHIP

§ 15009. Partner as agent of partnership; authority

(1) Every partner is an agent of the partnership for the purpose of its business, and the act of every partner, including the execution in the partnership name of any instrument, for apparently carrying on in the usual way the business of the partnership of which he is a member binds the partnership, unless the partner so acting has in fact no authority to act for the partnership in the particular matter, and the person with whom he is dealing has knowledge of the fact that he has no such authority. For purposes of this subdivision, "knowledge" includes constructive notice pursuant to Section 15010.7.

(2) An act of a partner which is not apparently for carrying on of the business of the partnership in the usual way does not bind the partnership unless authorized by the other partners.

(3) Unless authorized by the other partners or unless they have abandoned the business, one or more but less than all the partners have no authority to:

(a) Assign the partnership property in trust for creditors or on the assignee's promise to pay the debts of the partnership.

(b) Dispose of the goodwill of the business.

(c) Do any other act which would make it impossible to carry on the ordinary business of a partnership.

(d) Confess a judgment.

(e) Submit a partnership claim or liability to arbitration or reference.

(4) No act of a partner in contravention of a restriction on authority shall bind the partnership to persons having knowledge of the restriction. *(Added by Stats. 1949, c. 383, § 1. Amended by Stats.1984, c. 477, § 1.)*

§ 15010. Conveyance of title to realty

(1) Where title to real property is in the partnership name, any partner may convey title to such property by a conveyance executed in the partnership name; but the partnership may recover such property unless the partner's act binds the partnership under the provisions of subdivision (1) of Section 15009, or unless such property has been conveyed to a bona fide purchaser for value without knowledge that the partner in executing the conveyance has exceeded his authority. For purposes of this subdivision, "knowledge" includes constructive notice pursuant to Section 15010.7.

(2) Where title to real property is in the name of the partnership, a conveyance executed by a partner, in his own name, passes the equitable interest of the partnership, provided the act is one within the authority of the partner under the provisions of subdivision (1) of Section 15009.

(3) Where title to real property is in the name of one or more of the partners, whether or not the record discloses the right of the partnership, the partners in whose name the title stands may convey title to such property, but the partnership may recover such property unless the partner's act binds the partnership under the provisions of subdivision (1) of Section 15009, or unless the property has been conveyed to a bona fide purchaser for value without knowledge that the partner in executing the conveyance has exceeded his authority.

(4) Where the title to real property is in the name of one or more or all the partners, or in a third person in trust for the partnership, a conveyance executed by a partner in the partnership name, or in his own name, passes the equitable interest of the partnership, provided the act is one within the authority of the partner under the provisions of subdivision (1) of Section 15009.

(5) Where the title to real property is in the names of all the partners a conveyance executed by all the partners passes all their rights in such property. *(Added by Stats.1949, c. 383, § 1. Amended by Stats.1984, c. 477, § 2.)*

§ 15010.5. Recording statement of partnership; definitions

(1) Recording with county recorder; execution of statement; contents; effect of recordation. A statement of partnership, in the name of the partnership, signed, acknowledged and verified by two or more of the partners, or such a statement signed by two or more of the partners as individuals, acknowledged and verified by each signing partner, may be recorded in the office of the county recorder of any county. Such recorded statement, or a copy thereof certified by any recorder in whose office it or a copy thereof so certified is recorded, may be recorded in any other county or counties. The statement shall set forth the name of the partnership and the name of each of the partners, and shall state that the partners named are all of the partners. If a partnership is not dissolved by the death or by the withdrawal of a partner by reason of an agreement provided for in subdivision (4) or (7) of Section 15031 the statement or amended statement may state the name and date of death or withdrawal of such deceased or withdrawing (whether voluntarily or involuntarily according to the terms of the agreement) partner and that the partnership was not dissolved by reason of such death or withdrawal because of the existence of such agreement.

It shall be conclusively presumed, in favor of any bona fide purchaser for value of the partnership real property located in a county in which such statement or such certified copy thereof has been recorded, that the persons named as partners therein are members of the partnership named and that they are all of the members of the partnership, and that any partner stated to be dead is deceased, and any partner stated to have withdrawn has withdrawn therefrom, and that the partnership was not dissolved by reason of such death or withdrawal, unless there is recorded by anyone claiming to be a partner, or a personal representative, whether executor, administrator, guardian or conservator, of such partner, a statement of partnership, verified and acknowledged by the person executing it, which shall set forth the name of the partnership, a statement that such person claims to be a member of such partnership, or a personal representative of such member, or a statement that any of the persons named in a previously recorded statement of partnership are not members of such partnership.

(2) Conveyance, convey and purchaser defined. As used in this section and in Section 15010, "conveyance" includes every instrument in writing by which any estate or interest in real estate is created, aliened, mortgaged, or encumbered, or by which the title to any real property may be affected, except wills; "convey" includes the execution of any such instrument; and "purchaser" includes any person acquiring an interest under any such instrument. *(Added by Stats.1949, c. 383, § 1. Amended by Stats.1957, c. 1233, § 1; Stats.1961, c. 747, § 1; Stats.1963, c. 718, § 1; Stats.1970, c. 606, § 1.)*

§ 15010.6. Recording statement of partnership after death of partner

Where no statement of partnership as provided in Section 15010.5 has been recorded prior to the death of one or more of the partners, such statement may be signed, acknowledged and verified by two or more of the surviving partners, in the form and manner specified in said section; provided that if all of the partners except one are deceased, the statement may be signed, acknowledged and verified by the last survivor of the partners only; and provided further that such statement shall specify the date of creation of the partnership, which of the partners are deceased and the date of death of each deceased partner.

Nothing in this section shall be construed to affect the provisions of Section 15031 of this code. *(Added by Stats.1963, c. 718, § 2.)*

§ 15010.7. Restrictions on partner's authority contained in statement of partnership; constructive notice

A statement of partnership, as authorized in Section 15010.5, may also contain restrictions upon the authority of individual partners to convey, encumber, or transfer interest in partnership real property, so long as it is otherwise valid under the law, and it is signed, acknowledged, and verified by all of the partners.

Such a statement, provided that it is signed, acknowledged, and verified by all of the partners and so long as title to the real property appears in the partnership name or otherwise indicates ownership by the partnership, shall constitute constructive notice of the contents of the restrictions and shall be conclusive as to any real property located in each county in which such a statement, or certified copy thereof, is duly recorded. Such a statement shall remain effective until there is recorded, with respect to the same partnership, a subsequent statement of partnership, signed, acknowledged, and verified by all the existing partners, as provided in Section 15010.5. *(Added by Stats.1984, c. 477, § 3. Amended by Stats.1985, c. 138, § 1.)*

§ 15011. Partner's admission or representation; evidence against partnership

An admission or representation made by any partner concerning partnership affairs within the scope of his authority as conferred by this act is evidence against the partnership. *(Added by Stats.1949, c. 383, § 1).*

§ 15012. Notice to and knowledge of partner; imputation to partnership

Notice to any partner of any matter relating to partnership affairs, and the knowledge of the partner acting in the particular matter, acquired while a partner or then present to his mind, and the knowledge of any other partner who reasonably could and should have communicated it to the acting partner, operate as notice to or knowledge of the partnership, except in the case of a fraud on the partnership committed by or with the consent of that partner. *(Added by Stats.1949, c. 383, § 1.)*

§ 15013. Liability of partnership for wrongs of partner

Where, by any wrongful act or omission of any partner acting in the ordinary course of the business of the partnership or with the authority of his copartners, loss or injury is caused to any person, not being a partner in the partnership, or any penalty is incurred, the partnership is liable therefor to the same extent as the partner so acting or omitting to act. *(Added by Stats.1949, c. 383, § 1.)*

§ 15014. Liability of partnership for partner's misapplication of money or property

The partnership is bound to make good the loss:

(a) Where one partner acting within the scope of his apparent authority receives money or property of a third person and misapplies it; and

(b) Where the partnership in the course of its business receives money or property of a third person and the money or property so received is misapplied by any partner while it is in the custody of the partnership. *(Added by Stats.1949, c. 383, § 1.)*

§ 15015. Joint and several liability of partners

All partners are liable

(a) Jointly and severally for everything chargeable to the partnership under Sections 15013 and 15014.

(b) Jointly for all other debts and obligations of the partnership; but any partner may enter into a separate obligation to perform a partnership contract. *(Added by Stats.1949, c. 383, § 1.)*

§ 15016. Liability for misrepresentation of person as a partner

(1) Liability of person misrepresenting self as a partner. When a person, by words spoken or written or by conduct, represents himself, or consents to another representing him to any one, as a partner in an existing partnership or with one or more persons not actual partners, he is liable to any such person to whom such representation has been made, who has, on the faith of such representation, given credit to the actual or apparent partnership, and if he has made such representation or consented to its being made in a public manner he is liable to such person, whether the representation has or has not been made or communicated to such person so giving credit by or with the knowledge of the apparent partner making the representation or consenting to its being made.

(a) When a partnership liability results, he is liable as though he were an actual member of the partnership.

(b) When no partnership liability results, he is liable jointly with the other persons, if any, so consenting to the contract or representation as to incur liability, otherwise separately.

(2) Liability of persons consenting to misrepresentation. When a person has been thus represented to be a partner in an existing partnership, or with one or more persons not actual partners, he is an agent of the persons consenting to such representation to bind them to the same extent and in the same manner as though he were a partner in fact, with respect to persons who rely upon the representation. Where all the members of the existing partnership consent to the representation, a partnership act or obligation results; but in all other cases it is the joint act or obligation of the person acting and the persons consenting to the representation. *(Added by Stats.1949, c. 383, § 1.)*

§ 15017. Liability of new partner for partnership obligations

A person admitted as a partner into an existing partnership is liable for all the obligations of the partnership arising before his admission as though he had been a partner when such obligations were incurred, except that this liability shall be satisfied only out of partnership property. *(Added by Stats.1949, c. 383, § 1.)*

ARTICLE 4. RELATIONS OF PARTNERS TO ONE ANOTHER

§ 15018. Rights and duties of partners

The rights and duties of the partners in relation to the partnership shall be determined, subject to any agreement between them, by the following rules:

(a) Each partner shall be repaid his contributions, whether by way of capital or advances to the partnership property and share equally in the profits and surplus remaining after all liabilities, including those to partners, are satisfied; and must contribute towards the losses, whether of capital or otherwise, sustained by the partnership according to his share in the profits.

(b) The partnership must indemnify every partner in respect of payments made and personal liabilities reasonably incurred by him in the ordinary and proper conduct of its business, or for the preservation of its business or property.

(c) A partner, who in aid of the partnership makes any payment or advance beyond the amount of the capital which he agreed to contribute, shall be paid interest from the date of the payment or advance.

(d) A partner shall receive interest on the capital contributed by him only from the date when repayment should be made.

(e) All partners have equal rights in the management and conduct of the partnership business.

(f) No partner is entitled to remuneration for acting in the partnership business, except that a surviving partner is entitled to reasonable compensation for his services in winding up the partnership affairs.

(g) No person can become a member of a partnership without the consent of all the partners.

(h) Any difference arising as to ordinary matters connected with the partnership business may be decided by a majority of the partners; but no act in contravention of any agreement between the partners may be done rightfully without the consent of all the partners. *(Added by Stats.1949, c. 383, § 1.)*

§ 15019. Partnership books; right to inspect

The partnership books shall be kept, subject to any agreement between the partners, at the principal place of business of the partnership, and every partner shall at all times have access to and may inspect and copy any of them. *(Added by Stats.1949, c. 383, § 1.)*

§ 15020. Disclosure of information on demand

Partners shall render on demand true and full information of all things affecting the partnership to any partner or the legal representative of any deceased partner or partner under legal disability. *(Added by Stats.1949, c. 383, § 1.)*

§ 15021. Accounting of partner to partnership; personal representatives of deceased last surviving partner

(1) Every partner must account to the partnership for any benefit, and hold as trustee for it any profits derived by him without the consent of the other partners from any transaction connected with the formation, conduct, or liquidation of the partnership or from any use by him of its property.

(2) This section applies also to the representatives of a deceased partner engaged in the liquidation of the affairs of the partnership as the personal representatives of the last surviving partner. *(Added by Stats.1949, c. 383, § 1.)*

§ 15022. Partner's right to formal accounting

Any partner shall have the right to a formal account as to partnership affairs:

(a) If he is wrongfully excluded from the partnership business or possession of its property by his copartners,

(b) If the right exists under the terms of any agreement,

(c) As provided by Section 15021,

(d) Whenever other circumstances render it just and reasonable. *(Added by Stats.1949, c. 383, § 1.)*

§ 15023. Continuation of terminated partnership

(1) When a partnership for a fixed term or particular undertaking is continued after the termination of such term or particular undertaking without any express agreement, the rights and duties of the partners remain the same as they were at such termination, so far as is consistent with a partnership at will.

(2) A continuation of the business by the partners or such of them as habitually acted therein during the term, without any settlement or liquidation of the partnership affairs, is prima facie evidence of a continuation of the partnership. *(Added by Stats.1949, c. 383, § 1.)*

ARTICLE 5. PROPERTY RIGHTS OF A PARTNER

§ 15024. Property rights

The property rights of a partner are (1) his rights in specific partnership property, (2) his interest in the partnership, and (3) his right to participate in the management. *(Added by Stats.1949, c. 383, § 1.)*

§ 15025. Ownership of specific partnership property

(1) A partner is coowner with the other partners of specific partnership property holding as a tenant in partnership.

(2) The incidents of this tenancy are such that:

(a) A partner, subject to the provisions of this chapter and to any agreement between the partners, has an equal right with the other partners to possess specific partnership property for partnership purposes; but a partner has no right to possess such property for any other purpose without the consent of the other partners.

(b) A partner's right in specific partnership property is not assignable except in connection with the assignment of rights of all the partners in the same property.

(c) A partner's right in specific partnership property is not subject to enforcement of a money judgment, except on a claim against the partnership. When partnership property is levied upon for a partnership debt, the partners, or any of them, or the representatives of a deceased partner, cannot claim any right under the exemption laws.

(d) On the death of a partner, the partner's right in specific partnership property vests in the surviving partner or partners, except where the deceased was the last surviving partner, when the deceased partner's right in such property vests in his or her legal representative. Such surviving partner or partners, or the legal representative of the last surviving partner, has no right to possess the partnership property for any but a partnership purpose.

(e) A partner's right in specific partnership property is not subject to dower, curtesy, or allowances to widows, heirs, or next of kin, and is not community property. *(Added by Stats. 1949, c. 383, § 1. Amended by Stats.1982, c. 497, § 84.)*

Section 185 of Stats.1982, c. 497, provides:

"This act shall become operative only if Assembly Bill No. 707 [Stats.1982, c. 1364] is chaptered and becomes effective January 1, 1983, and in such case this act shall become operative on July 1, 1983, the same as Assembly Bill No. 707."

§ 15026. Interest in partnership

A partner's interest in the partnership is his share of the profits and surplus, and the same is personal property. *(Added by Stats.1949, c. 383, § 1.)*

§ 15027. Conveyance of interest in partnership

(1) Effect of conveyance; assignee's rights. A conveyance by a partner of his interest in the partnership does not of itself dissolve the partnership, nor, as against the other partners in the absence of agreement, entitle the assignee, during the continuance of the partnership, to interfere in the management or administration of the partnership business or affairs, or to require any information or account of partnership transactions, or to inspect the partnership books; but it merely entitles the assignee to receive in accordance with his contract the profits to which the assigning partner would otherwise be entitled.

(2) Assignee's rights upon dissolution. In case of a dissolution of the partnership, the assignee is entitled to receive his assignor's interest and may require an account from the date only of the last account agreed to by all the partners. *(Added by Stats.1949, c. 383, § 1.)*

§ 15028. Creditor's remedy to reach partner's interest in partnership

(1) Application by judgment creditor; charge on partner's interest; appointment of receiver. On due application to a competent court by any judgment creditor of a partner, the court which entered the judgment, order, or decree, or any other court, may charge the interest of the debtor partner with payment of the unsatisfied amount of such judgment debt with interest thereon; and may then or later appoint a receiver of his share of the profits, and of any other money due or to fall due to him in respect of the partnership, and make all other orders, directions, accounts, and inquiries which the debtor partner might have made, or which the circumstances of the case may require.

(2) Redemption; purchase at judicial sale. The interest charged may be redeemed at any time before foreclosure, or in case of a sale being directed by the court may be purchased without thereby causing a dissolution:

(a) With separate property, by any one or more of the partners, or

(b) With partnership property, by any one or more of the partners with the consent of all the partners whose interests are not so charged or sold.

(3) Application of exemption laws. Nothing in this act shall be held to deprive a partner of his right, if any, under the exemption laws, as regards his interest in the partnership. *(Added by Stats.1949, c. 383, § 1.)*

ARTICLE 6. DISSOLUTION AND WINDING UP

§ 15029. Dissolution defined

The dissolution of a partnership is the change in the relation of the partners caused by any partner ceasing to be associated in the carrying on as distinguished from the winding up of the business. *(Added by Stats.1949, c. 383, § 1.)*

§ 15030. Effect of dissolution

On dissolution the partnership is not terminated, but continues until the winding up of partnership affairs is completed. *(Added by Stats.1949, c. 383, § 1.)*

§ 15031. Causes of dissolution

Dissolution is caused:

(1) Without violation of the agreement between the partners,

(a) By the termination of the definite term or particular undertaking specified in the agreement,

(b) By the express will of any partner when no definite term or particular undertaking is specified,

(c) By the express will of all the partners who have not assigned their interests or suffered them to be charged for their separate debts, either before or after the termination of any specified term or particular undertaking,

(d) By the expulsion of any partner from the business bona fide in accordance with such a power conferred by the agreement between the partners;

(2) In contravention of the agreement between the partners, where the circumstances do not permit a dissolution under any other provision of this section, by the express will of any partner at any time;

(3) By any event which makes it unlawful for the business of the partnership to be carried on or for the members to carry it on in partnership;

(4) By the death of any partner unless otherwise provided in an agreement in writing signed by all the partners before such death or in a court order made pursuant to Section 9762 of the Probate Code;

(5) By the bankruptcy of any partner or the partnership;

(6) By decree of court under Section 15032;

(7) By withdrawal of a partner or admission of a new partner unless otherwise provided in an agreement in writing signed by all of the partners, including any such withdrawing partner or any such newly admitted partner, before such withdrawal or admission; provided that in the case of a newly admitted partner he or she may become a party to any such preexisting agreement by signing the same upon such admission.

None of the provisions of any other section of this chapter shall prevent, or impair the effect or enforceability of, any agreement in writing that a partnership will not be dissolved as provided for in subdivision (4) or (7) of this section. *(Added by Stats.1949, c. 383, § 1. Amended by Stats.1961, c. 1913, § 1; Stats.1963, c. 718, § 3; Stats.1987, c.923, § 1.5, operative July 1, 1988.)*

§ 15032. Decree of dissolution

(1) Application by partner. On application by or for a partner the court shall decree a dissolution whenever:

(a) A partner has been declared a lunatic in any judicial proceeding or is shown to be of unsound mind,

(b) A partner becomes in any other way incapable of performing his part of the partnership contract,

(c) A partner has been guilty of such conduct as tends to affect prejudicially the carrying on of the business,

(d) A partner wilfully or persistently commits a breach of the partnership agreement, or otherwise so conducts himself in matters relating to the partnership business that it is not reasonably practicable to carry on the business in partnership with him,

(e) The business of the partnership can only be carried on at a loss,

(f) Other circumstances render a dissolution equitable.

(2) Application by purchaser of partner's interest. On the application of the purchaser of a partner's interest under Sections 15027 and 15028:

(a) After the termination of the specified term or particular undertaking,

(b) At any time if the partnership was a partnership at will when the interest was assigned or when the charging order was issued. *(Added by Stats.1949, c. 383, § 1.)*

§ 15033. Effect of dissolution on partner's authority

Except so far as may be necessary to wind up partnership affairs or to complete transactions begun but not then finished, dissolution terminates all authority of any partner to act for the partnership,

(1) With respect to the partners,

(a) When the dissolution is not by the act, bankruptcy or death of a partner; or

(b) When the dissolution is by such act, bankruptcy or death of a partner in cases where Section 15034 so requires;

(2) With respect to persons not partners, as declared in Section 15035. *(Added by Stats.1949, c. 383, § 1.)*

§ 15034. Liability of partner to copartners when dissolution caused by act, death, or bankruptcy of partner

Where the dissolution is caused by the act, death or bankruptcy of a partner, each partner is liable to his copartners for his share of any liability created by any partner acting for the partnership as if the partnership had not been dissolved unless

(a) The dissolution being by act of any partner, the partner acting for the partnership had knowledge of the dissolution, or

(b) The dissolution being by the death or bankruptcy of a partner, the partner acting for the partnership had knowledge or notice of the death or bankruptcy. *(Added by Stats.1949, c. 383, § 1.)*

§ 15035. Authority and liability after dissolution

(1) Partner's authority. After dissolution a partner can bind the partnership except as provided in paragraph three,

(a) By any act appropriate for winding up partnership affairs or completing transactions unfinished at dissolution;

(b) By any transaction which would bind the partnership if dissolution had not taken place, provided, the other party to the transaction:

I. Had extended credit to the partnership prior to dissolution and had no knowledge or notice of the dissolution; or

II. Though he had not so extended credit, had nevertheless known of the partnership prior to dissolution, and, having no knowledge or notice of dissolution, the fact of dissolution had not been advertised in a newspaper of general circulation in the place (or in each place if more than one) at which the partnership business was regularly carried on.

(2) Satisfaction of partner's liability out of partnership assets. The liability of a partner under paragraph 1(b) shall be satisfied out of partnership assets alone when such partner had been prior to dissolution

(a) Unknown as a partner to the person with whom the contract is made; and

(b) So far unknown and inactive in partnership affairs that the business reputation of the partnership could not be said to have been in any degree due to his connection with it.

(3) Liability of partnership. The partnership is in no case bound by any act of a partner after dissolution

(a) Where the partnership is dissolved because it is unlawful to carry on the business, unless the act is appropriate for winding up partnership affairs; or

(b) Where the partner has become bankrupt; or

(c) Where the partner has no authority to wind up partnership affairs; except by a transaction with one who

I. Had extended credit to the partnership prior to dissolution and had no knowledge or notice of his want of authority; or

II. Had not extended credit to the partnership prior to dissolution, and, having no knowledge or notice of his want of authority, the fact of his want of authority has not been advertised in the manner provided for advertising the fact of dissolution in paragraph (1bII).

(4) Liability for misrepresentation of person as a partner. Nothing in this section shall affect the liability under Section 15016 of any person who after dissolution represents himself or consents to another representing him as a partner in a partnership engaged in carrying on business. *(Added by Stats.1949, c. 383, § 1.)*

§ 15035.5. Notice of dissolution; publication

Whenever a partnership is dissolved, a notice of the dissolution shall be published at least once in a newspaper of general circulation in the place, or in each place if more than one, at which the partnership business was regularly carried on, and an affidavit showing the publication of such notice shall be filed with the county clerk within thirty days after such publication. *(Added by Stats.1949, c. 1210, § 3.)*

§ 15036. Discharge of partner's liability

(1) Effect of dissolution alone. The dissolution of the partnership does not of itself discharge the existing liability of any partner.

(2) Agreement to discharge. A partner is discharged from any existing liability upon dissolution of the partnership by an agreement to that effect between himself, the partnership creditor and the person or partnership continuing the business; and such agreement may be inferred from the course of dealing between the creditor having knowledge of the dissolution and the person or partnership continuing the business.

(3) Assumption of partnership obligations. Where a person agrees to assume the existing obligations of a dissolved partnership, the partners whose obligations have been assumed shall be discharged from any liability to any creditor of the partnership who, knowing of the agreement, consents to a material alteration in the nature or time of payment of such obligations.

(4) Deceased partner. The individual property of a deceased partner shall be liable for all obligations of the partnership incurred while he was a partner but subject to the prior payment of his separate debts. *(Added by Stats.1949, c. 383, § 1.)*

§ 15037. Right to wind up partnership affairs

Unless otherwise agreed the partners who have not wrongfully dissolved the partnership or the legal representative of the last surviving partner, not bankrupt, has the right to wind up the partnership affairs; provided, however, that any partner, his legal representative, or his assignee, upon cause shown, may obtain winding up by the court. *(Added by Stats.1949, c. 383, § 1.)*

§ 15038. Rights of partners upon dissolution

(a) Dissolution in accordance with partnership agreement; application of partnership property; expelled partner. When dissolution is caused in any way, except in contravention of the partnership agreement, each partner, as against the copartners and all persons claiming through them in respect of their interests in the partnership, unless otherwise agreed, may have the partnership property applied to discharge its liabilities, and the surplus applied to pay in cash the net amount owing to the respective partners. But if dissolution is caused by expulsion of a partner, bona fide under the partnership agreement and if the expelled partner is discharged from all partnership liabilities, either by payment or agreement under Section 15036(2), the expelled partner shall receive in cash only the net amount due from the partnership.

(b) Dissolution in violation of partnership agreement. When dissolution is caused in contravention of the partnership agreement the rights of the partners shall be as follows:

(1) Rights of partner not causing dissolution. Each partner who has not caused dissolution wrongfully shall have:

(A) All the rights specified in subdivision (a).

(B) The right, as against each partner who has caused the dissolution wrongfully, to damages for breach of the agreement.

(2) Continuation of partnership business. The partners who have not caused the dissolution wrongfully, if they all desire to continue the business in the same name, either by themselves or jointly with others, may do so, during the agreed term for the partnership and for that purpose may possess the partnership property; provided, they secure the payment by bond or pay to any partner who has caused the dissolution wrongfully, the value of the partner's interest in the partnership at the dissolution, less any damages recoverable under subdivision (b)(1)(B), and in like manner indemnify the partner against all present or future partnership liabilities.

(3) Rights of partner causing dissolution. A partner who has caused the dissolution wrongfully shall have:

(A) If the business is not continued under the provisions of subdivision (b)(2), all the rights of a partner under subdivision (a), subject to subdivision (b)(1)(B).

(B) If the business is continued under subdivision (b)(2) the right as against the copartners and all claiming through them in respect of their interests in the partnership, to have the value of the partner's interest in the partnership, less any damages caused to the copartners by the dissolution, ascertained and paid to the partner in cash, or the payment secured by bond, and to be released from all existing liabilities of the partnership; but in ascertaining the value of the partner's interest the value of the good will of the business shall not be considered. *(Added by Stats. 1949, c. 383, § 1. Amended by Stats. 1982, c. 517, § 191.)*

§ 15039. Rights of partner entitled to rescind partnership

Where a partnership contract is rescinded on the ground of the fraud or misrepresentation of one of the parties thereto the party entitled to rescind is, without prejudice to any other right, entitled,

(a) To a lien on, or right of retention of, the surplus of the partnership property after satisfying the partnership liabilities to third persons for any sum of money paid by him for the purchase of an interest in the partnership and for any capital or advances contributed by him; and

(b) To stand, after all liabilities to third persons have been satisfied, in the place of the creditors of the partnership for any payments made by him in respect of the partnership liabilities; and

(c) To be indemnified by the person guilty of the fraud or making the representation against all debts and liabilities of the partnership. *(Added by Stats. 1949, c. 383, § 1.)*

§ 15040. Rules for settling accounts between partners

In settling accounts between the partners after dissolution, the following rules shall be observed, subject to any agreement to the contrary:

(a) Partnership assets. The assets of the partnership are:

I. The partnership property,

II. The contributions of the partners necessary for the payment of all the liabilities specified in clause (b) of this paragraph.

(b) Order of payment of liabilities. The liabilities of the partnership shall rank in order of payment, as follows:

I. Those owing to creditors other than partners,

II. Those owing to partners other than for capital and profits,

III. Those owing to partners in respect of capital,

IV. Those owing to partners in respect of profits.

(c) Order of application of assets to liabilities. The assets shall be applied in the order of their declaration in clause (a) of this paragraph to the satisfaction of the liabilities.

(d) Contribution by partners. The partners shall contribute, as provided by Section 15018(a) the amount necessary to satisfy the liabilities; but if any, but not all, of the partners are insolvent, or, not being subject to process, refuse to contribute, the other partners shall contribute their share of the liabilities, and, in the relative proportions in which they share the profits, the additional amount necessary to pay the liabilities.

(e) Who may enforce contribution. An assignee for the benefit of creditors or any person appointed by the court shall have the right to enforce the contributions specified in clause (d) of this paragraph.

(f) Partner's right to enforce contribution. Any partner or his legal representative shall have the right to enforce the contributions specified in clause (d) of this paragraph, to the extent of the amount which he has paid in excess of his share of the liability.

(g) Contribution from individual property of deceased partner. The individual property of a deceased partner shall be liable for the contributions specified in clause (d) of this paragraph.

(h) Priorities between partnership and separate creditors. When partnership property and the individual properties of the partners are in possession of a court for distribution, partnership creditors shall have priority on partnership property and separate creditors on individual property, saving the rights of lien or secured creditors as heretofore.

(i) Priorities against separate property of bankrupt or insolvent partner. Where a partner has become bankrupt or his estate is insolvent the claims against his separate property shall rank in the following order:

I. Those owing to separate creditors,

II. Those owing to partnership creditors,

III. Those owing to partners by way of contribution. *(Added by Stats. 1949, c. 383, § 1.)*

§ 15041. Creditors' rights against person or partnership continuing business of dissolved partnership

(1) Admission of new partner; retirement of partner and assignment of rights to two or more partners or to one or more partners and one or more third persons.

When any new partner is admitted into an existing partnership, or when any partner retires and assigns (or the representative of the deceased partner assigns) his rights in partnership property to two or more of the partners, or to one or more of the partners and one or more third persons, if the business is continued without liquidation of the partnership affairs, creditors of the first or dissolved partnership are also creditors of the partnership so continuing the business.

(2) Retirement of all but one partner and assignment of rights to remaining partner. When all but one partner retire and assign (or the representative of a deceased partner assigns) their rights in partnership property to the remaining partner, who continues the business without liquidation of partnership affairs, either alone or with others, creditors of the dissolved partnership are also creditors of the person or partnership so continuing the business.

(3) Retirement or death of partner and continuance of business with consent but without assignment. When any partner retires or dies and the business of the dissolved partnership is continued as set forth in paragraphs (1) and (2) of this section, with the consent of the retired partners or the representative of the deceased partner, but without any assignment of his right in partnership property, rights of creditors of the dissolved partnership and of the creditors of the person or partnership continuing the business shall be as if such assignment had been made.

(4) Assignment of rights of all partners to third persons who assume partnership debts. When all the partners or their representatives assign their rights in partnership property to one or more third persons who promise to pay the debts and who continue the business of the dissolved partnership, creditors of the dissolved partnership are also creditors of the person or partnership continuing the business.

(5) Continuance of business by remaining partners after dissolution by wrongful act of partner. When any partner wrongfully causes a dissolution and the remaining partners continue the business under the provisions of Section 15038(2b), either alone or with others, and without liquidation of the partnership affairs, creditors of the dissolved partnership are also creditors of the person or partnership continuing the business.

(6) Continuance of business by remaining partners after expulsion of partner. When a partner is expelled and the remaining partners continue the business either alone or with others, without liquidation of the partnership affairs, creditors of the dissolved partnership are also creditors of the person or partnership continuing the business.

(7) Liability of new partner to creditors of dissolved partnership. The liability of a third person becoming a partner in the partnership continuing the business, under this section, to the creditors of the dissolved partnership shall be satisfied out of partnership property only.

(8) Creditors' priority to claim of retired or deceased partner against person or partnership continuing business. When the business of a partnership after dissolution is continued under any conditions set forth in this section the creditors of the dissolved partnership, as against the separate creditors of the retiring or deceased partner or the representative of the deceased partner, have a prior right to any claim of the retired partner or the representative of the deceased partner against the person or partnership continuing the business, on account of the retired or deceased partner's interest in the dissolved partnership or on account of any consideration promised for such interest or for his right in partnership property.

(9) Right to set aside fraudulent assignment. Nothing in this section shall be held to modify any right of creditors to set aside any assignment on the ground of fraud.

(10) Use of deceased partner's name; liability of deceased partner's separate property for new debts. The use by the person or partnership continuing the business of the partnership name, or the name of a deceased partner as part thereof, shall not of itself make the individual property of the deceased partner liable for any debts contracted by such person or partnership. *(Added by Stats.1949, c. 383, § 1.)*

§ 15042. Rights of retiring or deceased partner against person or partnership continuing business

When any partner retires or dies, and the business is continued under any of the conditions set forth in Section 15041(1, 2, 3, 5, 6), or Section 15038(2b) without any settlement of accounts as between him or his estate and the person or partnership continuing the business, unless otherwise agreed, he or his legal representative as against such persons or partnership may have the value of his interest at the date of dissolution ascertained, and shall receive as an ordinary creditor an amount equal to the value of his interest in the dissolved partnership with interest, or, at his option or at the option of his legal representative, in lieu of interest, the profits attributable to the use of his right in the property of the dissolved partnership; provided, that the creditors of the dissolved partnership as against the separate creditors, or the representative of the retired or deceased partner, shall have priority on any claim arising under this section, as provided by Section 15041(8) of this act. *(Added by Stats.1949, c. 383, § 1.)*

§ 15043. Partner's right to account of his interest

The right to an account of his interest shall accrue to any partner, or his legal representative, as against the winding up partners or the surviving partners or the person or partnership continuing the business, at the date of dissolution, in the absence of any agreement to the contrary. *(Added by Stats.1949, c. 383, § 1.)*

ARTICLE 7. MISCELLANEOUS PROVISIONS

§ 15044. General partnerships and partners

Every partnership that is not formed in accordance with the law concerning special, limited, or mining partnerships, and every special or limited partnership, so far only as those partners who are not special partners are concerned, is a general partnership. Every partner who is not a special or limited partner nor a member of a mining partnership is a general partner. *(Added by Stats.1949, c. 383, § 1.)*

§ 15045. Application of Probate Code

The rights and duties of surviving partners, the legal representatives of deceased partners, the creditors of such partners, and the creditors of the partnership created by or defined in this chapter shall be given full force and effect notwithstanding any provision inconsistent therewith in the Probate Code, but nothing in this chapter shall otherwise affect any provision of the Probate Code. *(Added by Stats.1949, c. 383, § 1.)*

2. California Revised Limited Partnership Act

§ 15533. Force and effect of chapter

This chapter shall be of no force and effect except as provided by Article 11 (commencing with Section 15710) or Article 12 (commencing with Section 15721) of Chapter 3. *(Added by Stats.1983, c. 1223, § 8.)*

Section 15 of Stats.1983, c. 1223, provides:

"Sections 8 to 13, inclusive, of this act shall become operative on July 1, 1984."

CHAPTER 3. CALIFORNIA REVISED LIMITED PARTNERSHIP ACT

ARTICLE 1. GENERAL PROVISIONS

§ 15611. Definitions

As used in this chapter, unless the context otherwise requires:

(a) "Acknowledged" means that an instrument is either of the following:

(1) Formally acknowledged as provided in Article 3 (commencing with Section 1180) of Chapter 4 of Title 4 of Part 4 of Division 2 of the Civil Code.

(2) Executed to include substantially the following wording preceding the signature: It is hereby declared that I am the person who executed this instrument, which execution is my act and deed.

Any certificate of acknowledgment taken without this state before a notary public or a judge or clerk of a court of record having an official seal need not be further authenticated.

(b) "Capital account" of a partner, unless otherwise provided in the partnership agreement, means the amount of the capital interest of that partner in the partnership consisting of that partner's original contribution, as (1) increased by any additional contributions and by that partner's share of the partnership's profits and (2) decreased by any distribution to that partner and by that partner's share of the partnership's losses.

(c) "Certificate of limited partnership" or "certificate" means the certificate referred to in Section 15621, including all amendments thereto.

(d) "Constituent limited partnership" means a limited partnership which is merged with one or more other limited partnerships and includes the surviving limited partnership.

(e) "Contribution" means any money, property or services rendered, or a promissory note or other binding obligation to contribute money or property, or to render services as permitted in this chapter, which a partner contributes to a limited partnership as capital in that partner's capacity as a partner pursuant to an agreement between the partners, including an agreement as to value.

(f) "Disappearing limited partnership" means a constituent limited partnership which is not the surviving limited partnership.

(g) "Distribution" means the transfer of money or property by a partnership to its partners without consideration.

(h) "Foreign limited partnership" means a partnership formed under the laws of any state other than this state or under the laws of a foreign country and having as partners one or more general partners and one or more limited partners (or their equivalents under any name).

(i) "General partner" means a person who has been admitted to a limited partnership as a general partner in accordance with the partnership agreement or a person who has been admitted as a general partner pursuant to Section 15641.

(j) "Interests of limited partners" means the aggregate interests of all limited partners in their respective capacities as limited partners in the current profits derived from business operations of the partnership.

(k) "Limited partner" means a person who has been admitted to a limited partnership as a limited partner in accordance with the partnership agreement, or an assignee of a limited partnership interest who has become a limited partner pursuant to Section 15674, or, to the extent provided in subdivision (b) of Section 15662, a former general partner who has ceased to be a general partner.

(*l*) "Limited partnership" or "domestic limited partnership" means a partnership formed by two or more persons under the laws of this state and having one or more general partners and one or more limited partners.

(m) "Mail," unless otherwise provided in the partnership agreement, means first-class mail, postage prepaid, unless registered mail is specified. Registered mail includes certified mail.

(n) "Majority-in-interest of the limited partners," unless otherwise provided in the partnership agreement, means more than 50 percent of the interests of limited partners.

(*o*) "Parent" of a specified limited partnership means each general partner of the limited partnership, each person possessing, directly or indirectly, the power to direct or cause the direction of the management and policies of a general partner of the limited partnership, and a person owning, directly or indirectly, limited partnership interests possessing more than 50 percent of the aggregate voting power of the specified limited partnership.

(p) "Partner" means a limited or general partner. "Partner of record" means a partner named as a partner on the list maintained in accordance with subdivision (a) of Section 15615.

(q) "Partnership agreement" means any valid agreement of the partners as to the affairs of a limited partnership and the conduct of its business, including all amendments thereto.

(r) "Person" means an individual, partnership, limited partnership (domestic or foreign), trust, estate, association, corporation, or other entity.

(s) "Proxy" means a written authorization signed by a partner or the partner's attorney-in-fact giving another person the power to vote with respect to the interest of that partner. "Signed," for the purpose of this section, means the placing of the partner's name on the proxy (whether by manual signature, typewriting, telegraphic transmission, or otherwise) by the partner or partner's attorney-in-fact.

(t) "Return of capital," unless otherwise provided in the partnership agreement, means any distribution to a partner to the extent that the partner's capital account, immediately after the distribution, is less than the amount of that partner's contributions to the partnership as reduced by prior distributions which were a return of capital.

(u) "State" means a state, territory, or possession of the United States, the District of Columbia, or the Commonwealth of Puerto Rico.

(v) "Surviving limited partnership" means a limited partnership into which one or more other limited partnerships are merged.

(w) "Time a notice is given or sent," unless otherwise expressly provided, means the time a written notice to a partner or the limited partnership is deposited in the United States mails; or the time any other written notice is personally delivered to the recipient or is delivered to a common carrier for transmission, or actually transmitted by the person giving the notice by electronic means, to the recipient; or the time any oral notice is communicated, in person or by telephone or wireless, to the recipient or to a person at the office of the recipient who the person giving the notice has reason to believe will promptly communicate it to the recipient.

(x) (1) "Transact intrastate business" means entering into repeated and successive transactions of business in this state, other than interstate or foreign commerce.

(2) A foreign limited partnership shall not be considered to be transacting intrastate business merely because it is a limited partner of a foreign limited partnership transacting intrastate business or because it is a limited partner of a domestic limited partnership.

(3) Without excluding other activities which may not constitute transacting intrastate business, a foreign limited partnership shall not be considered to be transacting intrastate business within the meaning of paragraph (1) solely by reason of carrying on in this state any one or more of the following activities:

(A) Maintaining or defending any action or suit or any administrative or arbitration proceeding, or effecting the settlement thereof or the settlement of claims and disputes.

(B) Holding meetings of its partners or carrying on other activities concerning its internal affairs.

(C) Maintaining bank accounts.

(D) Maintaining offices or agencies for the transfer, exchange, and registration of its securities or depositaries with relation to its securities.

(E) Effecting sales through independent contractors.

(F) Soliciting or procuring orders, whether by mail or through employees or agents or otherwise, where such orders require acceptance without this state before becoming binding contracts.

(G) Creating evidences of debt or mortgages, liens, or security interests on, real or personal property.

(H) Conducting an isolated transaction completed within a period of 180 days and not in the course of a number of repeated transactions of like nature. *(Added by Stats.1983, c. 1223, § 10. Amended by Stats. 1984, c. 103, § 1; Stats.1987, c. 1364, § 1; Stats.1990, c. 1088 (S.B.2575), § 1.)*

§ 15612. Partnership name

The name of each limited partnership as set forth in its certificate of limited partnership:

(a) Shall contain the words "limited partnership" or the abbreviation "L.P." at the end of its name.

(b) May contain the name of a limited partner.

(c) May not be a name which the Secretary of State determines is likely to mislead the public and may not be the same as, or resemble so closely as to tend to deceive (1) a name which is under reservation for another limited partnership pursuant to Section 15613 or (2) the name of any limited partnership which has previously filed a certificate pursuant to Section 15621 or of a foreign limited partnership registered pursuant to Section 15692, except that a limited partnership may adopt a name that is substantially the same as that of an existing domestic limited partnership or foreign limited partnership which is registered pursuant to Section 15692, upon proof of consent by such domestic limited partnership or foreign limited partnership and a finding by the Secretary of State that under the circumstances the public is not likely to be misled.

(d) May not contain the words "bank," "insurance," "trust," "trustee," "incorporated," "inc.," "corporation," or "corp.".

(e) The use by a limited partnership or a foreign limited partnership of a name in violation of this section may be enjoined notwithstanding the filing of its certificate of limited partnership or its registration with the Secretary of State. *(Added by Stats.1983, c. 1223, § 10. Amended by Stats. 1984, c. 103, § 2; Stats.1987, c. 1364, § 2; Stats.1990, c. 1088 (S.B.2575), § 2.)*

§ 15613. Certificate of reservation of name

Any applicant may, upon payment of the fee prescribed therefor in the Government Code, obtain from the Secretary of State a certificate of reservation of any name not prohibited by Section 15612, and upon the issuance of the certificate the name stated therein shall be reserved for a period of 60 days. The Secretary of State shall not, however, issue certificates reserving the same name for two or more consecutive 60-day periods to the same applicant or for the use or benefit of the same person; nor shall consecutive reservations be made by or for the use or benefit of the same person of names so similar as to fall within the prohibitions of subdivision (c) of Section 15612. *(Added by Stats.1983, c. 1223, § 10.)*

§ 15614. Office and agent for service of process

Each limited partnership shall continuously maintain in this state each of the following:

(a) An office at which shall be kept the records required by Section 15615 to be maintained.

(b) An agent in this state for service of process on the limited partnership. *(Added by Stats.1983, c. 1223, § 10. Amended by Stats.1987, c. 1364, § 3.)*

§ 15615. Documents, books and records to be kept

Each limited partnership shall keep at the office referred to in subdivision (a) of Section 15614 all of the following:

(a) A current list of the full name and last known business or residence address of each partner set forth in alphabetical order together with the contribution and the share in profits and losses of each partner.

(b) A copy of the certificate of limited partnership and all certificates of amendment thereto, together with executed copies of any powers of attorney pursuant to which any certificate has been executed.

(c) Copies of the limited partnership's federal, state, and local income tax or information returns and reports, if any, for the six most recent taxable years.

(d) Copies of the original partnership agreement and all amendments thereto.

(e) Financial statements of the limited partnership for the six most recent fiscal years.

(f) The partnership's books and records as they relate to the internal affairs of the partnership for at least the current and past three fiscal years. *(Added by Stats. 1983, c. 1223, § 10. Amended by Stats.1987, c. 1364, § 3.5.)*

§ 15616. Nature of business

A limited partnership may carry on any business that a partnership without limited partners may carry on except the banking, insurance or trust company business. *(Added by Stats.1983, c. 1223, § 10.)*

§ 15617. Business transactions of partner with partnership

Except as otherwise provided in the partnership agreement, a partner may lend money to and transact other business with the limited partnership and, subject to other applicable law, has the same rights and obligations with respect thereto as a person who is not a partner. *(Added by Stats.1983, c. 1223, § 10.)*

§ 15618. Agreement varying effects of chapter

The effect of the provisions of this chapter may be varied as among the partners by the partnership agreement, except to the extent expressly provided to the contrary in this chapter and except that Sections 15642, 15694, 15701, and 15702, Article 2 (commencing with Section 15621), and Article 8 (commencing with Section 15681) may be varied by the partnership agreement only to the extent expressly provided in those sections. The presence in certain provisions of this chapter of the words "unless otherwise provided in the partnership agreement" or words of similar import does not imply that the effect of other provisions may not be varied as among the partners by agreement under this section. *(Added by Stats.1987, c. 1364, § 4.)*

ARTICLE 2. FORMATION: CERTIFICATE OF LIMITED PARTNERSHIP

§ 15621. Partnership agreement; certificate; execution, acknowledgment, and filing; form; contents; formation of partnership; evidence; recording certificate; presumptions created; dishonored filing fee payment; cancellation of filing; notice

(a) In order to form a limited partnership the general partners shall execute, acknowledge, and file a certificate of limited partnership and, either before or after the filing of a certificate, the partners shall have entered into a partnership agreement. The certificate shall be filed in the office of, and on a form prescribed by, the Secretary of State and shall set forth all of the following:

(1) The name of the limited partnership.

(2) The street address of the principal executive office.

(3) The names and addresses of the general partners.

(4) The name and address of the agent for service of process required to be maintained by Section 15614, unless a corporate agent is designated, in which case only the name of the agent shall be set forth.

(5) Any other matters the person filing the certificate determines to include.

(b) A limited partnership is formed at the time of the filing of the certificate of limited partnership in the office of the Secretary of State. There shall be no requirement that any partner have a preexisting relationship with any other partner in order to form a limited partnership.

(c) For all purposes, a copy of the certificate of limited partnership duly certified by the Secretary of State is conclusive evidence of the formation of a limited partnership and prima facie evidence of its existence.

(d) A limited partnership may record in the office of the county recorder of any county in this state a certified copy of the certificate of limited partnership, or any amendment thereto, which has been filed in the office of the Secretary of State. A foreign limited partnership may record in the office of the county recorder of any county in the state a certified copy of the application for registration, together with the certificate of registration, referred to in Section 15692, or any amendment thereto, which has been filed in the office of the Secretary of State. The recording shall create a conclusive presumption in favor of any bona fide purchaser or encumbrancer for value of the partnership real property located in the county in which the certified copy has been recorded, that the persons named as general partners therein are the general partners of the partnership named and that they are all of the general partners of the partnership, and the recording shall also create such other presumptions as provided in Section 15010.5.

(e) The Secretary of State may cancel the filing of certificates of limited partnership if a check or other remittance accepted in payment of the filing fee is not paid upon presentation. Upon receiving written notification that the item presented for payment has not been honored for payment, the Secretary of State shall give a first written notice of the applicability of this section to the agent for service of process or to the person submitting the instrument. Thereafter, if the amount has not been paid by cashier's check or equivalent, the Secretary of State shall give a second written notice of cancellation and the cancellation shall thereupon be effective. The second notice shall be given 20 days or more after the first notice and 90 days or less after the original filing. *(Added by Stats.1983, c. 1223, § 10. Amended by Stats. 1984, c. 103, § 3; Stats.1985, c. 171, § 1; Stats.1987, c. 1364, § 5.)*

§ 15622. Amendment of certificate; liability for misstatement or failure to file amendment

(a) A certificate of limited partnership is amended by filing a certificate of amendment thereto executed and acknowledged by all general partners (unless a lesser number is provided in the certificate of limited partnership) and by each general partner designated in the certificate of amendment as a new partner, unless filed by any other partner pursuant to Section 15625. The certificate of amendment shall be filed in the office of, and on a form prescribed by, the Secretary of State. The certificate of amendment shall set forth all of the following:

(1) The name and the Secretary of State's file number of the limited partnership.

(2) The text of the amendment to the certificate.

(b) The general partners shall cause to be filed, within 30 days after the happening of any of the following events, an amendment to a certificate of limited partnership reflecting the occurrence of any of the following events:

(1) A change in name of the limited partnership.

(2) A change in the street address of the principal executive office.

(3) A change in the address of a general partner or a change in the address of the agent for service of process, unless a corporate agent is designated, or appointment of a new agent for service of process.

(4) The admission of a general partner and that partner's address or the cessation of a general partner to be a general partner.

(5) The discovery by any of the general partners of any false or erroneous material statement contained in the certificate or any amendment thereto.

(c) A certificate of limited partnership may also be amended at any time in any other respect that the general partners determine.

(d) Any general partner, or any limited partner executing a certificate pursuant to Section 15633, shall be liable for any statement materially inconsistent with the partnership agreement or any material misstatement of fact contained in the certificate if the partner knew or should have known that the statement was false when made and an amendment required by subdivision (b) was not filed, and the person suffering the loss relied on the statement or misstatement. A limited partner executing and filing a certificate shall send a copy of the certificate so filed to each general partner at the general partner's last known address. Any general partner shall be liable for any statement materially inconsistent with the partnership agreement or any material misstatement of fact contained in the certificate if the general partner knew or should have known that the statement became false and an amendment required by subdivision (b) was not filed, and the person suffering the loss relied on the statement or misstatement.

(e) Except as otherwise provided in Section 15642, no person has any liability because an amendment to a certificate of limited partnership has not been filed to reflect the occurrence of any event referred to in subdivision (b) if the amendment is filed within the time specified in subdivision (b).

(f) Except as provided in subdivision (d), no limited partner shall incur any liability for any misstatement contained in the certificate or for the failure to file an amendment to a certificate of limited partnership pursuant to subdivision (b). *(Added by Stats. 1983, c. 1223, § 10. Amended by Stats. 1984, c. 103, § 4; Stats. 1984, c. 474, § 1; Stats. 1986, c. 344, § 1; Stats. 1987, c. 1364, § 6.)*

Section 5 of Stats. 1984, c. 474, provided:

"This act shall become operative on July 1, 1984."

Section 6 of Stats. 1984, c. 474, provided, in part:

"The California Revised Limited Partnership Act (Act), as added by Chapter 1223 of the Statutes of 1983, becomes operative on July 1, 1984. The technical amendments to this act made by this bill will directly affect interpretations and application of this new law as it relates to third party dealings with, and distributions of assets of, limited partnerships. In order to preserve the rights of California citizens dealing with and participating in, limited partnerships operating under the act, it is essential that this act take effect immediately."

§ 15623. Certificate of dissolution; certificate of cancellation of certificate of limited partnership; certificate of continuation

(a) (1) The general partners shall cause to be filed in the office of, and on a form prescribed by, the Secretary of State, a certificate of dissolution upon the dissolution of the limited partnership pursuant to Article 8 (commencing with Section 15681), unless the event causing the dissolution is that specified in subdivision (c) of Section 15681, in which case the partners conducting the winding up of the partnership affairs under Section 15683 shall have the obligation to file the certificate of dissolution.

(2) The certificate of dissolution shall set forth all of the following:

(A) The name of the limited partnership and the Secretary of State's file number.

(B) The event causing, and the date of, the dissolution.

(C) Any other information the partners filing the certificate of dissolution determine to include.

(b) (1) The general partners shall cause to be filed in the office of, and on a form prescribed by, the Secretary of State, a certificate of cancellation of certificate of limited partnership upon the completion of the winding up of the affairs of the limited partnership, pursuant to Article 8 (commencing with Section 15681), unless the event causing the dissolution is that specified in subdivision (c) of Section 15681, in which case the partners conducting the winding up of the partnership affairs under Section 15683 shall have the obligation to file the certificate of cancellation of certificate of limited partnership.

(2) The certificate of cancellation of certificate of limited partnership shall set forth all of the following:

(A) The name of the limited partnership and the Secretary of State's file number.

(B) Any other information the partners filing the certificate of cancellation of certificate of limited partnership determine to include.

(c) (1) Notwithstanding the filing of a certificate of dissolution, the general partners may cause to be filed, in the office of, and on a form prescribed by, the Secretary of State, a certificate of continuation, in any of the following circumstances:

(A) The business of the partnership is to be continued pursuant to the written consent of all partners.

(B) The dissolution of the partnership was by written consent of the partners pursuant to subdivision (b) of Section 15681 and each partner who consented to the dissolution has agreed in writing to revoke the partner's consent to the dissolution.

(C) The partnership was not, in fact, dissolved.

The form prescribed by the Secretary of State may be a separate form or may be part of the certificate of amendment.

(2) The certificate of continuation shall set forth all of the following:

(A) The name of the limited partnership and the Secretary of State's file number.

(B) The grounds provided by paragraph (1) that are the basis for filing the certificate of continuation.

(3) Upon the filing of a certificate of continuation, the certificate of dissolution shall be of no effect from the time of the filing of the certificate of dissolution except to the extent provided in subdivision (d) of Section 15622. *(Added by Stats.1983, c. 1223, § 10. Amended by Stats.1987, c. 1364, § 7.)*

§ 15624. Execution of certificates

(a) Each certificate required by this article to be filed in the office of the Secretary of State shall be executed in the following manner:

(1) A certificate referred to in Section 15621 shall be executed by all general partners, unless filed by a limited partner pursuant to Section 15633.

(2) A certificate of amendment shall be executed by all general partners (or a lesser number provided in the certificate of limited partnership) and by each general partner designated in the certificate as a new partner, provided that if the amendment states the cessation of a general partner to be a general partner, it need not be signed by that former general partner if it is signed as otherwise required in this paragraph or in Section 15625.

(3) A certificate of dissolution shall be executed by all general partners (or a lesser number provided in the certificate of limited partnership).

(4) A certificate of cancellation of certificate of limited partnership shall be executed by all general partners (or a lesser number provided in the certificate of limited partnership).

(5) A certificate of continuation shall be executed by all general partners (or a lesser number provided in the certificate of limited partnership).

(6) A certificate of merger shall be executed by all general partners of each domestic constituent limited partnership (or a lesser number as provided in the certificate of limited partnership of the constituent limited partnership) and by one or more general partners of each foreign constituent limited partnership.

(7) A certificate filed by a limited partner pursuant to Section 15633 shall be signed by the limited partner.

(b) Any person may execute any certificate referred to in this section by an attorney-in-fact. *(Added by Stats. 1983, c. 1223, § 10. Amended by Stats. 1984, c. 103, § 5; Stats.1987, c. 1364, § 8; Stats.1990, c. 1088 (S.B. 2575), § 3.)*

§ 15625. Failure or refusal to execute or file required certificates; execution or filing by others; court order; reimbursement of expenses; attorney fees

If a general partner required by this article to execute or file a certificate of limited partnership * * * fails after demand to do so within a reasonable time or refuses to do so, any other partner, or any person appointed by a court of competent jurisdiction, may prepare, execute, and file with the Secretary of State a certificate of limited partnership. If a general partner required by this article to execute any certificate fails to do so within a reasonable time or refuses to do so, or if there is any dispute concerning the filing of a certificate of amendment, a certificate of continuation, a certificate of dissolution, or a certificate of cancellation of limited partnership, or the failure to file any such certificate, any partner may petition the superior court to direct the execution of the certificate. If the court finds that it is proper for the certificate to be executed and that any person so designated has failed or refused to execute the certificate, or if the court determines that any certificate should be filed, it shall order a party to file a certificate on the appropriate form prescribed by the Secretary of State, as ordered by the court. In any action under this section, if the court finds the failure of the general partner to comply with the requirement to file any certificate to have been without justification, the court may award an amount sufficient to reimburse the partners bringing the action for the reasonable expenses incurred by the partners, including attorneys' fees, in connection with the action or proceeding. Any partner, other than a general partner, or person filing any certificate under this chapter, shall state the statutory authority after the signature on the appropriate certificate. *(Added by Stats.1983, c. 1223, § 10.*

Amended by Stats.1986, c. 344, § 2; Stats.1987, c. 1364, § 9.)

§ 15626. Filing of certificate of amendment or cancellation; effect

Upon the filing of a certificate of amendment in the office of the Secretary of State, the certificate of limited partnership is amended as set forth therein, and upon the filing of a certificate of cancellation of certificate of limited partnership pursuant to paragraph (1) of subdivision (b) of Section 15623, the certificate of limited partnership is canceled. *(Added by Stats.1983, c. 1223, § 10.)*

§ 15627. Service of process; production of books and records

(a) In addition to Chapter 4 (commencing with Section 413.10) of Title 5 of Part 2 of the Code of Civil Procedure, process may be served upon limited partnerships and foreign limited partnerships as provided in this section.

(b) Personal service of a copy of any process against the limited partnership or the foreign limited partnership by delivery (1) to any individual designated by it as agent or, if a limited partnership, to any general partner or (2) if the designated agent or, if a limited partnership, general partner is a corporation, to any person named in the latest certificate of the corporate agent filed pursuant to Section 1505 at the office of the corporate agent or to any officer of the general partner, shall constitute valid service on the limited partnership or the foreign limited partnership. No change in the address of the agent for service of process or appointment of a new agent for service of process shall be effective (1) for a limited partnership until an amendment to the certificate of limited partnership is filed pursuant to paragraph (3) of subdivision (b) of Section 15622 or (2) for a foreign limited partnership until an amendment to the application for registration is filed pursuant to Section 15695. In the case of a foreign limited partnership that has appointed the Secretary of State as agent for service of process by reason of subdivision (e) of Section 15697, process shall be delivered by hand to the Secretary of State, or to any person employed in the capacity of assistant or deputy, which shall be one copy of the process for each defendant to be served, together with a copy of the court order authorizing the service and the fee therefor. The order shall include and set forth an address to which such process shall be sent by the Secretary of State.

(c)(1) If an agent for service of process has resigned and has not been replaced or if the agent designated cannot with reasonable diligence be found at the address designated for personal delivery of the process, and it is shown by affidavit to the satisfaction of the court that process against a limited partnership or foreign limited partnership cannot be served with reasonable diligence upon the designated agent or, if a foreign limited partnership, upon any general partner by hand in the manner provided in Section 415.10, subdivision (a) of Section 415.20 or subdivision (a) of Section 415.30, of the Code of Civil Procedure, the court may make an order that the service shall be made upon a domestic limited partnership which has filed a certificate pursuant to Section 15621 or upon a registered foreign limited partnership by delivering by hand to the Secretary of State, or to any person employed in the Secretary of State's office in the capacity of assistant or deputy, one copy of the process for each defendant to be served, together with a copy of the order authorizing the service. Service in this manner shall be deemed complete on the 10th day after delivery of the process to the Secretary of State.

(2) Upon receipt of any such copy of process and the fee therefor, the Secretary of State shall give notice of the service of the process to the limited partnership or foreign limited partnership, at its principal executive office, by forwarding to that office, by registered mail with request for return receipt, the copy of the process.

(3) The Secretary of State shall keep a record of all process served upon the Secretary of State under this chapter and shall record therein the time of service and the Secretary of State's action with reference thereto. A certificate under the Secretary of State's official seal, certifying to the receipt of process, the giving of notice thereof to the limited partnership or foreign limited partnership, and the forwarding of the process pursuant to this section, shall be competent and prima facie evidence of the matters stated therein.

(d)(1) The certificate of a limited partnership and the application for registration of a foreign limited partnership shall designate, as the agent for service of process, an individual residing in this state or a corporation which has complied with Section 1505 and whose capacity to act as an agent has not terminated. If an individual is designated, the statement shall set forth that person's complete business or residence address in this state.

(2) An agent designated for service of process may file with the Secretary of State a signed and acknowledged written statement of resignation as an agent. Thereupon the authority of the agent to act in that capacity shall cease and the Secretary of State forthwith shall give written notice of the filing of the statement of resignation by mail to the limited partnership or foreign limited partnership addressed to its principal executive office.

(3) If an individual who has been designated agent for service of process dies or resigns or no longer resides in the state or if the corporate agent for that purpose, resigns, dissolves, withdraws from the state, forfeits its right to transact intrastate business, has its corporate rights, powers and privileges suspended or ceases to exist, (A) the limited partnership shall promptly file an amend-

ment to the certificate pursuant to paragraph (3) of subdivision (b) of Section 15622 designating a new agent or (B) the foreign limited partnership shall promptly file an amendment to the application for registration pursuant to Section 15695.

(e) In addition to any other discovery rights which may exist, in any case pending in a California court having jurisdiction in which a party seeks records from a partnership formed under this chapter, whether or not the partnership is a party, the court shall have the power to order the production in California of the books and records of the partnership on the terms and conditions that the court deems appropriate. *(Added by Stats.1983, c. 1223, § 10. Amended by Stats.1987, c. 1364, § 10.)*

§ 15628. Filing with secretary of state; date; endorsement; microfilming or reproduction

Upon receipt of any instrument accompanied by the fee prescribed therefor in the Government Code by the Secretary of State for filing pursuant to this chapter, it shall be filed by, and in the office of, the Secretary of State and the date of filing endorsed thereon. The date of filing shall be the date the instrument is received by the Secretary of State unless withheld from filing for a period of time not to exceed 90 days pursuant to a request by the party submitting it for filing or unless in the judgment of the Secretary of State the filing is intended to be coordinated with the filing of some other document which cannot be filed. The Secretary of State shall file a document as of any requested future date not more than 90 days after its receipt, including a Saturday, Sunday or legal holiday, if that document is received in the Secretary of State's office at least one business day prior to the requested date of filing. Upon receipt and after filing of any document under this chapter the Secretary of State may microfilm or reproduce by other techniques any such filings or documents and destroy the original filing or document. The microfilm or other reproduction of any document under the provision of this section shall be admissible in any court of law. *(Added by Stats.1983, c. 1223, § 10.)*

ARTICLE 3. LIMITED PARTNERS

§ 15631. Admission of additional limited partners

(a) After the filing of a certificate referred to in Section 15621, a person may become a limited partner:

(1) In the case of a person acquiring a limited partnership interest directly from the limited partnership, upon the compliance with the partnership agreement or, if the partnership agreement does not so provide, upon the written consent of all of the partners.

(2) In the case of an assignee of a partnership interest, upon compliance with subdivision (a) of Section 15674.

(b) In each case under subdivision (a), the person acquiring the partnership interest shall be added by the general partners as a limited partner to the list required by subdivision (a) of Section 15615. *(Added by Stats. 1983, c. 1223, § 10. Amended by Stats. 1984, c. 103, § 6.)*

§ 15632. Liability

(a) A limited partner is not liable for any obligation of a limited partnership unless named as a general partner in the certificate or, in addition to the exercise of the rights and powers of a limited partner, the limited partner participates in the control of the business. If a limited partner participates in the control of the business without being named as a general partner, that partner may be held liable as a general partner only to persons who transact business with the limited partnership with actual knowledge of that partner's participation in control and with a reasonable belief that the partner is a general partner at the time of the transaction. Nothing in this chapter shall be construed to affect the liability of a limited partner to third parties for the limited partner's participation in tortious conduct.

(b) A limited partner does not participate in the control of the business within the meaning of subdivision (a) solely by doing one or more of the following:

(1) Being a contractor for or an agent or employee of the limited partnership or of a general partner, or an officer, director, or shareholder of a corporate general partner.

(2) Consulting with and advising a general partner with respect to the business of the limited partnership.

(3) Acting as surety for the limited partnership or guaranteeing one or more specific debts of the limited partnership.

(4) Approving or disapproving an amendment to the partnership agreement.

(5) Voting on or calling a meeting of the partners for one or more of the following matters:

(A) The dissolution and winding up of the limited partnership.

(B) The merger of the limited partnership or sale, exchange, lease, mortgage, pledge, or other transfer of all or a substantial part of the assets of the limited partnership other than in the ordinary course of its business.

(C) The incurrence of indebtedness by the limited partnership other than in the ordinary course of its business.

(D) A change in the nature of the business.

(E) Transactions in which the general partners have an actual or potential conflict of interest with the limited partners or the partnership.

(F) The removal of a general partner.

(G) An election to continue the business of the limited partnership other than under the circumstances described in subparagraph (I) or (J).

(H) The admission of a general partner other than under the circumstances described in subparagraph (I) or (J).

(I) The admission of a general partner or an election to continue the business of the limited partnership after a general partner ceases to be a general partner other than by removal where there is no remaining or surviving general partner.

(J) The admission of a general partner or an election to continue the business of the limited partnership after the removal of a general partner where there is no remaining or surviving general partner.

(K) Matters related to the business of the limited partnership not otherwise enumerated in this subdivision, which the partnership agreement states in writing may be subject to the approval or disapproval of limited partners.

(6) Winding up the partnership pursuant to Section 15683.

(7) Executing and filing a certificate pursuant to Section 15625 or a certificate of dissolution pursuant to paragraph (1) of subdivision (a) of Section 15623 or a certificate of cancellation of certificate of limited partnership pursuant to paragraph (1) of subdivision (b) of Section 15623.

(8) Serving on an audit committee or committee performing the functions of an audit committee.

(9) Exercising any right or power permitted to limited partners under this chapter and not specifically enumerated in this subdivision.

(c) The enumeration in subdivision (b) does not mean that any other conduct or the possession or exercise of any other power by a limited partner constitutes participation by the limited partner in the control of the business of the limited partnership. *(Added by Stats. 1983, c. 1223, § 10. Amended by Stats. 1984, c. 103, § 7; Stats.1987, c. 1364, § 11; Stats.1990, c. 1088 (S.B.2575), § 4.)*

§ 15633. Person erroneously believing himself or herself to be limited partner

(a) Except as provided in subdivision (b), if a certificate of limited partnership has not been filed, a person who makes a contribution to the purported limited partnership and in good faith believes that that person has become a limited partner is not liable for the obligations of the purported limited partnership, if, on ascertaining that the certificate has not been filed and after a failure of the general partner or partners to file the certificate within a reasonable time after request, that person promptly files the certificate of limited partnership.

(b) A person who makes a contribution to the purported limited partnership and in good faith believes that that person has become a limited partner is liable only to any third party who transacted business with the purported limited partnership before the certificate is filed and who reasonably believed that the person was a general partner at the time of the transaction. *(Added by Stats.1983, c. 1223, § 10.)*

§ 15634. Rights to information, statements, returns, and reports; enforcement

(a) Upon the request of a limited partner, the general partners shall promptly deliver to the limited partner, at the expense of the partnership, a copy of the information required to be maintained by subdivision (a), (b), or (d) of Section 15615.

(b) Each limited partner has the right upon reasonable request to each of the following:

(1) Inspect and copy during normal business hours any of the partnership records required to be maintained by Section 15615.

(2) Obtain from the general partners, promptly after becoming available, a copy of the limited partnership's federal, state and local income tax or information returns for each year.

(c) In the case of any limited partnership with more than 35 limited partners:

(1) The general partners shall cause an annual report to be sent to each of the partners not later than 120 days after the close of the fiscal year. That report shall contain a balance sheet as of the end of the fiscal year and an income statement and statement of changes in financial position for the fiscal year.

(2) Limited partners representing at least 5 percent of the interests of limited partners may make a written request to a general partner for an income statement of the limited partnership for the initial three-month, six-month, or nine-month period of the current fiscal year ended more than 30 days prior to the date of the request and a balance sheet of the partnership as of the end of

that period. The statement shall be delivered or mailed to the limited partners within 30 days thereafter.

(3) The financial statements referred to in this section shall be accompanied by the report thereon, if any, of the independent accountants engaged by the partnership or, if there is no such report, the certificate of a general partner of the partnership that such financial statements were prepared without audit from the books and records of the limited partnership.

(d) The general partners shall promptly furnish to a limited partner a copy of any amendment to the partnership agreement executed by a general partner pursuant to a power of attorney from the limited partner.

(e) The general partners shall send to each of the partners within 90 days after the end of each taxable year such information as is necessary to complete federal and state income tax or information returns, and, in the case of a limited partnership with 35 or fewer limited partners, a copy of the limited partnership's federal, state, and local income tax or information returns for the year.

(f) In addition to any other remedies, a court of competent jurisdiction may enforce the duty of making and mailing or delivering the information and financial statements required by this section and, for good cause shown, may extend the time therefor.

(g) In any action under this section, if the court finds the failure of the partnership to comply with the requirements of this section to have been without justification, the court may award an amount sufficient to reimburse the partners bringing the action for the reasonable expenses incurred by the partners, including attorneys' fees, in connection with the action or proceeding.

(h) Any waiver by a partner of the rights provided in this section shall be unenforceable.

(i) Any request, inspection, or copying by a limited partner may be made by the limited partner or by the limited partner's agent or attorney. *(Added by Stats. 1983, c. 1223, § 10. Amended by Stats.1987, c. 1364, § 12.)*

§ 15635. Failure to comply with § 15634 or give partners rights under partnership agreement; complaint to attorney general; notice; answer not received or unsatisfactory; remedies; joinder of parties

(a) The Attorney General, upon complaint that a limited partnership is failing to comply with the provisions of Section 15634, or to afford to the partners rights given to them in the partnership agreement, may in the name of the people of the State of California send to the principal executive office, as specified pursuant to paragraph (2) of subdivision (a) of Section 15621, notice of the complaint.

(b) If the answer of the limited partnership is not received within 30 days of the date the notice was transmitted, or if the answer is not satisfactory, and if the enforcement of the rights of the aggrieved persons by private civil action, by class action or otherwise, would be so burdensome or expensive as to be impracticable, the Attorney General may institute, maintain, or intervene in their suits, actions or proceedings in any court of competent jurisdiction or before any administrative agency for relief by way of injunction, the dissolution of entities, the appointment of receivers, or any other temporary, preliminary, provisional, or final remedies as may be appropriate to protect the rights of partners or to restore the position of the partners for the failure to comply with the requirements of Section 15634 or the partnership agreement. In any such action, suit, or proceeding there may be joined as parties all persons and entities responsible for or affected by the activity. *(Added by Stats.1983, c. 1223, § 10.)*

§ 15636. Rights and duties; rules

The rights and duties of the partners in relation to the limited partnership shall be determined, subject to any provision in the partnership agreement to the contrary, by the following rules:

(a) No limited partner shall be required to make any additional contribution to the limited partnership.

(b) Except for distributions made pursuant to Section 15664, no limited partner shall have a priority over any other limited partner, as to return of contributions or as to compensation as a limited partner by way of income.

(c) The obligation of a partner to make a contribution or return money or property distributed in violation of this chapter may be compromised only by the written consent of all the partners.

(d) No limited partner shall have the right to receive property other than money upon any distribution.

(e) A partner may not be compelled to accept a distribution of any asset in kind from a limited partnership in lieu of a proportionate distribution of money being made to other partners.

(f) The limited partners shall have the right to vote on all matters specified in subparagraphs (A) to (G), inclusive, of paragraph (5) of subdivision (b) of Section 15632 and the actions specified therein may be taken by the general partners only with the affirmative vote of a majority in interest of the limited partners.

The limited partners shall also have the right to vote on matters specified in subparagraphs (H) and (I) of paragraph (5) of subdivision (b) of Section 15632. Notwithstanding any other provision of this chapter or any provision of the partnership agreement to the contrary, the actions specified in subparagraph (H) may only be taken by the affirmative vote of a majority in interest of the limited partners or such greater interest as is provided in the partnership agreement, and the actions specified in that subparagraph (I) may only be taken by the affirmative vote of all of the limited partners. *(Added by Stats.1983, c. 1223, § 10. Amended by Stats.1984, c. 103, § 8; Stats.1987, c. 1364, § 13.)*

§ 15637. Meetings; place; call; notice and report; adjournment; approval of actions; validity; quorum; proxies; record date

(a) Meetings of partners may be held at any place within or without this state selected by the person or persons calling the meeting or as may be stated in or fixed in accordance with the partnership agreement. If no other place is stated or so fixed, partners' meetings shall be held at the principal executive office of the partnership.

(b) A meeting of the partners may be called by any of the general partners or by limited partners representing more than 10 percent of the interests of limited partners for any matters on which the limited partners may vote.

(c)(1) Whenever partners are required or permitted to take any action at a meeting, a written notice of the meeting shall be given not less than 10, nor more than 60, days before the date of the meeting to each partner entitled to vote at the meeting. The notice shall state the place, date, and hour of the meeting and the general nature of the business to be transacted, and no other business may be transacted.

(2) Notice of a partners' meeting or any report shall be given either personally or by mail or other means of written communication, addressed to the partner at the address of the partner appearing on the books of the partnership or given by the partner to the partnership for the purpose of notice, or, if no address appears or is given, at the place where the principal executive office of the partnership is located or by publication at least once in a newspaper of general circulation in the county in which the principal executive office is located. The notice or report shall be deemed to have been given at the time when delivered personally or deposited in the mail or sent by other means of written communication. An affidavit of mailing of any notice or report in accordance with the provisions of this article, executed by a general partner, shall be prima facie evidence of the giving of the notice or report.

If any notice or report addressed to the partner at the address of the partner appearing on the books of the partnership is returned to the partnership by the United States Postal Service marked to indicate that the United States Postal Service is unable to deliver the notice or report to the partner at the address, all future notices or reports shall be deemed to have been duly given without further mailing if they are available for the partner at the principal executive office of the partnership for a period of one year from the date of the giving of the notice or report to all other partners.

(3) Upon written request to the general partners by any person entitled to call a meeting of partners, the general partners immediately shall cause notice to be given to the partners entitled to vote that a meeting will be held at a time requested by the person calling the meeting, not less than 10, nor more than 60, days after the receipt of the request. If the notice is not given within 20 days after receipt of the request, the person entitled to call the meeting may give the notice or, upon the application of such person, the superior court of the county in which the principal executive office of the limited partnership is located, or if the principal executive office is not in this state, the county in which the limited partnership's address in this state is located, shall summarily order the giving of the notice, after notice to the partnership giving it an opportunity to be heard. The procedure provided in subdivision (c) of Section 305 of the Corporations Code shall apply to the application. The court may issue any order as may be appropriate, including, without limitation, an order designating the time and place of the meeting, the record date for determination of partners entitled to vote, and the form of notice.

(d) When a partners' meeting is adjourned to another time or place, unless the partnership agreement otherwise requires and, except as provided in this subdivision, notice need not be given of the adjourned meeting if the time and place thereof are announced at the meeting at which the adjournment is taken. At the adjourned meeting the partnership may transact any business which might have been transacted at the original meeting. If the adjournment is for more than 45 days or if after the adjournment a new record date is fixed for the adjourned meeting, a notice of the adjourned meeting shall be given to each partner of record entitled to vote at the meeting.

(e) The transactions of any meeting of partners, however called and noticed, and wherever held, are as valid as though had at a meeting duly held after regular call and notice, if a quorum is present either in person or by proxy, and if, either before or after the meeting, each of the persons entitled to vote, not present in person or by proxy, signs a written waiver of notice or a consent to the holding of the meeting or an approval of the minutes thereof. All waivers, consents, and approvals shall be filed with the partnership records or made a part of the minutes of the meeting. Attendance of a person at a meeting shall constitute a waiver of notice of the meeting, except when the person objects, at the beginning of the meeting to the transaction of any business because the meeting is not lawfully called or convened and except that attendance at a meeting is not a waiver of any right to object to the consideration of matters required by this chapter to be included in the notice but not so included, if the objection is expressly made at the meeting. Neither the business to be transacted at nor the purpose of any meeting of partners need be specified in any written waiver of notice, unless otherwise provided in the partnership agreement, except as provided in subdivision (f).

(f) Any partner approval at a meeting, other than unanimous approval by those entitled to vote, pursuant to paragraph (5) of subdivision (b) of Section 15632 shall be valid only if the general nature of the proposal so approved was stated in the notice of meeting or in any written waiver of notice.

(g)(1) Unless otherwise provided in the partnership agreement, a majority in interest of the limited partners represented in person or by proxy shall constitute a quorum at a meeting of partners.

(2) The partners present at a duly called or held meeting at which a quorum is present may continue to transact business until adjournment notwithstanding the withdrawal of enough partners to leave less than a quorum, if any action taken (other than adjournment) is approved by the requisite percentage of interests of limited partners specified in this chapter or in the partnership agreement.

(3) In the absence of a quorum, any meeting of partners may be adjourned from time to time by the vote of a majority of the interests represented either in person or by proxy, but no other business may be transacted, except as provided in paragraph (2).

(h) Unless otherwise provided in the partnership agreement, any action which may be taken at any meeting of the partners may be taken without a meeting if a consent in writing, setting forth the action so taken, shall be signed by partners having not less than the minimum number of votes that would be necessary to authorize or take that action at a meeting at which all entitled to vote thereon were present and voted. In the event the limited partners are requested to consent on a matter without a meeting, each partner shall be given notice of the matter to be voted upon in the same manner as described in subdivision (c). In the event any general partner, or limited partners representing more than 10 percent of the interests of the limited partners, request a meeting for the purpose of discussing or voting on the matter, the notice of a meeting shall be given in accordance with subdivision (c) and no action shall be taken until the meeting is held. Unless delayed in accordance with the provisions of the preceding sentence, any action taken without a meeting will be effective 15 days after the required minimum number of voters have signed the consent, however, the action will be effective immediately if all general partners and limited partners representing at least 90 percent of the interests of the limited partners have signed the consent.

(i) The use of proxies in connection with this section will be governed in the same manner as in the case of corporations formed under the General Corporation Law.

(j) In order that the limited partnership may determine the partners of record entitled to notices of any meeting or to vote, or entitled to receive any distribution or to exercise any rights in respect of any other lawful action, the general partners, or limited partners representing more than 10 percent of the interests of limited partners, may fix, in advance, a record date, which is not more than 60 or less than 10 days prior to the date of the meeting and not more than 60 days prior to any other action. If no record date is fixed:

(1) The record date for determining partners entitled to notice of or to vote at a meeting of partners shall be at the close of business on the business day next preceding the day on which notice is given or, if notice is waived, at the close of business on the business day next preceding the day on which the meeting is held.

(2) The record date for determining partners entitled to give consent to partnership action in writing without a meeting shall be the day on which the first written consent is given.

(3) The record date for determining partners for any other purpose shall be at the close of business on the day on which the general partners adopt it, or the 60th day prior to the date of the other action, whichever is later.

(4) The determination of partners of record entitled to notice of or to vote at a meeting of partners shall apply to any adjournment of the meeting unless the general partners, or the limited partners who called the meeting, fix a new record date for the adjourned meeting, but the general partners, or the limited partners wno called the meeting, shall fix a new record date if the meeting is adjourned for more than 45 days from the date set for the original meeting. *(Added by Stats.1983, c. 1223, § 10. Amended by Stats. 1984, c. 103, § 9; Stats.1987, c. 1364, § 14.)*

§ 15638. Certificates of interest

The partnership agreement may provide that the interest of a partner or assignee in a limited partnership may be evidenced by a certificate of interest issued by the limited partnership, may provide for the assignment or transfer of any interest represented by such a certificate and the admission of transferees of certificates as additional or substituted limited partners, and may make other provisions with respect to the form of those certificates not inconsistent with this chapter. A certificate of interest may be, but is not required to be, a security as defined in Section 8102 of the Commercial Code. *(Added by Stats.1987, c. 1364, § 15.)*

ARTICLE 4. GENERAL PARTNERS

§ 15641. Admission of additional general partners

Unless otherwise provided in the partnership agreement, after the filing of a certificate referred to in Section 15621, a general partner may be admitted only (a) with the written consent of each general partner and such affirmative vote of limited partners as is required in accordance with the provisions of subdivision (f) of Section 15636 and the last paragraph of Section 15636 or (b) with the written consent of each partner in accordance with the provisions of subdivision (c) of Section 15681. *(Added by Stats.1983, c. 1223, § 10. Amended by Stats. 1984, c. 103, § 10.)*

§ 15642. Cessation as general partner; specified events; acting as general partner until filing of amended certificate

A person ceases to be a general partner of a limited partnership upon the happening of any of the following events:

(a) The general partner withdraws from the limited partnership.

(b) The general partner is removed as a general partner.

(c) Unless otherwise provided in the partnership agreement, an order for relief against the general partner is entered under Chapter 7 of the federal bankruptcy law, or the general partner: (1) makes a general assignment for the benefit of creditors, (2) files a voluntary petition under the federal bankruptcy law, (3) files a petition or answer seeking for that partner any reorganization, arrangement, composition, readjustment, liquidation, dissolution or similar relief under any statute, law, or regulation, (4) files an answer or other pleading admitting or failing to contest the material allegations of a petition filed against that partner in any proceeding of this nature, or (5) seeks, consents to, or acquiesces in the appointment of a trustee, receiver, or liquidator of the general partner or of all or any substantial part of that partner's properties.

(d) Unless otherwise provided in the partnership agreement, 60 days after the commencement of any proceeding against the general partner seeking reorganization, arrangement, composition, readjustment, liquidation, dissolution or similar relief under any statute, law, or regulation, the proceeding has not been dismissed, or if within 60 days after the appointment without that partner's consent or acquiescence of a trustee, receiver, or liquidator of the general partner or of all or any substantial part of that partner's properties, the appointment is not vacated or stayed, or within 60 days after the expiration of any such stay, the appointment is not vacated.

(e) In the case of a general partner who is an individual, either of the following:

(1) The death of that partner.

(2) The entry by a court of competent jurisdiction of an order adjudicating the partner incompetent to manage the general partner's person or estate.

(f) Unless otherwise provided in the partnership agreement, in the case of a general partner who is acting as a general partner by virtue of being a trustee of a trust, the termination of the trust (but not merely the substitution of a new trustee, in which case the new trustee automatically becomes the new general partner).

(g) Unless otherwise provided in the partnership agreement, in the case of a general partner that is a separate partnership, the dissolution of the separate partnership.

(h) In the case of a general partner that is a corporation, the filing of a certificate of dissolution, or its equivalent, for the corporation.

(i) In the case of a general partner that is an estate, the distribution by the fiduciary of the estate's entire interest in the limited partnership.

Notwithstanding the provisions of this section, a person who ceases to be a general partner of a limited partnership, shall be deemed to be acting as a general partner with respect to a third party doing business with the limited partnership, until an amended certificate of limited partnership is filed with the Secretary of State pursuant to Section 15622. *(Added by Stats.1983, c. 1223, § 10. Amended by Stats. 1984, c. 474, § 2.)*

§ 15643. Rights, powers, restrictions, and liabilities

(a) Except as otherwise provided in this chapter or in the partnership agreement, a general partner of a limited partnership has the rights and powers and is subject to the restrictions of a partner in a partnership without limited partners.

(b) Except as provided in this chapter, a general partner of a limited partnership has the liabilities of a partner in a partnership without limited partners to persons other than the partnership and the other partners. Except as provided in this chapter or in the partnership agreement, a general partner of a limited partnership has the liabilities of a partner in a partnership without limited partners to the partnership and to the other partners. *(Added by Stats.1983, c. 1223, § 10.)*

§ 15644. Contributions by general partner; share of profits, losses, and distributions

A general partner of a limited partnership may make contributions to the limited partnership and share in the profits and losses of, and in distributions from, the limited partnership as a general partner. A general partner also may make contributions, and share in the profits and losses and distributions, as a limited partner, if the general partner's interest as a limited partner is separately designated in the partnership agreement. A person who is both a general partner and a limited partner has the rights and powers, and is subject to the restrictions and liabilities, of a general partner and, except as otherwise provided in the partnership agreement, also has the powers, and is subject to the restrictions, of a limited partner to the extent of his participation in the limited partnership as a limited partner. *(Added by Stats.1983, c. 1223, § 10.)*

ARTICLE 5. FINANCE

§ 15651. Form of contribution

The contribution of a partner may be in money, property, or services rendered, or a promissory note or other obligation to contribute money or property or to render services. A limited partner may not make a contribution of an obligation to render future services in consideration of the receipt of a partnership interest. *(Added by Stats.1983, c. 1223, § 10.)*

§ 15652. Claims; contribution or return of distribution; conditional obligation of limited partner; capital contribution payable upon discretionary call; third-party creditors; fraudulent transfers

Notwithstanding the compromise of a claim referred to in subdivision (c) of Section 15636, a person whose claim against a limited partnership arises before the receipt of notice of the compromise may enforce the original obligation of a partner to make a contribution to the partnership or to return a distribution to the partnership if the person had knowledge of the original obligation prior to the time the claim arose and if the compromise occurred after the time the claim arose. Any other person with a claim against a limited partnership may enforce only the existing obligation of a partner to make a contribution to the partnership or to return a distribution to the partnership. A person with a claim against a limited partnership may not enforce a conditional obligation of a limited partner unless the conditions have been satisfied or waived. Conditional obligations include, without limitation, a capital contribution payable upon a discretionary call of the partnership or a general partner prior to the time the call occurs. Nothing in this section shall be construed to affect the rights of third-party creditors of the partnership to seek equitable remedies nor any rights existing under the Uniform Fraudulent Transfer Act (Chapter 1 (commencing with Section 3439) of Title 2 of Part 2 of Division 4 of the Civil Code). *(Added by Stats.1983, c. 1223, § 10. Amended by Stats.1987, c. 1364, § 16; Stats.1990, c. 1088 (S.B.2575), § 5.)*

§ 15653. Allocation of profits and losses

The profits and losses of a limited partnership shall be allocated among the partners in the manner provided in the partnership agreement. If the partnership agreement does not otherwise provide, profits and losses shall be allocated in proportion to the contributions of each partner. *(Added by Stats.1983, c. 1223, § 10. Amended by Stats. 1984, c. 103, § 11.)*

§ 15654. Distributions

Distributions of the money or property of a limited partnership shall be made to the partners in the manner provided in the partnership agreement. If the partnership agreement does not otherwise provide, distributions which are a return of capital shall be made in proportion to the contributions of each partner and distributions which are not a return of capital shall be made in proportion to the allocation of profits. *(Added by Stats.1983, c. 1223, § 10. Amended by Stats. 1984, c. 103, § 12.)*

ARTICLE 6. DISTRIBUTIONS AND WITHDRAWALS

§ 15661. Interim distributions

Except as provided in this article, a partner is entitled to receive distributions from a limited partnership before the withdrawal of that partner from the limited partnership and before the dissolution and winding up thereof, subject to the limitations contained in Section 15666, to the extent and at the times or upon the happening of the events specified in the partnership agreement. *(Added by Stats.1983, c. 1223, § 10.)*

§ 15662. Withdrawal of general partner

(a) A general partner may withdraw from a limited partnership at any time by giving written notice to the other partners, but if the withdrawal violates the partnership agreement the limited partnership may recover from the withdrawing general partner damages for breach of the partnership agreement and, in addition to any other remedies, shall have the right to offset the damages against any amounts otherwise distributable to the general partner. Unless otherwise provided in the partnership agreement, in the case of a partnership for a fixed term, a withdrawal by a general partner prior to the expiration of that term is a breach of the partnership agreement.

(b) Unless otherwise provided in the partnership agreement, and subject to the liability created under subdivision (a), a general partner who ceases to be a general partner under Section 15642 shall:

(1) Retain the same interest in that partner's capital account, profits, losses, and distributions, but that interest shall be that of a limited partner.

(2) Not be personally liable for partnership debts incurred after the person ceases to be a general partner, other than any debts incurred by reason of that person's being deemed to be acting as a general partner, pursuant to Section 15642.

(3) Be entitled to vote as a limited partner on all matters except the admission and compensation of a general partner.

(4) Have the partner's interest in profits, losses, and distributions reduced pro rata with all other partners to provide compensation, or an interest in the partnership, or both, to a new general partner. *(Added by Stats.1983, c. 1223, § 10. Amended by Stats. 1984, c. 474, § 3.)*

§ 15663. Withdrawal of limited partner

A limited partner may withdraw from a limited partnership at the time or upon the happening of events specified in the partnership agreement. If the partnership agreement does not specify the time or the events upon the happening of which a limited partner may withdraw or a definite time for the dissolution and winding up of the limited partnership, a limited partner may withdraw upon not less than six months' prior written notice to each general partner at his address set forth in the certificate. *(Added by Stats.1983, c. 1223, § 10.)*

§ 15664. Distribution upon withdrawal

Upon withdrawal, any withdrawing limited partner is entitled to receive any distribution to which that partner is entitled under the partnership agreement and, if not otherwise provided in the partnership agreement, the limited partner is entitled to receive, within a reasonable time after withdrawal, the fair value of the limited partner's interest in the limited partnership as of the date of withdrawal based upon the limited partner's right to share in distributions from the limited partnership. *(Added by Stats.1983, c. 1223, § 10.)*

§ 15665. Remedies of partner with respect to distribution

Subject to Section 15684, at the time a partner becomes entitled to receive a distribution, that partner has the status of, and is entitled to all remedies available to a creditor of the limited partnership with respect to the distribution. *(Added by Stats.1983, c. 1223, § 10.)*

§ 15666. Obligation to return distribution

(a) A partner is obligated to return a distribution from a limited partnership to the extent that (1) the partner had knowledge of facts indicating the impropriety of the distribution, and (2) immediately after giving effect to the distribution, and notwithstanding the compromise of a claim referred to in subdivision (c) of Section 15636, all liabilities of the limited partnership, other than liabilities to partners on account of their interest in the limited partnership and liabilities as to which recourse of creditors is limited to specified property of the limited partnership, exceed the fair value of the partnership assets, provided that the fair value of any property that is subject to a liability as to which recourse of creditors is so limited shall be included in the partnership assets only to the extent that the fair value of the property exceeds this liability.

(b) A cause of action with respect to an obligation to return a distribution pursuant to subdivision (a) is extinguished unless the action is brought within four years after the distribution is made. *(Added by Stats. 1983, c. 1223, § 10. Amended by Stats. 1984, c. 474, § 4; Stats.1990, c. 1088 (S.B.2575), § 6.)*

ARTICLE 7. ASSIGNMENT OF PARTNERSHIP INTERESTS

Section

§ 15671. Nature of partnership interest

An interest in a limited partnership is personal property and a partner has no interest in specific partnership property. *(Added by Stats.1983, c. 1223, § 10.)*

§ 15672. Assignment of partnership interest

Except as otherwise provided in the partnership agreement, a limited partnership interest is assignable in whole or in part. An assignment of a limited partnership interest does not dissolve a limited partnership or, other than as set forth in this chapter or in the partnership agreement, entitle the assignee to become or to exercise any rights of a partner. An assignment entitles the assignee to receive, to the extent assigned, the distributions and the allocations of income, gain, loss, deduction, credit, or similar item, to which the assignor would be entitled. Except as otherwise provided in the assignment, an assignee of a limited partnership interest in a limited partnership with over 100 limited partners also shall be entitled to all of the rights granted to a limited partner pursuant to Section 15634. A limited partner remains a partner upon assignment of all or part of the limited partner's limited partnership interest, with such rights as the assignee does not acquire or possess, subject to the assignee becoming a limited partner pursuant to subdivision (a) of Section 15674. *(Added by Stats.1983, c. 1223, § 10. Amended by Stats.1987, c. 1364, § 17; Stats.1990, c. 1088 (S.B.2575), § 7.)*

§ 15673. Rights of creditor

On application to a court of competent jurisdiction by any judgment creditor of a partner, the court may charge the limited partnership interest of the partner with payment of the unsatisfied amount of the judgment with interest. To the extent so charged, the judgment creditor has only the rights of an assignee of the limited partnership interest. This chapter does not deprive any partner of the benefit of any exemption laws applicable to the partner's limited partnership interest. *(Added by Stats. 1983, c. 1223, § 10.)*

§ 15674. Assignee becoming limited partner; removal of general partner upon assignment of interest

(a) An assignee of a partnership interest, including an assignee of a general partner, may become a limited partner if and to the extent that (1) the partnership agreement so provides or (2) all partners consent.

(b) An assignee who has become a limited partner has, to the extent assigned, the rights and powers, and is subject to the restrictions and liabilities, of a limited partner under the partnership agreement and this chapter. An assignee who becomes a limited partner also is liable for the obligations of the assignor to make contributions as provided in Article 5 (commencing with Section 15651). However, the assignee is not obligated for liabilities unknown to the assignee at the time the assignee became a limited partner and which could not be ascertained from the partnership agreement.

(c) If an assignee of a limited partnership interest becomes a limited partner, the assignor is not released from the assignor's liability to the limited partnership under subdivision (d) of Section 15622, and Sections 15652 and 15666.

(d) If the general partner assigns all of the general partner's interest in the partnership to a third party, the limited partners may remove that general partner, unless otherwise provided by the partnership agreement. *(Added by Stats.1983, c. 1223, § 10. Amended by Stats.1987, c. 1364, § 18.)*

§ 15675. Deceased or incompetent partner; exercise of rights by legal representative

If a limited partner who is an individual dies or a court of competent jurisdiction adjudges the limited partner to be incompetent to manage the limited partner's person or property, the partner's executor, administrator, guardian, conservator, or other legal representative may exercise all the partner's rights for the purpose of settling the partner's estate or administering the partner's property. *(Added by Stats.1983, c. 1223, § 10.)*

ARTICLE 7.5. MERGER

Section

§ 15678.1. Limited partnerships

Two or more limited partnerships may be merged into one of such limited partnerships pursuant to this article. *(Added by Stats.1990, c. 1088 (S.B.2575), § 8.)*

§ 15678.2. Agreement; approval; parties; contents; limited partnership interests; distributions; conversions; amendment; abandonment; delivery

(a) Each limited partnership which desires to merge shall approve an agreement of merger. The agreement of merger shall be approved by all general partners of each constituent limited partnership and the principal terms of the merger shall be approved by a majority in interest of each class of limited partners of each constituent limited partnership, unless otherwise provided in the partnership agreement of the constituent limited partnership. Other persons, including a parent of a constituent limited partnership, may be parties to the agreement of merger. The agreement of merger shall state:

(1) The terms and conditions of the merger.

(2) The name of the surviving limited partnership, and of each disappearing limited partnership, and the agreement of merger may change the name of the surviving limited partnership, which new name may be the same as or similar to the name of a disappearing domestic or foreign limited partnership, subject to Section 15612.

(3) The manner of converting the partnership interests of each of the constituent limited partnerships into partnership interests or other securities of the surviving limited partnership and, if partnership interests of any of the constituent limited partnerships are not to be converted solely into partnership interests or other securities of the surviving limited partnership, the cash, property, rights, or securities which the holders of the partnership interests are to receive in exchange for the partnership interests, which cash, property, rights, or securities may be in addition to or in lieu of partnership interests or other securities of the surviving limited partnership.

(4) Such other details or provisions as are desired, including, without limitation, a provision for the treatment of fractional partnership interests.

(b) Each limited partnership interest of the same class of any constituent limited partnership (other than the cancellation of limited partnership interests held by a constituent limited partnership or its parent or a limited partnership of which the constituent limited partnership is a parent in another constituent limited partnership) shall, unless all limited partners of the class consent, be treated equally with respect to any distribution of cash, property, rights, or securities. Notwithstanding this subdivision (b), except in a merger of a limited partnership with a limited partnership in which it controls at least 90 percent of the limited partnership interests entitled to vote with respect to the merger, the nonredeemable limited partnership interests of a constituent limited partnership may be converted only into nonredeemable limited partnership interests of the surviving limited partnership or a parent if a constituent limited partnership or its parent owns, directly or indirectly, limited partnership interests of another constituent limited partnership representing more than 50 percent of the limited partnership interests entitled to vote with respect to the merger of the other constituent limited partnership prior to the merger, unless all of the limited partners of the class consent. This subdivision shall apply only to constituent limited partnerships with over 35 limited partners.

(c) Notwithstanding its prior approval, an agreement of merger may be amended prior to the filing of the certificate of merger if the amendment is approved by the general partners of each constituent limited partnership in the same manner as required for approval of the original agreement of merger and, if the amendment changes any of the principal terms of the agreement of merger, the amendment is approved by the limited partners of each constituent limited partnership in the same manner and to the same extent as required for the approval of the original agreement of merger.

(d) The general partners of a limited partnership may, in their discretion, abandon a merger, subject to the contractual rights, if any, of third parties, including other constituent limited partnerships, without further approval by the limited partnership interests, at any time before the merger is effective.

(e) The surviving limited partnership shall keep the agreement of merger at the office referred to in subdivision (a) of Section 15614, and, upon the request of a limited partner of a constituent limited partnership, the general partners of the surviving limited partnership shall promptly deliver to the limited partner, at the expense of the surviving limited partnership, a copy of the agreement of merger. A waiver by a partner of the rights provided in this subdivision shall be unenforceable. *(Added by Stats.1990, c. 1088 (S.B.2575), § 8.)*

§ 15678.3. Approval of terms and conditions of transaction by commissioner; inapplication of subdivision (b) of § 15678.2

Subdivision (b) of Section 15678.2 shall not apply to any transaction if the commissioner has approved the terms and conditions of the transaction and the fairness of such terms and conditions pursuant to Section 25142. *(Added by Stats.1990, c. 1088 (S.B.2575), § 8.)*

§ 15678.4. Certificate of merger; filing; execution; contents; effect

(a) After approval of a merger by the constituent limited partnerships, the constituent limited partnerships shall file a certificate of merger in the office of, and on a form prescribed by, the Secretary of State. The certificate of merger shall be executed and acknowledged by each domestic constituent limited partnership by all general partners (unless a lesser number is provided in the certificate of limited partnership of the domestic constituent limited partnership) and by each foreign constituent limited partnership by one or more general partners. The certificate of merger shall set forth all of the following:

(1) The names and the Secretary of State's file numbers of each of the constituent limited partnerships, if any, separately identifying the disappearing limited partnerships and the surviving limited partnership.

(2) If a vote of the limited partners was required under Section 15678.2, a statement setting forth the total number of outstanding interests of each class entitled to vote on the merger and that the principal terms of the agreement of merger were approved by a vote of the number of interests of each class which equaled or exceeded the vote required, specifying each class entitled to vote and the percentage vote required of each class.

(3) Any change required to the information set forth in the certificate of limited partnership of the surviving

limited partnership resulting from the merger, including any change in the name of the surviving limited partnership resulting from the merger. The filing of a certificate of merger setting forth any such changes to the certificate of limited partnership of the surviving limited partnership shall have the effect of the filing of a certificate of amendment by the surviving limited partnership, and the surviving limited partnership need not file a certificate of amendment under Section 15622 to reflect such changes.

(4) The future effective date or time (which shall be a date or time certain not more than 90 days subsequent to the date of filing) of the merger, if the merger is not to be effective upon the filing of the certificate of merger with the office of the Secretary of State.

(b) A certificate of merger shall have the effect of the filing of a certificate of cancellation for each disappearing limited partnership, and no disappearing limited partnership need file a certificate of dissolution or a certificate of cancellation under Section 15623 as a result of the merger. *(Added by Stats.1990, c. 1088 (S.B.2575), § 8.)*

§ 15678.5. Effective date of merger; conclusive evidence of merger

(a) Unless a future effective date or time is provided in a certificate of merger, in which event the merger shall be effective at such future effective date or time, a merger shall be effective upon the filing of the certificate of merger in the office of the Secretary of State.

(b) For all purposes, a copy of the certificate of merger duly certified by the Secretary of State is conclusive evidence of the merger of the constituent limited partnerships into the surviving limited partnership. *(Added by Stats.1990, c. 1088 (S.B.2575), § 8.)*

§ 15678.6. Surviving limited partnership; succession to rights and property, and debt and liabilities of disappearing entity; liens on property; pending actions

(a) Upon a merger of limited partnerships pursuant to this chapter, the separate existence of the disappearing limited partnerships ceases and the surviving limited partnership shall succeed, without other transfer, act or deed, to all the rights and property, whether real, personal, or mixed, of each of the disappearing limited partnerships and shall be subject to all the debts and liabilities of each in the same manner as if the surviving limited partnership had itself incurred them.

(b) All rights of creditors and all liens upon the property of each of the constituent limited partnerships shall be preserved unimpaired and may be enforced against the surviving limited partnership to the same extent as if the debt, liability or duty which gave rise to such lien had been incurred or contracted by it, provided that such liens upon the property of a disappearing limited partnership shall be limited to the property affected thereby immediately prior to the time the merger is effective.

(c) Any action or proceeding pending by or against any disappearing limited partnership may be prosecuted to judgment, which shall bind the surviving limited partnership, or the surviving limited partnership may be proceeded against or be substituted in the disappearing limited partnership's place. *(Added by Stats.1990, c. 1088 (S.B.2575), § 8.)*

§ 15678.7. Foreign limited partnerships; merger with domestic entities; conditions; surviving partnership; law governing; effective date

(a) The merger of any number of domestic limited partnerships with any number of foreign limited partnerships may be effected if the foreign limited partnerships are authorized by the laws under which they are organized to effect such a merger.

(b) If the surviving limited partnership is a domestic limited partnership, the merger proceedings with respect to that limited partnership and any domestic disappearing limited partnership shall conform to the provisions of this chapter governing the merger of domestic limited partnerships, but if the surviving limited partnership is a foreign limited partnership, then, subject to the requirements of subdivision (d) and Article 7.6 (commencing with Section 15679.1), the merger proceedings may be in accordance with the laws of the state or place of organization of the surviving limited partnership.

(c) If the surviving limited partnership is a domestic limited partnership, a certificate of merger shall be filed as provided in Section 15678.4, and thereupon, subject to subdivision (a) of Section 15678.5, the merger shall be effective as to each domestic constituent limited partnership.

(d) If the surviving limited partnership is a foreign limited partnership, the merger shall become effective in accordance with the law of the jurisdiction in which the surviving limited partnership is organized, but shall be effective as to any domestic disappearing limited partnership as of the time of effectiveness in such foreign jurisdiction upon the filing in this state of a certificate of merger as provided in Section 15678.4.

(e) If a merger described in subdivision (c) or (d) also includes a foreign disappearing limited partnership previously registered for the transaction of intrastate business in this state pursuant to Section 15692, the filing of the certificate of merger automatically has the effect of a cancellation of registration for that foreign limited partnership pursuant to Section 15696 without the necessity of the filing of a certificate of cancellation.

(f) The provisions of subdivision (b) of Section 15678.2 and Article 7.6 (commencing with Section 15679.1) apply to the rights of the limited partners of any of the constituent limited partnerships which are domestic limited partnerships and of any domestic limited partnership which is a parent of any foreign constituent limited partnership. *(Added by Stats.1990, c. 1088 (S.B.2575), § 8.)*

§ 15678.8. Real property rights; record of ownership; filing requirements

Whenever a domestic or foreign limited partnership having any real property in this state merges with another limited partnership pursuant to the laws of this state or of the state or place in which any constituent limited partnership was organized, and the laws of the state or place of organization (including this state) of any disappearing limited partnership provide substantially that the making and filing of the agreement of merger or certificate of merger vests in the surviving limited partnership all the real property of any disappearing limited partnership, the filing for record in the office of the county recorder of any county in this state in which any of the real property of such disappearing limited partnership is located of either (a) a certificate of merger certified by the Secretary of State, or (b) a copy of the agreement of merger or certificate of merger, certified by the Secretary of State or an authorized public official of the state or place pursuant to the laws of which the merger is effected, shall evidence record ownership in the surviving limited partnership of all interest of such disappearing limited partnership in and to the real property located in that county. *(Added by Stats.1990, c. 1088 (S.B.2575), § 8.)*

§ 15678.9. Recording of certificate; conclusive presumption of merger

Recording of the certificate of merger in accordance with Section 15678.8 shall create, in favor of bona fide purchasers or encumbrancers for value, a conclusive presumption that the merger was validly completed. *(Added by Stats.1990, c. 1088 (S.B.2575), § 8.)*

ARTICLE 7.6. DISSENTING LIMITED PARTNERS' RIGHTS

§ 15679.1. Reorganization; control

(a) For purposes of this article, "reorganization" refers to either of the following:

(1) A merger pursuant to Article 7.5 (commencing with Section 15678.1).

(2) The acquisition by one limited partnership in exchange in whole or part for its partnership interests (or the partnership interests or equity securities of a partnership or other entity that is in control of the acquiring limited partnership) of partnership interests of another limited partnership if, immediately after the acquisition, the acquiring limited partnership has control of the other limited partnership.

(3) The acquisition by one limited partnership in exchange in whole or in part for its partnership interests (or the partnership interests or equity securities of a partnership or other entity which is in control of the acquiring limited partnership) or for its debts securities (or debt securities of a limited partnership or other entity which is in control of the acquiring limited partnership) which are not adequately secured and which have a maturity date in excess of five years after the consummation of the acquisition, or both, of all or substantially all of the assets of another limited partnership.

(b) For purposes of this article, "control" means the possession, direct or indirect, of the power to direct or cause the direction of the management and policies of a limited partnership. *(Added by Stats.1990, c. 1088 (S.B.2575), § 9.)*

§ 15679.2. Purchase of dissenting partnership interests; fair market value; dissenting interest; dissenting limited partner

(a) If the approval of outstanding limited partnership interests is required for a limited partnership to participate in a reorganization, pursuant to the limited partnership agreement of the partnership, or otherwise, then each limited partner of the limited partnership holding such interests may, by complying with this article, require the limited partnership to purchase for cash, at its fair market value, the interest owned by the limited partner in the limited partnership, if such interest is a dissenting interest as defined in subdivision (b). The fair market value shall be determined as of the day before the first announcement of the terms of the proposed reorganization, excluding any appreciation or depreciation in consequence of the proposed reorganization.

(b) As used in this article, "dissenting interest" means the interest of a limited partner that satisfies all of the following conditions:

(1) Either:

(A) The interest was not, immediately prior to the reorganization, either (i) listed on any national securities exchange certified by the Commissioner of Corporations under subdivision (*o*) of Section 25100, or (ii) listed on the list of OTC margin stocks issued by the Board of Governors of the Federal Reserve System, provided that in either such instance the limited partnership whose outstanding interests are so listed provides, in its notice to limited partners requesting their approval of the proposed reorganization, a summary of the provisions of this section and Sections 15679.3, 15679.4, 15679.5, and 15679.6.

(B) Demands for payment are filed with respect to 5 percent or more of the outstanding interests of any class of interests described in clause (i) or (ii) of subparagraph (A).

(2) Which was outstanding on the date for the determination of limited partners entitled to vote on the reorganization.

(3) (i) Which was not voted in favor of the reorganization, or (ii) if such interest is described in clause (i) or (ii) of subparagraph (A) of paragraph (1), was voted against the reorganization; provided, however, that clause (i) rather than clause (ii) of this paragraph applies in any case where the approval for the proposed reorganization is sought by written consent rather than at a meeting.

(4) Which the limited partner has demanded that the limited partnership purchase at its fair market value in accordance with Section 15679.3.

(5) Which the limited partner submits for endorsement, if applicable, in accordance with Section 15679.4.

(c) As used in this article, "dissenting limited partner" means the recordholder of a dissenting interest, and includes an assignee of record of such an interest. *(Added by Stats.1990, c. 1088 (S.B.2575), § 9.)*

§ 15679.3. Notice of approval of reorganization by outstanding interests; statement of price; written demand for purchase; contents of demand

(a) If limited partners have a right under Section 15679.2, subject to compliance with paragraphs (4) and (5) of subdivision (b) thereof, to require the limited partnership to purchase their limited partnership interests for cash, such limited partnership shall mail to each such limited partner a notice of the approval of the reorganization by the requisite vote or consent of the limited partners, within 10 days after the date of such approval, accompanied by a copy of this section and Sections 15679.2, 15679.4, 15679.5, and 15679.6, a statement of the price determined by the limited partnership to represent the fair market value of its outstanding interests, and a brief description of the procedure to be followed if the limited partner desires to exercise the limited partner's rights under such sections. The statement of price constitutes an offer by the limited partnership to purchase at the price stated any dissenting interests as defined in subdivision (b) of Section 15679.2, unless they lose their status as dissenting interests under Section 15679.11.

(b) Any limited partner who has a right to require the limited partnership to purchase the limited partner's interest for cash under Section 15679.2, subject to compliance with paragraphs (4) and (5) of subdivision (b) thereof, and who desires the limited partnership to purchase such interest, shall make written demand upon the limited partnership for the purchase of such interest and the payment to the limited partner in cash of its fair market value. The demand is not effective for any purpose unless it is received by the limited partnership or any transfer agent thereof (1) in the case of interests described in clause (i) or (ii) of subparagraph (A) of paragraph (1) of subdivision (b) of Section 15679.2, not later than the date of the limited partners' meeting to vote upon the reorganization, or (2) in any other case, within 30 days after the date on which notice of the approval of the reorganization by the requisite vote or consent of the limited partners is mailed by the limited partnership to the limited partners.

(c) The demand shall state the number or amount of the limited partner's interest in the limited partnership and shall contain a statement of what such limited partner claims to be the fair market value of that interest on the day before the announcement of the proposed reorganization. The statement of fair market value constitutes an offer by the limited partner to sell the interest at such price. *(Added by Stats.1990, c. 1088 (S.B.2575), § 9.)*

§ 15679.4. Notice of the number or amount of interest demanded to be purchased; conditions; transfers of interests; new certificates or statements

Within 30 days after the date on which notice of the approval of the outstanding interests of the limited partnership is mailed to the limited partner pursuant to subdivision (a) of Section 15679.3, the limited partner shall submit to the limited partnership at its principal office or at the office of any transfer agent thereof, (a) if the interest is evidenced by a certificate, the limited partner's certificate representing the interest which the limited partner demands that the limited partnership purchase, to be stamped or endorsed with a statement that the interest is a dissenting interest or to be exchanged for certificates of appropriate denominations so stamped or endorsed, or (b) if the interest is not evidenced by a certificate, written notice of the number or amount of interest which the limited partner demands that the limited partnership purchase. Upon subsequent transfers of the dissenting interest on the books of the limited partnership, the new certificates or other written statement issued therefor shall bear a like statement, together with the name of the original holder of the dissenting interest. *(Added by Stats.1990, c. 1088 (S.B. 2575), § 9.)*

§ 15679.5. Agreements fixing fair market value of dissenting interest; payment

(a) If the limited partnership and the dissenting limited partner agree that such limited partner's interest is a dissenting interest and agree upon the price to be paid for the dissenting interest, the dissenting limited partner is entitled to the agreed price with interest thereon at the legal rate on judgments from the date of consummation of the reorganization. All agreements fixing the fair market value of any dissenting limited partner's interest as between the limited partnership and such limited partner shall be in writing and filed in the records of the limited partnership.

(b) Subject to the provisions of Section 15679.8, payment of the fair market value for a dissenting interest shall be made within 30 days after the amount thereof has been agreed or within 30 days after any statutory or contractual conditions to the reorganization are satisfied, whichever is later, and in the case of dissenting interests evidenced by certificates of interest, subject to surrender of such certificates of interest, unless provided otherwise by agreement. *(Added by Stats.1990, c. 1088 (S.B.2575), § 9.)*

§ 15679.6. Denial of status as dissenting interest; failure to agree upon fair market value; complaint; filing; joinder of parties; trial of action

(a) If the limited partnership denies that a limited partnership interest is a dissenting interest, or the limited partnership and a dissenting limited partner fail to agree upon the fair market value of a dissenting interest, then such limited partner or any interested limited partnership, within six months after the date on which notice of the approval of the reorganization by the requisite vote or consent of the limited partners was mailed to the limited partner, but not thereafter, may file a complaint in the superior court of the proper county praying the court to determine whether the interest is a dissenting interest, or the fair market value of the dissenting interest, or both, or may intervene in any action pending on such a complaint.

(b) Two or more dissenting limited partners may join as plaintiffs or be joined as defendants in any such action and two or more such actions may be consolidated.

(c) On the trial of the action, the court shall determine the issues. If the status of the limited partnership interest as a dissenting interest is in issue, the court shall first determine that issue. If the fair market value of the dissenting interest is in issue, the court shall determine, or shall appoint one or more impartial appraisers to determine, the fair market value of the dissenting interest. *(Added by Stats.1990, c. 1088 (S.B.2575), § 9.)*

§ 15679.7. Appraisals; appointment of appraiser; report; submission to court; confirmation; failure to file report; determination by court; judgment; appeal; costs

(a) If the court appoints an appraiser or appraisers, they shall proceed forthwith to determine the fair market value per interest of the outstanding limited partnership interests of the limited partnership, by class if necessary. Within the time fixed by the court, the appraisers, or a majority of them, shall make and file a report in the office of the clerk of the court. Thereupon, on the motion of any party, the report shall be submitted to the court and considered on such additional evidence as the court considers relevant. If the court finds the report reasonable, the court may confirm it.

(b) If a majority of the appraisers appointed fails to make and file a report within 30 days from the date of their appointment, or within such further time as may be allowed by the court, or the report is not confirmed by the court, the court shall determine the fair market value per interest of the outstanding limited partnership interests of the limited partnership, by class if necessary.

(c) Subject to Section 15679.8, judgment shall be rendered against the limited partnership for payment of an amount equal to the fair market value, as determined by the court, of each dissenting interest which any dissenting limited partner who is a party, or has intervened, is entitled to require the limited partnership to purchase, with interest thereon at the legal rate on judgments from the date of consummation of the reorganization.

(d) Any such judgment shall be payable forthwith, provided, however, that with respect to limited partnership interests evidenced by transferable certificates of interest, only upon the endorsement and delivery to the limited partnership of those certificates representing the interests described in the judgment. Any party may appeal from the judgment.

(e) The costs of the action, including reasonable compensation for the appraisers, to be fixed by the court, shall be assessed or apportioned as the court considers equitable, but, if the appraisal exceeds the price offered by the limited partnership, the limited partnership shall pay the costs (including, in the discretion of the court, if the value awarded by the court for the dissenting interest is more than 125 percent of the price offered by the limited partnership under subdivision (a) of Section 15679.3, attorneys' fees and fees of expert witnesses). *(Added by Stats.1990, c. 1088 (S.B.2575), § 9.)*

§ 15679.8. Extent payment to dissenting partners would require return of portion thereof by reason of Uniform Fraudulent Transfer Act; dissenting partners as creditors

To the extent that the payment to dissenting limited partners of the fair market value of their dissenting interests would require the dissenting limited partners to return such payment or a portion thereof by reason of Section 15666 or the Uniform Fraudulent Transfer Act (Chapter 1 (commencing with Section 3439) of Title 2 of Part 2 of Division 4 of the Civil Code), then that payment or portion thereof shall not be made and the dissenting limited partners shall become creditors of the limited partnership for the amount not paid, together with interest thereon at the legal rate on judgments until the date of payment, but subordinate to all other creditors in any proceeding relating to the winding up and dissolution of the limited partnership, such debt to be payable when permissible. *(Added by Stats.1990, c. 1088 (S.B.2575), § 9.)*

§ 15679.9. Cash distributions to dissenting partner after reorganization, but prior to payments by limited partner; credit

Any cash distributions made by a limited partnership to a dissenting limited partner after the date of consummation of the reorganization, but prior to any payment by the limited partnership for such dissenting limited partner's interest, shall be credited against the total amount to be paid by the limited partnership for such dissenting interest. *(Added by Stats.1990, c. 1088 (S.B. 2575), § 9.)*

§ 15679.10. Dissenting limited partners; rights and privileges; withdrawal of demand for payment

Except as expressly limited by this article, dissenting limited partners shall continue to have all the rights and privileges incident to their interests, until payment by the limited partnership for their dissenting interests. A dissenting limited partner may not withdraw a demand for payment unless the limited partnership consents thereto. *(Added by Stats.1990, c. 1088 (S.B.2575), § 9.)*

§ 15679.11. Dissenting interests; loss of status

A dissenting interest loses its status as a dissenting interest and the holder thereof ceases to be a dissenting limited partner and ceases to be entitled to require the limited partnership to purchase the interest upon the happening of any of the following:

(a) The limited partnership abandons the reorganization. Upon abandonment of the reorganization, the limited partnership shall pay, on demand, to any dissenting limited partner who has initiated proceeding in good faith under this article, all reasonable expenses incurred in such proceedings and reasonable attorneys' fees.

(b) The interest is transferred prior to its submission for endorsement in accordance with Section 15679.4.

(c) The dissenting limited partner and the limited partnership do not agree upon the status of the interest as a dissenting interest or upon the purchase price of the dissenting interest, and neither files a complaint nor intervenes in a pending action, as provided in Section 15679.6, within six months after the date upon which notice of the approval of the reorganization by the requisite vote or consent of limited partners was mailed to the limited partner.

(d) The dissenting limited partner, with the consent of the limited partnership, withdraws such limited partner's demand for purchase of the dissenting interest. *(Added by Stats.1990, c. 1088 (S.B.2575), § 9.)*

§ 15679.12. Litigation; suspension of proceedings pursuant to §§ 15679.6 and 15679.7

If litigation is instituted to test the sufficient or regularity of the vote or consent of the limited partners in authorizing a reorganization, any proceedings under Sections 15679.6 and 15679.7 shall be suspended until final determination of that litigation. *(Added by Stats. 1990, c. 1088 (S.B.2575), § 9.)*

§ 15679.13. Application of article

(a) This article applies to the following:

(1) A domestic limited partnership formed on or after January 1, 1991.

(2) A foreign limited partnership if (A) the foreign limited partnership was formed on or after January 1, 1991, or filed an application to qualify to do business on or after January 1, 1991, and (B) limited partners holding more than 50 percent of the voting power held by all limited partners of the foreign limited partnership reside in this state.

(3) A limited partnership if the partnership agreement so provides or if all general partners and a majority in interest of the limited partners determine that this article shall apply.

(b) This article does not apply to limited partnership interests governed by limited partnership agreements whose terms and provisions specifically set forth the amount to be paid in respect of such interests in the event of a reorganization of the limited partnership, or to limited partnerships with 35 or fewer limited partners, unless the partnership agreement provides that this article shall apply or unless all general partners and a majority in interest of the limited partners agree that this article shall apply. *(Added by Stats.1990, c. 1088 (S.B.2575), § 9.)*

§ 15679.14. Right to attach validity of reorganization; action to set aside or rescind

(a) No limited partner of a limited partnership who has a right under this article to demand payment of cash for the interest owned by such limited partner in a limited partnership shall have any right at law or in equity to attack the validity of the reorganization, or to have the reorganization set aside or rescinded, except in an action to test whether the vote or consent of limited partners required to authorize or approve the reorganization has been obtained in accordance with the procedures established therefor by the partnership agreement of the limited partnership.

(b) If one of the parties to a reorganization is directly or indirectly controlled by, or under common control with, another party to the reorganization, subdivision (a) shall not apply to any limited partner of such controlled party who has not demanded payment of cash for such limited partner's interest pursuant to this article; but if such limited partner institutes any action to attack the validity of the reorganization or to have the reorganization set aside or rescinded, the limited partner shall not thereafter have any right to demand payment of cash for such limited partner's interest pursuant to this article.

(c) If one of the parties to a reorganization is directly or indirectly controlled by, or under common control with, another party to the reorganization, then, in any action to attack the validity of the reorganization or to have the reorganization set aside or rescinded, (1) a party to a reorganization which controls another party to a reorganization shall have the burden of proving that the transaction is just and reasonable as to the limited partners of the controlled party, and (2) a person who controls two or more parties to a reorganization shall have the burden of proving that the transaction is just and reasonable as to the limited partners of any party so controlled.

(d) Subdivisions (b) and (c) shall not apply if a majority in interest of the limited partners other than limited partners who are directly or indirectly controlled by, or under common control with, another party to the reorganization approve or consent to the reorganization.

(e) This section shall not prevent a partner of a limited partnership that is a party to a reorganization from bringing an action against a general partner of the limited partnership, the limited partnership, or any person controlling a general partner at law or in equity as to any matters (including, without limitation, an action for breach of fiduciary obligation or fraud) other than to attack the validity of the reorganization or to have the reorganization set aside or rescinded. *(Added by Stats. 1990, c. 1088 (S.B.2575), § 9.)*

ARTICLE 8. DISSOLUTION

Section

§ 15681. Nonjudicial dissolution

A limited partnership is dissolved and its affairs shall be wound up upon the happening of the first to occur of the following:

(a) At the time or upon the happening of events specified in the partnership agreement.

(b) Except as otherwise provided in the partnership agreement, written consent of all general partners and a majority in interest of the limited partners.

(c) A general partner ceases to be a general partner under Section 15642 (other than by removal), unless (1) at the time there is at least one other general partner and the partnership agreement permits the business of the limited partnership to be continued by the remaining general partner or partners, if any, and such partner or partners do so, or (2) all partners agree in writing to continue the business of the limited partnership and to admit one or more general partners.

(d) Entry of a decree of judicial dissolution under Section 15682. *(Added by Stats.1983, c. 1223, § 10.)*

§ 15682. Judicial dissolution

Pursuant to an action filed by a partner, a court of competent jurisdiction may decree the dissolution of a limited partnership whenever any of the following occurs:

(a) It is not reasonably practicable to carry on the business in conformity with the partnership agreement.

(b) The general partners have been guilty of or have knowingly countenanced persistent and pervasive fraud or abuse of authority or persistent unfairness toward any partner, or the property of the limited partnership is being misapplied or wasted by the general partners.

(c) Dissolution is reasonably necessary for the protection of the rights or interest of the complaining partners. *(Added by Stats.1983, c. 1223, § 10.)*

§ 15683. Winding up

In the event of a dissolution of a limited partnership:

(a) Except as provided in the partnership agreement, the general partners who have not wrongfully dissolved a limited partnership or, if none, the limited partners, may wind up the limited partnership's affairs, unless the dissolution occurs pursuant to subdivision (d) of Section 15681, in which event the winding up shall be conducted in accordance with the decree of dissolution.

(b) Upon the petition of limited partners representing 5 percent or more of the interests of limited partners, or three or more creditors, a court of competent jurisdiction may enter a decree ordering the winding up of the limited partnership if that appears necessary for the protection of any parties in interest. The decree shall designate the partners who are to wind up the limited partnership's affairs.

(c) Unless otherwise provided in the partnership agreement, the limited partners winding up the affairs of the partnership pursuant to this section, shall be entitled to reasonable compensation. *(Added by Stats.1983, c. 1223, § 10.)*

§ 15684. Distribution of assets

Upon the winding up of a limited partnership, the assets shall be distributed in the following order:

(a) To creditors, including partners who are creditors to the extent permitted by law, in satisfaction of liabilities of the limited partnership other than liabilities for distributions to partners under Section 15661, 15664 or 15665.

(b) Except as provided in the partnership agreement, to partners and former partners in satisfaction of liabilities for distributions under Sections 15661, 15664, and 15665.

(c) To partners in accordance with their rights under the partnership agreement and Section 15636. *(Added by Stats.1983, c. 1223, § 10.)*

§ 15685. Binding partnership after dissolution

After dissolution, a general partner can bind the partnership as follows:

(a) By any act appropriate for winding up partnership affairs or completing transactions unfinished at dissolution.

(b) By any transaction which would bind the partnership if dissolution had not taken place, if the other party to the transaction:

(1) Had extended credit to the partnership prior to dissolution and had no actual knowledge or notice of the dissolution.

(2) Though not so extending credit, had nevertheless known of the partnership prior to dissolution, and, had no actual knowledge or notice of dissolution, and a certificate of dissolution has not been filed as provided in subdivision (a) of Section 15623. *(Added by Stats.1983, c. 1223, § 10. Amended by Stats. 1984, c. 103, § 13.)*

ARTICLE 9. FOREIGN LIMITED PARTNERSHIPS

Section

§ 15691. Law governing

Subject to Section 15694, (a) the laws of the state or country under which a foreign limited partnership is organized govern its organization and internal affairs and the liability of its limited partners, and (b) a foreign limited partnership may not be denied registration by reason of any difference between those laws and the laws of this state. *(Added by Stats.1983, c. 1223, § 10.)*

§ 15692. Registration

Before transacting intrastate business in this state, a foreign limited partnership shall register with the Secretary of State. In order to register, a foreign limited partnership shall submit to the Secretary of State an application for registration as a foreign limited partnership, signed and acknowledged by a general partner on a form prescribed by the Secretary of State and setting forth all of the following:

(a) The name of the foreign limited partnership and, if different, the name under which it proposes to register and transact business in this state.

(b) The state or country and date of its formation and a statement that the foreign limited partnership is authorized to exercise its powers and privileges in such state or country of formation.

(c) The name and address of an agent for service of process on the foreign limited partnership meeting the qualifications specified in paragraph (1) of subdivision (d) of Section 15627.

(d) A statement that the Secretary of State is appointed the agent of the foreign limited partnership for service of process if the agent has resigned and has not been replaced or if the agent cannot be found or served with the exercise of reasonable diligence.

(e) The address of the principal executive office of the foreign limited partnership and of its principal office in this state, if any.

(f) The names and business or residence addresses of the general partners.

(g) The Secretary of State may cancel the application and certificate of registration of a foreign limited partnership if a check or other remittance accepted in payment of the filing fee is not paid upon presentation. Upon receiving written notification that the item presented for payment has not been honored for payment, the Secretary of State shall give a first written notice of the applicability of this section to the agent for service of process or to the person submitting the instrument. Thereafter, if the amount has not been paid by cashier's check or equivalent, the Secretary of State shall give a second written notice of cancellation and the cancellation shall thereupon be effective. The second notice shall be given 20 days or more after the first notice and 90 days or less after the original filing. *(Added by Stats.1983, c. 1223, § 10. Amended by Stats.1985, c. 171, § 2.)*

§ 15693. Issuance of certification of registration

If the Secretary of State finds that an application for registration conforms to law and all requisite fees have been paid, the Secretary of State shall issue a certificate of registration to transact intrastate business in this state. However, no certificate of registration shall be issued for a foreign limited partnership to transact intrastate business in this state under a name which falls within the prohibitions of subdivision (c) of Section 15612. *(Added by Stats.1983, c. 1223, § 10.)*

§ 15694. Information and rights provided in § 15634

If the limited partners of a foreign limited partnership residing in this state represent 25 percent or more of the interests of limited partners of that partnership, those limited partners shall be entitled to all information and rights provided in Section 15634. *(Added by Stats.1983, c. 1223, § 10.)*

§ 15695. Amendment to application for registration

If any statement in the application for registration of a foreign limited partnership was false when made or any statements made have become erroneous, the foreign limited partnership shall promptly file in the office of the Secretary of State an amendment to the application for registration, signed and acknowledged by a general partner, amending the statement. *(Added by Stats.1983, c. 1223, § 10.)*

§ 15696. Cancellation of registration

A foreign limited partnership may cancel its registration by filing with the Secretary of State a certificate of cancellation signed and acknowledged by a general partner. A cancellation does not terminate the authority of the Secretary of State to accept service of process on the foreign limited partnership with respect to causes of action arising out of the transaction of business in this state. *(Added by Stats.1983, c. 1223, § 10.)*

§ 15697. Transaction of business without registration; penalty

(a) A foreign limited partnership transacting intrastate business in this state may not maintain any action, suit, or proceeding in any court of this state until it has registered in this state.

(b) Any foreign limited partnership which transacts intrastate business in this state without registration is subject to a penalty of twenty dollars ($20) for each day that such unauthorized intrastate business is transacted, up to a maximum of ten thousand dollars ($10,000). An action to recover such penalty may be brought, and any recovery shall be paid, as provided in Section 2258.

(c) The failure of a foreign limited partnership to register in this state does not impair the validity of any contract or act of the foreign limited partnership or prevent the foreign limited partnership from defending any action, suit, or proceeding in any court of this state.

(d) A limited partner of a foreign limited partnership is not liable as a general partner of the foreign limited partnership solely by reason of its having transacted intrastate business in this state without registration.

(e) A foreign limited partnership, transacting intrastate business in this state without registration, appoints the Secretary of State as its agent for service of process with respect to causes of action arising out of the transaction of business in this state. *(Added by Stats. 1983, c. 1223, § 10.)*

§ 15698. Action by attorney general to restrain violations

The Attorney General may bring an action to restrain a foreign limited partnership from transacting intrastate business in this state in violation of this article. *(Added by Stats.1983, c. 1223, § 10.)*

§ 15699. Foreign lending institutions; registration with secretary of state; conditions

No foreign lending institution organized as a foreign limited partnership and the activities of which in this state are limited as provided in subdivision (d) of Section 191 and which has on file the statement provided for in Section 2104 shall be required to register with the Secretary of State as may otherwise be provided in Section 15692. *(Added by Stats.1990, c. 1088 (S.B.2575), § 10.)*

§ 15700. Repealed by Stats. 1983, c. 1223, § 11, operative July 1, 1984

See, now, § 15800.

ARTICLE 10. CLASS ACTIONS AND DERIVATIVE ACTIONS

Section

§ 15701. Class actions

Any limited partner of a foreign or domestic limited partnership may bring a class action on behalf of all or a class of limited partners to enforce any claim common to those limited partners and any such action shall be governed by the law governing class actions generally, provided that in order to maintain the class action there shall be no requirement that the class be so numerous that joinder of all members is impracticable. *(Added by Stats.1983, c. 1223, § 10. Amended by Stats.1987, c. 1364, § 19.)*

§ 15702. Derivative actions

(a) No action may be instituted or maintained in right of any domestic or foreign limited partnership by any partner of the limited partnership unless both of the following conditions exist:

(1) The plaintiff alleges in the complaint that plaintiff was a partner of record or beneficially, at the time of the transaction or any part thereof of which plaintiff complains or that plaintiff's interest thereafter devolved upon plaintiff by operation of law from a partner who was a partner at the time of the transaction or any part thereof complained of. Any partner who does not meet these requirements may nevertheless be allowed in the discretion of the court to maintain the action on a preliminary showing to and determination by the court, by motion and after a hearing at which the court shall consider any evidence, by affidavit or testimony, as it deems material, that (A) there is a strong prima facie case in favor of the claim asserted on behalf of the limited partnership, (B) no other similar action has been or is likely to be instituted, (C) the plaintiff acquired the interest before there was disclosure to the public or to the plaintiff of the wrongdoing of which plaintiff complains, (D) unless the action can be maintained the defendant may retain a gain derived from defendant's willful breach of a fiduciary duty, and (E) the requested relief will not result in unjust enrichment of the limited partnership or any partner of the limited partnership.

(2) The plaintiff alleges in the complaint with particularity plaintiff's efforts to secure from the general partners such action as plaintiff desires or the reasons for not making that effort, and alleges further that plaintiff has either informed the limited partnership or the general partners in writing of the ultimate facts of each cause of action against each defendant or delivered to the limited partnership or the general partners a true copy of the complaint which plaintiff proposes to file.

(b) In any action referred to in subdivision (a), at any time within 30 days after service of summons upon the limited partnership or upon any defendant who is a general partner of the limited partnership or held that position at the time of the acts complained of, the limited partnership or the defendant may move the court for an order, upon notice and hearing, requiring the plaintiff to furnish security as hereinafter provided. The motion shall be based upon one or both of the following grounds:

(1) That there is no reasonable possibility that the prosecution of the cause of action alleged in the complaint against the moving party will benefit the limited partnership or its partners.

(2) That the moving party, if other than the limited partnership, did not participate in the transaction complained of in any capacity. The court on application of the limited partnership or any defendant may, for good cause shown, extend the 30-day period for an additional period not exceeding 60 days.

(c) At the hearing upon any motion pursuant to subdivision (b), the court shall consider evidence, written or oral, by witnesses or affidavit, as may be material (1) to the ground upon which the motion is based, or (2) to a determination of the probable reasonable expenses, including attorneys' fees, of the limited partnership and the moving party which will be incurred in the defense of the action. If the court determines after hearing the evidence adduced by the parties, that the moving party has established a probability in support of any of the grounds upon which the motion is based, the court shall fix the nature and amount of security, not to exceed fifty thousand dollars ($50,000) to be furnished by the plaintiff for reasonable expenses, including attorneys' fees, which may be incurred by the moving party and the limited partnership in connection with the action. A ruling by the court on the motion shall not be a determination of any issue in the action or of the merits thereof. The amount of the security may thereafter be increased or decreased in the discretion of the court upon a showing that the security provided has or may become inadequate or is excessive, but the court may not in any event increase the total amount of the security beyond fifty thousand dollars ($50,000) in the aggregate for all defendants. If the court, upon any such motion, makes a determination that security shall be furnished by the plaintiff as to any one or more defendants, the action shall be dismissed as to such defendant or defendants, unless the security required by the court shall have been furnished within any reasonable time as may be fixed by the court. The limited partnership and the moving party shall have recourse to the security in such amount as the court shall determine upon the termination of the action.

(d) If the plaintiff shall, either before or after a motion is made pursuant to subdivision (b), or any order or determination pursuant to such motion, post good and sufficient bond or bonds in the aggregate amount of fifty thousand dollars ($50,000) to secure the reasonable expenses of the parties entitled to make the motion, the plaintiff has complied with the requirements of this section and with any order for security theretofore made pursuant hereto, and any such motion then pending shall be dismissed and no further or additional bond or other security shall be required.

(e) If a motion is filed pursuant to subdivision (b), no pleadings need be filed by the limited partnership or any other defendant and the prosecution of the action shall be stayed until 10 days after the motion has been disposed of. *(Added by Stats.1983, c. 1223, § 10.)*

ARTICLE 11. TRANSITION PROVISIONS

Section

§ 15710. Prior limited partnerships; filings

Notwithstanding the provisions of Section 15712 or 15713, any limited partnership organized under the laws of this state or any foreign limited partnership existing on March 1, 1984, which has recorded its existence with a county recorder, may file under the provisions of Section 15712 or 15713 as provided therein for the purpose of permitting the Secretary of State to establish a name availability file for the implementation of the provisions of Section 15612 on July 1, 1984, and to establish other files pertaining to these limited partnerships to permit an orderly implementation of the California Revised Limited Partnership Act on July 1, 1984. Filings with the Secretary of State under the provisions of this section may only be made on or after March 1, 1984. Those documents acceptable for filing shall be filed as of July 1, 1984. *(Added by Stats.1983, c. 1223, § 10.)*

§ 15711. Prior limited partnerships; continuation under prior law

Except as provided in Section 15712, this Chapter 3 shall not apply to any limited partnership organized under the laws of this state and existing on the effective date, which shall continue to be governed by the law previously applicable to it. *(Added by Stats.1983, c. 1223, § 10.)*

§ 15712. Prior limited partnerships; law governing; election to be governed by this chapter; certificate filing; certificate forms

(a) A limited partnership organized under the laws of this state and existing on the effective date:

(1) Shall be governed by the law previously applicable to it unless it elects to be governed by this chapter instead of by the law previously applicable to it. The election shall be made by the written consent of all partners, or of the lesser number provided by the partnership agreement for this election. The election shall be prospective only and shall not affect preexisting rights of third parties.

(2) Shall file a certificate as provided by subdivision (a) of Section 15621, including therein the date that the limited partnership filed or recorded under the law previously applicable to it, and shall thereafter be governed by Article 2 (commencing with Section 15621), and not by the law previously applicable to it relating to filing or recording requirements. When a certificate has been filed pursuant to Article 2 (commencing with Section 15621), the limited partnership shall not be required to make any further filings or record any documents pursuant to the Uniform Limited Partnership Act (Chapter 2 (commencing with Section 15501) of Title 2) and no person may rely on the accuracy or completeness of information filed or recorded pursuant to that act subsequent to the filing by the partnership of a certificate pursuant to subdivision (a) of Section 15621.

(3) Shall not be subject to the requirement of subdivision (a) of Section 15612 or to the limitations of subdivision (c) of Section 15612 if a certificate as required by paragraph (2) of this subdivision is filed prior to July 1, 1985.

(4) May not maintain any action, suit, or proceeding in any court of this state until it has filed a certificate as required by paragraph (2).

(b) To the extent that the provisions of the certificate filed under the law previously applicable to a limited partnership governed the rights and obligations of the partners and the limited partnership among each other, those provisions shall continue to govern those rights and obligations except (1) as they may subsequently be affected by amendments to the partnership agreement or by the terms of a certificate filed pursuant to paragraph (6) of subdivision (a) of Section 15621 or by the terms of a certificate of amendment filed pursuant to subdivision (c) of Section 15622, and (2) for the effect upon those rights and obligations of an election to be governed by this chapter pursuant to this section.

(c) The Secretary of State may adopt new forms of certificates, continue to use previously adopted forms, or both, for filings required pursuant to Article 2 (commencing with Section 15621), provided the certificate to be filed contains the information required to be included in such a certificate by that article. No partnership that has filed a certificate pursuant to Article 2 (commencing with Section 15621) shall be required to refile, to amend, or to take any other action with respect to any certificate unless an act amending this chapter expressly so requires. *(Added by Stats.1983, c. 1223, § 10. Amended by Stats.1985, c. 106, § 12; Stats.1987, c. 1364, § 20.)*

§ 15713. Operative date and application of certain provisions

(a) A foreign limited partnership existing on the effective date shall not be subject to the limitations of subdivision (c) of Section 15612 if a certificate of registration referred to in Section 15693 is issued prior to July 1, 1985.

(b) The provisions of subdivision (b) of Section 15697 shall not be operative until July 1, 1985. *(Added by Stats.1983, c. 1223, § 10.)*

§ 15714. Effective date

As used in this article, "effective date" means July 1, 1984. *(Added by Stats.1983, c. 1223, § 10.)*

ARTICLE 12. MISCELLANEOUS

Section

§ 15721. Short title

This chapter may be cited as the California Revised Limited Partnership Act. *(Added by Stats.1983, c. 1223, § 10.)*

§ 15722. Cases not provided for in this chapter; application of Uniform Partnership Act

In any case not provided for in this chapter, the provisions of the Uniform Partnership Act, Chapter 1 (commencing with Section 15001), govern. *(Added by Stats.1983, c. 1223, § 10.)*

§ 15723. . Alteration or repeal of provisions; rights of partners

All provisions of this chapter and all provisions that may hereafter be added to this chapter may be altered from time to time or repealed and all rights of partners are subject to this reservation. *(Added by Stats.1983, c. 1223, § 10.)*

CHAPTER 4. PROCESS AGENTS FOR CERTAIN FOREIGN CORPORATIONS [PARTNERSHIPS]

§ 15800. Designation of agent; service of process

Every partnership, other than a foreign limited partnership subject to Chapter 3 (commencing with Section 15691) of Title 2 of the Corporations Code or a commercial or banking partnership established and transacting business in a place without the United States, which is domiciled without this state and has no regular place of business within this state, shall, within 40 days from the time it commences to do business in this state, file a statement in the office of the Secretary of State in accordance with Section 24003 designating some natural person or corporation as the agent of the partnership upon whom process issued by authority of or under any law of this state directed against the partnership may be served. A copy of the designation, duly certified by the Secretary of State, is sufficient evidence of the appointment.

The process may be served in the manner provided in subdivision (e) of Section 24003 on the person so designated, or, in the event that no such person has been designated, or if the agent designated for the service of process is a natural person and cannot be found with due diligence at the address stated in the designation, or if the agent is a corporation and no person can be found with due diligence to whom the delivery authorized by subdivision (e) of Section 24003 may be made for the purpose of delivery to the corporate agent, or if the agent designated is no longer authorized to act, then service may be made by personal delivery to the Secretary of State, Assistant Secretary of State, or a Deputy Secretary of State of the process, together with a written statement signed by the party to the action seeking the service, or by the party's attorney, setting forth the last known address of the partnership and a service fee of fifty dollars ($50). The Secretary of State shall forthwith give notice of the service to the partnership by forwarding the process to it by registered mail, return receipt requested, at the address given in the written statement.

Service on the person designated, or personal delivery of the process and statement of address together with a service fee of fifty dollars ($50) to the Secretary of State, Assistant Secretary of State, or a Deputy Secretary of State, pursuant to this section is a valid service on the partnership. The partnership so served shall appear within 30 days after service on the person designated or within 30 days after delivery of the process to the Secretary of State, Assistant Secretary of State, or a Deputy Secretary of State. *(Added by Stats.1983, c. 1223, § 12. Amended by Stats. 1984, c. 103, § 14; Stats.1987, c. 1348, § 15.)*

3. California Corporations Code—Corporate Formation Sections*

§ 200. Formation; articles; signatures and acknowledgments; commencement and perpetuity of existence

(a) One or more natural persons, partnerships, associations or corporations, domestic or foreign, may form a corporation under this division by executing and filing articles of incorporation.

(b) If initial directors are named in the articles, each director named in the articles shall sign and acknowledge the articles; if initial directors are not named in the articles, the articles shall be signed by one or more persons described in subdivision (a) who thereupon are the incorporators of the corporation.

(c) The corporate existence begins upon the filing of the articles and continues perpetually, unless otherwise expressly provided by law or in the articles. *(Added by Stats.1975, c. 682, § 7. Amended by Stats.1983, c. 1223, § 1.)*

§ 200.5. Business associations organized as trust; incorporation; articles

(a) An existing business association organized as a trust under the laws of this state or of a foreign jurisdiction may incorporate under this division upon approval by its board of trustees or similar governing body and approval by the affirmative vote of a majority of the outstanding voting shares of beneficial interest (or such greater proportion of the outstanding shares of beneficial interest or the vote of such other classes of shares of beneficial interest as may be specifically required by its declaration of trust or bylaws) and the filing of articles of incorporation with certificate attached pursuant to this chapter.

(b) In addition to the matters required to be set forth in the articles pursuant to Section 202, the articles in the case of an incorporation authorized by subdivision (a) shall set forth that an existing unincorporated associa-

*Excerpts from the California Corporations Code; sections relating to corporate formation.

tion, stating its name, is being incorporated by the filing of the articles.

(c) The articles filed pursuant to this section shall be signed by the president, or any vice president, and the secretary, or any assistant secretary, of the existing association and shall be accompanied by a certificate signed and verified by such officers signing the articles and stating that the incorporation of the association has been approved by the trustees and by the required vote of holders of shares of beneficial interest in accordance with subdivision (a).

(d) Upon the filing of articles of incorporation pursuant to this section, the corporation shall succeed automatically to all of the rights and property of the association being incorporated and shall be subject to all of its debts and liabilities in the same manner as if the corporation had itself incurred them. The incumbent trustees of the association shall constitute the initial directors of the corporation and shall continue in office until the next annual meeting of the shareholders, unless they die, resign or are removed prior thereto. All rights of creditors and all liens upon the property of the association shall be preserved unimpaired. Any action or proceeding pending by or against the association may be prosecuted to judgment, which shall bind the corporation, or the corporation may be proceeded against or substituted in its place.

(e) The filing for record in the office of the county recorder of any county in this state in which any of the real property of the association is located of a copy of the articles of incorporation filed pursuant to this section, certified by the Secretary of State, shall evidence record ownership in the corporation of all interests of the association in and to the real property located in that county. *(Added by Stats.1978, c. 370, § 2.5.)*

§ 201. Names; use of "bank", "trust" or "trustee"; misleading or deceptive; certificate of reservation

(a) The Secretary of State shall not file articles setting forth a name in which "bank", "trust", "trustee" or related words appear, unless the certificate of approval of the Superintendent of Banks is attached thereto. This subdivision does not apply to the articles of any corporation subject to the Banking Law on which is endorsed the approval of the Superintendent of Banks.

(b) The Secretary of State shall not file articles which set forth a name which is likely to mislead the public or which is the same as, or resembles so closely as to tend to deceive, the name of a domestic corporation, the name of a foreign corporation which is authorized to transact intrastate business or has registered its name pursuant to Section 2101, a name which a foreign corporation has assumed under subdivision (b) of Section 2106, a name which will become a record name of a domestic or foreign corporation upon the effective date of a filed corporate instrument where there is a delayed effective date pursuant to subdivision (c) of Section 110 or subdivision (c) of Section 5008, or a name which is under reservation for another corporation pursuant to this section, Section 5122, Section 7122, or Section 9122, except that a corporation may adopt a name that is substantially the same as an existing domestic corporation or foreign corporation which is authorized to transact intrastate business or has registered its name pursuant to Section 2101, upon proof of consent by such domestic or foreign corporation and a finding by the Secretary of State that under the circumstances the public is not likely to be misled.

The use by a corporation of a name in violation of this section may be enjoined notwithstanding the filing of its articles by the Secretary of State.

(c) Any applicant may, upon payment of the fee prescribed therefor in the Government Code, obtain from the Secretary of State a certificate of reservation of any name not prohibited by subdivision (b), and upon the issuance of the certificate the name stated therein shall be reserved for a period of 60 days. The Secretary of State shall not, however, issue certificates reserving the same name for two or more consecutive 60-day periods to the same applicant or for the use or benefit of the same person, partnership, firm or corporation; nor shall consecutive reservations be made by or for the use or benefit of the same person, partnership, firm or corporation of names so similar as to fall within the prohibitions of subdivision (b). *(Added by Stats.1975, c. 682, § 7. Amended by Stats.1978, c. 370, § 2.6; Stats.1978, c. 1305, § 2.)*

§ 201.5. Insurers, approval of corporate name

The Secretary of State shall not file articles in which the business is to be an insurer unless the certificate of the Insurance Commissioner approving the corporate name is attached thereto. *(Added by Stats.1979, c. 737, § 1.)*

§ 202. Articles of incorporation; required provisions

The articles of incorporation shall set forth:

(a) The name of the corporation; provided, however, that in order for the corporation to be subject to the provisions of this division applicable to a close corporation (Section 158), the name of the corporation must contain the word "corporation", "incorporated" or "limited" or an abbreviation of one of such words.

(b)(1) The applicable one of the following statements:

(i) The purpose of the corporation is to engage in any lawful act or activity for which a corporation may be organized under the General Corporation Law of California other than the banking business, the trust company business or the practice of a profession permitted to be incorporated by the California Corporations Code; or

(ii) The purpose of the corporation is to engage in the profession of ______ (with the insertion of a profession permitted to be incorporated by the California Corporations Code) and any other lawful activities (other than the banking or trust company business) not prohibited to a corporation engaging in such profession by applicable laws and regulations.

(2) In case the corporation is a corporation subject to the Banking Law, the articles shall set forth a statement

of purpose which is prescribed in the applicable provision of the Banking Law.

(3) In case the corporation is a corporation subject to the Insurance Code as an insurer, the articles shall additionally state that the business of the corporation is to be an insurer.

The articles shall not set forth any further or additional statement with respect to the purposes or powers of the corporation, except by way of limitation or except as expressly required by any law of this state other than this division or any federal or other statute or regulation (including the Internal Revenue Code and regulations thereunder as a condition of acquiring or maintaining a particular status for tax purposes).

(c) The name and address in this state of the corporation's initial agent for service of process in accordance with subdivision (b) of Section 1502.

(d) If the corporation is authorized to issue only one class of shares, the total number of shares which the corporation is authorized to issue.

(e) If the corporation is authorized to issue more than one class of shares, or if any class of shares is to have two or more series:

(1) The total number of shares of each class the corporation is authorized to issue, and the total number of shares of each series which the corporation is authorized to issue or that the board is authorized to fix the number of shares of any such series;

(2) The designation of each class, and the designation of each series or that the board may determine the designation of any such series; and

(3) The rights, preferences, privileges and restrictions granted to or imposed upon the respective classes or series of shares or the holders thereof, or that the board, within any limits and restrictions stated, may determine or alter the rights, preferences, privileges and restrictions granted to or imposed upon any wholly unissued class of shares or any wholly unissued series of any class of shares. As to any series the number of shares of which is authorized to be fixed by the board, the articles may also authorize the board, within the limits and restrictions stated therein or stated in any resolution or resolutions of the board originally fixing the number of shares constituting any series, to increase or decrease (but not below the number of shares of such series then outstanding) the number of shares of any such series subsequent to the issue of shares of that series. In case the number of shares of any series shall be so decreased, the shares constituting such decrease shall resume the status which they had prior to the adoption of the resolution originally fixing the number of shares of such series. *(Added by Stats.1975, c. 682, § 7. Amended by Stats.1978, c. 370, § 2.7; Stats.1979, c. 737, § 2.)*

§ 203. Distinctions between classes or series of shares or holders thereof

Except as specified in the articles or in any shareholders' agreement, no distinction shall exist between classes or series of shares or the holders thereof. *(Added by Stats.1975, c. 682, § 7.)*

§ 203.5. Number of shares for series within a class; amendment of articles

(a) If the articles include the designation and number of shares of one or more series within a class, the stated number of shares for all series within the class shall not exceed, and may be less than, the stated number of shares for the class.

(b) If so authorized in the articles and if the articles state the number of shares of the class, the articles may be amended by approval of the board alone to increase or decrease (but not below the number of shares of the series then outstanding) the number of shares of a series.

(c) If the articles authorize a class of shares which is stated to be issuable in series, the articles shall include either the designation and number of shares for at least one series within that class or an authorization of common shares. *(Added by Stats.1988, c. 919, § 2.)*

§ 204. Articles of incorporation; optional provisions

The articles of incorporation may set forth:

(a) Any or all of the following provisions, which shall not be effective unless expressly provided in the articles:

(1) Granting, with or without limitations, the power to levy assessments upon the shares or any class of shares.

(2) Granting to shareholders preemptive rights to subscribe to any or all issues of shares or securities.

(3) Special qualifications of persons who may be shareholders.

(4) A provision limiting the duration of the corporation's existence to a specified date.

(5) A provision requiring, for any or all corporate actions (except as provided in Section 303, subdivision (b) of Section 402.5, subdivision (c) of Section 708 and Section 1900) the vote of a larger proportion or of all of the shares of any class or series, or the vote or quorum for taking action of a larger proportion or of all of the directors, than is otherwise required by this division.

(6) A provision limiting or restricting the business in which the corporation may engage or the powers which the corporation may exercise or both.

(7) A provision conferring upon the holders of any evidences of indebtedness, issued or to be issued by the corporation, the right to vote in the election of directors and on any other matters on which shareholders may vote.

(8) A provision conferring upon shareholders the right to determine the consideration for which shares shall be issued.

(9) A provision requiring the approval of the shareholders (Section 153) or the approval of the outstanding shares (Section 152) for any corporate action, even though not otherwise required by this division.

(10) Provisions eliminating or limiting the personal liability of a director for monetary damages in an action brought by or in the right of the corporation for breach of a director's duties to the corporation and its shareholders, as set forth in Section 309, provided, however, that

(A) such a provision may not eliminate or limit the liability of directors (i) for acts or omissions that involve intentional misconduct or a knowing and culpable violation of law, (ii) for acts or omissions that a director believes to be contrary to the best interests of the corporation or its shareholders or that involve the absence of good faith on the part of the director, (iii) for any transaction from which a director derived an improper personal benefit, (iv) for acts or omissions that show a reckless disregard for the director's duty to the corporation or its shareholders in circumstances in which the director was aware, or should have been aware, in the ordinary course of performing a director's duties, of a risk of serious injury to the corporation or its shareholders, (v) for acts or omissions that constitute an unexcused pattern of inattention that amounts to an abdication of the director's duty to the corporation or its shareholders, (vi) under Section 310, or (vii) under Section 316, (B) no such provision shall eliminate or limit the liability of a director for any act or omission occurring prior to the date when the provision becomes effective, and (C) no such provision shall eliminate or limit the liability of an officer for any act or omission as an officer, notwithstanding that the officer is also a director or that his or her actions, if negligent or improper, have been ratified by the directors.

(11) A provision authorizing, whether by bylaw, agreement, or otherwise, the indemnification of agents (as defined in Section 317) in excess of that expressly permitted by Section 317 for those agents of the corporation for breach of duty to the corporation and its stockholders, provided, however, that the provision may not provide for indemnification of any agent for any acts or omissions or transactions from which a director may not be relieved of liability as set forth in the exception to paragraph (10) or as to circumstances in which indemnity is expressly prohibited by Section 317.

Notwithstanding this subdivision, in the case of a close corporation any of the provisions referred to above may be validly included in a shareholders' agreement. Notwithstanding this subdivision, bylaws may require for all or any actions by the board the affirmative vote of a majority of the authorized number of directors. Nothing contained in this subdivision shall affect the enforceability, as between the parties thereto, of any lawful agreement not otherwise contrary to public policy.

(b) Reasonable restrictions upon the right to transfer or hypothecate shares of any class or classes or series, but no restriction shall be binding with respect to shares issued prior to the adoption of the restriction unless the holders of such shares voted in favor of the restriction.

(c) The names and addresses of the persons appointed to act as initial directors.

(d) Any other provision, not in conflict with law, for the management of the business and for the conduct of the affairs of the corporation, including any provision which is required or permitted by this division to be stated in the bylaws. *(Added by Stats.1975, c. 682, § 7. Amended by Stats.1976, c. 641, § 6.2; Stats.1977, c. 235, § 1.5; Stats.1983, c. 1223, § 2; Stats.1987, c. 1201, § 5; Stats.1987, c. 1203, § 1, eff. Sept. 27, 1987.)*

§ 204.5. Director liability; limiting provision in articles; wording; disclosure to shareholders regarding provision

(a) If the articles of a corporation include a provision reading substantially as follows: "The liability of the directors of the corporation for monetary damages shall be eliminated to the fullest extent permissible under California law"; the corporation shall be considered to have adopted a provision as authorized by paragraph (10) of subdivision (a) of Section 204 and more specific wording shall not be required.

(b) This section shall not be construed as setting forth the exclusive method of adopting an article provision as authorized by paragraph (10) of subdivision (a) of Section 204.

(c) This section shall not change the otherwise applicable standards or duties to make full and fair disclosure to shareholders when approval of such a provision is sought. *(Added by Stats. 1987, c. 1203, § 1.5, eff. Sept. 27, 1987.)*

§ 205. Par value of shares

Solely for the purpose of any statute or regulation imposing any tax or fee based upon the capitalization of a corporation, all authorized shares of a corporation organized under this division shall be deemed to have a nominal or par value of one dollar ($1) per share. If any federal or other statute or regulation applicable to a particular corporation requires that the shares of such corporation have a par value, such shares shall have the par value determined by the board in order to satisfy the requirements of such statute or regulation. *(Added by Stats.1975, c. 682, § 7.)*

§ 206. Authorized business activities

Subject to any limitation contained in the articles and to compliance with any other applicable laws, any corporation other than a corporation subject to the Banking Law or a professional corporation may engage in any business activity; and a corporation subject to the Banking Law or a professional corporation may engage in any business activity not prohibited by the respective statutes and regulations to which it is subject. *(Added by Stats.1975, c. 682, § 7. Amended by Stats.1978, c. 370, § 2.8.)*

§ 207. Powers

Subject to any limitations contained in the articles and to compliance with other provisions of this division and any other applicable laws, a corporation shall have all of the powers of a natural person in carrying out its business activities, including, without limitation, the power to:

(a) Adopt, use and at will alter a corporate seal, but failure to affix a seal does not affect the validity of any instrument.

(b) Adopt, amend and repeal bylaws.

(c) Qualify to do business in any other state, territory, dependency or foreign country.

(d) Subject to the provisions of Section 510, issue, purchase, redeem, receive, take or otherwise acquire, own, hold, sell, lend, exchange, transfer or otherwise dispose of, pledge, use and otherwise deal in and with its own shares, bonds, debentures and other securities.

(e) Make donations, regardless of specific corporate benefit, for the public welfare or for community fund, hospital, charitable, educational, scientific, civic or similar purposes.

(f) Pay pensions, and establish and carry out pension, profit-sharing, share bonus, share purchase, share option, savings, thrift and other retirement, incentive and benefit plans, trusts and provisions for any or all of the directors, officers and employees of the corporation or any of its subsidiary or affiliated corporations, and to indemnify and purchase and maintain insurance on behalf of any fiduciary of such plans, trusts or provisions.

(g) Subject to the provisions of Section 315, assume obligations, enter into contracts, including contracts of guaranty or suretyship, incur liabilities, borrow and lend money and otherwise use its credit, and secure any of its obligations, contracts or liabilities by mortgage, pledge or other encumbrance of all or any part of its property, franchises and income.

(h) Participate with others in any partnership, joint venture or other association, transaction or arrangement of any kind, whether or not such participation involves sharing or delegation of control with or to others. *(Added by Stats.1975, c. 682, § 7. Amended by Stats. 1977, c. 235, § 1.7.)*

§ 208. Limitations on business, purposes or powers; enforcement; contracts or conveyances; enforcement

(a) No limitation upon the business, purposes or powers of the corporation or upon the powers of the shareholders, officers or directors, or the manner of exercise of such powers, contained in or implied by the articles or by Chapters 18 [1], 19 [2] and 20 [3] or by any shareholders' agreement shall be asserted as between the corporation or any shareholder and any third person, except in a proceeding (1) by a shareholder or the state to enjoin the doing or continuation of unauthorized business by the corporation or its officers, or both, in cases where third parties have not acquired rights thereby, or (2) to dissolve the corporation or (3) by the corporation or by a shareholder suing in a representative suit against the officers or directors of the corporation for violation of their authority.

(b) Any contract or conveyance made in the name of a corporation which is authorized or ratified by the board, or is done within the scope of the authority, actual or apparent, conferred by the board or within the agency power of the officer executing it, except as the board's authority is limited by law other than this division, binds the corporation, and the corporation acquires rights thereunder, whether the contract is executed or wholly or in part executory.

(c) This section applies to contracts and conveyances made by foreign corporations in this state and to all conveyances by foreign corporations of real property situated in this state. *(Added by Stats.1975, c. 682, § 7.)*

1 Section 1800 et seq.

2 Section 1900 et seq.

3 Section 2000 et seq.

§ 209. Certified copies of articles of incorporation; conclusive evidence of formation and prima facie evidence of existence

For all purposes other than an action in the nature of quo warranto, a copy of the articles of a corporation duly certified by the Secretary of State is conclusive evidence of the formation of the corporation and prima facie evidence of its corporate existence. *(Added by Stats. 1975, c. 682, § 7.)*

§ 210. Incorporators; powers

If initial directors have not been named in the articles, the incorporator or incorporators, until the directors are elected, may do whatever is necessary and proper to perfect the organization of the corporation, including the adoption and amendment of bylaws of the corporation and the election of directors and officers. *(Added by Stats.1975, c. 682, § 7.)*

§ 211. Bylaws; adoption, amendment or repeal

Bylaws may be adopted, amended or repealed either by approval of the outstanding shares (Section 152) or by the approval of the board, except as provided in Section 212. Subject to subdivision (a)(5) of Section 204, the articles or bylaws may restrict or eliminate the power of the board to adopt, amend or repeal any or all bylaws. *(Added by Stats.1975, c. 682, § 7.)*

§ 212. Bylaws; contents

(a) The bylaws shall set forth (unless such provision is contained in the articles, in which case it may only be changed by an amendment of the articles) the number of directors of the corporation; or that the number of directors shall be not less than a stated minimum nor more than a stated maximum (which in no case shall be greater than two times the stated minimum minus one), with the exact number of directors to be fixed, within the limits specified, by approval of the board or the shareholders (Section 153) in the manner provided in the bylaws, subject to paragraph (5) of subdivision (a) of Section 204. The number or minimum number of directors shall not be less than three; provided, however, that (1) before shares are issued, the number may be one, (2) before shares are issued, the number may be two, (3) so long as the corporation has only one shareholder, the number may be one, (4) so long as the corporation has only one shareholder, the number may be two, and (5) so long as the corporation has only two shareholders, the number may be two. After the issuance of shares, a bylaw specifying or changing a fixed number of directors or the maximum or minimum number or changing from a fixed to a variable board or vice versa may only be adopted by approval of the outstanding shares (Section 152); provided, however, that a bylaw or amendment of the articles reducing the fixed number or the minimum number of directors to a number less than five cannot be adopted if the votes cast against its adoption at a meeting or the shares not consenting in the case of action by written consent are equal to more than 16⅔ percent of the outstanding shares entitled to vote.

(b) The bylaws may contain any provision, not in conflict with law or the articles for the management of the business and for the conduct of the affairs of the corporation, including but not limited to:

(1) Any provision referred to in subdivision (b), (c) or (d) of Section 204.

(2) The time, place and manner of calling, conducting and giving notice of shareholders', directors' and committee meetings.

(3) The manner of execution, revocation and use of proxies.

(4) The qualifications, duties and compensation of directors; the time of their annual election; and the requirements of a quorum for directors' and committee meetings.

(5) The appointment and authority of committees of the board.

(6) The appointment, duties, compensation and tenure of officers.

(7) The mode of determination of holders of record of its shares.

(8) The making of annual reports and financial statements to the shareholders. *(Added by Stats.1975, c. 682, § 7. Amended by Stats.1976, c. 641, § 6.6; Stats.1977, c. 235, § 1.8.)*

§ 213. Bylaws; inspection by shareholders

Every corporation shall keep at its principal executive office in this state, or if its principal executive office is not in this state at its principal business office in this state, the original or a copy of its bylaws as amended to date, which shall be open to inspection by the shareholders at all reasonable times during office hours. If the principal executive office of the corporation is outside this state and the corporation has no principal business office in this state, it shall upon the written request of any shareholder furnish to such shareholder a copy of the bylaws as amended to date. *(Added by Stats.1975, c. 682, § 7.)*

4. Equal Credit Opportunity

PART 202—EQUAL CREDIT OPPORTUNITY

Sec.

REGULATION B (EQUAL CREDIT OPPORTUNITY)

Regulation B (Equal Credit Opportunity)

§ 202.1 Authority, scope and purpose.

(a) *Authority and scope.* This regulation is issued by the Board of Governors of the Federal Reserve System pursuant to title VII (Equal Credit Opportunity Act) of the Consumer Credit Protection Act, as amended (15 USC 1601 et seq.). Except as otherwise provided herein, the regulation applies to all persons who are creditors, as defined in § 202.2(1). Information collection requirements contained in this regulation have been approved by the Office of Management and Budget under the provisions of 44 USC 3501 et seq. and have been assigned OMB No. 7100-0201.

(b) *Purpose.* The purpose of this regulation is to promote the availability of credit to all creditworthy applicants without regard to race, color, religion, national origin, sex, marital status, or age (provided the applicant has the capacity to contract); to the fact that all or part of the applicant's income derives from a public assistance program; or to the fact that the applicant has in good faith exercised any right under the Consumer Credit Protection Act. The regulation prohibits creditor practices that discriminate on the basis of any of these factors. The regulation also requires creditors to notify applicants of action taken on their applications; to report credit history in the names of both spouses on an account; to retain records of credit applications; and to collect information about the applicant's race and other personal characteristics in applications for certain dwelling-related loans.

§ 202.2 Definitions.

For the purposes of this regulation, unless the context indicates otherwise, the following definitions apply.

(a) *Account* means an extension of credit. When employed in relation to an account, the word *use* refers only to open-end credit.

(b) *Act* means the Equal Credit Opportunity Act (title VII of the Consumer Credit Protection Act).

(c) *Adverse action.* (1) The term means:

(i) A refusal to grant credit in substantially the amount or on substantially the terms requested in an application unless the creditor makes a counteroffer (to grant credit in a different amount or on other terms) and the applicant uses or expressly accepts the credit offered;

(ii) A termination of an account or an unfavorable change in the terms of an account that does not affect all or a substantial portion of a class of the creditor's accounts; or

(iii) A refusal to increase the amount of credit available to an applicant who has made an application for an increase.

(2) The term does not include:

(i) A change in the terms of an account expressly agreed to by an applicant.

(ii) Any action or forbearance relating to an account taken in connection with inactivity, default, or delinquency as to that accounnt;

(iii) A refusal or failure to authorize an account transaction at a point of sale or loan, except when the refusal is a termination or an unfavorable change in the terms of an account that does not affect all or a substantial portion of a class of the creditor's accounts, or when the refusal is a denial of an application for an increase in the amount of credit available under the account;

(iv) A refusal to extend credit because applicable law prohibits the creditor from extending the credit requested; or

(v) A refusal to extend credit because the creditor does not offer the type of credit or credit plan requested.

(3) An action that falls within the definition of both paragraphs (c)(1) and (c)(2) of this section is governed by paragraph (c)(2).

(d) *Age* refers only to the age of natural persons and means the number of fully elapsed years from the date of an applicant's birth.

(e) *Applicant* means any person who requests or who has received an extension of credit from a creditor, and includes any person who is or may become contractually liable regarding an extension of credit. For purposes of § 202.7(d), the term includes guarantors, sureties, endorsers and similar parties.

(f) *Application* means an oral or written request for an extension of credit that is made in accordance with procedures established by a creditor for the type of credit requested. The term does not include the use of an account or line of credit to obtain an amount of credit that is within a previously established credit limit. A *completed application* means an application in connection with which a creditor has received all the information that the creditor regularly obtains and considers in evaluating applications for the amount and type of credit requested (including, but not limited to, credit reports, any additional information requested from the applicant, and any approvals or reports by governmental agencies or other persons that are necessary to guarantee, insure, or provide security for the credit or collateral). The creditor shall exercise reasonable diligence in obtaining such information.

(g) *Business credit* refers to extensions of credit primarily for business or commercial (including agricultural) purposes, but excluding extensions of credit of the types described in § 202.3 (a), (b), and (d).

(h) *Consumer credit* means credit extended to a natural person primarily for personal, family, or household purposes.

(i) *Contractually liable* means expressly obligated to repay all debts arising on an account by reason of an agreement to that effect.

(j) *Credit* means the right granted by a creditor to an applicant to defer payment of a debt, incur debt and defer its payment, or purchase property or services and defer payment therefor.

(k) *Credit card* means any card, plate, coupon book, or other single credit device that may be used from time to time to obtain money, property, or services on credit.

(l) *Creditor* means a person who, in the ordinary course of business, regularly participates in the decision of whether or not to extend credit. The term includes a creditor's assignee, transferee, or subrogee who so participates. For purposes of §§ 202.4 and 202.5(a), the term also includes a person who, in the ordinary course of business, regularly refers applicants or prospective applicants to creditors, or selects or offers to select creditors to whom requests for credit may be made. A person is not a creditor regarding any violation of the act or this regulation committed by another creditor unless the person knew or had reasonable notice of the act, policy, or practice that constituted the violation before becoming involved in the credit transaction. The term does not include a person whose only participation in a credit transaction involves honoring a credit card.

(m) *Credit transaction* means every aspect of an applicant's dealings with a creditor regarding an application for credit or an existing extension of credit (including, but not limited to, information requirements; investigation procedures; standards of creditworthiness; terms of credit; furnishing of credit information; revocation, alteration, or termination of credit; and collection procedures).

(n) *Discriminate against an applicant* means to treat an applicant less favorably than other applicants.

(o) *Elderly* means age 62 or older.

(p) *Empirically derived and other credit scoring systems*—(1) *A credit scoring system* is a system that evaluates an applicant's creditworthiness mechanically, based on key attributes of the applicant and aspects of the transaction, and that determines, alone or in conjunction with an evaluation of additional information about the applicant, whether an applicant is deemed creditworthy. To qualify as an *empirically derived, demonstrably and statistically sound, credit scoring system*, the system must be:

(i) Based on data that are derived from an empirical comparison of sample groups or the population of creditworthy and noncreditworthy applicants who applied for credit within a reasonable preceding period of time;

(ii) Developed for the purpose of evaluating the creditworthiness of applicants with respect to the legitimate business interests of the creditor utilizing the system (including, but not limited to, minimizing bad debt losses and operating expenses in accordance with the creditor's business judgment);

(iii) Developed and validated using accepted statistical principles and methodology; and

(iv) Periodically revalidated by the use of appropriate statistical principles and methodology and adjusted as necessary to maintain predictive ability.

(2) A creditor may use an empirically derived, demonstrably and statistically sound, credit scoring system obtained from another person or may obtain credit experience from which to develop such a system. Any such system must satisfy the criteria set forth in paragraph (p)(1) (i) through (iv) of this section; if the creditor is unable during the development process to validate the system based on its own credit experience in accordance with paragraph (p)(1) of this section, the system must be validated when sufficient credit experience becomes available. A system that fails this validity test is no longer an empirically derived, demonstrably and statistically sound, credit scoring system for that creditor.

(q) *Extend credit* and *extension of credit* mean the granting of credit in any form (including, but not limited to, credit granted in addition to any existing credit or credit limit; credit granted pursuant to an open-end credit plan; the refinancing or other renewal of credit, including the issuance of a new credit card in place of an expiring credit card or in substitution for an existing credit card; the consolidation of two or more obligations; or the continuance of existing credit without any special effort to collect at or after maturity).

(r) *Good faith* means honesty in fact in the conduct or transaction.

(s) *Inadvertent error* means a mechanical, electronic, or clerical error that a creditor demonstrates was not intentional and occurred notwithstanding the maintenance of procedures reasonably adapted to avoid such errors.

(t) *Judgmental system of evaluating applicants* means any system for evaluating the creditworthiness of an applicant other than an empirically derived, demonstrably and statistically sound, credit scoring system.

(u) *Marital status* means the state of being unmarried, married, or separated, as defined by applicable state law. The term "unmarried" includes persons who are single, divorced, or widowed.

(v) *Negative factor or value*, in relation to the age of elderly applicants, means utilizing a factor, value, or weight that is less favorable regarding elderly applicants than the creditor's experience warrants or is less favorable than the factor, value, or weight assigned to the class of applicants that are not classified as elderly and are most favored by a creditor on the basis of age.

(w) *Open-end credit* means credit extended under a plan under which a creditor may permit an applicant to make purchases or obtain loans from time to time directly from the creditor or indirectly by use of a credit card, check, or other device.

(x) *Person* means a natural person, corporation, government or governmental subdivision or agency, trust, estate, partnership, cooperative, or association.

(y) *Pertinent element of creditworthiness*, in relation to a judgmental system of evaluating applicants, means any information about applicants that a creditor obtains and considers and that has a demonstrable relationship to a determination of creditworthiness.

(z) *Prohibited basis* means race, color, religion, national origin, sex, marital status, or age (provided that the applicant has the capacity to enter into a binding contract); the fact that all or part of the applicant's income derives from any public assistance program; or the fact that the applicant has in good faith exercised any right under the Consumer Credit Protection Act or any state law upon which an exemption has been granted by the Board.

(aa) *State* means any State, the District of Columbia, the Commonwealth of Puerto Rico, or any territory or possession of the United States.

[Reg. B, 50 FR 48026, Nov. 20, 1985, as amended at 54 FR 50485, Dec. 7, 1989]

§ 202.3 Limited exceptions for certain classes of transactions

(a) *Public utilities credit*—(1) *Definition.* Public utilities credit refers to extensions of credit that involve public utility services provided through pipe, wire, or other connected facilities, or radio or similar transmission (including extensions of such facilities), if the charges for service, delayed payment, and any discount for prompt payment are filed with or regulated by a government unit.

(2) *Exceptions.* The following provisions of this regulation do not apply to public utilities credit:

(i) Section 202.5(d)(1) concerning information about marital status;

(ii) Section 202.10 relating to furnishing of credit information; and

(iii) Section 202.12(b) relating to record retention.

(b) *Securities credit*—(1) *Definition.* Securities credit refers to extensions of credit subject to regulation under section 7 of the Securities Exchange Act of 1934 or extensions of credit by a broker or dealer subject to regulation as a broker or dealer under the Securities Exchange Act of 1934.

(2) *Exceptions.* The following provisions of this regulation do not apply to securities credit:

(i) Section 202.5(c) concerning information about a spouse or former spouse;

(ii) Section 202.5(d)(1) concerning information about marital status;

(iii) Section 202.5(d)(3) concerning information about the sex of an applicant;

(iv) Section 202.7(b) relating to designation of name, but only to the extent necessary to prevent violation of rules regarding an account in which a broker or dealer has an interest, or rules necessitating the aggregation of accounts of spouses for the purpose of determining controlling interests, beneficial interests, beneficial ownership, or purchase limitations and restrictions;

(v) Section 202.7(c) relating to action concerning open-end accounts, but only to the extent the action taken is on the basis of a change of name or marital status;

(vi) Section 202.7(d) relating to the signature of a spouse or other person;

(vii) Section 202.10 relating to furnishing of credit information; and

(viii) Section 202.12(b) relating to record retention.

(c) *Incidental credit.* (1) *Definition.* Incidental credit refers to extensions of consumer credit other than credit of the types described in paragraphs (a) and (b) of this section:

(i) That are not made pursuant to the terms of a credit card account;

(ii) That are not subject to a finance charge (as defined in Regulation Z, 12 CFR 226.4); and

(iii) That are not payable by agreement in more than four installments.

(2) *Exceptions.* The following provisions of this regulation do not apply to incidental credit:

(i) Section 202.5(c) concerning information about a spouse or former spouse;

(ii) Section 202.5(d)(1) concerning information about marital status;

(iii) Section 202.5(d)(2) concerning information about income derived from alimony, child support, or separate maintenance payments;

(iv) Section 202.5(d)(3) concerning information about the sex of an applicant, but only to the extent necessary for medical records or similar purposes;

(v) Section 202.7(d) relating to the signature of a spouse or other person;

(vi) Section 202.9 relating to notifications;

(vii) Section 202.10 relating to furnishing of credit information; and

(viii) Section 202.12(b) relating to record retention.

(d) *Government credit*—(1) *Definition.* Government credit refers to extensions of credit made to governments or governmental subdivisions, agencies, or instrumentalities.

(2) *Applicability of regulation.* Except for section 202.4, the general rule prohibiting discrimination on a prohibited basis, the requirements of this regulation do not apply to government credit.

[Reg. B, 50 FR 48026, Nov. 20, 1985, as amended at 54 FR 50485, Dec. 7, 1989]

§ 202.4 General rule prohibiting discrimination.

A creditor shall not discriminate against an applicant on a prohibited basis regarding any aspect of a credit transaction.

§ 202.5 Rules concerning taking of applications.

(a) *Discouraging applications.* A creditor shall not make any oral or written statement, in advertising or otherwise, to applicants or prospective applicants that would discourage on a prohibited basis a reasonable person from making or pursuing an application.

(b) *General rules concerning requests for information.* (1) Except as provided in paragraphs (c) and (d) of this section, a creditor may request any information in connection with an application.[1]

(2) *Required collection of information.* Notwithstanding paragraphs (c) and (d) of this section, a creditor shall request information for monitoring purposes as required by § 202.13 for credit secured by the applicant's dwelling. In addition, a creditor may obtain information required by a regulation, order, or agreement issued by, or entered into with, a court or an enforcement agency (including the Attorney General of the United States or a similar state official) to monitor or enforce compliance with the act, this regulation, or other federal or state statute or regulation.

(3) *Special purpose credit.* A creditor may obtain information that is otherwise restricted to determine eligibility for a special purpose credit program, as provided in §§ 202.8 (c) and (d).

(c) *Information about a spouse or former spouse.* (1) Except as permitted in this paragraph, a creditor may not request any information concerning the spouse or former spouse of an applicant.

(2) *Permissible inquiries.* A creditor may request any information concerning an applicant's spouse (or former spouse under paragraph (c)(2)(v)) that may be requested about the applicant if:

(i) The spouse will be permitted to use the account;

(ii) The spouse will be contractually liable on the account;

(iii) The applicant is relying on the spouse's income as a basis for repayment of the credit requested;

(iv) The applicant resides in a community property state or property on which the applicant is relying as a basis for repayment of the credit requested is located in such a state; or

(v) The applicant is relying on alimony, child support, or separate maintenance payments from a spouse or former spouse as a basis for repayment of the credit requested.

(3) *Other accounts of the applicant.* A creditor may request an applicant to list any account upon which the applicant is liable and to provide the name and address in which the account is carried. A creditor may also ask the names in which an applicant has previously received credit.

(d) *Other limitations on information requests*—(1) *Marital status.* If an applicant applies for individual unsecured credit, a creditor shall not inquire about the applicant's marital status unless the applicant resides in a community property state or is relying on property located in such a state as a basis for repayment of the credit requested. If an application is for other than individual unsecured credit, a creditor may inquire about the applicant's marital status, but shall use only the terms "married," "unmarried," and "separated." A creditor may explain that the category "unmarried" includes single, divorced, and widowed persons.

(2) *Disclosure about income from alimony, child support, or separate maintenance.* A creditor shall not inquire whether income stated in an application is derived from alimony, child support, or separate maintenance payments unless the creditor discloses to the applicant that such income need not be revealed if the applicant does not want the creditor to consider it in determining the applicant's creditworthiness.

(3) *Sex.* A creditor shall not inquire about the sex of an applicant. An applicant may be requested to designate a title on an application form (such as Ms., Miss, Mr., or Mrs.) if the form discloses that the designation of a title is optional. An application form shall otherwise use only terms that are neutral as to sex.

(4) *Childbearing, childrearing.* A creditor shall not inquire about birth control practices, intentions concerning the bearing or rearing of children, or capability to bear children. A creditor may inquire about the number and ages of an applicant's dependents or about dependent-related financial obligations or expenditures, provided such information is requested without regard to sex, marital status, or any other prohibited basis.

(5) *Race, color, religion, national origin.* A creditor shall not inquire about the race, color, religion, or national origin of an applicant or any other person in connection with a credit transaction. A creditor may inquire about an applicant's permanent residence and immigration status.

[1] This paragraph does not limit or abrogate any federal or state law regarding privacy, privileged information, credit reporting limitations, or similar restrictions on obtainable information.

(e) *Written applications.* A creditor shall take written applications for the types of credit covered by § 202.13(a), but need not take written applications for other types of credit.

§ 202.6 Rules concerning evaluation of applications.

(a) *General rule concerning use of information.* Except as otherwise provided in the Act and this regulation, a creditor may consider any information obtained, so long as the information is not used to discriminate against an applicant on a prohibited basis.[1]

(b) *Specific rules concerning use of information.* (1) Except as provided in the act and this regulation, a creditor shall not take a prohibited basis into account in any system of evaluating the creditworthiness of applicants.

(2) *Age, receipt of public assistance.* (i) Except as permitted in this paragraph (b)(2), a creditor shall not take into account an applicant's age (provided that the applicant has the capacity to enter into a binding contract) or whether an applicant's income derives from any public assistance program.

(ii) In an empirically derived, demonstrably and statistically sound, credit scoring system, a creditor may use an applicant's age as a predictive variable, provided that the age of an elderly applicant is not assigned a negative factor or value.

(iii) In a judgmental system of evaluating creditworthiness, a creditor may consider an applicant's age or whether an applicant's income derives from any public assistance program only for the purpose of determining a pertinent element of creditworthiness.

(iv) In any system of evaluating creditworthiness, a creditor may consider the age of an elderly applicant when such age is used to favor the elderly applicant in extending credit.

(3) *Childbearing, childrearing.* In evaluating creditworthiness, a creditor shall not use assumptions or aggregate statistics relating to the likelihood that any group of persons will bear or rear children or will, for that reason, receive diminished or interrupted income in the future.

(4) *Telephone listing.* A creditor shall not take into account whether there is a telephone listing in the name of an applicant for consumer credit, but may take into account whether there is a telephone in the applicant's residence.

(5) *Income.* A creditor shall not discount or exclude from consideration the income of an applicant or the spouse of an applicant because of a prohibited basis or because the income is derived from part-time employment or is an annuity, pension, or other retirement benefit; a creditor may consider the amount and probable continuance of any income in evaluating an applicant's creditworthiness. When an applicant relies on alimony, child support, or separate maintenance payments in applying for credit, the creditor shall consider such payments as income to the extent that they are likely to be consistently made.

(6) *Credit history.* To the extent that a creditor considers credit history in evaluating the creditworthiness of similarly qualified applicants for a similar type and amount of credit, in evaluating an applicant's creditworthiness a creditor shall consider:

(i) The credit history, when available, of accounts designated as accounts that the applicant and the applicant's spouse are permitted to use or for which both are contractually liable;

(ii) On the applicant's request, any information the applicant may present that tends to indicate that the credit history being considered by the creditor does not accurately reflect the applicant's creditworthiness; and

(iii) On the applicant's request, the credit history, when available, of any account reported in the name of the applicant's spouse or former spouse that the applicant can demonstrate accurately reflects the applicant's creditworthiness.

(7) *Immigration status.* A creditor may consider whether an applicant is a permanent resident of the United States, the applicant's immigration status, and any additional information that may be necessary to ascertain the creditor's rights and remedies regarding repayment.

(c) *State property laws.* A creditor's consideration or application of state property laws directly or indirectly affecting creditworthiness does not constitute unlawful discrimination for the purposes of the Act or this regulation.

§ 202.7 Rules concerning extensions of credit.

(a) *Individual accounts.* A creditor shall not refuse to grant an individual account to a creditworthy applicant on the basis of sex, marital status, or any other prohibited basis.

(b) *Designation of name.* A creditor shall not refuse to allow an applicant to open or maintain an account in a birth-given first name and a surname that is the applicant's birth-given surname, the spouse's surname, or a combined surname.

(c) *Action concerning existing open-end accounts*—(1) *Limitations.* In the absence of evidence of the applicant's inability or unwillingness to repay, a creditor shall not take any of the following actions regarding an applicant who is contractually liable on an existing open-end account on the basis of the applicant's reaching a certain age or retiring or on the basis of a change in the applicant's name or marital status:

(i) Require a reapplication, except as provided in paragraph (c)(2) of this section;

(ii) Change the terms of the account; or

(iii) Terminate the account.

(2) *Requiring reapplication.* A creditor may require a reapplication for an open-end account on the basis of a change in the marital status of an applicant who is contractually liable if the credit granted was based in whole or in part on income of the applicant's spouse and if information available to the creditor indicates that the applicant's income may not support the amount of credit currently available.

(d) *Signature of spouse or other person*—(1) *Rule for qualified applicant.* Except as provided in this paragraph, a creditor shall not require the signature of an applicant's spouse or other person, other than a joint applicant, on any credit instrument if the applicant qualifies under the creditor's standards of creditworthiness for the amount and terms of the credit requested.

(2) *Unsecured credit.* If an applicant requests unsecured credit and relies in part upon property that the applicant owns jointly with another person to satisfy the creditor's standards of creditworthiness, the creditor may require the signature of the other person only on the instrument(s) necessary, or reasonably believed by the creditor to be necessary, under the law of the state in which the property is located, to enable the creditor to reach the property being relied upon in the event of the death or default of the applicant.

(3) *Unsecured credit—community property states.* If a married applicant requests unsecured credit and resides in a community property state, or if the property upon which the applicant is relying is located in such a state, a creditor may require the signature of the spouse on any instrument necessary, or reasonably believed by the creditor to be necessary, under applicable state law to make the community property available to satisfy the debt in the event of default if:

(i) Applicable state law denies the applicant power to manage or control sufficient community property to qualify for the amount of credit requested under the creditor's standards of creditworthiness; and

(ii) The applicant does not have sufficient separate property to qualify for the amount of credit requested without regard to community property.

(4) *Secured credit.* If an applicant requests secured credit, a creditor may require the signature of the applicant's spouse or other person on any instrument necessary, or reasonably believed by the creditor to be necessary, under applicable state law to make the property being offered as security available to satisfy the debt in the event of default, for example, an instrument to create a valid lien, pass clear title, waive inchoate rights or assign earnings.

(5) *Additional parties.* If, under a creditor's standards of creditworthiness, the personal liability of an additional party is necessary to support the extension of the credit requested, a creditor may request a cosigner, guarantor, or the like. The applicant's spouse may serve as an additional party, but the creditor shall not require that the spouse be the additional party.

(6) *Rights of additional parties.* A creditor shall not impose requirements upon an additional party that the creditor is prohibited from imposing upon an applicant under this section.

(e) *Insurance.* A creditor shall not refuse to extend credit and shall not

[1]The legislative history of the Act indicates that the Congress intended an "effects test" concept, as outlined in the employment field by the Supreme Court in the cases of *Griggs* v. *Duke Power Co.*, 401 U.S. 424 (1971), and *Albemarle Paper Co.* v. *Moody*, 422 U.S. 405 (1975), to be applicable to a creditor's determination of creditworthiness.

terminate an account because credit life, health, accident, disability, or other credit-related insurance is not available on the basis of the applicant's age.

§ 202.8 Special purpose credit programs.

(a) *Standards for programs.* Subject to the provisions of paragraph (b) of this section, the act and this regulation permit a creditor to extend special purpose credit to applicants who meet eligibility requirements under the following types of credit programs:

(1) Any credit assistance program expressly authorized by federal or state law for the benefit of an economically disadvantaged class of persons;

(2) Any credit assistance program offered by a not-for-profit organization, as defined under section 501(c) of the Internal Revenue Code of 1954, as amended, for the benefit of its members or for the benefit of an economically disadvantaged class of persons; or

(3) Any special purpose credit program offered by a for-profit organization or in which such an organization participates to meet special social needs, if:

(i) The program is established and administered pursuant to a written plan that identifies the class of persons that the program is designed to benefit and sets forth the procedures and standards for extending credit pursuant to the program; and

(ii) The program is established and administered to extend credit to a class of persons who, under the organization's customary standards of creditworthiness, probably would not receive such credit or would receive it on less favorable terms than are ordinarily available to other applicants applying to the organization for a similar type and amount of credit.

(b) *Rules in other sections.* (1) *General applicability.* All of the provisions of this regulation apply to each of the special purpose credit programs described in paragraph (a) of this section unless modified by this section.

(2) *Common characteristics.* A program described in paragraph (a)(2) or (a)(3) of this section qualifies as a special purpose credit program only if it was established and is administered so as not to discriminate against an applicant on any prohibited basis; however, all program participants may be required to share one or more common characteristics (for example, race, national origin, or sex) so long as the program was not established and is not administered with the purpose of evading the requirements of the act or this regulation.

(c) *Special rule concerning requests and use of information.* If participants in a special purpose credit program described in paragraph (a) of this section are required to possess one or more common characteristics (for example, race, national origin, or sex) and if the program otherwise satisfies the requirements of paragraph (a) of this section, a creditor may request and consider information regarding the common characteristic(s) in determining the applicant's eligibility for the program.

(d) *Special rule in the case of financial need.* If financial need is one of the criteria under a special purpose program described in paragraph (a) of this section, the creditor may request and consider, in determining an applicant's eligibility for the program, information regarding the applicant's martial status; alimony, child support, and separate maintenance income; and the spouse's financial resources. In addition, a creditor may obtain the signature of an applicant's spouse or other person on an application or credit instrument relating to a special purpose program if the signature is required by Federal or State law.

§ 202.9 Notifications.

(a) *Notification of action taken, ECOA notice, and statement of specific reasons*—(1) *When notification is required.* A creditor shall notify an applicant of action taken within:

(i) 30 days after receiving a completed application concerning the creditor's approval of, counteroffer to, or adverse action on the application;

(ii) 30 days after taking adverse action on an incomplete application, unless notice is provided in accordance with paragraph (c) of this section;

(iii) 30 days after taking adverse action on an existing account; or

(iv) 90 days after notifying the applicant of a counteroffer if the applicant does not expressly accept or use the credit offered.

(2) *Content of notification when adverse action is taken.* A notification given to an applicant when adverse action is taken shall be in writing and shall contain: a statement of the action taken; the name and address of the creditor; a statement of the provisions of section 701(a) of the Act; the name and address of the Federal agency that administers compliance with respect to the creditor; and either:

(i) A statement of specific reasons for the action taken; or

(ii) A disclosure of the applicant's right to a statement of specific reasons within 30 days, if the statement is requested within 60 days of the creditor's notification. The disclosure shall include the name, address, and telephone number of the person or office from which the statement of reasons can be obtained. If the creditor chooses to provide the reasons orally, the creditor shall also disclose the applicant's right to have them confirmed in writing within 30 days of receiving a written request for confirmation from the applicant.

(3) *Notification to business credit applicants.* For business credit, a creditor shall comply with the requirements of this paragraph in the following manner:

(i) With regard to a business that had gross revenues of $1,000,000 or less in its preceding fiscal year (other than an extension of trade credit, credit incident to a factoring agreement, or other similar types of business credit), a creditor shall comply with paragraphs (a) (1) and (2) of this section, except that:

(A) The statement of the action taken may be given orally or in writing, when adverse action is taken;

(B) Disclosure of an applicant's right to a statement of reasons may be given at the time of application, instead of when adverse action is taken, provided the disclosure is in a form the applicant may retain and contains the information required by paragraph (a)(2)(ii) and the ECOA notice specified in paragraph (b)(1) of this section;

(C) For an application made solely by telephone, a creditor satisfies the requirements of this paragraph by an oral statement of the action taken and of the applicant's right to a statement of reasons for adverse action.

(ii) With regard to a business that had gross revenues in excess of $1,000,000 in its preceding fiscal year or an extension of trade credit, credit incident to a factoring agreement, or other similar types of business credit, a creditor shall:

(A) Notify the applicant, orally or in writing, within a reasonable time of the action taken; and

(B) Provide a written statement of the reasons for adverse action and the ECOA notice specified in paragraph (b)(1) of this section if the applicant makes a written request for the reasons within 60 days of being notified of the adverse action.

(b) *Form of ECOA notice and statement of specific reasons.*

(1) *ECOA notice.* To satisfy the disclosure requirements of paragraph (a)(2) of this section regarding section 701(a) of the Act, the creditor shall provide a notice that is substantially similar to the following:

The Federal Equal Credit Opportunity Act prohibits creditors from discriminating against credit applicants on the basis of race, color, religion, national origin, sex, marital status, age (provided the applicant has the capacity to enter into a binding contract); because all or part of the applicant's income derives from any public assistance program; or because the applicant has in good faith exercised any right under the Consumer Credit Protection Act. The Federal agency that administers compliance with this law concerning this creditor is (name and address as specified by the appropriate agency listed in Appendix A of this regulation).

(2) *Statement of specific reasons.* The statement of reasons for adverse action required by paragraph (a)(2)(i) of this section must be specific and indicate the principal reason(s) for the adverse action. Statements that the adverse action was based on the creditor's internal standards or policies or that the applicant failed to achieve the qualifying score on the creditor's credit scoring system are insufficient.

(c) *Incomplete applications*—(1) *Notice alternatives.* Within 30 days after receiving application that is incomplete regarding matters that an applicant can complete, the creditor shall notify the applicant either:

(i) Of action taken, in accordance with paragraph (a) of this section; or

(ii) Of the incompleteness, in accordance with paragraph (c)(2) of this section.

(2) *Notice of incompleteness.* If additional information is needed from an applicant, the creditor shall send a written notice to the applicant specifying the information needed, designating a reasonable period of time for the applicant to provide the information, and informing the applicant that fail-

ure to provide the information requested will result in no further consideration being given to the application. The creditor shall have no further obligation under this section if the applicant fails to respond within the designated time period. If the applicant supplies the requested information within the designated time period, the creditor shall take action on the application and notify the applicant in accordance with paragraph (a) of this section.

(3) *Oral request for information.* At its option, a creditor may inform the applicant orally of the need for additional information; but if the application remains incomplete the creditor shall send a notice in accordance with paragraph (c)(1) of this section.

(d) *Oral notifications by small-volume creditors.* The requirements of this section (including statements of specific reasons) are satisified by oral notifications in the case of any creditor that did not receive more than 150 applications during the preceding calendar year.

(e) *Withdrawal of approved application.* When an applicant submits an application and the parties contemplate that the applicant will inquire about its status, if the creditor approves the application and the applicant has not inquired within 30 days after applying, the creditor may treat the application as withdrawn and need not comply with paragraph (a)(1) of this section.

(f) *Multiple applicants.* When an application involves more than one applicant, notification need only be given to one of them, but must be given to the primary applicant where one is readily apparent.

(g) *Applications submitted through a third party.* When an application is made on behalf of an applicant to more than one creditor and the applicant expressly accepts or uses credit offered by one of the creditors, notification of action taken by any of the other creditors is not required. If no credit is offered or if the applicant does not expressly accept or use any credit offered, each creditor taking adverse action must comply with this section, directly or through a third party. A notice given by a third party shall disclose the identify of each creditor on whose behalf the notice is given.

[Reg. B, 50 FR 48026, Nov. 20, 1985, as amended at 54 FR 50485, Dec. 7, 1989]

§ 202.10 Furnishing of credit information.

(a) *Designation of accounts.* A creditor tht furnishes credit information shall designate:

(1) Any new account to reflect the participation of both spouses if the applicant's spouse is permitted to use or is contractually liable on the account (other than as a guarantor, surety, endorser, or similar party); and

(2) Any existing account to reflect such participation, within 90 days after receiving a written request to do so from one of the spouses.

(b) *Routine reports to consumer reporting agency.* If a creditor furnishes credit information to a consumer reporting agency concerning an account designated to reflect the participation of both spouses, the creditor shall furnish the information in a manner that will enable the agency to provide access to the information in the name of each spouse.

(c) *Reporting in response to inquiry.* If a creditor furnishes credit information in response to an inquiry concerning an account designated to reflect the participation of both spouses, the creditor shall furnish the information in the name of the spouse about whom the information is requested.

§ 202.11 Relation to state law.

(a) *Inconsistent state laws.* Except as otherwise provided in this section, this regulation alters, affects, or preempts only those state laws that are inconsistent with the act and this regulation and then only to the extent of the inconsistency. A state law is not inconsistent if it is more protective of an applicant.

(b) *Preempted provisions of state law.* (1) A state law is deemed to be inconsistent with the requirements of the Act and this regulation and less protective of an applicant within the meaning of section 705(f) of the Act to the extent that the law:

(i) Requires or permits a practice or act prohibited by the Act or this regulation;

(ii) Prohibits the individual extension of consumer credit to both parties to a marriage if each spouse individually and voluntarily applies for such credit;

(iii) Prohibits inquiries or collection of data required to comply with the act or this regulation;

(iv) Prohibits asking or considering age in an empirically derived, demonstrably and statistically sound, credit scoring system to determine a pertinent element of creditworthiness, or to favor an elderly applicant; or

(v) Prohibits inquiries necessary to establish or administer as special purpose credit program as defined by § 202.8.

(2) A creditor, state, or other interested party may request the Board to determine whether a state law is inconsistent with the requirements of the Act and this regulation.

(c) *Laws on finance charges, loan ceilings.* If married applicants voluntarily apply for and obtained individual accounts with the same creditor, the accounts shall not be aggregated or otherwise combined for purposes of determining permissible finance charges or loan ceilings under any federal or state law. Permissible loan ceiling laws shall be construed to permit each spouse to become individually liable up to the amount of the loan ceilings, less the amount for which the applicant is jointly liable.

(d) *State and Federal laws not affected.* This section does not alter or annul any provision of state property laws, laws relating to the disposition of decedents' estates, or Federal or state banking regulations directed only toward insuring the solvency of financial institutions.

(e) *Exemption for state-regulated transactions.* (1) *Applications.* A state may apply to the Board for an exemption from the requirements of the Act and this regulation for any class of credit transactions within the state. The Board will grant such an exemption if the Board determines that:

(i) The class of credit transactions is subject to state law requirements substantially similar to the Act and this regulation or that applicants are afforded greater protection under state law; and

(ii) There is adequate provision for state enforcement.

(2) *Liability and enforcement.* (i) No exemption will extend to the civil liability provisions of section 706 or the administrative enforcement provisions of section 704 of the Act.

(ii) After an exemption has been granted, the requirements of the applicable state law (except for additional requirements not imposed by Federal law) will constitute the requirements of the Act and this regulation.

§ 202.12 Record retention.

(a) *Retention of prohibited information.* A creditor may retain in its files information that is prohibited by the Act or this regulation in evaluating applications, without violating the Act or this regulation, if the information was obtained:

(1) From any source prior to March 23, 1977;

(2) From consumer reporting agencies, an applicant, or others without the specific request of the creditor; or

(3) As required to monitor compliance with the Act and this regulation or other Federal or state statutes or regulaticns.

(b) *Preservation of records*—(1) *Applications.* For 25 months (12 months for business credit) after the date that a creditor notifies an applicant of action taken on an application or of incompleteness, the creditor shall retain in original form or a copy thereof:

(i) Any application that it receives, any information required to be obtained concerning characteristics of the applicant to monitor compliance with the Act and this regulation or other similar law, and any other written or recorded information used in evaluating the application and not returned to the applicant at the applicant's request;

(ii) A copy of the following documents if furnished to the applicant in written form (or, if furnished orally, any notation or memorandum made by the creditor):

(A) The notification of action taken; and

(B) The statement of specific reasons for adverse action; and

(iii) Any written statement submitted by the applicant alleging a violation of the Act or this regulation.

(2) *Existing accounts.* For 25 months (12 months for business credit) after the date that a creditor notifies an applicant of adverse action regarding an existing account, the creditor shall retain as to that account, in original form or a copy thereof:

(i) Any written or recorded information concerning the adverse action; and

(ii) Any written statement submitted by the applicant alleging a violation of the act or this regulation.

(3) *Other applications.* For 25 months (12 months for business credit) after the date that a creditor receives an application for which the creditor is not required to comply with

the notification requirements of § 202.9, the creditor shall retain all written or recorded information in its possession concerning the applicant, including any notation of action taken.

(4) *Enforcement proceedings and investigations.* A creditor shall retain the information specified in this section beyond 25 months (12 months for business credit) if it has actual notice that it is under investigation or is subject to an enforcement proceeding for an alleged violation of the act or this regulation by the Attorney General of the United States or by an enforcement agency charged with monitoring that creditor's compliance with the act and this regulation, or if it has been served with notice of an action filed pursuant to section 706 of the Act and § 202.14 of this regulation. The creditor shall retain the information until final disposition of the matter, unless an earlier time is allowed by order of the agency or court.

(5) *Special rule for certain business credit applications.* With regard to a business with gross revenues in excess of $1,000,000 in its preceding fiscal year, or an extension of trade credit, credit incident to a factoring agreement or other similar types of business credit, the creditor shall retain records for at least 60 days after notifying the applicant of the action taken. If within that time period the applicant requests in writing the reasons for adverse action or that records be retained, the creditor shall retain records for 12 months.

[Reg. B, 50 FR 48026, Nov. 20, 1985, as amended at 54 FR 50486, Dec. 7, 1989]

§ 202.13 Information for monitoring purposes.

(a) *Information to be requested.* A creditor that receives an application for credit primarily for the purchase or refinancing of a dwelling occupied or to be occupied by the applicant as a principal residence, where the extension of credit will be secured by the dwelling, shall request as part of the application the following information regarding the applicant(s):

(1) Race or national origin, using the categories American Indian or Alaskan Native; Asian or Pacific Islander; Black; White; Hispanic; Other (Specify);

(2) Sex;

(3) Marital status, using the categories married, unmarried, and separated; and

(4) Age.

"Dwelling" means a residential structure that contains one to four units, whether or not that structure is attached to real property. The term includes, but is not limited to, an individual condominium or cooperative unit, and a mobile or other manufactured home.

(b) *Obtaining of information.* Questions regarding race or national origin, sex, marital status, and age may be listed, at the creditor's option, on the application form or on a separate form that refers to the application. The applicant(s) shall be asked but not required to supply the requested information. If the applicant(s) chooses not to provide the information or any part of it, that fact shall be noted on the form. The creditor shall then also note on the form, to the extent possible, the race or national origin and sex of the applicant(s) on the basis of visual observation or surname.

(c) *Disclosure to applicant(s).* The creditor shall inform the applicant(s) that the information regarding race or national origin, sex, marital status, and age is being requested by the Federal government for the purpose of monitoring compliance with Federal statutes that prohibit creditors from discriminating against appliants on those bases. The creditor shall also inform the applicant(s) that if the applicant(s) chooses note to provide the information, the creditor is required to note the race or national origin and sex on the basis of visual observation or surname.

(d) *Substitute monitoring program.* A monitoring program required by an agency charged with administrative enforcement under section 704 of the Act may be substituted for the requirements contained in paragraphs (a), (b), and (c).

§ 202.14 Enforcement, penalties and liabilities.

(a) *Administrative enforcement.* (1) As set forth more fully in section 704 of the Act, administrative enforcement of the Act and this regulation regarding certain creditors is assigned to the Comptroller of the Currency, Board of Governors of the Federal Reserve System, Board of Directors of the Federal Deposit Insurance Corporation, Office of Thrift Supervision, National Credit Union Administration, Interstate Commerce Commission, Secretary of Agriculture, Farm Credit Administration, Securities and Exchange Commission, Small Business Administration, and Secretary of Transportation.

(2) Except to the extent that administrative enforcement is specifically assigned to other authorities, compliance with the requirements imposed under the act and this regulation is enforced by the Federal Trade Commission.

(b) *Penalties and liabilities.* (1) Sections 706 (a) and (b) and 702(g) of the Act provide that any creditor that fails to comply with a requirement imposed by the Act or this regulation is subject to civil liability for actual and punitive damages in individual or class actions. Pursuant to sections 704 (b), (c), and (d) and 702(g) of the Act, violations of the Act or regulations also constitute violations of other Federal laws. Liability for punitive damages is restricted to nongovernmental entities and is limited to $10,000 in individual actions and the lesser of $500,000 or 1 percent of the creditor's net worth in class actions. Section 706(c) provides for equitable and declaratory relief and section 706(d) authorizes the awarding of costs and reasonable attorney's fees to an aggrieved applicant in a successful action.

(2) As provided in section 706(f), a civil action under the Act or this regulation may be brought in the appropriate United States district court without regard to the amount in controversy or in any other court of competent jurisdiction within two years after the date of the occurrence of the violation, or within one year after the commencement of an administrative enforcement proceeding or of a civil action brought by the Attorney General of the United States within two years after the alleged violation.

(3) Sections 706 (g) and (h) provide that, if an agency responsible for administrative enforcement is unable to obtain compliance with the Act or this regulation, it may refer the matter to the Attorney General of the United States. On referral, or whenever the Attorney General has reason to believe that one or more creditors are engaged in a pattern or practice in violation of the Act or this regulation, the Attorney General may bring a civil action.

(c) *Failure of compliance.* A creditor's failure to comply with §§ 202.6(b)(6), 202.9, 202.10, 202.12 or 202.13 is not a violation if it results from an inadvertent error. On discovering an error under §§ 202.9 and 202.10, the creditor shall correct it as soon as possible. If a creditor inadvertently obtains the monitoring information regarding the race or national origin and sex of the applicant in a dwelling-related transaction not overed by § 202.13, the creditor may act on and retain the application without violating the regulation.

[Reg. B, 50 FR 48026, Nov. 20, 1985, as amended at 54 FR 53539, Dec. 29, 1989]

Appendix A to Part 202—Federal Enforcement Agencies

The following list indicates the Federal agencies the enforce Regulation B for particular classes of creditors. Any questions concerning a particular creditor should be directed to its enforcement agency.

National Banks

Comptroller of the Currency, Consumer Examinations Division, Washington, DC 20219.

State Member Banks

Federal Reserve Bank serving the district in which the state member bank is located.

Nonmember Insured Banks

Federal Deposit Insurance Corporation Regional Director for the region in which the nonmember insured bank is located.

Savings institutions insured under the Savings Association Insurance Fund of the FDIC and federally chartered saving banks insured under the Bank Insurance Fund of the FDIC (but not including state-chartered savings banks insured under the Bank Insurance Fund).

The District Director of the Office of Thrift Supervision in the District in which the institution is located.

5a. A Guide to California Taxes: Your California Sellers Permit*

1. Obtaining a Seller's Permit

Who must obtain a seller's permit?

You must obtain a seller's permit if you:

- Are engaged in business in California and
- Intend to sell or lease tangible personal property that is ordinarily subject to sales tax

The requirement to obtain a seller's permit applies to individuals as well as corporations, firms, partnerships, and so forth. Both wholesalers and retailers must apply for a permit.

If you do not hold a seller's permit but will hold sales of a temporary nature (such as Christmas tree sales and rummage sales), you must apply for a temporary seller's permit. Temporary permits are issued to cover selling operations of a temporary nature—normally lasting no longer than 30 days at one location. Contact your local Board office for more information.

What does *engaged in business* mean?

You are considered to be engaged in business in California if you:

- Have an office, sales room, warehouse, or similar place of business in this state (even if the location is only temporary)
- Have a sales representative, agent, or canvasser operating in this state
- Receive rental payments from the lease of tangible personal property in this state

There are many other activities that *may* qualify a selling operation as being *engaged in business* in California—such as soliciting orders for tangible personal property through the mail or using television or other advertising methods to solicit sales in this state. Due to the various rules that apply, you should contact a local Board office to determine if you must obtain a permit.

What is meant by *ordinarily subject to sales tax*?

In general, retail sales of tangible personal property in California are subject to sales tax. Examples of tangible personal property include such items as furniture, giftware, toys, candy, antiques, clothing, and so forth.

In addition, some service and labor costs are taxable if they result in the creation of tangible personal property. For example, if you make a ring for a specific customer, you are creating tangible personal property. Therefore, the total amount you charge for the ring (including the charge for labor) would be taxable.

However, labor costs for making repairs (resetting a diamond, for example) are not taxable since they do not result in the creation of tangible personal property. You are only repairing or reconditioning existing property. Likewise, labor charges to install or apply property which has been sold is not ordinarily subject to sales tax (*note*: the labor charge should be stated separately on the bill).

There are many rules governing what is taxable. You are encouraged to contact a local Board office for information on what is taxable for your business. You may also order a tax tip booklet designed for your type of business or request copies of regulations which explain the law more fully. A listing of available publications appears at the back of this pamphlet.

How do I apply for a permit?

Contact a local Board office to request an application. You may have one mailed to you and complete your registration entirely by mail. Or, if you prefer, you may visit a nearby office to obtain an application. Board office telephone numbers are listed at the back of this publication.

What information is needed for an application?

You will be asked to furnish:

- Your social security number
- The name and location of banks where you have an account
- Your driver's license number
- Addresses of property owned, its value, the amount owed, and to whom payments are made
- Names of suppliers
- Name of bookkeeper or accountant
- Names and addresses of three personal references
- Estimated monthly operating expenses for your business (rent, payroll, payments on equipment, and so forth)
- Anticipated average monthly sales and the amount of those sales which are not taxable

Additional information may be required.

If you have business partners, or if the business is managed by corporation officers, those persons will also be asked to furnish some of the information listed above.

Note: The information shown on the face of your seller's permit and the closeout date of your business, if it is terminated, is public record and is furnished to the public.

Do I need more than one permit?

Yes. If you have more than one place of business, a separate permit must be obtained for each location.

Is there a fee charged for a seller's permit?

No. However, the Board may require a security deposit to cover any unpaid taxes that may be owed if, at a later date, the business closes. The amount of the security will be determined at the time you apply.

If I am no longer in business, can I keep my seller's permit?

No. Your permit is valid only so long as you are actively engaged in business. If you are no longer conducting business, you must return your permit to the Board for cancellation. Likewise, the Board may cancel your permit if it finds that you are no longer engaged in business as a seller.

What are my obligations as a permit holder?

As a permit holder, you are required to:

- **Pay sales and use taxes** (see chapters 3, 4, and 5)

---

*"Your California Seller's Permit," Pamphlet 73, is available from the State Board of Equalization. Contact the Board for the most recent information.

You are also required to notify the Board if you:

- **Change your business address**
- **Change business owners** (incorporating a business, forming a partnership, or changing partners is considered a change of ownership and must be reported)
- **Sell your business** (see Chapter 6)
- **Buy another business** (see Chapter 6)
- **Discontinue your business** (see Chapter 6)

2. Using a Resale Certificate

What is a resale certificate?

A resale certificate is a document you give to another seller to enable you to buy tangible personal property for resale without having to pay sales or use tax to that seller. As a retailer, you may also accept resale certificates from other retailers who wish to buy property from you for resale.

What information must a resale certificate include?

The certificate may be in any form, such as a note, letter, or memorandum. However, the certificate must contain the following information:

- The name and address of the purchaser
- The number of the seller's permit held by the purchaser
- A description of the property to be purchased
- A statement that the described property is being purchased for resale. (The certificate must contain words that state the property *will be resold* or is *for resale*. The use of words such as *nontaxable* or *exempt* or similar terms is not acceptable.)
- The date of the document
- The signature of the purchaser or someone approved to act in his or her behalf

The Board of Equalization does not furnish resale certificate forms. However, certificates are available in many office supply and stationery stores.

What are my responsibilities as a buyer using a resale certificate?

You are responsible for providing the seller with a resale certificate indicating your purchase is for resale. You should not use a resale certificate if there is any question the goods will not be resold.

If you are purchasing a combination of items where some are for resale and others are taxable (for personal use, for example), you must clearly indicate to the vendor which items are being purchased for resale.

There may be times when you are not sure whether the items you are purchasing are for resale or for personal use. In such cases, you should pay the sales or use tax to your supplier. If, at a later date, you resell an item before making personal use of it, you can take a credit on the tax return on which you report the sale.

Do I need to submit a resale certificate each time I make a purchase?

No. If you make several purchases from one vendor, you may file one resale certificate with that vendor to be kept on file. If purchase orders are used, in the part of the resale certificate where you describe the property being purchased, you may enter the words *see purchase order*. When you make purchases from that vendor, you must then clearly indicate on the purchase order which items are being purchased for resale. The Board assumes that items not marked for resale are being purchased for personal use and are therefore taxable.

What are my responsibilities as a seller accepting a resale certificate?

As a seller, you should always note the general character of the purchaser's business. If the nature of the business is such that the property purchased would not normally be resold, you should question the use of the certificate. For example, a resale certificate describing the business as a service station should not be accepted for the purchase of a sofa or a similar item not regularly sold by service stations. If the purchaser insists that the item is to be resold, you should either collect tax on the sale or ask for a resale certificate for that particular item.

You should not accept the certificate if you know or have reason to believe the property is being purchased for other than resale.

You are required to take a resale certificate in a timely fashion. That is, it must be taken:

- Before you bill the purchaser for the property, or
- At any time within your normal billing and payment cycle, or
- At any time prior to delivery of the property to the purchaser

You should retain resale certificates you accept from others to substantiate claims that a sale was for resale and therefore not subject to tax.

Can I find out if a seller's permit number is current?

Yes. To help you ensure that a seller's permit is valid, the Board has established a telephone verification service. The service is available Monday through Friday, except holidays, from 8:30 a.m. to 4:30 p.m.

When you call one of the numbers listed below, you will be asked to provide the number of the permit to be verified and the name and business address of the purchaser. To accommodate as many callers as possible, no more than three permit numbers may be verified at one time. Additional information cannot be given.

Hollywood area:	(213) 913-7814	San Jose area:	(408) 277-1003
Oakland area:	(510) 286-4321	Santa Ana area:	(714) 558-4296
Sacramento area:	(916) 324-2397	Van Nuys area:	(818) 901-5525
San Diego area:	(619) 525-4532		

Are there any penalties for the illegal use of a resale certificate?

Yes. It is a misdemeanor to use a resale certificate to avoid payment of tax if you are no longer actively engaged in business or if you know at the time of purchase that the property will not be resold. Each offense is punishable by a fine of $1,000 to $5,000 and imprisonment for up to one year.

In addition, you may have your seller's permit cancelled and may be required to pay:

- The taxes that would have been due on the transaction
- Interest payments
- A penalty of 10 percent or $500, whichever is greater
- A 25 percent penalty for fraud, or intent to evade the tax, on all unreported tax liability

3. Collecting Sales and Use Taxes

What is taxable?

As a retailer, you are required to:

- *Pay sales and use taxes for the products you sell*
- *File tax returns*

This chapter includes a discussion of your responsibilities in collecting taxes. Chapter 4 includes a description of how to report taxes to the Board.

As noted in Chapter 1, retail sales of tangible personal property in California are generally subject to *sales tax*. Examples of tangible personal property include such items as furniture, giftware, toys, antiques, clothing, and so forth. In addition, some service and labor costs are subject to sales tax if they result in the creation of tangible personal property.

In some instances, retailers must pay *use tax*, rather than sales tax, to the Board. The most common example of a purchase subject to the use tax is a purchase of an item for use in California from an out-of-state retailer who is not engaged in business in this state. Out-of-state retailers who are engaged in business in this state are required to collect the use tax, whenever applicable, from the consumer at the time of making the sale. The tax rate for sales and use taxes is the same.

Some sales and purchases are exempt from sales and use tax. Examples of exempt sales include, but are not limited to, sales of certain food products for human consumption, sales to the U.S. Government, and sales of prescription medicines. For more information on exempt sales, you should contact staff at your local Board office or request a copy of pamphlet 61, *Sales and Use Taxes: Exemptions and Exclusions.* (See Chapter 10 for information on how to order publications.)

Who is responsible for paying the correct amount of tax to the Board of Equalization?

As a seller, you are responsible for paying the correct amount of tax to the Board. If you do not pay the correct amount, you may be required to pay any taxes that are due, plus penalties and interest if applicable.

Although you are required to pay sales taxes directly to the Board, the law provides that you may be reimbursed for those taxes by your customers. It is presumed that the customer agrees to the addition of tax if:

- Sales tax reimbursement is shown on the sales check or other proof of sale
- The sales agreement specifically calls for the addition of sales tax reimbursement
- The retailer posts on the business premises in a location visible to purchasers, or includes on a price tag or in an advertisement or other printed material directed to purchasers, a notice to the effect that reimbursement for sales tax will be added to the sales price of all items or certain items, whichever is applicable

How much tax should be collected?

As of July 15, 1991, the standard sales and use tax rate is 7.25 percent statewide. However, in some counties the sales and use tax is 7.50, 7.75, or 8.25 percent. The reason for this difference is that voters in those counties have approved the creation of one or more special tax districts (each funded by a one-half or one-quarter percent tax rate) to provide revenue for transit projects or other government services. Examples of transit agencies supported by district taxes include the Los Angeles County Transportation Commission and the Bay Area Rapid Transit District. Nearly two-thirds of all businesses in the state are located in or do business in special tax districts.

How will I know if I must report special district taxes?

Pamphlet 44-A, *New District Taxes,* includes a list of those counties that have adopted ordinances creating special districts. If you have not already received a copy of Pamphlet 44-A, you may request a copy from one of the field offices listed at the back of this pamphlet. A listing of the special tax districts also appears on the back of the sales and use tax return which you will use to report taxes. (Tax returns are discussed in the next chapter.)

You are subject to special district taxes if you:

- Have a business location or are engaged in business within the district,
- Lease, store, or consume tangible personal property in the district, or
- Sell or lease vehicles, undocumented vessels, or aircraft that will be registered in the district

You are engaged in business in a district if you are a retailer who:

- Maintains, occupies, or uses any type of office, sales room, warehouse, or other place of business in the district, even if it is used temporarily, indirectly, or through an agent; or
- Has any kind of representative operating in the district for the purpose of making sales, making deliveries, or taking orders; or
- Receives rental income from leases of tangible personal property located in the district.

There are some differences between the rules that apply to the collection of taxes in special districts and the collection of sales and use taxes in general. You should refer to Pamphlet 44-A for more information.

What if I collect too much tax?

If you collect more than the amount of tax due, you must either return the excess tax to the customer or pay it to the state.

Are barters and exchanges taxable?

Yes. The use of barter or exchanges is considered the same as making sales or purchases under the sales and use tax law. The fair market value of the property received is normally the amount to which tax will apply.

For example, if you operate a furniture store and accept a television in exchange for a couch, and if the television has a fair market value of $200, you have made a $200 taxable sale. You would report and pay tax based on that amount.

Are trade-ins taxable?

Yes. The value of a trade-in is considered taxable. For example, if you sold a car for $20,000 and accepted a trade-in valued at $4,000 as partial payment, tax would be based on the $20,000 selling price (that is, you could not deduct the value of the trade-in from the sales price of the car being sold when computing sales tax).

If I accept foreign currency as payment, how do I figure tax?

Tax is measured in United States dollars based on the conversion rate of the foreign currency as of the date of the contract for the sale.

Where can I get more information?

It is not possible in the space available to explain what is taxable for every type of business. You are encouraged to use any of the resources listed below to obtain answers to your questions. You may:

- Contact your local Board office and talk to a staff member (see Chapter 8)
- Request a tax tip booklet designed to explain what is taxable for the type of business you are in (see Chapter 10)
- Request copies of the laws and regulations that apply to your business (see chapters 9 and 10)
- Write for advice regarding the taxability of a particular sale or transaction. Written requests should be sent to your local Board office or to the Board's headquarter offices. They should fully describe the facts and circumstances of the transaction.

  Note: If you rely on a written response from the Board regarding the taxability of a particular sale or transaction, you may be relieved of any tax, penalty, or interest related to that transaction if the Board determines that its written response included errors.
- Attend classes offered at some Board offices on how to apply and report taxes. Call your local Board office to find out whether they offer such classes (see Chapter 8)

4. Reporting Taxes

What is a sales and use tax return?

A sales and use tax return is a form used by holders of seller's permits to report the payment of sales and use taxes to the Board of Equalization. The complete title of the form is *State, Local & District Sales & Use Tax Return* (BT-401 series).

When do I file the tax return form?

When you obtain your seller's permit, you will be instructed to file your tax return on a monthly, quarterly, or annual basis (the determination is based on the volume of sales expected for your business). The Board will send you a tax return form to complete at the close of each reporting period.

Returns must be filed no later than the last day of the month following the reporting period. As an example, if your reporting period is quarterly and you are reporting taxes for the period ending March 31, your return must be filed no later than April 30. Or, if you report taxes on a monthly basis and are reporting sales made in July, you would be required to file your return by August 31.

If you do not receive your tax return form within 15 days after the end of the reporting period for your business, you should contact your nearest Board office. You must file a tax return; failure to receive a return from the Board does not excuse you from the requirement to file.

(If the Board notifies you to report taxes on a prepayment basis, you will have different reporting dates from those above. Prepayment accounts are discussed on the next page.)

If I don't owe taxes, do I still file a return?

Yes. You must file a tax return even if no taxes are owed for the reporting period. So, even if you have no sales for the period, or all your sales are nontaxable, you must still file a return.

How do I pay the taxes that are due?

You may pay at any Board office or through the mail. Payments should be by check or money order made payable to the State Board of Equalization. Please do not send cash in the mail.

Can I round to the nearest dollar?

Yes. You may round to the nearest whole dollar on your tax return. An amount of less than 50 cents would be rounded to the next lowest dollar, and an amount of 50 cents or more would be rounded to the next highest dollar. For example, $127.49 would be rounded as $127.00, and $127.50 would be rounded as $128.00.

What happens if I file a late return?

You will be required to pay interest and penalties on late payments. Information appearing on the sales and use tax return explains how to calculate interest and penalties. If you need help with the calculation, please contact your local Board office.

Under limited circumstances, the Board may allow additional time (up to one month) for filing a return. If the additional time is granted and payment is made within that time, you will owe interest on the payment but will not be required to pay a penalty. If you are unable to file your return on time, you should contact your local Board office to learn whether you qualify for an extension. (The law does not recognize lack of funds as good cause.)

What happens if I do not file a tax return?

Failure or refusal to file a tax return is a misdemeanor and punishable by a fine of $1,000 to $5,000 and may result in imprisonment for up to one year. In addition, your seller's permit could be cancelled.

What are prepayment accounts?

Businesses with average monthly taxable sales of $17,000 or more are required to make tax prepayments to the Board. You will be notified in writing if this requirement applies to you. Please do not make prepayments without written authorization

If a customer pays after the tax reporting period, when is the tax due?

Tax is due for the period in which the sale was made. This is not always the same as when payment is made for an item. For example, if a customer purchased an item on December 31 and paid for it on January 10, the tax would be due for the reporting period ending December 31.

I report taxes annually. If I close or sell my business, when do I report taxes?

You are required to file a final tax return when closing your business. If you close your business between January 1 and March 31, you must file your final sales and use tax return by April 30. If you close between April 1 and June 30, the filing date is July 31. If you close between July 1 and September 30, the filing date is October 30. If you close between October 1 and December 31, you must file by January 31.

You should contact your local Board office to obtain a sales and use tax return form to use at the time you close your business. Failure to file a timely return will result in interest and penalty charges.

Where can I get help in filling out a tax return?

You may phone or visit your local Board office for assistance. Staff will explain how to complete the tax return correctly. Although they cannot prepare the return for you or review your records to determine what amount to report, they will be glad to explain what information is required and how to enter it on the form. Chapter 5 includes additional information on sales and use tax returns.

5. Completing Your Tax Return

This chapter is designed to introduce you to the sales and use tax return (form BT 401 series). The return itself includes instructions that will help you complete the form. Since this chapter provides a general overview of the return and may not answer all your questions, you are encouraged to contact staff at your local Board office for more information.

What are the basic steps to follow to complete a tax return?

There are four basic steps to follow in completing your tax return:

- You must first report:
  (1) total gross sales for the reporting period (including lease and rental receipts), and
  (2) total purchases that are subject to use tax (such as purchases made for resale but used for personal use).
- You will then list all exemptions to which you are entitled.
- Third, to determine the dollar amount that is subject to tax, you must subtract the total for exemptions from the total for sales and purchases.
- Finally, using the result from step three, you will calculate the state and county, local, and special district taxes that must be paid to the Board.

What types of sales are included under gross sales?

The law requires that you report any sale of tangible personal property for which you have received or will receive a payment. Normally, payment for those sales will be in the form of money (such as cash and charge sales). However, there may be times when you will receive other forms of payment (such as exchanges of property), and the fair market value of those payments must be reported.

You are not required to include sales or use taxes collected as part of total gross sales. If you prefer, you can report the amount of the sale before tax has been added.

Do not include receipts for the following sales under total gross sales:

- California Lottery, Lotto, Little Lotto, or Decco sales
- Money order service charges

As mentioned in the previous chapter, you must report sales in the tax reporting period in which they occur, which may be different from the time when payment is made. For example, you may sell merchandise to a customer and allow the customer to take possession of the merchandise before paying for it. The sale is considered to have occurred at the time possession changed hands. So, if your customer took possession of the merchandise in April but paid for it in May, the sale is considered to have taken place in April and must be reported for that month.

What are "purchases subject to use tax"?

In general, purchases become subject to use tax under one of the following conditions:

The purchase is made for resale but used for another purpose. As a seller, if you use a resale certificate to purchase merchandise that you intend to resell, the purchase is not subject to California sales tax. However, if you use the merchandise for another purpose before you resell it, the purchase becomes subject to use tax and must be reported on your return.

The purchase is made from an out-of-state retailer. In general, if you purchase taxable merchandise from an out-of-state retailer and use the merchandise for a purpose other than for resale, the purchase is subject to use tax and must be reported.

If you paid another state's sales tax on the purchase, you may receive credit for the tax paid to the other state by reporting the amount under "taxes imposed by other states" at the bottom of your return. (You can be credited up to the amount of California tax due.)

You should be aware that some out-of-state retailers are authorized to collect and report use tax to California. If you have been furnished with a receipt indicating that California use tax has been collected on the sale, and if the amount collected is correct, you do not need to report the purchase on your return.

Can I deduct exempt transactions?

Yes. As mentioned earlier, you will report (1) the total gross sales for your business and (2) purchases that are subject to use tax. Some sales will include items that are exempt from tax and can be deducted to reduce the total amount subject to tax. For example, the total gross sales reported for your business may include certain labor charges that are not taxable. To ensure that you do not pay too much tax, you will need to claim a deduction for the nontaxable labor. There are many other types of deductions that can be claimed. Those deductions are explained in the following paragraphs.

Common Exemptions

The exemptions described below are arranged in the order in which they appear on form BT- 401-A, *State, Local & District Sales & Use Tax Return.* The information provided below is designed to provide an overview of the types of exemptions that can be deducted; it is not designed to provide detailed information about the requirements for each deduction. For additional information, you should contact your local Board office.

Note: You cannot claim deductions for transactions that have not been reported on your tax return. For example, you cannot claim a deduction for a sale to the U.S. Government unless that sale has been reported as part of total gross sales on your return. You must also keep documentation to support your claims for deductions (see Chapter 7 "Keeping Records").

Sales to Other Retailers for Purposes of Resale

Sales made to other retailers who purchased property from you using a resale certificate can be deducted. (If you sell taxable property to another retailer for resale, and if that retailer presents you with a valid resale certificate stating that the property will be resold, you do not collect sales tax from that retailer. Chapter 2 includes additional information on the use of resale certificates.)

Nontaxable Sales of Food Products

Sales of nontaxable food products can be deducted. However, some sales of food products, including most meals, are taxable and cannot be deducted.

For more information on the taxability of food products, you should contact your local Board office. You may also request one of the following booklets: *Tax Tips for the Dining and Beverage Industry; Tax Tips for Package (Off-Sale) Liquor Stores; Tax Tips for Grocery Stores.* (See Chapter 10, "Publications," for ordering information.) Or you can request copies of regulations that pertain to food products. (See Chapter 9, "Regulations," under "Food Products and Meals.")

Nontaxable Labor

Labor charges for repairing, reconditioning, or installing tangible personal property are not subject to tax and can be deducted. For example, labor charges for installing a premanufactured part such as a car radiator would be nontaxable. However, labor charges associated with the creation of tangible personal property (such as charges for making a ring or furniture) are taxable and cannot be deducted. Staff at your Board office can provide you with more information on the taxability of labor charges.

Sales to the United States Government and Other Entities

Sales to the U.S. Government or to some of its agencies and instrumentalities are exempt from tax and can be deducted if they have been reported in total gross sales. Examples of other exempt sales, such as those made to the American Red Cross and to qualified federal credit unions, are listed in the instructions that accompany your return.

Sales made to the state of California or to cities and counties and other local governments in the state are *not* exempt. They are treated like any other sale. That is, you report them under total gross sales and then claim any deductions that might apply. (For example, charges for nontaxable labor could be deducted.)

Interstate and Foreign Commerce Sales

In general, tangible personal property to be shipped to an out-of-state location for use outside of California is exempt from California sales tax and can be listed as a deduction on your tax return. For more information, you should refer to the instructions on your return or request a copy of Regulation 1620, *Interstate and Foreign Commerce.*

Sales Tax

Sales taxes included as part of total gross sales on your return can be deducted. (If you do not report sales taxes as part of total gross sales, you cannot claim a deduction for those taxes since you will have already excluded them from your reporting.)

Bad Debt Losses on Taxable Sales

You can deduct taxable sales that you have been unable to collect payment for (accounts considered worthless according to generally accepted accounting standards or uncollectible accounts and bad checks written off for income tax purposes).

You should claim the deduction on the return filed for the period in which the amount was found worthless and written off. If, at a later point, you do receive payment, you must report it on the sales and use tax return filed for the period in which the payment was made.

You can deduct the amount of a bad check you accepted as payment for taxable goods or services if all the following apply:

- The check is returned unpaid by the bank
- The check is uncollectible by you or your agent
- The amount of the check is charged off for income tax purposes

For more information on how to deduct worthless or uncollectible accounts, you should check with your local Board office.

Cost of Tax-Paid Purchases Resold Prior to Use

You may have purchased tangible personal property and paid sales or use tax on the purchase. Generally, if you sell the property prior to using it, you can deduct the cost of the purchase on your return.

Returned Merchandise

You can claim a deduction for returned merchandise or for orders that have been cancelled or rescinded (the sale must have been reported on your return as part of your total gross sales). In claiming a deduction for returned merchandise, claim only the amount of the purchase before tax was added. For example, if the returned merchandise had been sold for $15 plus tax, you would claim only $15 as a deduction.

Cash Discounts

Some businesses offer price discounts for cash payments or for payments that are made within specified time periods, such as 10 or 30 days. If your business offers such discounts, you may or may not be allowed to claim a cash discount on your return.

If you report the *reduced* selling price (the price after the cash discount) as part of your total gross sales, you cannot claim a cash discount deduction since you will have already excluded that amount from your total sales.

If you report the *full* price of the item (the price before the discount was given) as part of your total gross sales, you can claim a deduction for the cash discount since the price you are reporting overstates the actual selling price.

If a cash discount is given after the sale has been reported to the Board, you may have overpaid the tax due on the sale. To ensure that you receive proper credit, you will need to take a deduction for the discount given. If this situation applies to you, you should contact your local Board office for advice on how to report the cash discount.

Regardless of how you report a cash-discounted sale, sales tax must be based on the actual selling price of the property. Moreover, you cannot deduct a cash discount for nontaxable transactions, such as a cash discount on repair labor.

For more information on cash discounts, please request copies of Regulation 1671, *Trading Stamps and Related Promotional Plans* and Regulation 1700, *Reimbursement for Sales Tax.*

Other Deductions

The deductions listed above are the most common. There are other exemptions that may apply to your business, such as sales of prescribed medicine. If you would like additional information on exempt and deductible sales, you should contact your local Board office or request a copy of pamphlet 61, *Sales and Use Taxes: Exemptions and Exclusions*. For more information on how to request a publication, please see Chapter 10.

5b. A Guide to California Taxes: California Employment Taxes*

Are You An Employer?

Generally, an employer is a person or a legal entity, such as a partnership or a corporation, for whom a worker performs services as an employee. "Employer" can also include associations, trusts, charitable foundations, nonprofit organizations, public entities and other organizations. A person or organization paying wages to a former employee after the employment has ended is also an employer for employment tax purposes.

When Must An Employer Register And Begin Withholding Payroll Taxes?

Different rules apply to different types of employers in determining when each becomes "subject" to the employment tax laws of California. A subject employer is required to file a registration form, DE 1 (refer to pull out in the middle of this guide), within specified time limits (generally within fifteen days) after paying wages to one or more employees. No distinction is made between full-time, part-time, permanent or temporary employees in meeting this requirement or in subsequent reporting. Wages include cash payments, commissions and bonuses and the reasonable cash value for nonmonetary payments such as meals or housing.

Subject employers are required to pay the unemployment insurance (UI) tax and must also pay the employment training tax (ETT). However, different rules apply to the withholding of disability insurance (DI) contributions and personal income taxes (PIT) from employee wages. Not all subject employers are required to withhold PIT and DI for example:

1. Employers In General, Including Agricultural Employers

When wages paid exceed $100 in a calendar quarter an employer becomes subject for UI and DI purposes and must withhold for both DI and PIT. A registration form must be filed within 15 days. Once subject, an employer must report for the current and subsequent calendar years regardless of the amount of wages paid. An agricultural employer is not required to withhold PIT.

Example 1:

An individual proprietor hired a permanent employee during the month of March and paid the employee $75 per month. The employer is subject effective April 1, since the employer has not paid the employee over $100 during the first quarter but will pay over $100 during the second quarter.

Example 2:

A two-person partnership operates a business in which each partner draws a salary of $1,000 during the first quarter. When one partner goes on vacation, an employee is hired and paid $100 during the quarter. The partnership is not required to register as an employer since partnership draws are not considered wages and the employee was not paid wages over $100. (Coverage is available under Section 701. See "Elective Coverage.")

Example 3:

A corporation operates without any employees except for the corporate president. The corporation is an employer and is required to register if the corporate president is paid wages over $100 in a calendar quarter.

2. Nonprofit Entities

Religious, charitable, educational or other nonprofit organizations are also subject for UI, DI, ETT and PIT withholding. However, these entities have a choice of financing methods for unemployment insurance costs. They can either elect to be subject to UI taxes like those paid by commercial employers or they can reimburse the State for full cost of all UI benefits paid to their employees. To choose between the tax-rated or the cost of benefit methods, a nonprofit employer must file form DE 1SNP as well as the DE 1, when registering. Refer to the "BENEFIT COST REIMBURSEMENT" section for complete information. The forms are available from Employment Tax District Offices.

*Excerpted from "Employer's Guide," available from the Employment Development Department. Contact EDD for the most current information.

3. Public Entities

A public entity is defined in Section 135(a)(3) California Unemployment Insurance Code (CUIC) and includes the State of California, any county, city, district, public agency, public authority, school district or community college. A public entity must withhold PIT and provide for UI coverage through tax rated or reimbursable financing. DI withholding is not required but coverage may be extended upon request under certain circumstances. (See "Elective Coverage.")

A public entity must register within 15 days of paying any amount of wages. Special exclusions which apply to public entities are described in "Workers and Services Not Covered By Law." Optional financing is explained under "Benefit Cost Reimbursement."

4. Employers of Domestic Services

An employer of domestic services can be a private household, a local college club, or local chapter of a college fraternity or sorority that pays cash wages of $750 or more in a calendar quarter. Such an employer must withhold DI and report the wages. The employer must register with the Department within 15 days of payment.

When the employer pays cash wages of $1,000 or more in a quarter, the employer must also report for UI purposes and pay UI and ETT. Personal income tax withholding is not required on domestic wages.

Once an employer meets the above limits for **cash** wages, he must include as wages all cash and noncash payments, such as the value of meals and lodging. The employer must continue to report all amounts for the current and the subsequent calendar years. A Household Employers Guide (DE 8829) has been prepared for use by household employers. It may be requested by writing to the Employment Development Department, 805 R Street, Sacramento, CA 95814-6497 or by contacting your local Employment Tax District Office.

Sales And Use Tax

Sales or use tax may apply to your business activities. You may seek written advice regarding the application of tax to your particular business by writing to any State Board of Equalization Office. Requests for advice should fully describe the facts and circumstances of the business.

5c. A Guide to California Taxes: Employer Obligations*

How And Where To Register For An Account Number

Registration forms may be obtained from the nearest Employment Tax District Office. If you obtain a registration form from another source it may not be the latest version. If you are also applying for a sales tax permit at an office of the State Board of Equalization, that agency can assist you in filing for an employer account number. All registered employers must report any subsequent change in business name, address or legal entity, such as individual to partnership or corporation. For your convenience, a pull out registration form is provided in the middle of this guide.

Employers who are subject to only the personal income tax (PIT) withholding provisions are also required to register. Under Section 13070, CUIC, the employer is liable for the required PIT, whether or not it is withheld. The filing of Forms 1099 for their employees does not relieve them of a PIT liability if these 1099 individuals are later held to be subject employees.

When you register you will be assigned an eight-digit account number arranged as follows: 000-0000-0. This number will be on all reporting forms sent to you and on all notices relating to former employees. Use it in all correspondence with this department. If a bank or payroll service prepares your returns be sure to provide them your account number.

Include your nine-digit Federal Identification Number on the registration form so that tax credit can be properly applied when claimed on your Federal Form 940. For information on Federal filing requirements, contact your nearest Internal Revenue Service Office. Information on sales and use tax may be obtained from any State Board of Equalization Office.

When you have completed the registration process you will be sent notices that you must use to inform employees of their rights. These required notices are:

1. DE 1857A, Notice to Employees informing employees of their rights under Unemployment Insurance and Disability Insurance. Employers covered for Unemployment Insurance only receive form DE 1857D, those covered for Disability Insurance only receive form DE 7857A. Post these notices in a prominent location easily seen by your employees. You can request additional copies and a Spanish language translation is available.

2. Pamphlets explaining benefit rights to be given to employees at the time they become unemployed or are ill, injured or hospitalized due to causes not related to work. The pamphlet DE 2320 summarizes unemployment claims information and the pamphlet DE 2515 outlines the State program of disability insurance and must be given to each new employee hired on or after July 1, 1988. Effective July 1, 1989, the law also requires that this pamphlet be given to each employee leaving work due to pregnancy or nonoccupational sickness or injury. Both are available in Spanish. Voluntary plan insurers have similar literature. Voluntary plan employers must also supply claim forms to their employees when disabled.

   Additional State forms can be requested. You may use the order form in the back of this book, the DE 3274, Requisition Form or mail a request for forms to:

   Employment Development Department
805 R Street
Sacramento, CA 95814-6497

*Excerpted from "Employer's Guide," available from the Employment Development Department. Contact EDD for the most current information.

You must also give immediate notice to an employee of his/her discharge, fire, layoff or leave of absence. These notices are not furnished by the Department, but must be furnished by employers at their own expense. No written notice to an employee is required in any of the following situations:

1. Voluntary quit.
2. Promotion or demotion.
3. Change in work assignment or work location.
4. Cessation of work due to a trade dispute.

No format is prescribed. The following format would meet the requirements. You may wish to prepare the notice in duplicate and keep the second copy for your files.

Suggested Format

Notice to Employee as to Change in Relationship (Issued pursuant to provisions of Section 1089 of the California Unemployment Insurance Code).

Name ________________ SSA # ________________

1. You were laid off/discharged on ____________ 19 ____
2. You were on leave of absence starting __________ 19 ____

____
NAME OF EMPLOYER

____
BY

Recordkeeping

You are required to keep your payroll records for at least 4 years. Your books must provide a true and accurate record of all workers, employed or on layoff or leave of absence, and all wages paid. Records must also include:

1. Money wages paid, the dates and amounts of payment and the period covered.
2. For each employee, name, social security number, date hired, date released, occupation and place of work.
3. The fair market value of in-kind wages paid.
4. Special payments such as annual bonuses, gifts, the nature of the payment and the period of employment covered by the special payment.
5. The amounts withheld from employee wages. You may be required to make withholding deposits.

Each year the books of many employers are audited. Other records that you must keep and which could be required during such audits are:

1. Amounts and dates of payment to employees absent due to sickness or injury, whether you made the payment or a third party made the payment.
2. The value of fringe benefits provided to employees.
3. Tips reported by employees.
4. Meals and lodging furnished employees.
5. Amounts and dates of payments under pension and annuity plans and the plans and agreements themselves.
6. Copies of your State and federal payroll returns, income tax withholding certificates (W4s or DE 4s), copies of employees' yearly statements of wages and withholding (W2s).

An employing unit that considers it is not subject under the CUIC, or that it is engaged in exempt employment, or has only exempt employees, must also maintain records and keep them for at least 4 years.

Employers having a payroll processing office outside of California may maintain those records outside this State, provided the records are furnished to the Department upon request.

Multiple Location/Function Employers

When an employer maintains business at more than one physical location and/or conducts more than one business activity/function at the same location, that employer is considered to be a multiple establishment employer. In this case the employer is required to file on a quarterly basis a separate Multiple Worksite Report form to the Labor Market Information Division of EDD as well as their DE 3DP and DE 3B forms to the Tax Branch.

For more information regarding the Multiple Worksite Report and filing requirements, contact:

California Employment Development Department
Labor Market Information Division
BEL Editing Unit
P.O. Box 826220
Sacramento, California 94230-6220
(916) 427-4911

Depositing Withheld Taxes

Although your returns are due quarterly, the deductions taken from your employees' wages may have to be deposited more often. State deposit due dates may differ from federal deposit due dates. You will have to examine the state deposit requirements for each payroll to determine if and when a state deposit is required. State requirements are based on the amount of personal income tax (PIT) withheld, but state Disability Insurance contributions (DI) must also be deposited whenever a PIT deposit is required. Penalty and interest is charged on late deposits.

For additional information on **federal** deposit requirements please contact your nearest **Internal Revenue Service** office.

There are two sets of requirements for making deposits during any quarter; eighth-monthly and monthly. You may be subject to one or both of these requirements depending on the amount of PIT withholding for each payroll in any given quarter.

6. California Consumer Affairs Legislation

The California Consumer Affairs Act of 1970

Although there are many consumer protection laws that impact businesses in California, the 1970 act set the tone for many laws and regulations that followed.

STATE OF CALIFORNIA—STATE AND CONSUMER SERVICES AGENCY

DEPARTMENT OF Consumer Affairs

DIVISION OF CONSUMER SERVICES
LEGAL SERVICES UNIT
1020 N STREET, ROOM A-602
SACRAMENTO, CALIFORNIA 95814
TELEPHONE: (916) 445-5126

THE CALIFORNIA CONSUMER AFFAIRS ACT OF 1970

The Consumer Affairs Act of 1970 (1970 ch. 1394) gives the California Department of Consumer Affairs the broadest and deepest mandate of any government consumer agency.

In its declaration of intent, the Legislature expressed its finding "that vigorous representation and protection of consumer interests are essential to the fair and efficient functioning of a free enterprise market economy." (Bus. & Prof. Code §301.)

The Legislature stated that its intent and purpose in enacting the Consumer Affairs Act was "to promote and protect the interests of the people as consumers." (Bus. & Prof. Code §301.) The Legislature declared that "government advances the interests of consumers by facilitating the proper functioning of the free enterprise market economy through

> "(a) educating and informing the consumer to insure rational consumer choice in the marketplace;
>
> "(b) protecting the consumer from the sale of goods and services through the use of deceptive methods, acts, or practices which are inimical to the general welfare of consumers;
>
> "(c) fostering competition; and
>
> "(d) promoting effective representation of consumers' interests in all branches and levels of government." (Bus. & Prof. Code §301.)

In order to enable the Director of Consumer Affairs to implement these policies, the Consumer Affairs Act established a separate Division of Consumer Services (Bus. & Prof. Code

§303), and gave the Director the power to mobilize the staff of the Division of Consumer Services to --

> "(a) Recommend and propose the enactment of such legislation as necessary to protect and promote the interests of consumers.
>
> "(b) Represent the consumer's interests before federal and state legislative hearings and executive commissions.
>
> "(c) Assist, advise, and cooperate with federal, state, and local agencies and officials to protect and promote the interests of consumers.
>
> "(d) Study, investigate, research, and analyze matters affecting the interests of consumers.
>
> "(e) Hold public hearings, subpoena witnesses, take testimony, compel the production of books, papers, documents, and other evidence, and call upon other state agencies for information.
>
> "(f) Propose and assist in the creation and development of consumer education programs.
>
> "(g) Promote ethical standards of conduct for business and consumers and undertake activities to encourage public responsibility in the production, promotion, sale and lease of consumer goods and services.
>
> "(h) Advise the Governor and Legislature on all matters affecting the interests of consumers.
>
> "(i) Exercise and perform such other functions, powers and duties as may be deemed appropriate to protect and promote the interests of consumers as directed by the Governor or the Legislature.
>
> "(j) Maintain contact and liaison with consumer groups in California and nationally." (Bus. & Prof. Code §310.)

Recognizing the importance that court and administrative agency proceedings have and can have as a consumer law enforcement mechanism and in preserving and promoting consumer options, rights, benefits and interests, the Legislature also gave the Director power to intervene in (Bus. & Prof. Code §320) and institute (Bus. & Prof. Code §321) legal proceedings that may substantially affect the interests of consumers within California.

The Director was also given the power to develop educational materials and disseminate information regarding unsafe products and services, harmful trade practices, and other information relevant to consumers (Bus. & Prof. Code §335), and to receive and act upon individual consumer complaints (Bus. & Prof. Code §§325-326).

The Director was also required to establish a comprehensive library of books, documents, studies and other materials relating to consumers and consumer problems (Bus. & Prof. Code §313), and to publish a bibliography of consumer information available in the Department's library and elsewhere (Bus. & Prof. Code §313.5.)

In 1971, the first year of the Division of Consumer Services, the Director had a staff of ten in the Division to assist in carrying out the mandate of the Consumer Affairs Act.

The inability of such a limited staff to carry out the promises of the Consumer Affairs Act led some consumer activists to characterize the Department as "deceptive packaging". As a result, the Legislature increased the staff of the Division of Consumer Services from thirty-two in 1975 to its present fifty-seven.

The Division of Consumer Services handles consumer complaints, litigates issues which have a major impact on consumers, educates and informs consumers of their marketplace rights and responsibilities, reviews legislation, conducts studies of consumer issues, and represents consumers in various judicial and administrative forums.

RAE:vc
(3/10/83)

It is good business to keep informed about consumer rights. Each year, new legislation is passed that will affect your business. For example, the Consumer Legal Remedies Act protects consumers who run into problems with retailers, finance companies and the like. Under this act consumers may sue *and recoup legal fees* in certain cases where the business owner has violated the law. Another recent California provision says that a written copy of any contract negotiated in Spanish MUST be given to the parties, IN SPANISH. Any contract negotiated in any other language, such as Vietnamese, must be provided to the customer in the native language if requested. These are merely examples of the kind of consumer legislation you will want to stay aware of. Keep in contact with your local and State Chamber of Commerce, as well as the trade association for your line of business. Know who your elected officials are, at the local as well as state level, and ASK QUESTIONS when in doubt. Last of all, see the "Free Help" section of this book.

7. Information Regarding California Securities Laws*

260.102.1. Non-Public Offering Under Subdivision (a) of Section 25102

(a) For the purposes of subdivision (a) of Section 25102 of the Code, no public offering is involved in an offer made to not more than 35 persons. The number of offerees referred to above is exclusive of the following:

(1) Those persons described in Section 25102(i) of the Code and Sections 260.102.10 and 260.105.14 of these rules.

(2) Officers, directors and affiliates of the issuer and those persons described in Section 260.102.13, subject to the definitions and limitations contained in Sections 260.102.12 and 260.102.13.

(3) For the purposes of this section, a husband and wife (together with any custodian or trustee acting for the account of their minor children) are counted as one person and a partnership, corporation or other organization which was not specifically formed for the purpose of

*Excerpted from the California Corporations Code.

purchasing the security offered in reliance upon this exemption, is counted as one person.

(b) This section does not create any presumption that a public offering is involved in offers made to more than 35 persons and the determination of whether or not a transaction not covered by this section involves a public offering shall be made without reference to this section.

260.102.2. Non-Public Offering And Sale

For the purposes of subdivisions (e) and (g) of Section 25102 and subdivision (a) of Section 25104 of the Code, an offer or sale, does not involve any public offering if offers are not made to more than 25 persons and sales are not consummated to more than 10 of such persons, and if all of the offerees either have a preexisting personal or business relationship with the offeror or its partners, officers, directors or controlling persons or by reason of their business or financial experience could be reasonably assumed to have the capacity to protect their own interests in connection with the transaction. The number of offerees and purchasers referred to above is exclusive of any described in subdivision (i) of Section 25102 of the Code and a husband and wife (together with any custodian or trustee acting for the account of their minor children) are counted as one person. This section does not create any presumption that a public offering is involved in offers not conforming to this section, and the determination of whether or not a transaction not covered by this section involves a public offering shall be made without reference to this section.

260.102.3. Evidence of Indebtedness

The term "evidence of indebtedness" as used in subdivision (e) in Section 25102 of the Code does not include a debt security which is convertible into an equity security unless such debt security is convertible into an equity security of the same issuer and the offer and sale of such equity security would be exempt from the provisions of Section 25110 of the Code by any provision other than Section 25102(h) of the Code.

260.102.4. One Class of Stock

For the purposes of subdivision (h) of Section 25102 of the Code:

(a) Debt securities are not a "class of stock" though they may be determined to be "equity" for the purpose of income taxes with respect to either the corporation or the shareholders thereof or for the purpose of priorities in bankruptcy or otherwise among creditors of the corporation.

(b) A corporation does not have "only one class of stock" outstanding if, at the time its shares are issued, there exists or is presently intended to be executed a shareholders' agreement pursuant to which any of the rights, preferences, privileges, or restrictions upon its shares, as enumerated in Subdivision (e) of Section 25103 of the Code, are or would be modified as to any such shares, or as to the holders of any such shares, in a manner not applicable to all outstanding shares.

260.102.5. Beneficial Ownership of Securities

For the purpose of Subdivision (h) of Section 25102 of the Code:

(a) Securities held by a partnership or joint venture shall be considered to be owned beneficially by each of its partners or joint venturers and securities held by a trustee shall be considered to be owned beneficially by each of the beneficiaries, present, future, and contingent of the trust, provided, however, that a future or contingent beneficiary shall be disregarded if he or she is an ancestor, descendant or spouse of a present beneficiary, or a custodian or trustee for his or her account.

(b) In determining the number of persons owning shares beneficially, the provisions of Subdivision (d) of Section 158 of the Code are not controlling and reference should be made to this rule and to Subdivision (h)(5) of Section 25102 of the Code.

260.102.6. Transfer Restriction on Stock Issued under Small Offering Exemption

The issuer of any shares issued pursuant to the exemption contained in Subdivision (h) of Section 25102 of the Code shall comply with Section 260.141.11 of these rules, and it shall be unlawful for the holder of any such shares to make any disposition thereof in nonconformity with such rule, unless and until such conditions are removed pursuant to Section 260.141.12 of these rules.

260.102.7. Selling Expenses

For the purposes of Clause (2) of Subdivision (h) of Section 25102 of the Code, "selling expenses" means commissions, discounts or other compensation paid to any person as remuneration for selling the securities.

260.102.8. Notice of Issuance of Securities Pursuant to Small Offering Exemption

(a) The notice referred to in Clause (5) of Subdivision (h) of Section 25102 of the Code shall be in the following form on 8½" by 11" paper:

(Department of Corporations Use Only)	DEPARTMENT OF CORPORATIONS FILE NO., If Any
Fee Paid $____________	____________
Receipt No. ____________	(Insert File Number(s) of Previous Filings Before the Department, If Any)
____________	

FEE: $25.00 $35.00 $50.00 $150.00 $300.00

Circle or underline appropriate amount of fee. See Corporations Code Section 25608(c).

TO THE COMMISSIONER OF CORPORATIONS OF THE STATE OF CALIFORNIA

Notice of Issuance of Shares Pursuant to Subdivision (h) of Section 25102 of the Corporations Code or Rule 260.103, Title 10, Cal.Admin.Code.

Check one of the following:

( ) Notice pursuant to Section 25102(h) as to an issuance subject to qualification under Corp. Section 25110, unless exempted.

( ) Notice pursuant to Rule 260.103 as to an issuance subject to qualification under Corp. Code Section 25120, unless exempted.

Name of Issuer

State of incorporation

Address of Principal Place of Business

Number and Street City State Zip Code

---

1. Is the issuer a "close corporation" as defined in Section 260.001, Title 10, California Administrative Code? Yes ☐ No ☐

Instruction: Review Corporations Code Section 158 and Rule 260.001, Title 10, California Administrative Code.

---

2. Under the exemption provided by Section 25102(h), shares of voting common stock have been or are proposed to be issued pursuant to this Notice beneficially to not more than 35 persons, whose names are set forth below; together with the names of the corresponding record shareholders if other than the beneficial shareholders:

____________________ ____________________

____________________ ____________________

____________________ ____________________

If additional space is needed for the names of shareholders, check this box and attach a separate sheet of paper to the Notice. ☐

3. The value of the securities sold or proposed to be sold in the transaction, determined in accordance with the provisions of Section 25608(g) of the Corporations Code in connection with the fee required upon filing this notice, is:

(a) $__________ in money.

$__________ in consideration other than money.

(b) ( ) Change in rights, preferences, privileges or restrictions of or on outstanding securities under Rule 260.103 ($25 fee).

4. Immediately after the issuance and sale of such shares, the above-named issuer had or will have only one class of stock outstanding which was or will be owned beneficially by no more than 35 persons.

Instruction: Review Sections 260.102.4 and 260.102.5, Title 10, California Administrative Code.

5. The offer and sale of such shares was not nor will be accompanied by the publication of any advertisement and neither selling expenses nor promotional considerations were or will be given, paid or incurred in connection therewith.

6. To the best knowledge of the issuer, its shareholders (or proposed shareholders) have not entered into or granted, and presently do not intend entering into or granting, a shareholders' agreement, voting agreement, irrevocable proxy or other arrangement the effect of which would cause the statements contained herein to be incorrect.

Instruction: Review Sections 260.001 and 260.102.4, Title 10, California Administrative Code.

7. Pursuant to the requirements of Section 260.102.6 of Title 10 of the California Administrative Code, all certificates evidencing such shares bear or will bear on their face the legend required by Section 260.141.11, and a copy of Section 260.141.11 has been or will be delivered to each issuee or transferee of the shares.

The undersigned officer of the issuer hereby declares that the foregoing is true under penalty of perjury. Executed at __________, __________ this ______ day of ______, 19__.

____

Name

____

Title

NOTE: If the officer signs this form in a jurisdiction which does not permit verifications under penalty of perjury, there must be attached a verification executed and sworn to before a notary public.

OPINION OF COUNSEL

I certify that I am an active member of the State Bar of California. On the basis of the facts stated in the foregoing Notice and other information, including representations as to the type of consideration received or to be received, supplied to me by officials and shareholders of the issuer and by proposed issuees, it is my opinion that the exemption from qualification with the Commissioner of Corporations provided by Subdivision (h) of Section 25102 of the California Corporations Code is available for the offer and sale of the shares referred to in this Notice.

____________________________ ____________________________

Signature Firm Name

____________________________ ____________________________

Name of Member of the State Bar of California Address Tel. No.

(This opinion of counsel must be signed by an active member of the State Bar of California. Type name of attorney, address, phone number and firm name, if any.)

NOTE: If the issuer is a non-California corporation, a Consent to Service of Process as prescribed in the Commissioner's Rule 102.8(b) must be filed concurrently.

Copies of Section 260.141.11 suitable for attachment to share certificates are available from the Department (see Item 7).

(b) The consent to service of process form required by Clause (5) of Subdivision (h) of Section 25102 of the Code shall be in the following form on 8½" by 11" paper:

West's Cal.Corp.Code '91 Pamph.—17

TO THE COMMISSIONER OF CORPORATIONS OF
THE STATE OF CALIFORNIA

CONSENT TO SERVICE OF PROCESS

KNOW ALL MEN BY THESE PRESENTS:

That the undersigned, ____________________________,
(a corporation organized under the laws of the State of ____________________)
hereby irrevocably appoints the Commissioner of Corporations of the State of California, or the Commissioner's successor in office, to be its attorney to receive service of any lawful process in any noncriminal suit, action or proceeding against it, or its successor which arises under the California Corporate Securities Law of 1968 or any rule or order thereunder after this consent has been filed, with the same force and validity as if served personally on the undersigned.

For the purpose of compliance with the Corporations Code of the State of California, notice of the service and a copy of the process should be sent by registered or certified mail to the undersigned at the following address:

____

Name

____

Street Address

____

City State Zip Code

DATED: ____________, 19___.

____

By____________________________

Title____________________________

CORPORATE ACKNOWLEDGMENT

STATE OF ____________)
) ss.
COUNTY OF ____________)

On this _____ day of __________, in the year __________, before me __________, personally appeared __________ personally known to me (or proved to me on the basis of satisfactory evidence) to be the person that executed this instrument on behalf of the corporation and acknowledged to me that the corporation executed it.

IN WITNESS WHEREOF I have hereunto set my hand and official seal.

____

[NOTARIAL SEAL] Notary Public
My Commission expires: ____________

260.102.9. Proof of Mailing

The mailing of the notice referred to in Section 260.102.8 of these rules may be proved in the manner provided in Section 1013a of the California Code of Civil Procedure for proof of mailing of papers in civil actions, except that the affidavit of mailing need not be filed, but should be retained in duplicate in the records of the attorney and of the issuer.

260.102.10. Designation of Institutional Investors and Governmental Agencies and Instrumentalities by Class

The following institutional investors and governmental agencies and instrumentalities are hereby designated by class as persons to whom an offer or sale may be made without qualification pursuant to the exemption contained in Subdivision (i) of Section 25102 of the Code:

(a) Any organization described in Section 501(c)(3) of the Internal Revenue Code, as amended December 29, 1981, which has total assets (including endowment, annuity and life income funds) of not less than $5,000,000 according to its most recent audited financial statement.

(b) Any corporation which has a net worth on a consolidated basis according to its most recent audited financial statement of not less than $14,000,000, provided that, if the securities being acquired pursuant to an exemption under this subsection (b) are common stock of a corporation or securities exchangeable for or convertible into common stock of a corporation, (1) the holders of less than 25% of the outstanding shares of such common stock (computed as provided in Section 25103(d) of the Corporate Securities Law, but deeming outstanding all shares of common stock issuable upon exchange or conversion of securities presently exchangeable for or convertible into common stock) have addresses in this state according to the records of the issuer of such common stock as of the most recent record date of such issuer for any action requiring the determination of shareholders of record, or as of three months prior to such offer or sale, whichever is most recent; or (2) such securities (plus any other similar securities held by the purchaser) will not represent more than five per cent of the total number of outstanding shares of common stock of the issuer assuming the exchange or conversion of all securities exchangeable for or convertible into common stock (unless all such shares of common stock are owned by corporations meeting the net worth test of this subsection (b)) provided, however, that the foregoing limitations with respect to transactions in common shares or securities convertible into common shares shall not apply to a transaction (1) in which such securities are offered pro rata to the holders of the outstanding common shares, (2) which is approved by the holders of 75% or more of the outstanding common shares, or (3) there are no common shares or securities convertible into common shares outstanding prior to the transaction.

(c) Any wholly-owned subsidiary of any institutional investor designated in Subdivision (i) of Section 25102 of the Code or in this Section.

260.102.12. Limited Offering Exemption—Interpretations

(a) The provisions of this section apply to the provisions of Section 25102(f) of the Code.

(b) Integration. The term "transaction" does not include

(1) any offer or sale of a security made more than 6 months before the start of an offering under the exemption or made more than six months after completion of an offering under the exemption, so long as during those six month periods there are no offers or sales of securities by or for the issuer that are of the same or a similar class as those offered or sold pursuant to the exemption, other than those offers or sales of securities under any purchase, savings, option, bonus, appreciation, profit-sharing, thrift, incentive, pension or similar plan solely for employees, directors, trustees or officers of the issuer or a subsidiary of the issuer (note: Section 25102(f) is not available for an offer or sale of a security to a pension or profit-sharing trust of the issuer),

(2) any offer or sale of a security pursuant to a qualification under Section 25110 or 25120 which became effective after the filing of the notice of the transaction pursuant to Rule 260.102.14, or in which the application for qualification discloses the transaction under the exemption, whether past, current or proposed. This subsection does not create any presumption that offers and sales not excluded from the transaction by its provisions are to be integrated for the purposes of the exemption and that determination shall be made without reference to this subsection.

(c) Purchaser. The term "purchaser" means a person who acquires the beneficial ownership of the security, whether individually or in joint ownership, in the transaction under the exemption. Each person who takes in joint ownership with another is to be counted as one except as otherwise provided in Section 25102(f).

(d) Relationship.

(1) The term "preexisting personal or business relationship" includes any relationship consisting of personal or business contacts of a nature and duration such as would enable a reasonably prudent purchaser to be aware of the character, business acumen and general business and financial circumstances of the person with whom such relationship exists. A relationship of employer-employee, or as a security holder of the issuer, or as a customer of a broker-dealer, investment adviser or other person, does not necessarily involve contacts of a nature which are sufficient to establish a "preexisting personal or business relationship" within the meaning of Section 25102(f). This subsection does not create any presumption that relationships not falling within its terms are not within the statutory language, and the determination of whether or not such a relationship is within the statutory language shall be made without reference to this subsection.

(2) The phrase "all purchasers" used in Section 25102(f)(2) of the Code does not include purchasers excluded from the count of purchasers by virtue of Section 25102(f)(4) or Rule 260.102.13.

(e) Partners. The term "partners" in Section 25102(f)(2) means general partners.

(f) Controlling Person. The term "controlling person of the offeror" includes but is not limited to a person who, in connection with transactions within one year of the formation of the issuer, is a "promoter" of the issuer. "Promoter" means a person who, acting alone or in conjunction with one or more other persons, takes the initiative in founding and organizing the business or enterprise of an issuer.

(g) Professional Advisor. The term "professional advisor" means a person who, as a regular part of such person's business, is customarily relied upon by others for investment recommendations or decisions, and who is customarily compensated for such services, either specifically or by way of compensation for related professional services, and attorneys and certified public accountants.

(1) The foregoing includes but is not limited to persons licensed or registered as broker-dealers, agents, investment advisers, banks and savings and loan associations. The foregoing also includes licensed real estate brokers with respect to those securities referred to in Section 25206 of the Code.

(2) A person is not the professional advisor of a purchaser unless designated as such by the purchaser.

(h) Unaffiliated. The relationships which will render a person not "unaffiliated" include

(1) a present or intended relationship of employment, either as an employee, employer, independent contractor or principal,

(2) any relationship within the definition of the term "affiliate" or as an officer or director of an affiliate and

(3) the beneficial ownership by the professional advisor of securities of the issuer or its affiliates or selling agent, except that the ownership of 1% or less of such securities shall not render a professional advisor not unaffiliated.

(i) Affiliate. "Affiliate" of the issuer means a person controlling, controlled by or under common control with, the issuer. A person controls another person within the meaning of this subsection through the possession, direct or indirect, of the power to direct or cause the direction of the management, policies or actions of such other person.

(j) Publication of Advertising. Section 25102(f)(4) of the Code is to be interpreted so as to facilitate the circulation of disclosure materials to offerees and purchasers, so long as such materials are not disseminated to the public (see Sections 25002 and 25014 of the Code). Private placement memoranda, offering circulars and similar disclosure documents are not "disseminated to the public" for the purposes of Section 25102(f) of the Code if the issuer limits such circulation

(1) to persons reasonably believed to be interested in purchasing the securities or

(2) to persons whom the issuer believes may meet the qualifications required of purchasers pursuant to such section and the rules thereunder, provided with respect to clause (1) and clause (2) that neither the issuer nor any person acting on its behalf shall offer or sell the securities by any form of general solicitation or general advertising, including, but not limited to, the following:

(A) Any advertisement, article, notice or other communication published in any newspaper, magazine, or similar media or broadcast over television or radio; and

(B) Any seminar or meeting whose attendees have been invited by any general solicitation or general advertising. The preceding sentence does not create any presumption that a dissemination of materials otherwise than as described therein is a "publication of advertising", and the determination of that question shall be made without reference to that sentence.

(k) Institutional Investors. The reference in Section 25102(f) of the Code to purchasers described in Section 25102(i) includes those persons designated in Rule 260.-102.10.

(*l*) For purposes of Section 25102(f), when a person is both an "affiliate of the issuer" or a purchaser excluded by Rule 260.102.13 and a partnership, corporation or other organization which was specifically formed for the purpose of purchasing the security offered in reliance upon the exemption, each beneficial holder of its securities shall be counted or excluded from the count in accordance with the provisions of Section 25102(f).

260.102.13. Limited Offering Exemption—Excluded Purchasers

For the purposes of Section 25102(f) of the Code, the following purchasers are excluded from the count of purchasers for purposes of Subparagraph (1) of that subdivision, except as provided in Subsection (*l*) of Rule 260.102.12:

(a) The trustee of an issuer which is a trust and the general partner of an issuer which is a partnership, who exercise managerial functions with respect to such entities, and any officer, director or general partner of a general partner of an issuer which is a partnership.

(b) Any person who occupies a position with the issuer, or with a general partner of an issuer which is a partnership, with duties and authority substantially similar to those of an executive officer of a corporation.

(c) (1) Any relative, spouse or relative of the spouse of a purchaser who has the same principal residence as the purchaser;

(2) any trust or estate in which a purchaser and any of the persons related to such purchaser as specified in Clause (1) or Clause (3) collectively have more than 50% of the beneficial interest (excluding contingent interests); and

(3) any corporation or other organization of which a purchaser and any of the persons related to such purchaser as specified in Clause (1) or Clause (2) collectively are beneficial owners of more than 50% of the equity securities (excluding director's qualifying shares) or equity interests. "Relative" means a person related by blood, marriage or adoption.

(d) Any individual who is a "promoter" of the issuer, as defined in Subsection (f) of Section 260.102.12.

(e) Any person who purchases $150,000 or more of the securities offered in the transaction, provided each such purchaser meets any one of the following, or who the issuer reasonably believes comes within any one of the following:

(1) Such person, or such person's professional advisor, has the capacity to protect such person's own interests in connection with the transaction, as provided in Section 25102(f)(2).

(2) Such person is able to bear the economic risk of such person's investment in the transaction.

(3) The investment (including mandatory assessments) does not exceed 10% of such person's net worth or joint net worth with that person's spouse.

(f) A small business investment company licensed by the U.S. Small Business Administration under Section 301(c) or (d) of the Small Business Investment Company Act of 1958, and a business development company as defined in Section 2(a)(48) of the Investment Company Act of 1940, and a private business development company as defined in Section 202(a)(22) of the Investment Advisors Act of 1940.

(g) An individual whose net worth, or whose joint net worth with such individual's spouse, at the time of purchase exceeds $1,000,000, or an individual whose income, or whose joint income with such individual's spouse, exceeded $200,000 in each of the two most recent years and who reasonably expects an income in excess of $200,000 in the current year, provided in either case that such purchaser meets the provisions of, or the issuer reasonably believes that the purchaser meets the provisions of, subparagraph (1), (2), or (3) of subsection (e). For the purposes of this subsection, the terms "income" and "net worth" shall be interpreted in a manner consistent with the interpretation of those terms as used in subsections (6) and (7) of Rule 230.501(a) under the Securities Act of 1933 (17 CFR Part 230).

(h) Any entity in which all of the equity owners are persons specified in Section 25102(i) of the Code; Rule 260.102.10; or subsections (a), (b), (c), (d), (f) and (g) of this rule; or who are "officers, directors or affiliates of the issuer" as that term is used in Section 25102(f) of the Code.

260.102.14. Limited Offering Exemption—Notice of Transaction

(a) An issuer who conducts a transaction under Section 25102(f) of the Code shall file a notice with the Commissioner as follows:

(1) If in connection with the transaction the issuer is filing a notice with the Securities and Exchange Commission pursuant to Section 4(6) of the Securities Act of 1933 or Regulation D (Rule 230.503), the notice may be a copy of the form first filed pursuant to those provisions. The fee required by Section 25608(c) of the Code must accompany the filing. Each issuer (other than a California corporation) must also file a consent to service of process (Form 260.165), unless it already has a consent to service on file with the Commissioner. The filing should be accompanied with a cover letter indicating that the filing is pursuant to Section 25102(f), and if a consent to service is not included, a statement that the issuer already has a consent to service on file with the Commissioner.

(2) Unless a notice is filed pursuant to paragraph (1), the notice shall be in the form and contain the information specified by subsection (c) and in accordance with the instructions in subsection (d).

(b) A notice required by this section shall be filed with the Commissioner no later than 15 calendar days after the first sale of a security in the transaction in this state. No notice is required if none of the securities offered are purchased in this state.

(c) Form of Notice. The following form is to be used for transactions covered by subsection (a)(2):

(Department of Corporations Use Only) Fee paid $ ____________ ____________	DEPARTMENT OF CORPORATIONS FILE NO., if any: ____________ ____________
Receipt No. ____________ ____________ ____________	Insert File number(s) of Previous Filings Before the Department, if any.

FEE: $25.00 $35.00 $50.00 $150.00 $300.00

(Circle the appropriate amount of fee. See Corporations Code Section 25608(c))

COMMISSIONER OF CORPORATIONS
STATE OF CALIFORNIA

NOTICE OF TRANSACTION PURSUANT TO CORPORATIONS CODE SECTION 25102(f)

A. Check one: Transaction under ( ) Section 25102(f) ( ) Rule 260.103.

1. Name of Issuer:

____

2. Address of Issuer:

____

Street City State Zip

Mailing Address:

____

Street City State Zip

3. Area Code and Telephone Number: ______________________________
4. Issuer's state (or other jurisdiction) of incorporation or organization:

____

5. Title of class or classes of securities sold in transaction:

____

____

6. The value of the securities sold or proposed to be sold in the transaction, determined in accordance with Corporations Code Sec. 25608(g) in connection with the fee required upon filing this notice, is (fee based on amount shown in line (iii) under "Total Offering"):

	California	*Total Offering*
(a) (i) in money	$________	$________
(ii) in consideration other than money	$________	$________
(iii) total of (i) and (ii)	$________	$________

(b) ( ) Change in rights, preferences, privileges or restrictions of or on outstanding securities ($25.00 fee.) (See Rule 260.103.)

7. Type of filing under Securities Act of 1933, if applicable: ______________________________

____

8. Date of Notice: ______________ ______________
Issuer

( ) Check if issuer already has a consent to service of process on file with the Commissioner.

______________________________ ______________________________
Authorized Signature on behalf of issuer Print name and title of signatory

Name, Address and Phone number of contact person: ______________________________

Instruction: Each issuer (other than a California Corporation) filing a notice under Section 25102(f) must file a consent to service of process (Form 260.165), unless it already has a consent to service on file with the Commissioner.

(d) Instructions. The following instructions apply to the form specified in subsection (c):

COMMISSIONER OF CORPORATIONS
STATE OF CALIFORNIA

NOTICE OF TRANSACTION PURSUANT TO CORPORATIONS CODE SECTION 25102(f)

INSTRUCTIONS

1. This Notice is to provide information on transactions conducted under the section 25102(f) exemption from the qualification requirements of Section 25110 of the Corporate Securities Law of 1968 and under the Rule 260.103 exemption from the qualification requirements of Section 25120 of that Law. The form is not designed to indicate whether or not the transaction complies with the requirements of those exemptions but only to provide notice to the commissioner that the exemption is being relied on.

2. When to File Notice. The Notice must be filed with, or mailed to, the Commissioner within 15 calendar days after the first sale of a security in the transaction in this state, or, if the issuer has failed to file a notice, within 15 business days after demand by the Commissioner. The first sale in this state occurs when the issuer has obtained a contractual commitment in this state to purchase one or more of the securities the issuer intends to sell in connection with the transaction. No notice is required if none of the securities offered are purchased in this state. No subsequent notices are required for sales in connection with the same transaction. The information required by the form is to relate to the entire transaction, not just the first sale or sales in this state.

3. The Notice may be filed in person or by mail at any office of the Department.

The Heading. If the issuer has previously qualified securities with the Department, insert the file number of the qualification in the upper right hand corner of the form in the space provided. Circle the appropriate fee for filing this Notice. The fee is based on the value of all securities sold or intended to be sold in the entire transaction as follows (see Item 6 for valuing securities):

Value of Securities	Filing Fee
$25,000 or less	$25
$25,001–$100,000	$35
$100,001–$500,000	$50
$500,001–$1,000,000	$150
Over $1,000,000	$300

Item A. Check appropriate box for exemption being relied on.

Item 1. Give the issuer's legal name.

Item 2. Give the street address, and the mailing address if different, of the issuer's principal place of business.

Item 3. Give the telephone number of issuer's principal place of business.

Item 4. Give the name of the state or other jurisdiction under whose laws the issuer is incorporated or organized. If the issuer is not incorporated or organized under the laws of any jurisdiction, provide the name of the jurisdiction where issuer is domiciled and include parenthetical "(domicile)".

Item 5. Set forth the name or title of each class or type of security to be sold in the transaction.

Item 6. See Corp. Code Sec. 25608(g). Generally, the value of the securities shall be the price at which the issuer proposes to sell the securities, as alleged in the notice, or the actual value of the consideration (if other than money) to be received in exchange for the securities. See Sec. 25608(g) for valuing voting trust certificates, warrants, rights, and share dividends.

Item 7. If the transaction was registered under the Securities Act of 1933, insert "registered". If conducted pursuant to an exemption from registration under that Act which requires a filing with the Securities and Exchange Commission, indicate the number of the rule pursuant to which such filing was made. If no such filing was required, insert "none".

Item 8. Date and Signature. The notice should be signed by an authorized officer, director, general partner or trustee of the issuer (or a person occupying a position with the issuer of equivalent responsibility) or by the authorized attorney of the issuer. If the person the Department is to contact in the event of questions concerning the transaction or the notice is different than the signer, insert the contact person's name, telephone number and correspondence address in the spaces provided. Otherwise, provide this information with respect to the signer.

Filing Fee. Each notice, whether under 25102(f) or Rule 260.103, must be accompanied by the filing fee required by Section 25608(c) of the Code.

Corporations Code Section 25165 requires each issuer, other than a California corporation, to file a consent to service of process with the notice filed pursuant to Section 25102(f) unless it already has a consent to service on file with the Commissioner. Use Form 260.165 (see Rule 260.165, Title 10, California Administrative Code).

8. Information Regarding the Federal Securities Laws

What are the Federal securities laws?

The securities laws were, in large part, enacted as a reaction to the chaotic securities markets of the 1920's, when stocks and bonds were often sold on the basis of glittering promises of fantastic profits, without disclosure of any meaningful information to investors. These conditions were major contributors to the disastrous Stock Market Crash of 1929. In response, the Congress passed the Securities Act of 1933 (Securities Act) and the Securities Exchange Act of 1934 (Exchange Act), and set up the Securities and Exchange Commission (SEC) to administer those laws.

The Securities Act requires a company to make "full disclosure" of all material facts before it offers its securities to the public. In enforcing this law, the SEC has no authority to evaluate the quality of securities offered nor to pass judgement on the merits of each offering. Rather, the "disclosure" approach permits a company to offer its securities for sale, regardless of the merit of the investment, so long as it has disclosed sufficient, accurate information about the business it conducts or proposes to conduct.

The Exchange Act sets up requirements for continued disclosure by most publicly held companies on a periodic basis. The company has an obligation under the Exchange Act to keep its shareholders informed of its business operations, financial condition and management.

There are, however, alternatives to registration under the Securities Act, and exemptions from the Exchange Act reporting requirements, which are discussed elsewhere in this brochure.

Is any special help available for small businesses that want to sell securities?

The SEC's primary responsibility under the securities laws is to protect investors and ensure that the capital markets operate in a fair and orderly manner. However, the Commission believes that its regulations should not have the effect of inadvertently impairing capital formation by small businesses. Therefore, the SEC has for some time been examining steps that might be taken to facilitate capital raising by small businesses and reduce undue regulatory burdens arising from the Federal securities laws.

The Office of Small Business Policy

In furtherance of this effort, the SEC, in 1979, established the Office of Small Business Policy within its Division of Corporation Finance. The mission of this Office is to:

- spearhead the SEC's small business rulemaking initiatives;
- review and comment upon the impact of various SEC rule proposals on smaller issuers; and
- serve as a liaison with Congressional committees, government agencies, and other groups concerned with small business.

Registration Alternatives and Exemptions

The SEC has adopted a number of measures which are designed to facilitate capital formation by small business. Alternatives to, or exemptions from full registration are discussed in detail elsewhere in this brochure. It is hoped that these regulations will ease the burden of regulation for those small businesses which qualify to take advantage of them, and will enable these companies to raise needed capital.

Should my company "go public"?

The first thing to be considered when a small business is seeking additional capital is whether or not "going public" is the right step to take. There are both advantages and disadvantages to making a registered public offering of your securities and these should be carefully considered. Some of the factors to be weighed are listed below.

Advantages

- Your company may become more widely known.
- Future financing may be more easily obtainable since the company can offer investors a security that is liquid--more freely tradeable--and that has an ascertainable market value.
- Controlling shareholders of the company have a ready market for their shares, which means that they can more easily sell their interests at retirement or for some other reason.
- The company may be able to attract and retain more highly qualified personnel if it can offer stock options, bonuses, or other incentives that have an ascertainable market value.

Disadvantages

- The company assumes additional responsibilities to its shareholders and the general public, the most important of which is its continuing obligations to inform its shareholders of the company's business operations, financial condition, and management. Such disclosure may be expensive and time consuming, and exposes the company and its management to certain liabilities.
- The management of a company may lose some flexibility in directing the company's affairs, particularly with regard to actions requiring shareholder approval.

How does a small business "go public"?

Section 5 of the Securities Act requires that a registration statement be filed with the SEC before securities are offered for sale to the public, and prohibits the sale of those securities until the registration statement becomes "effective". The basic registration statement consists of two principal parts:

Part I is the legal offering or "selling" document, called the prospectus, which must be furnished to all purchasers of the securities. The company--the "issuer" of the securities--is required to put the essential facts regarding its business operations, financial condition, and management in the printed prospectus. This document must be made available to everyone who buys the new issue, and also to anyone who has been made an offer to purchase the securities.

Part II contains supplemental information which is available for inspection by the public at the SEC. (Copies of all disclosure documents filed with the SEC may be obtained by mail, for a nominal copying charge.)

Basic Registration of Securities

The basic registration form, Form S-1, requires, among other things, a description of the company's business; its properties; material transactions between the company and its officers and directors; competition; identification of officers and directors and their remuneration; certain pending legal proceedings; the plan for distributing the securities and the intended use of the proceeds. It is not prepared as a fill-in-the-blank form like a tax return, but, rather, is similar to a brochure, with the information provided in a narrative format. In addition, there are detailed requirements concerning financial statements, including that such statements be audited by an independent certified public accountant. In addition to the information expressly required by the form, the company must also provide any other information that is necessary to make the statements complete and not misleading. If there are sufficient adverse or risk factors concerning the offering and the issuer--such as lack of business operating history, adverse economic conditions in a particular industry, lack of market for the securities offered, dependence upon key personnel, etc.--they must be set forth prominently in the prospectus, usually in the beginning.

Alternative Registration for Small Issues

In April 1979, the SEC adopted a simplified registration form for use by certain domestic or Canadian issuers, as an alternative to Form S-1. Form S-18 is available for the registration of securities to be sold to the public for cash not exceeding an aggregate offering price of $5 million, provided such issuers are not subject to the SEC's continuous reporting requirements under the Exchange Act. Form S-18 provides for reduced disclosure requirements and has other attributes which are intended to result in a more timely and less expensive registration process for the smaller issuer who wishes to gain access to the public capital markets.

Although many of the requirements for an S-18 registration statement are the same as those for a full registration, Form S-18 permits the issuer:

- to provide audited financial statements for two fiscal years prepared in accordance with generally accepted accounting principals, whereas Form S-1 requires the issuer to provide audited financial statements for three fiscal years prepared in accordance with more detailed SEC regulations;
- to include less extensive narrative disclosure, particularly in the areas of the description of business, than that required by Form S-1;
- to file with either the SEC's Regional Office nearest the place where the company's principal business operations are conducted, or with the SEC's Division of Corporation Finance, in Washington, D.C., where all Form S-1 registration statements are filed and reviewed. The primary advantage of regional filing is that Regional Office personnel may be more familiar with local economic conditions, the business community, the financial environment, and, in some cases, the background and history of the company.

After a company becomes "public", what are its disclosure obligations?

The Exchange Act requires a company to file certain periodic reports once its registration statement has been declared effective. This obligation continues indefinitely unless, at the beginning of any subsequent fiscal year, the class of securities offered is held of record by less than 300 persons, or at the beginning of any subsequent fiscal year, other than the two fiscal years immediately succeeding the year the registration statement became effective, all securities offered are held of record by less than 500 persons and the issuer has had less than $3 million in total assets for each of its last three fiscal years. In these cases, the reporting obligation is suspended. This means that a company must continuously disclose certain information about its operations, its officers, directors and certain shareholders (including salary, various fringe benefits, and inside transactions between the company and management), the financial condition of the business (including audited financial statements by an independent certified public accountant), its competitive position, material terms of certain contracts or lease agreements, etc.

Even if a company has not filed a registration statement which has been declared effective, the Exchange Act requires all companies with total assets exceeding $3 million and a class of equity securities held by 500 or more persons, to register these securities, and file the same supplementary, periodic, and current reports as noted above. In addition, the Commission's rules require that if proxies are solicited from holders of securities registered under the Exchange Act, the company must furnish all shareholders proxy statements disclosing all of the material facts concerning the matters on which they are being asked to vote. If the proxy solicitation by management relates to an annual meeting at which directors are to be elected, the Commission's proxy rules require the company to furnish each shareholder an annual report that discloses certain information about the company, including audited financial statements for its latest fiscal year.

Are there ways to sell securities legally without registering with the SEC?

The Securities Act provides several exemptions from the registration requirements, and the most common of them are discussed below. It should be pointed out, however, that the purchase or sale of even an exempt security is subject to the antifraud provisions of the Federal securities laws. This means that there is a risk of exposure to private or government legal action, including criminal sanctions, for false or misleading statements, whether oral or written. It should also be noted that if all of the conditions of the exemptions discussed below are not met, each purchaser may seek to have his purchase price refunded. In addition, the fact that an offering may be exempt from certain provisions of the Federal securities laws does not necessarily mean that it is exempt from the notice and filing obligations of various state laws. Accordingly, an issuer is cautioned to check with the appropriate state authority before proceeding with an offering in reliance on any of the exemptions discussed below.

Intrastate Offering Exemption

Section 3(a)(11) of the Securities Act is generally known as the "intrastate offering exemption." It exempts from registration any security which is a part of an issue offered and sold only to persons who are residents of a single state or territory, where the issuer of such security is a person who is both a resident and is doing business within that state or territory. This exemption is intended to facilitate the local financing of local business operations. In order to qualify for the exemption, the company:

- must be incorporated in the state in which it is making the offering;
- must carry out a significant amount of its business in such state; and
- must make offers and sales only to residents of the state.

Although there is no fixed limit on the size of the offering or the number of purchasers, the company has the obligation to determine the residence of each purchaser. If any of the securities are offered or sold to one out-of-state purchaser, the exemption may be lost. In addition, if any of the securities are resold by an original resident purchaser to a person resident outside the state within nine months after the offering by the issuer is completed, the entire transaction may be in violation of the Securities Act. Therefore, there is usually no significant after-market for any securities issued in an intrastate offering during the nine month period following the initial sale and, consequently, they must normally be sold at a discount.

It is difficult for an issuer to rely on the intrastate exemption unless the company knows the purchasers and the sale is directly negotiated with them. In addition, a company that has some of its assets outside of the state or derives a substantial portion of its revenues outside of the state in which it proposes to offer its securities will, in all probability, have a difficult time in justifying the availability of the exemption.

The SEC has adopted Rule 147, a "safe-harbor" rule, which may be followed by companies that want to be certain they meet the requirements for this exemption. However, it is possible that transactions that do not meet all of the requirements of Rule 147 may still qualify for the exemption.

Private Offering Exemption

Section 4(2) of the Securities Act provides an exemption from registration for "transactions by an issuer not involving any public offering." There has been much uncertainty, however, as to the precise limits of this "private offering exemption". Generally, sales to persons directly managing the business fall within the intended scope of the exemption. However, as the number of purchasers increase, and their relationship to the company and its management becomes more remote, it becomes more difficult for an issuer to demonstrate that it does, in fact, qualify for the exemption.

Generally, in order to qualify the offering under this exemption, it is necessary that the persons to whom the security is sold:

- have sufficient knowledge and experience in financial and business matters that they are capable of evaluating the risks and merits of the investment, or are able to bear the economic risk of the investment;
- have access to the type of information that would normally be provided in a prospectus; and
- agree not to resell or distribute the securities.

In addition, the offering may not be made by means of any form of public solicitation or general advertising.

It should be noted that if the security is offered for sale to even one person who does not meet the necessary conditions, the entire offering may be in violation of the Securities Act.

The SEC has adopted Rule 506, a "safe-harbor" rule, which provides objective standards upon which businessmen may rely in order to be certain they meet the requirements of this exemption. Rule 506 is a part of Regulation D, which is described more fully below.

Regulation A

Section 3(b) of the Securities Act gives the SEC authority to exempt from registration certain offerings where the securities to be offered involve relatively small dollar amounts. Under this provision, the SEC has adopted Regulation A. Regulation A is a conditional exemption from registration for certain public offerings, not exceeding $1.5 million in any 12-month period. An offering statement, consisting of a notification, offering circular and exhibits, must be filed with the SEC's Regional Office in the region in which the company's principal business activities are conducted. Although Regulation A is technically an exemption from the registration requirements of the Securities Act, it is often referred to as a "short form" of registration, since the offering circular, which is similar in content to a prospectus, must be supplied to each purchaser, and the securities issued are freely tradeable in an aftermarket. The principal advantages of Regulation A offerings as opposed to full registration on either Form S-1 or S-18 are:

- the required financial statements are simpler and need not be audited, and
- there are no periodic SEC reporting requirements, other than sales reports following the sale of the securities, unless the issuer has more than $3 million in assets and more than 500 shareholders.

All types of companies may utilize Regulation A, with the exception of investment companies registered or required to be registered under the Investment Company Act of 1940. In addition, in most cases Regulation A may be utilized by shareholders for the resale of up to $100,000 of securities.

Regulation D

In March, 1982, the SEC adopted Regulation D under Sections 4(2) and 3(b) of the Securities Act to coordinate the various limited offering exemptions and to streamline the existing requirements applicable to private offers and sales of securities. The Regulation establishes three exemptions from registration in Rules 504, 505, and 506.

Rule 504 - Rule 504 provides an exemption for non-reporting companies for offerings up to $500,000. Under the Rule:

- The sale of up to $500,000 of securities is permitted in a 12-month period.
- No limitation is placed on the number of persons purchasing securities.
- The offering may not be made through any form of general solicitation or general advertising and the securities received in the offering are "restricted securities" unless the offering is made only in states which provide for the registration of the securities and the delivery of a disclosure document.
- Within 15 days after the first sale of securities under the Rule, a Form D notice must be filed with the headquarters office of the SEC.

Unlike Rules 505 and 506, Rule 504 does not mandate that specified disclosure must be provided to purchasers. However, the businessperson should take care that sufficient information is provided to meet the full disclosure obligations which exist under the antifraud provisions of the securities laws.

Rule 505 - Rule 505 was adopted by the SEC in order to provide small businesses more flexibility in raising capital than under Rule 504, but without the uncertainty of determining the quality of the purchasers that generally is involved in using Rule 506. The Rule provides a limited offering exemption for issuers for sales of securities totaling up to $5 million in any 12-month period. Under Rule 505:

- The total offering price of each issue of securities under Rule 505 may not exceed $5 million per issue.
- The issuer may sell the securities to an unlimited number of "accredited investors" and to 35 non-accredited persons. There are no requirements of "sophistication" or "wealth" for persons to whom the securities are sold.
- The offering may not be made by means of any form of general solicitation or general advertising.
- The term "accredited investor" is defined to include banks, insurance companies, registered investment companies, business development companies, or small business investment companies, and certain employee benefit plans for which investment decisions are made by a bank, insurance company, or registered investment adviser; any employee benefit plan within the meaning of Title I of the Employee Retirement Income Security Act with total assets in excess of $5 million; private business development companies; charitable organizations with assets in excess of $5 million; directors, executive officers and general partners of the issuer; persons purchasing at least $150,000 of securities, where the total purchase price does not exceed 20 percent of the purchaser's net worth; natural persons with a net worth of at least $1 million; and natural persons with an income of at least $200,000 per year for two years preceding the offering and for the year in which the offering is made.
- There is no specified information which the issuer must furnish to investors, if only accredited investors are involved in the offering. However, if the offering involves one or more non-accredited persons, the issuer must furnish all purchasers with the same kind of information as that specified in Part I of Form S-18. The information is normally referred to as an "offering memorandum" or "circular." Only financial statements for the most recent fiscal year need be certified by an independent public accountant. If an issuer, other than a limited partnership, cannot obtain audited financial statements without unreasonable effort or expense, then only the issuer's balance sheet, which shall be dated within 120 days of the start of the offering, must be audited. If the issuer is a limited partnership and cannot obtain the required financial statements without unreasonable effort or expense, it may furnish financial statements that have been prepared on the basis of federal income tax requirements and examined and reported on in accordance with generally accepted auditing standards by an independent public or certified accountant. The issuer must also be available to answer questions which prospective purchasers may have about the issuer or the offering.
- A company must take whatever steps are necessary to ensure that the purchasers are acquiring securities for investment only, and not with a view to resale. This means that the securities are "restricted" and investors must be informed that they may not be able to sell their investment for at least two years.
- The issuer is not required to file any offering materials with the Commission. Fifteen days after the first sale in the offering, the issuer must file a notice of sales on Form D. The notice also contains an undertaking by the issuer under Rule 505 to furnish the Commission, upon its staff's request, any information furnished to non-accredited purchasers in connection with the offering.

Rule 506 - Under Rule 506:

- There is no ceiling on the amount which may be raised.
- The issuer may sell its securities to an unlimited number of accredited investors and 35 non-accredited purchasers in reliance on the Rule. All non-accredited purchasers, either alone or with a purchaser representative, must have such knowledge and experience in financial and business matters that they are capable of evaluating the merits and risks of the prospective investment.
- No general solicitation or general advertising is permitted.
- The term "accredited investor" is defined the same as for Rule 505 (See discussion under Rule 505, above).

- There is no specified information which the issuer must furnish to investors, if only accredited investors are involved in the offering. However, if the offering involves one or more non-accredited persons, the issuer must furnish all purchasers with the same kind of information as they would receive if furnished a prospectus filed under a registration statement. In the case of an offering under $5 million, the information requirements would be the same as those for Rule 505, above. In the case of an offering over $5 million, the information would be the same kind as would be specified on the registration form the issuer would be entitled to use, except that if the issuer cannot obtain audited financial statements without unreasonable effort or expense, then the issuer may provide financial statements in accordance with the special treatment described under Rule 505, above. The issuer must also be available to answer questions which prospective purchasers may have about the issuer or the offering.
- The securities sold pursuant to Rule 506 are restricted securities, as under Rule 505.
- A company is required to file a notice of the offering on Form D at the SEC's headquarters office in Washington, D.C., within 15 days after the first sale in the offering. There is no requirement to file the offering memorandum with the Commission.

Accredited Investor Exemption: Section 4(6)

The Small Business Investment Incentive Act of 1980 created a new statutory exemption from registration under the Securities Act for transactions involving offers and sales of securities by any issuer solely to one or more "accredited investors." Under new Section 4(6):

- The total offering price of each issue of securities under the exemption may not exceed the limit on small offerings set by Section 3(b) the Securities Act, which currently is $5 million per issue.
- The offering may not be made by means of any form of advertising or public solicitation.
- The term "accredited investor" is defined to include the same individuals and entities as included for purposes of Rules 505 and 506.
- The issuer is required to file a notice of sales on Form D with the Commission 15 days after the initial sale is made in reliance on the exemption.
- The Section 4(6) exemption does not contain any specific disclosure requirements. The issuer is cautioned however, that, as in the case of the other exemptions, Section 4(6) does not exempt the issuer from the antifraud provisions of the securities laws.

Are there state law requirements in addition to those under the Federal securities laws?

The Federal government and the state governments each have separate and autonomous securities laws and regulations. Compliance with the laws and rules of one, does not constitute compliance with the laws and regulations of the other. A company selling securities must comply with the laws of each state in which it intends to offer its securities. At a minimum, it must comply with at least two sets of requirements--the Federal securities laws and the laws of the state in which the securities are to be sold (if sold in only one state). In addition, the fact that a particular offering may be exempt from certain provisions of the Federal securities laws does not necessarily mean that it is exempt from the notice and filing requirements of various state laws.

In certain states, the law permits a state official to judge the merits of an offering. In these "merit states", even though a company complies with the registration or filing procedures, the state may prohibit the offering because the state official does not consider it to be "fair, just and equitable" for purchase by citizens of his state. Consequently, an issuer of securities must be careful to make sure that there is compliance with all of the appropriate state requirements, as well as with the Federal securities laws.

Where can I go for more information?

The staff of the Office of Small Business Policy, as well as the personnel of the SEC's Regional Offices, will be glad to assist you with any questions you may have with respect to the Federal securities laws. For information regarding state securities laws, contact the appropriate state securities commissioner, whose office is usually located in the capital city.

The entire text of the Commission's rules and regulations is available through the U.S. Government Printing Office or from several private publishers of legal information. In addition, numerous books on this subject have been published, and some are available at most metropolitan public libraries. As of this writing, the following items were available from the Government Printing Office:

Title 17 of the Code of Federal Regulations *(The SEC's rules and regulations)* April 1, 1982

Vol. I – Parts 1 to 239. SEC Organization; Conduct & Ethics; Info & Requests; Rules of Practice; Regulation S-X and Securities Act of 1933.
Stock No. 022-003-94463-0. . . . . $8.50

Vol. II – Parts 240 to End. Securities Exchange Act of 1934; Public Utility Holding Company, Trust Indenture, Investment Company, Investment Advisers, and Securities Investor Protection Corporation Acts.
Stock No.022-003-94464-8 . . . . $8.00

To order the items on this page, send a check or money order to:

Superintendent of Documents
Government Printing Office
Washington, D.C. 20402

For advice concerning matters relating particularly to small business:

Office of Small Business Policy
U.S. Securities and Exchange Commission
450 Fifth Street, N.W.
Washington, D.C. 20549
Telephone: (202) 272-2644

For copies of Commission forms, and recently-adopted rules:

Publications Section
(same address as above)
Telephone: (202) 272-7460

For information concerning alternative ways of financing small business activities:

Office of Chief Counsel for Advocacy
U.S. Small Business Administration
1441 L Street, N.W.
Washington, D.C. 20416
Telephone: (202) 653-6533

For further information with regard to any aspect of the SEC's operations, you may contact the Regional Office listed on the following two pages, that is most convenient for you.

Regional and Branch offices

New York
Region 1

NEW YORK REGIONAL OFFICE
26 Federal Plaza New York, N.Y. 10278
212-264-1636
Region: New York and New Jersey

Boston
Region 2

BOSTON REGIONAL OFFICE
150 Causeway Street
Boston, Massachusetts 02114
617-223-2721
Region: Maine, New Hampshire, Vermont, Massachusetts, Rhode Island and Connecticut

Atlanta
Region 3

ATLANTA REGIONAL OFFICE
1375 Peachtree Street, N.E.
Suite 788
Atlanta, Georgia 30367
404-881-2524
Region: Tennessee, Virgin Islands, Puerto Rico, North Carolina, South Carolina, Georgia, Alabama, Mississippi, Florida and Louisiana east of the Atchafalaya River

MIAMI BRANCH OFFICE
Dupont Plaza Center
300 Biscayne Blvd., Way, Suite 500
Miami, Florida 33131
305-350-5765

Chicago
Region 4

CHICAGO REGIONAL OFFICE
Everett McKinley Dirksen Bldg.
219 South Dearborn Street, Room 1204
Chicago, Illinois 60604
312-353-7390
Region: Michigan, Ohio, Kentucky, Wisconsin, Indiana, Iowa, Minnesota, Missouri, and Illinois

DETROIT BRANCH OFFICE
1044 Federal Bldg.
Detroit, Michigan 48226
313-226-6070

Fort Worth
Region 5

FORT WORTH REGIONAL OFFICE
411 W. Seventh St.
Fort Worth, Texas 76102
817-334-3821
Region: Oklahoma, Arkansas, Texas, Louisiana west of the Atchafalaya River and Kansas

HOUSTON BRANCH OFFICE
7500 San Felipe, Suite 550
Houston, Texas 77063
713-266-3671

Denver
Region 6

DENVER REGIONAL OFFICE
410 17th Street, Suite 700
Denver, Colorado 80202
303-844-2071

Region: North Dakota, South Dakota, Wyoming, Nebraska, Colorado, New Mexico, and Utah

SALT LAKE BRANCH OFFICE
Boston Bldg. Suite 810
9 Exchange Place
Salt Lake City, Utah 84111
801-524-5796

Los Angeles
Region 7

LOS ANGELES REGIONAL OFFICE
5670 Wilshire Blvd., 11th Floor
Los Angeles, California 90036-3648
213-965-3998

Region: Nevada, Arizona, California, Hawaii, and Guam

SAN FRANCISCO BRANCH OFFICE
450 Golden Gate Avenue, Box 36042
San Francisco, California 94102
415-556-5264

Seattle
Region 8

SEATTLE REGIONAL OFFICE
3040 Federal Building
915 Second Avenue
Seattle, Washington 98174
206-442-7990
Region: Montana, Idaho, Washington, Oregon, and Alaska

Washington
Region 9

WASHINGTON REGIONAL OFFICE
Ballston Center Tower 3
4015 Wilson Blvd.
Arlington, Virginia 22203
703-235-3701
Region: Pennsylvania, Delaware, Maryland, Virginia, West Virginia, and District of Columbia

PHILADELPHIA BRANCH OFFICE
William J. Green, Jr. Federal Bldg.
600 Arch Street, Room 2204
Philadelphia, Pennsylvania 19106
215-597-3100

U.S. Securities and Exchange Commission

450 Fifth Street,
N. W. Washington, D. C.
20549

Office Locations

SEC 1753 3-85

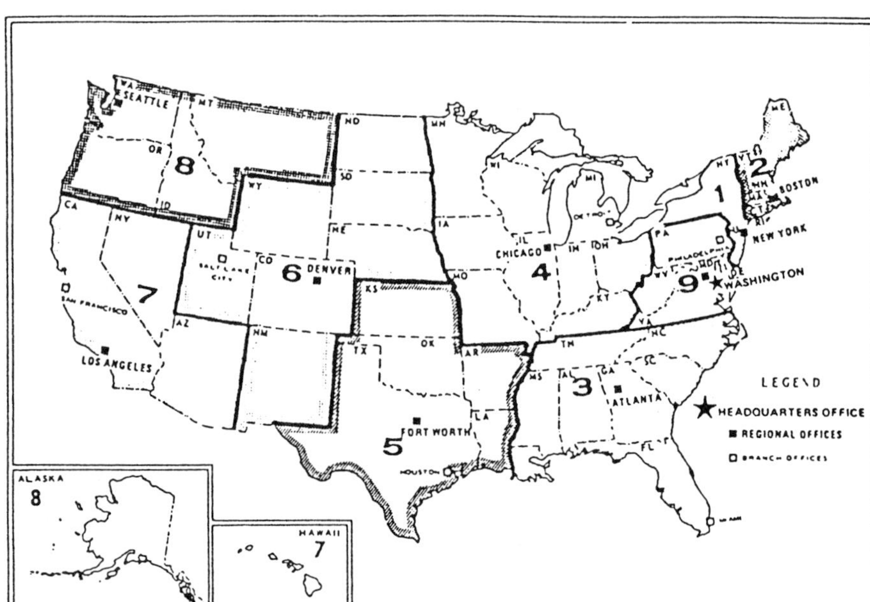

9. Magnuson-Moss Warranty Law—Rules*

SUBCHAPTER G—RULES, REGULATIONS, STATEMENTS AND INTERPRETATIONS UNDER THE MAGNUSON-MOSS WARRANTY ACT

PART 700—INTERPRETATIONS OF MAGNUSON-MOSS WARRANTY ACT

AUTHORITY: Magnuson-Moss Warranty Act, Pub. L. 93-637, 15 U.S.C. 2301.

SOURCE: 42 FR 36114, July 13, 1977, unless otherwise noted.

§ 700.1 Products covered.

(a) The Act applies to written warranties on tangible personal property which is normally used for personal, family, or household purposes. This definition includes property which is intended to be attached to or installed in any real property without regard to whether it is so attached or installed. This means that a product is a "consumer product" if the use of that type of product is not uncommon. The percentage of sales or the use to which a product is put by any individual buyer is not determinative. For example, products such as automobiles and typewriters which are used for both personal and commercial purposes come within the definition of consumer product. Where it is unclear whether a particular product is covered under the definition of consumer product, any ambiguity will be resolved in favor of coverage.

(b) Agricultural products such as farm machinery, structures and implements used in the business or occupation of farming are not covered by the Act where their personal, family, or household use is uncommon. However, those agricultural products normally used for personal or household gardening (for example, to produce goods for personal consumption, and not for resale) are consumer products under the Act.

(c) The definition of "Consumer product" limits the applicability of the Act to personal property, "including any such property intended to be attached to or installed in any real property without regard to whether it is so attached or installed." This provision brings under the Act separate items of equipment attached to real property, such as air conditioners, furnaces, and water heaters.

(d) The coverage of separate items of equipment attached to real property includes, but is not limited to, appliances and other thermal, mechanical, and electrical equipment. (It does not extend to the wiring, plumbing, ducts, and other items which are integral component parts of the structure.) State law would classify many such products as fixtures to, and therefore a part of, realty. The statutory definition is designed to bring such products under the Act regardless of whether they may be considered fixtures under state law.

(e) The coverage of building materials which are not separate items of equipment is based on the nature of the purchase transaction. An analysis of the transaction will determine whether the goods are real or personal property. The numerous products which go into the construction of a consumer dwelling are all consumer products when sold "over the counter," as by hardware and building supply retailers. This is also true where a consumer contracts for the purchase of such materials in connection with the improvement, repair, or modification of a home (for example, paneling, dropped ceilings, siding, roofing, storm windows, remodeling). However, where such products are at the time of sale integrated into the structure of a dwelling they are not consumer products as they cannot be practically distinguished from realty. Thus, for example, the beams, wallboard, wiring, plumbing, windows, roofing, and other structural components of a dwelling are not consumer products when they are sold as part of real estate covered by a written warranty.

(f) In the case where a consumer contracts with a builder to construct a home, a substantial addition to a home, or other realty (such as a garage or an in-ground swimming pool) the building materials to be used are not consumer products. Although the materials are separately identifiable at the time the contract is made, it is the intention of the parties to contract for the construction of realty which will integrate the component materials. Of course, as noted above, any separate items of equipment to be attached to such realty are consumer products under the Act.

(g) Certain provisions of the Act apply only to products actually costing the consumer more than a specified amount. Section 103 applies to consumer products actually costing the consumer more than $10, excluding tax. The $10 minimum will be interpreted to include multiple-packaged items which may individually sell for less than $10, but which have been packaged in a manner that does not permit breaking the package to purchase an item or items at a price less than $10. Thus, a written warranty on a dozen items packaged and priced for sale at $12 must be designated, even though identical items may be offered in smaller quantities at under $10. This interpretation applies in the same manner to the minimum dollar limits in section 102 and rules promulgated under that section.

(h) Warranties on replacement parts and components used to repair consumer products are covered; warranties on services are not covered. Therefore, warranties which apply solely to a repairer's workmanship in performing repairs are not subject to the Act. Where a written agreement warrants both the parts provided to effect a repair and the workmanship in making that repair, the warranty must comply with the Act and the rules thereunder.

(i) The Act covers written warranties on consumer products "distributed in commerce" as that term is defined in section 101(3). Thus, by its terms the Act arguably applies to products exported to foreign jurisdictions. However, the public interest would not be served by the use of Commission resources to enforce the Act with respect to such products. Moreover, the legislative intent to apply the requirements of the Act to such products is not sufficiently clear to justify such an extraordinary result. The Commission does not contemplate the enforcement of the Act with respect to consumer products exported to foreign jurisdictions. Products exported for sale at military post exchanges remain subject to the same enforcement standards as products sold within the United States, its territories and possessions.

§ 700.2 Date of manufacture.

Section 112 of the Act provides that the Act shall apply only to those consumer products manufactured after July 4, 1975. When a consumer purchases repair of a consumer product the date of manufacture of any replacement parts used is the measuring date for determining coverage under the Act. The date of manufacture of the consumer product being repaired is in this instance not relevant. Where a consumer purchases or obtains on an exchange basis a rebuilt consumer product, the date that the rebuilding process is completed determines the Act's applicability.

[42 FR 36114, July 13, 1977; 42 FR 38341, July 28, 1977]

*Excerpts from federal regulations regarding warranties.

§ 700.3 Written warranty.

(a) The Act imposes specific duties and liabilities on suppliers who offer written warranties on consumer products. Certain representations, such as energy efficiency ratings for electrical appliances, care labeling of wearing apparel, and other product information disclosures may be express warranties under the Uniform Commercial Code. However, these disclosures alone are not written warranties under this Act. Section 101(6) provides that a written affirmation of fact or a written promise of a specified level of performance must relate to a specified period of time in order to be considered a "written warranty."[1] A product information disclosure without a specified time period to which the disclosure relates is therefore not a written warranty. In addition, section 111(d) exempts from the Act (except section 102(c)) any written warranty the making or content of which is required by federal law. The Commission encourages the disclosure of product information which is not deceptive and which may benefit consumers, and will not construe the Act to impede information disclosure in product advertising or labeling.

(b) Certain terms, or conditions, of sale of a consumer product may not be "written warranties" as that term is defined in section 101(6), and should not be offered or described in a manner that may deceive consumers as to their enforceability under the Act. For example, a seller of consumer products may give consumers an unconditional right to revoke acceptance of goods within a certain number of days after delivery without regard to defects or failure to meet a specified level of performance. Or a seller may permit consumers to return products for any reason for credit toward purchase of another item. Such terms of sale taken alone are not written warranties under the Act. Therefore, suppliers should avoid any characterization of such terms of sale as warranties. The use of such terms as "free trial period" and "trade-in credit policy" in this regard would be appropriate. Furthermore, such terms of sale should be stated separately from any written warranty. Of course, the offering and performance of such terms of sale remain subject to section 5 of the Federal Trade Commission Act, 15 U.S.C. 45.

(c) The Magnuson-Moss Warranty Act generally applies to written warranties covering consumer products. Many consumer products are covered by warranties which are neither intended for, nor enforceable by, consumers. A common example is a warranty given by a component supplier to a manufacturer of consumer products. (The manufacturer may, in turn, warrant these components to consumers.) The component supplier's warranty is generally given solely to the product manufacturer, and is neither intended to be conveyed to the consumer nor brought to the consumer's attention in connection with the sale. Such warranties are not subject to the Act, since a written warranty under section 101(6) of the Act must become "part of the basis of the bargain between a supplier and a buyer for purposes other than resale." However, the Act applies to a component supplier's warranty in writing which is given to the consumer. An example is a supplier's written warranty to the consumer covering a refrigerator that is sold installed in a boat or recreational vehicle. The supplier of the refrigerator relies on the boat or vehicle assembler to convey the written agreement to the consumer. In this case, the supplier's written warranty is to a consumer, and is covered by the Act.

[1] A "written warranty" is also created by a written affirmation of fact or a written promise that the product is defect free, or by a written undertaking of remedial action within the meaning of section 101(6)(B).

§ 700.4 Parties "actually making" a written warranty.

Section 110(f) of the Act provides that only the supplier "actually making" a written warranty is liable for purposes of FTC and private enforcement of the Act. A supplier who does no more than distribute or sell a consumer product covered by a written warranty offered by another person or business and which identifies that person or business as the warrantor is not liable for failure of the written warranty to comply with the Act or rules thereunder. However, other actions and written and oral representations of such a supplier in connection with the offer or sale of a warranted product may obligate that supplier under the Act. If under State law the supplier is deemed to have "adopted" the written affirmation of fact, promise, or undertaking, the supplier is also obligated under the Act. Suppliers are advised to consult State law to determine those actions and representations which may make them co-warrantors, and therefore obligated under the warranty of the other person or business.

§ 700.5 Expressions of general policy.

(a) Under section 103(b), statements or representations of general policy concerning customer satisfaction which are not subject to any specific limitation need not be designated as full or limited warranties, and are exempt from the requirements of sections 102, 103, and 104 of the Act and rules thereunder. However, such statements remain subject to the enforcement provisions of section 110 of the Act, and to section 5 of the Federal Trade Commission Act, 15 U.S.C. 45.

(b) The section 103(b) exemption applies only to general policies, not to those which are limited to specific consumer products manufactured or sold by the supplier offering such a policy. In addition, to qualify for an exemption under section 103(b) such policies may not be subject to any specific limitations. For example, policies which have an express limitation of duration or a limitation of the amount to be refunded are not exempted. This does not preclude the imposition of reasonable limitations based on the circumstances in each instance a consumer seeks to invoke such an agreement. For instance, a warrantor may refuse to honor such an expression of policy where a consumer has used a product for 10 years without previously expressing any dissatisfaction with the product. Such a refusal would not be a specific limitation under this provision.

§ 700.6 Designation of warranties.

(a) Section 103 of the Act provides that written warranties on consumer products manufactured after July 4, 1975, and actually costing the consumer more than $10, excluding tax, must be designated either "Full (statement of duration) Warranty" or "Limited Warranty". Warrantors may include a statement of duration in a limited warranty designation. The designation or designations should appear clearly and conspicuously as a caption, or prominent title, clearly separated from the text of the warranty. The full (statement of duration) warranty and limited warranty are the exclusive designations permitted under the Act, unless a specific exception is created by rule.

(b) Section 104(b)(4) states that "the duties under subsection (a) (of section 104) extend from the warrantor to each person who is a consumer with respect to the consumer product." Section 101(3) defines a consumer as "a buyer (other than for purposes of resale) of any consumer product, any person to whom such product is transferred during the duration of an implied or written warranty (or service contract) applicable to the product, * * *." Therefore, a full warranty may not expressly restrict the warranty rights of a transferee during its stated duration. However, where the duration of a full warranty is defined solely in terms of first purchaser ownership there can be no violation of section 104(b)(4), since the duration of the warranty expires, by definition, at the time of transfer. No rights of a subsequent transferee are cut off as there is no transfer of ownership "during the duration of (any) warranty." Thus, these provisions do not preclude the offering of a full warranty with its duration determined exclusively by the period during which the first purchaser owns the product, or uses it in conjunction with another product. For example, an automotive battery or muffler warranty may be designated as "full warranty for as long as you own your car." Because this type of warranty leads the consumer to believe that proof of purchase is not needed so long as he or she owns the product a duty to furnish documentary proof may not be reasonably imposed on the consumer under this type of warranty. The burden is on the warrantor to prove that a particular claimant under this type of warranty is not the original purchaser or owner of the product. Warrantors or their designated agents may, however, ask consumers to state or affirm that they are the first purchaser of the product.

§ 700.7 Use of warranty registration cards.

(a) Under section 104(b)(1) of the Act a warrantor offering a full warranty may not impose on consumers any duty other than notification of a defect as a condition of securing remedy of the defect or malfunction, unless such additional duty can be demonstrated by the warrantor to be reasonable. Warrantors have in the past stipulated the return of a "warranty registration" or similar card. By "warranty registration card" the Commission means a card which must be returned by the consumer shortly after purchase of the product and which is stipulated or implied in the warranty to be a condition precedent to warranty coverage and performance.

(b) A requirement that the consumer return a warranty registration card or a similar notice as a condition of performance under a full warranty is an unreasonable duty. Thus, a provision such as, "This warranty is void unless the warranty registration card is returned to the warrantor" is not permissible in a full warranty, nor is it permissible to imply such a condition in a full warranty.

(c) This does not prohibit the use of such registration cards where a warrantor suggests use of the card as one possible means of proof of the date the product was purchased. For example, it is permissible to provide in a full warranty that a consumer may fill out and return a card to place on file proof of the date the product was purchased. Any such suggestion to the consumer must include notice that failure to return the card will not affect rights under the warranty, so long as the consumer can show in a reasonable manner the date the product was purchased. Nor does this interpretation prohibit a seller from obtaining from purchasers at the time of sale information requested by the warrantor.

§ 700.8 Warrantor's decision as final.

A warrantor shall not indicate in any written warranty or service contract either directly or indirectly that the decision of the warrantor, service contractor, or any designated third party is final or binding in any dispute concerning the warranty or service contract. Nor shall a warrantor or service contractor state that it alone shall determine what is a defect under the agreement. Such statements are deceptive since section 110(d) of the Act gives state and federal courts jurisdiction over suits for breach of warranty and service contract.

§ 700.9 Duty to install under a full warranty.

Under section 104(a)(1) of the Act, the remedy under a full warranty must be provided to the consumer without charge. If the warranted product has utility only when installed, a full warranty must provide such installation without charge regardless of whether or not the consumer originally paid for installation by the warrantor or his agent. However, this does not preclude the warrantor from imposing on the consumer a duty to remove, return, or reinstall where such duty can be demonstrated by the warrantor to meet the standard of reasonableness under section 104(b)(1).

§ 700.10 Section 102(c).

(a) Section 102(c) prohibits tying arrangements that condition coverage under a written warranty on the consumer's use of an article or service identified by brand, trade, or corporate name unless that article or service is provided without charge to the consumer.

(b) Under a limited warranty that provides only for replacement of defective parts and no portion of labor charges, section 102(c) prohibits a condition that the consumer use only service (labor) identified by the warrantor to install the replacement parts. A warrantor or his designated representative may not provide parts under the warranty in a manner which impedes or precludes the choice by the consumer of the person or business to perform necessary labor to install such parts.

(c) No warrantor may condition the continued validity of a warranty on the use of only authorized repair service and/or authorized replacement parts for non-warranty service and maintenance. For example, provisions such as, "This warranty is void if service is performed by anyone other than an authorized 'ABC' dealer and all replacement parts must be genuine 'ABC' parts," and the like, are prohibited where the service or parts are not covered by the warranty. These provisions violate the Act in two ways. First, they violate the section 102 (c) ban against tying arrangements. Second, such provisions are deceptive under section 110 of the Act, because a warrantor cannot, as a matter of law, avoid liability under a written warranty where a defect is unrelated to the use by a consumer of "unauthorized" articles or service. This does not preclude a warrantor from expressly excluding liability for defects or damage caused by such "unauthorized" articles or service; nor does it preclude the warrantor from denying liability where the warrantor can demonstrate that the defect or damage was so caused.

§ 700.11 Written warranty, service contract, and insurance distinguished for purposes of compliance under the Act.

(a) The Act recognizes two types of agreements which may provide similar coverage of consumer products, the written warranty, and the service contract. In addition, other agreements may meet the statutory definitions of either "written warranty" or "service contract," but are sold and regulated under state law as contracts of insurance. One example is the automobile breakdown insurance policies sold in many jurisdictions and regulated by the state as a form of casualty insurance. The McCarran-Ferguson Act, 15 U.S.C. 1011 et seq., precludes jurisdiction under federal law over "the business of insurance" to the extent an agreement is regulated by state law as insurance. Thus, such agreements are subject to the Magnuson-Moss Warranty Act only to the extent they are not regulated in a particular state as the business of insurance.

(b) "Written warranty" and "service contract" are defined in sections 101(6) and 101(8) of the Act, respectively. A written warranty must be "part of the basis of the bargain." This means that it must be conveyed at the time of sale of the consumer product and the consumer must not give any consideration beyond the purchase price of the consumer product in order to benefit from the agreement. It is not a requirement of the Act that an agreement obligate a supplier of the consumer product to a written warranty, but merely that it be part of the basis of the bargain between a supplier and a consumer. This contemplates written warranties by third-party non-suppliers.

(c) A service contract under the Act must meet the definitions of section 101(8). An agreement which would meet the definition of written warranty in section 101(6) (A) or (B) but for its failure to satisfy the basis of the bargain test is a service contract. For example, an agreement which calls for some consideration in addition to the purchase price of the consumer product, or which is entered into at some date after the purchase of the consumer product to which it applies, is a service contract. An agreement which relates only to the performance of maintenance and/or inspection services and which is not an undertaking, promise, or affirmation with respect to a specified level of performance, or that the product is free of defects in materials or workmanship, is a service contract. An agreement to perform periodic cleaning and inspection of a product over a specified period of time, even when offered at the time of sale and without charge to the consumer, is an example of such a service contract.

§ 700.12 Effective date of 16 CFR Parts 701 and 702.

The Statement of Basis and Purpose of the final rules promulgated on December 31, 1975, provides that Parts 701 and 702 of this chapter will become effective one year after the date of promulgation, December 31, 1976. The Commission intends this to mean that these rules apply only to written warranties on products manufactured after December 31, 1976.

PART 701—DISCLOSURE OF WRITTEN CONSUMER PRODUCT WARRANTY TERMS AND CONDITIONS

Sec.

AUTHORITY: 15 U.S.C. 2302 and 2309.

SOURCE: 40 FR 60188, Dec. 31, 1975, unless otherwise noted.

§ 701.1 Definitions.

(a) "The Act" means the Magnuson-Moss Warranty Federal Trade Commission Improvement Act, 15 U.S.C. 2301, et seq.

(b) "Consumer product" means any tangible personal property which is distributed in commerce and which is normally used for personal, family, or household purposes (including any such property intended to be attached to or installed in any real property without regard to whether it is so attached or installed. Products which are purchased solely for commercial or industrial use are excluded solely for purposes of this part.

(c) "Written warranty" means:

(1) Any written affirmation of fact or written promise made in connection with the sale of a consumer product by a supplier to a buyer which relates to the nature of the material or workmanship and affirms or promises that such material or workmanship is defect free or will meet a specified level of performance over a specified period of time, or

(2) Any undertaking in writing in connection with the sale by a supplier of a consumer product to refund, repair, replace, or take other remedial action with respect to such product in the event that such product fails to meet the specifications set forth in the undertaking, which written affirmation, promise or undertaking becomes part of the basis of the bargain between a supplier and a buyer for purposes other than resale of such product.

(d) "Implied warranty" means an implied warranty arising under State law (as modified by sections 104(a) and 108 of the Act) in connection with the sale by a supplier of a consumer product.

(e) "Remedy" means whichever of the following actions the warrantor elects:

(1) Repair,

(2) Replacement, or

(3) Refund; except that the warrantor may not elect refund unless: (i) The warrantor is unable to provide replacement and repair is not commercially practicable or cannot be timely made, or

(ii) The consumer is willing to accept such refund.

(f) "Supplier" means any person engaged in the business of making a consumer product directly or indirectly available to consumers.

(g) "Warrantor" means any supplier or other person who gives or offers to give a written warranty.

(h) "Consumer" means a buyer (other than for purposes of resale or use in the ordinary course of the buyer's business) of any consumer product, any person to whom such product is transferred during the duration of an implied or written warranty applicable to the product, and any other such person who is entitled by the terms of such warranty or under applicable State law to enforce against the warrantor the obligations of the warranty.

(i) "On the face of the warranty" means:

(1) Where the warranty is a single sheet with printing on both sides of the sheet or where the warranty is comprised of more than one sheet, the page on which the warranty text begins;

(2) Where the warranty is included as part of a larger document, such as a use and care manual, the page in such document on which the warranty text begins.

§ 701.2 Scope.

The regulations in this part establish requirements for warrantors for disclosing the terms and conditions of written warranties on consumer products actually costing the consumer more than $15.00.

§ 701.3 Written warranty terms.

(a) Any warrantor warranting to a consumer by means of a written warranty a consumer product actually costing the consumer more than $15.00 shall clearly and conspicuously disclose in a single document in simple and readily understood language, the following items of information:

(1) The identity of the party or parties to whom the written warranty is extended, if the enforceability of the written warranty is limited to the original consumer purchaser or is otherwise limited to persons other than every consumer owner during the term of the warranty;

(2) A clear description and identification of products, or parts, or characteristics, or components or properties covered by and where necessary for clarification, excluded from the warranty;

(3) A statement of what the warrantor will do in the event of a defect, malfunction or failure to conform with the written warranty, including the items or services the warrantor will pay for or provide, and, where necessary for clarification, those which the warrantor will not pay for or provide;

(4) The point in time or event on which the warranty term commences, if different from the purchase date, and the time period or other measurement of warranty duration;

(5) A step-by-step explanation of the procedure which the consumer should follow in order to obtain performance of any warranty obligation, including the persons or class of persons authorized to perform warranty obligations. This includes the name(s) of the warrantor(s), together with: The mailing address(es) of the warrantor(s), and/or the name or title and the address of any employee or department of the warrantor responsible for the performance of warranty obligations, and/or a telephone number which consumers may use without charge to obtain information on warranty performance;

(6) Information respecting the availability of any informal dispute settlement mechanism elected by the warrantor in compliance with Part 703 of this subchapter;

(7) Any limitations on the duration of implied warranties, disclosed on the face of the warranty as provided in section 108 of the Act, accompanied by the following statement:

Some States do not allow limitations on how long an implied warranty lasts, so the above limitation may not apply to you.

(8) Any exclusions of or limitations on relief such as incidental or consequential damages, accompanied by the following statement, which may be combined with the statement required in paragraph (a)(7) of this section:

Some States do not allow the exclusion or limitation of incidental or consequential damages, so the above limitation or exclusion may not apply to you.

(9) A statement in the following language:

This warranty gives you specific legal rights, and you may also have other rights which vary from State to State.

(b) Paragraphs (a)(1) through (9) of this section shall not be applicable with respect to statements of general policy on emblems, seals or insignias issued by third parties promising replacement or refund if a consumer product is defective, which statements contain no representation or assurance of the quality or performance characteristics of the product; *Provided* That: (1) The disclosures required by paragraphs (a)(1) through (9) of this section are published by such third parties in each issue of a publication with a general circulation, and (2) such disclosures are provided free of charge to any consumer upon written request.

§ 701.4 Owner registration cards.

When a warrantor employs any card such as an owner's registration card, a warranty registration card, or the like, and the return of such card is a condition precedent to warranty coverage and performance, the warrantor shall disclose this fact in the warranty. If the return of such card reasonably appears to be a condition precedent to warranty coverage and performance, but is not such a condition, that fact shall be disclosed in the warranty.

PART 702—PRE-SALE AVAILABILITY OF WRITTEN WARRANTY TERMS

Sec.

AUTHORITY: 15 U.S.C. 2302 and 2309.

SOURCE: 40 FR 60189, Dec. 31, 1975, unless otherwise noted.

§ 702.1 Definitions.

(a) "The Act" means the Magnuson-Moss Warranty Federal Trade Commission Improvement Act, 15 U.S.C. 2301, *et seq.*

(b) "Consumer product" means any tangible personal property which is distributed in commerce and which is normally used for personal, family, or household purposes (including any such property intended to be attached to or installed in any real property without regard to whether it is so attached or installed). Products which are purchased solely for commercial or industrial use are excluded solely for purposes of this part.

(c) "Written warranty" means—

(1) Any written affirmation of fact or written promise made in connection with the sale of a consumer product by a supplier to a buyer which relates to the nature of the material or workmanship and affirms or promises that such material or workmanship is defect free or will meet a specified level of performance over a specified period of time, or

(2) Any undertaking in writing in connection with the sale by a supplier of a consumer product to refund, repair, replace or take other remedial action with respect to such product in the event that such product fails to meet the specifications set forth in the undertaking,

which written affirmation, promise, or undertaking becomes part of the basis of the bargain between a supplier and a buyer for purposes other than resale of such product.

(d) "Warrantor" means any supplier or other person who gives or offers to give a written warranty.

(e) "Seller" means any person who sells or offers for sale for purposes other than resale or use in the ordinary course of the buyer's business any consumer product.

(f) "Supplier" means any person engaged in the business of making a consumer product directly or indirectly available to consumers.

[40 FR 60189, Dec. 31, 1975, as amended at 52 FR 7574, Mar. 12, 1987]

§ 702.2 Scope.

The regulations in this part establish requirements for sellers and warrantors for making the terms of any written warranty on a consumer product available to the consumer prior to sale.

§ 702.3 Pre-sale availability of written warranty terms.

The following requirements apply to consumer products actually costing the consumer more than $15.00:

(a) *Duties of seller.* Except as provided in paragraphs (c) through (d) of this section, the seller of a consumer product with a written warranty shall make a text of the warranty readily available for examination by the prospective buyer by:

(1) Displaying it in close proximity to the warranted product, or

(2) Furnishing it upon request prior to sale and placing signs reasonably calculated to elicit the prospective buyer's attention in prominent locations in the store or department advising such prospective buyers of the availability of warranties upon request.

(b) *Duties of the warrantor.* (1) A warrantor who gives a written warranty warranting to a consumer a consumer product actually costing the consumer more than $15.00 shall:

(i) Provide sellers with warranty materials necessary for such sellers to comply with the requirements set forth in paragraph (a) of this section, by the use of one or more by the following means:

(A) Providing a copy of the written warranty with every warranted consumer product; and/or

(B) Providing a tag, sign, sticker, label, decal or other attachment to the product, which contains the full text of the written warranty; and/or

(C) Printing on or otherwise attaching the text of the written warranty to the package, carton, or other container if that package, carton or other container is normally used for display purposes. If the warrantor elects this option a copy of the written warranty must also accompany the warranted product; and/or

(D) Providing a notice, sign, or poster disclosing the text of a consumer product warranty. If the warrantor elects this option, a copy of the written warranty must also accompany each warranted product.

(ii) Provide catalog, mail order, and door-to-door sellers with copies of written warranties necessary for such sellers to comply with the requirements set forth in paragraphs (c) and (d) of this section.

(2) Paragraph (a)(1) of this section shall not be applicable with respect to statements of general policy on emblems, seals or insignias issued by third parties promising replacement or refund if a consumer product is defective, which statements contain no representation or assurance of the quality or performance characteristics of the product; provided that

(i) The disclosures required by § 701.3(a) (1) through (9) of this part are published by such third parties in each issue of a publication with a general circulation, and

(ii) Such disclosures are provided free of charge to any consumer upon written request.

(c) *Catalog and mail order sales.* (1) For purposes of this paragraph:

(i) "Catalog or mail order sales", means any offer for sale, or any solicitation for an order for a consumer product with a written warranty, which includes instructions for ordering the product which do not require a personal visit to the seller's establishment.

(ii) "Close conjunction" means on the page containing the description of the warranted product, or on the page facing that page.

(2) Any seller who offers for sale to consumers consumer products with written warranties by means of a catalog or mail order solicitation shall:

(i) Clearly and conspicuously disclose in such catalog or solicitation in close conjunction to the description of warranted product, or in an information section of the catalog or solicitation clearly referenced, including a page number, in close conjunction to the description of the warranted product, *either:*

(A) The full text of the written warranty; or

(B) That the written warranty can be obtained free upon specific written request, and the address where such warranty can be obtained. If this option is elected, such seller shall promptly provide a copy of any written warranty requested by the consumer.

(d) *Door-to-door sales.* (1) For purposes of this paragraph:

(i) "Door-to-door sale" means a sale of consumer products in which the seller or his representative personally solicits the sale, including those in response to or following an invitation by a buyer, and the buyer's agreement to offer to purchase is made at a place other than the place of business of the seller.

(ii) "Prospective buyer" means an individual solicited by a door-to-door seller to buy a consumer product who indicates sufficient interest in that consumer product or maintains sufficient contact with the seller for the seller reasonably to conclude that the person solicited is considering purchasing the product.

(2) Any seller who offers for sale to consumers consumer products with written warranties by means of door-to-door sales shall, prior to the consummation of the sale, disclose the fact that the sales representative has copies of the warranties for the warranted products being offered for sale, which may be inspected by the prospective buyer at any time during the sales presentation. Such disclosure shall be made orally and shall be included in any written materials shown to prospective buyers.

[40 FR 60189, Dec. 31, 1975, as amended at 52 FR 7574, Mar. 12, 1987]

PART 703—INFORMAL DISPUTE SETTLEMENT PROCEDURES

AUTHORITY: 15 U.S.C. 2309 and 2310.

SOURCE: 40 FR 60215, Dec. 31, 1975, unless otherwise noted.

§ 703.1 Definitions.

(a) "The Act" means the Magnuson-Moss Warranty—Federal Trade Commission Improvement Act, 15 U.S.C. 2301, *et seq.*

(b) "Consumer product" means any tangible personal property which is distributed in commerce and which is normally used for personal, family, or household purposes (including any such property intended to be attached to or installed in any real property without regard to whether it is so attached or installed).

(c) "Written warranty" means:

(1) Any written affirmation of fact or written promise made in connection with the sale of a consumer product by a supplier to a buyer which relates to the nature of the material or workmanship and affirms or promises that such material or workmanship is defect free or will meet a specified level of performance over a specified period of time, or

(2) Any undertaking in writing in connection with the sale by a supplier of a consumer product to refund, repair, replace, or take other remedial action with respect to such product in the event that such product fails to meet the specifications set forth in the undertaking, which written affirmation, promise or undertaking becomes part of the basis of the bargain between a supplier and a buyer for purposes other than resale of such product.

(d) "Warrantor" means any person who gives or offers to give a written warranty which incorporates an informal dispute settlement mechanism.

(e) "Mechanism" means an informal dispute settlement procedure which is incorporated into the terms of a written warranty to which any provision of Title I of the Act applies, as provided in section 110 of the Act.

(f) "Members" means the person or persons within a Mechanism actually deciding disputes.

(g) "Consumer" means a buyer (other than for purposes of resale) of any consumer product, any person to whom such product is transferred during the duration of a written warranty applicable to the product, and any other person who is entitled by the terms of such warranty or under applicable state law to enforce against the warrantor the obligations of the warranty.

(h) "On the face of the warranty" means:

(1) If the warranty is a single sheet with printing on both sides of the sheet, or if the warranty is comprised of more than one sheet, the page on which the warranty text begins;

(2) If the warranty is included as part of a longer document, such as a use and care manual, the page in such document on which the warranty text begins.

§ 703.2 Duties of warrantor.

(a) The warrantor shall not incorporate into the terms of a written warranty a Mechanism that fails to comply with the requirements contained in §§ 703.3 through 703.8 of this part. This paragraph shall not prohibit a warrantor from incorporating into the terms of a written warranty the step-by-step procedure which the consumer should take in order to obtain performance of any obligation under the warranty as described in section 102(a) (7) of the Act and required by Part 701 of this subchapter.

(b) The warrantor shall disclose clearly and conspicuously at least the following information on the face of the written warranty:

(1) A statement of the availability of the informal dispute settlement mechanism;

(2) The name and address of the Mechanism, or the name and a telephone number of the Mechanism which consumers may use without charge;

(3) A statement of any requirement that the consumer resort to the Mechanism before exercising rights or seeking remedies created by Title I of the Act; together with the disclosure that if a consumer chooses to seek redress by pursuing rights and remedies not created by Title I of the Act, resort to the Mechanism would not be required by any provision of the Act; and

(4) A statement, if applicable, indicating where further information on the Mechanism can be found in materials accompanying the product, as provided in § 703.2(c) of this section.

(c) The warrantor shall include in the written warranty or in a separate section of materials accompanying the product, the following information:

(1) Either (i) a form addressed to the Mechanism containing spaces requesting the information which the Mechanism may require for prompt resolution of warranty disputes; or (ii) a telephone number of the Mechanism which consumers may use without charge;

(2) The name and address of the Mechanism;

(3) A brief description of Mechanism procedures;

(4) The time limits adhered to by the Mechanism; and

(5) The types of information which the Mechanism may require for prompt resolution of warranty disputes.

(d) The warrantor shall take steps reasonably calculated to make consumers aware of the Mechanism's existence at the time consumers experience warranty disputes. Nothing contained in paragraphs (b), (c), or (d) of this section shall limit the warrantor's option to encourage consumers to seek redress directly from the warrantor as long as the warrantor does not expressly require consumers to seek redress directly from the warrantor. The warrantor shall proceed fairly and expeditiously to attempt to resolve all disputes submitted directly to the warrantor.

(e) Whenever a dispute is submitted directly to the warrantor, the warrantor shall, within a reasonable time, decide whether, and to what extent, it will satisfy the consumer, and inform the consumer of its decision. In its notification to the consumer of its decision, the warrantor shall include the information required in § 703.2 (b) and (c) of this section.

(f) The warrantor shall: (1) Respond fully and promptly to reasonable requests by the Mechanism for information relating to disputes;

(2) Upon notification of any decision of the Mechanism that would require action on the part of the warrantor, immediately notify the Mechanism whether, and to what extent, warrantor will abide by the decision; and

(3) Perform any obligations it has agreed to.

(g) The warrantor shall act in good faith in determining whether, and to what extent, it will abide by a Mechanism decision.

(h) The warrantor shall comply with any reasonable requirements imposed by the Mechanism to fairly and expeditiously resolve warranty disputes.

Minimum Requirements of the Mechanism

§ 703.3 Mechanism organization.

(a) The Mechanism shall be funded and competently staffed at a level sufficient to ensure fair and expeditious resolution of all disputes, and shall not charge consumers any fee for use of the Mechanism.

(b) The warrantor and the sponsor of the Mechanism (if other than the warrantor) shall take all steps necessary to ensure that the Mechanism, and its members and staff, are sufficiently insulated from the warrantor and the sponsor, so that the decisions of the members and the performance of the staff are not influenced by either the warrantor or the sponsor. Necessary steps shall include, at a minimum, committing funds in advance, basing personnel decisions solely on merit, and not assigning conflicting warrantor or sponsor duties to Mechanism staff persons.

(c) The Mechanism shall impose any other reasonable requirements necessary to ensure that the members and staff act fairly and expeditiously in each dispute.

§ 703.4 Qualification of members.

(a) No member deciding a dispute shall be: (1) A party to the dispute, or an employee or agent of a party other than for purposes of deciding disputes; or

(2) A person who is or may become a party in any legal action, including but not limited to class actions, relating to the product or complaint in dispute, or an employee or agent of such person other than for purposes of deciding disputes. For purposes of this paragraph (a) a person shall not be considered a "party" solely because he or she acquires or owns an interest in a party solely for investment, and the acquisition or ownership of an interest which is offered to the general public shall be prima facie evidence of its acquisition or ownership solely for investment.

(b) When one or two members are deciding a dispute, all shall be persons having no direct involvement in the manufacture, distribution, sale or service of any product. When three or more members are deciding a dispute, at least two-thirds shall be persons having no direct involvement in the manufacture, distribution, sale or service of any product. "Direct involvement" shall not include acquiring or owning an interest solely for investment, and the acquisition or ownership of an interest which is offered to the general public shall be prima facie evidence of its acquisition or ownership solely for investment. Nothing contained in this section shall prevent the members from consulting with any persons knowledgeable in the technical, commercial or other areas relating to the product which is the subject of the dispute.

(c) Members shall be persons interested in the fair and expeditious settlement of consumer disputes.

§ 703.5 Operation of the Mechanism.

(a) The Mechanism shall establish written operating procedures which shall include at least those items specified in paragraphs (b) through (j) of this section. Copies of the written procedures shall be made available to any person upon request.

(b) Upon notification of a dispute, the Mechanism shall immediately inform both the warrantor and the consumer of receipt of the dispute.

(c) The Mechanism shall investigate, gather and organize all information necessary for a fair and expeditious decision in each dispute. When any evidence gathered by or submitted to the Mechanism raises issues relating to the number of repair attempts, the length of repair periods, the possibility of unreasonable use of the product, or any other issues relevant in light of Title I of the Act (or rules thereunder), including issues relating to consequential damages, or any other remedy under the Act (or rules thereunder), the Mechanism shall investigate these issues. When information which will or may be used in the decision, submitted by one party, or a consultant under § 703.4(b) of this part, or any other source tends to contradict facts submitted by the other party, the Mechanism shall clearly, accurately, and completely disclose to both parties the contradictory information (and its source) and shall provide both parties an opportunity to explain or rebut the information and to submit additional materials. The Mechanism shall not require any information not reasonably necessary to decide the dispute.

(d) If the dispute has not been settled, the Mechanism shall, as expeditiously as possible but at least within 40 days of notification of the dispute, except as provided in paragraph (e) of this section:

(1) Render a fair decision based on the information gathered as described in paragraph (c) of this section, and on any information submitted at an oral presentation which conforms to the requirements of paragraph (f) of this section (A decision shall include any remedies appropriate under the circumstances, including repair, replacement, refund, reimbursement for expenses, compensation for damages, and any other remedies available under the written warranty or the Act (or rules thereunder); and a decision shall state a specified reasonable time for performance);

(2) Disclose to the warrantor its decision and the reasons therefor;

(3) If the decision would require action on the part of the warrantor, determine whether, and to what extent, warrantor will abide by its decision; and

(4) Disclose to the consumer its decision, the reasons therefor, warrantor's intended actions (if the decision would require action on the part of the warrantor), and the information described in paragraph (g) of this section. For purposes of paragraph (d) of this section a dispute shall be deemed settled when the Mechanism has ascertained from the consumer that:

(i) The dispute has been settled to the consumer's satisfaction; and (ii) the settlement contains a specified reasonable time for performance.

(e) The Mechanism may delay the performance of its duties under paragraph (d) of this section beyond the 40 day time limit:

(1) Where the period of delay is due solely to failure of a consumer to provide promptly his or her name and address, brand name and model number of the product involved, and a statement as to the nature of the defect or other complaint; or

(2) For a 7 day period in those cases where the consumer has made no attempt to seek redress directly from the warrantor.

(f) The Mechanism may allow an oral presentation by a party to a dispute (or a party's representative) only if: (1) Both warrantor and consumer expressly agree to the presentation;

(2) Prior to agreement the Mechanism fully discloses to the consumer the following information:

(i) That the presentation by either party will take place only if both parties so agree, but that if they agree, and one party fails to appear at the agreed upon time and place, the presentation by the other party may still be allowed;

(ii) That the members will decide the dispute whether or not an oral presentation is made;

(iii) The proposed date, time and place for the presentation; and

(iv) A brief description of what will occur at the presentation including, if applicable, parties' rights to bring witnesses and/or counsel; and

(3) Each party has the right to be present during the other party's oral presentation. Nothing contained in this paragraph (b) of this section shall preclude the Mechanism from allowing an oral presentation by one party, if the other party fails to appear at the agreed upon time and place, as long as all of the requirements of this paragraph have been satisfied.

(g) The Mechanism shall inform the consumer, at the time of disclosure required in paragraph (d) of this section that:

(1) If he or she is dissatisfied with its decision or warrantor's intended actions, or eventual performance, legal remedies, including use of small claims court, may be pursued;

(2) The Mechanism's decision is admissible in evidence as provided in section 110(a) (3) of the Act; and

(3) The consumer may obtain, at reasonable cost, copies of all Mechanism records relating to the consumer's dispute.

(h) If the warrantor has agreed to perform any obligations, either as part of a settlement agreed to after notification to the Mechanism of the dispute or as a result of a decision under paragraph (d) of this section, the Mechanism shall ascertain from the consumer within 10 working days of the date for performance whether performance has occurred.

(i) A requirement that a consumer resort to the Mechanism prior to commencement of an action under section 110(d) of the Act shall be satisfied 40 days after notification to the Mechanism of the dispute or when the Mechanism completes all of its duties under paragraph (d) of this section, whichever occurs sooner. Except that, if the Mechanism delays performance of its paragraph (d) of this section duties as allowed by paragraph (e) of this section, the requirement that the consumer initially resort to the Mechanism shall not be satisfied until the period of delay allowed by paragraph (e) of this section has ended.

(j) Decisions of the Mechanism shall not be legally binding on any person. However, the warrantor shall act in good faith, as provided in § 703.2(g) of this part. In any civil action arising out of a warranty obligation and relating to a matter considered by the Mechanism, any decision of the Mechanism shall be admissible in evidence, as provided in section 110(a) (3) of the Act.

§ 703.6 Recordkeeping.

(a) The Mechanism shall maintain records on each dispute referred to it which shall include:

(1) Name, address and telephone number of the consumer;

(2) Name, address, telephone number and contact person of the warrantor;

(3) Brand name and model number of the product involved;

(4) The date of receipt of the dispute and the date of disclosure to the consumer of the decision;

(5) All letters or other written documents submitted by either party;

(6) All other evidence collected by the Mechanism relating to the dispute, including summaries of relevant and material portions of telephone calls and meetings between the Mechanism and any other person (including consultants described in § 703.4(b) of this part);

(7) A summary of any relevant and material information presented by either party at an oral presentation;

(8) The decision of the members including information as to date, time and place of meeting, and the identity of members voting; or information on any other resolution;

(9) A copy of the disclosure to the parties of the decision;

(10) A statement of the warrantor's intended action(s);

(11) Copies of follow-up letters (or summaries of relevant and material portions of follow-up telephone calls) to the consumer, and responses thereto; and

(12) Any other documents and communications (or summaries of relevant and material portions of oral communications) relating to the dispute.

(b) The Mechanism shall maintain an index of each warrantor's disputes grouped under brand name and subgrouped under product model.

(c) The Mechanism shall maintain an index for each warrantor as will show:

(1) All disputes in which the warrantor has promised some performance (either by settlement or in response to a Mechanism decision) and has failed to comply; and

(2) All disputes in which the warrantor has refused to abide by a Mechanism decision.

(d) The Mechanism shall maintain an index as will show all disputes delayed beyond 40 days.

(e) The Mechanism shall compile semi-annually and maintain statistics which show the number and percent of disputes in each of the following categories:

(1) Resolved by staff of the Mechanism and warrantor has complied;

(2) Resolved by staff of the Mechanism, time for compliance has occurred, and warrantor has not complied;

(3) Resolved by staff of the Mechanism and time for compliance has not yet occurred;
(4) Decided by members and warrantor has complied;
(5) Decided by members, time for compliance has occurred, and warrantor has not complied;
(6) Decided by members and time for compliance has not yet occurred;
(7) Decided by members adverse to the consumer;
(8) No jurisdiction;
(9) Decision delayed beyond 40 days under § 703.5(e)(1) of this part;
(10) Decision delayed beyond 40 days under § 703.5(e)(2) of this part;
(11) Decision delayed beyond 40 days for any other reason; and
(12) Pending decision.

(f) The Mechanism shall retain all records specified in paragraphs (a) through (e) of this section for at least 4 years after final disposition of the dispute.

§ 703.7 Audits.

(a) The Mechanism shall have an audit conducted at least annually, to determine whether the Mechanism and its implementation are in compliance with this part. All records of the Mechanism required to be kept under § 703.6 of this part shall be available for audit.

(b) Each audit provided for in paragraph (a) of this section shall include at a minimum the following:

(1) Evaluation of warrantors' efforts to make consumers aware of the Mechanism's existence as required in § 703.2(d) of this part;

(2) Review of the indexes maintained pursuant to § 703.6 (b), (c), and (d) of this part; and

(3) Analysis of a random sample of disputes handled by the Mechanism to determine the following:

(i) Adequacy of the Mechanism's complaint and other forms, investigation, mediation and follow-up efforts, and other aspects of complaint handling; and

(ii) Accuracy of the Mechanism's statistical compilations under § 703.6(e) of this part. (For purposes of this subparagraph "analysis" shall include oral or written contact with the consumers involved in each of the disputes in the random sample.)

(c) A report of each audit under this section shall be submitted to the Federal Trade Commission, and shall be made available to any person at reasonable cost. The Mechanism may direct its auditor to delete names of parties to disputes, and identity of products involved, from the audit report.

(d) Auditors shall be selected by the Mechanism. No auditor may be involved with the Mechanism as a warrantor, sponsor or member, or employee or agent thereof, other than for purposes of the audit.

§ 703.8 Openness of records and proceedings.

(a) The statistical summaries specified in § 703.6(e) of this part shall be available to any person for inspection and copying.

(b) Except as provided under paragraphs (a) and (e) of this section, and paragraph (c) of § 703.7 of this part, all records of the Mechanism may be kept confidential, or made available only on such terms and conditions, or in such form, as the Mechanism shall permit.

(c) The policy of the Mechanism with respect to records made available at the Mechanism's option shall be set out in the procedures under § 703.5(a) of this part; the policy shall be applied uniformly to all requests for access to or copies of such records.

(d) Meetings of the members to hear and decide disputes shall be open to observers on reasonable and nondiscriminatory terms. The identity of the parties and products involved in disputes need not be disclosed at meetings.

(e) Upon request the Mechanism shall provide to either party to a dispute:

(1) Access to all records relating to the dispute; and

(2) Copies of any records relating to the dispute, at reasonable cost.

(f) The Mechanism shall make available to any person upon request, information relating to the qualifications of Mechanism staff and members.

10. The Song-Beverly Act*

§ 1790. Short title

This chapter may be cited as the "Song-Beverly Consumer Warranty Act."

(Added by Stats.1970, c. 1333, p. 2478, § 1.)

§ 1790.1. Waiver, effect

Any waiver by the buyer of consumer goods of the provisions of this chapter, except as expressly provided in this chapter, shall be deemed contrary to public policy and shall be unenforceable and void.

(Added by Stats.1970, c. 1333, p. 2478, § 1.)

§ 1790.4. Cumulative remedies; applicability of other remedies

The remedies provided by this chapter are cumulative and shall not be construed as restricting any remedy that is otherwise available, and, in particular, shall not be construed to supplant the provisions of the Unfair Practices Act.[1]

[1] Bus. & Prof.C. § 17000 et seq.

(Added by Stats.1971, c. 1523, p. 3000, § 1, operative Jan. 1, 1972. Amended by Stats.1976, c. 416, p. 1068, § 1.)

*Excerpts from California state legislation regarding warranties.

§ 1791. Definitions

As used in this chapter:

(a) "Consumer goods" means any new product or part thereof that is used, bought, or leased for use primarily for personal, family, or household purposes, except for clothing and consumables. "Consumer goods" shall include new and used assistive devices sold at retail.

(b) "Buyer" or "retail buyer" means any individual who buys consumer goods from a person engaged in the business of manufacturing, distributing, or selling such goods at retail. As used in this subdivision, "person" means any individual, partnership, corporation, association, or other legal entity which engages in any such business.

(c) "Clothing" means any wearing apparel, worn for any purpose, including under and outer garments, shoes, and accessories composed primarily of woven material, natural or synthetic yarn, fiber, or leather or similar fabric.

(d) "Consumables" means any product which is intended for consumption by individuals, or use by individuals for purposes of personal care or in the performance of services ordinarily rendered within the household, and which usually is consumed or expended in the course of such consumption or use.

(e) "Distributor" means any individual, partnership, corporation, association, or other legal relationship which stands between the manufacturer and the retail seller in purchases, consignments, or contracts for sale of consumer goods.

(f) "Independent repair or service facility" or "independent service dealer" means any individual, partnership, corporation, association, or other legal entity, not an employee or subsidiary of a manufacturer or distributor, which engages in the business of servicing and repairing consumer goods.

(g) "Lease" means any contract for the lease or bailment for the use of consumer goods by an individual, for a term exceeding four months, primarily for personal, family, or household purposes, whether or not it is agreed that the lessee bears the risk of the consumer goods' depreciation.

(h) "Lessee" means an individual who leases consumer goods under a lease.

(i) "Lessor" means a person who regularly leases consumer goods under a lease.

(j) "Manufacturer" means any individual, partnership, corporation, association, or other legal relationship which manufactures, assembles, or produces consumer goods.

(k) "Place of business" means, for the purposes of any retail seller that sells consumer goods by catalog or mail order, the distribution point for such goods.

(*l*) "Retail seller," "seller," or "retailer" means any individual, partnership, corporation, association, or other legal relationship which engages in the business of selling or leasing consumer goods to retail buyers.

(m) "Return to the retail seller" means, for the purposes of any retail seller that sells consumer goods by catalog or mail order, the retail seller's place of business, as defined in subdivision (k).

(n) "Sale" means (1) the passing of title from the seller to the buyer for a price, or (2) a consignment for sale.

(*o*) "Service contract" means a contract in writing to perform, over a fixed period of time or for a specified duration, services relating to the maintenance or repair of a consumer product.

(p) "Assistive device" means any instrument, apparatus, or contrivance, including any component or part thereof or accessory thereto, which is used or intended to be used, to assist a physically disabled person in the mitigation or treatment of an injury or disease or to assist or affect or replace the structure or any function of the body of a physically disabled person, except that this term does not include prescriptive lenses and other ophthalmic goods unless they are sold or dispensed to a blind person, as defined in Section 19153 of the Welfare and Institutions Code and unless they are intended to assist the limited vision of the person so disabled.

(q) "Catalogue or similar sale" means a sale in which neither the seller nor any employee or agent of the seller nor any person related to the seller nor any person with a financial interest in the sale participates in the diagnosis of the buyer's condition or in the selection or fitting of the device.

§ 1791.1. Implied warranty; definition; duration; remedies of buyers

As used in this chapter:

(a) "Implied warranty of merchantability" or "implied warranty that goods are merchantable" means that the consumer goods meet each of the following:

(1) Pass without objection in the trade under the contract description.

(2) Are fit for the ordinary purposes for which such goods are used.

(3) Are adequately contained, packaged, and labeled.

(4) Conform to the promises or affirmations of fact made on the container or label.

(b) "Implied warranty of fitness" means (1) that when the retailer, distributor, or manufacturer has reason to know any particular purpose for which the consumer goods are required, and further, that the buyer is relying on the skill and judgment of the seller to select and furnish suitable goods, then there is an implied warranty that the goods shall be fit for such purpose and (2) that when there is a sale of an assistive device sold at retail in this state, then there is an implied warranty by the retailer that the device is specifically fit for the particular needs of the buyer.

(c) The duration of the implied warranty of merchantability and where present the implied warranty of fitness shall be coextensive in duration with an express warranty which accompanies the consumer goods, provided the duration of the express warranty is reasonable; but in no event shall such implied warranty have a duration of less than 60 days nor more than one year following the sale of new consumer goods to a retail buyer. Where no duration for an express warranty is stated with respect to consumer goods, or parts thereof, the duration of the implied warranty shall be the maximum period prescribed above.

(d) Any buyer of consumer goods injured by a breach of the implied warranty of merchantability and where applicable by a breach of the implied warranty of fitness has the remedies provided in Chapter 6 (commencing with Section 2601) and Chapter 7 (commencing with Section 2701) of Division 2 of the Commercial Code, and, in any action brought under such provisions, Section 1794 of this chapter shall apply.

§ 1791.2. Express warranty; definition

(a) "Express warranty" means:

(1) A written statement arising out of a sale to the consumer of a consumer good pursuant to which the manufacturer, distributor, or retailer undertakes to preserve or maintain the utility or performance of the consumer good or provide compensation if there is a failure in utility or performance; or

(2) In the event of any sample or model, that the whole of the goods conforms to such sample or model.

(b) It is not necessary to the creation of an express warranty that formal words such as "warrant" or "guarantee" be used, but if such words are used then an express warranty is created. An affirmation merely of the value of the goods or a statement purporting to be merely an opinion or commendation of the goods does not create a warranty.

(c) Statements or representations such as expressions of general policy concerning customer satisfaction which are not subject to any limitation do not create an express warranty.

§ 1791.3. Disclaimer of implied warranties; "as is" or "with all faults" sales

As used in this chapter, a sale "as is" or "with all faults" means that the manufacturer, distributor, and retailer disclaim all implied warranties that would otherwise attach to the sale of consumer goods under the provisions of this chapter.

§ 1792. Implied warranty of merchantability; manufacturers and retail sellers; indemnity

Unless disclaimed in the manner prescribed by this chapter, every sale of consumer goods that are sold at retail in this state shall be accompanied by the manufacturer's and the retail seller's implied warranty that the goods are merchantable. The retail seller shall have a right of indemnity against the manufacturer in the amount of any liability under this section.

§ 1792.1. Goods for particular purpose; implied warranty of fitness by manufacturer

Every sale of consumer goods that are sold at retail in this state by a manufacturer who has reason to know at the time of the retail sale that the goods are required for a particular purpose and that the buyer is relying on the manufacturer's skill or judgment to select or furnish suitable goods shall be accompanied by such manufacturer's implied warranty of fitness.

§ 1794. Actions by buyers; measure of damages; civil penalties; costs and expenses; attorney's fees

(a) Any buyer of consumer goods who is damaged by a failure to comply with any obligation under this chapter or under an implied or express warranty or service contract may bring an action for the recovery of damages and other legal and equitable relief.

(b) The measure of the buyer's damages in an action under this section shall be as follows:

(1) Where the buyer has rightfully rejected or justifiably revoked acceptance of the goods or has exercised any right to cancel the sale, Sections 2711, 2712, and 2713 of the Commercial Code shall apply.

(2) Where the buyer has accepted the goods, Sections 2714 and 2715 of the Commercial Code shall apply, and the measure of damages shall include the cost of repairs necessary to make the goods conform.

(c) If the buyer establishes that the failure to comply was willful, the judgment may include, in addition to the amounts recovered under subdivision (a), a civil penalty which shall not exceed two times the amount of actual damages. This subdivision shall not apply in any class action under Section 382 of the Code of Civil Procedure or under Section 1781, or with respect to a claim based solely on a breach of an implied warranty.

(d) If the buyer prevails in an action under this section, the buyer may be allowed by the court to recover as part of the judgment a sum equal to the aggregate amount of costs and expenses, including attorney's fees based on actual time expended, determined by the court to have been reasonably incurred by the buyer in connection with the commencement and prosecution of such action, unless the court in its discretion determines that such an award of attorney's fees would be inappropriate.

11. State Tax Information

It seems that every year the tax laws pertaining to small businesses change. Laws change at both federal and state levels. The best advice is for you to keep informed! The federal government's Internal Revenue Service, the friendly IRS, will be glad to furnish you a copy of Pamphlet 334, *Tax Guide for Small Businesses.* Call the IRS (see the front of your phone book, "Government Section" for the nearest number). While you have them on the phone, you might ask for the IRS "YBTK" package, or "*Your Business Tax Kit.*" The YBTK includes Pamphlet 334 plus some other up-to-date info.

Similarly, be sure to obtain the most recent copy of the *Employers Guide* published by the State of California's Employment Development Department. You can find them in the white pages of your phone book also, in that same "Government Section" where you found the IRS number.

Last but not least, contact the State Board of Equalization and ask for the most recent edition of Pamphlet 73, *Your California Seller's Permit.* Write to them at 1020 "N" Street, Sacramento, California 94279, or check the phone book once again for a number to call.

Appendix B

Forms and Sample Agreements

Form 1. General Partnership Agreement

GENERAL PARTNERSHIP AGREEMENT

This General Partnership Agreement is made and entered into as of the ______ day of ________, 1991, by and between (hereinafter sometimes referred to individually as respectively, or collectively as the "Partners").

WITNESSETH

WHEREAS, the Partners own the real property more particularly described in Exhibit "A" hereto (the "Real Estate"); and

WHEREAS, each of the Partners desires to enter into a general partnership agreement upon the terms and conditions hereinafter set forth;

NOW, THEREFORE, in consideration of the mutual promises and covenants herein contained, the parties hereto agree as follows:

1. Nature of Business. The Partners hereby create and establish a general partnership (the "Partnership") for the primary purpose of holding the Real Property for investment and doing all things related to or in furtherance of that business.

2. Name and Principal Place of Business. The name of this Partnership shall be ssociates, and initially its principal place of business shall be at provided that the business of the Partnership may be conducted at such other place or places as a majority in interest of the Partners may hereafter determine. After the execution of this agreement or a subsequent change in the membership of the Partnership, a Certificate of Fictitious Business Name, setting forth the name and residence of each Partner, shall be executed, filed and published as required by the provisions of the Business and Professions Code of California.

3. Term. The term of this Partnership shall commence as of the date hereof, and shall continue until dissolved or terminated as hereinafter provided or in accordance with applicable law.

4. Capital Contributions. The original capital of the Partnership shall consist of the entire interest of each of the Partners in the Real Estate. The Partners acknowledge that they have heretofore each expended money and contributed assets to the Partnership in addition to their interest in the Real Estate. The Partners hereby agree that the amount of such funds expended and the value of such property contributed by each shall be deemed to be proproportionate to their respective interests in the Real Estate, which constitute the original capital of the Partnership, and shall not result in any change in the capital account of any Partner nor shall the same be deemed to be a loan by the Partner to the Partnership. From and after the date hereof, the Partners shall from time to time contribute any additional capital in cash or property that may be necessary or desirable for the operation of the Partnership, in proportion to their respective interests in profits and losses.

5. Advances. If any Partner shall advance any moneys to the Partnership in excess of the capital agreed to be contributed by the Partners as provided in Paragraph 4 hereof, the amount of money so advanced shall be considered a loan to the Partnership and shall not be considered an increase in the Partner's capital account nor increase his share of the profits, unless a majority in interest of the Partners agree otherwise in writing. Such advance shall bear interest at the rate of 9% per annum. Repayment of each such advance shall be made within sixty (60) days following the date of the advance unless a majority in interest of the Partners agree otherwise.

6. Division of Profits and Losses. All profits and losses of the Partnership shall be allocated 50% to

7. Distributions. Within sixty (60) days after the end of each fiscal year of the Partnership there shall be distributed in cash to the Partners, in proportion to their respective shares in the Partnership's profits, an amount equal to the sum of the Partnership's net profit for that fiscal year as computed under this agreement, increased by the amounts deducted as depreciation, depletion, or amortization on the Partnership's federal income tax return, and increased by any payments received and reduced by any payments made by the Partnership during that fiscal year on account of the principal of all debt obligations (other than obligations for which provision was made in computing net profit), less a reasonable reserve for current operating requirements, emergencies, and forseeable capital improvements. Upon agreement by a majority in interest of the Partners, distributions may be made more or less frequently than as provided above.

8. Management. Each Partner shall have equal rights in the management and conduct of the business of the Partnership. No Partner shall, without the written consent of all Partners, knowingly suffer or cause anything to be done whereby Partnership property may be seized or attached or taken in execution, or its ownership or possession otherwise endangered. No Partner shall, without the written consent of a majority in interest of the Partners:

(a) Borrow money in the Partnership's name, other than in the ordinary course of the Partnership's business;

(b) Transfer, hypothecate, compromise, or release any Partnership claim except on payment in full;

(c) Subject to the provisions of Paragraph 12, sell or hypothecate the Real Estate or any interest therein, or enter into a lease of the Real Estate for a term of more than one year, or enter into any contract for any such purpose;

(d) Sell, lease or hypothecate any other Partnership property or enter into any contract for any such purpose, other than in the ordinary course of the Partnership's business.

9. Other Business Ventures. Each of the Partners may engage in other business ventures or make investments exclusively for his own account, whether or not involving real estate, and whether or not in competition with the business of the Partnership, and no Partner shall have any interest in the business ventures or investments of any other Partner. No Partner shall be obligated to offer any business opportunity to the Partnership or any other Partner, with the sole exception of opportunities to lease, sell, or otherwise dispose of the Real Estate.

10. Transfer of Partnership Interest.

(a) In the event of a proposed transfer by a Partner (the "Offering Partner") of all or any portion of his interest in the Partnership or any rights or interests therein, the other Partners shall have the option of purchasing the interest proposed to be transferred in accordance with the terms and provisions of this Paragraph 10. In the event the Offering Partner is a 50% Partner (as defined in Paragraph 19) each of the remaining Partners shall have the option to purchase the interest proposed to be transferred (the "First Option"). In the event more than one remaining Partner exercises the First Option, each remaining Partner who has done so shall be deemed to have elected to purchase a pro rata portion of the offered interest. In the event the Offering Partner is a Minority Partner (as defined in Paragraph 19), the other Minority Partner shall have the option to purchase the interest proposed to be transferred (the "First Option"), and in the event such other Minority Partner does not exercise said option, the 50% Partner shall have the option to purchase the interest (the "Second Option").

(b) At least sixty (60) days prior to a proposed transfer by the Offering Partner, the Offering Partner shall give written notice of such proposed transfer to the other Partners, which notice shall set forth the name of the proposed transferee and all terms and conditions of the proposed transfer. (The latest of the dates on which such notice is given is hereinafter referred to in this Paragraph 10(b) as the "Notice Receipt Date".) The option price hereunder and terms and conditions of purchase shall be the same as the purchase price and terms and conditions set forth in the notice from the Offering Partner. The remaining Partner or Partners having the First Option may exercise that option only giving notice of the exercise of said option to the Offering Partner within thirty (30) days after the Notice Receipt Date. In the event said option is not so exercised, the Offering Partner shall give notice of such fact to the remaining Partner having the Second Option (if any) within 35 days after the Notice Receipt Date, and said remaining Partners may exercise the Second Option only by giving notice thereof to the Offering Partner within 50 days after the Notice Receipt Date. In the event the options granted herein are not exercised within the times above-specified, the Offering Partner may transfer his Partnership interest, but only within one hundred twenty (120) days after the Notice Receipt Date and only to the person, at the price and on the terms specified in the notice of the intended transfer. Such transfer shall not constitute the transferee a partner or entitle him to any of the rights of a partner, other than the right to receive the Offering Partner's share of distributions from the Partnership. If such purchase is not consummated within said one hundred twenty (120) day period, the Partnership interest which was proposed to be transferred shall again become subject to all of the provisions of this agreement and may not thereafter be transferred except in the manner and on the terms herein provided.

11. Death of a Partner.

(a) The death of a Partner shall not cause the dissolution of the Partnership, provided the option granted herein is exercised.

(b) Upon the death of a Partner, the surviving Partners shall have the option to purchase the entire Partnership interest of the deceased Partner in accordance with the terms of this Paragraph 11, at the option price hereinafter provided. In the event the deceased Partner is a 50% Partner, each of the surviving Partners shall have the option to purchase the entire Partnership interest of the deceased Partner (the "First Option"). In the event more than one surviving Partner exercises the First Option, each surviving Partner who had done so shall be deemed to have elected to purchase a pro rata portion of the interest of the deceased Partner. In the event the deceased Partner is a Minority Partner, the surviving Minority Partner shall have the option to purchase the entire Partnership interest of the deceased Partner (the "First Option"), and in the event such Partner does not exercise said option, the surviving 50% Partner shall have the option to purchase the interest (the "Second Option").

(c) In the event of the death of a Partner, the executor or administrator of his estate (the "Executor") shall promptly give written notice thereof to the surviving Partners in the manner prescribed in Paragraph 18 hereof. (The date such notice is given is hereinafter referred to in this Paragraph 11 as the "Notice Receipt Date".) The First Option granted herein may be exercised only by delivering written notice of the exercise thereof to the Executor within 180 days after the Notice Receipt Date. In the event said option is not so exercised, the Executor shall give notice of such fact to the surviving Partner having the Second Option (if any) within 185 days after the Notice Receipt Date, and said Partner may exercise the Second Option only by giving notice thereof to the Executor within 200 days after the Notice Receipt Date.

(d) In the event a surviving Partner elects to purchase the Partnership interest of the deceased Partner, said surviving Partner and the Executor shall consummate the purchase and sale of the Partnership interest within 230 days after the Notice Receipt Date and shall execute and deliver all deeds, instruments and documents as are necessary in connection therewith. The option price may be paid by the surviving Partner, at his option, either in cash or fifty percent (50%) in cash and fifty percent (50%) by delivery of a promissory note in the amount of fifty percent (50%) of the option price, all principal of which shall be due and payable five (5) years after the date thereof with interest payable annually at the higher of nine percent (9%) per annum or the interest rate then being charged for eighty percent (80%), thirty (30) year home loans on homes in Beverly Hills, California by American Savings and Loan Association; provided, however, that in no event shall the interest rate provided exceed the maximum interest rate permitted by law; and provided further that said note may be prepaid at any time without penalty.

(e) The option price at which the surviving Partner shall have the option of purchasing the Partnership interest of the deceased Partner hereunder shall be an amount equal to the deceased Partner's percentage interest in profits and losses multiplied by the amount by which the Partnership's total assets exceeded its total liabilities at the end of first partial or full fiscal quarter ending after the date of death of the deceased Partner, as stated on the Partnership's balance sheet prepared in the regular course of business as of said date, whether or not audited; provided, however that for purposes of computing the option price the value at which the Real Estate shall be carried on said balance sheet shall be determined as follows: Within sixty (60) days after the Notice Receipt Date, the surviving Partners shall each appoint a qualified real estate appraiser by delivering notice thereof to the Executor. (If they choose, each surviving Partner may appoint the same real estate appraiser.) Appointment of a real estate appraiser hereunder shall not be deemed to be an election to exercise the option granted herein, but if a surviving Partner fails to make such appointment within such time, he shall be deemed to have elected not to exercise the option granted herein. Within seventy-five (75) days after the Notice Receipt Date, the Executor shall appoint a qualified real estate appraiser by delivering written notice thereof to the surviving Partners. In the event the Executor fails to do so, the surviving Partners shall name a second qualified real estate appraiser by delivering written notice thereof to the Executor within 90 days after the Notice Receipt Date. Each appraiser shall thereupon appraise the fair market value of the Real Estate in accordance with such generally recognized method or methods of appraisal as he shall select. Within one hundred twenty (120) days after the Notice Receipt Date each appraiser shall submit his written appraisal to the surviving Partner and the Executor. For purposes of computing the option price, the value at which the Real Estate shall be carried on the aforementioned balance sheet shall be the average of the appraisals submitted by the appraisers. The costs of the appraisals shall be divided equally between the surviving Partners and the estate of the deceased Partner (in the case of a deceased Partner who was a 50% Partner) or between the surviving Minority Partner and the estate of the deceased Partner (in the case of a deceased Partner who was a Minority Partner), regardless of whether or not the surviving Partner exercises the option granted herein.

12. The Real Estate. In the event a bona fide written offer to purchase the Real Estate at a purchase price equal to $255,000 plus fifteen percent (15%) per annum from July 1, 19 is received and a Partner or Partners having a 50% or more interest in the profits and losses of the Partnership desire to sell and the other Partner or Partners do not deliver their written acceptance of such offer to the Partners desiring to accept within 30 days after their receipt of such offer together with the written acceptance thereof by the Partner or Partners desiring to accept, the Partner or Partners refusing to sell shall be obligated to purchase the entire Partnership interest of the Partner or Partners desiring to sell at a purchase price equal to the percentage interest of the Partners desiring to sell multiplied by the amount by which the total assets of the Partnership exceeds its total liabilities at the end of the last fiscal quarter ending prior to the date the offer to purchase is received; provided, however, that for this purpose the value at which the Real Estate shall be carried on said balance sheet shall be the amount of the offer. In the event the Partner or Partners fail, within fifty (50) days after receipt of the aforementioned offer, so to purchase the Partnership interest of the Partner or Partners desiring to sell, the Partner or Partners desiring to sell shall in addition to any rights against the Partner or Partners refusing to sell, have the right to sell the Real Estate on behalf of the Partnership in accordance with such offer, and all Partners shall execute and deliver such deeds and other documents and instruments as may be necessary in connection therewith.

13. Services of
shall be responsible for the day-to-day contacts with tenants of the Real Estate and for arranging for the maintenance of and repairs to the Real Estate; provided, however, that any single expenditure exceeding $______________ and expenditures in any calendar month exceeding $______________ in the aggregate shall require the approval of a majority in interest of the Partners. The above services shall be provided by Mr: :y free of charge to the Partnership.

14. Dissolution and Termination. The Partnership shall be dissolved upon the first to occur of any of the following events:

(a) The written consent of a majority in interest of the Partners;

(b) The adjudicated bankruptcy of any Partner or the Partnership;

(c) Any event which makes it unlawful for the Partnership's business to be carried on, or for the Partners to carry it on in partnership; or

(d) A decree of a court of competent jurisdiction.

15. Distribution on Dissolution and Termination of Partnership. In the event the Partnership is dissolved and terminated for any cause, the Partners agree to make a true, just and final account of all matters relating to the business of the Partnership which shall thereupon be wound up and liquidated. Distribution of the Partnership assets shall then be made in the following order or priority:

(a) The payment of all debts and liabilities of the Partnership in the order of priority as provided by law;

(b) The payment of any debts of the Partnership to the Partners;

(c) The payment to the Partners of sums owing on account of their respective capital contributions;

(d) The payment to the Partners of undistributed profits and of any other surplus proceeds in the ratio of profits and losses as hereinabove set forth.

16. Salaries and Interest on Capital Accounts. No salaries shall be payable for any services rendered to the Partnership by the Partners, unless such salaries shall be agreed upon by a majority in interest of the Partners. The Partnership shall pay the reasonable expenses of each of the Partners incurred in connection with the business of the Partnership, including those expenses paid by any Partner himself, and as to the latter, a Partner shall be entitled to immediate reimbursement to the extent he paid such expenses. No interest shall be paid on the capital account of either Partner.

17. Records and Bank Accounts.

(a) The Partnership shall keep accurate books and records setting forth a true and correct copy of all transactions arising out of or connected with the conduct of the Partnership. All Partners shall have the right at all reasonable times to have access to and inspect and copy the Partnership's books and records.

(b) There shall be delivered to each Partner, within sixty (60) days after the end of each annual accounting period of the Partnership, a statement of profit and loss pertaining to said year, and a balance sheet prepared as of the close of said year, together with a copy of the Partnership information tax return (prior to filing thereof with the federal and state tax authorities), showing the profits and losses of the Partnership and distributions to each Partner for the preceding annual accounting period. All of the foregoing shall be prepared by the accountant designated by a majority in interest of the Partners and shall be prepared in accordance with generally accepted accounting principles.

(c) The Partnership shall maintain checking and savings accounts at such banks and other institutions as a majority in interest of the Partners shall agree. All funds shall be deposited in the name of the Partnership and may be withdrawn upon the signature of any Partner; provided, however, that checks exceeding $__________ shall require the signatures of a majority in interest of the Partners.

18. Notices. All notices, statements or other documents which any person shall be required or shall desire to give to another hereunder must be in writing and shall be given only in one of the following ways: (1) by personal delivery, or (2) by addressing the same as indicated below, and depositing it, registered or certified mail, postage prepaid, in the United States mail, or (3) by delivering it toll prepaid to a telegraph or cable company addressed as indicated below. If so delivered, mailed, telegraphed or cabled, each such notice, statement or other document shall be conclusively deemed to have been given when personally delivered or forty-eight (48) hours after the date of mailing, or on the date of delivery to the telegraph or cable company, as the case may be. The addresses of the Partners shall be as follows provided that either Partner may change the address to which notices to him are to be sent by giving notice thereof to the other in accordance herewith:

If to

If to Mr.

19. Definitions. As used herein the term "Minority Partner" means a Partner having less than a 50% interest in the profits and losses of the Partnership, and the term "50%

Partner" means a Partner having a 50% or greater interest in the profits and losses of the Partnership, and the term "majority in interest of the Partners" means a Partner or Partners having in the aggregate more than a 50% interest in the profits and losses of the Partnership.

20. Amendment. This Partnership Agreement may be amended only by a writing executed by all of the Partners.

21. Paragraph Headings. Paragraph headings are inserted herein solely for convenience and the same shall not be used to interpret or construe any provision hereof, nor shall the same be deemed a part hereof.

22. Integration. This agreement sets forth the entire agreement of the parties hereto with respect to the subject matter hereof.

23. Governing Law. This Agreement shall be governed by the Uniform Partnership Act

IN WITNESS WHEREOF, the parties hereto have executed this Partnership Agreement as of the _______day of _________,

Form 2. Limited Partnership Agreement

This Limited Partnership Agreement is executed this ____ day of __________, by and between (hereinafter referred to as the "general partner"), and _______________ (hereinafter individually and collectively referred to as the "limited partners"), to form a limited partnership (the "partnership") for the purposes and upon the terms, covenants, and conditions set forth herein.

1. Introductory Statement.

The objective of the partnership is to raise, from a total of no more than twenty (20) limited partner investors, the sum of Five Hundred Fifty Thousand Dollars ($550,000.00) (such amount, as it may be reduced by the general partner pursuant to this paragraph 1, is hereinafter referred to as the "Construction Fund") for the development, construction, and operation of a skateboard park (as hereinafter described) and incidental activities pursuant to paragraph 4 upon one of the four (4) prospective real estate properties listed on Exhibit "A" attached hereto. In addition, the general partner is authorized, but not required, in its discretion to raise an additional amount of up to, but not exceeding, Three Hundred Fifty Thousand Dollars ($350,000.00) (such amount is hereinafter referred to as the "Acquisition Fund") to be used exclusively for or toward the purchase of the real property upon which the park shall be situated. There need be no segregation of the Construction and Acquisition Funds, it being the intention of the parties that any funds in excess of the Construction Fund be applied, in the discretion of the general partner, exclusively for or toward the acquisition of the real property upon which the skateboard park shall be situated and for no other purpose whatsoever. Notwithstanding the foregoing, in the event that Four Hundred Fifty Thousand Dollars ($450,000.00) is raised, then, at the option of the general partner, the Construction Fund may thereupon be reduced, a skateboard park may be constructed, and the partnership may pursue the business purposes for which it is formed. With respect to both the Construction Fund and the Acquisition Fund, it is anticipated that one-third (1/3) of the monies raised will be in the form of capital contributions from the limited partners, and that two-thirds (2/3) of the monies raised will be in the form of loans from the limited partners to the partnership pursuant to the terms and conditions set forth in paragraph 7. This Agreement shall become binding and effective upon execution, but the partnership shall not engage in the actual construction of any skateboard park pursuant to paragraph 4 unless and until the Construction Fund is raised. Any contribution received from a limited partner shall be placed by the general partner in an interest-bearing trust account until the Construction Fund is raised. In the event that the Construction Fund is not raised by the partnership within one (1) month after the date of the execution of this Agreement, the limited partners shall receive a refund of their respective contributions, including any accrued interest at the rate of five percent (5%) per annum, and this Agreement shall be of no further force or effect. In addition, in the event that the Construction Fund is raised but the general partner, in its discretion, decides not to apply the Acquisition Fund to purchase the real property upon which the park shall be situated, the limited partners shall receive a refund of their contributions to the Acquisition Fund with accrued interest at the rate of five percent (5%) per annum. In the event that the funds raised by the partnership are more than are needed by the partnership, then the limited partners shall receive a refund of such excess pari passu with interest at the rate of five percent (5%) per annum. In all other instances, the interest rate and the terms set forth in paragraph 7(b) shall apply with respect to loans from the limited partners to the partnership.

2. Name.

The name of the partnership is Upon the execution of this Agreement, and upon any subsequent change in the partnership's membership, the partners shall sign, and shall cause to be filed and published in the county in which the principal place of business of the partnership is situated, a Fictitious Business Name Statement setting forth the name and residence of each partner and any other information as required by State law.

3. Place of Business.

The principal place of business of the partnership shall be located at until changed by designation of the general partner.

4. Purpose.

The principal purpose of this limited partnership is to develop and operate a skateboard park, and to engage in any and all general business activities related to or incidental to that purpose. The partnership shall obtain, by lease, by lease with option to purchase, or by outright purchase, real property upon which the skateboard park and any incidental activities shall be constructed, the site to be chosen from those properties listed on Exhibit "A" attached hereto, all of which are located in

5. Certificate of Limited Partnership.

The partners shall, concurrently with the execution of this Agreement, sign and acknowledge a Certificate of Limited Partnership They shall thereafter cause the certificate to be recorded in the office of the recorder for the county in which the principal place of business of the partnership is situated. A certified copy of that certificate shall be recorded in the office of the recorder for any other county in which the partnership shall have a place of business or in which real property it owns shall be situated

6. General Partner.

(a) Authority. The general partner shall have sole and complete charge of the affairs of the partnership, and shall operate the partnership business for the benefit of all of the partners. The general partner shall have the authority to act on behalf of the partnership in all matters respecting the partnership, its business, and its property. Without limiting the generality of the foregoing, the general partner shall have the authority: (1) to employ, at the partnership's expense, such agents, employees, independent contractors, management personnel, attorneys, and accountants as it considers reasonably necessary; (2) to acquire, by lease, by lease with option to purchase, or by purchase, such real or personal property as it considers appropriate to the purposes of the partnership; (3) to alter, improve, repair, raze, replace, and rebuild the partnership property; (4) to let or lease property for any period and for any purpose; (5) to obtain necessary insurance for the proper protection of the partnership and of either (a) the general and limited partners, or (b) the general partner or the limited partners; (6) to pay, collect, compromise, arbitrate, or otherwise adjust any and all claims or demands of or against the partnership; (7) to obtain loans for the partnership or in the partnership's name; (8) to enter the partnership into partnerships, joint ventures, or other business relationships; and (9) to act for the partnership in all other transactions concerning the partnership's real or personal property or business affairs, including the execution of contracts, deeds, options, loan obligations, deeds of trust, notes, and other documents.

(b) Duties and Compensation. The general partner shall not be required to devote its full time to the affairs of the partnership, but shall devote whatever time, effort, and skill may be necessary for the efficient and successful conduct and completion of the partnership's business. The general partner may manage the partnership business and property or may engage others to assist it or to work under its direction and control in the management of the partnership business and property. The general partner shall not be compensated for management services performed by it, except to the extent of its profit participation as set forth in paragraph 8, but shall be reimbursed, on demand, for its actual costs and expenses incurred on behalf of the partnership. If the general partner is not reimbursed within fourteen (14) days after demand, it shall be entitled to receive interest at the rate of eight percent (8%) per annum from the date the cost or expense was demanded. No person, firm, or company owned or controlled by the general partner may be compensated for the performance of management services except with the prior written consent of a majority of the limited partners.

(c) Finder's Fees. The general partner is hereby authorized to pay finder's fees out of the Construction Fund in an amount not to exceed Fifty Thousand Dollars ($50,000.00) to persons who are not principals, officers, or employees of the partnership or of the general partner and who substantially assist in procuring investors for the partnership.

7. Limited Partners.

(a) Capital Contributions. The capital of the partnership shall consist of contributions made by the limited partners. Any contribution made to the partnership by a limited partner shall be allocated one-third (1/3) as a capital contribution to the partnership, and two-thirds (2/3) as a loan to the partnership repayable in accordance with the provisions of paragraph 7(b). The minimum amount to be contributed and loaned by a limited partner pursuant to this paragraph 7(a) and pursuant to paragraph 7(b) shall be Twenty-Five Thousand Dollars ($25,000.00), payable upon or, pursuant to paragraph 1, within one (1) month after the execution of this Agreement; provided, however, that there shall be no more than twenty limited partners.

(b) Loans. In addition to a capital contribution, each limited partner shall make a loan to the partnership. The aggregate amount of all such loans shall be two-thirds (2/3) of the Construction Fund and two-thirds (2/3) of the Acquisition Fund, if any. Such loans shall be repaid only out of the Net Cash Flow of the partnership pursuant to the provisions of paragraph 8(c), or upon dissolution of the partnership in accordance with the provisions set forth in paragraphs 8(d) and 9(c), with interest at the rate of eight percent (8%) per annum, accruing from and after the date upon which the full amount of the Construction Fund or Acquisition Fund is raised, respectively, with respect to loans allocated to the Construction Fund or Acquisition Fund, respectively. The general partner shall have no liability in connection with such loans.

(c) No Additional Contributions. No limited partner shall be required to make any additional capital contribution or loan to the partnership. With the exception of the payments set forth in paragraph 6(c) all monies received by the partnership shall be devoted to the business of the partnership, including, without limitation, the construction and operation of a skateboard park and incidental activities. The general partner warrants and represents that the cost of the park currently existing at 4445 Emerald Street, Torrance, California, was approximately Five Hundred Thousand Dollars ($500,000.00) (as set forth on Exhibit "B" attached hereto), of which approximately Twenty-Three Thousand Dollars ($23,000.00) represents security deposits which are ultimately refundable. The general partner further warrants and represents that, unless the partnership is cancelled for insufficient funding pursuant to paragraph 1, the general partner shall use its best efforts to build a park from the Construction Fund in accordance with a design approved by a majority of the limited partners. In the event that any monies in excess of those in the Construction Fund are needed to complete the construction and to commence operation of a park approved by the limited partners, the general partner shall obtain the approval of a majority of the limited partners prior to obtaining and spending any such excess monies. If the approval of a majority of the limited partners is obtained, the general partner shall have the right to borrow on behalf of the partnership and any such debt shall be repaid pursuant to paragraph 8 prior to the distribution of any Net Cash Flow (as hereinafter defined) to the partners. The general partner warrants and represents that, if the consent of the limited partners is not obtained to expend more monies than are in the Construction Fund, the general partner shall nevertheless construct and open for operation a skateboard park of a reasonable design and capacity.

(d) Powers of Limited Partners. The limited partners shall take no part in the conduct or control of the partnership business and shall have no right or authority to act for or bind the partnership; provided, however, that the approval of the general partner and of the limited partners owning seventy-five percent (75%) of the contributed capital shall be necessary to effectuate: (1) the termination of the partnership, except as provided herein elsewhere; (2) amendment of the partnership agreement; or (3) sale of all or substantially all of the partnership assets.

8. Distributions and Allocations.

(a) Gross Receipts. The term "Gross Receipts" as used herein means all receipts from the conduct of the business of the partnership, except: (i) any net proceeds realized by the partnership from the sale, exchange, condemnation, or other disposition of its properties, or any portion thereof; (ii) any net proceeds from insurance payments (property or title) based upon damage, destruction, or loss of the partnership property or any portion thereof; (iii) all proceeds received from any borrowings or refinancings by the partnership; and (iv) contributions and advances made by the partners.

(b) Net Cash Flow. The term "Net Cash Flow" as used herein means the Gross Receipts of the partnership from all sources less the following: (i) all expenditures of any kind made by the partnership, including, without limitation, taxes, insurance, escrow payments, repair and maintenance expenses, expenditures made for capital improvements and replacements, accountants' and attorneys' fees, real estate commissions, lease payments, amortization payments of principal and interest and all other fees and charges paid with respect to indebtedness of the partnership (except with respect to the loans from the limited partners set forth in paragraph 7(b), and any staff salary or expense reimbursement payable pursuant to paragraph 6(b) hereof; (ii) reserves to pay anticipated expenses, including taxes, insurance, and other expenses or costs incident to the ownership of the skateboard park; and (iii) an amount equal to two percent (2%) of the Gross Receipts per month as a reserve (the "Reserve") for future expenditures for capital replacements and additions to the park. At any time the Reserve equals or exceeds the sum of Ten Thousand Dollars ($10,000.00), no further deduction from Gross Receipts shall be made until the Reserve has been depleted below such sum, in which event the general partner shall continue to reserve two percent (2%) of the Gross Receipts per month until the Reserve once again equals or exceeds the sum of Ten Thousand Dollars ($10,000.00).

(c) Distribution of Net Cash Flow and Allocation of Profit and Loss. The Net Cash Flow and the profit and loss of the partnership shall be determined on a quarterly basis in accordance with the accounting provisions set forth in paragraph 10. The Net Cash Flow, and all profit and loss (including all federal and state income and other tax deductions and credits) shall be distributed and allocated, respectively, as follows:

(i) All of the Net Cash Flow shall first be distributed, and all profit and loss (including all federal and state income and other tax deductions and credits) shall be allocated, entirely to the limited partners until the limited partners have been repaid in Net Cash Flow the amount of their respective loans to the partnership plus accrued interest at the rate of eight percent (3%) per annum, accruing pursuant to the provisions set forth in paragraph 7(b).

(ii) When all of the foregoing loans are repaid, all of the Net Cash Flow shall be distributed, and all profit and loss (including all federal and state income and other tax deductions and credits) allocated, entirely to the limited partners until the limited partners have received in Net Cash Flow an amount equal to their respective capital contributions to the partnership without interest.

(iii) When the amounts set forth in paragraphs 8(c)(i) and 6(c)(ii) have been paid in full, the Net Cash Flow shall be distributed, and the profit and loss (including all federal and state income and other tax deductions and credits) allocated, fifty percent (50%) to the general partner, and fifty percent (50%) to the limited partners collectively. The amount distributed or allocated under the immediately preceding sentence to the limited partners shall be distributed or allocated among the limited partners in a proportion corresponding to their respective capital contributions.

(d) Distributions on Sale of Partnership Assets. The sale, condemnation, or destruction of all or substantially all of the partnership property shall be an event causing the dissolution of the partnership. Upon such event there shall be first deducted from the proceeds received by the partnership such sums as are needed to pay the obligations of the partnership, other than those obligations set forth in paragraphs 8(d)(i), (ii), and (iii), and other than loans assumed by a purchaser of the partnership assets in the event of a sale, and there shall be further deducted from the proceeds such reserves as the general partner may deem reasonably necessary for the expenses of liquidation. The balance of such proceeds shall be distributed in the manner provided below:

(i) First, each limited partner shall receive a sum equal to the loan made by each such limited partner not theretofore repaid, plus interest of eight percent (8%) per annum thereon, accruing pursuant to the provisions set forth in paragraph 7(b). If the net proceeds are insufficient to allocate to each limited partner the portion thereof to which he is entitled hereunder, then the limited partners shall share the net proceeds prorata in the ratio which each such limited partner's loan bears to the total of all loans made by the limited partners.

(ii) After repayment of the loans under paragraph 8(d)(i), each limited partner shall receive a sum equal to the capital contribution made by each such limited partner not theretofore returned, less prior Net Cash Flow distributions paid to each such limited partner. If the net proceeds are insufficient to allocate to each limited partner the portion thereof to which he is entitled hereunder, then the limited partners shall share the net proceeds prorata in the ratio which each such limited partner's capital contribution bears to the total of all capital contributions of the limited partners.

(iii) After repayment of the amounts set forth in paragraphs 8(d)(i) and 8(d)(ii), any remaining net sales proceeds shall be distributed fifty percent (50%) to the general partner, and fifty percent (50%) to the limited partners prorata in the ratio which each such limited partner's capital contribution bears to the total of all capital contributions of the limited partners.

(e) Losses. No limited partner shall be required under any circumstances to contribute further sums to the capital or creditors of the partnership beyond the amount of his capital contribution as provided in paragraph 7(a) and the amount of loans as provided in paragraph 7(b).

9. Term, Dissolution, and Continuation.

(a) Term. The partnership shall dissolve on the 30th anniversary of the date of the first filing for record in Los Angeles County of the Certificate of Limited Partnership.

(b) Dissolution. The partnership shall dissolve upon the bankruptcy, dissolution, or withdrawal of the general partner; provided, however, that the partnership business shall be continued thereafter upon the written consent, made within sixty (60) days after such event, of the limited partners owning in the aggregate two-thirds (2/3) of the total contributed capital, and the election within that time of a new general partner by the same percentage of limited partners. If the partnership business is continued upon the happening of the event described in the preceding sentence, then the general partner or its legal representative shall become a limited partner of the partnership with the same interest in Net Cash Flow and distributions pursuant to paragraphs 8(d) and 9(c) which such general partner would have had had it remained the general partner, except that it shall not bear any losses in excess of its capital account as it exists from time to time.

(c) Winding Up. On dissolution of the partnership, unless it continues as provided in paragraph 9(b) above, the general partner shall wind up the partnership's affairs, liquidate the assets of the partnership, and apply its funds in the manner provided for in paragraph 8(d).

10. Books of Account.

(a) Maintenance of Records. The partnership shall maintain, at the office of the partnership or of its accountant, books, records, and accounts showing separately, in accordance with generally accepted accounting principles applied on a consistent basis, all items which in any way affect the financial and tax computations called for by this Agreement, and shall make the books, records, and accounts available for inspection by any partner, general or limited, at any reasonable time.

(b) Profit and Loss. The net profit or net loss of the partnership for each year shall be determined for accounting purposes on a quarterly basis in accordance with generally accepted accounting practices consistently applied as soon as possible after the end of each calendar quarter.

(c) Periodic Report or Audit. Within thirty (30) days after the close of each accounting period as set forth in paragraph 10(b), the general partner shall, at the expense of the partnership, cause to be prepared a report by an independent certified public accountant qualified to act as such and shall, within sixty (60) days after the close of the accounting period, cause a copy of the report to be furnished to each member of the partnership.

The report shall include a balance sheet as of the last day of the accounting period and a statement of income or profit and loss for the period. The balance sheet or accompanying comments shall set forth all of the following:

(i) The basis used in stating the valuation of assets and any changes in basis during the accounting period.

(ii) The amount, sources, and any changes in capital during the period.

(iii) The names of the partners and their prorata share of the partnership capital and losses at the beginning and at the end of the period.

(iv) Any amounts of loans or advances to or from the general partner.

(v) Any allocated but unpaid distributions to the general partner.

(vi) Total Net Cash Flow and distributions, and the amounts distributed to each partner.

The statement of income or profit and loss shall disclose the amount of and any changes in income or loss and the Net Cash Flow available for distribution compared to the immediate prior period, and shall show in particular the amounts of depreciation, depletion, amortization, interest, and extraordinary income or charges, whether or not included in operating income.

11. Bank Account. The partnership funds shall be deposited in the name of the partnership in one or more banks to be designated by the general partner and shall be withdrawn on the signature of an officer of the general partner.

12. Transfer of Interest.

(a) Assignment by Living Partners. The interest of the general partner shall not be assignable in whole or in part, except when a substitution is made pursuant to paragraph 9(b). Each limited partner may sell his interest (defined herein to include both his capital account and his loan to the partnership), subject to the provisions of this paragraph 12. Partial assignments shall not be allowed. If any limited partner (referred to in this paragraph as the "seller") desires to sell his interest in the partnership, he shall give each of the other partners thirty (30) days' written notice of the election to sell (referred to in this paragraph as the "option period"), and the other partners shall then have an option to purchase the seller's interest during the option period at the price and on the terms stated in the notice, subject to the following conditions:

(i) The interest may be purchased during the option period, with first option to each of the remaining limited partners in the proportion which the contributed capital of each bears to the total contributed capital of the partnership (less the seller's interest). If, however, any of the limited partners does not elect to purchase his share of the seller's interest, the general partner may purchase that share. If the general partner fails to exercise its option, the remaining limited partners may purchase the share, in the proportion that the contributed capital of each of those who elects to purchase the share bears to the total contributed capital of all those who so elect. The seller shall not be required to sell to the partners, however, unless his entire interest is purchased by the remaining partners. In the event the seller's interest is purchased by any of the remaining partners, then the amounts of the seller's outstanding capital contribution and loan shall be allocated prorata among the purchasers.

(ii) If the seller's entire interest is not purchased by the other partners, the seller may sell or transfer it to any person, whether or not a party to this Agreement, at not less than the price and the terms stated in the notice of election to sell. The transferee of the seller's interest shall not be a substituted limited partner and shall have only a right, upon the same terms and conditions as are applicable to the seller, to receive the distributions and allocations set forth in paragraph 8 and a share of distribution on termination of the partnership. With the consent of the general partner, however, the transferee shall become a substituted limited partner, on the same basis as the seller by an appropriate amendment of the Certificate of Limited Partnership.

(iii) If a seller is unable to sell his partnership interest to any person at not less than the price and the terms offered to the remaining partners, the seller shall, before any attempt to sell at a lower price or on more favorable terms, give the remaining partners a new notice of election to sell in accordance with the requirements stated above, and the procedure for purchase and sale shall again be followed.

(iv) Notwithstanding the foregoing, any limited partner may transfer his interest to a trust for the benefit of himself or his spouse or children, and the trust may become a substituted limited partner in the manner and on the conditions described for transferees of living partners.

(b) Transfer on Death. The heirs, devisees, and legatees of a deceased limited partner shall have the rights of a transferee of a living partner pursuant to paragraph 12(a)(ii), subject to administration of the deceased's estate, but may become substituted limited partners in lieu of the deceased partner only with the consent of the general partner pursuant to, and in the manner and on the conditions described in, paragraph 12(a)(ii).

(c) Adjustment of Basis. The partnership may elect, at the option of the general partner, pursuant to Internal Revenue Code Section 754, to adjust the basis of partnership property under the circumstances and in the manner provided in Internal Revenue Code Sections 734 and 743. The general partner shall take all necessary steps to effect the election.

13. Covenant to Sign Documents.

Each party covenants on behalf of himself and his successors and assigns to execute, with acknowledgement or affidavit if required, any and all documents and writings that may be necessary or expedient in the creation of this partnership, the achievement of the purposes of this partnership, or the consummation of any matter covered by this Agreement, specifically including, without limitation, the Certificate of Limited Partnership, any amendment to it, and any cancellation of it.

14. Power of Attorney.

Each of the limited partners irrevocably constitutes and appoints the general partner as his true and lawful attorney-in-fact, in his name, place, and stead, to make, execute, acknowledge, and file any of the following documents, this authority to be limited, however, solely to such documents as the limited partners have agreed elsewhere in this Agreement to execute and deliver:

(a) The original and any modification or amendment of the Certificate of Limited Partnership;

(b) The Fictitious Business Name Statement; and

(c) Any other instrument that may be required to be filed by the partnership under the laws of the State

This paragraph does not supersede any other paragraph of this Agreement, nor is it to be used to deprive any limited partner of his rights under this Agreement, but is intended only to provide a simplified system for the execution of documents. This power of attorney is coupled with an interest and shall survive the delivery of an assignment of a limited partnership interest.

15. Legal Fees.

It is hereby acknowledged that Esq. is a shareholder, officer, and director of each of the corporations comprising the general partner and is a partner of the law firm of It is hereby acknowledged and approved that the general partner has retained the law firm of to provide the legal services relating to the formation of the partnership, the acquisition on a lease or purchase basis of the land on which the park is to be situated, and the construction of the skateboard park, including, without limitation, the drafting of this Agreement and the architects' and contractors' agreements. A fee of Fifteen Thousand Dollars ($15,000.00) has been budgeted for such services and is hereby authorized and approved.

16. Notices.

All notices that may be required under this Agreement shall be given in writing and shall be given either personally or by prepaid certified mail directed to the parties' respective addresses as shown in the Certificate of Limited Partnership, or as later entered in the books of the partnership pursuant to written notification to the general partner. Each notice shall be signed by the party or parties giving notice. A copy of any such notice shall be sent to

17. Recovery of Attorney's Fees.

In any action between the parties to enforce any of the terms of this Agreement or of any other contract relating to the partnership, or in an action in any other way pertaining to the partnership affairs or to this Agreement, the prevailing party shall be entitled to recover expenses, including, without limitation, a reasonable attorney's fee.

18. Right to Purchase Other Property.

It is hereby expressly acknowledged that the general partner has built and operates an existing skateboard park and may build and operate, alone or with others, other skateboard parks in the future. Nothing contained in this Agreement shall preclude the general partner from building, purchasing, operating, or investing in other skateboard parks or real property of any nature whatsoever, including, without limitation, a skateboard park or real property in the locality of any skateboard park built by this partnership. Any such purchase or investment may be made without notice to the other partners, without participation by the other partners, and without liability to them or to any of them. Each limited partner waives any rights he may have against the general partner for utilizing or profiting upon information learned as a consequence of its connection with the affairs of this partnership.

19. Entire Agreement.

This Agreement contains the entire agreement between the parties and supersedes all prior writings or representations. It is binding on the parties, their executors, administrators, heirs, successors, legal representatives, and assigns.

20. Counterparts.

This partnership agreement may be executed in counterparts, and as executed shall constitute one Agreement, binding on all of the parties, even though all the parties do not sign the original or the same counterpart.

IN WITNESS WHEREOF, the parties sign this Limited Partnership Agreement.

GENERAL PARTNER

General Partnership

By ____________________

By ____________________

LIMITED PARTNERS

	AMOUNT OF CAPITAL CONTRIBUTION	AMOUNT OF LOAN
[Name]		
[Address]		
[Name]		
[Address]		

Form 3. Joint Venture Agreement

JOINT VENTURE AGREEMENT

This Joint Venture Agreement ("Agreement") is made and entered into as of the 21st day of December, by and between CORPORATION, a corporation (hereinafter "PPC", or a "Venturer"), on the one hand, and (hereinafter "Malick") and (hereinafter "TFMP"), on the other hand. Malick and TFMP shall hereinafter sometimes collectively be referred to as "Malick/TFMP", or a "Venturer".

WHEREAS, PPC and TFMP are concurrently herewith entering into an agreement (hereinafter the "Picture Agreement") for the development and possible financing, production and distribution of a theatrical motion picture (the "Picture");

WHEREAS, Malick has heretofore developed an idea for a device and/or process (hereinafter referred to as the "Process") with possible applications in motion picture technology or otherwise;

WHEREAS, the parties desire to form this venture for the purposes of further developing and exploiting the Process, all on the terms and conditions hereinbelow set forth:

NOW, THEREFORE, it is hereby agreed:

1. Formation of Joint Venture; Name.

The parties hereby form a joint venture (hereinafter the "Venture") under the firm name and style of ____________.

2. Business of the Venture.

The Venture is formed for the principal purpose of engaging in the development, manufacture, distribution, sale, license, or other exploitation of the Process, a description of which is set forth in Schedule "A" attached hereto.

3. Principal Office.

The principal office of the Venture shall be:

The parties may change such principal office and may establish such branch offices as they may deem necessary or appropriate for the proper conduct of the Venture's business.

4. Capital Contributions.

A. Initial Contributions.

(1) Malick/TFMP. Malick/TFMP hereby contribute to the capital of the Venture their entire right, title and interest, whether acquired before or after the date of this Agreement, in and to the concept, designs, specifications, and other information, data and proprietary rights relating to, or in, the Process and all rights related thereto, including but not limited to all rights in and to any and all derivative processes, and modifications and/or refinements of the Process, whether created before or after the date of this Agreement.

(2) PPC. PPC shall contribute cash to the capital of the Venture (whether by reimbursement or otherwise) subject to the following limitations:

a. PPC's contributions, when aggregated with expenditures and/or reimbursements to TFMP in connection with preproduction and development of the Picture pursuant to paragraph I-C of the Picture Agreement, shall not exceed $250,000.00;

b. PPC shall have the right to discontinue its contributions to the Venture at the Initial Election Point (as hereinbelow defined), notwithstanding that the aggregated expenditures or reimbursements at such point are less than $250,000; and

c. PPC shall have no obligation to furnish, or cause to be furnished, any sums in excess of the initial contributions herein specified.

B. Additional Contributions. Any additional contributions to the capital of the Venture shall be made in accordance with the terms and conditions of Paragraph 5 below.

C. Capital Accounts. For the purposes of this Agreement, the initial capital contributions of PPC, on the one hand, and Malick/TFMP, on the other hand, shall be deemed to be equal. The capital account of each party shall be equal to the value of such party's initial contribution, increased by the amount of any additional contributions made by such party and such party's share of any profits of the Venture and decreased by the amount of any distributions to such party and such party's share of any losses of the Venture.

5. Election to Proceed.

A. The Initial Election Point shall be defined as that time at which PPC approves or disapproves the budget of the Picture in accordance with the terms of paragraph II-A of the Picture Agreement. At said Initial Election Point, PPC shall elect whether or not to go forward with the development of the Process. PPC's aforesaid election shall be totally independent of PPC's election to approve or disapprove the budget of the Picture, i.e., PPC shall be entitled to go forward with the Picture and not the Process, to go forward with the Process and not the Picture, to go forward with both, or to go forward with neither.

B. If, at the Initial Election Point, PPC determines in good faith that additional monetary or other contributions are required for the further development or exploitation of the Process, PPC shall so notify Malick/TFMP in writing within ten (10) days after said Initial Election Point. Within two (2) business days after such notice is given, PPC and Malick/TFMP shall commence negotiations in good faith with regard to the manner and amount in which such contributions shall be made and the effects thereof upon the parties' respective interests in the Venture, including, without limitation, the parties' equity interests therein, it being understood that it is the intent of the parties that there shall be a reallocation of such equity interests if monies or other property, in addition to that specified in paragraph 4A above, are contributed to the Venture other than in equal amounts by both Venturers.

C. If no agreement is reached within five (5) business days after the commencement of the negotiations described in paragraph 5B above, then PPC shall have the right, at any time thereafter, to either:

(1) Refrain from making any additional contributions to the Venture; or

(2) To make, or cause to be made, additional contributions to the Venture, in which event the respective equity interests of the Venturers shall be adjusted as follows: PPC's percentage interest in the capital, profits and losses of the Venture shall be increased at the rate of one percentage point per $10,000 of additional contributions made or caused to be made by PPC and Malick/TFMP's percentage interest in the capital, profits and losses of the Venture shall be decreased in like amount; provided, however, that in no event shall Malick/TFMP's percentage interest in the capital, profits and losses of the Venture be reduced pursuant to this paragraph 5C(2) to less than ten percent (10%). Notwithstanding the foregoing, it is understood and agreed that in the event PPC elects to make additional contributions to the Venture pursuant to this paragraph 5C, it shall have no obligation to contribute any sum or sums certain and it shall at all times have the right to discontinue, or refrain from making, any further additional contributions.

6. Admission of Additional Joint Ventures.

The sole members of the Venture shall be the parties to this Agreement. No other party may be admitted to the Venture without the written consent of all members of the Venture.

7. Expenses; Compensation.

A. PPC shall reimburse Malick/TFMP for its reasonable out-of-pocket expenses incurred in connection with the business of the Venture, provided that such reimbursement and any out-of-pocket expense reasonably incurred by PPC in connection with the business of the Venture shall constitute a part of PPC's initial capital contribution and shall be subject to the provisions of paragraph 4A(2) above. After PPC shall have satisfied its obligation with respect to the initial contribution of capital, the extent to which the expenses of either party shall be reimbursed shall be determined by the management of the Venture.

B. Except as otherwise provided in this Agreement and except for its share of the profits of the Venture, no party shall be entitled to any compensation or other payment for services rendered or provided to the Venture.

8. Profit and Loss.

A. Subject to the provisions of paragraph 5 above, the profits and losses of the Venture shall be divided among and borne by the parties hereto as follows:

PPC	-	50%
MALICK/TFMP	-	50%

B. Determination of the profits and losses of the Venture, to the extent not otherwise specifically provided for in this Agreement, shall be made in the same manner as that used in preparation of the Venture's information tax return for Federal Income Tax purposes.

9. Distributions.

A. At such time or times as the Venture, in the opinion of PPC, shall have cash in excess of its foreseeable needs, the Venture shall distribute such excess cash. Such distributions shall be made wholly to PPC until such time as the aggregate of such distributions and any amounts recouped by PPC pursuant to subparagraph B. below shall equal the entire amount of PPC's contributions to the Venture, and thereafter such distributions shall be made to the Venturers in the same ratio as profits and losses are shared.

B. All sums contributed or caused to be contributed by PPC to the Venture prior to the Initial Election Point shall be included as an item of negative cost of the Picture and shall be recouped by PPC in the manner provided for the recoupment of the negative cost of the Picture pursuant to the Picture Agreement. If PPC elects to go forward with the development and/or exploitation of the Process after the Initial Election Point, such sums contributed or caused to be contributed by PPC to the Venture in connection with such development and/or exploitation as are properly chargeable to the negative cost of the Picture in accordance with generally accepted accounting principles shall be so charged. All contributions not properly chargeable to the negative cost of the Picture shall be recouped by PPC out of any amounts payable to TFMP pursuant to sections 1 and 2 of paragraph III-C of the Picture Agreement after such time as TFMP shall have received Two Hundred Fifty Thousand Dollars ($250,000.00) pursuant to said sections 1 and 2.

10. Rights/Control.

The management and control of the Venture shall be vested solely in PPC. Without limiting the generality of the foregoing, PPC shall be authorized to sell, license or otherwise dispose of any assets of the Venture, or make any other commitment on behalf of the Venture without the consent of Malick/TFMP.

11. Duties.

Malick shall be required to render services diligently and in good faith in connection with the development of the Process during the entire period of his participation in the Venture. Except for his duties in connection with the Picture, Malick shall be exclusive to the Venture until PPC's Initial Election, and in the event PPC elects to go forward with the Picture and the Process, he shall be exclusive until completion of the final answer print of the Picture. In the event PPC elects to go forward with the Process but not the Picture, Malick shall cease to be exclusive to the Venture, but he shall continue diligently to render such services as are necessary to expeditiously develop and/or exploit the Process as and when required by the Venture. Nothing herein contained shall be deemed to modify or enlarge PPC's obligation to make, or cause to be made, contributions to the Venture.

12. Books And Records; Annual Accountings, Bank Accounts.

A. The financial books and records of the Venture shall, unless otherwise agreed by each of the parties, be maintained in accordance with generally accepted accounting principles applied on a consistent basis and in a manner acceptable to the Venture's accountants. The annual accounting period of the Venture shall be the calendar year. Each party shall have full access to the books and records of the Venture.

B. Each Venturer shall receive an accounting statement from the Venture and a copy of the Venture's tax returns annually on a date to be determined by the Venturers.

C. The Venture shall maintain checking and/or savings accounts at such banks as PPC shall determine. All funds shall be deposited in the name of the Venture and may be withdrawn upon the signature of such person or persons as PPC may, in its sole discretion, designate.

13. Liability; Other Interests.

A. Liability.

Neither party shall be liable to the other party or to the Venture for any act or omission performed, or omitted to be performed by such party in good faith and on behalf of the Venture and in a manner reasonably believed by such party to be within the scope of the authority granted to such party hereunder, unless such party was guilty of gross negligence, willful misconduct or breach of this Agreement; provided, however, that Malick/TFMP shall have full responsibility and liability for, and shall indemnify the Venture and PPC in respect of, any loss, cost, damage, demand, expense, liability, claim or suit (including all attorneys' fees incurred in any such suit), or judgment incurred or suffered as a result of, or based on, the claim that the design or operation of the Process constitutes an actual or alleged infringement of a patent or other property right of a third party.

B. Other Interests.

(1) Except as otherwise provided herein, either party hereto may engage in or possess an interest in other business ventures of every nature and description, independently or with others, and neither the

Venture, nor the other party hereto shall have any right by virtue of this Agreement in and to such ventures or to the income and profits derived therefrom.

(2) No party shall be obligated to offer any business opportunity to the others or to the Venture, except opportunities which relate to the Process.

(3) Malick acknowledges that, in the event PPC goes forward with the Picture and with the Process, it is anticipated that the Process will be used in connection with the filming and/or exhibition of the Picture. Malick/TFMP hereby agrees that the Process may be used in connection with the Picture without payment of any kind to the Venture.

(4) In the event PPC abandons the Picture but goes forward with the development of the Process and Malick/TFMP sets up the Picture elsewhere pursuant to Paragraph IIB of the Picture Agreement, PPC hereby agrees that the Venture shall license the Process for use in connection with the Picture for an amount to be determined in good faith between the Venturers on the one hand, and the producer of the Picture, on the other hand. In the event of a dispute as to the value of the licensing of the Process for use in connection with the Picture after good faith negotiations, the dispute shall be submitted to and determined by arbitration in accordance with the rules of the American Arbitration Association.

14. Option To Purchase Interest.

A. The death, bankruptcy, or appointment of a guardian or conservator for the person or estate of Malick or the bankruptcy or assignment for the benefit of creditors of TFMP, or the bankruptcy or assignment for the benefit of creditors of PPC (the party suffering such event being referred to as the "Selling Venturer"), shall give rise to the right of exercise by the other party of the option hereinbelow set forth. For purposes hereof, consistent with the definition of the term "party" hereinabove contained, Malick and TFMP are considered a single party and the occurrence of the above with respect to either Malick or TFMP shall entitle PPC to exercise the option hereinbelow set forth.

B. Upon the occurrence of an event specified in subparagraph A hereof, the other party ("Buying Venturer") shall have the option (the "Option") to purchase the entire Venture interest of the Selling Venturer, including the right to return of capital, share of profit and loss and distributions in accordance with the terms of this Paragraph 14, at the price hereinafter provided.

C. Upon the occurrence of any event giving rise to the option set forth in subparagraph B hereof, the Selling Venturer, or a representative thereof, (hereinafter referred to as the "Representative"), shall promptly give written notice thereof to the Buying Venturer in the manner prescribed elsewhere in this Agreement, provided that the failure to give such notice by the Representative shall not entitle the Buying Venturer to any damages, nor prevent the Buying Venturer from exercising the Option nor have any other effect other than to extend the time to exercise the Option. (The date such notice is given is hereinafter referred to in this Paragraph 14 as the "Notice Receipt Date"). The Option may be exercised only by delivering written notice of the exercise thereof to the Representative within the period commencing upon the date of the occurrence of the event giving rise to the Option and ending, if at all, one hundred twenty (120) days after the Notice Receipt Date. In the event the Buying Venturer exercises the Option, said Buying Venturer and the Representative shall consummate the purchase and sale of the Venture interest within ninety (90) days after exercise of the Option and shall execute and deliver all instruments and documents as are necessary in connection therewith. The option price shall be payable by the Buying Venturer in cash and shall be determined in accordance with paragraph D below.

D. The option price at which the Buying Venturer shall purchase the Venture interest of the Selling Venturer hereunder shall be an amount equal to the appropriate percentage interest of the Selling Venturer in the Venture multiplied by the amount by which the Venture's total assets exceeded its total liabilities at the end of the calendar month during which the event occurred making the option first exercisable, as stated on the Venture's balance sheet prepared in the regular course of business as of said date, whether or not audited, less the amount of any distributions to the Selling Venturer made after the date of the said balance sheet.

15. Dissolution And Termination.

The Venture shall be dissolved upon the first to occur of any of the following events:

A. The written consent of all parties;

B. Any event which makes it unlawful for the Venture's business to be carried on, or for the parties to carry it on as a joint venture;

C. A decree of a court of competent jurisdiction; or

D. Thirty (30) days after receipt of all proceeds from the sale of all or substantially all of the assets of the Venture.

16. Distribution On Dissolution And Termination Of Venture.

In the event the Venture is dissolved and terminated for any cause, the parties agree to make a true, just and final account of all matters relating to the business of the Venture which shall thereupon be wound up and liquidated. All assets of the Venture (other than any patents on the Process, and the proprietary rights in the Process) shall be converted to cash as quickly as is commercially prudent and reasonable. Distribution of the Venture's assets shall then be made in the following order of priority:

A. The payment of all debts and liabilities of the Venture in the order of priority as provided by law;

B. The payment of any debts of the Venture to the parties hereto (other than for capital or profits);

C. To the parties hereto in payment of the balances in their respective capital accounts; and

D. To the extent of any excess, to the parties hereto in the same proporation as the parties share profit and loss.

17. Representations And Warranties Of Parties.

A. PPC and TFMP each represents and warrants that it is a duly organized and validly existing California corporation, with full corporate power and authority to enter into this Agreement and perform its obligations hereunder, and that this Agreement has been duly authorized, executed and delivered and constitutes PPC's and TFMP's binding agreement and obligation.

B. Malick represents and warrants that he has full capacity and right to enter into this Agreement and perform his obligations hereunder and that this Agreement constitutes his binding agreement and obligation.

C. Malick/TFMP represents and warrants that it owns all rights being contributed by it, or to be contributed by it, to the Venture free and clear of any and all liens, claims, encumbrances, rights or interest of third persons, that neither the execution, delivery or performance of this Agreement by it will be prohibited by, cause a default under, or require the consent of any person to, any agreement, instrument, court order, decree or injunction binding upon Malick or TFMP or upon the assets of either, nor has it done any act or suffered any event or condition to exist as a consequence of which any of the assets of the Venture, or its interest in the Venture, will be, or is, subject to any lien, claim, charge, encumbrance or interest of a third person.

D. Each party indemnifies and agrees to hold each other party and the Venture harmless from any loss, cost, damage, expense, claim, demand, suit, liability, or cause of action (and any and all legal fees and expenses incurred in connection therewith) which an indemnified party may suffer, or which may be asserted against an indemnified party, as a result or consequence of any breach of any warranty hereunder, and will defend the indemnified parties against any claim, suit, action or proceeding commenced, which, if successful, would require the indemnifying party to indemnify the indemnified parties.

18. Notices.

All notices, statements or other documents which any party shall be required or shall desire to give to another hereunder must be in writing and shall be given only in one of the following ways: (1) by personal delivery, or (2) by addressing the same as indicated below, and depositing it, registered or certified mail, postage prepaid, in the United States mail, or (3) by delivering it toll prepaid to a telegraph or cable company addressed as indicated below. If so delivered, mailed, telegraphed or cabled, each such notice, statement or other document shall be conclusively deemed to have been given when personally delivered or forty-eight (48) hours after the date of mailing, or on the date of delivery to the telegraph or cable company, as the case may be. The addresses of the parties shall be as follows provided that any party may change the address to which notices to him are to be sent by giving notice thereof to the others in accordance herewith:

If to PPC:

With A Copy To:

If to Malick/TFMP:

19. Amendment.

This Agreement may be amended, modified, supplemented or terminated only by a writing executed by all of the parties.

20. No Violation of Law.

Nothing herein contained shall be construed so as to require the commission of any act contrary to law, and wherever there is any conflict between any provision of this Agreement and any statute, law or ordinance contrary to which the parties have no legal right to contract, the latter shall prevail, but in such event the provision of this Agreement so affected shall be curtailed and limited only to the extent necessary to bring it within the legal requirements.

21. Further Assurances.

Malick and TFMP hereby individually and collectively agree to duly execute, acknowledge and deliver to the Venture, or procure the due execution, acknowledgment and delivery to the Venture of, any and all agreements, assignments and/or other instruments, in a form approved by counsel for PPC, necessary or expedient to carry out and effectuate the purposes and intent of the parties as expressed in this Agreement, and to convey to the Venture all rights herein granted and agreed to be granted to the Venture. Malick and TFMP, individually and collectively, further agree to procure for the Venture properly executed documents and other proof, if such is required, to establish a clear chain of title in themselves to the rights herein granted. Without limiting in any way the generality of the foregoing, in the event the Venture elects to attempt to obtain patent protection with respect to the Process, or any derivative process, application or refinement relating thereto, Malick and TFMP shall, upon request, execute all assignments and other instruments as may be required to evidence the Venture's ownership and Malick/TFMP shall use its best efforts to have the inventor execute such patent applications or other instruments as may be required in order to obtain such patent protection, vesting ownership of any and all rights in the patent application and any resulting patent in the Venture. If Malick or TFMP or both shall fail, refuse, or neglect to so execute and deliver, or cause to be so executed and delivered any such agreement, assignment or other instrument herein provided for, PPC shall be deemed, and Malick and TFMP hereby each appoint PPC, the true-and-lawful attorney-in-fact of Malick and TFMP, respectively, with full right of substitution and delegation to execute and deliver any and all documents, and to do or perform any and all acts and things, reasonably required in the premises in the name of Malick and TFMP or both or otherwise, Malick and TFMP, individually and collectively, hereby acknowledging that the power hereby granted is coupled with an interest and is irrevocable.

22. Confidentiality.

The Venturers shall use their best efforts to maintain in secrecy the Process and all derivative Processes, applications, and refinements thereof. The Venturers each recognize that the other would be seriously damaged if the Process or any information relating thereto should come into the possession of any unauthorized person, and each of them accordingly agrees to use its best efforts to prevent this from happening. In this connection, each Venturer agrees to use its best efforts to prevent any information regarding the Process from coming into the possession of any of its officers or employees except only those who are necessarily called upon to render services in connection with the development and/or exploitation of the Process and each of the Venturers shall exercise care in the selection of its employees who may be authorized to handle, use or otherwise deal with the Process. Each of the Venturers shall maintain close control over all documents, devices, or other information or equipment relating to the Process in its possession.

23. Paragraph Headings.

Paragraph headings are inserted herein solely for convenience and the same shall not be used to interpret or construe any provision hereof, nor shall the same be deemed a part hereof.

24. Integration.

This Agreement and the Picture Agreement set forth the entire agreement of the parties hereto with respect to the subject matter hereof and supersede in full all discussions, agreements or understandings of the parties respecting the subject matter hereof.

25. Governing Law.

This Agreement shall be governed by the Uniform Partnership Act

26. Successors And Assigns.

A. This Agreement shall be binding upon, and inure to the benefit of, the parties hereto and their respective heirs, successors and assigns. No person other than the parties hereto, and their respective successors and assigns, shall have any rights against any of the members of the Venture, or the Venture, by virtue of this Agreement.

B. Notwithstanding the terms of the preceding Paragraph A, Malick/TFMP shall not be entitled to assign any of its rights or obligations under this Agreement without PPC's prior written consent in each instance. Furthermore, as an essential consideration to the execution of this Agreement, without which Malick/TFMP acknowledges PPC would not enter into this Agreement, Malick/TFMP agrees that if it shall propose to enter into any transaction with a third party whereby any of Malick/TFMP's interest in the Venture or distributions from the Venture shall or may be assigned, transferred, hypothecated or encumbered, Malick/TFMP shall give PPC notice in writing of all material details and terms of such proposed transaction, including without limitation the names of the third parties, and such notice shall constitute an offer to enter into an identical transaction with PPC. PPC shall have ten (10) business days thereafter to give written notice of its acceptance or rejection of such offer, and failure to give such written notice shall be deemed rejection. If PPC shall reject such offer, Malick/TFMP shall be free for a period of thirty (30) calendar days after such rejection, but not thereafter, to consummate the proposed transaction on the terms described in said notice, but not on any other or different terms, with the third parties named in such notice, but not with anyone else.

C. PPC shall be entitled to assign this Agreement or any of its rights or obligations hereunder to any subsidiary, parent or affiliate corporation or to any person, firm or corporation which shall succeed to all or to substantially all of PPC's assets, or to all or substantially all of PPC's theatrical distribution facilities, or possessing substantially equivalent theatrical distribution facilities regardless of whether it succeeds to the remainder of PPC's assets, provided that such assignees shall, in any event, assume in writing and agree to perform all of the terms and conditions to be performed by PPC hereunder. Notwithstanding the foregoing, nothing herein contained shall be deemed or construed to limit or prevent PPC from assigning or hypothecating all or a portion of its interests in the Venture.

27. References.

All references to the singular shall, if appropriate, refer to the plural as well, and any references to the masculine shall, if appropriate, refer to the feminine and neuter, and in each case vice versa.

28. Nature of Obligations.

Each and every agreement, covenant, obligation, liability, representation, warranty and responsibility expressed herein as that of "Malick/TFMP" shall be that of Malick and TFMP jointly and severally.

29. Security Interest.

For the purpose of securing the performance of Malick/TFMP's obligations hereunder, Malick/TFMP hereby grant PPC a security interest in all of Malick/TFMP's rights, title and interest in and to, or arising under, this Agreement.

IN WITNESS WHEREOF, the parties hereto have executed this Agreement as of the 21st day of December,

By____________________

By____________________

Form 4. Stock Certificate

SAMPLE STOCK CERTIFICATE

Certificate number _____ (1) _____
For ____ (Number of) ____ Shares
Issued To:
____ (Name of shareholder) ____
____ (Address of shareholder) ____
Dated ____ (Date of issuance) ____ 19__

From whom transferred
(4) ________________
Dated ____________ 19__

No. Original Shares	No. Original Certificate	No. of Shares Transferred

Received certificate number _____
For ____ (Number of) ____ Shares
(Date of issuance)
This ____ day of ____ 19__
____ (Shareholder's signature) ____

INCORPORATED UNDER THE LAWS OF THE STATE OF

NO. _____

____ (name of corporation as given in articles) ____

Shares (number of shares represented by certificate)

The Corporation Is Authorized To Issue _____ Common Shares — Par Value $____ Each

THE SHARES REPRESENTED BY THIS CERTIFICATE HAVE NOT BEEN REGISTERED UNDER ANY FEDERAL OR STATE SECURITIES LAW. THEY HAVE BEEN ACQUIRED FOR INVESTMENT AND MAY NOT BE TRANSFERRED WITHOUT AN EFFECTIVE REGISTRATION STATEMENT PURSUANT TO SUCH LAWS OR AN OPINION OF LEGAL COUNSEL SATISFACTORY TO THE CORPORATION THAT REGISTRATION IS NOT REQUIRED.

THIS CERTIFIES THAT ____ (name of shareholder) ____
is the owner of ____ (number of shares represented by certificate) ____
fully paid and non-assessable Shares of the above Corporation transferable only on the books of the Corporation by the holder hereof in person or by duly authorized Attorney upon surrender of this Certificate properly endorsed.

IN WITNESS WHEREOF, the said Corporation has caused this Certificate to be signed by its duly authorized officers and to be sealed with the Seal of the Corporation.

DATED ____________

____________ President

____________ Secretary

Form 5a. Articles of Incorporation (Short Form)

ARTICLES OF INCORPORATION

I

The name of this corporation is ____.

II

The purpose of the corporation is to engage in any lawful act or activity for which a corporation may be organized under the General Corporation Law of California other than the banking business, the trust company business or the practice of a profession permitted to be incorporated by the California Corporations Code.

III

The name and address in the State of California of this corporation's initial agent for service of process is:

Name ____

STREET Address ____

City ______________________ State CALIFORNIA ZIP ____________

IV

This corporation is authorized to issue only one class of shares of stock; and the total number of shares which this corporation is authorized to issue is ______________.

(Signature of Incorporator)

____

(Typed Name of Incorporator)

Form 5b. Articles of Incorporation (Long Form)

ARTICLES OF INCORPORATION

I

The name of this corporation is ____.

II

The purpose of the corporation is to engage in any lawful act or activity for which a corporation may be organized under the General Corporation Law of California other than the banking business, the trust company business or the practice of a profession permitted to be incorporated by the California Corporations Code.

III

The name and address in the State of California of this corporation's initial agent for service of process is:

Name ____

STREET Address ____

City ______________________ State CALIFORNIA ZIP ____________

(continued on next page)

IV

The names and address of the persons who are appointed to act as the first directors of this corporation are:

Name	Address
(Typed Name of Director)	*(Street, City and State)*
(Typed Name of Director)	*(Street, City and State)*
(Typed Name of Director)	*(Street, City and State)*

V

This corporation is authorized to issue only one class of shares of stock; and the total number of shares which this corporation is authorized to issue is ________________.

(Signature of Director)
____
(Typed Name of Director)

(Signature of Director)
____
(Typed Name of Director)

(Signature of Director)
____
(Typed Name of Director)

We declare that we are the persons who executed the foregoing articles of incorporation which execution is our act and deed.

(Signature of Director)
____

(Signature of Director)
____

(Signature of Director)
____

Form 5c. Statement of Officers

STATEMENT OF OFFICERS

ALL corporations **in active status on the records of the Secretary of State's office**, are required to file an annual statement setting forth specific information. All newly formed stock and nonprofit domestic corporations are also required **to file a statement within 90 days after the file date of the Articles of Incorporation.** The statement for all corporations is to be filed annually by the last day of the month of the anniversary month of incorporation or qualification, or within the five month period preceding the anniversary month, and whenever the agent for service of process or the agent's address is changed. Additionally, some qualified foreign corporations are required to file annually an Officer's Certificate.

STATEMENT BY DOMESTIC STOCK CORPORATION

Statements, pursuant to Section 1502, must be filed on behalf of all domestic stock corporations in active status on the records of the Secretary of State's office. The first such filing is **due within 90 days of incorporation.** Subsequent filings are required annually by the anniversary month of incorporation.

Statement information is to be completed on a form prescribed by, and available from, the office of the Secretary of State. Pre-printed forms, with self-addressed return envelopes, are mailed to the corporation at the time of the initial filing of the articles, for the 90-day requirement, and thereafter, are mailed automatically by this office, to each active stock corporation to the last mailing address of record, for completion and return to the office of the Secretary of State prior to the annual due date. Additional statement forms for the filing of updated information, between the required filing periods, may be obtained at any of the Secretary of State offices (all locations are listed on pages 3 and 4 of this booklet). Failure to file the required statements will result in the assessment of a $250.00 penalty and, ultimately, in the suspension of the corporation's powers, rights and privileges, including the right to the name for corporate use.

State of California
March Fong Eu
Secretary of State

P.O. Box 944230
Sacramento, CA 94244-0230
Phone: (916) 445-2020

STATEMENT BY DOMESTIC STOCK CORPORATION

THIS STATEMENT MUST BE FILED WITH CALIFORNIA SECRETARY OF STATE (SEC. 1502, CORPORATIONS CODE)

A $5 FILING FEE MUST ACCOMPANY THIS STATEMENT.

WHEN COMPLETING FORM, PLEASE USE BLACK TYPEWRITER RIBBON OR BLACK INK

IMPORTANT—Please Read Instructions On Back Of Form

1.

DO NOT ALTER PREPRINTED NAME. IF ITEM NO. 1 IS BLANK, PLEASE ENTER CORPORATE NAME

DO NOT WRITE IN THIS SPACE

THE CALIFORNIA CORPORATION NAMED HEREIN, MAKES THE FOLLOWING STATEMENT

2. STREET ADDRESS OF PRINCIPAL EXECUTIVE OFFICE	ROOM NO.	2A. CITY AND STATE	2B. ZIP CODE
3. STREET ADDRESS OF PRINCIPAL BUSINESS OFFICE IN CALIFORNIA (IF ANY)	ROOM NO.	3A. CITY CA	3B. ZIP CODE
4. MAILING ADDRESS	ROOM NO.	4A. CITY AND STATE	4B. ZIP CODE

THE NAMES OF THE FOLLOWING OFFICERS ARE:

5. CHIEF EXECUTIVE OFFICER	5A. STREET ADDRESS (SEE REVERSE SIDE)	5B. CITY AND STATE	5C. ZIP CODE
6. SECRETARY	6A. STREET ADDRESS (SEE REVERSE SIDE)	6B. CITY AND STATE	6C. ZIP CODE
7. CHIEF FINANCIAL OFFICER	7A. STREET ADDRESS (SEE REVERSE SIDE)	7B. CITY AND STATE	7C. ZIP CODE

INCUMBENT DIRECTORS, INCLUDING DIRECTORS WHO ARE ALSO OFFICERS (Attach supplemental list if necessary)

8. NAME	8A. STREET ADDRESS (SEE REVERSE SIDE)	8B. CITY AND STATE	8C. ZIP CODE
9. NAME	9A. STREET ADDRESS (SEE REVERSE SIDE)	9B. CITY AND STATE	9C. ZIP CODE
10. NAME	10A. STREET ADDRESS (SEE REVERSE SIDE)	10B. CITY AND STATE	10C. ZIP CODE

11. THE NUMBER OF VACANCIES ON THE BOARD OF DIRECTORS, IF ANY: ____________

DESIGNATED AGENT FOR SERVICE OF PROCESS (Only one agent may be named)

12. NAME

13. CALIFORNIA STREET ADDRESS IF AGENT IS AN INDIVIDUAL. (DO NOT USE P.O. BOX) DO NOT INCLUDE ADDRESS IF AGENT IS A CORPORATION.

14. DESCRIBE TYPE OF BUSINESS OF THE CORPORATION NAMED IN ITEM 1.

15. I DECLARE THAT I HAVE EXAMINED THIS STATEMENT AND TO THE BEST OF MY KNOWLEDGE AND BELIEF, IT IS TRUE, CORRECT AND COMPLETE.

TYPE OR PRINT NAME OF SIGNING OFFICER OR AGENT — SIGNATURE — TITLE — DATE

16. I DECLARE THERE HAS BEEN NO CHANGE IN THE INFORMATION CONTAINED IN THE LAST STATEMENT OF THE CORPORATION WHICH IS ON FILE IN THE SECRETARY OF STATE'S OFFICE. DOES NOT APPLY ON INITIAL FILING.

(READ INSTRUCTIONS BEFORE COMPLETING THIS ITEM)

☐ (CHECK HERE) — TYPE OR PRINT NAME OF SIGNING OFFICER OR AGENT — SIGNATURE — TITLE — DATE

SO-200 (REV. 6/88)

Form 6. Corporate Bylaws

ARTICLE ONE

OFFICES

Registered Office

1.01 The registered office of the corporation is located at ____ ____.

Registered Agent

1.02 The name of the registered agent of the corporation at such address is ____.

Principal Office

1.03 The principal office for the transaction of the business of this corporation is located at ______________________________ ____.

Other Offices

1.04 The corporation may also have offices at such other places, within or without the State of where the corporation is qualified to do business, as the Board of Directors may from time to time designate, or as the business of the corporation may require.

ARTICLE TWO

SHAREHOLDERS' MEETINGS

Place of Meetings

2.01 Meetings of shareholders shall be held at any place within or without the State of designated by the Board of Directors pursuant to authority hereinafter granted to the Board, or by the written consent of all persons entitled to vote thereat. In the absence of any such designation, shareholders' meetings shall be held at the principal office of the corporation. Any meeting is valid wherever held if held by the written consent of all the persons entitled to vote thereat, which consent may be given either before or after the meeting and filed with the Secretary of the corporation.

Time of Annual Meeting - Business Transacted

2.02 The annual meeting of shareholders shall be held on the first Tuesday of February of each year, at the hour of 10:00 a.m.; however, should said day fall upon a legal holiday, then at the same time on the next business day thereafter. At such meetings Directors shall be elected, reports of the affairs of the corporation shall be considered, and any other business may be transacted which is within the powers of the shareholders.

Notice of Meetings

2.03 (1) Notice of all meetings of shareholders shall be given in writing to shareholders entitled to vote by the President or Secretary or by the officer or person calling the meeting, or, in case of his neglect or refusal, or if there is no person charged with the duty of giving notice, by any Director or shareholder. The notice shall be given to each shareholder, either personally or by prepaid mail, addressed to the shareholder at his address appearing on the transfer books of the corporation.

Time of Notice

(2) Notice of any meeting of shareholders shall be sent to each shareholder entitled thereto not less than ten (10) nor more than fifty (50) days before the meeting, except in the case of a meeting for the purpose of approving a merger or consolidation agreement, in which case the notice must be given not less than twenty (20) days prior to the date of the meeting.

Contents of Notice

(3) Notice of any meeting of shareholders shall specify the place, date, and hour of the meeting. The notice shall also specify the purpose of the meeting if it is a special meeting, or if its purpose, or one of its purposes, will be to consider a proposed amendment of the articles of incorporation, to consider a proposed reduction of stated capital without amendment, to consider a proposed merger or consolidation, to consider a voluntary dissolution or the revocation of a voluntary dissolution by act of the corporation, or to consider a proposed disposition of all, or substantially all, of the assets of the corporation outside of the ordinary course of business.

Notice of Adjourned Meeting

(4) When a shareholders' meeting is adjourned for thirty (30) days or more, notice of the adjourned meeting shall be given as in the case of an original meeting. When a meeting is adjourned for less than thirty (30) days, it is not necessary to give any notice of the time and place of the adjourned meeting or of the business to be transacted thereat other than by announcement at the meeting at which the adjournment is taken.

Calling of Special Meeting

2.04 (1) On request in writing to the President, Vice-President, or Secretary, sent by registered mail or delivered to the officer in person, by any persons entitled to call a meeting of shareholders, the officer forthwith shall cause notice to be given to the shareholders entitled to vote that a meeting will be held at a time, fixed by the officer, not less than ten (10) days after the receipt of the request. If the notice is not given within seven (7) days after the date of delivery, or the date of mailing of the request, the persons calling the meeting may fix the time of meeting and give the notice in the manner provided in these bylaws. Nothing contained in this section shall be construed as limiting, fixing, or affecting the time or date when a meeting of shareholders called by action of the Board of Directors may be held.

Persons Entitled to Call Special Meetings

(2) Special meetings of the shareholders, for any purpose whatsoever, may be called at any time by any of the following: (1) the President; (2) the Board of Directors; (3) one or more shareholders holding not less than one-tenth of all the shares entitled to vote at the meetings; (4) the Executive Committee.

Quorum of Shareholders

2.05 (1) The presence in person or by proxy of the persons entitled to vote a majority of the voting shares at any meeting constitutes a quorum for the transaction of business.

Adjournment for Lack or Loss of Quorum

(2) In the absence of a quorum or the withdrawal of enough shareholders to leave less than a quorum, any meeting of shareholders may be adjourned from time to time by the vote of a majority of the shares, the holders of which are either present in person or represented by proxy thereat, but no other business may be transacted.

Closing Transfer Books

2.06 (1) For the purpose of determining shareholders entitled to notice of or to vote at any meeting of shareholders or any adjournment thereof, or entitled to receive payment of any dividend, or in order to make a determination of shareholders for any other proper purpose, the Board of Directors may provide that the share transfer books shall be closed for a stated period not to exceed, in any case, fifty (50) days. If the transfer books shall be closed for the purpose of determining shareholders entitled to notice of or to vote at a meeting of shareholders, such books shall be closed for at least ten (10) days immediately preceding such meeting.

Record Date for Determination of Shareholders

(2) In lieu of closing the share transfer books, the Board of Directors may fix in advance a date as the record date for any such determination of shareholders, such date in any case to be not more than fifty (50) days and, in case of a meeting of shareholders, not less than ten (10) days prior to the date on which the particular action, requiring such determination of shareholders, is to be taken.

Date of Notice or Resolution for Determination of Shareholders

(3) If the share transfer books are not closed and no record date is fixed for determination of sharenolders entitled to notice of or to vote at a meeting of shareholders, or shareholders entitled to receive payment of a dividend, the date on which notice of the meeting is mailed or the date on which the resolution of the Board of Directors declaring such dividend is adopted, as the case may be, is the record date for such determination of shareholders.

(4) When any determination of shareholders entitled to vote at any meeting of shareholders has been made as provided in this Paragraph, such determination shall apply to any adjournment thereof except where the determination has been made through closing of the transfer books and the stated period of closing has expired, in which case the Board of Directors shall make a new determination as hereinbefore provided.

Voting List

2.07 At least ten (10) days before each meeting of shareholders, the officer or agent having charge of the stock transfer books for shares of the corporation shall make a complete list of the shareholders entitled to vote at such meeting or any adjournment thereof, arranged in alphabetical order, with the address of and the number of shares held by each, which list, for a period of ten (10) days prior to such meeting, shall be kept on file at the office of the corporation and shall be subject to inspection by any shareholder at any time during usual business hours. Such list shall also be produced and kept open at the time and place of the meeting. The original share transfer books shall be prima facie evidence as to who are the shareholders entitled to examine such list or transfer books or to vote at any meeting of shareholders. However, failure to prepare such a list shall not affect the validity of any action taken at the meeting.

Votes Per Share

2.08 Each outstanding share, regardless of class, shall be entitled to one vote on each matter submitted to a vote at a meeting of shareholders, except to the extent that the voting rights of shares of any class or classes are limited by the articles of incorporation.

Cumulative Voting

2.09 Unless prohibited by the articles of incorporation every shareholder entitled to vote at any election for Directors may cumulate his votes and give one candidate a number of votes equal to the number of Directors to be elected multiplied by the number of votes to which his shares are entitled, or distribute his votes on the same principle among any number of candidates. The candidates receiving the highest number of votes up to the number of Directors to be elected are elected. No shareholder may cumulate his votes unless he shall have given written notice of his intention so to do to the Secretary of the corporation on or before the day preceding the election at which such votes will be cumulated. If any shareholder gives written notice as provided above, all shareholders may cumulate their votes.

Voting by Voice and Ballot

2.10 Elections for Directors need not be by ballot unless a shareholder demands election by ballot at the election and before the voting begins.

Proxies

2.11 A shareholder may vote either in person or by proxy executed in writing by the shareholder or by his duly authorized attorney in fact. No proxy shall be valid after eleven (11) months from the date of its execution unless otherwise provided in the proxy. Each proxy shall be revocable unless expressly provided therein to be irrevocable, and in no event shall it remain irrevocable for a period of more than eleven (11) months.

Waiver of Notice

2.12 Any notice required by law or these bylaws may be waived by the execution by the person entitled to the notice of a written waiver of such notice, which may be signed before or after the time stated in the notice.

Action Without Meeting

2.13 Any action which, under any provision of the Business Corporation Act may be taken at a meeting of the shareholders, may be taken without a meeting if authorized by a writing signed by all of the persons who would be entitled to vote on such action a meeting, and filed with the Secretary of the corporation. Any such signed consent, or a signed copy thereof, shall be placed on the minute book of the corporation.

Appointment of Inspectors of Election

2.14 (1) In advance of any meeting of shareholders, the Board of Directors may appoint any persons, other than nominees for office, as inspectors of election to act at such meeting or any adjournment thereof. If inspectors of election are not so appointed, the chairman of any such meeting may, and on the request of any shareholder or his proxy shall, appoint inspectors of election at the meeting. The number of inspectors shall be either one or three. If appointed at a meeting on the request of one or more shareholders or proxies, the majority of shares present shall determine whether one or three inspectors are to be appointed. In case any person appointed as inspector fails to appear or fails or refuses to act, the vacancy may be filled by appointment by the Board of Directors in advance of the meeting, or at the meeting by the person acting as chairman.

Duties of Inspectors

(2) The inspectors of election shall determine the number of shares outstanding and the voting power of each, the shares represented at the meeting, the existence of a quorum, the authenticity, validity, and effect of proxies, receive votes, ballots, or consents, hear and determine all challenges and questions in any way arising in connection with the right to vote, count and tabulate all votes or consents, determine the result, and do such acts as may be proper to conduct the election or vote with fairness to all shareholders. The inspectors of election shall perform their duties impartially, in good faith, to the best of their ability and as expeditiously as is practical.

Vote of Inspectors

(3) If there are three inspectors of election, the decision, act or certificate of a majority is effective in all respects as the decision, act, or certificate of all.

Report of Inspectors

(4) On request of the chairman of the meeting or of any shareholder or his proxy the inspectors shall make a report in writing of any challenge or question or matter determined by them and execute a certificate of any fact found by them. Any report or certificate made by them is prima facie evidence of the facts stated therein.

Conduct of Meetings

2.15 At every meeting of the shareholders, the President, or in his absence, the Vice-President designated by the President, or, in the absence of such designation, a chairman (who shall be one of the Vice Presidents, if any is present) chosen by a majority in interest of the shareholders of the corporation present in person or by proxy and entitled to vote, shall act as chairman. The Secretary of the corporation, or in his absence, an Assistant Secretary, shall act as secretary of all meetings of the shareholders. If no Secretary or Assistant Secretary is present, the chairman may appoint another person to act as secretary of the meeting.

ARTICLE THREE

DIRECTORS

Directors Defined

3.01 "Directors" or "Board", when used in relation to any power or duty requiring collective action, means "Board of Directors".

Powers

3.02 The business and affairs of the corporation and all corporate powers shall be exercised by or under authority of the Board of Directors, subject to limitations imposed by the Business Corporation Act, the articles of incorporation, or these bylaws as to action which requires authorization or approval by the shareholders.

Number of Directors

3.03 The number of Directors of this corporation shall be ________, none of whom need be shareholders or residents of the State of . The number of Directors may be increased or decreased from time to time by amendment to these bylaws, but no decrease shall have the effect of shortening the term of any incumbent Director.

Term of Office

3.04 The Directors named in the articles shall hold office until their successors are elected by the shareholders and the successors are qualified. Directors other than those named in the articles shall hold office until the next annual meeting and until their successors are elected and qualified.

Vacancies

3.05 (1) Vacancies in the Board of Directors shall exist in the case of the happening of any of the following events: (a) the death, resignation, or removal of any Director; (b) the authorized number of Directors is increased; or (c) at any annual, regular, or special meeting of shareholders at which any Director is elected, the shareholders fail to elect the full authorized number of Directors to be voted for at that meeting.

Declaration of Vacancy

(2) The Board of Directors may declare vacant the office of a Director in either of the following cases: (a) if he is adjudged incompetent by an order of court, or finally convicted of a felony; or (b) if within sixty (60) days after notice of his election, he does not accept the office either in writing or by attending a meeting of the Board of Directors.

Filling Vacancies by Directors

(3) Vacancies may be filled by a majority of the remaining Directors, though less than a quorum, or by a sole remaining Director. Each Director so elected shall hold office until his successor is elected at an annual, regular, or special meeting of the shareholders.

Filling Vacancies by Shareholders - Reduction of Authorized Number of Directors

(4) The shareholders may elect a Director at any time to fill any vacancy not filled by the Directors. If the Board of Directors accepts the resignation of a Director tendered to take effect at a future time, the Board or the shareholders may elect a successor to take office when the resignation becomes effective. A reduction of the authorized number of Directors does not remove any Director prior to the expiration of his term of office.

Removal of Directors

3.06 The entire Board of Directors or any individual Director may be removed from office by a vote of shareholders holding a majority of the outstanding shares entitled to vote at an election of Directors. However, unless cumulative voting has been denied by statute or by the Articles of Incorporation, and if less than the entire Board is to be removed, no one of the Directors may be removed if the votes cast against his removal would be sufficient to elect him if cumulatively voted at an election of the entire Board of Directors, or if there be classes of Directors, at an election of the class of Directors of which he is a part. If any or all Directors are so removed, new Directors may be elected at the same meeting. Whenever a class or series of shares is entitled to elect one or more Directors under authority granted by the articles, the provisions of this paragraph apply to the vote of that class or series and not to the vote of the outstanding shares as a whole.

Place of Meetings

3.07 Regular meetings of the Board of Directors shall be held at any place within or without the State of which has been designated from time to time by resolution of the Board or by written consent of all members of the Board. In the absence of such designation, regular meetings shall be held at the principal office of the corporation. Special meetings of the Board may be held either at a place so designated or at the principal office. Any regular or special meeting is valid, wherever held, if held on written consent of all members of the Board given either before or after the meeting and filed with the Secretary of the corporation.

Regular Meetings

3.08 (1) Regular meetings of the Board of Directors shall be held at such time and place as shall from time to time be determined by the Board.

Call of Regular Meetings

(2) All regular meetings of the Board of Directors of this corporation shall be called by the President or, if he is

absent or is unable or refuses to act, by any Vice President or by any two Directors.

Notice of Regular Meetings

(3) Written notice of the time and place of the regular meetings of the Board of Directors shall be delivered personally to each Director, or sent to each Director by mail or by other form of written communication at least seven (7) days before the meeting. If the address of a Director is not shown on the records and is not readily ascertainable, notice shall be addressed to him at the corporation's office located in the city or place in which the meetings of the Directors are regularly held. Notice of the time and place of holding an adjourned meeting of a meeting need not be given to absent Directors if the time and place are fixed at the meeting adjourned.

Validation of Meeting Defectively Called or Noticed

(4) The transactions of any meeting of the Board of Directors, however called and noticed or wherever held, are as valid as though effected at a meeting duly held after regular call and notice, if a quorum is present and if, either before or after the meeting, each of the Directors not present signs a waiver of notice, a consent to holding the meeting, or an approval of the minutes thereof. All such waivers, consents, or approvals shall be filed with the corporate records or made a part of the minutes of the meeting. Attendance by a Director at a meeting shall constitute a waiver of notice of the meeting, unless the express purpose for such attendance is to present the objection that the meeting is not lawfully called or convened.

Call of Special Meeting

3.09 (1) Special meetings of the Board of Directors of this corporation shall be called by the President or, if he is absent or is unable or refuses to act, by any Vice President or by any two Directors.

(2) Written notice of the time, place, and purpose of special meetings of the Board of Directors shall be delivered personally to each Director, or sent to each Director by mail or by other form of written communication, at least seven (7) days before the meeting. If the address of a Director is not shown on the records and is not readily ascertainable, notice shall be addressed to him at the city or place in which the meetings of the Directors are regularly held. Notice of the time and place of holding an adjourned meeting of a meeting need not be given to absent Directors if the time and place are fixed at the meeting adjourned.

Quorum

3.10 A majority of the authorized number of Directors constitutes a quorum of the Board for the transaction of business.

Majority Action

3.11 Every act or decision done or made by a majority of the Directors present at any meeting duly held at which a quorum is present is the act of the Board of Directors, unless an act of a greater number is required by the articles of incorporation or these bylaws. Each Director who is present at a meeting will be deemed to have assented to any action taken at such meeting unless his dissent to the action is entered in the minutes of the meeting, or unless he shall file his written dissent thereto with the Secretary of the meeting or shall forward such dissent by registered mail to the Secretary of the corporation immediately after such meeting.

Action by Consent of Board Without Meeting

3.12 Any action required or permitted to be taken by the Board of Directors under any provision of the Business Corporation Act may be taken without a meeting, if all members of the Board shall individually or collectively consent in writing to such action. Such written consent or consents shall be filed with the minutes of the proceedings of the Board. Such action by written consent shall have the same force and effect as a unanimous vote of such Directors. Any certificate or other document filed under any provision of the Business Corporation Act which relates to action so taken shall state that the action was taken by unanimous written consent of the Board of Directors without a meeting and that these bylaws authorize the Directors to so act, and such statement shall be prima facie evidence of such authority.

Adjournment

3.13 (1) In the absence of a quorum a majority of the Directors present may adjourn from time to time until the time fixed for the next regular meeting of the Board.

Notice of Adjourned Meeting

(2) Notice of the time and place of holding an adjourned meeting of a meeting need not be given to absent Directors if the time and place are fixed at the meeting adjourned.

Conduct of Meetings

3.14 At every meeting of the Board of Directors, the Chairman of the Board of Directors, if there shall be such an officer, and if not, the President, or in his absence, the Vice President designated by him, or in the absence of such designation, a chairman chosen by a majority of the Directors present, shall preside. The Secretary of the corporation shall act as Secretary of the Board of Directors. In case the Secretary shall be absent from any meeting, the chairman may appoint any person to act as Secretary of the meeting.

Compensation

3.15 Directors shall receive such compensation for their services as Directors as shall be determined from time to time by resolution of the Board. Any Directors may serve the corporation in any other capacity as an officer, agent, employee or otherwise and receive compensation therefor.

Indemnification of Directors and Officers

3.16 The Board of Directors shall authorize the corporation to pay or reimburse any present or former Director or officer of the corporation any costs or expenses actually and necessarily incurred by him in any action, suit, or proceeding to which he is made a party by reason of his holding such position; provided, however, that he shall not receive such indemnification if he be finally adjudicated therein to be liable for negligence or misconduct in office, or if such indemnification would violate law. The indemnification herein provided shall also extend to good faith expenditures incurred in anticipation of, or preparation for, threatened or proposed litigation. The Board of Directors may, in proper cases, extend the indemnification to cover the good faith settlement of any such action, suit, or proceeding, whether formally instituted or not.

Interested Directors

3.17 Any contract or other transaction between the corporation and any of its Directors (or any corporation or firm in which any of its Directors is directly or indirectly interested) shall be valid for all purposes notwithstanding the presence of such Director at the meeting authorizing such contract or transaction, or his participation in such meeting. The foregoing shall, however, apply only if the interest of each such Director is known or disclosed to the Board of Directors and it shall nevertheless authorize or ratify such contract or transaction by a majority of the Directors present, each such interested Director to be counted in determining whether a quorum is present but not in calculating the majority necessary to carry such vote. This section shall not be construed to invalidate any contract or transaction which would be valid in the absence of this paragraph.

Executive Committee

3.18 The Board of Directors may at any time appoint from among its members an executive committee and one or more other committees, each of which so appointed shall have such power and authority to conduct the business and affairs of the corporation as is vested by law, the articles of incorporation, and these bylaws in the Board of Directors as a whole, except that it may not take any action that is specifically required by statute to be taken by the entire Board of Directors. Each Director shall be deemed to have assented to any action of the executive committee unless he shall, within seven (7) days after receiving actual or constructive notice of such action, deliver his written dissent thereto to the Secretary of the corporation. Members of the executive committee shall serve at the pleasure of the Board of Directors.

Other Committees

3.19 The Board of Directors, by an affirmative vote of a majority of the members constituting the Board of Directors, may appoint other committees which shall have and may exercise such powers as shall be conferred or authorized by resolution of the Board. A majority of any such committee may determine its action and fix the time and place of its meetings unless the Board of Directors shall otherwise provide. The Board of Directors, by affirmative vote, shall have the power at any time to change the powers and members of any committee of the Board, to fill vacancies, to determine the compensation of such committee members, and to dissolve any such committee.

ARTICLE FOUR

OFFICERS

Number and Titles

4.01 The officers of the corporation shall be a President, a Vice President, a Secretary, and a Treasurer. The corporation may also have, at the discretion of the Board of Directors, a Chairman of the Board, one or more additional Vice Presidents, one or more Assistant Secretaries, one or more Assistant Treasurers, and such other officers as may be appointed in accordance with the provisions of Paragraph 4.03 of this Article. One person may hold two or more offices.

Election

4.02 The officers of the corporation, except such officers as may be appointed in accordance with the provisions of Paragraph 4.03 or Paragraph 4.05 of this Article, shall be chosen annually by the Board of Directors, and each shall hold his office until he shall resign or shall be removed or otherwise disqualified to serve, or his successor shall be elected and qualified.

Subordinate Officers

4.03 The Board of Directors may appoint such other officers or agents as the business of the corporation may require, each of whom shall hold office for such period, have such authority, and perform such duties as are provided in these bylaws or as the Board of Directors may from time to time determine. The Board of Directors may delegate to any officer or committee the power to appoint any such subordinate officers, committees or agents, to specify their duties and to determine their compensation.

Removal and Resignation

4.04 Any officer may be removed, either with or without cause, by a majority of the Directors at the time in office, at any regular or special meeting of the Board, or, except in case of an officer chosen by the Board of Directors, by any committee or officer upon whom such power of removal may be conferred by the

Board of Directors; provided, however, that such removal shall not be without prejudice to the contract rights, if any, of the person removed. Any officer may resign at any time by giving written notice to the Board of Directors or the President, or to the Secretary of the corporation. Any such resignation shall take effect at the date of the receipt of such notice or at any later time specified therein; and, unless otherwise specified therein, the acceptance of such resignation shall not be necessary to make it effective.

Vacancies

4.05 If the office of the President, Vice President, Secretary, Treasurer, Assistant Secretary (if any), or Assistant Treasurer (if any) becomes vacant by reason of death, resignation, removal, or otherwise, the Board of Directors shall elect a successor who shall hold office for the unexpired term, and until his successor is elected.

Chairman of the Board

4.06 The Chairman of the Board, if there shall be such an officer, shall, if present, preside at all meetings of the Board of Directors and exercise and perform such other powers and duties as may be from time to time assigned to him by the Board of Directors or prescribed by the bylaws.

President

4.07 Subject to such supervisory powers, if any, as may be given by the Board of Directors to the Chairman of the Board, if there be such an officer, the President shall be the chief executive officer of the corporation and shall, subject to the control of the Board of Directors, have general supervision, direction, and control of the business and officers of the corporation, and shall have the general powers and duties of management usually vested in the office of the President of a corporation, and shall have such other powers and duties as may be prescribed by the Board of Directors or the bylaws. Within this authority and in the course of his duties he shall:

Conduct Meetings

(1) Preside at all meetings of the shareholders, and in the absence of the Chairman of the Board, or, if there be none, at all meetings of the Board of Directors, and shall be ex officio a member of all the standing committees, including the executive committee, if any.

Sign Share Certificates

(2) Sign all certificates of stock of the corporation, in conjunction with the Secretary or Assistant Secretary, unless otherwise ordered by the Board of Directors.

(3) When authorized by the Board of Directors or required by law, execute, in the name of the corporation, deeds, conveyances, notices, leases, checks, drafts, bills of exchange, warrants, promissory notes, bonds, debentures, contracts, and other papers and instruments in writing, and unless the Board of Directors shall order otherwise by resolution, make such contracts as the ordinary conduct of the corporation's business may require.

Hire and Fire Employees

(4) Appoint and remove, employ and discharge, and prescribe the duties and fix the compensation of all agents, employees, and clerks of the corporation other than the duly appointed officers, subject to the approval of the Board of Directors, and control, subject to the direction of the Board of Directors, all of the officers, agents, and employees of the corporation.

Meetings of Other Corporations

(5) Unless otherwise directed by the Board of Directors, attend, or designate a substitute representative to attend all meetings of the shareholders of any corporation in which this corporation holds stock.

Vice President

4.08 In the absence or disability of the President, the Vice Presidents, in order of their rank as fixed by the Board of Directors or, if not ranked, the Vice President designated by the Board of Directors, shall perform all the duties of the President, and when so acting shall have all the powers of, and be subject to all the restrictions on, the President. The Vice Presidents shall have such other powers and perform such other duties as from time to time may be prescribed for them respectively by the Board of Directors or the bylaws.

Secretary

4.09 The Secretary shall:

Sign Share Cerfificates

(1) Sign, with the President or a Vice President, certificates for shares of the corporation.

Attest Bylaws

(2) Attest and keep at the principal office of the corporation the original or a copy of its bylaws, as amended.

Minutes of Meetings

(3) Keep at the principal office of the corporation, or such other place as the Board of Directors may order, a book of minutes of all meetings of its Directors and shareholders, executive committee, and other committees, with the time and place of holding, whether regular or special, and, if special, how authorized, the notice thereof given, the names of those present at directors' meetings, the number of shares or members present or represented at shareholders' meetings, and the proceedings thereof.

Sign or Attest Documents and Affix Seal

(4) Sign or attest such documents as may be required by law or the business of the corporation, and to keep the corporate seal and affix it to such instruments as may be necessary or proper.

Notices

(5) See that all notices are duly given in accordance with the provisions of these bylaws or as required by law. In case of the absence or disability of the Secretary, or his refusal or neglect to act, notice may be given and served by an Assistant Secretary or by the President or Vice President or by the Board of Directors.

Custodian of Records and Seal

(6) Be custodian of the records and of the seal of the corporation and see that it is engraved, lithographed, printed, stamped, impressed upon or affixed to all certificates for shares prior to their issuance and to all documents, the execution of which on behalf of the corporation under its seal is duly authorized in accordance with the provisions of these bylaws.

Share Register

(7) Keep at the principal office of the corporation a share register or duplicate share register showing the names of the shareholders and their addresses; the number, date of issue, and class of shares represented by each outstanding share certificate; and the number and date of cancellation of each certificate surrendered for cancellation.

Reports and Statements

(8) See that the books, reports, statements, certificates and all other documents and records required by law are properly kept and filed.

Exhibit Records

(9) Exhibit at all reasonable times to any Director on application, or on written demand stating the purpose thereof of any person who has been a shareholder of record for at least six (6) months immediately preceding his demand or who is the holder of record of at least five (5) percent of all of the outstanding shares of the corporation, upon application, the bylaws, the share register, and minutes of proceedings of the shareholders and Directors of the corporation.

Other Duties

(10) In general, perform all duties incident to the office of Secretary, and such other duties as from time to time may be assigned to him by the Board of Directors.

Absence of Secretary

(11) In case of the absence or disability of the Secretary or his refusal or neglect to act, the Assistant Secretary, or if there be none, the Treasurer, acting as Assistant Secretary, may perform all of the functions of the Secretary. In case of the absence or disability of, or the refusal or neglect to act of both the Secretary, the Assistant Secretary and Treasurer, any person thereunto authorized by the President or Vice President or by the Board of Directors may perform the functions of the Secretary.

Assistant Secretary

4.10 At the request of the Secretary, or in his absence or disability, the Assistant Secretary, designated as set forth in preceding Subparagraph 4.10(11) of these bylaws, shall perform all the duties of the Secretary, and when so acting, he shall have all the powers of, and be subject to all the restrictions on, the Secretary. The Assistant Secretary shall perform such other duties as from time to time may be assigned to him by the Board of Directors or the Secretary.

Treasurer

4.11 The Treasurer shall:

Funds--Custody and Deposit

(1) Have charge and custody of, and be responsible for, all funds and securities of the corporation, and deposit all such funds in the name of the corporation in such banks, trust companies, or other depositaries as shall be selected by the Board of Directors.

Funds--Receipt

(2) Receive, and give receipt for, moneys due and payable to the corporation from any source whatever.

Funds--Disbursements

(3) Disburse, or cause to be disbursed, the funds of the corporation as may be directed by the Board of Directors, taking proper vouchers for such disbursements.

Maintain Accounts

(4) Keep and maintain adequate and correct accounts of the corporation's properties and business transactions including account of its assets, liabilities, receipts, disbursements, gains, losses, capital, surplus, and shares. Any surplus, including earned surplus, paid-in surplus, and surplus arising from a reduction of stated capital, shall be classified according to source and shown in a separate account.

Exhibit Records

(5) Exhibit at all reasonable times the books of account and records to any director on application, or to any person who has been a shareholder of record for a least six (6) months immediately preceding his demand or who is the holder of record of at least five (5) percent of all the outstanding shares of the

corporation, on written demand stating the purpose thereof, during business hours at the office of the corporation where such books and records are kept.

Reports to President and Directors

(6) Render to the President and Directors, whenever they request it, an account of all his transactions as Treasurer and of the financial condition of the corporation.

Financial Report to Shareholders

(7) Prepare, or cause to be prepared, and certify the financial statements to be included in the annual report to shareholders and statements of the affairs of the corporation when requested by shareholders holding at least ten (10) percent of the number of outstanding shares of the corporation.

Bond

(8) Give to the corporation a bond, if required by the Board of Directors or by the President, in a sum, and with one or more sureties, or a surety company satisfactory to the Board, for the faithful performance of the duties of his office and for the restoration to the corporation, in case of his death, resignation, retirement, or removal from office, of all books, papers, vouchers, money, and other property of whatever kind in his possession or under his control belonging to the corporation.

Other Duties

(9) In general, perform all the duties incident to the office of Treasurer and such other duties as from time to time may be assigned to him by the Board of Directors.

Absence of Treasurer

(10) In case of the absence or disability of the Treasurer or his refusal or neglect to act, the Assistant Treasurer or the Secretary acting as Assistant Treasurer, may perform all of the functions of the Treasurer. In the absence or inability to act, or refusal or neglect to act, of the Treasurer, the Assistant Treasurer, and the Secretary, any person thereunto authorized by the President or Vice President or by the Board of Directors may perform the functions of the Treasurer.

Assistant Treasurer

4.12 The Assistant Treasurer, if required so to do by the Board of Directors, shall give bond for the faithful discharge of his duties, in such sum, and with such sureties as the Board of Directors shall require. At the request of the Treasurer, or his absence or disability, the Assistant Treasurer designated as set forth in preceding Subparagraph 4.11(10) of these bylaws shall perform all the duties of the Treasurer, and when so acting, he shall have all the powers of, and be subject to all the restrictions on, the Treasurer. He shall perform such other duties as from time to time may be assigned to him by the Board of Directors or the Treasurer.

Salaries

4.13 The salaries of the officers shall be fixed from time to time by the Board of Directors, and no officer shall be prevented from receiving such salary by reason of the fact that he is also a Director of the corporation.

ARTICLE FIVE

EXECUTION OF INSTRUMENTS AND DEPOSIT OF FUNDS

Authority for Execution of Instruments

5.01 The Board of Directors, except as otherwise provided in these bylaws, may authorize any officer or officers, agent or agents, to enter into any contract or execute and deliver any instrument in the name of and on behalf of the corporation, and such authority may be general or confined to specific instances; and, unless so authorized, no officer, agent, or employee shall have any power or authority to bind the corporation by any contract or engagement or to pledge its credit or to render it liable pecuniarily for any purpose or in any amount.

Execution of Instruments

5.02 Unless otherwise specifically determined by the Board of Directors or otherwise required by law, formal contracts of the corporation, promissory notes, deeds of trust, mortgages and other evidences of indebtedness of the corporation, and other corporate instruments or documents, and certificates of shares of stock owned by the corporation, shall be executed, signed or endorsed by the President or any Vice President and by the Secretary or the Treasurer, or any Assistant Secretary or Assistant Treasurer, and may have the corporate seal affixed thereto.

Bank Accounts and Deposits

5.03 (1) All funds of the corporation shall be deposited from time to time to the credit of the corporation with such banks, trust companies, or other depositaries as the Board of Directors may select or as may be selected by any officer or officers, agent or agents of the corporation to whom such power may be delegated from time to time by the Board of Directors.

Endorsement Without Countersignature

(2) Endorsements for deposit to the credit of the corporation in any of its duly authorized depositaries may be made without countersignature by the President or any Vice President, or the Treasurer or any Assistant Treasurer, or by any other officer or agent of the corporation to whom the Board of Directors, by resolution, shall have delegated such power, or by hand stamped impression in the name of the corporation.

Signing of Checks, Drafts, Etc.

(3) All checks, drafts or other order for payment of money notes or other evidences of indebtedness, issued in the name of or payable to the corporation, shall be signed or endorsed by such person or persons and in such manner as shall be determined from time to time by resolution of the Board of Directors.

ARTICLE SIX

ISSUANCE AND TRANSFER OF SHARES

Classes and Series of Shares

6.01 The corporation may issue one or more classes or series of shares, or both, any of which classes or series may be with par value or without par value and with full limited or no voting rights, and with such other preferences, rights, privileges, and restrictions as are stated or authorized in the articles of incorporation. All shares of any one class shall have the same voting rights, conversion, redemption, and other rights, preferences, privileges, and restrictions, unless the class is divided into series. If a class is divided into series, all the shares of any one series shall have the same voting rights, conversion, redemption, and other rights, preferences, privileges, and restrictions. There shall always be a class or series of shares outstanding which has complete voting rights except as limited or restricted by voting rights conferred on some other class or series of outstanding shares.

Certificates for Fully Paid Shares

6.02 Neither shares nor certificates representing such shares may be issued by the corporation until the full amount of the consideration has been paid. When such consideration has been paid to the corporation, the shares shall be deemed to have been issued and the certificate representing such shares shall be issued to the shareholder.

Consideration for Shares

6.03 The consideration paid for the issuance of shares shall consist of money paid, labor done, or property actually received; neither promissory notes nor the promise of future services shall constitute payment or part payment for shares of the corporation.

Contents of Share Certificates

6.04 (1) Certificates for shares shall be of such form and style, printed or otherwise, as the Board of Directors may designate, and each certificate shall state all the following facts:

(a) The corporation is organized under the appropriate state laws.

(b) The name of the person to whom issued.

(c) The number and class of shares and the designation of the series, if any, which such certificate represents;

(d) The par value of each share represented by such certificate, or a statement that the shares are without par value.

Shares in Classes or Series

(2) If the corporation is authorized to issue shares of more than one class, the certificate shall set forth, either on the face or back of the certificate, a full summary statement of all the designation, preferences, limitations, and relative rights of the shares of each class authorized to be issued and, if the corporation is authorized to issue any preferred or special class in series, the variations in the relative rights and preferred or special class in series, the variations in the relative rights and preferences of the shares of each such series so far as the same have been fixed and determined and the authority of the Board of Directors to fix and determine the relative rights and preferences of subsequent series. In lieu of providing such a statement in full of the certificate may provide that the corporation will furnish such information to any shareholder without charge upon written request to the corporation as its principal place of business or registered office and that copies of the information are on file in the office of the Secretary of State.

Restriction on Transfer

(3) Any restrictions imposed by the corporation on the sale or other disposition of its shares and on the transfer thereof must be copied at length or in summary form on the face, or so copied on the back and referred to on the face, of each certificate representing shares to which the restriction applies. The certificate may however state on the face or back that such a restriction exists pursuant to a specified document and that the corporation will furnish a copy of the document to the holder of the certificate without charge upon written request to the corporation at its principal place of business.

Preemptive Rights

(4) Any preemptive rights of a shareholder to acquire unissued or treasury shares of the corporation which are limited or denied by the articles of incorporation must be set forth at length on the face or back of the certificate representing shares subject thereto. In lieu of providing such a statement in full

on the certificate, a statement on the face or back of the certificate may provide that the corporation will furnish such information to any shareholder without charge upon written request to the corporation at its principal place of business and that a copy of such information is on file in the office of the Secretary of State.

Signing Certificates-Facsimile Signatures

6.05 All such certificates shall be signed by the President or a Vice President and the Secretary or an Assistant Secretary. The signatures of the President or Vice President, Secretary or Assistant Secretary may be facsimiles if the certificate is countersigned by a transfer agent or registered by a registrar either of which is not the corporation itself or an employee of the corporation. If the officer who has signed or whose facsimile signature has been placed on the certificate has ceased to be such officer before the certificate is issued, the certificate may be issued by the corporation with the same effect as if he were such officer at the date of its issuance.

Transfer of Lost or Destroyed Shares

6.06 (1) Where a share certificate has been lost, apparently destroyed, or wrongfully taken and the owner fails to notify the corporation of that fact within a reasonable time after he has notice of it, and the corporation registers a transfer of the share represented by the certificate before receiving such a notification, the owner is precluded from asserting against the corporation any claim for registering the transfer or any claim to a new certificate.

Replacement of Lost or Destroyed Certificates

(2) Where the holder of a share certificate claims that the certificate has been lost, destroyed, or wrongfully taken, the corporation shall issue a new certificate in place of the original certificate if: (i) the owner so requests before the corporation has notice that the share has been acquired by a bona fide purchaser; (ii) files with the corporation a sufficient indemnity bond; and (iii) satisfies any other reasonable requirements imposed by the Board of Directors.

Transfer After Replacement

(3) If, after the issue of a new security as a replacement for a lost, destroyed, or wrongfully taken certificate, a bona fide purchaser of the original certificate presents it for registration of transfer, the corporation must register the transfer unless registration would result in overissue. In addition to any rights on the indemnity bond, the corporation may recover the new security from the person to whom it was issued or any person taken under him except a bona fide purchaser.

Transfer Agents and Registrars

6.07 The Board of Directors may appoint one or more transfer agents or transfer clerks, and one or more registrars which shall be an incorporated bank or trust company, either domestic or foreign, who shall be appointed at such times and places as the requirements of the corporation may necessitate and the Board of Directors may designate.

Conditions of Transfer

6.08 A person in whose name shares of stock stand on the books of the corporation shall be deemed the owner thereof as regards the corporation; provided that whenever any transfer of shares shall be made for collateral security, and not absolutely, and written notice thereof shall be given to the Secretary of the corporation or its transfer agent, if any, such fact shall be stated in the entry of the transfer.

Reasonable Doubts as to Right to Transfer

6.09 When a transfer of shares is requested and there is reasonable doubt as to the right of the person seeking the transfer, the corporation or its transfer agent, before recording the tranfer of the shares on its books or issuing any certificate therefore, may require from the person seeking the transfer reasonable proof of his right to the transfer. If there remains a reasonable doubt of the right to the transfer, the corporation may refuse a transfer unless the person gives adequate security or a bond of indemnity executed by a corporate surety or by two individual sureties satisfactory to the corporation as to form, amount, and responsibility of sureties. The bond shall be conditioned to protect the corporation, its officers, transfer agents, and registrars, or any of them, against any loss, damage, expense, or other liability to the owner of the shares by reason of the recordation of the transfer or the issuance of a new certificate for shares.

ARTICLE SEVEN

CORPORATE RECORDS, REPORTS AND SEAL

Minutes of Corporate Meetings

7.01 The corporation shall keep at the principal office, or such other place as the Board of Directors may order, a book of minutes of all meetings of its Directors and of its shareholders or members, with the time and place of holding, whether regular or special, and, if special, how authorized, the notice thereof given, the names of those present at Directors' meetings, the number of shares or members present or represented at shareholders' or members' meetings, and the proceedings thereof.

Books of Account

7.02 The corporation shall keep and maintain adequate and correct accounts of its properties and business transactions, including accounts of its assets, liabilities, receipts, disbursements, gains, losses, capital, surplus, and shares. Any surplus, including earned surplus, paid-in surplus, and surplus arising from a reduction of stated capital, shall be classified according to source and shown in a separate account.

Share Register

7.03 The corporation shall keep at the principal office, or at the office of the transfer agent, a share register, showing the names of the shareholders and their addresses, the number and classes of shares held by each, the number and date of certificates issued for shares, and the number and date of cancellation of every certificate surrendered for cancellation. The above specified information may be kept by the corporation on punchcards, magnetic tape, or any other information storage device is capable of reproducing the information in clearly legible form for the purposes of inspection as provided in Section 7.04 of these bylaws.

Inspection of Records by Shareholders

7.04 (1) Any person who shall have been a shareholder of record for at least six (6) months immediately preceding his demand, or who is the holder of record of at least five (5) percent of all of the outstanding shares of the corporation, on written demand stating the purpose thereof, has the right to examine, in person, or by agent, accountant, or attorney, at any reasonable time or times, for any proper purpose, its books and records of account, minutes, and record of shareholders, and is entitled to make therefrom.

Inspection of Records by Directors

(2) Every Director shall have the absolute right at any reasonable time to inspect all books, records, documents of every kind, and the physical properties of the corporation, and all of its subsidiary corporations, domestic or foreign. Such inspection by a Director may be made in person or by agent or attorney, and the right of inspection includes the right to make extracts.

Annual Report to Shareholders

7.05 (1) The Board of Directors shall cause an annual report to be sent to the shareholders not later than 90 days after the close of the fiscal or calendar year.

Contents of Annual Reports

(2) The annual report shall include the following financial statements:

(a) A balance sheet as of closing date;
(b) A statement of income or profit and loss for the year ended on such closing date.
(c) Such other information as the Directors shall determine.

Preparation of Financial Statements

(3) The financial statements shall be prepared from the books and shall be in accordance therewith and shall be certified by the President, Secretary, Treasurer, or a public accountant. They shall be prepared in a form sanctioned by sound accounting practice for the particular kind of business carried on by the corporation.

Fiscal Year

7.06 The fiscal year of the corporation shall be determined by the Board of Directors.

Corporate Seal

7.07 The Board of Directors may adopt, use, and thereafter alter, the corporate seal.

ARTICLE EIGHT

AMENDMENT OF BYLAWS

Adoption, Amendment, Repeal of Bylaws by Directors

8.01 Bylaws may be altered, amended, or repealed, and new bylaws may be adopted, by the Directors, subject to repeal or change by action of the shareholders.

Certificate of Adoption of Bylaws

This is to certify:

That I am the duly elected, qualified and acting Secretary of _______________________________________, and that the above bylaws were duly adopted as the bylaws of said corporation by the Board of Directors of said corporation.

Dated:________________________

____

___________________, Secretary

The undersigned, being all the Directors of the Corporation, hereby consent to all the foregoing this ______ day of ___________, 19___

____

____

Form 7. Corporate Minutes of First Meeting

ORGANIZATIONAL CONSENT OF DIRECTORS

OF

____

The undersigned, being all the members of the Board of Directors of ________________________, (the "Corporation"), pursuant to Article 9.10B of the Business Corporation Act, hereby consent to the adoption of the following resolutions and to the action authorized in such resolutions being taken by the Board of Directors in lieu of an Organizational Meeting thereof:

1. ADOPTION OF BYLAWS

RESOLVED, that the form of Bylaws attached to these resolutions be and the same are hereby approved and adopted as the Bylaws of the Corporation and the Secretary of the Corporation is directed to cause the originals thereof to be placed in the Minute Book of the Corporation.

2. ELECTION OF OFFICERS

RESOLVED, that the following named persons be and they are hereby elected to the office set opposite their respective names to serve until the next annual meeting of Directors or until their successors are elected and qualified:

President
Vice President
Secretary
Treasurer

3. ADOPTION OF CORPORATE SEAL

RESOLVED, that the Seal, an impression of which is shown below, be and the same is hereby adopted as the Corporate Seal of the Corporation.

4. ADOPTION OF STOCK CERTIFICATES

RESOLVED, that the attached form of stock certificate be and the same is hereby approved and adopted as the Stock Certificate of the Corporation.

5. AUTHORITY TO EXECUTE INSTRUMENTS AS MAY BE REQUIRED BY LAW

RESOLVED, that the proper officers of the Corporation be and they are hereby authorized and directed on behalf of the Corporation and under its Corporate Seal, to make and file such certificate or certificates, report or reports, or other instrument or instruments as may be required by law to be filed in the State of ___, or any other state in which the Corporation is authorized to transact business, and the purpose for which the Corporation was incorporated.

6. QUALIFICATION IN OTHER STATES

RESOLVED, that the proper officers of the Corporation be and they are hereby authorized and directed on behalf of the Corporation and under its Corporate Seal (where a seal is required by the recipient, law or regulation under which filed) to make and file such certificates, reports, or other instruments as may be required by law to be filed in any State, Territory, Colony or Dependency of the United States, or in any foreign country, in which said officers shall find it necessary or expedient to file the same to authorize the Corporation to transact business in such State, Territory, Colony, Dependency, or foreign country.

7. PAYMENT OF ORGANIZATION FEES

RESOLVED, that the President or Treasurer is hereby authorized to pay all fees and expenses incident to and necessary for the organization of the Corporation.

8. AUTHORITY TO ISSUE SHARES OF COMMON STOCK

RESOLVED, that the proper officers of the Corporation be and they hereby are authorized to issue certificates for stock of the Corporation to the following persons for the number of shares set opposite their respective names in consideration of the cash payment by each person of $_____ per share:

____________ ______ shares
____________ ______ shares
____________ ______ shares

9. BANKING AUTHORITY

RESOLVED, that the President of the Corporation be and is hereby authorized and directed to execute and deliver such form resolutions of ________________________, as may be required to establish such checking accounts and borrowing accounts as the President of the Corporation shall deem necessary and appropriate; and

RESOLVED FURTHER, that such form resolutions be attached to this Consent, and incorporated herein for all purposes as the official resolutions of the Corporation; and

RESOLVED FURTHER, that this resolution and the form resolutions to which it is applicable shall continue in full force and effect until official written notice of the rescission thereof by the Board of Directors of the Corporation has been given to the Bank.

10. FISCAL YEAR

RESOLVED, that the fiscal year of the Corporation shall end on ____________ of each year.

11. ADOPTION OF SHAREHOLDERS' AGREEMENT

RESOLVED, that the Corporation shall enter into a Shareholders' Agreement, containing provisions substantially similar to those contained in the sample Shareholders' Agreement attached hereto as Exhibit ____, which includes, among other provisions, restrictions on the transfer of the Corporation's shares by and between all the shareholders of the Corporation; and

FURTHER RESOLVED, that a counterpart of the Agreement shall be placed on file by the Corporation at its principal place of business and its registered office and that the same shall be subject to the same right of examination by a Shareholder of the Corporation, in person or by agent, attorney, or accountant, as are the books and records of the Corporation; and

RESOLVED, that the officers and directors of the Corporation be, and they hereby are, authorized to do any and all acts and things and to execute any and all agreements, consents and documents as in their opinion, or in the opinion of counsel to the Corporation, may be necessary or appropriate in order to carry out the purposes and intent of any of the foregoing resolutions; and

12. DATE OF ANNUAL SHAREHOLDERS' MEETING

RESOLVED, that the annual meeting of the shareholders commencing with the year 19___, shall be held each year at 10:00 A.m. on the 10th day of DECEMBER. If such day is a legal holiday, then the meeting shall be held on the next secular day following.

13. NUMBER OF DIRECTORS

RESOLVED, that the number of directors of the Corporation shall be ___ ________.

14. RESOLVED, that the directors be, and they hereby are, authorized to execute this consent in multiple counterparts.

The undersigned, being all the Directors of the Corporation, hereby consent to all the foregoing this ______ day of ___________, 19___

____

____

Form 8. Shareholders' Agreement

SHAREHOLDERS' AGREEMENT
(Redemption and Buy-Sell)
FOR
X CORPORATION

AGREEMENT, made as of this ____ day of ________, 19__, by and among X CORPORATION, a __________ corporation (hereinafter referred to as the "Corporation"), and A, B, D and D, each of __________________ County, _______ (hereinafter referred to separately and collectively as the "Shareholder" and the "Shareholders" respectively), and among the shareholders themselves.

W I T N E S S E T H:

WHEREAS, the Shareholders are the owners of all of the outstanding shares of capital sotck in the Corporation; and

WHEREAS, for good and valuable consideration, the Corporation and the Shareholders have agreed to impose certain restrictions on said capital stock; and

WHEREAS, the Shareholders mutually agree that it is to their mutual benefit and in the best interests of the Corporation to restrict the assignability of the capital stock of the Corporation, to provide for the control and disposition of the Corporation, to provide for the orderly transition of ownership in the event of death, disability or retirement of a Shareholder, or other termination of a Shareholder's interest in the Corporation, to provide for the purchase of a Shareholder's capital stock under certain specified conditions, and to provide the funds necessary to carry out such purchases.

NOW, THEREFORE, in consideration of the mutual agreements contained herein and for other valuable consideration, the sufficiency and receipt of which is hereby acknowledged, it is mutually agreed by and among the parties to this Agreement as follows:

I. DEFINITIONS

The following definitions shall control the meanings of the repective terms:

A. "Disability" or "Disabled" means with respect to Shareholders, physical or mental disability, or both, determined to be (or reasonably expected to be, based upon then available medical information) of not less than twelve (12) calendar months' duration or more. The determination (or reasonable expectancy) shall rest upon the opinion of the physician regularly attending the Shareholder who is Disabled ("Disabled Shareholder"). If the Continuing Shareholders disagree with said physician's opinion, the Continuing Shareholders may engage at their own expense a physician to examine the Disabled Shareholder, and each Shareholder a party hereto hereby consents to such examination and to waive, if applicable, any privilege between the physician and the Shareholder that may arise as a result of said examination. If, after conferring, the two physicians cannot concur on a final opinion, they shall choose a third consulting physician whose opinion shall control. The expense of the third consulting physician shall be borne equally by the Disabled Shareholder and the Continuing Shareholders. "Physician" means a medical doctor.

B. "Termination or "Terminating" means, to the extent applicable according to the provisions hereof, death, disability, severance of employment, whether voluntarily or by action of the Corporation, cessation of functioning as a Shareholder, including the loss of any rights or license necessary to continue in the employment of the Corporation, abandonment of duties or position as an officer, director, or employee of the Corporation, retirement (whether voluntary or not, or with consent of or by action of the employer), or Assignment or other transfer of an Ownership Interest (or any part thereof), and includes dissolution of marriage or permanent separation. A call to military service shall be a "termination" only to the extent allowed under the Soldiers and Sailors Relief Act.

C. "Assignment of other transfer" includes, but is not limited to, sale, exchange, hypothecation, collateral assignment, subjecting the ownership interest to a security interest. Attachment, judgment, creditor execution, bankruptcy, or other similar occurrence sanctioned by law, without the advance consent in writing of the Continuing Shareholders.

"Assignment or other transfer" shall not include a transfer or assignment by way of gift (directly or in trust) of up to but not exceeding a cumulative total of fifty percent (50%) of the Ownership Interest of a Shareholder in the Corporation to his spouse, children, or other lineal descendants, or to other employees of the Corporation or other Shareholders, however, any such assignee, transferee or donee shall be subject to the terms hereof.

D. "Continuing Shareholders" means those Shareholders who are not terminating their interest in the Corporation or who are not making an Assignment or other transfer of their Ownership Interest.

E. "Terminating Shareholder" or "Offering Shareholder" means the Shareholder who is terminating his interest in the Corporation. It includes, as required, the estate of a deceased Shareholder acting through its personal representative, which shall also be referred to as "Deceased Shareholder," or the extate of a Disabled Shareholder acting through its guardian or conservator, or, if same are not appointed, through the adult spouse of said Disabled Shareholder, or the Trustee (by trust, or in bankruptcy), receiver, or other legal representative of the Terminating Shareholder who has the power to act.

F. "Ownership Interest" means the equity interest that each Shareholder has in the Corporation which is reflected by stock ownership, regardless of class or series.

G. "Debt" means the obligation of the Corporation to repay a loan made to the Corporation by a Shareholder. Unless otherwise expressly stated herein, the debt shall be repaid according to its terms at the interest rate, interest dates, and maturity date fixed in the note, but if the note is payable on demand, is in default at the termination date, or past maturity, the debt shall be repaid upon the terms, at the interest rate, and upon the dates on which the payments in exchange for the Terminating Shareholder's Ownership Interest are made: being, for example, prorated over the installments due for the Terminating Shareholder's Ownership Interest.

H. "Receipt" or "received" refers to the date received. In the event of a dispute as to the date received, if mailed by ordinary mail, the date of receipt is three days afer the postmark date; otherwise it is the date shown on the return ship receipt. If more than two Continuing Shareholders are involved, the date received by the Shareholder who makes up the majority in number of the Continuing Shareholders shall be the receipt date for all the Continuing Shareholders, so that, for example, if three Continuing Shareholders are involved, A, B, and C, if A has received, but B and C have not, then the date that either B or C receives first is the date of receipt.

Unless otherwise stated specifically herein, any time period shall commence, run, and expire at 12:00 midnight, __________ time, within the stated days or months, whether the offer acceptance, or other act is to or by the Terminating Shareholder, the Corporation, or the Continuing Shareholders, acting jointly or separately, simultaneously or consecutively, and regardless of which party or parties is entitled to the first offer. All "days" shall refer to calendar days.

I. "Offerees" shall refer to the Corpoation or the Continuing Shareholders, or both, but such reference shall not alter or change any rights of the parties, and the term "Offerees" shall mean that the offer shall first be made to the Corporation and the next offers shall be made to the Continuing Shareholders, if that be required.

J. "Closing" or "Closing Date" shall mean the first business day or after the tenth day after the acceptance of an offer hereunder.

II. GENERAL TERMS

A. Delegation to Other Contractual Arrangements. Unless expressly provided herein otherwise, nothing contained in this Agreement shall discharge, release, or otherwise change, amend, or alter any sums due, or rights under any employment contract or other employment arrangement between the Corporation and any Shareholder. Further, no other contractual relationship between the Corporation and a Shareholder or among any or all of them shall be affected by this Agreement save one that attempts to define or speak to the terms of this Agreement, in which case the other contract shall be null and void unless it is in writing, it expressly indicates that it is amending this Agreement, and it is signed by the Corporation and all the Shareholders.

B. Redemption Agreement. This Agreement is intended to be a redemption agreement, and all offers required to be made hereunder shall first be made to the Corporation. If the Corporation is willing to accept the offer but does not have the financial means to accomplish the acceptance, then the Continuing Shareholders shall have the right, but not the duty, to provide to the Corporation sufficient funding, in the amounts and in the manner agreed upon between themselves, so that the Corporation may accept the offer in the first instance.

If the Corporation is for any reason unable or unwilling to accept the offer, the offer shall next be made to the Continuing Shareholders, who shall accept same, on the terms and conditions as provided herein.

C. Status of Assignees, Transferees, etc. All (i) assignees, transferees, trustees, receivers, or others who obtain an interest in the shares, whether by attachment, execution, bankruptcy law, receivership law, or otherwise by operation of law, and (ii) assignees, transferees, secured parties, creditors, and others who obtain an interest in the shares, whether or not said Assignment or other transfer occurred with the consent of the Continuing Shareholders, take subject to the terms and conditions of this Agreement. Any such act of Assignment or other transfer, whether by operation of law, voluntarily or involuntarily, or by act of a Shareholder if not consented to by the Continuing Shareholders, or, if consented to, any act, demand, or attempt to realize upon the collateral security of the shares, shall consitute the party succeeding to or attempting to succeed to the Ownership Interest of such Shareholder, a Terminating Shareholder, and the act, as described in this sentence, a termination event, so that the terms and conditions of this Agreement shall apply.

D. Rights of Continuing Shareholders. Any rights of the Continuing Shareholders shall be shared among them proportionately according to the Ownership Interest that each owns in relation to the total owned by all Continuing Shareholders. If, with the consent of the other Continuing Shareholder, one or more Continuing Shareholders decline to participate in the exercise of a right, the Continuing Shareholders so participating shall share the right proportionately according to the Ownership Interest that each owns in relation to the total owned by all of the Continuing Shareholders who exercise the right. If only one Continuing Shareholder desires to exercise the right, he may do so, and, by reason of such exercise, he shall be under no fiduciary duty to the other Continuing Shareholders wo delined to participate, and the Continuing Shareholder who elects to act may purchase control.

E. Offers, Acceptances and Communications. All offers, acceptances, communications, and the like between the Corporation, a Terminating Shareholder, and the Continuing Shareholders, or among themselves, shall be in writing. Such writing shall contain all pertinent particulars, including, as applicable, selling price, dates, terms, and conditions. A writing directed to the Corporation concerning a right that the Continuing Shareholders may exercise under this Agreement shall be sufficient as to the Continuing Shareholders, and a different or additional writing need not be directed to the Continuing Shareholders.

F. Status of Spouses. It is recognized that none of the Shareholders are married, however, in the event one of more of them shall become married, their respective spouses may have an interest in any or all shares of capital stock of the Cororation held by them to the extent such shares constitute or become community property, or are held in joint tenancy or as tenants by the entireties (included herein as "Community Property") by reason of their respective souses' rights to acquire, manage, control, or dispose of Community Property. Therefore, each of the Shareholders hereby agree and consent to the requirement that upon their marriage, they will cause their respective spouses to consent to the terms hereof, as such may affect the interest of their respective spouses and evidence such consent in writing by executing a copy of this Agreement. Furthermore, in the event of the marriage of any of the Shareholders, unless shares are issued by the Corporation to a spouse of the Shareholder, in such spouse's own name, or shares are transferred to a spouse in such spouse's own name pursuant to paragraph C of Section I hereof or otherwise, any and all references to a Shareholder or Shareholders, including the specific references incorporating such terms in Section I hereof, shall not include and shall not be interpreted to include any spouse of any of the Shareholders. In the event that circumstances cause the terms of this Agreement to be operative, whereby a Terminating Shareholder is required to offer his Ownership Interest to the Offerees, the spouse of the Terminating Shareholder shall in like manner and upon the same terms and conditions as provided herein offer any Ownership Interest and that owned by his spouse.

III CERTAIN TERMINATING EVENTS

The following terms and conditions shall control upon the occurrence of any of the following Terminating events with respect to a Shareholder:

A. Disability.

If a Shareholder is or becomes Disabled, he must offer (or be deemed to have offered automatically) to the Offerees his Ownership Interest within thirty (30) days after his Diability is finally determined; provided, however, notwithstanding any other provisions hereof, the purchase of a Disabled Shareholder's interest by the Offerees shall be optional and evidence of the Offeree's decision to accept or decline such purchase shall be communicated to the Disabled Shareholder pursuant to part iii hereof, and the following provisions shall apply:

i. The purchase price, the terms of purchase, the interest rate, the security, and the like shall be as provided in Section VII hereof.

ii. Unless the Disabled Shareholder shall consent otherwise, the Corporation, if it elects to purchase, shall purchase all (100%) of the Disabled Shareholder's Ownership Interest. If the Disabled Shareholder so consents, the Corporation and the Continuing Shareholders may purchase jointly such amounts of the Disabled Shareholder's Ownership Interst as they shall mutually agree provided that 100% of the Disabled Shareholder's Ownership Interest is so purchased.

iii. Acceptance of the offer by the Offerees shall be delivered to the Disabled Shareholder on or before the sixtieth (60th) day next succeeding the date the Offerees receive the Disabled Shareholder's offer.

B. Retirement

If a Shareholder is at the date hereof an employee of the Corporation, or thereafter becomes an employee of the Corporation and subsequently retires from such employment, the same terms and conditions as are provided in respect of the Disability of a Shareholder in subparagraphs i-iii of paragraph A of this Section III shall apply, with the term "Retired Shareholder" being substituted for the term "Disabled Shareholder". The offer period shall be measured from the date the Shareholder actually retires according to payroll records or the date mutually agreed upon by the Retired Shareholder and the Offerees.

C. Severance of employment.

If a Shareholder is at the date hereof an employee of the corporation or thereafter becomes an employee of the Corpoation and subsequently such employment is severed for eeasons other than retirement or Disability, whether or not the severance is by mutual consent or otherwise, the Terminating Shareholder shall offer (or be deemed to have offered automatically) his ownership Interest to the Offerees. The offer period shall be measured from the date of the last day of his employment, and the same terms and conditions as are provided in respect of the Disability of a Shareholder in subparagraphs i-iii of paragraph A to this Section III shall apply, with the term "Terminating Shareholder" being substituted for the term "Disabled Shareholder".

D. Divorce or Permanent Separation

In the event that a petition is filed in a court of competent jurisdiction seeking a divorce or permanent separation, by or against a Shareholder, such Terminating Shareholder shall offer (or be deemed to have offered automatically) his ownership Interest to the Offerees. The Off period shall be measured from the date of the filing of such peititon, or the date the Terminating Shareholder shall have received notice of same, whichever is later, and the same terms and conditions as are provided in respect of the Disability of a Shareholder in subparagraphs i-iii of paragraph A of this Section III shall apply with the term "Terminating Shareholder" being substituted for the term "Disabled Shareholder".

IV. ASSIGNMENT OR OTHER TRANSFER

If a Shareholder receives a bona fide offer for all or any part of his Ownership Interest from an unaffiliated third party and he desires to sell and make an Assignment or other transfer of his Ownership Interest pursuant to such offer, he shall offer to the Offerees his Ownership Interest within ten (10) calendar days after receiving the outside offer, on the following terms and conditions:

i. The purchase price, the terms of purchase, the interest rate, the security, and the like shall be as provided in Section VII hereof, except that if in the sole discretion of the Continuing Shareholders, the bona fide offer is on more favorable terms or the purchase price is less than the purchase price of the shares being offered as determined under Section VII hereof, the terms or the purchase price of the bona fide offer may be accepted by the Offerees.

ii. The Offerees shall have the period of thirty (30 days after the receipt of the Offering Shareholder's offer to elect to purchase the Offering Shareholder's Ownership Interest. The Ownership Interest offered by the Offering Shareholder to the Offerees shall be the same Ownership Interest that the Offering Shareholder proposes to sell or otherwise transfer, and the Offerees shall have the right to purchase such Ownership Interest, and no more or less, except as the Offering Shareholder shall permit.

iii. The Offering Shareholder's offer must be accepted by the Offerees in writng received by the Offering Shareholder on or before thirty (30) days after receipt of the offer. If the Offerees do not accept the offer within the thirty (30) days acceptance period, the Offering Shareholder shall be at liberty to accept the outside bona fide offer.

iv. Unless the Offering Shareholder consents otherwise, the Corporation, if it elects to purchase, shall purchase all (100%) of the Ownership Interest being offered by the Offering Shareholder. If the Offering Shareholder so consents, the Offerees may purchase jointly such amounts of the Ownership Interest being offered as they shall mutually agree provided that all (100%) of the Ownership Interest being offered by the Offering Shareholder is so purchased.

v. This first option or right in the Offerees shall be a continuing right. If the Offering Shareholder does not sell his Ownership Interest pursuant to the outside offer that is the initial offer which initiated his offer to the Offerees, within forty-five days from the date the Offering Shareholder is first entitled to make such sale, the Offering Shareholder may not sell or otherwise transfer his ownership Interest without first offering again his Ownership Interest to the Offerees as provided above.

V. DEATH AS A TERMINATING EVENT

If a Shareholder dies, the Deceased Shareholder shall offer (or be deemd to have offered automatically) to the Offerees his Ownership Interest in the Corporation, and the following provisions shall apply:

A. Offer. The offer shall be made as soon as practical after the appointment of the decedent's personal representative, but in no event later than one hundred and twenty (120) days after the decedent's death.

B. Purchase Price. The purchase price, the terms of purchase, the interest, the security, and the like shall be as provided in Section VII hereof.

C. Purchase. Unless the Deceased Shareholder shall consent otherwise, the Corporation, if it elects to purchase, shall purchase all (100%) of the Deceased Shareholder's Ownership Interest. If the Deceased Shareholder so consents, the Corporation and the Continuing Shareholders may purchase jointly such amounts of the Deceased Shareholder's Ownership Interest as they shall mutually agree provided that 100% of the Disabled Shareholder's Ownership Interest is so purchased.

D. Acceptance. Acceptance of the offer by the Offerees shall be delivered to the Deceased Shareholder on or before the thirtieth (30th day) next succeeding the later of (a) the date Offerees received the Deceased Shareholder's offer, or (b) one hundred and twenty (120) days after the death of the Shareholder.

VI. FIRST LIEN

A. First Lien. The rights to purchase or redistribute an Ownership Interest resting in the Continuing Shareholders, as above provided, shall be a first lien or encumbrance upon the Ownership Interst of each Shareholder. This lien shall be evidence upon the books and records of the Corporation, and all indicia of an Ownership Interest shall bear a legend to that effect. Any attempted or purported transfer of an Ownership Interest in violation of this Agreement shall be deemed a termination of the Ownership Interest concerned, and the terms of this Agreement as to Disability shall apply.

B. Effect on Transfers. No transfer of an Ownership Interest pursuant to this Agreement shall be recognized by the Corporation or by the Continuing Shareholders until it is duly entered upon the books and records of the Corporation and all indicia of such Ownership Interest are changed accordingly.

C. Legend. The share certificates shall bear the following legend or a legend to the following effect:

> "The transfer of these shares is restricted. These shares may be restricted under the terms of the Securities Act of 1933, the Securities and Exchange Act of 1934, or the Securities Act of (collectively called the "Securities Acts"). The restriction may involve limitations required under an exemption from said Security Acts, such as an investment representation, a residence requirement, or a holding period requirement under the Intrastate Offering exemption."
>
> "Further, the transfer of these shares is restricted under the terms of a Stock Redemption and under the terms of a Stock Redemption and Buy-Sell Agreement between the holder of this certificate and the Corporation or other shareholders, or both. Said shares may not be sold, transferred, assigned, given away, pledged, encumbered, or otherwise disposed of except in strict accordance with the terms of that agreement, and no transfer will be recognized by the Corporation until, as the case may be, counsel to the Corporation is satisfied there is no violation of the Security Acts, the other shareholders consent to the transfer, or both."
>
> "A copy of said Stock Redemption and Buy-Sell Agreement will be furnished without charge to the holder of this certificate upon receipt by the Corporation at its principal place of business or registered office of a written request from the holder hereof requesting such a copy."

VII. PURCHASE PRICE AND TERMS

A. Valuation. The value of the Corporation shall be determined as provided in Exhibit A attached hereto. Except as otherwise provided in paragraph F hereof, the purchase price payable to the Terminating Shareholder shall be the value of the Terminating Shareholder's Ownership Interest in the Corporation, without discount or adjustment. Thus, if the Terminating Shareholder's Ownership Interest is ten percent (10%) of the Corporation and the Corporation's value is one hundred dollars ($100), the purchase price shall be ten dollars ($10).

B. Payment. In the case of a Termination other than by reason of death, the purchase price shall be paid as follows: fifteen percent (15%) of the purchase price paid at Closing, with the palance paid in five (5) equal and consecutive annual installments, to commence on the first business day of the next succeeding fiscal year of the Corporation after the Closing. The unpaid principal shall bear simple annual interest payable on each principal installment date at the rate payable on the Closing Date by ____________ Bank, ______________ on passbook accounts, but in no event shall the interest rate be less than ___ percent (___%). In default of either a principal installment or the interest due in respect thereof, the remaining balance of the purchase price shall become due and payable at the option of the noteholder. The entire principal balance or any part thereof, other than in the year of the Closing my be prepaid without penalty. All costs and expenses which arise in connection with collection of any amounts due shall be borne by the maker of the note, including a reasonable attorney's fee. The note to be used shall be in substantially the form attached as Exhibit B hereto.

C. Escrow. The Ownership Interest being sold to the Corporation or the Continuing Shareholders, as the case may be, and all indicia thereof, shall, at the election of the Terminating Shareholder, be retained in escrow by a disinterested third party selected by mutual agreement between the Terminating Shareholder and the Corporation or the Contintuing Shareholdes, as the case may be, with appropriate escrow instructions to the effect that the Ownership Interest shall be delivered to the Corporation or the Continuing Shareholders, as the case may be, when the purchase price, together with any accrued interest, has been paid in full, and, in the event of default thereof, the Ownership Interest shall revert to the Terminating Shareholder. However, so long as no default occurs any voting rights or oghter interests accruing to the Contintuing Shareholders by reason of their purchase of such stock shall be fully exercisable by them.

D. Secured Transaction. The terms of Article 9 of the Uniform Commercial Code, dealing with default and the taking of acollateral, then applying in the State of ________ shall govern the Terminating Shareholder' the Corpoartion's, or the Continuing Shareholders', rights and remedies in the event of default.

E. Tax Status. All proceeds payable to a Terminating Shareholder shall be regarded for income tax purposes as paid from the following sources, in the order of priority shown:

i. First, to the extent thereof, the Terminating Shareholder shall receive the balance of his salary or other employee compensation, including expense reimbursement but excluding a qualified employee plan distribution, due and owing to him for the period involved.

ii. Second, as to the balance, the Terminating Shareholder shall receive payment for his shares.

F. Death. In the case of a Termination by reason of death, all of the proceeds of any insurance owned by the Corporation or Continuing Shareholders on the life of the Deceased Shareholder shall be paid by the Corporation or Continuing Shareholders to the Deceased Shareholder in reduction or payment of the purchase price, without regard to B above. In no event shall the purchase price be less than the value of the insurance proceeds. In the event the purchase price as calculated pursuant to paragraph A hereof exceeds the value of any insurance proceeds described above, the provisions of this Section VII shall apply except that under paragraph B hereof the purchase price shall be paid at closing, with the balance paid in three equal and consecutive annual installments, to commence on the first business day of the next succeeding fiscal year of the Corporation after the Closing.

VIII. RESIGNATIONS

Effective upon the occurrence of a Terminating event, the Terminating Shareholder and his spouse will automatically be deemed to have resigned as a director or officer of the Corporation as the case may be, and such resignation shall be effective without further act of the Terminating Shareholder or his spouse. Each Shareholder confers a power of attorney upon every Continuing Shareholder and agrees that upon the occurrence of the above events, every Continuing Shareholder shall thereafter have the power to do the things and perform the acts which may be necessary to reflect the fact that neither the Terminating Shareholder nor his spouse is an officer or director of the Corporation. This power of attorney shall not be affected by the disability of the Terminating Shareholder or the lack of information as to whether he is dead or alive.

Nothing herein, however, shall act as a waiver of or release of any claim, demand, or assertion of the Terminating Shareholder against the Corporation for salary, expense reimbursement, or similar employee benefits, to the extent he is entitled to the same.

IX. NON-INTERFERENCE

A. Covenants of Terminating Shareholder. Notwithstanding that the balance of the purchase price may be due and payable to the Terminating Shareholder and the Ownership Interest is held in escrow as collateral security, the continuing interest of the Terminating Shareholer shall be solely a secured interest protecting a debt due. The Terminating Shareholder shall not have any say or right in management, and he agrees to execute whatever documents, instruments, and papers shall resonably be required by the attorney for the Corporation or the Continuing Shareholders, as the case may be, to reflect that the Terminating Shareholder has severed all relationship and connection with the Corporation save as a creditor. The Corporation or the Continuing Shareholders, as the case may be, and the Terminating Shareholder shall each have the right to send notices of the severance of the relationship.

B. Mutual Covenants. The Corporation, the Continuing Shareholders, and the Terminating Shareholder hereby mutually exchange convenants of non-interference and each agrees to refrain from any conduct, by word or act, that will reflect negatively on the character or conduct of the other.

C. Non-Competition. The terminating Shareholder, recognizing that a covenant not to compete is required to protect the business interests of the Corporation and the Continuing Shareholders, agrees that unless the Corporation or the Continuing Shareholders, as the case may be, consent in writing to the contrary, such Terminating Shareholder shall not engage in a competing business in any of the metropolitan areas surrounding cities in which the Corporation is then conducting business, for three years (1095 successive calendar days) after the Closing of the purchase transaction. A "competing business" shall mean and include a business similar or directly reltaed to the active trade or business of the Corporation or any subsidiary of the Corporation, including but not limited to, the design, manufacture and marketing of fashions, but shall not include inactive activities such as an investment not for use in the trade or business conducted by the Corporation it shall cover employment, management, and investment in any such competing business.

D Reasonableness. The Corporation and all the Shareholders expressly agree that because of the nature of the business of the Corporation, the above restrictions in paragraph C as to area and time are reasonable.

E. Preservation of Name. The Corporation now has and shall continue to have, the sole and exclusive right to use the name "X Corporation" as its corporate name and title. This right shall not be affected by the termination of asociation with the Corporation of any Shareholder, either as a shareholder, officer, director, or employee, nor by any other cause. In the event that any Shareholder ceases to be associated with or employed by the Corporation for any reason, they agree herein and hereby to not thereafter use or permit the use of the name "X Corporation" in the name or trademerk of any corporation, partnership, or other business with which they are associated in any capacity, directly or indirectly, and which is engaged in a business similar in any repect to that conducted the Corporation, unless such name or trademark includes other words denoting that such business is a separate organization, business, or entity entirely distinct from and not to be confused with the Corporation, and unless such name or trademark does not contain any words stating or suggesting prior or current affiliation or connection with, or comparison in age, business, or otherwise with the Corporation.

F. Confidentiality. It is also recognized and acknowledged by the Shareholders that confidential information pertaining to the Corporation's customers and manufacturing processes which may be available to them is valuable, special and unique except as such may be in the public domain. Accordingly, each Shareholder hereby agrees that he will not at any time disclose any of such information to any person, firm, corporation, association or other entity for any reason or purpose whatsoever or make use in any other way to his advantage of such information.

IX. MISCELLANEOUS MATTERS

A. Mutual Release. The Terminating Shareholder, for his part, and the Corporation and the Continuing Shareholders, for their part, do each release and acquit the other of any and all claims that each may have against the other, save and except the obligations set forth in this Agreement. It is the intention of the parties hereto that once this Agreement becomes effective, each of the parties will look only to the rights that he or they have under this Agreement.

B. Access to Books and Records. The Corporation and each Shareholder agree that the accountant or bookkeeper, or both, regularly engaged by the Corporation to keep the Corporation's books and records and report in respect thereto, acts for the Corporation and each Shareholder, and that each Shareholder shall have free and open access to the books and records of the Corporation. As against the Corporation or any Shareholder, said accountnat may not claim an accountant-client privilege, and said accountant shall be under a duty to report all information to all Shareholders and shall be under a further affirmative duty to report any matter of concern to him, which comes to his attention in the course of his duties, to all shareholders.

C. Insurance Policies. If the Corporation is the owner and beneficiary of insurance policies on the lives of the Shareholders, the Corporation may continue to maintain such incurance in force and effect during the lifetime of each insured Shareholder. The Corporation shall have the right to obtain additional insurance on the lives of the Shareholders whenever, in the opinion of the Corporation, additional insurance may be required for the benefit of the Corporation or to enable it to carry out its obligations under this Agreement. During the term of this Agreement, the Corporation shall pay premiums on all insurance policies carried by it pursuant to this Agreeemnt as they may become due. If any premium is not paid within twenty (20) days after its due date, the Shareholder whose life is insured may pay the premium or cause it to be paid, and shall be entitled to reimbursement from the Corporation. The Corporation shall apply any dividends declared on any such policy to the payment of premiums.

D. Rights to Purchase Policies. A Terminating Shareholder shall have the right to purchase the policy or policies carried by the Corporation on his own life by paying to the Corporation an amount equal to the then net cash surrender value of such policy or policies plus the unearned portion of any premiums that may have been paid thereon. Such right of purchase shall be exercised by notice given to the Corporation, in writing, within thrty (30) days after the Closing Date of the purchase of such Terminating Shareholder's Ownership Interest and the purchase price of the issuance shall be paid in full, in cash, within such period of time. On receipt of the entire purchase price, the Corporation will deliver the policies of insurance and will execute all necessary instruments of transfer.

E. Continuation of Business. Upon the occurrence of an event of Termination for any reason whatsoever, the Continuing Shareholders shall be entitled to utilize the corporate name and to continue to conduct the business of the Corporation at the premises utilized by the Corporation at the time of the Termination event, except as provided otherwise by law.

F. Entire Agreement. This instrument contains the entire agreement of the parties hereto and supersedes all prior agreements made between the shareholders and the Corporation affecting the capital stock of the Corporation and all such prior agreements are hereby terminated. No modification, amendment, change, or discharge of any term or provision of this Agreement shall be valid or binding unless the same is in writing and signed by all the parties hereto. No waiver of any of the terms of this Agreement shall be valid unless signed by the party against whom such waiver is asserted.

G. Termination. This Agreement shall terminate on the occurrence of any of the following events:

a. Bankruptcy, receivership, or dissolution of the Corporation.

b. Death of all the Shareholders simultaneously or within a period of ninety (90) days of each other.

c. The voluntary agreement of all of the Shareholders.

H. Binding Effect. This Agreement shall be binding upon and inure to the benefit of the Shareholders and their heirs, legal representatives, successors, and assigns, and the Shareholders agree for themselves and their heirs, legal representatives, successors, and assigns, to execute any instruments in writing which may be neceasary or proper in carrying out the purposes of this Agreement.

I. Applicable Law. The Shareholders mutually covenant and agree that this Agreement shall be subject to and governed by the laws of the State of __________, irrespective of the fact that one or more of the parties now is or may become a resident of a different state.

J. Damages. The parties hereby declare that it is impossible to measure in money the damages which will accrue to a party hereto or to the personal representatives of a Deceased Shareholder by reason of a failure to perform any of the obligations under this Agreement. Therefore, if any party thereto or the personal representatives of a Deceased Shareholder shall institute any action or proceeding to enforce the provisions hereof, any person (including the Corporation) against whom such action or proceeding is brought hereby waives the claim or defense therein that such party or such personal representative has or have an adequate remedy at law, and such person shall not urge in any such action or proceeding the claim or defense that such remedy at law exists.

K. Invalidity. The invalidity or unenforceability of any particular provision of this Agreement shall not affect the other provisions hereof, and the Agreement shall be construed in all respects as if such invalid or unenforceable provisions were omitted.

L. Gender. Words of any gender used in this Agreement shall be held and construed to include any other gender, and words in the singular shall be held and constured to include the plural, unless the context otherwise requires.

M. Headings. The captions or headings contained in this Agreement are inserted and included solely for convenience and shall never be considered or given any effect in construing the provisions hereof it any question of intent should arise.

N. Disability Insurance. If, during any period of Disability, the Bank or the Disabled Shareholder shall receive any proceeds of any disability insurance policy owned by the Corporation on the Disabled Shareholder, then any such payments so received by the Bank shall be paid to the Disabled Shareholder and all such payments to the Disabled Shareholder shall be applied on the purchase price as determined in accordance with the terms of this Agreement.

O. Repurchase After Divorce. In the event a Shareholder's Ownership Interest is purchased by the Offerees by reason of the Terminating Shareholder's divorce or permanent separation pursuant to the terms of this Agreement, such terminatin Shareholder shall have the exclusive right to repurchase his or her entire ownership interest in the Bank, including that of his spouse or any donees, following the entry of a final judgment and decree of divorce and the lapse of time allowed for any appeal thereof, provided no other terminating event occurs or has occurred. Such purchase shall be effected by said Terminating Shareholder giving written notice to the Offerees of his election to purchase all or any part of his Ownership Interest as provided herein within thirty (30) days of the entry of a final judgment and decree of divorce and the lapse of time allowed for any appeal thereof. If the Terminating Shareholder elects to purchase all or any part of his ownership interest as herein provided and written notice thereof is given as provided above and actually received by the Offerees within one (1) year from the date of Termination (which for purposes of this paragraph shall mean the date of the filing of any legal action regarding the Terminating Shareholder's divorce or permanent separation), the purchase price shall be the price originally paid by the Offerees to the Terminating Shareholders, otherwise the purchase price shall be determined as provided in Exhibit __ hereto, as of the date of the written notice of election.

P. Exhibits. All exhibits, attachments, annexed instruments and addenda referred to herein shall be considered a part hereof for all purposes with the same force and effect as if copied at full length herein.

Q. Dispute Resolution. Each of the Shareholders hereby agree that in the event any deadlock should arise, either among all of the holders of the Corporation's capital stock with voting rights or among all of the members of the Corporation's Board of Directors, then in the event the deadlock is among the holders of the Corporation's capital stock, the Corporation shall issue one share of a specially denominated series of Unclassified Preferred Stock, Five Dollars ($5.00) par value, which shall have full voting rights, to [Name] who shall vote such share in accordance with his best judgment. In the event the deadlock is among the Corporation's Board of Directors, the Shareholders and Common Shareholders hereby agree to increase the size of the Board of Directors by one and to elect [NAME] to the Board of Directors who shall exercise his rights as a member thereof in accordance with his best judgment. The Shareholders and the Corporation hereby agree to indemnify and hold [NAME] harmless for any action taken by him either as a holder of shares of the Corporation's capital stock or as a member of the Board of Directors.

IN WITNESS WHEREOF, the parties hereto warrant each to the other that they have read this Agreement in its entirety, understand all its terms, and execute this Agreement as of the date first above written with full knowledge of its significance.

SHAREHOLDERS:	RESPECTIVE SPOUSES:
______________________	______________________
______________________	______________________
______________________	______________________

ATTEST:	X CORPORATION
______________________ Secretary (CORPORATE SEAL)	By ______________________ President

Form 9a. Employment Agreement (Short Form)

For various considerations from ______________________ (hereinafter "Company"), I agree as follows:

1. Full Time Work for Company.

During my employment with Company:

(a) I will devote my full working time and best efforts to the service of Company and will comply with Company policies; and

(b) I will not participate in any planning, operation or management of any activity competitive with Company's interest and will not otherwise engage in any activity potentially in conflict with the interest of the Company except as authorized in writing by an officer of Company.

2. Obligation to Disclose to Company.

At Company's expense, I will both during or after my employment promptly disclose to Company all ideas, information, inventions and discoveries (whether or not patentable):

(i) which directly or indirectly relate to any of the business interests of Company in connection with which I have worked or carried responsibility or received Company confidential disclosures, and

(ii) which are conceived, made or learned by me alone or jointly with others during the term of my employment.

3. Title to Information, Ideas.

I assign unto Company all my right and title in such (see §2) ideas, information, inventions or discoveries. I will, at Company expense, cooperate both during and after my employment, in all lawful acts which may be desirable in the judgment of Company to protect for and in the name of either Company or its nominee all such ideas, information, inventions and discoveries.

4. Keep Information Proprietary and Confidential.

During my employment I may develop or be exposed to confidential or trade secret information of Company or others with whom Company does business, and maintenance of the confidential and proprietary character of such information is known to be important to Company. Accordingly, for so long either during or after my employment as any such confidential information or trade secrets may remain confidential, secret or otherwise totally or partially protectable or proprietary, I will not use or divulge such information except as permitted or required by the duties of my Company employment; and I will at all times exercise diligence to maintain any confidential, secret or proprietary character of all Company information, documents and things.

5. Restraint on Use of Company Information.

Without limitation on the obligation of section 4 above, for so long (up to two years after terminaton of my employment) as may be lawful, consistent with the place and circumstances: I will not take any employment wherein I would be aiding competition with Company and I will not undertake any owner, consultant or employment role competitive or in conflict with any interest of Company wherein the complete unhampered fulfillment of the duties of that employment would inherently or inevitably call upon me to reveal, to base judgments upon or to use any such Company confidential information or trade secrets.

6. Restraint on Diversion of Trade.

Both during and for two years after my employment I will not, within the State of ______ directly or indirectly or by aid to others, do anything which would tend to divert from Company any trade of business (i) with any customer with whom I have any contacts or association during one year next preceding termination of my Company employment, or (ii) with any party whose identity or potential as a customer was confidential and learned by me during my employment.

7. Restraint on Soliciting Employees to Leave Company.

During my employment and for so long (up to two years after termination of my employment) as may be lawful, consistent with the time, place and circumstances, I will not either directly or indirectly induce, attempt to induce or aid others in inducing any person with whom I was acquainted while in the employ of Company, to leave the employment of Company.

8. Return of Tangible Items.

I will return to Company upon termination of my employment all documents and things, produced by me or coming into my possession by or through my employment, and which are not my personal property.

9. Other Remedies Retained by Company.

The undertakings herein shall not be construed as any limitation upon the remedies Company might have at law or equity in the absence of this Agreement.

10. Freedom to Enter into this Agreement.

I am aware of no legal obligations of mine which are inconsistent with the terms of this Agreement or with my undertaking employment with Company.

11. Severability.

If in any place or circumstance any portion of this Agreement shall be deemed wholly or partially unenforceable, I agree nevertheless to be bound by all other provisions hereof to the full lawful extent.

______________________ Date	______________________ Employee
______________________ Place of Execution	
	Company
	By: ______________________

Form 9b. Employment Agreement (Long Form)

This Employment Agreement is executed by and between ______________ ______________, a ______________ corporation (hereinafter referred to as the "Company") and ______________ (hereinafter referred to as "Employee").

WITNESSETH:

1. The Company hereby agrees to employ Employee, and the Employee hereby agrees to render exclusive service to the Company and perform such duties as may be assigned from time to time by the Board of Directors, or the President of the Company for a period of ______ years commencing on the date of this Agreement, subject to earlier termination as hereinafter provided.

2. Employee shall be compensated by the Company at an initial base rate of ______________ Dollars ($__________) per month, payable semimonthly on the fifteenth and final days of each month during the period of Employee's employment under this greement, subject to such modifications as may be determined from ime to time by the management of the Company in its discretion. Such compensation shall be in addition to any group insurance, pension, profit sharing, and other fringe benefits which are extended from time to time to Employee in the discretion of the Board of Directors of the Company. Subject to such rules and procedures as are from time to time specified by the Company, the Company shall also reimburse Employee for all reasonable expenses incurred on behalf of the Company.

3. Employee shall devote Employee's full working time to the business of the Company; however, Employee shall be excused from performing any services for the Company hereunder during periods of temporary incapacity and during vacations conforming to the Company's standard vacation policy, without thereby in any way affecting the compensation to which Employee is entitled hereunder.

4. Without prior written consent of the Company, Employee shall not, during the period of employment herein provided, directly or indirectly invest or engage in any business which is competitive with that of the Company or accept employment with or render services to a competitor as a director, officer, agent, employee or consultant, or take any action inconsistent with the fiduciary relationship of an employee to his or her corporation.

5. In the event that the employment of Employee hereunder shall terminate for any reason, whether because of the expiration of this Agreement or otherwise, Employee agrees that during the period of ______ (____) months following the termination of his or her employment Employee will not, directly or indirectly, either through any kind of ownership (other than ownership of securities of publicly held corporations of which Employee owns less than one percent (1%) of any class of outstanding securities) or as a director, officer, agent, employee or consultant, engage in a business which is competitive with the business of the Company at the time such employment is terminated, within a radius of ______ miles from the office address where Employer was employed at the time of his termination of employment. It is expressly agreed that the remedy at law for breach of this covenant is inadequate and that injunctive relief shall be available to prevent the breach thereof.

6. All information relating to the business of the Company, including but not limited to the identity of the customers and suppliers of the Company, its arrangements with such suppliers and customers, and technical data relating to its products and services, hall be treated as confidential by Employee both during and after .e termination of Employee's employment under this Agreement. Except with the prior approval of the Company, Employee shall not disclose any of such information at any time to any person except authorized personnel of the Company or its subsidiary corporations. In the event of a breach or threatened breach by the Employee of the provisions of this paragraph, the Company shall, in addition to any other available remedies, be entitled to an injunction restraining Employee from disclosing, in whole or in part, any such information or from rendering any services to any person, firm or corporation to whom any of such information may have been disclosed or is threatened to be disclosed.

7. All data, drawings and other records and written material prepared or compiled by Employee or furnished to Employee while in the employ of the Company shall be the sole and exclusive property of the Company, and none of such data, drawings or other records, or copies thereof, shall be retained by Employee upon termination of his employment.

8. The provisions of Sections 5, 6, and 7 of this Agreement shall continue to be binding upon Employee in accordance with their terms, notwithstanding termination of Employee's employment hereunder for any reason.

9. The Board of Directors of the Company may, without cause and without advance notice, terminate Employee's employment hereunder at any time during the term of this Agreement, provided that within ten (10) days after such termination the Company shall pay to Employee all compensation earned but not previously paid prior to termination (prorated for any partial compensation period) plus the sum of ______________ Dollars ($__________), as a severance payment.

10. It is agreed and understood that, except as provided in Section 9 or upon the death of Employee, the Company cannot terminate the employment of Employee under this Agreement except for good cause, and that, without prejudice to the generality of the right to terminate for good cause, each of the following contingencies shall be good cause:

(a) Should Employee by reason of injury or illness become incapable for more than thirty (30) substantially consecutive days of satisfactorily performing his or her duties as an employee under this Agreement;

(b) Should Employee for reasons other than illness or injury be absent from his or her duties without the consent of the Company for more than ten (10) consective days;

(c) Should Employee be adjudicated a bankrupt or be convicted of a crime punishable by imprisonment;

(d) Should the Employee engage in any activity that would in the opinion of the Board of Directors of the Company constitute a conflict of interest with the Company; or

(e) Should Employee be negligent or inefficient in the performance of his or her duties hereunder, or otherwise fail to comply with the terms and conditions of this Agreement.

The Company may for good cause terminate Employee's employment under this Agreement without advance notice. Termination shall not affect any of the Company's other rights and remedies.

11. Employee represents and warrants that Employee has not previously assumed any obligations inconsistent with those of this Agreement.

12. This Agreement supersedes all previous agreements, written or oral, relating to Employee's employment by the Company, and shall not be changed orally, but only by a written instrument to which the Company and the Employee are both parties.

13. This Agreement and the rights and obligations hereunder shall be binding upon and inure to the benefit of the parties hereto and their respective legal representatives, and shall also bind and inure to the benefit of any successor of the Company by merger or consolidation or any assignee of all or substantially all of its properties, but, except to any such successor or assignee of the Company, neither this Agreement nor any rights or benefits hereunder may be assigned by either party hereto.

Executed this ______ day of ______________, 19____.

____
Employee

____

By: ______________________________
President

Form 10. Non-Disclosure Agreement Form

As an employee of ______________________ ("Company"), I am aware that Company is embarking on a program of rapid expansion and development of unique concepts and techniques in management, marketing and production control. I am also aware that Company contemplates allowing me to come into contact with highly confidential information concerning Company's business and that I, have a fiduciary responsibility to Company and its shareholders to not divulge this information to third parties. Accordingly, in consideration of Company allowing me access to confidential information in my continued employment with Company, I hereby agree that if I ever leave my employment with Company, I will not disclose or reveal to any other person, firm or corporation, any of the business practices, trade secrets, operating methods, techniques, or other confidential information revealed to me during my employment with Company.

Signed this ______ day of ______________, 19____.

By: ______________________________
Employee

Form 11. Invention and Patent Agreement

_____________ COMPANY, INC.

INVENTION AND PATENT AGREEMENT WITH

____

In view of the fact that we are employing you in a position where you have the opportunity to become familiar with our business and to use our facilities, which may enable you to make inventions and improvements relating to this company's business, we have made the following agreement:

1. All ideas, discoveries and inventions, whether patentable or not, which you make or conceive during your employment by this company which relate to the business of this company, or the contemplated business of this company, shall be the sole and exclusive property of this company and you will fully disclose such to this company.

2. You will promptly advise your supervisor of all inventions and improvements, whether patentable or not, which you, or you and another, or others, may make during your employment by this company, which in any way relate to the business, or contemplated business this company during your employment by it.

3. You will assist in the preparation of patent applications, both domestic and foreign, upon all such inventions and improvements; sign all papers and take all oaths required in connection with such applications or applications for reissue of patents, or any divisions, continuations, continuations-in-part or substitutes of such applications; and will assist in their prosecution and in any proceedings relating to them or to patents issuing them; it being understood, however, that you will not be subjected to financial expense in connection with any of this assistance.

4. You will assign to this company your entire right, title and interest in all such inventions and improvements, and in all domestic and foreign patent applications on them , so that this company may, if it desires, obtain domestic and foreign patents on these inventions and improvements, but they shall remain the property of this company whether patented or not.

5. It is understood that you have not heretofore made any inventions or improvements which in any way relate to the business of this company and to which it is not entitled, unless those inventions and improvements are identified on the reverse side of this form.

6. You agree that you will not disclose to anyone other than authorized individuals of this company, whether during or after your employment by us, any confidential information obtained by you while in our employ, without the written consent, any technical reports, drawings, blueprints, or other reproductions, or any papers of this company, and will not employ any such papers or any such confidential information except for the benefit of this company. Nothing in this agreement will prevent you, however, from disclosing or using any information which has become public knowledge.

7. It is understood that the salary which you receive while in our employ is in full payment for your services and for acts done in performance of this agreement.

8. This agreement is binding upon you, your administrators and executors, and upon this company, its successors and assigns, and will continue during your employment and as long thereafter as may be necessary to carry out the terms of this agreement.

9. Your signature below will indicate your agreement to the provisions of this agreement.

_____________ COMPANY, INC.

By:______________________

ACCEPTED:

____
Employee

DATED this ____ day of ___________, 198___.

Form 12a. Promissory Notes

SIMPLE PROMISSORY NOTE
Form I

[Date]

[Period of time] after date [or on (date)], I promise to pay to the order of [name of payee] at [place of payment, including county] the sum of [amount].

____
[Signature of maker]

Form II

$______________ Date ______________

______________after the above date I promise to pay to the order of ______________________________the sum of ____________________($___________), together with interest at _________percent per annum, payable at______________
____.

The maker and guarantor of this note further agree to waive demand, notice of nonpayment and protest, and in case suit shall be brought for the collection hereof, or the same has to be collected upon demand of an attorney, to pay reasonable attorney's fees for making such collection. Deferred interest payments to bear interest from maturity at ________________ percent per annum, payable semiannually.

(Signed) ______________________
Maker

(Signed) ______________________
Co-Maker [or Guarantor]

Due ________________

PROMISSORY NOTE
Form 3

Date:
Maker: (Debtor)
Maker's Mailing Address (including county):

Payee: (Person to be paid)
Place for Payment (including county):

Principal Amount:
Annual Interest Rate on Unpaid Principal from Date:
Annual Interest Rate on Matured, Unpaid Amounts:
Terms of Payment (principal and interest):

Maker promises to pay to the order of Payeee at the place for payment and according to the terms of payment the principal amount plus interest at the rates stated above. All unpaid amounts shall be due by the final scheduled payment date.

On default in the payment of this note, the unpaid principal balance and earned interest on this note shall become immediately due at the election of Payee. Maker and each endorser, and guarantor waive all demands for payment, presentations for payment, notices of intention to accelerate maturity, notices of acceleration of maturity, protests, and notices of protest.

If this note is given to an attorney for collection, or if suit is brought for collection, or if it is collected through probate, bankruptcy, or other judicial proceeding, then Maker shall pay Payee all costs of collection, including reasonably attorney's fees and court costs, in addition to other amounts due. Reasonable attorney's fees shall be 10% of all amounts due unless either party pleads otherwise.

Interest on the debt evidenced by this note shall not exceed the maximum amount of nonusurious interest that may be contracted for, taken, reserved, charged, or received under law; any inter- est in excess of that maximum amount shall be credited on the principal of the debtor or, if that has been paid, refunded. On any acceleration or required or permitted prepayment, any such excess shall be canceled automatically as of the acceleration or prepayment or, if already paid, credited on the principal of the debt or, if the principal of the debt has been paid, refunded. This provision overrides other provisions in this and all other instruments concerning the debt.

Each Maker is responsible for all obligations represented by this note.

____
Maker

____
Co-Maker [Guarantor]

Form 12b. Promissory Note (with Security Interest)

PROMISSORY NOTE
(to accompany Security Agreement)

Date:
Maker:
Maker's Mailing Address:

Payee:
Place for Payment:

Principal Amount:
Annual Interest Rate on Unpaid Principal from Date:
Annual Interest Rate on Matured, Unpaid Amounts:
Terms of Payment (principal and interest):

Security for Payment
A Security Interest Created and Granted in the Following Security Agreement:

Date:
Debtor:
Secured Party: Payee
County Where Collateral Located:
Collateral:

Maker promises to pay to the order of Payee at the place for payment and according to the terms of payment the principal amount plus interest at the rates stated above. All unpaid amounts shall be due by the final scheduled payment date.

On default in the payment of this note or in the performance of any obligation in any instrument securing or collateral to it, the unpaid principal balance and earned interest on this note shall become immediately due at the election of Payee. Maker and each surety, endorser, and guarantor waive all demands for payment, presentations for payment, notices of intention to accelerate maturity, notices of acceleration of maturity, protests, and notices of protest.

If this note or any instrument securing or collateral to it is given to an attorney for collection or enforcement, or if suit is brought for collection or enforcement, or if it is collected or enforced through probate, bankruptcy, or other judicial proceeding, then Maker shall pay Payee all costs of collection and enforcement, including reasonable attorney's fees and court costs, in addition to other amounts due. Reasonable attorney's fees shall be 10% of all amounts due unless either party pleads otherwise.

Interest on the debt evidenced by this note shall not exceed the maximum amount of nonusurious interest that may be contracted for, taken, reserved, charged, or received under law; any interest in excess of that maximum amount shall be credited on the principal of the debtor or, if that has been paid, refunded. On any acceleration or required or permitted prepayment, any such excess shall be canceled automatically as of the acceleration or prepayment or, if already paid, credited on the principal of the debt or, if the principal of the debt has been paid, refunded. This provision overrides other provisions in this and all other instruments concerning the debt.

Each Maker is responsible for all obligations represented by this note.

____
Maker

____
Co-Maker (or Guarantor)

Form 13. Loan Guaranty

_______________, 1991

In consideration of the loan by BUDGET FINANCIAL CORPORATION, a California personal property broker, ("Budget") to Borrower, a California partnership ("Borrower"), of the sum of $500,000 on the date hereof, which loan is evidenced by a certain promissory note, of even date, executed by BORROWER and payable to BUDGET on demand (the "Note"), the undersigned jointly and severally guarantee the prompt payment in full of the Note (and all extensions, renewals or novations thereof). A copy of the Note is attached hereto as Exhibit A.

The undersigned jointly and severally further guarantee BORROWER'S prompt payment of all obligations arising under, and BORROWER'S full performance of all of the terms, conditions, and covenants contained in, any instrument of security securing the Note or arising under, or contained in, any other agreement now existing, or hereafter entered into, between BORROWER and BUDGET whereby any indebtedness is now owing, or hereafter becomes owing, by BORROWER to BUDGET.

The undersigned jointly and severally further guarantee prompt payment and performance of any and all other liabilities or obligations according to the terms thereof, which BORROWER may now or hereafter owe or incur to BUDGET, without limitation as to amount, arising in any manner whatever, whether from dealings between BORROWER and BUDGET or from other dealings by which BUDGET may be or become in any manner whatever, a creditor of BORROWER.

BORROWER and BUDGET (and any other parties thereto) may make renewals and extensions of the time of payment or performance of any liability, obligation, contract or promissory note guaranteed hereby, and may change or otherwise alter the time or manner for performance contained therein, or enter into any amendment or novation, and BORROWER and BUDGET (and all parties thereto) may freely deal with each other in all respects without in any manner whatever affecting the liability hereunder of the undersigned. BUDGET may take, surrender, or modify, vary, exchange, renew, or abstain from perfecting or taking advantage of any security, accept or make compositions or other arrangements, discharge or release any party or guarantor without in any manner whatever affecting the liability hereunder of the undersigned.

The undersigned each waives:

(a) presentment, demand, protest, notice of protest, notice of dishonor, and notice of non-payment and notices of every kind or nature, including those of any action or non-action on the part of BORROWER, or of BUDGET, or of any other person or firm;

(b) the right, if any, to the benefit of, or to direct the application of, any security hypothecated to/or for BUDGET until all indebtedness of BORROWER to BUDGET, however arising, shall have been paid;

(c) the right to require BUDGET to proceed against BORROWER, or to pursue any other remedy available to BUDGET.

(d) The right to plead any and all statutes of limitation as a defense in any action or proceeding pertaining to this Note.

Upon default by BORROWER (or by any other party required to render performance) in performance of the terms of any liability, obligation, contract or promissory note guaranteed hereby, BUDGET may proceed, without notice, directly and independently of BORROWER against the undersigned, or any of them, to collect and recover the full amount hereby guaranteed, or any portion thereof. The cessation of the liability of BORROWER for any reason other than full payment, or any extension, renewal, forbearance, change of rate of interest, amendments, novation, or acceptance, release or substitution of security, or any impairment or suspension of the remedies or rights of BUDGET against BORROWER, shall not in any manner whatever affect the liability of the undersigned, or any of them, hereunder.

The undersigned jointly and severally agree to pay reasonable attorneys' fees and all other costs and expenses which may be incurred by BUDGET in the enforcement of this Guaranty and in collection of any of said liabilities from, or the enforcement of any obligation against, BORROWER or the undersigned, or any of them.

A married woman who signs this Guaranty agrees that her separate property shall be liable for all of her obligations hereunder regardless of whether or not any such obligation is secured by a mortgage, deed of trust or other hypothecation of community property.

This Guaranty shall inure to the benefit of the assigns and successors in interest of BUDGET and each of them, and shall be binding upon the heirs, administrators, executors and assigns of the undersigned and each of them.

Any legal action or proceeding pertaining to this Guaranty shall be brought in the courts of the State of California. By the execution and delivery of this Guaranty, each of the undersigned irrevocably and expressly (i) submits to the jurisdiction of said courts, (ii) designates, appoints and empowers Phlip F. Marantz, Esq., whose address is Suite 530, One Shell 123 Main St., Anywhere, CA 90000, as the agent for service of process in any legal action or proceeding pertaining to this Guaranty, (iii) waives any right he or she may have to object to the jurisdiction or venue of said courts in which any such action or proceeding is commenced, and (iv) consents to the service of process of said courts in any such action or proceeding by the mailing thereof by air mail, postage prepaid, to the undersigned at the address set forth after the signature of the undersigned below.

This Guaranty (including, without limitation, the validity, construction and enforcement hereof) shall be governed by the internal laws of the State of California.

________________	________________
John Jones	Sam Smith
Address: 5000 Montrose Blvd. Anywhere, CA 90000	Address: 4306 University Blvd Anywhere, CA 90000

Form 14a. Truth-in-Lending Sale Disclosure

TRUTH-IN-LENDING (SALE) DISCLOSURE STATEMENT

(Adapted from 12 C.F.R. pt. 226 app. H (1985) for use with mechanic's lien documents prepared by the State Bar of

CREDITOR	CONSUMER

ANNUAL PERCENTAGE RATE	FINANCE CHARGE	AMOUNT FINANCED	TOTAL OF PAYMENTS	TOTAL SALE PRICE
The cost of your credit as a yearly rate.	The dollar amount the credit will cost you.	The amount of credit provided to you or on your behalf.	The amount you will have paid after you have made all payments as scheduled.	The total cost of your purchase on credit, including your down payment of $__________
%	$	$	$	$

You have the right to receive at this time an itemization of the Amount Financed:
☐ I want an itemization. ☐ I do not want an itemization.

Your payment schedule will be:

Number of Payments	Amount of Payments	When Payments Are Due

Security: You are giving a security interest in:
☐ the goods or property being purchased.
☐

Filing Fees $ __________ **Nonfiling Insurance $** __________

Late Charge: If a payment is late, you will be charged __________ % per annum of the late payment.

Prepayment: If you pay off early, you
(check if the loan is at simple interest) ☐ may ☐ will not have to pay a penalty.

(check if private mortgage insurance premiums are charged to the consumer) ☐ may ☐ will not be entitled to a refund of part of the finance charge.

See your contract documents for any additional information about nonpayment, default, any required repayment in full before the scheduled date, and prepayment refunds and penalties.

Additional Disclosures:

"e" means an estimate

INSURANCE DISCLOSURES

Property Insurance. You may obtain property insurance from anyone that is authorized to transact business in . If you get the insurance from ____________________, you will pay $__________ for _____ months.
(creditor)

Credit Insurance. If you want, the creditor may provide you with credit insurance for the credit term. Credit life insurance and credit disability insurance are not required to obtain credit and will not be provided unless you sign and agree to pay the additional cost. You understand that if your credit term exceeds 59 months, the premium rates for credit insurance are not fixed or approved by the State Board of Insurance. If you desire insurance, you should indicate the type desired and sign below.

_____ I want credit life insurance on the life of the Consumer only for a premium of $__________.
_____ I want credit life insurance on the lives of the Consumer and Co-Borrower for a premium of $__________.
_____ I want credit disability insurance (available only to Consumer) for a premium of $__________.

____________________ (Consumer's signature) ____________________ (Co-Borrower's signature)

I have received a copy of this statement.

Signature __________ Date __________ Signature __________ Date __________

Form 14b. Truth-in-Lending Loan Disclosure

TRUTH-IN-LENDING (LOAN) DISCLOSURE STATEMENT

(Adapted from 12 C.F.R. pt. 226 app. H (1985) for use with mechanic's lien documents prepared by the State Bar of

CREDITOR	CONSUMER

ANNUAL PERCENTAGE RATE The cost of your credit as a yearly rate.	FINANCE CHARGE The dollar amount the credit will cost you.	AMOUNT FINANCED The amount of credit provided to you or on your behalf.	TOTAL OF PAYMENTS The amount you will have paid after you have made all payments as scheduled.
%	$	$	$

You have the right to receive at this time an itemization of the Amount Financed:
☐ I want an itemization. ☐ I do not want an itemization.

Your payment schedule will be:

Number of Payments	Amount of Payments	When Payments Are Due

Security: You are giving a security interest in:
☐ the goods or property being purchased.
☐

Filing Fees $ ______________ **Nonfiling Insurance $** ____________

Late Charge: If a payment is late, you will be charged ______________ % per annum of the late payment.

Prepayment: If you pay off early, you
(check if the loan is at simple interest) ☐ may ☐ will not have to pay a penalty.

(check if private mortgage insurance premiums are charged to the consumer) ☐ may ☐ will not be entitled to a refund of part of the finance charge.

See your contract documents for any additional information about nonpayment, default, any required repayment in full before the scheduled date, and prepayment refunds and penalties.

Additional Disclosures:

"e" means an estimate

INSURANCE DISCLOSURES

Property Insurance. You may obtain property insurance from anyone that is authorized to transact business in If you get the insurance from ______________________________, you will pay $______________ for _____ months.
(creditor)

Credit Insurance. If you want, the creditor may provide you with credit insurance for the credit term. Credit life insurance and credit disability insurance are not required to obtain credit and will not be provided unless you sign and agree to pay the additional cost. You understand that if your credit term exceeds 59 months, the premium rates for credit insurance are not fixed or approved by the State Board of Insurance. If you desire insurance, you should indicate the type desired and sign below.

_____ I want credit life insurance on the life of the Consumer only for a premium of $______________.

_____ I want credit life insurance on the lives of the Consumer and Co-Borrower for a premium of $______________.

_____ I want credit disability insurance (available only to Consumer) for a premium of $______________.

______________________________ ______________________________
(Consumer's signature) (Co-Borrower's signature)

I have received a copy of this statement.

______________________ __________ ______________________ __________
Signature Date Signature Date

Form 14c. Truth-in-Lending Right of Rescission

TRUTH-IN-LENDING NOTICE OF RIGHT OF RESCISSION

(Notice of Right To Cancel—Refinancing)

____

(Identification of Transaction)

Your Right To Cancel

You are entering into a new transaction to increase the amount of credit provided to you. We acquired a lien on your home under the original transaction and will retain that lien in the new transaction. You have a legal right under federal law to cancel the new transaction, without cost, within three business days from whichever of the following events occurs last:

1. the date of the new transaction, which is ______________________ ; or
2. the date you received your new Truth-in-Lending disclosures; or
3. the date you received this notice of your right to cancel.

If you cancel the new transaction, your cancellation will apply only to the increase in the amount of credit. It will not affect the amount that you presently owe or the lien we already have on your home. If you cancel, the lien as it applies to the increased amount is also canceled. Within 20 calendar days after we receive your notice of cancellation of the new transaction, we must take the steps necessary to reflect the fact that our lien on your home no longer applies to the increase of credit. We must also return any money you have given to us or anyone else in connection with the new transaction.

You may keep any money we have given you in the new transaction until we have done the things mentioned above, but you must then offer to return the money at the address below. If we do not take possession of the money within 20 calendar days of your offer, you may keep it without further obligation.

How To Cancel

If you decide to cancel the new transaction, you may do so by notifying us in writing, at

(Creditor's name and business address)

You may use any written statement that is signed and dated by you and states your intention to cancel, or you may use this notice by dating and signing below. Keep one copy of this notice because it contains important information about your rights.

If you cancel by mail or telegram, you must send the notice no later than midnight of ______________________ (or midnight of the third business day following the latest of the three events listed above). If you send or deliver your written notice to cancel in some other way, it must be delivered to the above address no later than that time.

In this agreement "you" and "your" refer to the consumer, and "we" and "us" refer to the creditor.

I WISH TO CANCEL.

______________________________ Consumer's Signature ______________ Date

______________________________ Consumer's Signature

____

Consumer acknowledges receipt of the Truth-in-Lending Notice of Right of Rescission with appropriate blanks completed.

______________________________ Consumer's Signature ______________ Date

______________________________ Consumer's Signature

from 12 C.F.R. pt. 226 app. H (1985)

Form 15. Bill of Sale

Date ___________________

1. ____________________, Seller, hereby sells the goods described in paragraph 2 to ________________________, Buyer.

2. The goods being sold under this bill of sale (Goods) are: ____

3. The purchase price for Goods is $_________. In exchange for Goods, Buyer has paid Seller:

(choose one)

[] the full purchase price.

[] $_________ as a down payment, balance due in ____ days.

[] $_________ as a down payment and has/have executed a promissory note for the balance of the purchase price.

4. Seller(s) warrant(s) that Seller(s) is/are legal owner(s) of Goods and that Goods are free of all liens and encumbrances except ______________________________________

5. Seller(s) believe(s) Goods to be in good condition except for the following defects:____________________________
____

6. Other than the warranty of ownership in Clause 4 and the representations in Clause 5, seller makes no express warranties. THE BUYER TAKES ALL GOODS AS IS. Seller hereby disclaims the implied warranty of merchantability and all other implied warranties which may apply to the extent that such disclaimers are permitted.

7. Goods shall be delivered to Buyer in the following manner:

(choose one and fill in information if Box b or c is checked)

a. [] Buyer shall take immediate possession of Goods.

b. [] Buyer(s) assume(s) responsibility for picking up goods from ______________________ within ______ days.

c. [] In exchange for an additional delivery charge of $______, receipt of which is hereby acknowledged, Seller will deliver Goods within _______ days to the following location: ________________________.

8. Additional terms of sale for Goods are as follows:
____

Signed (Seller): ____________ Signed (Buyer):____________

Address: ____________________ Address:____________________

____________________________ ____________________________

Form 16. Security Agreement

SIMPLE SECURITY AGREEMENT

STATE OF CALIFORNIA)
)
COUNTY OF ____________)

That I, ____,

of ____
Street Address Apt. No. City State Zip

hereinafter called "Debtor," hereby grant to_______________,

____,
Street Address Apt. No. City State Zip

hereinafter called the "Secured Party," a security interest in the following described property and all its proceeds as collateral to secure payment of the obligation described herein.

Collateral:
Obligation:

Note: Date
Amount
Maker
Payee
Terms of payment

Default in the payment of all or any part of the obligation described, or the failure to perform as agreed, is a default under this Agreement. Upon such default the Secured Party may declare all of the above-described obligation(s) immediately due and payable and shall have the remedies of a secured party under provisions of the California Business and Commerce Code. In the event legal action is required to enforce any provision of this Agreement, the prevailing party shall be entitled to recover reasonable attorney's fees and costs.

The Debtor hereby agrees to exercise reasonable caution and care in use of the herein-described collateral; to adequately insure or keep insured the described collateral; not to attempt to sell, assign or dispose of said collateral or his/her interest therein; not to encumber nor to permit any encumbrance against same; and not to remove said collateral from the county where the Debtor resides without written permission of the Secured Party.

EXECUTED this _________ day of _______________, 19____.

(Signed)________________________
Debtor

(Signed)________________________
Secured Party

Form 17. Fictitious Name Certificate

RETURN TO

Name ______________________

Address ______________________

City ______________________

Telephone ______________________

1 DO NOT SEPARATE — SUBMIT ALL ATTACHED COPIES
2 FILING FEE IS $21.00 FOR THE FIRST NAME AND $2.00 FOR EACH ADDITIONAL BUSINESS AND OWNER NAME ON THE SAME STATEMENT
3 PROVIDE RETURN ENVELOPE, IF MAILED
4 MUST BE TYPED.

SEE REVERSE SIDE FOR INSTRUCTIONS

GALE S. ENSTAD
COUNTY CLERK
County of Kern
1415 Truxtun Avenue
Bakersfield, California 93301
(805) 861-2621

FICTITIOUS BUSINESS NAME STATEMENT

COUNTY CLERK USE ONLY

THE FOLLOWING PERSON(S) IS (ARE) DOING BUSINESS AS:

1 • **FICTITIOUS BUSINESS NAME** (S) (Type)

2 •• **Street Address of Principal Place of business** City State Zip Code

Mailing Address City State Zip Code

3 •• **FULL NAME OF REGISTRANT** (Type only) **(If corporation, show State of Incorporation)**

Residence Address: (P.O. Box not acceptable) City State Zip Code

FULL NAME OF REGISTRANT (Type only) **(If corporation, show State of Incorporation)**

Residence Address: (P.O. Box not acceptable) City State Zip Code

FULL NAME OF REGISTRANT (Type only) **(If corporation, show State of Incorporation)**

Residence Address: (P.O. Box not acceptable) City State Zip Code

FULL NAME OF REGISTRANT (Type only) **(If corporation, show State of Incorporation)**

Residence Address: (P.O. Box not acceptable) City State Zip Code

FULL NAME OF REGISTRANT (Type only) **(If corporation, show State of Incorporation)**

Residence Address: (P.O. Box not acceptable) City State Zip Code

FULL NAME OF REGISTRANT (Type only) **(If corporation, show State of Incorporation)**

Residence Address: (P.O. Box not acceptable) City State Zip Code

4 •••• **THIS BUSINESS IS CONDUCTED BY:** (Check ONE Only)

A. ☐ An Individual	E. ☐ A Corporation	I. ☐ Joint Venture
B. ☐ A General Partnership	F. ☐ A Business Trust	J. ☐ Other - specify below
C. ☐ A Limited Partnership	G. ☐ Copartners	______________
D. ☐ An Unincorporated Association other than a Partnership	H. ☐ Husband and Wife	______________

5. **THE REGISTRANT COMMENCED TO TRANSACT BUSINESS UNDER THE FICTITIOUS BUSINESS NAME OR NAMES LISTED ABOVE ON** ______________.

6. ______________ Signed

______________ (Type Signature)

If registrant a corporation sign below

Corporation Name ______________

Signature and Title ______________

THIS STATEMENT FILED WITH THE COUNTY CLERK OF KERN COUNTY ON: ______________

GALE S. ENSTAD, County Clerk

By ______________, Deputy

THE FILING OF THIS STATEMENT DOES NOT OF ITSELF AUTHORIZE THE USE IN THIS STATE OF A FICTITIOUS BUSINESS NAME IN VIOLATION OF THE RIGHTS OF ANOTHER UNDER FEDERAL, STATE, OR COMMON LAW (SEE SECTION 14400 ET SEQ., BUSINESS AND PROFESSIONS CODE).

DO NOT PUBLISH CERTIFICATION

( ) Statement must be published once a week for four successive weeks (publication to start within 30 days of file date) and an affidavit of publication filed with the County Clerk within 30 days after publication has been accomplished.

( ) Publication is not required, pursuant to Bus. & Prof. Code Sec. 17917(c)
Additional certified copies may be requested for a statutory additional fee of $2.00 each.

CERTIFICATION
I hereby certify that the foregoing is a correct copy of the original on file in my office.

Date: ______________ GALE S. ENSTAD, County Clerk

By ______________, Deputy

FOR USE BY COUNTY CLERK ONLY

Abandonment filed ______________ Forced Expiration ______________

Dissolution filed ______________ New Statement No. ______________

Previous File No ______________ ( ) RENEWAL ( ) INITIAL FILING

FILE NO. ______________

NOTICE: THIS FICTITIOUS BUSINESS NAME STATEMENT EXPIRES FIVE YEARS FROM THE DATE IT WAS FILED IN THE OFFICE OF THE COUNTY CLERK.

CLERK 580 2170 **FN-1** (Rev. 1/91)(Front)

FILE WITH COUNTY CLERK

PUBLISH

THE BELOW INSTRUCTIONS ARE NOT TO BE PUBLISHED (Sec. 17924 B & P)

NOTICE TO REGISTRANT PURSUANT TO SECTION 17924 BUSINESS & PROFESSIONS CODE

(1) Your fictitious business name statement must be published in a newspaper within 30 days after the statement has been filed with the county clerk. The statement must be published once a week for four successive weeks and an affidavit of publication filed with the county clerk within 30 days after publication has been completed. The statement should be published in a newspaper of general circulation in the county where the principal place of business is located. The statement should be published in such county in a newspaper that circulates in the area where the business is to be conducted. (Sec. 17917, B & P Code)

(2) Any person who executes, files, or publishes any fictitious business name statement, knowing that such statement is false, in whole or in part, is quilty of a misdemeanor and upon conviction thereof shall be fined not to exceed five hundred dollars ($500). (Sec. 17930 B & P Code)

NOTE: This statement filed under Chapter 5 (commencing with Section 17900 of Part 3 of Division 7 of the Business and Professions Code need not be published if it is being filed because a prior statement has,expired under subdivision (a) of Section 17920 of the Business and Professions Code unless there has been a change in the information required in the expired statement. (Section 17917(c) Business and Professions Code.)

INSTRUCTIONS FOR COMPLETION OF STATEMENT

Please type

*(1) Insert the fictitious business name or names if more than one name is being filed.

**(2) If the registrant has a place of business in this state, insert the street address of his principal place of business in this state. If the registrant has no place of business in this state, insert the street address of his principal place of business outside this state. (P.O. Box not acceptable).

***(3) If registrant is an individual or husband and wife, insert the full name and residence address.

If registrant is a general partnership, limited partnership, copartners, or other association of persons, insert the full name and address of each general partner.

If registrant is an unincorporated association other than a partnership, insert the full name and principal place of business of the association.

If registrant is a joint venture, insert the name of each joint venturer and the principal place of business of each.

If registrant is a corporation, insert the name of the corporation as set forth in its articles of incorporation, the state of incorporation and the principal business address.

If registrant is a business trust, insert the name of the trust and its principal place of business.

(P.O. Box not acceptable for residence address.)

****(4) Check box provided, whichever best describes the nature of the business.

(5) Insert date in which registrant started doing business under this fictitious business name or names.

(6) If registrant is an individual or husband and wife, the statement shall be signed by an individual.

If registrant is a general or limited partnership or copartnership, the statemen't shall be signed by a general partner.

If registrant is business trust, the statement shal be signed by a trustee.

If registrant is a corporation, unincorporated association or joint venturer, the statement shall be signed by an officer. State title of officer.

A FICTITIOUS BUSINESS NAME STATEMENT EXPIRES 5 YEARS FROM THE DATE IT WAS FILED IN THE OFFICE OF THE COUNTY CLERK. Except as provided in Section 17923, B & P Code, it expires **40 days after any change in the facts set forth in the statement,** except that a change in the residence address of an individual or husband and wife, general partner, or trustee does not cause the statement to expire.

This statement expires upon the filing of a statement of abandonment.

ARTICLE 1.5 TRADE NAME REGISTRATION

Section 14411, Business and Professions Code (1972)

The filing of any fictitious business name statement by a person required to file such statement pursuant to Section 17910 shall establish a rebuttable presumption that the registrant has the exclusive right to use as a trade name the fictitious business name, as well as any confusing similar trade name, in the county in which the statement is filed, if the registrant is the first to file such a statement containing the fictitious business name in that county, and is actually engaged in a trade or business utilizing such fictitious business name or a confusingly similar name in that county.

The rebuttable presumption created by this section shall be one affecting the burden of producing evidence.

Clerk 580 2170 FN-1 (Rev 3-90) (Back)

Form 18. EDD Registration Form

DE-1 REGISTRATION FORM

INSTRUCTION SHEET

FILING A REGISTRATION FORM
Form DE-1 should be used for all registrations.
An employer is required by law to file a Registration Form with the Employment Development Department (any Employment Tax District Office) within 15 days after paying wages for employment in any calendar quarter.

If you are found to be subject to the Unemployment Insurance Code, you will be assigned an account number and notified. Each new employer should receive an Employer's Guide which is a yearly publication distributed to promote your understanding of the UI Code and to explain the administrative procedures involved. It should also help you understand your tax withholding and filing responsibilities under the law. Questions concerning problems or circumstances not covered in this guide should be directed to the appropriate Employment Tax District Office (ETDO). A listing of ETDO's is provided on the bottom of page 2. The following instructions will assist you in completing this registration form. Please detach and submit DE 1, Registration Form only.

A. OWNERS
Enter the full given name, middle initial, surname, social security account number and driver's license number. If a corporation, give name exactly as spelled and registered with the Secretary of State. Enter Corporate Identification and Federal Identification numbers in Sections J and N.

PRINCIPAL CORPORATION OFFICERS
Enter the full name of each officer and his/her social security account number and driver's license number. *NOTE: The disclosure of social security account numbers is mandatory under the Federal Tax Reform Act of 1976. The number will be used for identification purposes and will be available only to authorized personnel within the Employment Development Department and other government agencies as permitted in Sections 322 and 1095 of the California Unemployment Insurance Code.*

B. BUSINESS NAME
Give the name by which your business is known to the public (this name may be your own — John Jones; or a combination of name and descriptive term — Jones' Grocery; or a selected descriptive name — Best Value Market, etc.). Enter "None" if no business name is used.

C. MAILING ADDRESS
Enter the address to which your correspondence and forms should be sent.

D. BUSINESS PHONE
Provide day time business phone number.

E. BUSINESS TYPE
Provide a brief description of your principal business or primary industry. If you are engaged in more than one activity, describe the activity which is expected to utilize the largest number of workers during the subsequent 12-month period.

The description should consist of two parts:

First, place a check in the block opposite the item that applies to your business.

Second, describe the particular product handled or service rendered. Include liquor license number or contractor license number, if applicable.

The following examples indicate suitable entries in this item:

Agriculture — list the primary crops or agricultural services performed, also veterinary services or farm labor contractor.

Mining — describe the type, such as ores-iron, copper, lead, gold, silver, or list crude petroleum, natural gas or quarrying a type of stone.

Construction — general residential building, highway and bridge building, electrical contracting.

Manufacturing — prepared meat products, women's wear/dresses, sawing rough lumber, book printing, electronic/industrial controls. List products in order of importance.

Transportation — list the type; such as railroad, bus, trucking, water, air.

Communications — telephone, telegraph, radio and television broadcasting.

Services — motel, industrial laundering, management counsulting, auto repair, dental laboratory, barber shop, law offices, physician's offices.

Utilities — electric, gas, sanitary services.

Retail trade — list the primary products sold; such as automobiles, lumber, groceries, paper products, furniture, clothing, shoes.

Wholesale trade — same as retail trade.

Finance — list the type of financial institution; such as bank, credit union, mortgage company, security brokers, security traders.

Insurance — life, title, surety, pension funds.

Real Estate — real estate operators, and owners and lessors of real property, as well as buyers, sellers, developers, agents, and brokers.

Other — timber tracts, tree farms, forest nurseries, commercial fishing, wildlife management, government agency, domestic: household, local college club, fraternity or sorority; also complete Section "S".

F. SUPPORTIVE SERVICES
If you are part of a larger organization and you are primarily engaged in providing supportive services to other establishments of the same company rather than for the general public or other business firms, check one of the first four boxes. If you check "Other," please indicate what Supportive Services you provide to other establishments of your company, such as automotive repair, equipment repair, training or engineering support. If you are part of a larger organization, but do not provide supportive services as described above, or your organization is not primarily engaged in providing supportive services to other establishments of the same company, check the "No" box.

G. HAVE YOU PAID WAGES IN EXCESS OF $100 IN ANY CALENDAR QUARTER?
The payroll in excess of $100 must be entirely within ONE of the following calendar quarters: January-March; April-June; July-September; or October-December. (The date block checked should be the calendar quarter in which the payroll first totaled more than $100). If Employer Type from Section H is 5 — Domestic, complete Section S instead of Section G. If Employer Type from Section H is subject to Personal Income Tax only, complete Section V instead of Section G.

H. EMPLOYER TYPE
Examine the list and check the box next to the category which best describes the type of employer you are. Employer types are used to determine the employer's Unemployment Insurance (UI), Disability Insurance (DI), and Personal Income Tax (PIT) fund reporting requirements.

If you are considered to be nonprofit and exempt under Section 501(c)(3) of the Internal Revenue Code, a DE 1SNP, Selection of Financing Method By A Nonprofit Organization Exempt Under Section 501(c)(3) of the Internal Revenue Code, must also be completed. If you are a public entity, A DE 1 PE, Selection of Financing Method and Election to Cover Excluded Services, must be completed. For more information please call (916) 322-4688.

If you are a public school, a DE 1 SE, Selection of Financing Method and Election to Cover Excluded Services, must be completed. For more information please call (916) 445-9623.

If you checked box 5, Domestic, complete Section "S" and if you checked box 9, Agricultural, complete Section "T". If you checked box 10, Church, or box 12, Annuitant Payer, you are required to report PIT only and should complete Section "V".

I. ORGANIZATION TYPE
Check the term which best describes the legal form of your organization. If both spouses are engaged in the operation and/or management of a business that is community property, enter each spouse's name in Item A and check block marked "Husband/Wife Co-ownership" in Section I. If yours is a special type such as Association, Joint Venture, Receivership, Bankruptcy, Liquidation, Trusteeship, or Estate Administration, check the appropriate box. If yours is a LIMITED PARTNERSHIP, the General Partners should be so identified; use the space in Item A.

J. DO YOU HAVE MORE THAN ONE ESTABLISHMENT?
"Establishment" means a physical location where business is conducted or services or industrial operations are performed: e.g., a factory, mill, store, or mine.

K. DATE THIS OWNERSHIP BEGAN OPERATING
Enter date the new ownership, shown in Section A, started at the address shown in Section C or Z.

L. PERSONAL INCOME TAX WITHHOLDING
Indicate the first month that Personal Income Tax withheld will exceed $350.

M. EIGHTY-MONTHLY DEPOSITS
When required under Section 6302 of the Internal Revenue Code (IRC) to make deposits of federal income and social security (FICA) taxes on the basis of eighth-monthly periods, and California PIT withheld is more than $75, YOU MUST ALSO remit all DI and PIT withholdings to the Employment Development Department (EDD). Remittance must be made within the number of days specified by the IRC.

N. ENTER FEDERAL IDENTIFICATION NUMBER(S)
If not assigned, enter "Applied For".

O. OWNERSHIP RECORD OF BUSINESS YOU ARE NOW REGISTERING
When you take over all or part of a going business you may acquire all or part of the reserve account and the rate of the former owner. (Changes in partnership interests should be considered as having the same effect since they result in a new combination of ownership. The same is true of changes in form — partnership to corporation, sole proprietorship to partnership, etc.) Contact your nearest Employment Tax District Office for instructions on filing a DE 4453, Application for Transfer of Reserve Account.

P. WHO OPERATED THIS BUSINESS BEFORE YOU TOOK OVER?
This information is needed to close out the account of the former ownership.

Q. DID YOU ACQUIRE ALL OR ONLY A PART OF THE SELLER'S BUSINESS ACTIVITIES?
"All" means the entire business activity of the former owner within California. Acquisition of a complete establishment or all operations within an area is frequently misunderstood to be "entire". However, if the former owner continues to operate any other business, or in any other locality in the State, the acquisition is not entire. If there is any doubt on this point, check with the former owner or his agent.

R. HAVE YOU EVER OPERATED A BUSINESS OTHER THAN THE ONE YOU ARE NOW REGISTERING?
If the ownership now being registered is operating or has ever operated at another location, check "yes" and complete the other items.

Proper completion of these items will help prevent erroneous assignment of account numbers.

S. DOMESTIC SERVICE
Complete this section, not Section G, if you employ domestic workers in a private home, local college club, or local chapter of a college fraternity or sorority; and meet the requirements of 1 or 2.

1. DISABILITY INSURANCE ONLY (CASH wages ACTUALLY PAID between $750 and $999.99 inclusive).

   The payroll between $750 and $999.99 inclusive must be entirely within ONE of the following calendar quarters:

   January-March; April-June; July-September; or October-December. The date block checked should be the last month of the calendar quarter in which the payroll FIRST totaled between $750 and $999.99 inclusive.

2. UNEMPLOYMENT INSURANCE AND DISABILITY INSURANCE (CASH wages ACTUALLY PAID of $1,000 or more).

   The payroll of $1,000 or more must be entirely within ONE of the following calendar quarters: January-March; April-June; July-September; or October-December. The date block checked should be the last month of the calendar quarter in which the payroll FIRST totaled $1,000.

T. AGRICULTURAL EMPLOYERS

1. Place a check in the block opposite the item that applies to your activities, and describe the crops, commodities, or activities. The following examples indicate suitable entries in this item:

   Farm owner or operator — Oranges, vineyard, dairy, cotton, string beans.

   Farm labor contractor — Place check in block.

   Farm labor association — Oranges, cotton, vegetables.

   Commodity organization — Oranges, vegetables, nuts.
   Operator of agricultural services — Threshing, bailing, road siding hay.
   Other — Residential farms, feed lot operation, livestock feeding farms.

2. List each county in which you are engaged in agricultural activities.

U. PUBLIC ENTITIES
Nature of Activity — Describe the kind of activities carried on by organization. The following is an example:

Governmental — State type of governmental organization, whether a federal, state, county, municipality, etc., or relationship to such entities; i.e., City Library, County Hospital, etc.

V. EMPLOYERS SUBJECT TO PERSONAL INCOME TAX ONLY

1. Nature of Activity — Describe the kind of activites carried on by organization. The following are examples:
   Governmental — State type of governmental organization, whether a federal, state, county, school district, municipality, etc., or relationship to such entites; i.e., City Library, County Hospital, etc.
   Nonprofit (other than governmental) — State whether organization for religious, charitable, scientific, literary, educational, or humane purposes and state the principal activity; i.e., religious organization — hospital; charitable organization — home for aged; etc.
   Other — describe type of activity; i.e., railroad, pensions, annuities and independent contractor payer, etc.
2. Indicate if you make payments which are subject to personal income tax withholding.
   Indicate the number of employees.
   If the payment is to a family member, indicate what relationship to you. Also list birthdate if payment is to son or daughter.
3. Indicate first quarter and year in which personal income tax is withheld.

W. BOOKKEEPER/ACCOUNTANT INFORMATION
Enter the name of your bookkeeper or accountant and phone number.

X. LOCATION OF BUSINESS
If the address of the business you are now registering is different from your mailing address (Line C), please enter the location of your business here. (California location, if an out-of-state employer.)

Y. BANK INFORMATION

1. Enter the name of your bank.
2. Enter your bank account number.
3. Enter the branch address of your bank.

Z. DECLARATION
This declaration must be signed by one of the owners listed under Section A. The signature of a general partner is required for a limited partnership.

NEED MORE HELP OR INFORMATION?
For more information or help in registration, reporting of wages, or payment of contributions, contact one of the Employment Tax District Offices or write to the Employment Development Department, P.O. Box 826880, Sacramento, CA 94280-0001.

EMPLOYER ASSISTANCE

EMPLOYMENT TAX DISTRICT OFFICES

(Addresses and telephone numbers are listed in the telephone directory under California, State of . . . Taxes, Employment Development Department)
*Out-of-state employers refer to Interstate.

Bakersfield	(805) 395-2896	Los Angeles	(213) 669-7670	Sacramento	(916) 427-4068	Santa Monica	(310) 576-6400
Chico	(916) 895-4401	Merced	(209) 723-3061	San Bernardino	(714) 383-4176	Santa Rosa	(707) 576-2094
Downey	(310) 923-1237	Modesto	(209) 576-6207	San Diego	(619) 284-8615	Stockton	(209) 948-7634
El Monte	(818) 575-6751	Monterey	(408) 649-2902	San Francisco	(415) 557-1898	Vallejo	(707) 648-4040
Escondido	(619) 747-2200	Oakland	(510) 577-2396	San Jose	(408) 452-7175	Van Nuys	(818) 901-5208
Eureka	(707) 445-6522	Orange	(714) 558-4202	San Luis Obispo	(805) 549-3512	Ventura	(805) 654-4505
Fresno	(209) 445-5132	Placerville	(916) 622-2529	San Mateo	(415) 358-4102	Visalia	(209) 734-8126
*Interstate	(916) 322-7186	Pleasant Hill	(510) 977-8265	San Rafael	(415) 472-5651	Yuba City	(916) 741-4020
Laguna Hills	(714) 768-6103	Redding	(916) 225-2207	Santa Barbara	(805) 564-0390		
Long Beach	(310) 595-6321	Riverside	(714) 782-3260	Santa Cruz	(408) 464-6293		

EDD
Serving the People of California

This form will be the basic record of YOUR ACCOUNT. Please read the attached INSTRUCTION SHEET before filling it out. **PLEASE PRINT OR TYPE.** Proper completion of this form may save you and us a future phone call or letter. Return this form to:

DE-1 REGISTRATION FORM

EMPLOYMENT TAX DISTRICT OFFICE
1001 Tower Way, SU 240/P.O. Box 9836
Bakersfield, CA 93309
Telephone (805) 395-2871

ACCOUNT NUMBER	QUARTER	ETDO	FED CODE

SENT FORMS: | ON-LINE PROCESS DATE | DICTATOR CODE

A. OWNERS OR CORPORATION NAME — **List Partners* and Corporation Officers below.**	SOCIAL SECURITY NUMBER	DRIVER'S LICENSE NUMBER

*If entity is a **Limited Partnership,** indicate General Partner with an (*). List additional partners on a separate sheet.

List all partners or corporation officers names	TITLE Indicate partner or officer title	SOCIAL SECURITY NUMBER	DRIVER'S LICENSE NUMBER

B. BUSINESS NAME

C. MAILING ADDRESS P.O. Box or Street and Number | City or Town | State | ZIP Code | County

In Care of:

D. BUSINESS PHONE

E. BUSINESS TYPE Check one

☐ Agriculture (A) ☐ Communications (B) ☐ Finance (F)
☐ Mining (N) ☐ Services (S) ☐ Insurance (I)
☐ Construction (C) ☐ Utilities (L) ☐ Real Estate (E)
☐ Manufacturing (M) ☐ Wholesale Trade (W) ☐ Other
☐ Transportation (T) ☐ Retail Trade (R) ________

1) Describe kind of product or type of service: (See INSTRUCTION SHEET, Item E.)

2) IF MANUFACTURING, list the principal products in order of importance:

3) If applicable: Contractor License # ________

Liquor License # ________

F. SUPPORTIVE SERVICES
If you are part of a larger organization and you are primarily engaged in providing supportive services to other establishments of the larger organization, check one of these boxes.
☐ Control Administrative (headquarters, etc.) (1) ☐ Research, development, or testing (2) ☐ Storage (warehouse) (3) ☐ Other (specify) (9)
Otherwise, check ☐ No (5) ________

G. INDICATE FIRST QUARTER AND YEAR IN WHICH WAGES EXCEEDED $100. (e.g. JAN-MAR 83)
(Complete Section R if you meet the requirements of a domestic employer.)
(Complete Section U if you have employees subject to Personal Income Tax withholding only.)
☐ Jan.-Mar. 19 ____ ☐ July-Sept. 19 ____
☐ Apr.-June 19 ____ ☐ Oct.-Dec. 19 ____

H. EMPLOYER TYPE — No. of Employees:

☐ Commercial (01) ☐ Domestic (05) ☐ Church (10) ☐ Red Cross (20)
☐ Non Profit (02) ☐ Public School (07) ☐ Indian Reservation (11) ☐ Public Entity (21) ☐ State Hospital (28)
☐ Non Profit 501 C3 (03) ☐ District Hospital (08) ☐ Annuitant Payer (12) ☐ Pacific Maritime (22)
☐ Non Profit School (04) ☐ Agricultural (09) ☐ District Fair (16) ☐ Fishing Boat (25)

I. ORGANIZATION TYPE

☐ INDIVIDUAL OWNER (IW) ☐ JOINT VENTURE (JV) ☐ LIQUIDATION (LQ) ☐ GOVERNMENTAL (GO)
☐ HUS/WIFE CO-OWNERSHIP (HW) ☐ RECEIVERSHIP (RC) ☐ LIMITED PARTNERSHIP (LP) ☐ SCHOOL DISTRICT (ST)
☐ GENERAL PARTNERSHIP (GP) ☐ BANKRUPTCY (BK) ☐ TRUSTEESHIP (TR) ☐ OTHER (Specify) (OT)
☐ CORPORATION (CP) ☐ ASSOCIATION (AS) ☐ ESTATE ADMINISTRATION (EA) ________

J. DO YOU HAVE MORE THAN ONE ESTABLISHMENT IN CA? ☐ Yes ☐ No
Corporate ID No.: Incorporated in State of:

K. DATE THIS OWNERSHIP BEGAN OPERATING: Month Day Year

L. INDICATE FIRST MONTH THAT CALIFORNIA PERSONAL INCOME TAX WITHHELD EXCEEDS $350. Enter year ________
☐ Jan. ☐ Feb. ☐ Mar. ☐ Apr. ☐ May ☐ June
☐ July ☐ Aug. ☐ Sep. ☐ Oct. ☐ Nov. ☐ Dec. ☐ None

M. WILL YOU BE SUBJECT TO FEDERAL EIGHTH-MONTHLY DEPOSITS?
☐ Yes ☐ No (See instruction sheet)

N. FEDERAL EMPLOYER I.D. NO.: __ __ – __ __ __ __ __ __ __

O. OWNERSHIP RECORD OF BUSINESS YOU ARE REGISTERING (Please check the statement that most nearly applies in your case)
☐ 1. This is a new business — No previous ownership
☐ 2. This is a going business which has been — or is being — acquired by purchase
☐ 3. Change in partners ☐ Partner added ☐ Partner dropped
☐ 4. Change in form — sole proprietor to partnership; partnership to corporation, merger, etc.
☐ 5. Other change (See Instruction P)

CONTINUE ON THE REVERSE OF THIS FORM AND SIGN THE DECLARATION INCLUDED IN SECTION Z.

DE-1 Rev. 61 (1-92) State of California / Employment Development Department 91 63112

P. WHO OPERATED THIS BUSINESS BEFORE YOU TOOK OVER? → (If no previous owner please enter "New Business" below, and skip Item Q)

	PURCHASE PRICE	DATE OF TRANSFER	ACCOUNT NUMBER WITH DEPARTMENT
NAME			
BUSINESS NAME			

Q. DID YOU ACQUIRE ALL OR ONLY A PART OF THE SELLER'S BUSINESS? ☐ All ☐ Part (See INSTRUCTION SHEET, Item Q)

R. 1. HAVE YOU EVER OPERATED A BUSINESS OTHER THAN THE ONE YOU ARE NOW REGISTERING? ☐ No ☐ Yes → BUSINESS NAME

2. WAS THAT BUSINESS REGISTERED WITH THE DEPARTMENT? ☐ No ☐ Yes ADDRESS
Employer Account No. ______ CITY/STATE ZIP CODE

3. IS THAT BUSINESS STILL BEING OPERATED BY YOU? ☐ Yes ☐ No → IF NOT, WHEN DID IT CLOSE? (If exact date is not known please give approximate date) Month Year

COMPLETE SECTIONS S. THROUGH V. IF APPLICABLE

S. DOMESTIC SERVICE (See Instruction Sheet, Item S for examples.) No. of Employees

1. Indicate First Quarter and Year in Which Wages between $750 and $999.99 were ACTUALLY PAID in Cash.
☐ Jan.-Mar. 19 ___ ☐ Apr.-June 19 ___ ☐ July-Sep. 19 ___ ☐ Oct.-Dec. 19 ___

2. Indicate First Quarter and Year in Which $1,000 or More Total Payroll was ACTUALLY PAID in Cash. No. of Employees
☐ Jan.-Mar. 19 ___ ☐ Apr.-June 19 ___ ☐ July-Sep. 19 ___ ☐ Oct.-Dec. 19 ___

T. AGRICULTURAL EMPLOYERS

1. INDICATE TYPE OF AGRICULTURAL EMPLOYERS
☐ Farm owner or operator — Enter principal crops or commodities:
☐ Commodity organization — Enter commodity:
☐ Farm labor contractor
☐ Farm labor association — Enter commodity:
☐ Farm Cooperative
☐ Farm Association
☐ Operator of agricultural services (including custom work) — Enter type i.e., land leveling, mechanical cotton picking, spraying, etc.:
☐ Other (please specify):

Do you dry, pack, process, or change the agricultural commodity from its original state? ☐ Yes ☐ No

If yes, are less than fifty percent of the crops grown by this particular entity? ☐ Yes ☐ No

2. COUNTY OR COUNTIES IN WHICH YOU OPERATE: (List here)

3. DO YOU EMPLOY NONAGRICULTURAL WORKERS? ☐ No ☐ Yes If "Yes", see "4" across.

4. IF BUSINESS NAME DIFFERENT FROM ITEM B, PAGE 1, GIVE NAME AND ADDRESS OF THE BUSINESS:

5. IF REGISTERED FOR NONAGRICULTURAL PAYROLL, ENTER THAT EMPLOYER ACCOUNT NO.:

U. PUBLIC ENTITIES
NATURE OF ACTIVITY

V. EMPLOYERS SUBJECT TO PERSONAL INCOME TAX ONLY (Including Payers of Pensions and Annuities)

1. NATURE OF ACTIVITY

2. Do you have employees (annuitants) subject to only Personal Income Tax Withholdings? ☐ Yes ☐ No No. of Employees:

If that employee is a family member, what is the relationship to you? If that employee is a son or daughter, list the birthdate.

3. INDICATE FIRST QUARTER AND YEAR IN WHICH PERSONAL INCOME TAX IS WITHHELD.
☐ Jan.-Mar. 19 ___ ☐ Apr.-June 19 ___ ☐ July-Sep. 19 ___ ☐ Oct.-Dec. 19 ___

W. BOOKKEEPER/ACCOUNTANT **NAME:** **PHONE:**

X. LOCATION OF CALIFORNIA BUSINESS (if different from item C)

Street and Number	City or Town	State	ZIP Code	County

Y. BANK INFORMATION

1. Bank: ______
2. Acct. No. ______
3. Branch Address: ______ Street ______ City State ZIP Code

Z. DECLARATION

These statements are hereby declared to be correct to the best knowledge and belief of the undersigned. It is understood that this registration is not an application for a reserve account transfer to which I might be entitled. (See instruction P)

Signature ______ Date ______ Residence phone ( )
Title (Owner, Accountant, etc.) ______ Residence Address ______
Street City State ZIP Code

Form 19. OSHA Information

Digests and Standards

The Occupational Safety and Health Administration (OSHA) has prepared a series of pocket digests covering the following areas:

- Construction Industry
- General Industry
- Longshoring Industry
- Shipyard Industry

These digests have been compiled to aid employers, supervisors, and safety and health personnel in their efforts to comply with OSHA standards in the workplace.

Unless otherwise noted, a single free copy of each these digests are available from OSHA regional and area offices or from the OSHA publications office, 200 Constitution Avenue NW, Room N-3101, Washington, D.C. 20120.

The information contained in these digests should in no way be considered as a complete substitute for any provisions of the Occupational Safety and Health Act of 1970 or for any standards promulgated under the Act. The actual source standards are noted in the indexes to these booklets and should be consulted for complete reference to OSHA standards in their entirety.

Explanation of Contents

The *Construction Industry Digest* (OSHA 2202) and the *General Industry Digest* (OSHA 2201) contain those standards most frequently overlooked by employers, and those that are particularly hazardous. These two booklets only summarize the basic applicable standards; they do not list OSHA standards verbatim. The actual standards, in their entirety, are sold by the Superintendent of Documents, U.S. Government Printing Office, Washington, D.C. 20402-0325 (fax number 202-275-0019).

The *Shipyard Industry Digest* (OSHA 2268) contains all the safety and health standards in Title 29 Code of Regulations (CFR) Part 1915, as of January 31, 1989. Hazards not covered by the shipyard industry standards may be covered by general industry standards in 29 CFR Part 1910.

The *Longshoring Industry Digest* (OSHA 2232) contains all the safety and health standards to marine terminals (29 CFR 1917) and longshoring (29 CFR 1918) operations, as of September 1985. Consequently, the current digest does not include single-piece rim wheels or hazard communication. Other booklets on these topics are available from the OSHA Publications Office. Ask for "Chemical Hazard Communications (OSHA 3084)" or "Safe Operating Procedures: Single-Piece Rim Wheels (OSHA 3086)."

Form 20. California OSHA Offices

OFFICE	LOCATION	PUBLIC PHONE
HEADQUARTERS:	455 Golden Gate Ave., Rm. 5202, San Francisco 94102	
	John Howard, Chief	(415) 703–4341
	Frank R. Ciofalo, Ph.D., Deputy Chief - Health	(415) 703–4341
	Mark Carleson, Deputy Chief - Field Operations	(415) 703–4341
REGIONAL:		
Anaheim	2100 E. Katella Avenue, Suite 125, Anaheim 92806	(714) 939-8611
Los Angeles	3550 West 6th Street, Room 413, Los Angeles 90020	(213) 736-4911
Sacramento	2424 Arden Way, Suite 125, Sacramento 95825	(916) 263-2803
San Francisco	1390 Market St., Suite 822 San Francisco 94102	(415) 557–8640
DISTRICT:		
Anaheim	2100 E. Katella Avenue, Suite 140, Anaheim 92806	(714) 939-0145
Bakersfield	4800 Stockdale Hwy, Suite 212, Bakersfield 93309	(805) 395-2718
Concord	1465 Enea Circle, Bldg.E., Suite 900, Concord 94520	(510) 676-5333
Covina	1123 South Parkview, Suite 100, Covina 91724	(818) 966-1166
Fresno	2550 Mariposa St., Room 4000, Fresno 93721	(209) 445-5302
Los Angeles	3550 W. Sixth St., Room 431, Los Angeles 90020	(213) 736-3041
Oakland	7700 Edgewater Drive, Suite 125, Oakland 94621	(510) 568-8602
Pico Rivera	9455 E. Slauson Ave.,Pico Rivera 90660	(310) 949-7827
Redding	381 Hemsted, Redding 96002	(916) 224-4743
Sacramento	2424 Arden Way, Suite 165, Sacramento 95825	(916) 263-2800
San Bernardino	242 E. Airport Drive, Suite 103, San Bernardino 92408	(714) 383-4321
San Diego	7807 Convoy Court, Suite 140, San Diego 92111	(619) 237-7325
San Francisco	1390 Market St., Suite 718, San Francisco 94102	(415) 557-1677
San Jose	2010 N. First St.,Suite 401, San Jose 95131	(408) 452-7288
Santa Rosa	1221 Farmers Lane, Suite 300, Santa Rosa 95405	(707) 576-2388
Torrance/Long Beach/South Bay	680 Knox Street, Suite 100, Torrance 90502	(310) 516-3734
Van Nuys	6150 Van Nuys Blvd., Suite 405, Van Nuys 91401-3379	(818) 901-5403
Ventura	1655 Mesa Verde, Room 150, Ventura 93003	(805) 654-4581
FIELD:		
Chico	555 Rio Lindo, Suite A, Chico 95926	(916) 895-4761
Eureka	619 Second St., Room 109, Eureka 95501	(707) 445-6611
Modesto	1209 Woodrow, Suite C-4, Modesto 95350	(209) 576-6260
Salinas	1164 Monroe Street, Suite 1, Salinas 93906-3564	(408) 443-3050
San Mateo	1900 So. Norfolk St., Suite 215, San Mateo 94403	(415) 573-3812
Stockton	31 E. Channel St., Room 418, Stockton 95202	(209) 948-7762
Ukiah	620 Kings Court, Suite 5, Ukiah 95482	(707) 463-4783

Form 21a. List of IRS Publications

Instructions

Tax Practitioner Program

The purpose of this program is to provide: **two** informational copies of most tax forms and schedules; **one** copy of instructions and publications and Practitioner **newsletters** relating to recent law changes. We accept only one request per firm/company, per address, **for ordering forms and bulk shipments of Package X, and Publications 17 and 334.** Orders from different practitioners within the same firm will be removed at the discretion of IRS without further notification. However, we **will** accept multiple names per firm to receive **Practitioner Newsletters.** A Form 3975 must be completed for each person wishing to receive a newsletter.

Package X bulk distribution from the contractor is being expanded in order to process your order more efficiently. If you are requesting more than 40 copies, please order in increments of 5.

Federal agencies are required by law (Joint Committee on Printing (JCP) Regulation, Title III) to update their mailing list periodically. You **must** submit **Form 3975** to remain on the mailing list, even if you only want to receive the newsletter. Failure to annually submit Form 3975 will result in the removal of your name from the Tax Practitioner Mailing List.

Responsibilities of Return Preparers—The importance of the roles of income tax preparers is recognized in the Internal Revenue Code which contains provisions that regulate their conduct. For more information, see Notice 90-20, 1990-1 C.B. 328, IRC Sections 6060, 6109, 6694, 6695, 7216.

Paperwork Reduction Notice—We ask for the information on this form to furnish you information and to send you the items you ordered. Your compliance is voluntary.

The time needed to complete and file this form will vary depending on individual circumstances. The estimated average time is 3 minutes.

If you have comments concerning the accuracy of this time estimate or suggestions for making this form more simple, we would be happy to hear from you. You can write to both the **Internal Revenue Service,** Washington, DC 20224, Attn: IRS Reports Clearance Officer T:FP; and **Office of Management and Budget,** Paperwork Reduction Project (1545-0351), Washington, DC 20503. **DO NOT** send the form to either of these offices. Instead, see the instructions for information on where to mail your Form 3975.

Other Items

After December 15, 1991, written requests on company letterhead may be submitted for items **not listed on pages 2–7.** We cannot honor requests before this date. Send requests to the distribution center for your state (see page 12), or call 1-800-829-3676 and ask for the practitioner gate. You will receive the maximum quantity of two copies of tax forms and one copy of publications. You can also use this toll free number if you have a problem with your order.

The forms **listed** on pages 2–7 will be available only in **Package X** and the **Reproducible Kits.**

Bulk Quantities Of Forms

Multiple copies of tax forms which exceed our quantity limits, may be obtained by: (1) ordering from Superintendent of Documents using GPO Form 3565 on page 13, (2) ordering from a commercial forms broker or private printer, or (3) photocopy using the reproducible masters provided in the kits (page 10).

Superintendent of Documents (Sup Docs)

The Superintendent of Documents is part of the Government Printing Office and **is not affiliated with the Internal Revenue Service.** Sup. Docs. is the only government agency authorized to sell printed materials. Use GPO Form 3565 (page 13) for bulk forms requests and send directly to Sup. Docs., **not to the IRS.** All orders received at IRS will be returned to the requestor, thus delaying the processing time of your order. Checks must be included with your order and made payable to the Superintendent of Documents. If there is a problem with your GPO Form 3565 order, you should contact Sup. Docs. at (301) 953-2298. Partial shipments will begin as soon as forms become available.

Titles For Items Listed On Form 3975 (Refer to "Other Items" when requesting items not listed)

Tax Practitioner Kits
Reproducible Copies of Various Tax Forms (refer to pages 3-7 for items listed).

Package X
Informational Copies of Federal Tax Forms (refer to pages 3-7 for items listed).

Publication 1 *
Your Rights as a Taxpayer

Publication 15
Circular E—Employer's Tax Guide

Publication 17
Your Federal Income Tax

Publication 51 †
Circular A—Agricultural Employer's Tax Guide

Publication 54
Tax Guide for U.S. Citizens and Resident Aliens Abroad

Publication 225
Farmer's Tax Guide

Publication 334
Tax Guide for Small Business

Publication 393 †
Federal Employment Tax Forms

Publication 463 *
Travel, Entertainment, and Gift Expenses

Publication 501 *
Exemptions, Standard Deductions, Filing Information

Publication 502 *
Medical and Dental Expenses

Publication 503 *
Child and Dependent Care Expenses

Publication 504 *
Tax Information for Divorced or Separated Individuals

Publication 505 *
Tax Withholding and Estimated Tax

Publication 508 *
Educational Expenses

Publication 509 *
Tax Calendar for 1992

Publication 520 *
Scholarships and Fellowships

Publication 521 *
Moving Expenses

Publication 523 *
Tax Information on Selling Your Home

Publication 524 *
Credit for the Elderly or the Disabled

Publication 525 *
Taxable and Nontaxable Income

Publication 526 *
Charitable Contributions

Publication 527 *
Residential Rental Property

* Item also available in Pub. 1194.

† New item added this year.

Publication 529 *
Miscellaneous Deductions

Publication 530 *
Tax Information for Homeowners

Publication 531 *
Reporting Income From Tips

Publication 533 *
Self-Employment Tax

Publication 534 *
Depreciation

Publication 535 *
Business Expenses

Publication 537
Installment Sales

Publication 538
Accounting Periods and Methods

Publication 541 *
Tax Information on Partnerships

Publication 542 *
Tax Information on Corporations

Publication 544 *
Sales and Other Dispositions of Assets

Publication 545 * †
Interest Expense

Publication 547 *
Nonbusiness Disasters, Casualties, and Thefts

Publication 550 *
Investment Income and Expenses

Publication 551 *
Basis of Assets

Publication 552 *
Recordkeeping for Individuals

Publication 553 *
Highlights of 1991 Tax Changes

Publication 554 *
Tax Information for Older Americans

Publication 556 *
Examination of Returns, Appeal Rights, and Claims for Refund

Publication 559 *
Tax Information for Survivors, Executors, and Administrators

Publication 560 *
Retirement Plans For The Self-Employed

Publication 561
Determining the Value of Donated Property

Publication 564 *
Mutual Fund Distributions

Publication 570
Tax Guide for Individuals in U.S. Possessions

Publication 575 *
Pension and Annuity Income

Publication 583
Taxpayers Starting a Business

Publication 584
Nonbusiness, Disaster, Casualty and Theft Loss Workbook

Publication 587 *
Business Use of Your Home

Publication 589 *
Tax Information on S Corporations

Publication 590 *
Individual Retirement Arrangements (IRAs)

Publication 596 *
Earned Income Credit

Publication 776 † (Foreign Accounts Only)
Overseas Filers of Form 1040

Publication 907 *
Tax Information for Handicapped and Disabled Individuals

Publication 908
Bankruptcy and Other Debt Cancellation

Publication 909 *
Alternative Minimum Tax for Individuals

Publication 910 *
Guide to Free Tax Services

Publication 915 *
Social Security Benefits and Equivalent Railroad Retirement Benefits

Publication 917 *
Business Use of a Car

Publication 925 *
Passive Activity and At-Risk Rules

Publication 929 *
Tax Rules for Children and Dependents

Publication 936 *
Limits on Home Mortgage Interest Deduction

Publication 937 *
Business Reporting (Employment Taxes, Information Returns)

Publication 1167
Substitute Printed Computer-Prepared and Computer-Generated Tax Forms and Schedules

Publication 1220
Requirements for Filing Forms 1098,1099, 5498 & W-2G on Magnetic Tape 5¼ & 3½ Inch Diskettes

Publication 1345
Revenue Procedure for Electronic Filing of Individual Income Tax Returns (Tax Year 1991)

List of Various Tax Forms, Schedules and Instructions

The following list of tax forms, schedules and related instructions are **anticipated to be included in Package X and the Tax Practitioner Kits. Do not order items individually.** This list of items may vary due to the availability and approval to print.

SS-4
Application for Employer Identification Number

SS-4 Instructions

W-2 (1991)
Wage and Tax Statement
See W-2 Instructions (1991)

W-2 Instructions (1991)

W-2c
Statement of Corrected Income and Tax Amounts

W-3 (1991)
Transmittal of Income and Tax Statements

W-3c
Transmittal of Corrected Income and Tax Statements

W-4
Employee's Withholding Allowance Certificate

W-4P
Withholding Certificate for Pension or Annuity Payments

W-4S
Request for Federal Income Tax Withholding from Sick Pay

W-5
Earned Income Credit Advance Payment Certificate

W-9
Request for Taxpayer Identification Number and Certification

W-10
Dependent Car Provider's Identification and Certification

706
United States Estate (and Generation-Skipping Transfer) Tax Return

706 Instructions

709
United States Gift (and Generation-Skipping Transfer) Tax Return

* Item also available in Pub. 1194.
† New item added this year.

709 Instructions

720 (4th Qtr. 1991)
Quarterly Federal Excise Tax Return

843
Claim

843 Instructions

851
Affiliations Schedule

911
Application for Taxpayer Assistance Order To Relieve Hardship

940
Employer's Annual Federal Unemployment (FUTA) Tax Return

940 Instructions

940EZ
Employer's Annual Federal Unemployment (FUTA) Tax Return

Sch. A (Form 941)
Record of Federal Backup Withholding Tax Liability

942 (4th Qtr. 1991)
Employer's Quarterly Tax Return for Household Employees

943
Employer's Annual Tax Return for Agricultural Employees

943A
Agricultural Employer's Record of Federal Tax Liability

990
Return of Organization Exempt From Income Tax (Except Black Lung Benefit Trust or Private Foundation)

990 Instructions

990EZ
Short Form Return of Organization Exempt From Income Tax

990EZ Instructions

Sch. A (Form 990)
Organization Exempt Under Section 501(c)(3) (Supplementary Information)

Sch. A (Form 990) Instructions

990W
Estimated Tax on Unrelated Business Taxable Income for Tax-Exempt Organizations

1040
U.S. Individual Income Tax Return

1040 Instructions

Schs. A&B (Form 1040)
Itemized Deductions, Interest and Dividend Income
See 1040 Instructions

Sch. C (Form 1040)
Profit or Loss from Business
See 1040 Instructions

Sch. D (Form 1040)
Capital Gains and Losses
See 1040 Instructions

Sch. D-1 (Form 1040)
Continuation Sheet for Sch. D (Form 1040)
See 1040 Instructions

Sch. E (Form 1040)
Supplemental Income and Loss
See 1040 Instructions

Sch. EIC (Form 1040)
Earned Income Credit

Sch. F (Form 1040)
Farm Income and Expenses
See 1040 Instructions

Sch. R (Form 1040)
Credit for the Elderly or the Disabled

Sch. R (Form 1040) Instructions

Sch. SE (Form 1040)
Social Security Self-Employment Tax
See 1040 Instructions

1040A
U.S. Individual Income Tax Return

1040A Instructions

Sch. 1 (Form 1040A)
Interest and Dividend Income for Form 1040A Filers
See 1040A Instructions

Sch. 2 (Form 1040A)
Child and Dependent Care Expenses for Form 1040A Filers
See 1040A Instructions

Sch. 3 (Form 1040A)
Credit for the Elderly or the Disabled for Form 1040A Filers
See Sch. 3 (Form 1040A) Instructions

Sch. 3 (Form 1040A) Instructions

Sch. 4 (Form 1040A)
Earned Income Credit

1040-ES (1991)
Estimated Tax for Individuals

1040EZ
Income Tax Return for Single Filers With No Dependents
See 1040EZ Instructions

1040EZ Instructions

1040NR
U.S. Nonresident Alien Income Tax Return

1040NR Instructions

1040X
Amended U.S. Individual Income Tax Return

1040X Instructions

1041
U.S. Fiduciary Income Tax Return

1041 Instructions

Sch. D (Form 1041)
Capital Gains and Losses
See 1041 Instructions

Sch. J (Form 1041)
Information Return—Trust Allocation of an Accumulation Distribution (IRC Section 665)
See 1041 Instructions

Sch. K-1 (Form 1041)
Beneficiary's Share of Income, Deductions, Credits, etc.
See 1041 Instructions

1041-ES (1991)
Estimated Tax for Fiduciaries

1045
Application for Tentative Refund

1065
U.S. Partnership Return of Income

1065 Instructions

Sch. D (Form 1065)
Capital Gains and Losses

Sch. K-1 (Form 1065)
Partner's Share of Income, Credits, Deductions, etc.

Sch. K-1 (Form 1065) Instructions

1096 (1991)
Annual Summary and Transmittal of U.S. Information Returns
See 1099 Instructions (1991)

1098 (1991)
Mortgage Interest Statement
See 1099 Instructions (1991)

1099 Instructions (1991)
For Forms 1099, 1098, 5498, 5754, 1096, and W-2G

1099-A (1991)
Information Return for Acquisition or Abandonment of Secured Property
See 1099 Instructions (1991)

1099-B (1991)
Statement for Recipients of Proceeds From Broker and Barter Exchange Transactions
See 1099 Instructions (1991)

1099-DIV (1991)
Statement for Recipients of Dividends and Distributions
See 1099 Instructions (1991)

1099-G (1991)
Statement for Recipients of Certain Government Payments
See 1099 Instructions (1991)

1099-INT (1991)
Statement for Recipients of Interest Income
See 1099 Instructions (1991)

1099-MISC (1991)
Statement for Recipients of Miscellaneous Income
See 1099 Instructions (1991)

1099-OID (1991)
Statement for Recipients of Original Issue Discount
See 1099 Instructions (1991)

1099-PATR (1991)
Statement for Recipients (Patrons) of Taxable Distributions Received From Cooperatives
See 1099 Instructions (1991)

1099-R (1991)
Statement for Recipients of Total Distributions From Profit-Sharing, Retirement Plans, Individual Retirement Arrangements, Insurance Contracts, etc.
See 1099 Instructions (1991)

1099-S (1991)
Statement for Recipients of Proceeds From Real Estate Transactions
See 1099 Instructions (1991)

1116
Computation of Foreign Tax Credit (Individual, Fiduciary, or Nonresident Alien Individual)

1116 Instructions

1118
Computation of Foreign Tax Credit—Corporation

1118 Instructions

1120
U.S. Corporation Income Tax Return

1120 and 1120-A Instructions

Sch. D (Form 1120)
Capital Gains and Losses

Sch. PH (Form 1120)
U.S. Personal Holding Company Tax

Sch. PH (Form 1120) Instructions

1120-A
U.S. Corporation Short-Form Income Tax Return

1120S
U.S. Income Tax Return for an S Corporation

1120S Instructions

Sch. D (Form 1120S)
Capital Gains and Losses and Built-in Gains

Sch. D (Form 1120S) Instructions

Sch. K-1 (Form 1120S)
Shareholder's Share of Income, Credits, Deductions, etc.

Sch. K-1 (Form 1120S) Instructions

1120-W
Corporation Estimated Tax

1120X
Amended U.S. Corporation Income Tax Return

1127
Application for Extension of Time for Payment of Tax

1310
Statement of Person Claiming Refund Due a Deceased Taxpayer

2106
Employee Business Expenses

2106 Instructions

2119
Sale of Your Home

2119 Instructions

2120
Multiple Support Declaration

2210
Underpayment of Estimated Tax by Individuals

2210 Instructions

2220
Underpayment of Estimated Tax by Corporations

2220 Instructions

2290
Heavy Vehicle Use Tax Return

2350
Application for Extension of Time To File U.S. Income Tax Return

2441
Credit for Child and Dependent Care Expenses

2441 Instructions

2553
Election by a Small Business Corporation

2553 Instructions

2688
Application for Additional Extension of Time To File U.S. Individual Income Tax Return

2758
Application for Extension of Time To File Certain Excise, Income, Information and Other Returns

2848
Power of Attorney and Declaration of Representative

3115
Application for Change in Accounting Method

3115 Instructions

3468
Investment Credit

3468 Instructions

3800
General Business Credit

3800 Instructions

3903
Moving Expenses

3903 Instructions

3911
Taxpayer Statement Regarding Refund

4136
Computation of Credit for Federal Tax on Fuels

4137
Computation of Social Security Tax on Unreported Tip Income

4255
Recapture of Investment Credit

4506
Request for Copy of Tax Form

4562
Depreciation and Amortization

4562 Instructions

4626
Alternative Minimum Tax—Corporations

4626 Instructions

4684
Casualties and Thefts

4684 Instructions

4782
Employee Moving Expense Information

4797
Sale of Business Property

4797 Instructions

4804
Transmittal of Information Returns Reported on Magnetic Media

4835
Farm Rental Income and Expenses

4852
Substitute for Form W-2, Wage and Tax Statement for Recipients of Annuities, Pensions, Retired Pay, or IRS Payments

4868
Application for Automatic Extension of Time To File U.S. Individual Income Tax Return

4952
Investment Interest Expense Deduction

4952 Instructions

4970
Tax on Accumulation of Distribution of Trusts

4972
Tax on Lump-Sum Distribution

4972 Instructions

5329
Return for Additional Taxes Attributable to Qualified Retirement Plan (Including IRA's), Annuities and Modified Endowment Contracts

5329 Instructions

5498 (1991)
Individual Retirement Arrangement Information
See 1099 Instructions (1991)

5500
Annual Return/Report of Employee Benefit Plan (with 100 or more participants)

5500 Instructions

Sch. A (Form 5500)
Insurance Information

Sch. B (Form 5500)
Actuarial Information

Sch. B (Form 5500) Instructions

Sch. C (Form 5500)
Service Provider Information

Sch. P (Form 5500)
Annual Return of Fiduciary of Employee Benefit Trust

Sch. SSA (Form 5500)
Annual Registration Statement Identifying Separated Participants with Deferred Vested Benefits

5500-C/R
Return/Report of Employee Benefit Plan (with fewer than 100 participants)

5500-C/R Instructions

5500EZ
Annual Return of One-Participant (owners and their spouses) Pension Benefit Plan

5500EZ Instructions

5558
Application for Extension of Time to File Certain Employee Plan Returns

5754
Statement By Person(s) Receiving Gambling Winnings
See 1099 Instructions (1991)

5884
Jobs Credit

6198
At-Risk Limitations

6198 Instructions

6251
Alternative Minimum Tax Individuals

6251 Instructions

6252
Installment Sale Income

6252 Instructions

6781
Gains and Losses from Section 1256 Contracts and Straddles

7004
Application for Automatic Extension of Time To File Corporation Income Tax Return

8027
Employer's Annual Information Return of Tip Income and Allocated Tips

8027 Instructions

8082
Notice of Inconsistent Treatment or Amended Return (Administrative Adjustment Request (AAR))

8082 Instructions

8264
Application for Registration of Tax Shelter

8264 Instructions

8271
Investor Reporting of Tax Shelter Registration Number

8275
Disclosure Statement Under Section 6661

8275 Instructions

8283
Non-cash Charitable Contributions

8283 Instructions

8300
Report of Cash Payments Over $10,000 Received in a Trade or Business

8308
Report of a Sale or Exchange of Certain Partnership Interests

8332
Release of Claim to Exemption for Child of Divorced or Separated Parents

8379
Injured Spouse Allocation

8453
U.S. Individual Income Tax Declaration for Electronic Filing

8582
Passive Activity Loss Limitations

8582 Instructions

8582-CR
Passive Activity Credit Limitations

8582-CR Instructions

8586
Low-Income Housing Credit

8594
Asset Acquisition Statement

8606
Nondeductible IRA Contributions, IRA Basis, and Nontaxable IRA Distributions

8609
Low-Income Housing Credit Allocation Certification

Sch. A (Form 8609)
Annual Statement

8615
Computation of Tax for Children Under Age 14 Who Have Investment Income of More Than $1,000

8633
Electronic Filer Application to File 1991 Individual Income Tax Return Electronically

8656
Alternative Minimum Tax—Fiduciaries

8656 Instructions

8716
Election To Have a Tax Year Other Than a Required Tax Year

8717
User Fee for Employee Plan Determination Letter Request

8736
Application for Automatic Extension of Time To File Return/U.S. Partnerships or for Certain Trusts

8800
Application for Additional Extension of Time To File Return for U.S. Partnerships or Certain Trusts

8801
Credit for Prior Year Minimum Tax

8803
Limit on Alternative Minimum Tax for Children Under Age 14

8809
Requests for Extension of Time To File Information Returns

8810
Corporate Passive Activity Loss and Credit Limitations

8810 Instructions

8814
Parent's Election To Report Child's Interest and Dividends

8815
Exclusion of Interest From Series EE U.S. Savings Bonds Issued After 1989

8817
Allocation of Patronage and Nonpatronage Income and Deductions

8818
Redemption of College Savings Bonds, Optional Form To Record

8821
Taxed Information Authorization

8822
Change of Address

8824
Like-Kind Exchanges

8824 Instructions

8825
Rental Real Estate Income & Expenses of a Partnership S Corporation

9041
Application for Electronic/Magnetic Tape Filing of Tax Year 1991 Forms 1041, 1065, and 5500 C/R

TD F 90-22.1
Report of Foreign Bank and Financial Accounts

Form 21b. Form 3975-A—Tax Practitioner Annual Mailing List Application and Order Blank

Form **3975**
Department of the Treasury Internal Revenue Service

Tax Practitioner Annual Mailing List Application and Order Blank
▶ **For Paperwork Reduction Notice, see Instructions in Publication 1045.**

OMB No. 1545-0351
Expires: 6-30-94

199

Section A

Attach peel off label from front cover here.

Section B—Nature of Request (must be completed).

1 ☐ New application 2 ☐ Reapplication no change 3 ☐ Reapplication with change 4 ☐ Delete record

Section C—List daytime office phone number.

Office Telephone Number ☐☐☐ ☐☐☐ - ☐☐☐☐

Section D—Number of professional tax return preparers in your firm.

Section E—Mailing adddress information for the months of **October through April.**

First name

Last name

Firm/Company

Firm/Company street address

City or Town

State or Province

ZIP code (left justified)

(Foreign Countries)

Section F—Job Code

What is your principal occupation or business? (Check ONLY ONE.)

1 ☐ Association
4 ☐ CPA
7 ☐ Enrolled agent
2 ☐ Attorney
5 ☐ Accountant
8 ☐ Other
3 ☐ Banker
6 ☐ Preparer of tax returns

Section G—Purpose for being on the Tax Practitioner Mailing List? (Check ONLY ONE.)
Complete order blank (page 10) if you checked Box 1 or 3.

1 ☐ To order information copies of tax forms only 2 ☐ To receive the practitioner newsletter only 3 ☐ Both

Section H—Check if you **do not** want your firm/company name and address released to the public as part of a practitioner mailing list . . . . ☐ No

Section I—Check if you share office space at the same address with another practitioner firm? ☐ Yes

Cat. No. 41235N

Form 3975 (1991) Page 2

Section J—Tax Practitioner Order Blank (See pages 2-7 for Titles).
(Items are listed in numerical order, reading from left to right.)

ID No.	Pub.	X	ID No.	Pub.	X	ID No.	Pub.	X	ID No.	Pub.	X
001	1		002	15		003	51		004	54	
005	225		006	393		007	463		008	501	
009	502		010	503		011	504		012	505	
013	508		014	509		015	520		016	521	
017	523		018	524		019	525		020	526	
021	527		022	529		023	530		024	531	
025	533		026	534		027	535		028	537	
029	538		030	541		031	542		032	544	
033	545		034	547		035	550		036	551	
037	552		038	553		039	554		040	556	
041	559		042	560		043	561		044	564	
045	570		046	575		047	583		048	584	
049	587		050	589		051	590		052	596	
053	776		054	907		055	908		056	909	
057	910		058	915		059	917		060	925	
061	929		062	936		063	937		064	1167	
065	1220		066	1345		067	KITS				

Section K—Request For Miscellaneous Products

ID No.	ITEM	Quantity	ID No.	ITEM	Quantity	ID No.	ITEM	Quantity
071	Pub. 17		072	Pub. 334		073	Pkg. X	

Section L—1991 Informational Return Forms

ID No.	Form	Quantity	ID No.	Form	Quantity	ID No.	Form	Quantity	ID No.	Form	Quantity
075	W-2		076	W-3		077	1096		078	1098	
079	1099-A		080	1099-B		081	1099-DIV		082	1099-G	
083	1099-INT		084	1099-MISC		085	1099-OID		086	1099-PATR	
087	1099-R		088	1099-S		089	5498				

Form 22. SEC Form D

FORM D

UNITED STATES
SECURITIES AND EXCHANGE COMMISSION
Washington, D.C. 20549

FORM D

NOTICE OF SALE OF SECURITIES PURSUANT TO REGULATION D, SECTION 4(6), AND/OR UNIFORM LIMITED OFFERING EXEMPTION

OMB APPROVAL	
OMB Number:	3235-0076
Expires:	April 30, 19
Estimated average burden hours per response . . . 16.00	

SEC USE ONLY	
Prefix	Serial
DATE RECEIVED	

Name of Offering (☐ check if this is an amendment and name has changed, and indicate change.)

Filing Under (Check box(es) that apply): ☐ Rule 504 ☐ Rule 505 ☐ Rule 506 ☐ Section 4(6) ☐ ULOE

Type of Filing: ☐ New Filing ☐ Amendment

A. BASIC IDENTIFICATION DATA

1. Enter the information requested about the issuer

Name of Issuer (☐ check if this is an amendment and name has changed, and indicate change.)

Address of Executive Offices (Number and Street, City, State, Zip Code)	Telephone Number (Including Area Code)
Address of Principal Business Operations (Number and Street, City, State, Zip Code) (if different from Executive Offices)	Telephone Number (Including Area Code)

Brief Description of Business

Type of Business Organization

☐ corporation ☐ limited partnership, already formed ☐ other (please specify):

☐ business trust ☐ limited partnership, to be formed

Month Year

Actual or Estimated Date of Incorporation or Organization: ☐☐ ☐☐ ☐ Actual ☐ Estimated

Jurisdiction of Incorporation or Organization: (Enter two-letter U.S. Postal Service abbreviation for State: CN for Canada; FN for other foreign jurisdiction) ☐☐

GENERAL INSTRUCTIONS

Federal:

Who Must File: All issuers making an offering of securities in reliance on an exemption under Regulation D or Section 4(6), 17 CFR 230.501 et seq. or 15 U.S.C. 77d(6).

When To File: A notice must be filed no later than 15 days after the first sale of securities in the offering. A notice is deemed filed with the U.S. Securities and Exchange Commission (SEC) on the earlier of the date it is received by the SEC at the address given below or, if received at that address after the date on which it is due, on the date it was mailed by United States registered or certified mail to that address.

Where to File: U.S. Securities and Exchange Commission, 450 Fifth Street, N.W., Washington, D.C. 20549.

Copies Required: Five (5) copies of this notice must be filed with the SEC, one of which must be manually signed. Any copies not manually signed must be photocopies of the manually signed copy or bear typed or printed signatures.

Information Required: A new filing must contain all information requested. Amendments need only report the name of the issuer and offering, any changes thereto, the information requested in Part C, and any material changes from the information previously supplied in Parts A and B. Part E and the Appendix need not be filed with the SEC.

Filing Fee: There is no federal filing fee.

State:

This notice shall be used to indicate reliance on the Uniform Limited Offering Exemption (ULOE) for sales of securities in those states that have adopted ULOE and that have adopted this form. Issuers relying on ULOE must file a separate notice with the Securities Administrator in each state where sales are to be, or have been made. If a state requires the payment of a fee as a precondition to the claim for the exemption, a fee in the proper amount shall accompany this form. This notice shall be filed in the appropriate states in accordance with state law. The Appendix to the notice constitutes a part of this notice and must be completed.

ATTENTION

Failure to file notice in the appropriate states will not result in a loss of the federal exemption. Conversely, failure to file the appropriate federal notice will not result in a loss of an available state exemption unless such exemption is predicated on the filing of a federal notice.

SEC 1972 (2-89) 1 of 8

A. BASIC IDENTIFICATION DATA

2. Enter the information requested for the following:
   - Each promoter of the issuer, if the issuer has been organized within the past five years;
   - Each beneficial owner having the power to vote or dispose, or direct the vote or disposition of, 10% or more of a class of equity securities of the issuer;
   - Each executive officer and director of corporate issuers and of corporate general and managing partners of partnership issuers; and
   - Each general and managing partner of partnership issuers.

Check Box(es) that Apply: ☐ Promoter ☐ Beneficial Owner ☐ Executive Officer ☐ Director ☐ General and/or Managing Partner

Full Name (Last name first, if individual)

Business or Residence Address (Number and Street, City, State, Zip Code)

Check Box(es) that Apply: ☐ Promoter ☐ Beneficial Owner ☐ Executive Officer ☐ Director ☐ General and/or Managing Partner

Full Name (Last name first, if individual)

Business or Residence Address (Number and Street, City, State, Zip Code)

Check Box(es) that Apply: ☐ Promoter ☐ Beneficial Owner ☐ Executive Officer ☐ Director ☐ General and/or Managing Partner

Full Name (Last name first, if individual)

Business or Residence Address (Number and Street, City, State, Zip Code)

Check Box(es) that Apply: ☐ Promoter ☐ Beneficial Owner ☐ Executive Officer ☐ Director ☐ General and/or Managing Partner

Full Name (Last name first, if individual)

Business or Residence Address (Number and Street, City, State, Zip Code)

Check Box(es) that Apply: ☐ Promoter ☐ Beneficial Owner ☐ Executive Officer ☐ Director ☐ General and/or Managing Partner

Full Name (Last name first, if individual)

Business or Residence Address (Number and Street, City, State, Zip Code)

Check Box(es) that Apply: ☐ Promoter ☐ Beneficial Owner ☐ Executive Officer ☐ Director ☐ General and/or Managing Partner

Full Name (Last name first, if individual)

Business or Residence Address (Number and Street, City, State, Zip Code)

Check Box(es) that Apply: ☐ Promoter ☐ Beneficial Owner ☐ Executive Officer ☐ Director ☐ General and/or Managing Partner

Full Name (Last name first, if individual)

Business or Residence Address (Number and Street, City, State, Zip Code)

(Use blank sheet, or copy and use additional copies of this sheet, as necessary.) 2 of 8

B. INFORMATION ABOUT OFFERING

	Yes	No
1. Has the issuer sold, or does the issuer intend to sell, to non-accredited investors in this offering?	☐	☐
Answer also in Appendix, Column 2, if filing under ULOE.		
2. What is the minimum investment that will be accepted from any individual?	$______	
	Yes	No
3. Does the offering permit joint ownership of a single unit?	☐	☐

4. Enter the information requested for each person who has been or will be paid or given, directly or indirectly, any commission or similar remuneration for solicitation of purchasers in connection with sales of securities in the offering. If a person to be listed is an associated person or agent of a broker or dealer registered with the SEC and/or with a state or states, list the name of the broker or dealer. If more than five (5) persons to be listed are associated persons of such a broker or dealer, you may set forth the information for that broker or dealer only.

Full Name (Last name first, if individual)

Business or Residence Address (Number and Street, City, State, Zip Code)

Name of Associated Broker or Dealer

States in Which Person Listed Has Solicited or Intends to Solicit Purchasers

(Check "All States" or check individual States) . . . . ☐ All States

[AL]	[AK]	[AZ]	[AR]	[CA]	[CO]	[CT]	[DE]	[DC]	[FL]	[GA]	[HI]	[ID]
[IL]	[IN]	[IA]	[KS]	[KY]	[LA]	[ME]	[MD]	[MA]	[MI]	[MN]	[MS]	[MO]
[MT]	[NE]	[NV]	[NH]	[NJ]	[NM]	[NY]	[NC]	[ND]	[OH]	[OK]	[OR]	[PA]
[RI]	[SC]	[SD]	[TN]	[TX]	[UT]	[VT]	[VA]	[WA]	[WV]	[WI]	[WY]	[PR]

Full Name (Last name first, if individual)

Business or Residence Address (Number and Street, City, State, Zip Code)

Name of Associated Broker or Dealer

States in Which Person Listed Has Solicited or Intends to Solicit Purchasers

(Check "All States" or check individual States) .... ☐ All States

[AL]	[AK]	[AZ]	[AR]	[CA]	[CO]	[CT]	[DE]	[DC]	[FL]	[GA]	[HI]	[ID]
[IL]	[IN]	[IA]	[KS]	[KY]	[LA]	[ME]	[MD]	[MA]	[MI]	[MN]	[MS]	[MO]
[MT]	[NE]	[NV]	[NH]	[NJ]	[NM]	[NY]	[NC]	[ND]	[OH]	[OK]	[OR]	[PA]
[RI]	[SC]	[SD]	[TN]	[TX]	[UT]	[VT]	[VA]	[WA]	[WV]	[WI]	[WY]	[PR]

Full Name (Last name first, if individual)

Business or Residence Address (Number and Street, City, State, Zip Code)

Name of Associated Broker or Dealer

States in Which Person Listed Has Solicited or Intends to Solicit Purchasers

(Check "All States" or check individual States) .... ☐ All States

[AL]	[AK]	[AZ]	[AR]	[CA]	[CO]	[CT]	[DE]	[DC]	[FL]	[GA]	[HI]	[ID]
[IL]	[IN]	[IA]	[KS]	[KY]	[LA]	[ME]	[MD]	[MA]	[MI]	[MN]	[MS]	[MO]
[MT]	[NE]	[NV]	[NH]	[NJ]	[NM]	[NY]	[NC]	[ND]	[OH]	[OK]	[OR]	[PA]
[RI]	[SC]	[SD]	[TN]	[TX]	[UT]	[VT]	[VA]	[WA]	[WV]	[WI]	[WY]	[PR]

(Use blank sheet, or copy and use additional copies of this sheet, as necessary.)

C. OFFERING PRICE, NUMBER OF INVESTORS, EXPENSES AND USE OF PROCEEDS

1. Enter the aggregate offering price of securities included in this offering and the total amount already sold. Enter "0" if answer is "none" or "zero." If the transaction is an exchange offering, check this box ☐ and indicate in the columns below the amounts of the securities offered for exchange and already exchanged.

Type of Security	Aggregate Offering Price	Amount Already Sold
Debt	$______	$______
Equity	$______	$______
☐ Common ☐ Preferred		
Convertible Securities (including warrants)	$______	$______
Partnership Interests	$______	$______
Other (Specify __________)	$______	$______
Total	$______	$______

Answer also in Appendix, Column 3, if filing under ULOE.

2. Enter the number of accredited and non-accredited investors who have purchased securities in this offering and the aggregate dollar amounts of their purchases. For offerings under Rule 504, indicate the number of persons who have purchased securities and the aggregate dollar amount of their purchases on the total lines. Enter "0" if answer is "none" or "zero."

	Number Investors	Aggregate Dollar Amount of Purchases
Accredited Investors	______	$______
Non-accredited Investors	______	$______
Total (for filings under Rule 504 only)	______	$______

Answer also in Appendix, Column 4, if filing under ULOE.

3. If this filing is for an offering under Rule 504 or 505, enter the information requested for all securities sold by the issuer, to date, in offerings of the types indicated, in the twelve (12) months prior to the first sale of securities in this offering. Classify securities by type listed in Part C - Question 1.

Type of offering	Type of Security	Dollar Amount Sold
Rule 505	______	$______
Regulation A	______	$______
Rule 504	______	$______
Total	______	$______

4. a. Furnish a statement of all expenses in connection with the issuance and distribution of the securities in this offering. Exclude amounts relating solely to organization expenses of the issuer. The information may be given as subject to future contingencies. If the amount of an expenditure is not known, furnish an estimate and check the box to the left of the estimate.

Transfer Agent's Fees	☐	$______
Printing and Engraving Costs	☐	$______
Legal Fees	☐	$______
Accounting Fees	☐	$______
Engineering Fees	☐	$______
Sales Commissions (specify finders' fees separately)	☐	$______
Other Expenses (identify) ______	☐	$______
Total	☐	$______

4 of 8

C. OFFERING PRICE, NUMBER OF INVESTORS, EXPENSES AND USE OF PROCEEDS

b. Enter the difference between the aggregate offering price given in response to Part C - Question 1 and total expenses furnished in response to Part C - Question 4.a. This difference is the "adjusted gross proceeds to the issuer." .... $______

5. Indicate below the amount of the adjusted gross proceeds to the issuer used or proposed to be used for each of the purposes shown. If the amount for any purpose is not known, furnish an estimate and check the box to the left of the estimate. The total of the payments listed must equal the adjusted gross proceeds to the issuer set forth in response to Part C - Question 4.b above.

	Payments to Officers, Directors, & Affiliates	Payments To Others
Salaries and fees	☐ $______	☐ $______
Purchase of real estate	☐ $______	☐ $______
Purchase, rental or leasing and installation of machinery and equipment	☐ $______	☐ $______
Construction or leasing of plant buildings and facilities	☐ $______	☐ $______
Acquisition of other businesses (including the value of securities involved in this offering that may be used in exchange for the assets or securities of another issuer pursuant to a merger)	☐ $______	☐ $______

Repayment of indebtedness	☐ $______	☐ $______
Working capital	☐ $______	☐ $______
Other (specify): ______	☐ $______	☐ $______
______		
______	☐ $______	☐ $______
Column Totals	☐ $______	☐ $______
Total Payments Listed (column totals added)	☐ $______	

D. FEDERAL SIGNATURE

The issuer has duly caused this notice to be signed by the undersigned duly authorized person. If this notice is filed under Rule 505, the following signature constitutes an undertaking by the issuer to furnish to the U.S. Securities and Exchange Commission, upon written request of its staff, the information furnished by the issuer to any non-accredited investor pursuant to paragraph (b)(2) of Rule 502.

Issuer (Print or Type)	Signature	Date
Name of Signer (Print or Type)	Title of Signer (Print or Type)	

ATTENTION

Intentional misstatements or omissions of fact constitute federal criminal violations. (See 18 U.S.C. 1001.)

E. STATE SIGNATURE

1. Is any party described in 17 CFR 230.252(c), (d), (e) or (f) presently subject to any of the disqualification provisions of such rule? Yes ☐ No ☐

See Appendix, Column 5, for state response.

2. The undersigned issuer hereby undertakes to furnish to any state administrator of any state in which this notice is filed, a notice on Form D (17 CFR 239.500) at such times as required by state law.

3. The undersigned issuer hereby undertakes to furnish to the state administrators, upon written request, information furnished by the issuer to offerees.

4. The undersigned issuer represents that the issuer is familiar with the conditions that must be satisfied to be entitled to the Uniform limited Offering Exemption (ULOE) of the state in which this notice is filed and understands that the issuer claiming the availability of this exemption has the burden of establishing that these conditions have been satisfied.

The issuer has read this notification and knows the contents to be true and has duly caused this notice to be signed on its behalf by the undersigned duly authorized person.

Issuer (Print or Type)	Signature	Date
Name (Print or Type)	Title (Print or Type)	

Instruction:
Print the name and title of the signing representative under his signature for the state portion of this form. One copy of every notice on Form D must be manually signed. Any copies not manually signed must be photocopies of the manually signed copy or bear typed or printed signatures.

APPENDIX

1	2		3	4				5	
	Intend to sell to non-accredited investors in State (Part B-Item 1)		Type of security and aggregate offering price offered in state (Part C-Item1)	Type of investor and amount purchased in State (Part C-Item 2)				Disqualification under State ULOE (if yes, attach explanation of waiver granted) (Part E-Item1)	
State	Yes	No		Number of Accredited Investors	Amount	Number of Non-Accredited Investors	Amount	Yes	No
AL									
AK									
AZ									
AR									
CA									
CO									
CT									
DE									
DC									
FL									
GA									
HI									
ID									
IL									
IN									
IA									
KS									
KY									
LA									
ME									
MD									
MA									
MI									
MN									
MS									
MO									

APPENDIX

1	2		3	4				5	
	Intend to sell to non-accredited investors in State (Part B-Item 1)		Type of security and aggregate offering price offered in state (Part C-Item1)	Type of investor and amount purchased in State (Part C-Item 2)				Disqualification under State ULOE (if yes, attach explanation of waiver granted) (Part E-Item1)	
State	Yes	No		Number of Accredited Investors	Amount	Number of Non-Accredited Investors	Amount	Yes	No
MT									
NE									
NV									
NH									
NJ									
NM									
NY									
NC									
ND									
OH									
OK									
OR									
PA									
RI									
SC									
SD									
TN									
TX									
UT									
VT									
VA									
WA									
WV									
WI									
WY									
PR									

Form 23. Application for Sales Tax Permit

BT-400-MIP REV. 5 (10-92)

STATE OF CALIFORNIA
BOARD OF EQUALIZATION

APPLICATION FOR SELLER'S PERMIT AND REGISTRATION AS A RETAILER (INDIVIDUALS/PARTNERS)

Who Must Have a Permit

Generally, if you sell taxable merchandise or provide a taxable service in California, such as renting merchandise or fabrication labor, you must have a seller's permit. Wholesalers as well as retailers **must have a separate permit for each place of business.**

This application includes information you need to obtain a permit as well as a brief description of your rights and responsibilities once the permit is obtained.

If you have specific questions about information contained in this application, please contact any Board of Equalization office listed on the back of this page.

How To Obtain a Permit

To obtain a seller's permit, you must complete the attached application. Directions for completing the application follow.

1. **Type or print neatly in ink.** The application is organized into sections. To help us issue your permit quickly and accurately, be sure the information you include in each section is correct and legible. Your application will become a part of your permanent file with us, and the information you included in your application — except for your name, business name and address, permit number, and status (active or closed out) — is confidential and may not be furnished to the public.

2. **Complete only the unshaded portions of the application.** In addition, the application is printed on both the front and reverse. Be sure to complete both sides.

3. **Be sure to indicate the type of ownership of your business.** If you check Partnership and if the Board requests, please include a copy of the partnership agreement with your application. If you do not supply the necessary documents, your permit may be delayed.

4. **Be sure the Certification Section is completed and signed by the owner or one partner.** The application should also be signed in Section I by the owner. In the case of a partnership all partners should also sign in Section I.

5. **Return the completed application to the Board office from which this application was obtained.** Locations, mailing addresses, and telephone numbers of Board offices may be found on the back of this page. Once your application is reviewed and found in order, you will be issued a permit without charge. In addition, copies of pertinent regulations, forms, and returns will be returned to you. However, depending on the type of business and conditions surrounding ownership, you may be required to post a security deposit.

Your Rights and Responsibilities as a Seller

When you obtain a seller's permit, you acquire valuable rights and privileges as well as responsibilities. Information about some of those rights and responsibilities follows.

- **You may purchase property for resale without paying tax.** By providing the vendor with a completed resale certificate, you are not required to pay sales tax on tangible personal property you purchase for resale. However, you should not use a resale certificate if you intend to use the property prior to or instead of selling it. If you intend to use the property, you must pay sales tax.
- **You must keep records.** To substantiate your sales, any deductions you report on your returns, and any purchases you have made for your business, you must keep adequate records. Generally, records must be kept for four years.
- **You must file returns.** Returns must be filed on or before the last day of the month following your reporting period. <u>You must file your return even if you did not sell any merchandise.</u>
- **You must pay taxes.** As a seller, you must pay taxes on gross receipts from retail sales. However, you are allowed by law to be reimbursed by collecting the tax from your customers.
- **You must notify the Board if you move, change ownership of, or sell your business.** Your permit is valid only at the address and for the type of ownership specified on the permit. Unless you notify the Board of any change in ownership, you could be held liable for the successor's operations. In addition, you should notify the Board immediately if you discontinue your business. Your notification will help us to close your account and return any security you may have deposited.

92 95294

CALIFORNIA STATE BOARD OF EQUALIZATION OFFICES

10-92

BOARD MEMBERS

DISTRICT	MEMBER	OFFICE ADDRESS	AREA CODE	TELEPHONE NUMBER
First	William M. Bennett	1020 N Street, PO Box 942879, Sacramento, 94279-0001	916	445-4081
Second	Brad Sherman	901 Wilshire Boulevard, Suite 210, Santa Monica, 90401-1856	310	451-5777
			818	360-3186
Third	Ernest J. Dronenburg, Jr.	110 West C Street, Suite 1709, San Diego, 92101-3966	619	237-7844
Fourth	Matthew K. Fong	13200 Crossroads Pkwy. No., Ste 450, City of Industry, 91746-3497	310	908-0524
EXECUTIVE DIRECTOR				
	Burton W. Oliver	1020 N Street, PO Box 942879, Sacramento, 94279-0001	916	445-6464

SACRAMENTO HEADQUARTERS 1020 N Street, PO Box 942879, Sacramento 94279-0001 916 445-6464

BUSINESS TAXES FIELD OFFICES

CALIFORNIA CITIES	OFFICE HOURS 8-5 UNLESS OTHERWISE LISTED BELOW	OFFICE ADDRESS	AREA CODE	TELEPHONE NUMBER
Arcadia		20 East Foothill Boulevard, PO Box 900, 91066-0900	818	350-6401
		From LA	213	681-6675
Arroyo Grande		1303 Grand Avenue, Suite 115, 93420-2461	805	489-6293
Auburn	8-12 & 1-5 M thru F	11714 Enterprise Drive, 95603	916	885-8408
Bakersfield		525 18th Street, PO Box 1728, 93302-1728	805	395-2880
Bishop	8-12 & 1-5 M thru F	407 West Line Street, 93514-3321	619	872-3701
Chico	8-12 & 1-5 M thru F	8 Williamsburg Lane, 95926-2225	916	895-5322
Concord		1001 Galaxy Way, 94520 (PO Box 5965, Concord 94524)	510	687-6962
Covina		233 North Second Avenue, PO Box 4489, 91723-4489	818	331-6401
		From LA	213	686-2990
Crescent City	8-12 & 1-5 M thru F	555 101 So. Highway, Suite B, PO Box 367, 95531-0367	707	464-2321
Culver City		3861 Sepulveda Boulevard, 2nd Floor, PO Box 3652, 90231-3652	310	313-7111
		From LA	213	879-0600
Downey		11229 Woodruff Avenue, PO Box 4018, 90241-1018	310	803-3471
		From LA	213	773-3480
El Centro		1295 State Street, Suite 201, 92243-2879	619	352-3431
Eureka	8-12 & 1-5 M thru F	134 D Street, Suite 301, PO Box 4884, 95502-4884	707	445-6500
Fresno		2550 Mariposa Street, Rm 2020, PO Box 1827, 93717-2219	209	445-5285
Hollywood		5110 Sunset Boulevard, PO Box 27310, 90027-0310	213	913-7800
Laguna Hills		23141 Moulton Parkway, Suite 100, PO Box 30890, 92654-0890	714	770-2157
Lakewood		4040 Paramount Boulevard, Suite 101, PO Box 879, 90712-0879	310	421-3295
		From LA	213	636-2466
Lancaster		43301 North Division Street, Suite 206, PO Box 5149, 93539-5149	805	940-7383
Marysville		922 G Street, PO Box 700, 95901-0700	916	741-4301
Merced	8-12 & 1-5 M thru F	635 Olivewood Drive, P.O. Box 192, 95341-0192	209	726-6527
Modesto		3340 Tully Road, Suite A, PO Box 5237, 95352-5237	209	576-6360
Nevada City	8-12 & 1-5 M thru F	301 Broad Street, PO Box 247, 95959-0247	916	265-4628
Oakland		2101 Webster Street, Suite 210, Box 46, 94612	510	286-0347
Ontario		320 West G Street, Suite 105, 91762-3230	714	983-5969
Oroville	8-12 & 1-5 M thru F	2445 Oro Dam Boulevard, Suite 3A, 95966-6035	916	538-2246
Placerville	8-12 & 1-5 M thru F	344 Placerville Drive, Suite 12, PO Box 965, 95667-0965	916	622-1101
Quincy	9-1 M thru F	546 Lawrence Street, PO Box 938, 95971-0938	916	283-1070
Rancho Mirage		42-700 Bob Hope Drive, Suite 301, 92270-4473	619	346-8096
Redding		391 Hemstead Drive, PO Box 492529, 96049-2529	916	224-4729
Riverside		6700 Indiana Avenue, Suite 225, 92506-4204	714	782-4330
Sacramento		9823 Old Winery Place, Suite 1, 95827-1731	916	855-7528
Salinas		21 West Laurel Drive, Suite 79, 93906-3485	408	443-3008
San Bernardino		303 West Third Street, Suite 500, PO Box 1305, 92402-1305	714	383-4701
San Diego		1350 Front Street, Rm 5047, 92101-3612	619	525-4526
San Francisco		50 Fremont Street, Suite 1400, 94105-2234	415	396-9800
San Jose		100 Paseo de San Antonio, Rm 307, 95113-1477	408	277-1231
San Marcos		334 Via Vera Cruz, Suite 107, 92069-2637	619	744-1330
San Mateo		177 Bovet Road, Suite 250, PO Box 5530, 94402-5530	415	573-3800
San Rafael		7 Mt. Lassen Drive, Suite B136, 94903-0248	415	472-1513
Santa Ana		28 Civic Center Plaza, Rm 239, PO Box 12040, 92712-2040	714	558-4059
Santa Barbara		411 East Canon Perdido Street, Room 11, 93101-1589	805	564-7731
Santa Cruz		8030 Soquel Avenue, Suite 100, 95062-2094	408	462-9496
Santa Rosa		50 D Street, Rm 215, PO Box 730, 95402-0730	707	576-2100
Sonora	8-12 & 1-5 M thru F	1194 N. Highway 49, PO Box 385, 95370-0385	209	532-6979
South Lake Tahoe	8-12 & 1-5 M thru F	2489 Lake Tahoe Boulevard, Suite 7, 96150-7729	916	544-4816
Stockton		31 East Channel Street, Rm 264, PO Box 1890, 95201-1890	209	948-7720
Susanville	9-1 M thru F	63 North Roop Street, PO Box 639, 96130-0639	916	257-3429
Torrance		690 W. Knox Street, PO Box T, 90507-0270	310	516-4300
		From LA	213	770-4148
Ukiah		620 Kings Court, Suite 110, PO Box 939, 95482-0939	707	463-4731
Union City		32145 Alvarado-Niles Road, PO Box 1887, 94587-6887	510	429-7090
Vallejo		704 Tuolumne Street, 94590-0625	707	648-4065
Van Nuys		6150 Van Nuys Boulevard, Rm 205, PO Box 7735, 91409-7735	818	901-5293
Ventura		1001 Partridge Drive, Suite 200, 93003-5599	805	654-4523
Visalia		111 South Johnson Street, Suite E, PO Box 1109, 93279-1109	209	732-5641
Woodland	8-12 & 1-5 M thru F	96 West Main Street, Suite 2, 95695-3016	916	662-7331
Yreka	8-12 & 1-5 M thru F	1217 South Main Street, PO Box 435, 96097-0435	916	842-7439
OUT-OF-STATE FIELD OFFICES				
Sacramento (Hqtrs.)		1820 14th Street, PO Box 188269, 95818-0268	916	322-2010
Chicago, Illinois		150 North Wacker Drive, Rm 1400, 60606-1606	312	201-5300
New York, N.Y.		675 Third Avenue, Rm 520, 10017-4015	212	697-4680
Houston, Texas		9800 Northwest Freeway, Brookhollow Two, Suite 204, 77092-8807	713	681-1106

BT-400-MIP (FRONT) REV. 5 (10-92)

STATE OF CALIFORNIA
BOARD OF EQUALIZATION

APPLICATION FOR SELLER'S PERMIT AND REGISTRATION AS A RETAILER (INDIVIDUALS/PARTNERS)

FOR BOARD USE ONLY		
TAX	OFFICE	NUMBER
S		—

Business Code ____
Area Code ____
Preparer ____

Section I: Ownership Information

1. Please check type of ownership.
☐ Sole Owner ☐ Husband/Wife co-ownership ☐ Partnership

Use additional sheet to include information about additional co-owners or partners

	Owner or Partner	Co-owner or partner
2. Full name (first, middle, last)		
3. Address (residence)		
4. Telephone (residence)	( )	( )
5. Social Security no.		
6. Driver's license no. Date of birth		
7. Present/past employer		
8. Name of spouse		
9. Social Security No. of spouse		
10. Driver's license no. of spouse		
11. Name, address and telephone number of two personal references	1. 2.	1. 2.
12. Signature		

Section II: Business Information

1. Business name — Business telephone ( )

2. Business address (Do not list P.O. Box or mailing service) — City — State — ZIP Code

3. Mailing address (if different from No. 2 above) — City — State — ZIP Code

4. Date you will begin sales: Month — Day — Year

Days and hours of operation	Sun.	Mon.	Tue.	Wed.	Thurs.	Fri.	Sat.

5. Description of business
a. What will you sell?

b. Check the appropriate box
☐ Retail ☐ Whole-sale ☐ Manufac-turing ☐ Repair ☐ Service ☐ Construction Contractor

c. Check the appropriate box
☐ Full-time ☐ Part-time ☐ Mail-order

d. Are you
☐ Starting a new business? ☐ Adding/dropping partner? ☐ Buying a business? ☐ Other?

If buying a business, please indicate name and account no. of former owner ____

e. Purchase Price $ ____ Value of Fixtures and Equipment $ ____

6. How many selling locations will you have? (If 2 or more attach list of all locations) ____

7. If alcoholic beverages are sold, please list your Alcoholic Beverage Control License No. and type:

Continued

BT-400-MIP (BACK) REV. 5 (10-92)

STATE OF CALIFORNIA
BOARD OF EQUALIZATION

8. Name of accountant/bookkeeper	Address	Telephone ( )
9. Name of business landlord	Address	Telephone ( )
10. Name of bank or other financial institution (checking and savings account)	Location	Account number
11. Name of major suppliers	Address	Products purchased
12. Other account numbers issued to you by the Board		

Section III: Income and Expenses

1. Projected Monthly Business Expenses	2. Projected Monthly Business Revenue
Rent $ ______	Total Gross Revenue $ ______
Payroll $ ______	Non-taxable $ ______
Misc. $ ______	Taxable $ ______
Total $ ______	Tax $ ______

3. Information concerning Employment Development Department (EDD)

a. Are you registered with EDD?	☐ Yes	☐ No
b. If no, will your payroll exceed $100 per quarter? If yes, you must make application with EDD. Number of employees ______ See pamphlet DE 4525, "Employer Guide."	☐ Yes	☐ No
c. I have already received pamphlet DE 4525.	☐ Yes	☐ No
d. I have already received pamphlet DE 44, "Employer's Withholding Guide."	☐ Yes	☐ No

Section IV: Certification

The statements contained hereon are hereby certified to be correct to the best knowledge and belief of the undersigned who is duly authorized to sign this application.

______________________ SIGNATURE ______________________ TITLE

______________________ NAME (TYPED OR PRINTED) ______________________ DATE

FOR BOARD USE ONLY
Furnished to Applicant

Reporting Basis ______	☐ GA-324A	☐ REG. 1668	REGULATIONS
Security Review ☐ BT-1009	☐ BT-400Y	☐ REG. 1698	______
☐ BT-598 $ ______	☐ BT-467	☐ REG. 1700	______
By ______	☐ BT-519	☐ DE-44	PAMPHLETS
Approved By ______	☐ BT-741	☐ DE-4525	______
Remote Input Date ______	☐ BT-968	☐ ______	RETURNS
By ______	☐ BT-1241C	☐ ______	______
Permit Issued ☐ Date ______			______

SAMPLE

BT-400-MIP (FRONT) REV. 5 (10-92)

STATE OF CALIFORNIA
BOARD OF EQUALIZATION

APPLICATION FOR SELLER'S PERMIT AND REGISTRATION AS A RETAILER (INDIVIDUALS/PARTNERS)

FOR BOARD USE ONLY			
TAX	OFFICE	NUMBER	
S			—
Business Code			
Area Code			
Preparer			

Section I: Ownership Information

1. Please check type of ownership.

[X] Sole Owner [ ] Husband/Wife co-ownership [ ] Partnership

Use additional sheet to include information about additional co-owners or partners

	Owner or Partner	Co-owner or partner
2. Full name (first, middle, last)	Alexander James Hanson	
3. Address (residence)	123 Crabtree Ln., Sacramento, CA 95813	
4. Telephone (residence)	(916) 555-2376	( )
5. Social Security no.	120-26-3366	
6. Driver's license no. Date of birth	A2801266 10-22-50	
7. Present/past employer	Target	
8. Name of spouse	Sharon Marie Hanson	
9. Social Security No. of spouse	544-99-3355	
10. Driver's license no. of spouse	D664234	
11. Name, address and telephone number of two personal references	1. Janet Hanson 445-8792, 768 Maple Dr., Sacramento 2. John Hills 555-9030, 414 Vernon St. Roseville	1. 2.
12. Signature		

Section II: Business Information

1. Business name: Frames By Alex — Business telephone: (916) 555-2376

2. Business address (Do not list P.O. Box or mailing service): 123 Crabtree Ln. — City: Sacramento — State: CA — ZIP Code: 95813

3. Mailing address (if different from No. 2 above): — City: — State: — ZIP Code:

4. Date you will begin sales — Month 10 Day 20 Year 92

Days and hours of operation	Sun.	Mon.	Tue.	Wed.	Thurs.	Fri.	Sat.
			3-6	3-6	3-6	3-9	12-3

5. Description of business
 a. What will you sell? Frames & Artwork

 b. Check the appropriate box
 [X] Retail [ ] Wholesale [ ] Manufacturing [ ] Repair [ ] Service [ ] Construction Contractor

 c. Check the appropriate box
 [ ] Full-time [X] Part-time [ ] Mail-order

 d. Are you
 [X] Starting a new business? [ ] Adding/dropping partner? [ ] Buying a business? [ ] Other?

If buying a business, please indicate name and account no. of former owner ______

e. Purchase Price $ ______ Value of Fixtures and Equipment $ ______

6. How many selling locations will you have? (if 2 or more attach list of all locations) 1

7. If alcoholic beverages are sold, please list your Alcoholic Beverage Control License No. and type:

Continued

BT-400-MIP (BACK) REV. 5 (10-92) SAMPLE

STATE OF CALIFORNIA
BOARD OF EQUALIZATION

8. Name of accountant/bookkeeper	Address	Telephone
Self		( )
9. Name of business landlord	Address	Telephone
None (from home)		( )
10. Name of bank or other financial institution (checking and savings account)	Location	Account number
Wells Fargo	Citrus Heights	710-803070
11. Name of major suppliers	Address	Products purchased
California Lumber Co.	3160 J St. Sacramento	Wood
Wholesale Art Supplies	44 Brannon St. S.F.	Art Prints
12. Other account numbers issued to you by the Board		

Section III: Income and Expenses

1. Projected Monthly Business Expenses		2. Projected Monthly Business Revenue	
Rent	$ from Home	Total Gross Revenue	$ 10,000
Payroll	$	Non-taxable	$
Misc.	$ 2500	Taxable	$ 10,000
Total	$ 2,500	Tax	$

3. Information concerning Employment Development Department (EDD)

	Yes	No
a. Are you registered with EDD?	☐	☒
b. If no, will your payroll exceed $100 per quarter? If yes, you must make application with EDD. Number of employees ______ See pamphlet DE 4525, "Employer Guide."	☐	☒
c. I have already received pamphlet DE 4525.	☐	☒
d. I have already received pamphlet DE 44, "Employer's Withholding Guide."	☐	☒

Section IV: Certification

The statements contained hereon are hereby certified to be correct to the best knowledge and belief of the undersigned who is duly authorized to sign this application.

Alexander J. Hanson — SIGNATURE

Owner — TITLE

Alexander J. Hanson — NAME (TYPED OR PRINTED)

10-1-92 — DATE

FOR BOARD USE ONLY
Furnished to Applicant

Reporting Basis ______

Security Review ☐ BT-1009

☐ BT-598 $______

By ______

Approved By ______

Remote Input Date ______

By ______

Permit Issued ☐ Date ______

☐ GA-324A
☐ BT-400Y
☐ BT-467
☐ BT-519
☐ BT-741
☐ BT-968
☐ BT-1241C

☐ REG. 1668
☐ REG. 1698
☐ REG. 1700
☐ DE-44
☐ DE-4525
☐ ______
☐ ______

REGULATIONS

PAMPHLETS

RETURNS

STATE OF CALIFORNIA

BOARD OF EQUALIZATION
DEPARTMENT OF BUSINESS TAXES

SCHEDULE B—DETAILED ALLOCATION BY COUNTY OF 1% UNIFORM LOCAL SALES AND USE TAX

FOR — PERIOD — YEAR

PARTIAL PERIOD

BUSINESS CODE | AREA CODE | ACCOUNT NUMBER

NAME: Billy's Bikes, Inc.

BUSINESS ADDRESS

CITY: Irvine — STATE: CA — ZIP CODE — REPORTING BASIS

PLEASE READ INSTRUCTIONS ON REVERSE SIDE BEFORE COMPLETING THIS SCHEDULE.

Uniform local sales and use tax on retail sales of merchandise (not involving installation) made at your permanent place of business in California or local tax on property purchased ex-tax and used at this place of business, should be entered on Line B2 below the county schedule. Enter local tax on all other transactions in Column C of the schedule after the name of the county where the sale or use occurred.

A COUNTY IN WHICH TAXABLE TRANSACTION OCCURRED	B CODE	C AMOUNT OF 1% LOCAL TAX	A COUNTY IN WHICH TAXABLE TRANSACTION OCCURRED	B CODE	C AMOUNT OF 1% LOCAL TAX
ALAMEDA	01		PLACER	31	
ALPINE	02		PLUMAS	32	
AMADOR	03		RIVERSIDE	33	
BUTTE	04		SACRAMENTO	34	
CALAVERAS	05		SAN BENITO	35	
COLUSA	06		SAN BERNARDINO	36	
CONTRA COSTA	07		SAN DIEGO	37	
DEL NORTE	08		SAN FRANCISCO	38	
EL DORADO	09		SAN JOAQUIN	39	
FRESNO	10		SAN LUIS OBISPO	40	
GLENN	11		SAN MATEO	41	
HUMBOLDT	12		SANTA BARBARA	42	
IMPERIAL	13		SANTA CLARA	43	
INYO	14		SANTA CRUZ	44	
KERN	15		SHASTA	45	
KINGS	16		SIERRA	46	
LAKE	17		SISKIYOU	47	
LASSEN	18		SOLANO	48	
LOS ANGELES	19		SONOMA	49	
MADERA	20		STANISLAUS	50	
MARIN	21		SUTTER	51	
MARIPOSA	22		TEHAMA	52	
MENDOCINO	23		TRINITY	53	
MERCED	24		TULARE	54	
MODOC	25		TUOLUMNE	55	
MONO	26		VENTURA	56	
MONTEREY	27		YOLO	57	
NAPA	28		YUBA	58	
NEVADA	29				
ORANGE	30	580			

B1. Total local tax for all counties listed above .... $ 580

B2. Local tax on sales made and merchandise consumed at your permanent place of business in California. (Do not include any tax allocated to the above counties) ..... $ -0-

BOARD USE ONLY — Tax Area Code

B3. Total local tax liability (Line B1 plus Line B2) This total must agree with Line 17 on the return form .... $ 580

BE SURE TO ENCLOSE THIS SCHEDULE WITH YOUR SALES AND USE TAX RETURN—MAKE A COPY FOR YOUR RECORDS

BT-401-AC2 (S2F) REV. 36 (4-91)

BT-401-AC2 (S1B) REV. 36 (4-91)

SCHEDULE A—COMPUTATION SCHEDULE FOR DISTRICT TAX

A1.	AMOUNT ON WHICH LOCAL TAX APPLIES (Enter amount from Line 16 on the front of the return)		$ 58,000 .00
A2.	DEDUCT—Sales made from locations outside districts and delivered to any point not in a district.	000	- -0- .00
A3.	DEDUCT—Sales made from locations inside districts and delivered to any point not in a district.		- -0- .00
A4.	AMOUNT OF DISTRICT TRANSACTIONS (Line A1 minus Lines A2 and A3) (Allocate this amount to the correct district(s) in Column A5)		$ 58,000 .00

READ INSTRUCTIONS BEFORE PREPARING THIS SCHEDULE

Please round cents to the nearest whole dollar

* Transactions in a county with two districts must be reported in Column A5 for both districts.

DISTRICTS BY COUNTY	A5. ALLOCATE LINE A4 TO CORRECT DISTRICTS	A6. ADD (+) ADJUSTMENTS	A7. DEDUCT (−) ADJUSTMENTS	A8. TAXABLE AMOUNT A5 plus A6 minus A7	A9. TAX RATE	A10. DISTRICT TAX DUE Multiply A8 by A9
* ALAMEDA Co. 020 Bay Area Rapid Transit 011	.00	.00	.00	.00	.005	$ .00
* ALAMEDA Co. 010 Transportation Authority	.00	.00	.00	.00	.005	.00
* CONTRA COSTA Co. 021 Bay Area Rapid Transit 025	.00	.00	.00	.00	.005	.00
* CONTRA COSTA Co. 024 Transportation Authority	.00	.00	.00	.00	.005	.00
FRESNO Co. 012 Transportation Authority	.00	.00	.00	.00	.005	.00
IMPERIAL Co. 029 Local Transportation Authority	.00	.00	.00	.00	.005	.00
INYO Co. 014 Inyo Co. Transactions Tax	.00	.00	.00	.00	.005	.00
* LOS ANGELES Co. 005 LACT Effective 7-1-82 036	.00	.00	.00	.00	.005	.00
* LOS ANGELES Co. 035 LATC Effective 4-1-91	.00	.00	.00	.00	.005	.00
MADERA Co. 034 Transportation Authority	.00	.00	.00	.00	.005	.00
MONTEREY Co. 032 Public Repair & Improvement	.00	.00	.00	.00	.005	.00
ORANGE Co. 037 Transportation Authority	58,000 .00	-0- .00	-0- .00	58,000 .00	.005	290 .00
RIVERSIDE Co. 026 Transportation Commission	.00	.00	.00	.00	.005	.00
SACRAMENTO Co. 023 Transportation Authority	.00	.00	.00	.00	.005	.00
SAN BENITO Co. 015 Council of Governments	.00	.00	.00	.00	.005	.00
SAN BERNARDINO Co. 031 Transportation Authority	.00	.00	.00	.00	.005	.00
* SAN DIEGO Co. 013 Regional Transportation 017	.00	.00	.00	.00	.005	.00
* SAN DIEGO Co. 016 Regional Justice Facilities	.00	.00	.00	.00	.005	.00
* SAN FRANCISCO Co. 022 Bay Area Rapid Transit 028	.00	.00	.00	.00	.005	.00
* SAN FRANCISCO Co. 027 Transportation Authority	.00	.00	.00	.00	.005	.00
SAN JOAQUIN Co. 038 Transportation Authority	.00	.00	.00	.00	.005	.00
* SAN MATEO Co. 002 Transit District 019	.00	.00	.00	.00	.005	.00
* SAN MATEO Co. 018 Transportation Authority	.00	.00	.00	.00	.005	.00
SANTA BARBARA Co. 030 Local Transportation Authority	.00	.00	.00	.00	.005	.00
* SANTA CLARA Co. 006 Traffic Authority 007	.00	.00	.00	.00	.005	.00
* SANTA CLARA Co. 003 Transit District	.00	.00	.00	.00	.005	.00
* SANTA CRUZ Co. 004 Metropolitan Transit 041	.00	.00	.00	.00	.005	.00
* SANTA CRUZ Co. 040 Earthquake Recovery	.00	.00	.00	.00	.005	.00
SONOMA Co. 039 Open Space Authority	.00	.00	.00	.00	.0025	.00

A11.	TOTAL DISTRICT TAX. Add Column A10. (Enter here and on Line 18 on front of return)	$ 290 .00

Form 24. Sales and Use Tax Return

BT-401-AC2 (S1F) REV. 36 (4-91)

STATE OF CALIFORNIA
BOARD OF EQUALIZATION—Department of Business Taxes
STATE, LOCAL and DISTRICT SALES and USE TAX RETURN

DUE ON OR BEFORE

FOR PERIOD YEAR

PARTIAL PERIOD

Mail to:

STATE BOARD OF EQUALIZATION
P.O. BOX 942879
SACRAMENTO, CA 94279-0001

BUSINESS CODE | AREA CODE | ACCOUNT NUMBER

NAME: Billy's Bikes, Inc.

BUSINESS ADDRESS

CITY: Irvine STATE: CA ZIP CODE REPORTING BASIS

READ INSTRUCTIONS BEFORE PREPARING

PLEASE ROUND CENTS TO THE NEAREST WHOLE DOLLAR

1.	TOTAL GROSS SALES		$ 100,000.00
2.	PURCHASES SUBJECT TO USE TAX		2,500.00
3.	TOTAL (Line 1 plus Line 2)		102,500.00
4.	SALES TO OTHER RETAILERS FOR PURPOSES OF RESALE	50 $ 20,000.00	
5.	NONTAXABLE SALES OF FOOD PRODUCTS	51 0 .00	
6.	NONTAXABLE LABOR (Repair and Installation)	52 2,500.00	
7.	SALES TO THE UNITED STATES GOVERNMENT	53 2,000.00	
8.	SALES IN INTERSTATE OR FOREIGN COMMERCE	54 20,000.00	
9.	SALES TAX (IF ANY) INCLUDED ON LINE 1	55 0 .00	
10.	(a) BAD DEBT LOSSES ON TAXABLE SALES	56 0 .00	
	(b) COST OF TAX PAID PURCHASES RESOLD PRIOR TO USE	57 0 .00	
	(c) RETURNED MERCHANDISE	58 0 .00	
	(d) CASH DISCOUNTS	59 0 .00	
	(e) OTHER (Clearly explain)	90 0 .00	
11.	TOTAL OF EXEMPT TRANSACTIONS REPORTED ON LINES 4 thru 10e (Add Lines 4 thru 10e)		44,500.00
12.	TAXABLE TRANSACTIONS (Line 3 minus Line 11)		58,000.00
13.	STATE & COUNTY TAX 5% (Multiply Amount on Line 12 by .05)		2,900.00
14.	ENTER AMOUNT FROM LINE 12		58,000.00
15.	ADJUSTMENTS (See Instructions 15)		0 .00
16.	TAXABLE TRANSACTIONS (Line 14 plus or minus Line 15)		58,000.00
17.	LOCAL TAX 1% (Multiply amount on Line 16 by .01)		580.00
18.	DISTRICT TAX (From Schedule A Line A11) YOU MUST COMPLETE SCHEDULE A IF YOU ARE ENGAGED IN BUSINESS IN A TRANSACTIONS TAX DISTRICT		290.00
19.	TOTAL STATE, COUNTY, LOCAL AND DISTRICT TAX (Total of Lines 13, 17, & 18)		3,770.00
20.	DEDUCT sales or use tax imposed by other states and paid on the purchase price of tangible personal property. Purchase price must be included in Line 2		0 .00
21.	NET TAX (Line 19 minus Line 20)		3,770.00
22.	Less PREPAYMENTS — 1ST PREPAYMENT $ 1,000; 2ND PREPAYMENT $ 1,000	Total Prepayment	$ 2,000.00
23.	REMAINING TAX (Line 21 minus Line 22)		1,770.00
24.	PENALTY OF 10% (.10) if payment is made after due date shown above	PENALTY	0 .00
25.	INTEREST is due on tax for each month or fraction of a month that payment is delayed after the due date; refer to Notice of Interest Rate Change, Form BT-581, for current rate	INTEREST	0 .00
26.	TOTAL AMOUNT DUE AND PAYABLE (Line 23 plus 24 & 25)		$ 1,770.00

I hereby certify that this return, including any accompanying schedules and statements, has been examined by me and to the best of my knowledge and belief is a true, correct and complete return.

SIGNATURE AND TITLE .... (Sign Here) ( ) PHONE NUMBER

MAKE CHECK OR MONEY ORDER PAYABLE TO STATE BOARD OF EQUALIZATION
Always Write Your Account Number on Your Check or Money Order

MAKE A COPY FOR YOUR RECORDS

Form 25. Unemployment Tax Return

CONTRIBUTION RETURN AND REPORT OF WAGES DE 3DP

PURPOSE: To obtain quarterly payments for unemployment and disability insurance contributions and withheld personal income tax and wage reporting for benefit and tax purposes.

WHEN FURNISHED: March, June, September, and December of each year.

WHEN DUE: January 1, April 1, July 1, and October 1 of each year, together with payment due, if any. This report must be submitted even if no wages were paid during the calendar quarter.

REFER TO: Pages 16 and 17.

Note: Up to 25 copies of the DE 3DP continuous forms for computers may be obtained from the local Employment Tax District Offices. Larger volumes should be requested from Employment Development Department, Forms Management Unit. (Refer to Page 18, "How to Obtain Forms.")

EDD
Serving the People of California

State of California / Employment Development Department
P.O. Box 826847, Sacramento, CA 94247-0001

DE 3DP QUARTERLY CONTRIBUTION RETURN

QUARTER ENDED ______ DUE ______ DELINQUENT IF NOT POSTMARKED OR RECEIVED BY ______ QTR

H ☐ CHECK THIS BLOCK if corrections in name, address, or ownership are reported on the Request For Change form - see page three.

DO NOT ALTER PREPRINTED INFORMATION

DO NOT ALTER THIS AREA

DEPT. USE ONLY: P1 P2 C P U S W A

Employer Account No.

EFFECTIVE DATE Mo. Day Yr WIC

You must FILE this return even though you had no payroll this quarter. If you had no payroll show "0" in Item B. Enter a check mark in the block on the return envelope and sign the declaration on line K.

A. 1st Month ______ 2nd Month ______ 3rd Month ______
Enter in the boxes above the number of employees earning wages during pay periods that include the 12th day of the calendar month. (Enter numerals only)

PLEASE TYPE THIS FORM

B. TOTAL WAGES IN SUBJECT EMPLOYMENT . . . . . (B)

C. UNEMPLOYMENT INSURANCE TAXABLE WAGES (UI) (Individual Employee Wages to $ ______) . . . . . (C)

D. DISABILITY INSURANCE TAXABLE WAGES (DI) (Individual Employee Wages to $ ______) . . . . . (D)

E. EMPLOYER'S UI CONTRIBUTIONS ______ % Times C . . . . . (E)

E1. EMPLOYMENT TRAINING TAX ______ % Times C . . . . . (E1)

F. EMPLOYEE CONTRIBUTIONS (DI) WITHHELD ______ % Times D . . (F1) DI Employee Contributions ______ LESS (F2) DI Previously Paid This Quarter ______ (F3)

G. CALIFORNIA PERSONAL INCOME TAX (PIT) WITHHELD (G1) Total PIT Withheld this Quarter ______ LESS (G2) PIT Previously Paid This Quarter ______ (G3)

H. ADJUSTMENT TO PRIOR QUARTERS
A FORM DE 938, QUARTERLY REPORT ADJUSTMENT, MUST BE ATTACHED . . . . . (H)

J. TOTAL TAXES DUE (Add Items E, E1, F3 G3 and H)

J1. Make check payable to EMPLOYMENT DEVELOPMENT DEPARTMENT Bank No. ______ (J)
INCLUDE EMPLOYER ACCOUNT NUMBER ON YOUR CHECK. Do not staple check to return

DEPT USE

K. *BE SURE TO SIGN THIS DECLARATION: I DECLARE that the information herein is true and correct to the best of my knowledge and belief.*

Signature ______ Title (Owner, Accountant, Preparer, etc.) ______ Phone ( ) ______ Date ______

NOTE - IMPORTANT	DEPT USE	L. SOCIAL SECURITY ACCOUNT NUMBER	M. EMPLOYEE NAME First Initial Last Name	N1	N2. TOTAL WAGES PAID THIS QUARTER
Use form DE 3B REPORT OF WAGES, instead of this form if;					
1. You have more than seven (7) employees, OR					
2. Your employees are subject to Unemployment Insurance only, OR					
3. Your employees are subject to Disability Insurance only.					
Please check the appropriate box below:					
Individual employees' wages are reported on form DE 3B. ☐					
Individual employees' wages are reported on magnetic media. ☐		N3. Total of this page OR total of DE 3Bs attached →		(N3)	

DE 3DP REV. 13 (1-90)

Form 26. Sales Tax Resale Certificate

California Resale Certificate

____

(Name of Purchaser)

I HEREBY CERTIFY: That I hold valid seller's permit No. ________ issued pursuant to the Sales and Use Tax Law; that I am engaged in the business of selling

____;

that the tangible personal property described herein which I shall purchase from

____

____

will be resold by me in the form of tangible personal property; provided, however, that in the event any of such property is used for any purpose other than retention, demonstration, or display while holding it for sale in the regular course of business, it is understood that I am required by the Sales and Use Tax Law to report and pay tax, measured by the purchase price of such property or other authorized amount. Description of property to be purchased:

____

____

Date: ________ 19___ ______________________________

(Signature of Purchaser or Authorized Agent)

____

(Title)

Form 27. Sales and Use Tax Bond—Security Information

BT-598 REV. 15 (8-86)

NOTICE OF SECURITY REQUIREMENTS

STATE BOARD OF EQUALIZATION
DEPARTMENT OF BUSINESS TAXES

NOTE: Ownership name on security documents must be EXACTLY as underlined below WITHOUT reference to fictitious firm name or address.

To: ______________________________

Date ______________________________

Account No. ______________________________

You are notified that this Board requires you to deposit:

☐ Security ☐ Additional Security ☐ Replacement Security In the amount of $ ______________

For: ☐ Sales & Use Tax ☐ Use Fuel Tax ☐ Vendor Use Fuel Tax

Security is required because of:

☐ Need to secure state taxes
☐ Late filing; partial payments; returned check; account cited or revoked
☐ Understated estimated sales
☐ Surety bond cancellation
☐ (Other) ______________________________
____
____

Formula used to set amount of security:

YOUR REPORTING BASIS	AMOUNT
☐ Quarterly	2 x Qtr. Est.
☐ Quarterly Pre-payment	3 x Mo. Est.
☐ Monthly	3 x Mo. Est.
☐ Qtr. Acct. cited or revoked	3 x Qtr. Est.
☐ Qtr. Pre-pay Accts. cited or revoked	6 x Mo. Est.
☐ Mo. Acct. cited or revoked	5 x Mo. Est.
☐ User Use Fuel Tax account	6 x Mo. Est.
☐ Vendor Use Fuel account	4 x Mo. Est.

For additional information/clarification, contact the office listed above.

Failure to comply with this notice by ______________________ may result in the revocation of your permit.

The security must be surrendered to or mailed to any Board office and be one of the following types:

INTEREST BEARING:

a. Automatically renewable time certificates of deposit made payable to the "State Board of Equalization" which are issued by banks doing business in California and covered by Federal Depository Insurance. The original certificate is required for the Board's files.

b. Accounts issued in the name of the above ownership by insured savings and loan associations doing business in California and assigned to the "State Board of Equalization". *NOTE: The assignment and evidence of the account (in the form of either a certificate, passbook, identification card, etc.) are required for the Board's files. If the seller is a corporation, the savings and loan associations may require a resolution by the corporation's directors authorizing the account and assignment.*

c. Shares issued in the name above by credit unions doing business in California and assigned to the "State Board of Equalization". The assignment is required for the Board's files.

NON INTEREST BEARING:

a. Cash deposit.

b. Surety bond issued by an insurer duly authorized to write such bonds in California. The original bond is required for the Board's files. Bonds must be accompanied by a copy of the attorney in fact's power of attorney authorizing him or her to execute bonds on behalf of surety.

Form 28. Publications Available from the California State Board of Equalization

The publications listed at the right relate to sales and use taxes and other subjects. You may obtain copies of pamphlets and regulations from any field office (see Chapter 8). If you plan to visit a field office, you should call ahead to confirm that the publication you need is in stock.

The Board issues publications pertaining to other taxes, such as alcoholic beverage and motor vehicle fuel taxes. If you are interested in obtaining other publications, you should request a copy of *List of Board of Equalization Publications Available to the Public.*

If you are unable to obtain a publication or regulation through a field office, you should write to
Board of Equalization
Document Design
and Control Unit
P.O. Box 942879
Sacramento, CA 94279-0001

Pamphlets Available at No Charge [1]

General

No.	Title
1	Sales and Use Tax Law
2	Uniform Local Sales & Use Tax Law and Transactions & Use Tax Law
17	Appeals Procedures
21	State Board of Equalization
28	Business Tax & Property Tax Information for City and County Officials
44	Tax Tips for District Taxes
44-A	New District Taxes
61	Sales and Use Taxes: Exemptions and Exclusions
70	The California Taxpayers' Bill of Rights
71	California City and County Sales and Use Tax Rates

Tax Tip Booklets for Specific Types of Business Activities

No.	Title
9	Tax Tips for Construction and Building Contractors
18	Tax Tips: Sales Tax Guide for Volunteer and Nonprofit Fund Raising Organizations
22	Tax Tips for the Dining and Beverage Industry
24	Tax Tips for Package (Off-Sale) Liquor Stores
25	Tax Tips for Auto Repair Garages and Service Stations
27	Tax Tips for Drug Stores
31	Tax Tips for Grocery Stores
32	Tax Tips for Sellers Making Sales for Resale or Export to Purchasers from Mexico
34	Tax Tips for Motor Vehicle Dealers (New & Used)
35	Tax Tips for Interior Designers and Decorators
36	Tax Tips for Veterinarians
37	Tax Tips for the Graphic Arts Industry
38	Tax Tips for Advertising Agencies
40	Tax Tips for the Watercraft Industry
45	Tax Tips for Hospitals
46	Tax Tips for Leasing of Tangible Personal Property in California
47	Tax Tips for Mobilehomes and Factory-Built Housing
62	Tax Tips for Locksmiths
64	Tax Tips for Jewelry Stores
66	Tax Tips for Retail Feed and Farm Supply Stores
68	Tax Tips for Photographers, Photo Finishers and Film Processing Laboratories

Tax Schedules, Newsletters, Calendars, and Reports

- Tax Information Bulletin (published quarterly) [2]
- State of California Sales Tax Reimbursement Schedules
- Annual Calendar of Board Meetings
- List of Board of Equalization Publications Available to the Public
- Taxable Sales in California (published quarterly) [2]
- Annual Report of the State Board of Equalization
- Hearing Procedures of the State Board of Equalization

Publications Available at Cost [3]

- Business Taxes Law Guide
- Business Taxes Audit Manual
- Compliance Policy and Procedures Manual

---

[1] Single copies of these publications are available at no charge.

[2] When requesting this publication, please indicate the specific issue you need.

[3] For information and price quotes, write to the California State Board of Equalization, Document Design and Control Unit, P.O. Box 942879, Sacramento, CA 94279-0001.

STATE OF CALIFORNIA

STATE BOARD OF EQUALIZATION
23141 MOULTON PKWY., STE. 100
P.O. BOX 30890
LAGUNA HILLS, CA. 92653-0890
(714) 770-2157

WILLIAM M. BENNETT
First District, Kentfield

CONWAY H. COLLIS
Second District, Los Angeles

ERNEST J. DRONENBURG, JR.
Third District, San Diego

PAUL CARPENTER
Fourth District, Los Angeles

GRAY DAVIS
Controller, Sacramento

CINDY RAMBO
Executive Director

INVITATION TO

BASIC SALES TAX SEMINAR

The Board of Equalization offers free sales tax seminars designed to give taxpayers a basic understanding of the Sales and Use Tax Law. The seminar covers your obligations as a seller which include the responsibility for correctly reporting the tax. the course includes a demonstration on how to prepare a Sales and Use Tax return. Each seminar lasts approximately two hours.

If you are interested in attending a basic sales tax seminar, please complete and return the bottom portion of this invitation with your express registration documents. You will be notified of the next scheduled seminar.

I AM INTERESTED IN ATTENDING AN INTRODUCTORY SALES AND USE TAX SEMINAR.

NAME: --

ADDRESS: ---

CITY: ----------------- STATE: ------------------ ZIP: -----------

NUMBER IN YOUR GROUP ---------

Mail this form to the Board of Equalization nearest you. This form is an example, provided by the Board's Laguna Hills Office. See the address list on page 239, or consult your phone book for up-to-date information.

A sample of the Requisition for Employment Development Department Forms (DE 3274) is shown below. You may use the form on this page simply by cutting on the dotted line and mail to the address shown. A new requisition will be sent with your shipment.

DO NOT use this form to reorder preprinted tax deposit forms (eighth-monthly/monthly). Use the reorder form enclosed with your tax deposit coupon booklet. If you have not received a tax deposit coupon booklet and desire one, please contact your nearest Employment Tax District Office.

EDD Serving the People of California

REQUISITION FOR EMPLOYMENT DEVELOPMENT DEPARTMENT FORMS

Use this order blank to request frequently-used Employment Development Department forms. A new requisition form will be sent with each shipment of supplies.

*You may order up to a six months' supply of the forms you need. Overstocking forms may result in your using obsolete information.

Wage report forms (DE 3B) are also available from your nearest Employment Tax District Office where you may also obtain assistance regarding reporting problems. These offices are listed in the "white pages" of the telephone directory under "State Government Offices, Employment Development Department, Employment Tax District Office."

MAIL THIS ORDER FORM TO: EMPLOYMENT DEVELOPMENT DEPARTMENT
805 R Street, Sacramento, California 95814-6497

DE 3274 Rev. 19 (4-87)

Fill in Your Name and Address:

NAME ______________________

STREET ______________________

CITY ______ STATE ______ ZIP ______

**For efficiency and cost savings, please order only what you need: (Indicate quantity)*

_____ DE 3B Wage Report
_____ DE 3DP Contribution Return
_____ DE 4 Withholding Statement
_____ DE 44 Employer's Tax Guide
_____ DE 938 Claim for Credit or Refund
_____ DE 1857A Notice to Employees
_____ DE 2320 Unemployment Insurance
_____ DE 2320 S Unemployment Insurance (Span.)
_____ DE 2515 Disability Insurance
_____ DE 2515 S Disability Insurance (Span.)
_____ DE 4525 Employer's Guide

Other Forms (Specify)

_____ ______________________
_____ ______________________
_____ ______________________

Appendix C

Immigration Law Supplement

1. Employment Eligibility Verification Form

EMPLOYMENT ELIGIBILITY VERIFICATION (Form I-9)

1 EMPLOYEE INFORMATION AND VERIFICATION: (To be completed and signed by employee.)

Name: (Print or Type) Last	First	Middle	Birth Name
Address: Street Name and Number	City	State	ZIP Code
Date of Birth (Month/Day/Year)		Social Security Number	

I attest, under penalty of perjury, that I am (check a box):

☐ 1. A citizen or national of the United States.
☐ 2. An alien lawfully admitted for permanent residence (Alien Number A ______________).
☐ 3. An alien authorized by the Immigration and Naturalization Service to work in the United States (Alien Number A ______________, or Admission Number ______________, expiration of employment authorization, if any ______________).

I attest, under penalty of perjury, the documents that I have presented as evidence of identity and employment eligibility are genuine and relate to me. I am aware that federal law provides for imprisonment and/or fine for any false statements or use of false documents in connection with this certificate.

Signature	Date (Month/Day/Year)

PREPARER/TRANSLATOR CERTIFICATION (To be completed if prepared by person other than the employee). I attest, under penalty of perjury, that the above was prepared by me at the request of the named individual and is based on all information of which I have any knowledge.

Signature	Name (Print or Type)		
Address (Street Name and Number)	City	State	Zip Code

2 EMPLOYER REVIEW AND VERIFICATION: (To be completed and signed by employer.)

Instructions:
Examine one document from List A and check the appropriate box, ***OR*** examine one document from List B ***and*** one from List C and check the appropriate boxes. Provide the ***Document Identification Number*** and ***Expiration Date*** for the document checked.

List A
Documents that Establish Identity and Employment Eligibility

☐ 1. United States Passport
☐ 2. Certificate of United States Citizenship
☐ 3. Certificate of Naturalization
☐ 4. Unexpired foreign passport with attached Employment Authorization
☐ 5. Alien Registration Card with photograph

Document Identification
\# ______________
Expiration Date (if any)
____

List B
Documents that Establish Identity

☐ 1. A State-issued driver's license or a State-issued I.D. card with a photograph, or information, including name, sex, date of birth, height, weight, and color of eyes. (Specify State) ______________)
☐ 2. U.S. Military Card
☐ 3. Other (Specify document and issuing authority)
____

Document Identification
\# ______________
Expiration Date (if any)
____

and

List C
Documents that Establish Employment Eligibility

☐ 1. Original Social Security Number Card (other than a card stating it is not valid for employment)
☐ 2. A birth certificate issued by State, county, or municipal authority bearing a seal or other certification
☐ 3. Unexpired INS Employment Authorization
Specify form
\# ______________

Document Identification
\# ______________
Expiration Date (if any)
____

CERTIFICATION: I attest, under penalty of perjury, that I have examined the documents presented by the above individual, that they appear to be genuine and to relate to the individual named, and that the individual, to the best of my knowledge, is eligible to work in the United States.

Signature	Name (Print or Type)	Title
Employer Name	Address	Date

Employment Eligibility Verification

NOTICE:	Authority for collecting the information on this form is in Title 8, United States Code, Section 1324A, which requires employers to verify employment eligibility of individuals on a form approved by the Attorney General. This form will be used to verify the individual's eligibility for employment in the United States. Failure to present this form for inspection to officers of the Immigration and Naturalization Service or Department of Labor within the time period specified by regulation, or improper completion or retention of this form, may be a violation of the above law and may result in a civil money penalty.

Section 1. Instructions to Employee/Preparer for completing this form

Instructions for the employee.

All employees, upon being hired, must complete Section 1 of this form. Any person hired after November 6, 1986 must complete this form. (For the purpose of completion of this form the term "hired" applies to those employed, recruited or referred for a fee.)

All employees must print or type their complete name, address, date of birth, and Social Security Number. The block which correctly indicates the employee's immigration status must be checked. If the second block is checked, the employee's Alien Registration Number must be provided. If the third block is checked, the employee's Alien Registration Number ***or*** Admission Number must be provided, as well as the date of expiration of that status, if it expires.

All employees whose present names differ from birth names, because of marriage or other reasons, must print or type their birth names in the appropriate space of Section 1. Also, employees whose names change after employment verification should report these changes to their employer.

All employees must sign and date the form.

Instructions for the preparer of the form, if not the employee.

If a person assists the employee with completing this form, the preparer must certify the form by signing it and printing or typing his or her complete name and address.

Section 2. Instructions to Employer for completing this form

(For the purpose of completion of this form, the term "employer" applies to employers and those who recruit or refer for a fee.)

Employers must complete this section by examining evidence of identity and employment eligibility, and:
- checking the appropriate box in List A ***or*** boxes in both Lists B and C;
- recording the document identification number and expiration date (if any);
- recording the type of form if not specifically identified in the list;
- signing the certification section.

NOTE: Employers are responsible for reverifying employment eligibility of employees whose employment eligibility documents carry an expiration date.

Copies of documentation presented by an individual for the purpose of establishing identity and employment eligibility may be copied and retained for the purpose of complying with the requirements of this form and no other purpose. Any copies of documentation made for this purpose should be maintained with this form.

Name changes of employees which occur after preparation of this form should be recorded on the form by lining through the old name, printing the new name and the reason (such as marriage), and dating and initialing the changes. Employers should not attempt to delete or erase the old name in any fashion.

RETENTION OF RECORDS.

The completed form must be retained by the employer for:
- three years after the date of hiring; or
- one year after the date the employment is terminated, whichever is later.

Employers may photocopy or reprint this form as necessary.

U.S. Department of Justice
Immigration and Naturalization Service

OMB #1115-0136
Form I-9 (05/07/87)
★ U.S.G.P.O.: 1987- 183-918/69085

For sale by the Superintendent of Documents, U.S. Government Printing Office
Washington, D.C. 20402

2. Employer Instructions for Completing Employment Eligibility Verification Form

M-274 (5-87)

Handbook for Employers

Instructions for Completing Form I-9

(Employment Eligibility Verification Form)

To American Employers:

When the Congress passed and the President signed into law the Immigration Reform and Control Act of 1986, the result was the first major revision of America's immigration laws in decades. The new law seeks to preserve jobs for those who are legally entitled to them: American citizens and aliens who are authorized to work in our country.

The Immigration and Naturalization Service is responsible for implementing this new law. Public cooperation is crucial to the success of this national effort.

Put briefly, the law says that you should hire only American citizens and aliens who are authorized to work in the United States. You will need to verify employment eligibility of anyone hired after November 6, 1986, and complete and retain a one-page form (I-9) contained in this handbook.

We have worked to make the process as simple as possible. This handbook provides a step-by-step explanation of what you must do. We hope you will find it helpful.

All Americans stand to benefit from the successful implementation of the Immigration Reform and Control Act. We seek your cooperation.

Alan C. Nelson

Alan C. Nelson
Commissioner
U.S. Immigration and Naturalization Service

Contents

This Handbook is divided into nine parts:

This Handbook includes two copies of the Form I-9. At the back, you will also find a list of INS offices for you to contact if you need more information.

Part One

Why Employers Must Verify Employment Eligibility of New Employees

The Immigration Reform and Control Act of 1986 is the most comprehensive reform of our immigration laws since 1952. In recent years, our nation has been increasingly affected by illegal immigration. This law, passed by Congress through a bipartisan effort, preserves our tradition of legal immigration while closing the back door to illegal entry. By combining prohibitions against employing illegal entrants (or those aliens, such as tourists, who legally enter the United States but are not authorized to work while they are here) with increased border enforcement, the law represents a step forward in the effort to secure our nation's borders.

Employment is often the magnet that attracts persons to come to or stay in the United States illegally. The purpose of the new law is to remove the magnet by requiring employers to hire only citizens and aliens who are authorized to work here.

This new law was strongly supported by the American public. Employers will want to join the effort to protect our heritage of legal immigration and to preserve jobs for those who are legally entitled to them. This cooperation will make jobs available to American citizens and to aliens who are authorized to work in our country. It also can be a means to help people get off welfare and into jobs. Further it is a good business practice for you to verify the identity of your workers. The law deserves your support.

The Form I-9 has been developed for verifying that persons are eligible to work in the United States. The following instructions will help you assess your responsibilities for completing the Form and understanding the law.

The law requires you as an employer to do five things:

1. Have your employees fill out their part of the Form I-9 when they start to work;
2. Check documents establishing employees' identity and eligibility to work;
3. Properly complete the Form I-9;
4. Retain the Form for at least three years (if you employ the person for more than three years, you must retain the Form until one year after the person leaves your employment); and
5. Present the Form for inspection to an INS or Department of Labor (DOL) officer upon request. You will be given at least three days advance notice.

Part Two

When You Must Complete Form I-9

IF YOU EMPLOY PERSONS TO PERFORM LABOR OR SERVICES IN RETURN FOR WAGES OR OTHER PAY, **YOU MUST COMPLETE FORM I-9 FOR:**

Persons hired after May 31, 1987. For these employees, you must complete a Form I-9 within three business days of the date of the hire. (If you employ the person for less than three days, you must complete the Form I-9 before the end of the employee's first working day.)

Persons hired between November 7, 1986 and May 31, 1987. For these employees, you must complete Form I-9 before September 1, 1987.

NOTE: If you employ people for domestic work in your private home on a regular (such as weekly) basis, these requirements also apply to you.

YOU **DO NOT** NEED TO COMPLETE FORM I-9 FOR:

—Persons hired before November 7, 1986.

—Persons hired after November 6, 1986, who left your employment before June 1, 1987.

—Persons you employ for domestic work in a private home on an intermittent or sporadic basis.

—Persons who provide labor to you who are employed by a contractor providing contract services (e.g., employee leasing).

—Persons who are independent contractors.

Persons who are self-employed do not need to complete Form I-9.

Part Three

How to Complete Form I-9

Form I-9 contains two sections. The **employee** completes the first section (Steps 1, 2, and 3). If a preparer or translator assists the individual, he or she completes Step 4. The second section (Steps 5 and 6) should be completed by the **employer**.

When completing the Form I-9, the employee will need to provide a document or documents that establish identity and employment eligibility. Some documents establish *both* identity and employment eligibility. These documents appear in *List A* on the bottom half of the Form. Other documents establish identity alone (*List B*) or employment eligibility alone (*List C*). If the person does not provide a document from List A, he or she must produce one from List B *and* one from List C. A complete list of acceptable documents appears in Part Nine.

The employer should review the document or documents provided by the person. Documents should appear to be genuine and to relate to the individual.

If employees cannot complete Section 1 by themselves or need the Form translated, someone may assist them. The preparer or translator should read the Form to the employee, help with Step 1 and Step 2 as needed, have the employee sign or mark the Form, and follow Step 4.

Until September 1, 1987, if an employee indicates that he or she intends to or has applied for legalization, Special Agricultural Worker (SAW), or Cuban/Haitian entrant status, the employee is covered by a "special rule" and the employer should follow the instructions on page 4.

If a minor (under age 16) cannot produce a List A document or one of the identity documents listed in Part Nine (List B), he or she is exempt from producing one if: (1) a parent or legal guardian completes Section 1 and writes in the space for the minor's signature the words, "minor under age 16;" (2) the parent or legal guardian completes the "Preparer/Translator Certification," and (3) the employer writes in Section 2 the words, "minor under age 16" under List B in the space after the words "Document Identification #." If this procedure is followed, the minor must still produce a List C document showing employment eligibility.

SECTION 1: TO BE COMPLETED BY THE **EMPLOYEE**

STEP 1
Fill in the personal information.

STEP 2
Check the box for work eligibility. Give other information where needed.

STEP 3
Read, sign, and date.

STEP 4
(Preparer/Translator only)
Read, fill in information, and sign.

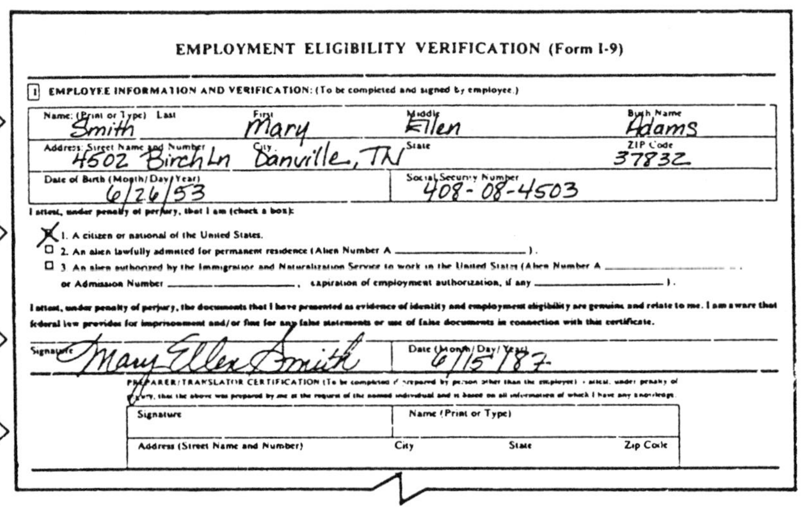

EMPLOYMENT ELIGIBILITY VERIFICATION (Form I-9)

1 EMPLOYEE INFORMATION AND VERIFICATION: (To be completed and signed by employee.)

Name: (Print or Type) Last Smith First Mary Middle Ellen Birth Name Adams

Address: Street Name and Number 4502 Birch Ln City Danville, State TN ZIP Code 37832

Date of Birth (Month/Day/Year) 6/26/53 Social Security Number 408-08-4503

I attest, under penalty of perjury, that I am (check a box):

☒ 1. A citizen or national of the United States.

☐ 2. An alien lawfully admitted for permanent residence (Alien Number A ______).

☐ 3. An alien authorized by the Immigration and Naturalization Service to work in the United States (Alien Number A ______ or Admission Number ______, expiration of employment authorization, if any ______).

I attest, under penalty of perjury, the documents that I have presented as evidence of identity and employment eligibility are genuine and relate to me. I am aware that federal law provides for imprisonment and/or fine for any false statements or use of false documents in connection with this certificate.

Signature Mary Ellen Smith Date (Month/Day/Year) 6/15/87

PREPARER/TRANSLATOR CERTIFICATION (To be completed if prepared by person other than the employee). I attest, under penalty of perjury, that the above was prepared by me at the request of the named individual and is based on all information of which I have any knowledge.

Signature | Name (Print or Type)

Address (Street Name and Number) | City | State | Zip Code

SECTION 2: TO BE COMPLETED BY THE **EMPLOYER**

STEP 5
Examine the document and check the box that corresponds to the document. Fill in document number and expiration date.

STEP 6
Read, fill in information, and sign.

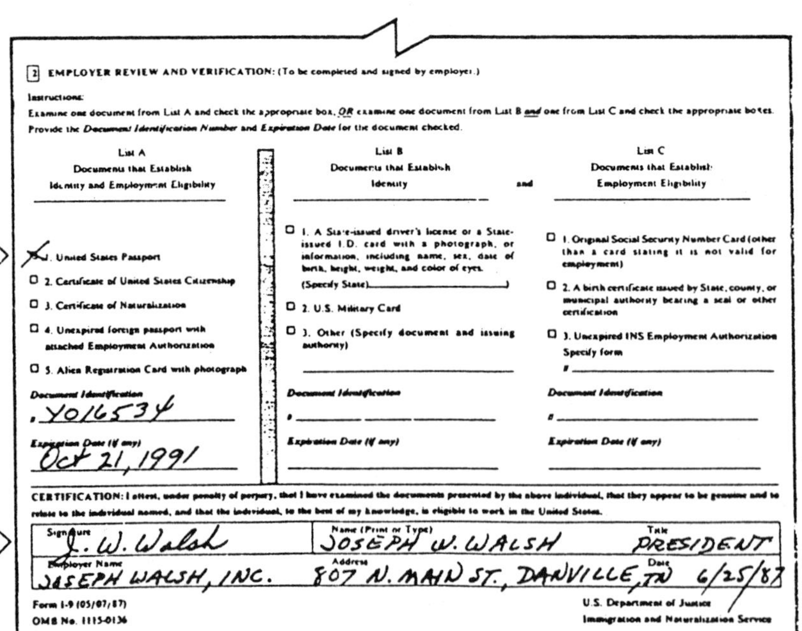

2 EMPLOYER REVIEW AND VERIFICATION: (To be completed and signed by employer.)

Instructions:
Examine one document from List A and check the appropriate box, *OR* examine one document from List B *and* one from List C and check the appropriate boxes.
Provide the *Document Identification Number* and *Expiration Date* for the document checked.

List A Documents that Establish Identity and Employment Eligibility	List B Documents that Establish Identity	and	List C Documents that Establish Employment Eligibility
☒ 1. United States Passport	☐ 1. A State-issued driver's license or a State-issued I.D. card with a photograph, or information, including name, sex, date of birth, height, weight, and color of eyes. (Specify State) ______		☐ 1. Original Social Security Number Card (other than a card stating it is not valid for employment)
☐ 2. Certificate of United States Citizenship	☐ 2. U.S. Military Card		☐ 2. A birth certificate issued by State, county, or municipal authority bearing a seal or other certification
☐ 3. Certificate of Naturalization	☐ 3. Other (Specify document and issuing authority) ______		☐ 3. Unexpired INS Employment Authorization Specify form # ______
☐ 4. Unexpired foreign passport with attached Employment Authorization			
☐ 5. Alien Registration Card with photograph			
Document Identification # Y016534	*Document Identification* # ______		*Document Identification* # ______
Expiration Date (if any) Oct 21, 1991	*Expiration Date (if any)* ______		*Expiration Date (if any)* ______

CERTIFICATION: I attest, under penalty of perjury, that I have examined the documents presented by the above individual, that they appear to be genuine and to relate to the individual named, and that the individual, to the best of my knowledge, is eligible to work in the United States.

Signature J. W. Walsh | Name (Print or Type) JOSEPH W. WALSH | Title PRESIDENT

Employer Name JOSEPH WALSH, INC. | Address 807 N. MAIN ST., DANVILLE, TN | Date 6/25/87

Form I-9 (05/07/87)
OMB No. 1115-0136

U.S. Department of Justice
Immigration and Naturalization Service

HOW TO FILL OUT FORM I-9 IF THE SPECIAL RULE APPLIES

The new immigration law also provides that certain qualified aliens who have resided illegally in the United States can legalize their status. In order to legalize their status, aliens must apply under the legalization, Special Agricultural Worker (SAW), or Cuban/Haitian entrant programs.

Employers may hire applicants or prospective applicants for legalization, SAW, or Cuban/Haitian entrant status. *Until September 1, 1987*, these applicants are covered by a "special rule" that authorizes them to work without providing employment eligibility documents. "Special rule" employees will need to fill out the I-9 as shown below and provide one of the specified documents that establish identity (see List B in Part Nine). The employer should review the identity document. It should appear to be genuine and to relate to the individual.

After September 1, 1987, the "special rule" expires, and these applicants will need to show a work authorization document to be hired or to continue to work. Employers must update the Form I-9 by recording the work authorization document information on the Form.

STEP 1
Fill in the personal information.

STEP 2
Check box #3. Write "special rule" in the space for alien number and "September 1, 1987" for the expiration date.

STEP 3
Read, sign, and date.

STEP 4
(Preparer/Translator only)
Read, fill in information, and sign.

STEP 5
Under List B, check the box that corresponds to the identity document and fill in document number and expiration date. Under List C, write "special rule" in the space for document number, and "September 1, 1987" for the expiration date.

STEP 6
Read, fill in information, and sign.

EMPLOYMENT ELIGIBILITY VERIFICATION (Form I-9)

1 EMPLOYEE INFORMATION AND VERIFICATION: (To be completed and signed by employee.)

Name: (Print or Type) Last JONES First DAVID Middle ALAN Birth Name

Address: Street Name and Number 407 ELM ST. City HARRISON State RHODE ISLAND ZIP Code 02912

Date of Birth (Month/Day/Year) NOVEMBER 19, 1955 Social Security Number

I attest, under penalty of perjury, that I am (check a box):

☐ 1. A citizen or national of the United States.
☐ 2. An alien lawfully admitted for permanent residence (Alien Number A ________).
☒ 3. An alien authorized by the Immigration and Naturalization Service to work in the United States (Alien Number A SPECIAL RULE or Admission Number ________, expiration of employment authorization, if any SEPT 1, 1987).

I attest, under penalty of perjury, the documents that I have presented as evidence of identity and employment eligibility are genuine and relate to me. I am aware that federal law provides for imprisonment and/or fine for any false statements or use of false documents in connection with this certificate.

Signature David A. Jones Date (Month/Day/Year) 7/14/87

PREPARER/TRANSLATOR CERTIFICATION (To be completed if prepared by person other than the employee). I attest, under penalty of perjury, that the above was prepared by me at the request of the named individual and is based on all information of which I have any knowledge.

Signature Name (Print or Type)

Address (Street Name and Number) City State Zip Code

2 EMPLOYER REVIEW AND VERIFICATION: (To be completed and signed by employer.)

Instructions:
Examine one document from List A and check the appropriate box, OR examine one document from List B and one from List C and check the appropriate boxes.
Provide the *Document Identification Number* and *Expiration Date* for the document checked.

List A Documents that Establish Identity and Employment Eligibility	List B Documents that Establish Identity	and	List C Documents that Establish Employment Eligibility
☐ 1. United States Passport	☒ 1. A State-issued driver's license or a State-issued I.D. card with a photograph, or information, including name, sex, date of birth, height, weight, and color of eyes. (Specify State) Rhode Island		☐ 1. Original Social Security Number Card (other than a card stating it is not valid for employment)
☐ 2. Certificate of United States Citizenship	☐ 2. U.S. Military Card		☐ 2. A birth certificate issued by State, county, or municipal authority bearing a seal or other certification
☐ 3. Certificate of Naturalization	☐ 3. Other (Specify document and issuing authority)		☐ 3. Unexpired INS Employment Authorization Specify form #
☐ 4. Unexpired foreign passport with attached Employment Authorization			
☐ 5. Alien Registration Card with photograph			
Document Identification #	*Document Identification* # 323-750-1031		*Document Identification* # Special Rule
Expiration Date (if any)	*Expiration Date (if any)* February 26, 1989		*Expiration Date (if any)* September 1, 1987

CERTIFICATION: I attest, under penalty of perjury, that I have examined the documents presented by the above individual, that they appear to be genuine and to relate to the individual named, and that the individual, to the best of my knowledge, is eligible to work in the United States.

Signature Barbara Evans Name (Print or Type) Barbara Evans Title Personnel Officer

Employer Name Apex Corporation Address 8204 Oak St, Harrison, RI 02912 Date 7/14/87

Form I-9 (05/07/87)
OMB No. 1115-0136

U.S. Department of Justice
Immigration and Naturalization Service

Part Four

Unlawful Discrimination

The new immigration law also prohibits discrimination. Under this law, if you have four or more employees, you may not discriminate against any individual (other than an unauthorized alien) in hiring, discharging, or recruiting or referring for a fee because of that individual's national origin or, in the case of a citizen or intending citizen, because of his or her citizenship status.

Title VII of the Civil Rights Act of 1964 and the remedies against discrimination it provides also remain in effect. Title VII prohibits discrimination against any individual on the basis of national origin in hiring, discharge, recruitment, assignment, compensation, and other terms and conditions of employment with respect to employers subject to its coverage. Claims of national origin discrimination against employers with fifteen or more employees should be filed with the Equal Employment Opportunity Commission.

Under the new immigration law, charges of national origin discrimination against employers with four through fourteen employees and charges of citizenship discrimination against employers with four or more employees should be filed with the Office of Special Counsel in the Department of Justice. Discrimination charges may be filed either by persons who believe they were discriminated against in employment on the basis of national origin or citizenship status (or by a person on their behalf) or by INS officers who have reason to believe that discrimination has occurred. Discrimination charges must be filed within 180 days of the discriminatory act. The Office of the Special Counsel will notify the employer by certified mail within ten days upon receipt of a charge of discrimination. After investigating the charge, the Special Counsel may file a complaint with an administrative law judge. If the Special Counsel does not file a complaint within 120 days of receiving the charge, the person making the charge (other than an INS officer) may initiate filing a complaint with an administrative law judge. The administrative law judge will conduct a hearing and issue a decision.

Employers found to have engaged in discriminatory practices under the new immigration law will be ordered to stop the prohibited practice. They may also be ordered to hire, with or without back pay, individuals directly injured by the discrimination; pay a fine of up to $1,000 for each individual discriminated against (up to $2,000 for each such individual in cases of employers previously fined); and keep certain records regarding the hiring of applicants and employees. If a court decides that the losing party's claim has no reasonable basis in fact or law, the court may award attorneys' fees to prevailing parties other than the United States.

For more information concerning the antidiscrimination section of the new immigration law, write the Office of the Special Counsel for Immigration-Related Unfair Employment Practices, P.O. Box 65490, Washington, D.C. 20035-5490 or call (202) 653-8121.

For more information on Title VII and policies and procedures of the Equal Employment Opportunity Commission, call 1-800-USA-EEOC.

Part Five

Penalties for Prohibited Practices

1. Civil Penalties

If an investigation reveals that an employer has violated the new immigration law with respect to employees hired after November 6, 1986, INS may take action. During the first year of implementation (June 1, 1987–May 31, 1988) INS will continue to assist employers in complying with the law. In addition, INS will only issue a citation for first violations. Further violations during this period may result in the penalties described below. When INS intends to impose those penalties, the Service first issues a Notice of Intent to Fine. Employers who receive a Notice may request a hearing before an administrative law judge. If a hearing is not requested within 30 days, the penalty will be imposed. After May 31, 1988, INS will no longer issue warning citations, and first violations may result in penalties.

- *Hiring or continuing to employ unauthorized employees.* Employers determined to have knowingly hired unauthorized employees (or to be continuing to employ persons knowing that they are or have become unauthorized) may be fined as follows:

  —*First Violation.* Not less than $250 and not more than $2,000 for each unauthorized employee.

  —*Second Violation.* Not less than $2,000 and not more than $5,000 for each unauthorized employee.

  —*Subsequent Violations.* Not less than $3,000 and not more than $10,000 for each unauthorized employee.

- *Failing to comply with record-keeping requirements.* Employers who fail to properly complete, retain, and present for inspection the Form I-9 as required by law may face civil fines of not less than $100 and not more than $1000 for each employee for whom the Form was not completed, retained, or presented. In determining penalties, consideration shall be given to the size of the business, good faith efforts to comply, the seriousness of the violation, and whether the violation involved unauthorized employees.

- *Requiring indemnification.* Employers found to have required a bond or indemnity from an individual against liability under the new law may be fined $1000 and ordered to make restitution, either to the person who was required to pay the indemnity, or, if that person cannot be located, to the United States Treasury.

- *Recruiting unauthorized seasonal agricultural workers outside the United States.* Employers who knowingly recruit unauthorized workers outside the United States to perform seasonal agricultural labor may face the same penalties as for hiring unauthorized workers, unless the workers recruited have been granted Special Agricultural Worker (SAW) status.

2. Criminal Penalties.

- *Engaging in a pattern or practice of knowingly hiring or continuing to employ unauthorized employees.* Employers convicted for having engaged in a pattern or practice of knowingly hiring unauthorized aliens after November 6, 1986, may face fines of up to $3000 per employee and/or six months imprisonment. The same penalties apply to engaging in a pattern or practice of recruiting unauthorized seasonal agricultural workers outside the United States. Criminal sanctions will be reserved for serious or repeated violations.

- *Engaging in fraud or false statements, or otherwise misusing visas, immigration permits, and identity documents.* Persons who use fraudulent identification or employment eligibility documents or documents that were lawfully issued to another, or who make a false statement or attestation, for purposes of satisfying the employment eligibility requirements may be imprisoned for up to five years or fined or both.

Part Six

Timetable for Employer Verification Requirements

December 1, 1986 through May 31, 1987

Public Education Period. This is an initial period established by law for the publication of regulations and dissemination of forms and information. During this period, citations are not issued and fines are not levied.

June 1, 1987 through May 31, 1988

Citation Period. This is a one-year period for public education, voluntary compliance and initial enforcement. INS will work with employer associations, labor unions, and others to provide assistance, develop voluntary cooperation, and encourage efforts to hire legal employees. Penalties are not imposed for first-offense violations during this time. Instead, a warning citation is issued which explains the nature of the violation. For subsequent or repeated violations, civil or in some cases criminal penalties can be imposed.

June 1, 1987 through September 1, 1987

Special Rule Period. Employers may hire or continue to employ employees who attest on the Form I-9 that they have applied or intend to apply for legalization, Special Agricultural Worker, or Cuban/Haitian status even if the workers have not yet received work authorization documents from the INS.

June 1, 1988

Effective Date for Full Enforcement. As of this date, citations will no longer be issued for first violations. Employers who violate the law may face civil or criminal penalties.

June 1, 1987 through November 30, 1988

Deferral Period for Employers of Seasonal Agricultural Workers. Penalties will not apply to employers of seasonal agricultural workers during this period. This deferral does not apply to the prohibition against recruitment of unauthorized employees who are outside the United States. As of December 1, 1988, INS will begin full enforcement of the law with respect to these agricultural employers.

Part Seven

Instructions for Recruiters and Referrers for a Fee

The provisions of the new law that apply to employers also apply to those who **recruit** persons and refer them to potential employers in return for a fee and those who **refer** or provide documents or information about persons to employers in return for a fee. The provisions do not apply to persons who recruit for their own company or business. In addition, union hiring halls that refer union members or non-union individuals who pay membership dues are not considered to be recruiters or referrers for a fee.

Recruiters and referrers for a fee are **not** required to verify the status of persons referred between November 6, 1986, and May 31, 1987. **Starting June 1, 1987, they should complete Form I-9 when a person they refer to an employer is hired by that employer.** The Form should be completed within three business days of the hire.

Recruiters and referrers for a fee may also refer individuals covered by the "special rule" and should follow the procedures for completing the Form I-9 on page 4.

Recruiters and referrers may designate agents to complete the verification procedures on their behalf, such as national associations, or employers. If the employer who hires the referred individual is designated as the agent, the employer needs only to provide the recruiter or referrer with a photocopy of the Form I-9. Recruiters or referrers who designate someone to complete the verification procedures on their behalf are still responsible for compliance with the law and may be found liable for violations of the law.

Recruiters and referrers must **retain** the Form I-9 for three years after the date the referred individual was hired by the employer. They must also present Forms for inspection to an INS or DOL officer after three days advance notice.

The penalties described in Part Five apply to recruiting and referring unauthorized employees for a fee which occurs on or after June 1, 1987.

Part Eight

Some Questions You May Have About the Form I-9

Q. Do United States citizens need to prove they are eligible to work?

A. Yes. While United States citizens are automatically eligible for employment, they too must provide the required documents and complete the Form I-9.

Q. Do I need to complete an I-9 for everyone who applies for a job with my company?

A. No. You need to complete I-9's only for people you actually hire. For purposes of the new law, a person is "hired" when he or she begins to work for you.

Q. If someone accepts a job with my company but will not start work for a month, can I complete the I-9 when the employee accepts the job?

A. Yes. While the law requires you to complete the I-9 when the person actually begins working, you may complete the Form when he or she accepts the job.

Q. Do I need to fill out an I-9 for independent contractors or their employees?

A. No. For example, if you contract with another company to provide temporary secretarial services, you do not have to complete I-9's for that company's employees. The other company is responsible for completing the I-9's for its own employees. However, you must not knowingly use contract labor to circumvent the law against hiring unauthorized workers.

Q. Do I need to complete an I-9 for people I hired after November 6, 1986, if they left the job before June 1, 1987?

A. No.

Q. Does the new law apply to my current employees if I hired them before it was passed?

A. No. You are not required to verify status or complete I-9's for current employees hired before November 7, 1986. However, if you choose to complete I-9's for these employees, you should do so for all your current employees hired before November 7, 1986.

Q. What if a current employee was hired before November 7, 1986, but has recently taken an approved leave of absence?

A. You do not need to complete an I-9 for that employee if he or she was temporarily absent from work for approved paid or unpaid leave, strike, or temporary layoff, or was transferred to another location of your business. However, if you rehire an employee who quit or was terminated, you should complete the employment verification process as you would for others hired after November 6, 1986. You must also verify employment eligibility and complete an I-9 if an employee leaves or is removed from the United States because of an order by a judge or INS.

Those conditions also apply to employees hired after November 6, 1986. Once you have completed an I-9 for those employees, you will not need to fill out a new Form if they have a temporary absence for approved leave, strike, layoff, or transfer.

Q. Will I be subject to employer sanctions penalties if a current employee I hired before November 7, 1986, is an illegal alien?

A. No. You will not be subject to employer sanctions penalties for merely retaining in your workforce an illegal alien hired before November 7, 1986. The fact that an illegal alien was on your payroll before November 7, 1986, does *not* give him or her any right to remain in the United States. Unless the alien is legalized or otherwise obtains permission from INS to remain in the United States, he or she is subject to apprehension and removal.

Q. What should I do if illegal alien employees ask me to help them in legalizing their status?

A. You can assist past and present employees who may qualify by providing documentation of employment history. Employment documentation furnished by employers and presented by legalization applicants will be used only to determine the applicant's eligibility for legal status. The government will not use the documents against the employer except in cases of fraud by the employer.

If aliens do not know how to apply for legal status, they may be able to get help from various organizations, such as churches, community groups, or business associations, which have been designated by INS to advise aliens and help them prepare applications.

You can also advise them that the Internal Revenue Service (IRS) may be able to provide them with documentation to verify residence. To obtain this documentation, employees should contact IRS in person or by correspondence to the service center where they filed their tax return(s). A letter to IRS should include name, address of filing, social security number (both spouses' numbers if a joint return was filed), tax year or years required and copies of any correspondence received from IRS relating to the requested years. IRS will then issue them a Form 6166 (Certification of Filing a Tax Return) if the tax information is verifiable.

Q. May I specify which documents I will accept for verification?

A. No. You must accept any document or combination of documents listed on the I-9 or in Part Nine of this Handbook that appear to be genuine.

Q. What should I do if the person I hire is unable to provide the required documents within three days?

A. If an employee is unable to provide the required document or documents within three days he or she must at least produce a receipt showing that he or she has applied for the document. The employee must produce the document itself within 21 days of the hire.

Q. What is my responsibility concerning the authenticity of documents?

A. You should examine the documents and if they appear to be genuine on their face and to relate to the person, you should accept them. If on their face the documents do not appear to be genuine or to relate to the person, you should not accept them. In addition, if the work authorization documents carry restrictions, you should abide by them.

You should also be aware that any social security number starting with a "9" is an invalid number. Employees who are using such numbers should be instructed to get a proper social security number using Form SS-5, available from the Social Security Administration.

Q. What identity documents are acceptable for minors?

A. If the minor does not have any of the identity documents listed in Part Nine, he or she does not have to produce an identity document if a parent or legal guardian completes the appropriate sections of the Form for the minor.

Q. When do I fill out the I-9 if I hire someone for less than three days?

A. You do need to complete an I-9 before the end of the employee's first working day. However, if the person is providing intermittent domestic service in your home, you do not need to complete an I-9.

Q. What if the person I hire after November 6, 1986, is an illegal alien who has applied or intends to apply for legalization?

A. There is a "special rule" for these applicants. Up until September 1, 1987, you should fill out the I-9 as illustrated on page 4.

After September 1, 1987 even these aliens must provide work authorization documents and you should update the I-9 to reflect the authorization.

Q. What if I rehire someone who previously filled out an I-9?

A. You do not need to complete a new I-9 if you rehire the person within three years of the initial hire, and the information on the Form indicates that the person is still authorized to work.

Q. Do I need to complete a new I-9 when one of my employees is promoted within my company or transfers from one of my company's offices to another at a different location?

A. No. You do not not need to complete a new I-9 if the employee is promoted or transferred within your company.

Q. What do I do when an employee's work authorization expires?

A. You will need to update the I-9 if you want to continue employing the person. At that time, the employee must present a document that either shows an extension of employment eligibility or that is a new grant of work authorization. If the employee cannot produce such a document, that person is no longer eligible to work. Continuing to employ that person is a violation of the law, even if the employee was previously authorized to work.

Q. As an employer, do I have to fill out all the I-9's myself?

A. No, you may designate someone to fill out the Form for you such as a personnel officer, foreman, agent, or anyone else acting in your interest. However, you are still responsible for compliance with the new law.

Q. Can I contract with someone to complete I-9's for my business?

A. Yes. You can contract with another person or business to verify employees' work eligibility and complete the I-9's for you. If you do so, of course, you are still responsible for the contractor's actions and could be liable for any violations of the new law.

Q. As an employer, can I negotiate my responsibility to complete the I-9's in a collective bargaining agreement with a union?

A. Yes. However, you are still responsible for compliance with the new law.

Q. When I review the identity and work authorization documents, should I make photocopies of them?

A. The law does not require you to photocopy documents. However, if you wish to make photocopies, you must retain them with the I-9. Photocopies must not be used for any other purpose.

Q. What are the requirements for retaining the I-9?

A. You must retain the Form for at least three years. If you employ the person for more than three years, you must retain the Form for one year after the person leaves your employment.

Q. Will I get any advance notice if an INS or DOL officer wishes to inspect my I-9's?

A. Yes. The officer will give you at least three days advance notice before the inspection. He or she will not need to show you a subpoena or warrant at that time. Failure to provide the I-9's for inspection could result in civil money penalties.

Q. What happens if I do everything the new law requires and INS discovers that one of my employees is not actually authorized to work?

A. Unless the government can show that you had actual knowledge of the illegal status of the employee, you will have an affirmative defense against the imposition of employer sanctions penalties if you have done the following things:

—Had employees fill out their part of the I-9 when they started to work;

—Checked the required documents (they should appear to be genuine and to relate to the individual);

—Properly completed the I-9;

—Retained the Form for the specified time; and

—Presented the Form upon request to an INS or Department of Labor officer. You will receive at least three days advance notice.

Q. How can I avoid discrimination while complying with the new immigration law?

A. Employers can avoid discrimination by applying the verification procedures of the Act to *all* newly hired employees and by hiring without respect to the national origin or citizenship status of those authorized to work in the United States. Seeking identity and employment eligibility documents only from individuals of a particular national origin or from those who appear or sound foreign violates the new immigration law and may also be a violation of Title VII of the Civil Rights Act of 1964. Employers should not discharge present employees, refuse to hire new employees, or otherwise discriminate on the basis of foreign appearance, language, or name. It is also a violation of Title VII to discriminate against employees or applicants for employment on the basis of national origin.

Q. I have heard that state employment agencies can certify that people they refer are eligible to work. Is that true?

A. Yes. State employment agencies may elect to provide individuals they refer to employers with a certification of employment eligibility. If one of these agencies refers potential employees to you and an employee presents you with one of these certifications, you do not have to check documents or complete an I-9 if you hire that person. However, you must retain the certification as you would an I-9 and present it for inspection if requested. Employers who hire people referred by state employment agencies should become familiar with what an authorized state employment agency certification looks like.

Q. Where can I get the Form I-9?

A. There are two copies of the Form I-9 in this Handbook. If you need more, you can photocopy or print the Forms. You may obtain a limited number of copies from INS. Or you may order them in bulk from the Superintendent of Documents at the following address:

Superintendent of Documents
U.S. Government Printing Office
Washington, D.C. 20402
Tel. (202) 783-3238

Q. What if one of my employees tells me that his or her Social Security Number is invalid?

A. You should tell the employee to get a proper Social Security Number by completing a Form SS-5. This Form is available from the Social Security Administration. You do not need to amend your employment tax returns. However, when the employee gives you the new number, you should file Form W-2C with the Social Security Administration for the years in which you reported income and withholding under the incorrect number.

Q. What advice should I give to my employees applying to legalize their status concerning their Federal Tax obligations?

A. You can advise employees that when they apply to INS for permanent resident status, they will be given an IRS publication explaining requirements for filing Form W-4 or W-4A to insure correct withholding of tax on wages, procedures for correcting prior year tax records (if an invalid social security number was used) and other guidelines relating to tax benefits.

Q. What advice should I give to newly-hired employees who ask about their Federal income tax obligations?

A. First, you can tell them it is important to have a valid social security number and to properly complete a W-4 or W-4A so that the employer can withhold the proper amount for income tax. Second, you can encourage employees to apply for social security numbers for their dependent children who will be five years old or older by the end of the year. Beginning in 1987, such numbers are required to be provided for dependents claimed on tax returns.

Part Nine

Acceptable Documents for Verifying Employment Eligibility

The following documents have been designated for determining employment eligibility by the Immigration Reform and Control Act of 1986 and the implementing regulations. As stated in Part Two, the employee will need to provide a document or documents that establish identity and employment eligibility. A complete list of acceptable documents is given on the next page. Samples of many of the acceptable documents appear on the following pages.

Some documents establish **both** identity and employment eligibility. These are listed on the Form I-9 under *List A*, "Documents that Establish Identity and Employment Eligibility."

If a person does not provide a document from *List A* he or she must provide one document that establishes identity **and** one document that establishes employment eligibility.

In order to establish **identity**, the person must provide a state-issued driver's license, a state-issued identification card, or one of the other documents in *List B*.

In order to establish **employment eligibility**, the person must provide a Social Security card, a United States birth certificate, or one of the immigration documents in *List C*.

If an employee is unable to provide the required document or documents within three days, he or she must at least produce (within three days) a receipt showing that he or she has applied for the document. The employee must produce the document itself within 21 days of the hire.

LIST A
Documents That Establish Identity and Employment Eligibility

- United States Passport
- Certificate of United States Citizenship. (INS Form N-560 or N-561)
- Certificate of Naturalization. (INS Form N-550 or N-570)
- Unexpired foreign passport which:
  —Contains an unexpired stamp which reads "Processed for I-551. Temporary Evidence of Lawful Admission for permanent residence. Valid until _____. Employment authorized;" or
  —Has attached thereto a Form I-94 bearing the same name as the passport and contains an employment authorization stamp, so long as the period of endorsement has not yet expired and the proposed employment is not in conflict with any restrictions or limitations identified on the Form I-94.
- Alien Registration Receipt Card (INS Form I-151) or Resident Alien Card (INS Form I-551), provided that it contains a photograph of the bearer.
- Temporary Resident Card. (INS Form I-688)
- Employment Authorization Card. (INS Form I-688A)

LIST B
Documents That Establish Identity

For individuals 16 years of age or older:

- State-issued driver's license or state-issued identification card containing a photograph. If the driver's license or identification card does not contain a photograph, identifying information should be included, such as name, date of birth, sex, height, color of eyes, and address.
- School identification card with a photograph
- Voter's registration card
- United States Military card or draft record
- Identification card issued by federal, state or local government agencies
- Military dependent's identification card
- Native American tribal documents
- United States Coast Guard Merchant Mariner Card
- Driver's license issued by a Canadian government authority

For individuals under age 16 who are unable to produce one of the documents listed above:

- School record or report card
- Clinic doctor or hospital record
- Daycare or nursery school record

LIST C
Documents That Establish Employment Eligibility

- Social Security number card, other than one which has printed on its face "not valid for employment purposes."
  Note: This must be a card issued by the Social Security Administration; a facsimile (such as a metal or plastic reproduction that people can buy) is not acceptable.
- An original or certified copy of a birth certificate issued by a state, county, or municipal authority bearing an official seal
- Unexpired INS employment authorization
- Unexpired re-entry permit. (INS Form I-327)
- Unexpired Refugee Travel Document. (INS Form I-571)
- Certification of Birth issued by the Department of State. (Form FS-545)
- Certification of Birth Abroad issued by the Department of State. (Form DS-1350)
- United States Citizen Identification Card. (INS Form I-197)
- Native American tribal document
- Identification Card for use of Resident Citizen in the United States. (INS Form I-179)

DOCUMENT LIST A.

United States Passport

Issued by the Department of State to United States citizens and nationals.

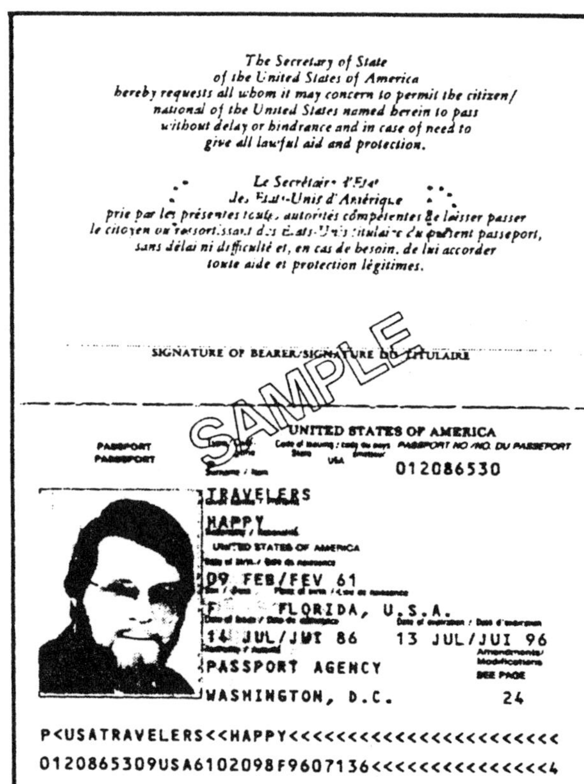

Certificate of United States Citizenship N-560

Issued by INS to individuals who derived citizenship through parental naturalization; acquired citizenship at birth abroad through a United States parent or parents; acquired citizenship through application by United States citizen adoptive parents; and who, pursuant to section 341 of the Act, have applied for a certificate of citizenship.

THE UNITED STATES OF AMERICA

No. A0000000

CERTIFICATE OF CITIZENSHIP

·ORIGINAL·

SAMPLE

Seal

IT IS PUNISHABLE BY U. S. LAW TO COPY, PRINT OR PHOTOGRAPH THIS CERTIFICATE.

DEPARTMENT OF JUSTICE

Certificate of Naturalization N-550 or N-570

Issued by INS to naturalized United States citizens.

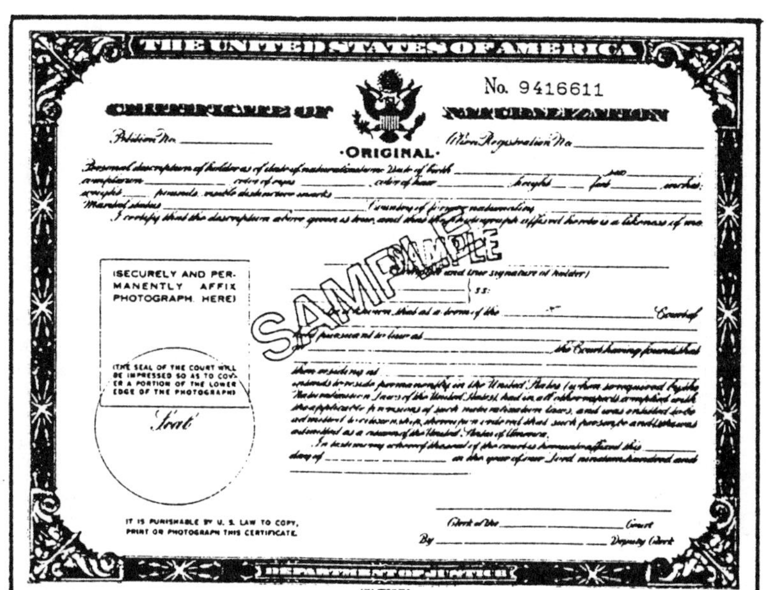

THE UNITED STATES OF AMERICA

No. 9416611

CERTIFICATE OF NATURALIZATION

·ORIGINAL·

SAMPLE

SECURELY AND PERMANENTLY AFFIX PHOTOGRAPH HERE

Seal

IT IS PUNISHABLE BY U. S. LAW TO COPY, PRINT OR PHOTOGRAPH THIS CERTIFICATE.

DEPARTMENT OF JUSTICE

I-94 Arrival-Departure Record

Arrival-departure record issued by INS to nonimmigrant aliens and attached to an unexpired foreign passport. An individual in possession of this document may only be employed if the document bears an employment authorization stamp. The expiration date is noted on the face of the document.

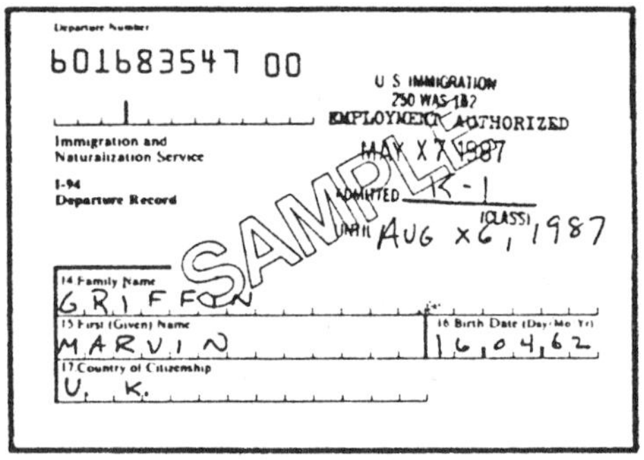

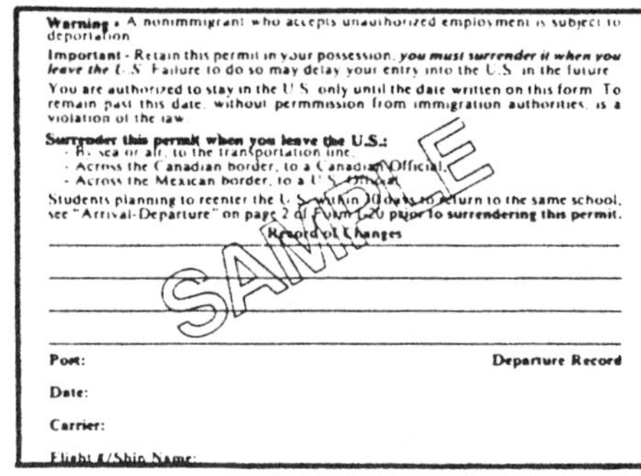

Alien Registration Receipt Card I-151

Issued by INS, prior to June 1978, to lawful permanent resident (lawful immigrant) aliens. There are numerous versions of this card because it was periodically revised. Although this card is no longer issued, it is valid indefinitely. This card is also commonly referred to as a "green card."

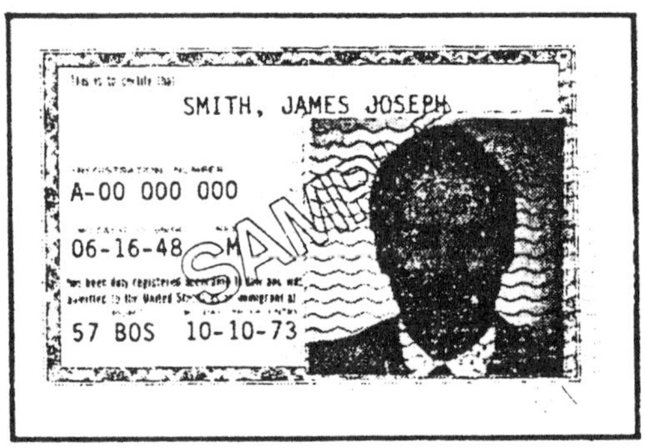

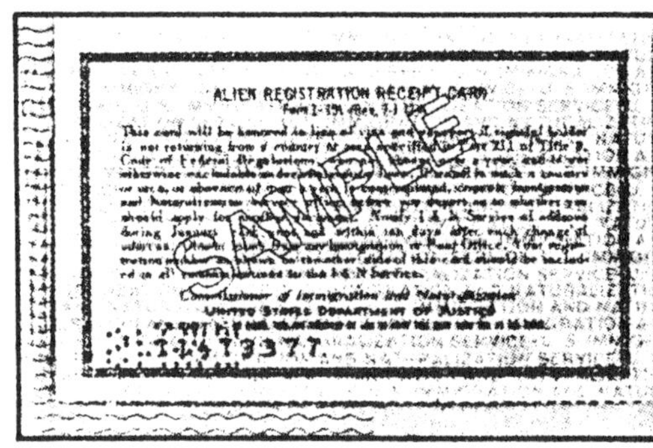

Alien Registration Receipt Card (Resident Alien Card) I-551

Issued by INS to lawful permanent resident (lawful immigrant) aliens. Valid indefinitely, this card is commonly referred to as a "green card" and is a revised edition of Form I-151.

Alien Registration Receipt Card (Conditional Resident Alien Card) I-551

Issued by INS to conditional permanent residents such as alien spouses of United States citizens or lawful permanent residents. Although it is the same card as the I-551 issued to permanent resident aliens, this card is valid for a limited period of time. The expiration date is stated on the back of the card.

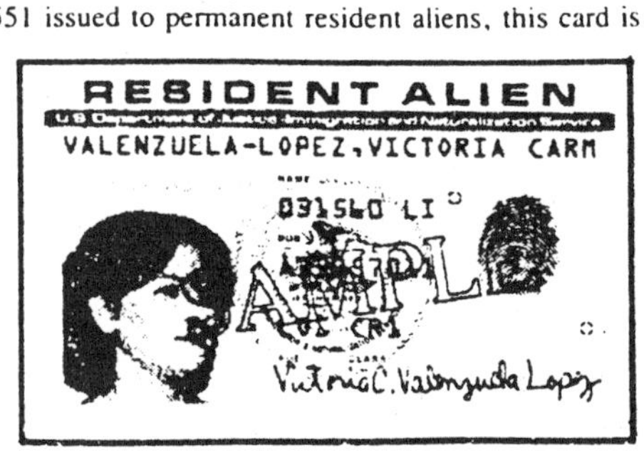

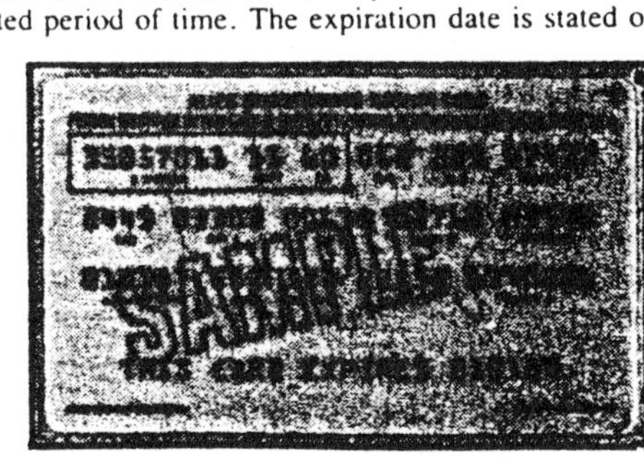

Temporary Resident Card I-688

Issued by INS to aliens granted temporary resident status under the legalization or SAW programs. It is valid until the expiration date stated on the face of the document.

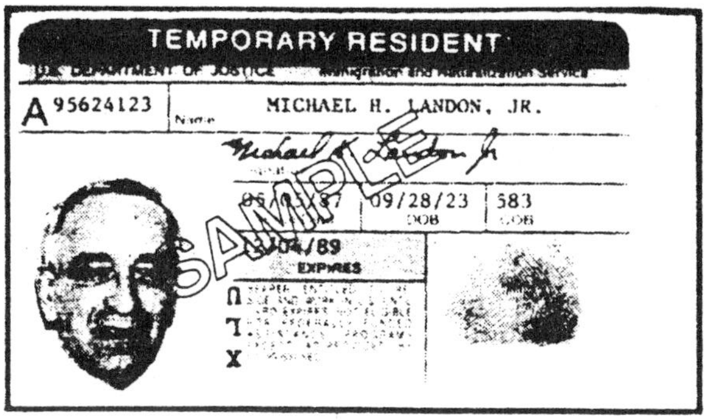

Employment Authorization Card I-688A

Issued by INS to applicants for temporary resident status after their interview for legalization or SAW status. It is valid for a period of six months from issuance and has the expiration date stated on the face of the card.

DOCUMENT LIST B.

Sample Driver's License

A driver's license issued by any state (including the District of Columbia, Puerto Rico, the Virgin Islands and Guam) or by a Canadian govern-ment authority is acceptable if it contains a photograph or other indentifying information such as name, date of birth, sex, height, color of eyes and address.

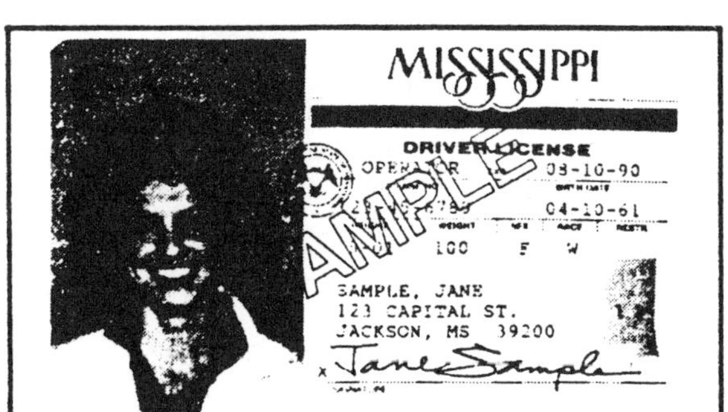

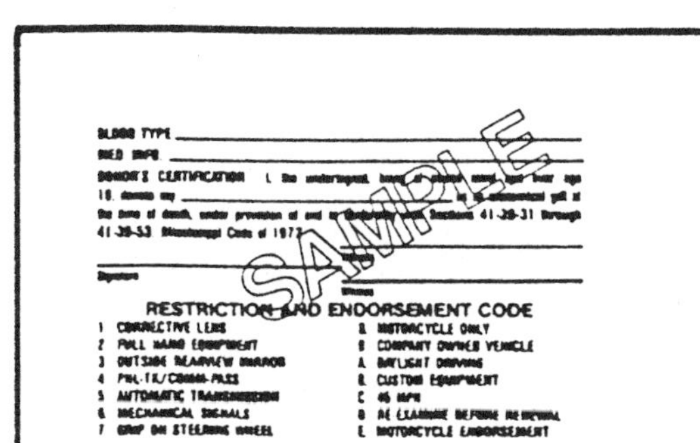

Sample State Identification Card

An identification card issued by any state (including the District of Columbia, Puerto Rico, the Virgin Islands and Guam) is acceptable if it contains a photograph or other identifying information such as name, date of birth, sex, height, color of eyes and address.

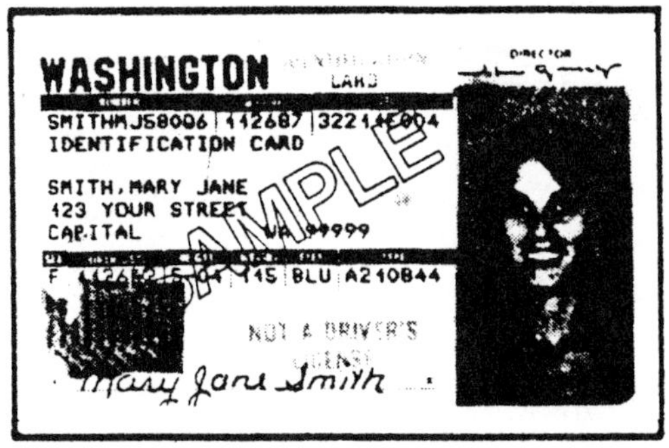

WASHINGTON
SMITHMJ580O6 | 112687 | 322144E004
IDENTIFICATION CARD
SMITH, MARY JANE
123 YOUR STREET
CAPITAL WA 99999
F 112687 5-04 115 BLU A210844
NOT A DRIVER'S LICENSE
SAMPLE

DOCUMENT LIST C.

Social Security Card

SOCIAL SECURITY
THIS NUMBER HAS BEEN ESTABLISHED FOR
SIGNATURE
SAMPLE

This card is invalid if laminated.

This card is invalid if not signed by the number holder unless health or age prevents signature.

Improper use of this card and/or number by the number holder or any other person is punishable by fine, imprisonment or both.

This card is the property of the Social Security Administration and must be returned upon request. If found, return to:
SSA—PO Box 17087
Baltimore, MD 21203
ATTN: FOUND SSN CARD (Return postage guaranteed)

Department of Health and Human Services
Social Security Administration
Form OA-702 (10-83)
B05193176

SAMPLE

Sample Birth Certificates

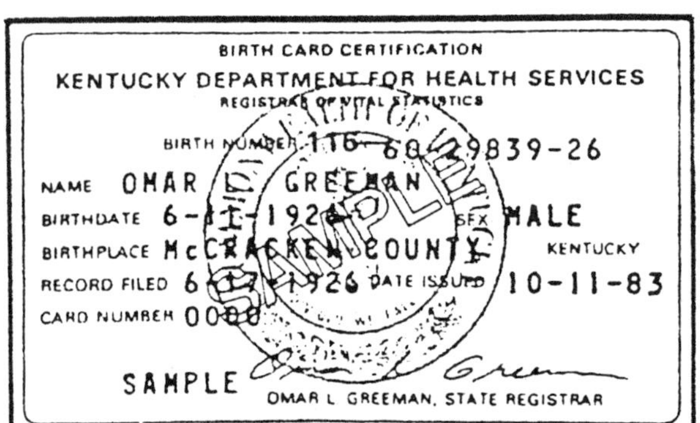

BIRTH CARD CERTIFICATION
KENTUCKY DEPARTMENT FOR HEALTH SERVICES
REGISTRAR OF VITAL STATISTICS
BIRTH NUMBER 116-60-29839-26
NAME OMAR L. GREEMAN
BIRTHDATE 6-11-1926 SEX MALE
BIRTHPLACE McCRACKEN COUNTY KENTUCKY
RECORD FILED 6-17-1926 DATE ISSUED 10-11-83
CARD NUMBER 0000
SAMPLE
OMAR L GREEMAN, STATE REGISTRAR

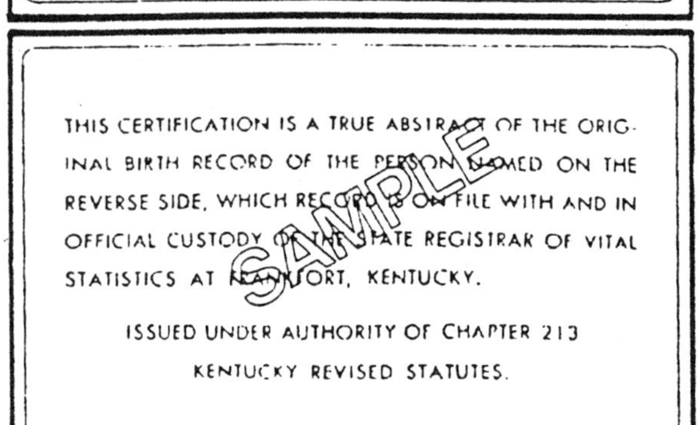

THIS CERTIFICATION IS A TRUE ABSTRACT OF THE ORIGINAL BIRTH RECORD OF THE PERSON NAMED ON THE REVERSE SIDE, WHICH RECORD IS ON FILE WITH AND IN OFFICIAL CUSTODY OF THE STATE REGISTRAR OF VITAL STATISTICS AT FRANKFORT, KENTUCKY.

ISSUED UNDER AUTHORITY OF CHAPTER 213 KENTUCKY REVISED STATUTES.

SAMPLE

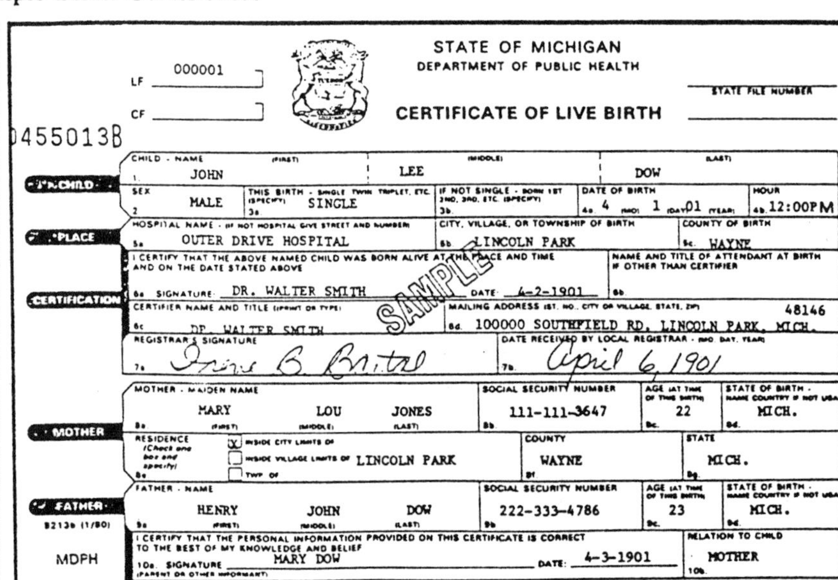

STATE OF MICHIGAN
DEPARTMENT OF PUBLIC HEALTH
CERTIFICATE OF LIVE BIRTH
LF 000001
CF
0455013B
STATE FILE NUMBER

CHILD: JOHN LEE DOW; SEX MALE; THIS BIRTH SINGLE; DATE OF BIRTH 4 1 01; HOUR 12:00PM
PLACE: OUTER DRIVE HOSPITAL; LINCOLN PARK; COUNTY WAYNE
CERTIFICATION: I CERTIFY THAT THE ABOVE NAMED CHILD WAS BORN ALIVE AT THE PLACE AND TIME AND ON THE DATE STATED ABOVE
SIGNATURE DR. WALTER SMITH DATE 4-2-1901
CERTIFIER NAME AND TITLE DR. WALTER SMITH
MAILING ADDRESS 100000 SOUTHFIELD RD. LINCOLN PARK, MICH. 48146
DATE RECEIVED BY LOCAL REGISTRAR April 6, 1901
MOTHER: MARY LOU JONES; SOCIAL SECURITY NUMBER 111-111-3647; AGE 22; STATE OF BIRTH MICH.
RESIDENCE LINCOLN PARK; COUNTY WAYNE; STATE MICH.
FATHER: HENRY JOHN DOW; SOCIAL SECURITY NUMBER 222-333-4786; AGE 23; STATE OF BIRTH MICH.
I CERTIFY THAT THE PERSONAL INFORMATION PROVIDED ON THIS CERTIFICATE IS CORRECT TO THE BEST OF MY KNOWLEDGE AND BELIEF
SIGNATURE MARY DOW DATE 4-3-1901 RELATION TO CHILD MOTHER
MDPH
SAMPLE

Unexpired Re-Entry Permit I-327

Issued by INS to lawful permanent resident (lawful immigrant) aliens before they leave the United States for a one to two year period.

UNITED STATES
DEPARTMENT OF JUSTICE
★
Immigration and Naturalization Service

PERMIT TO REENTER THE UNITED STATES
★

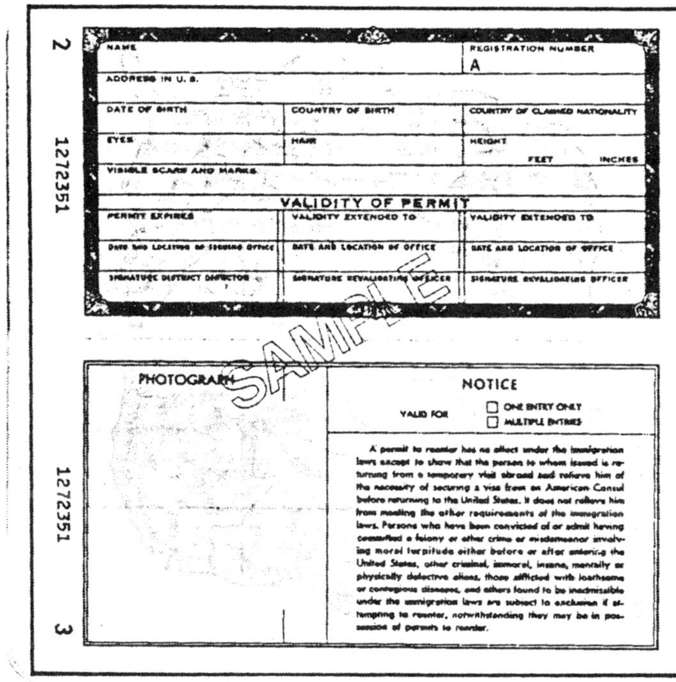

2 1272351

NAME | REGISTRATION NUMBER A
ADDRESS IN U. S.
DATE OF BIRTH | COUNTRY OF BIRTH | COUNTRY OF CLAIMED NATIONALITY
EYES | HAIR | HEIGHT FEET INCHES
VISIBLE SCARS AND MARKS
VALIDITY OF PERMIT
PERMIT EXPIRES | VALIDITY EXTENDED TO | VALIDITY EXTENDED TO
DATE AND LOCATION OF ISSUING OFFICE | DATE AND LOCATION OF OFFICE | DATE AND LOCATION OF OFFICE
SIGNATURE DISTRICT DIRECTOR | SIGNATURE REVALIDATING OFFICER | SIGNATURE REVALIDATING OFFICER

SAMPLE

PHOTOGRAPH

NOTICE

VALID FOR ☐ ONE ENTRY ONLY ☐ MULTIPLE ENTRIES

A permit to reenter has no effect under the immigration laws except to show that the person to whom issued is returning from a temporary visit abroad and relieve him of the necessity of securing a visa from an American Consul before returning to the United States. It does not relieve him from meeting the other requirements of the immigration laws. Persons who have been convicted of or admit having committed a felony or other crime or misdemeanor involving moral turpitude either before or after entering the United States, other criminal, immoral, insane, mentally or physically defective aliens, those afflicted with loathsome or contagious diseases, and others found to be inadmissible under the immigration laws are subject to exclusion if attempting to reenter, notwithstanding they may be in possession of permits to reenter.

1272351 3

Unexpired Refugee Travel Document I-571

Issued by INS to aliens who have been granted refugee status. The expiration date is stated on page four.

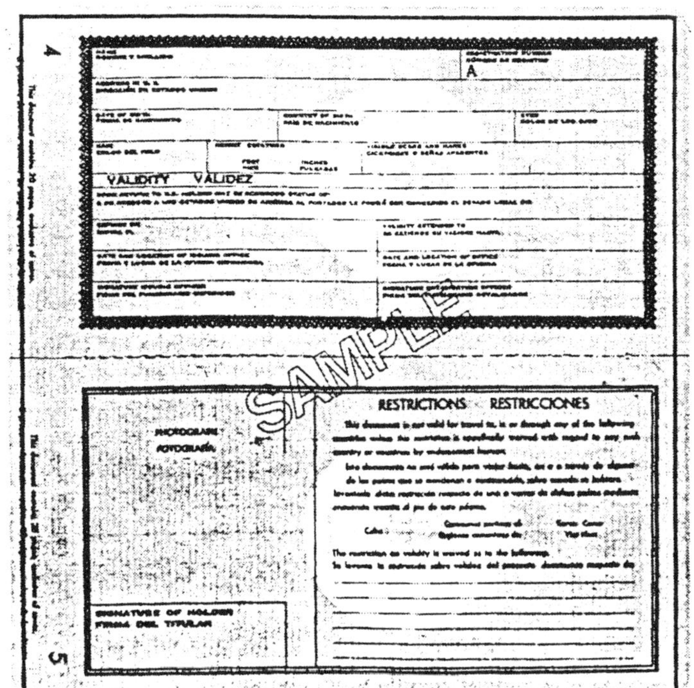

4

A

VALIDITY VALIDEZ

SAMPLE

RESTRICTIONS RESTRICCIONES

PHOTOGRAPH FOTOGRAFIA

SIGNATURE OF HOLDER FIRMA DEL TITULAR

5

Certification of Birth issued by the Department of State FS-545

Issued by U.S. embassies and consulates overseas to United States citizens born abroad.

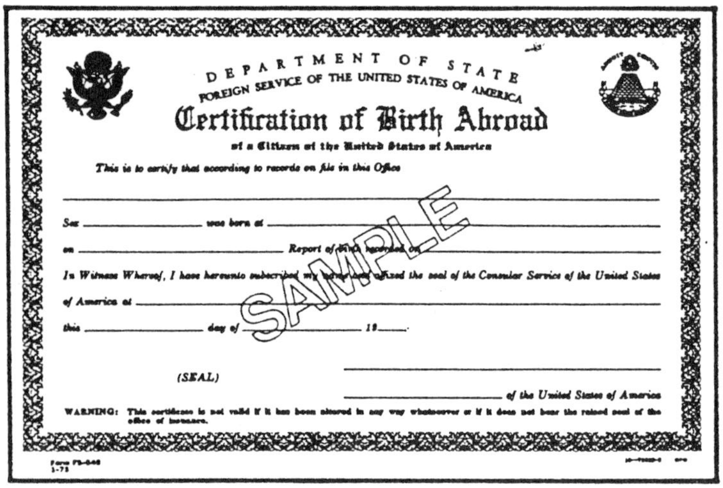

DEPARTMENT OF STATE
FOREIGN SERVICE OF THE UNITED STATES OF AMERICA
Certification of Birth Abroad
of a Citizen of the United States of America
This is to certify that according to records on file in this Office
Sex ______ was born at ______
on ______ Report of Birth recorded on ______
In Witness Whereof, I have hereunto subscribed my name and affixed the seal of the Consular Service of the United States of America at ______
this ______ day of ______ 19___.
(SEAL)
______ of the United States of America
WARNING: This certificate is not valid if it has been altered in any way whatsoever or if it does not bear the raised seal of the office of issuance.
SAMPLE

Certification of Birth issued by the Department of State DS-1350

Issued by the U.S. Department of State to United States citizens born abroad.

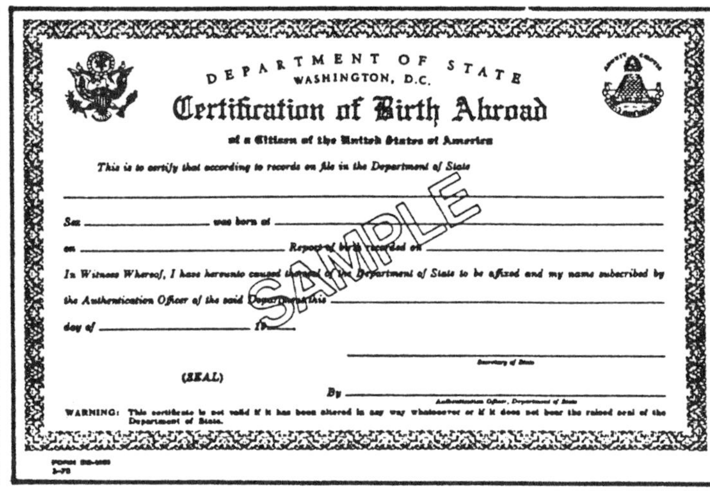

DEPARTMENT OF STATE
WASHINGTON, D.C.
Certification of Birth Abroad
of a Citizen of the United States of America
This is to certify that according to records on file in the Department of State
Sex ______ was born at ______
on ______ Report of Birth recorded on ______
In Witness Whereof, I have hereunto caused the seal of the Department of State to be affixed and my name subscribed by the Authentication Officer of the said Department, this ______
day of ______ 19___.
(SEAL)
Secretary of State
By ______
Authentication Officer, Department of State
WARNING: This certificate is not valid if it has been altered in any way whatsoever or if it does not bear the raised seal of the Department of State.
SAMPLE

United States Citizen Identification Card I-197

Issued by INS to United States citizens. INS no longer issues this card.

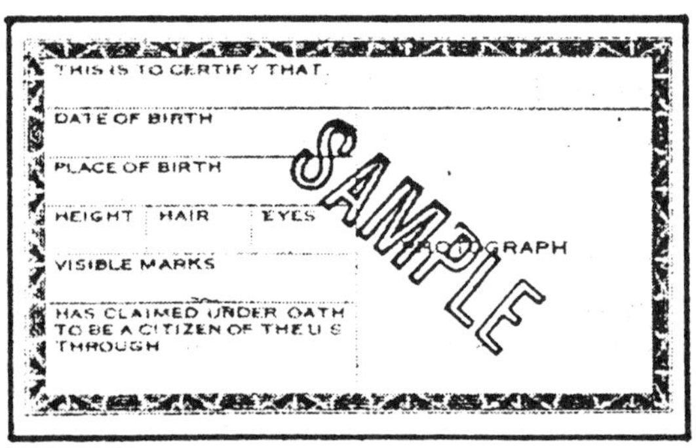

THIS IS TO CERTIFY THAT
DATE OF BIRTH
PLACE OF BIRTH
HEIGHT | HAIR | EYES
VISIBLE MARKS
HAS CLAIMED UNDER OATH TO BE A CITIZEN OF THE U S THROUGH
PHOTOGRAPH
SAMPLE

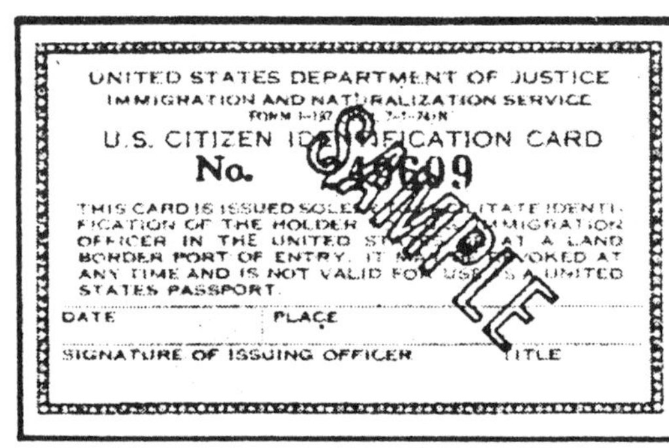

UNITED STATES DEPARTMENT OF JUSTICE
IMMIGRATION AND NATURALIZATION SERVICE
U.S. CITIZEN IDENTIFICATION CARD
No. 248609
THIS CARD IS ISSUED SOLELY TO FACILITATE IDENTIFICATION OF THE HOLDER TO AN IMMIGRATION OFFICER IN THE UNITED STATES AT A LAND BORDER PORT OF ENTRY. IT MAY BE REVOKED AT ANY TIME AND IS NOT VALID FOR USE AS A UNITED STATES PASSPORT.
DATE | PLACE
SIGNATURE OF ISSUING OFFICER | TITLE
SAMPLE

Identification Card for use of Resident Citizen in the United States I-179

Issued by INS to United States citizens who are residents of the United States. INS no longer issues this card.

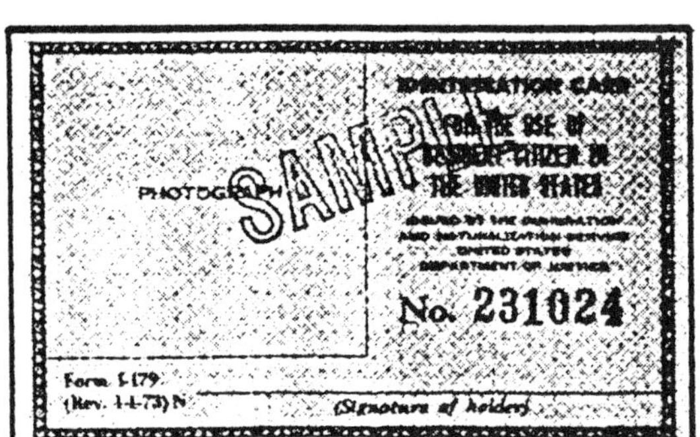

PHOTOGRAPH
IDENTIFICATION CARD
FOR THE USE OF RESIDENT CITIZEN IN THE UNITED STATES
ISSUED BY THE IMMIGRATION AND NATURALIZATION SERVICE
UNITED STATES DEPARTMENT OF JUSTICE
No. 231024
Form I-179
(Rev. 1-1-73) N
(Signature of holder)
SAMPLE

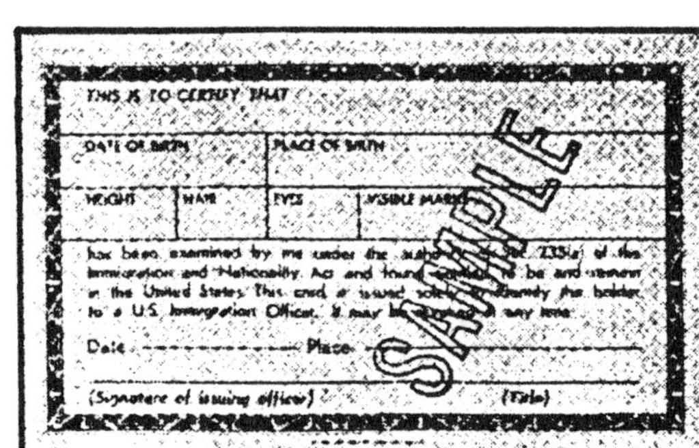

THIS IS TO CERTIFY THAT
DATE OF BIRTH | PLACE OF BIRTH
HEIGHT | HAIR | EYES | VISIBLE MARKS
has been examined by me under the authority of Sec. 235(a) of the Immigration and Nationality Act and found to be and remain in the United States. This card is issued solely to identify the holder to a U.S. Immigration Officer. It may be revoked at any time.
Date ______ Place ______
(Signature of issuing officer) | (Title)
SAMPLE

How to Obtain More Information

If you have questions after reviewing this Handbook, you may obtain information from one of the following local INS offices. Direct your letter to the attention of the *Employer Relations Officer*.

ALABAMA
75 Spring Street S.W.
Atlanta, GA 30303

ALASKA
701 "C" Street, Room D-251
Lock Box 16
Anchorage, AK 99513

ARIZONA
230 North First Avenue
Phoenix, AZ 85025

ARKANSAS
701 Loyola Avenue, Room T-8005
New Orleans, LA 70113

CALIFORNIA
300 North Los Angeles Street
Los Angeles, CA 90012

880 Front Street
San Diego, CA 92188

630 Sansome Street
San Francisco, CA 94111

COLORADO
1787 Federal Building
1961 Stout Street
Denver, CO 80202

CONNECTICUT
JFK Federal Building
Government Center
Boston, MA 02203

DELAWARE
601 Market Street
Room 1321, U.S. Courthouse
Philadelphia, PA 19106

DISTRICT OF COLUMBIA
4420 North Fairfax Drive
Arlington, VA 22203

FLORIDA
7880 Biscayne Boulevard
Miami, FL 33138

GEORGIA
75 Spring Street S.W.
Atlanta, GA 30303

GUAM
595 Ala Moana Boulevard
Honolulu, HI 96813

HAWAII
595 Ala Moana Boulevard
Honolulu, HI 96813

IDAHO
Federal Building, Room 512
310 South Park, Drawer 10036
Helena, MT 59626-0036

ILLINOIS
219 South Dearborn Street
Chicago, IL 60604

INDIANA
219 South Dearborn Street
Chicago, IL 60604

IOWA
Federal Building, Room 1008
106 South 15th Street
Omaha, NE 68102

KANSAS
9747 North Conant Avenue
Kansas City, MO 64153

KENTUCKY
701 Loyola Avenue, Room T-8005
New Orleans, LA 70113

LOUISIANA
701 Loyola Avenue, Room T-8005
New Orleans, LA 70113

MAINE
P.O. Box 578, Downtown Station
Portland, ME 04112

MARYLAND
101 West Lombard Street
Baltimore, MD 21201

MASSACHUSETTS
JFK Federal Building
Government Center
Boston, MA 02203

MICHIGAN
333 Mount Elliott Street
Detroit, MI 48207

MINNESOTA
927 Main Post Office Building
St. Paul, MN 55101

MISSISSIPPI
701 Loyola Avenue, Room T-8005
New Orleans, LA 70113

MISSOURI
9747 North Conant Avenue
Kansas City, MO 64153

MONTANA
Federal Building, Room 512
310 South Park, Drawer 10036
Helena, MT 59626-0036

NEBRASKA
Federal Building, Room 1008
106 South 15th Street
Omaha, NE 68102

NEVADA
230 North First Avenue
Phoenix, AZ 85025

NEW HAMPSHIRE
JFK Federal Building
Government Center
Boston, MA 02203

NEW JERSEY
970 Broad Street
Newark, NJ 07102

NEW MEXICO
343 U.S. Courthouse
P.O. Box 9398
El Paso, TX 79984

NEW YORK
68 Court Street
Buffalo, NY 14202

26 Federal Plaza
New York, NY 10278

NORTH CAROLINA
75 Spring Street S.W.
Atlanta, GA 30303

NORTH DAKOTA
927 Main Post Office Building
St. Paul, MN 55101

OHIO
1240 East 9th Street, Room 1917
Cleveland, OH 44199

OKLAHOMA
Federal Building, Room 6A 21
1100 Commerce Street
Dallas, TX 75242

OREGON
511 N.W. Broadway
Portland, OR 97209

PENNSYLVANIA
601 Market Street
Room 1321, U.S. Courthouse
Philadelphia, PA 19106

PUERTO RICO
GPO Box 5068
San Juan, Puerto Rico 00936

RHODE ISLAND
JFK Federal Building
Government Center
Boston, MA 02203

SOUTH CAROLINA
75 Spring Room S.W.
Atlanta, GA 30303

SOUTH DAKOTA
927 Main Post Office Building
St. Paul, MN 55101

TENNESSEE
701 Loyola Avenue, Room T-8005
New Orleans, LA 70113

TEXAS
Federal Building, Room 6A 21
1100 Commerce Street
Dallas, TX 75242

P.O. Box 9398
El Paso, TX 79984

2102 Teege Road
Harlingen, TX 78550

2627 Caroline Street
Houston, TX 77004

727 East Durango, Suite A301
San Antonio, TX 78206

UTAH
1787 Federal Building
1961 Stout Street
Denver, CO 80202

VERMONT
P.O. Box 578, Downtown Station
Portland, ME 04112

VIRGINIA
4420 North Fairfax Drive
Arlington, VA 22203

VIRGIN ISLANDS
GPO Box 5068
San Juan, Puerto Rico 00936

WASHINGTON
815 Airport Way South
Seattle, WA 98134

WEST VIRGINIA
601 Market Street
Room 1321, U.S. Courthouse
Philadelphia, PA 19106

WISCONSIN
219 South Dearborn Street
Chicago, IL 60604

WYOMING
1787 Federal Building
1961 Stout Street
Denver, CO 80202

BORDER PATROL HEADQUARTERS

1590 H Street
P.O. Drawer V
Blaine, WA 98230

P.O. Box 2020
Del Rio, TX 78841-2020

P.O. Box 32639
Detroit, MI 48232

1111 North Imperial Avenue
P.O. Box 60
El Centro, CA 92243

P.O. Box 9578
El Paso, TX 79986

P.O. Box 1657
Grand Forks, ND 58206-1657

P.O. Box 112
Havre, MT 59501

P.O. Box 706
Houlton, ME 04730

207 West Del Mar Boulevard
Laredo, TX 78041

P.O. Box 1
Marfa, TX 79843

2301 South Main Street
McAllen, TX 78501

161 N.E. 183rd Street
P.O. Box 3663 Norland Branch
Miami, FL 33169

P.O. Box 6218
New Orleans, LA 70174

P.O. Box 880
Pleasanton, CA 94566

3752 Beyer Boulevard
San Ysidro, CA 92073-9022

P.O. Box 18930
Spokane, WA 99208

Grand Avenue
P.O. Box 705
Swanton, VT 05488

1970 West Ajo Way
Tucson, AZ 85713

231 Grand Island Boulevard
Tonawanda, NY 14150

P.O. Box 2708
Yuma, AZ 85364

Appendix D

Free Help

Think about it: you will end up putting a lot on the line by having your own business. Even if you have not put in a lot of money, you are investing your ideas, your reputation, and your energy. The time you put into your business could be put elsewhere, making money working for someone else. This shows again the truth of the old adage "time is money."

With all you have to lose, it makes sense to do what you can to make your business succeed. A thousand dollars not spent on planning may cost you ten thousand later. That's why smart California business folks don't mind asking for help. But even the smart ones may not think of all the possible help available. Luckily, a lot of that help is available free.

Talk to People

It is amazing what you can learn by asking questions. Consider the following:

Say you are considering buying an automobile muffler repair shop. First, you could get on the phone and call a couple of suppliers. Call the big muffler manufacturers back East. Ask them to tell you why you should carry their mufflers if you start a muffler repair business. Who knows what you may learn! For one thing, you may actually find a new supplier. If someone offers to help set you up in business, and offers to extend credit, you may find an offer you can't refuse. More likely, you will learn something about the muffler industry, and about the strengths and weaknesses of the products of your potential future competitors.

What about your banker? Maybe you have never thought of a banker as a source of business advice, but you should. Tell him or her that you are considering going into business and you want to know what this bank has to offer a small business. Banks want new business, so it should be easy to find someone who will be happy to talk to you. Then, after you establish rapport, mention the muffler business you are considering. See if the banker volunteers any ideas, good or bad. Maybe the banker will even mention a "muffler shop that is going broke." If you listen closely, you may find that the exact muffler shop you plan to buy is not the gold mine you thought it was, but on the verge of going out of business. If so, it may be time to reconsider the deal.

You will need insurance for your new business, right? Shop around for an insurance agent who knows business, and while you are talking to them, mention your muffler shop idea. You have a legitimate interest in finding an insurance agent who may know the special insurance needs of muffler shops. But, there is an added benefit here if you do this checking *before* you buy your muffler shop: Once you have found an insurance agent who knows the muffler business, you have another potential source of information. Your insurance agent may know why such-and-such muffler shop went out of business. Any stories you hear about "the muffler shop that got into trouble" or "the muffler shop owner who got rich and retired in Palm Springs" will help you judge your chances of success. And, again, the insurance agent stories amount to free help.

Also, check your local board of Realtors or the phone book for names of business brokers. Every town has some real estate agents who specialize in sales of *businesses* as opposed to residences. Even if you have your exact muffler shop in mind, why not check a couple of business brokers? Who knows, they may have a muffler shop or two for sale. If the shop they try to sell you costs twice your price and appears to be earning half as much, you have learned something useful. On the other hand, if the broker has a muffler shop that looks twice as good as your gold mine but is selling for half the price, maybe it is time to reconsider. Incidentally, you might want to consider visiting with a business broker in a bigger city nearby. Two possible benefits may come your way. First, the broker may offer you such a deal (on a pet shop, maybe!) that you completely drop your muffler shop idea. Second, the deals that the broker offers you will give you benchmarks against which to measure your gold mine of a muffler shop.

You will probably want a bookkeeper or accountant to help you with your business sooner or later. Early on, before you start your business, talk to a few listed in the phone book. Ask how much it would cost to handle the books of a muffler shop business. Meanwhile, watch the person's eyes, and look for other body language clues. Maybe the look on their face will tell you that this accountant thinks for this town at this time, any muffler shop is an incredibly stupid business. If you get this kind of message, you have learned something that you need to consider. And, as with all the people you talked to described above, the knowledge came to you free!

Small Business Institutes

You probably know that many college business professors do consulting, for a fee. You may not think of your local college as a source of *free* consulting, but it is possible. Dozens of California schools have Small Business Institutes. SBIs receive support from the U.S. Small Business Administration, and send teams of seniors or graduate students to help evaluate your business. Sometimes SBI teams will focus on marketing, other times on your bookkeeping, and sometimes on your overall business strategy. The cost to you? Absolutely nothing!

Although the list of colleges that have Small Business Institutes changes from time to time, the following colleges had SBI programs as of 1993:

Los Angeles District

Antelope Valley College
Small Business Institute
3041 W. Ave. K
Lancaster, CA 93536
(805) 943-3241

California Lutheran College
Small Business Institute
60 W. Olsen Road
Thousand Oaks, CA 91360
(805) 493-3361

Cal Poly Pomona
Small Business Institute
3801 W. Temple Avenue
Pomona, CA 91768
(714) 869-2359

Cal State Dominguez Hills
Small Business Institute
1000 E. Victoria
Dominguez Hills, CA 90747
(310) 516-3551

Cal State Long Beach
Small Business Institute
6101 E. Seventh St.
Long Beach, CA 90840
(310) 985-4111

Cal State Los Angeles
Small Business Institute
5151 State University Drive
Los Angeles, CA 90032
(213) 343-2972

Cal State Northridge
Small Business Institute
18111 Nordhoff Street
Northridge, CA 91330
(818) 885-2070

Loyola Marymount University
Small Business Institute
7101 W. 80th
Los Angeles, CA 90045
(310) 338-2700

UCLA
Small Business Institute
405 Hilgard
Los Angeles, CA 90024
(213) 825-3045

Westmont College
Small Business Institute
955 La Paz Road
Santa Barbara, CA 93108
(805) 565-6182

Orange County District

Cal State Fullerton
Small Business Institute
800 N. State College Blvd.
Fullerton, CA 92634
(714) 773-2251

Cal State San Bernardino
Management Department
5500 State College Parkway
San Bernardino, CA 92407
(714) 880-5740

Rancho Santiago College
Small Business Institute
17th at Bristol
Santa Ana, CA 92706
(714) 564-6000

San Diego District

Point Loma Nazarene College
Small Business Institute
3900 Lomaland Drive
San Diego, CA 92106
(619) 221-2328

San Diego State University
Small Business Institute
San Diego, CA 92182-0092
(619) 594-5328

San Francisco District

Cal State Chico
Small Business Institute
School of Business
Third & Chestnut
Chico, CA 95929
(916) 898-5193

Cal State Hayward
Small Business Institute
22800 Carlos Bee Blvd.
Hayward, CA 94542
(510) 881-3000

Cal State Sacramento
Small Business Institute
6000 "J" Street
Sacramento, CA 95819
(916) 278-6203

De Anza College
Small Business Institute
21250 Stevens Creek Blvd.
Cupertino, CA 95014
(408) 864-5678

Humboldt State University
Small Business Institute
Arcata, CA 95521
(707) 826-4762

San Francsisco State University
Small Business Institute
1600 Holloway
San Francisco, CA 94132
(415) 338-2397

Fresno District

Cal-Poly San Luis Obispo
Small Business Institute
San Luis Obispo, CA 93407
(805) 756-2657

Cal State Bakersfield
Small Business Institute
9001 Stockdale Highway
Bakersfield, CA 93301
(805) 664-2175

Cal State Fresno
Small Business Institute
Fresno, CA 93740
(209) 278-2496

Cal State Stanislaus
Small Business Institute
800 Norte Vista Avenue
Turlock, CA 95380
(209) 667-3672

Small Business Development Centers

While Small Business Institutes have a good price (free), they do not usually help businesses in the start-up phase. Usually you must be in business a year or so before an SBI is willing to send students to look at your business. The idea is that student consultants can help in many ways, but start-ups are so difficult that it may be a bit much to ask for students to give advice before that first critical year has been conquered. Not to worry: there is another source of free help that has no "one-year survivor" restrictions. California has a series of Small Business Development Centers (SBDCs), and SBDCs will talk to you even if your business is still in the planning stage. The price for the consulting help is the same, free, but the consultants will most likely be professionals, employed on a consulting basis by the SBDC. It is free to you, but the consultant you get is a paid professional. By all means, run your business idea past the folks at one of the following locations (as of 1993):

Accelerate Technology Assistance Small Business Development Center
Graduate School of Management
University of California Irvine
Irvine, CA 92717-4125
(714) 856-8366
Tiffany Haugen, Interim Director
Fax # (714) 725-2978

Butte College Tri-County Small Business Development Center
260 Cohasset Avenue
Chico, CA 95926
(916) 895-9017
Kay Zimmerlee, Director
Fax # (916) 895-9099
Provides services in Butte, Glenn, and Tehama Counties.

Central California Small Business Development Center
2208 Tuolumne Street
Fresno, CA 93721
(209) 237-0660
Dennis Winans, Director
Fax # (209) 278-6964
Provides services in Fresno, Madera, Kings, and Tulare Counties.

Central Coast Small Business Development Center
6500 Soquel Drive
Aptos, CA 95003
(408) 479-6136
Elza Minor, Director
Fax # (408) 479-5743
Provides services in Santa Cruz and Monterey County west of Highway 101.

East Bay Small Business Development Center
2201 Broadway, Suite 701
Oakland, CA 94612

(510) 893-4114
Selma Taylor, Director
Fax # (510) 893-5532
Provides services in Alameda County.

East Los Angeles County Small Business Development Center
363 S. Park Avenue, Suite 100
Pomona, CA 91766
(909) 629-2247
Toni Valdez, Director
Fax # (909) 629-8310
Provides services in East Los Angeles (East L.A., Pasadena, Glendale, West Covina, and Pomona)

Export Small Business Development Center of Southern California
110 E. 9th, Suite A761
Los Angeles, CA 90079
(213) 892-1111
Gladys Moreau, Director
Fax # (213) 892-8232
Provides services in Los Angeles, Ventura, and Santa Barbara counties.

Export Satellite Center
300 Esplanade Drive, Suite 1010
Oxnard, CA 93030
(805) 981-4633
Jana Goldsworthy, Director
Fax # (805) 988-1862
Provides services in Ventura County.

Gavilan College Small Business Development Center
5055 Santa Teresa Boulevard
Gilroy, CA 95020
(408) 847-0373
Peter Graff, Director
Fax # (408) 847-0393
Provides services in southern Santa Clara, San Benito, and Monterey County east of Highway 101 counties.

Greater Sacramento Small Business Development Center
1787 Tribute Road, Suite A
Sacramento, CA 95815
(916) 263-6580
Helder Sebastiao, Interim Director
Fax # (916) 263-6571
Provides services in Sacramento, El Dorado, and Yolo Counties.

Greater San Diego Chamber of Commerce Small Business Development Center
4275 Executive Square, Suite 920
La Jolla, CA 92037
(619) 453-9388
Maria Morris, Director
Fax # (619) 450-1997
Provides services in northern San Diego County.

Inland Empire Small Business Development Center
1860 Chicago Avenue, Bldg. I, Suite 1
Riverside, CA 92507
(909) 781-2345
Teri Corrazini, Director
Fax # (909) 781-2353
Provides services in Riverside and San Bernardino counties.

Napa Valley College Small Business Development Center
1556 First Street, Suite 103
Napa, CA 94559
(707) 253-3210
Michael Kauffman, Director
Fax # (707) 253-3068
Provides services in Napa County.

North Coast Small Business Development Center
779 9th Street
Crescent City, CA 95531
(707) 464-2168
Fran Clark, Director
Fax # (707) 465-6008
Provides services in Del Norte and Humboldt counties.

North Coast Small Business Development Center
408 7th Street, Suite "E"
Eureka, CA 95501
(707) 445-9720
Duff Heuttner, Business Counselor
Fax # (707) 445-9652

North Los Angeles Small Business Development Center
14540 Victory Boulevard, Suite #206
Van Nuys, CA 91411
(818) 373-7092
Fax # (818) 373-7740
Provides services in Burbank, Van Nuys, and San Fernando Valley.

Orange County Small Business Development Center
901 East Santa Ana Boulevard, Suite 108
Santa Ana, CA 92701
(714) 647-1172

Gregory Kishel, Director
Fax # (714) 835-9008
Provides service in Orange County.

Redwood Empire Small Business Development Center
2300 County Center Drive, Suite B177
Santa Rosa, CA 95403
(707) 527-2132
Helder Sebastiao, Interim Director
Fax # (707) 527-2407
Provides service in the Santa Rosa metropolitan area, and Lake and Mendocino counties.

Lake County Satellite
341 North Main Street
Lakeport, CA 95453
(707) 263-6180
Dana Parker, Secretary
Fax # (707) 263-0920
Provides service in Lake county.

San Joaquin Delta College
Small Business Development Center
814 N. Hunter
Stockton, CA 95202
(209) 474-5089
Gillian Murphy, Director
Fax # (209) 474-5605
Providing services in San Joaquin, Calaveras, Amador, and Alpine counties.

Sierra College Small Business Development Center
560 Wall Street, Suite J
Auburn, CA 95603
(916) 885-5488
Mary Wollesen, Director
Fax # (916) 823-4704
Provides services in Sierra, Placer, and Nevada counties.

Silicon Valley/San Mateo County Small Business Development Center
111 N. Market Street, #150
San Jose, CA 95113
(408) 298-7694
Daniel Aloot, Director
Fax # (408) 971-0680
Provides services in San Mateo and Northern Santa Clara counties.

Silicon Valley/San Mateo County Small Business Development Center
1730 S. Amphlett Blvd., Suite 208
San Mateo, CA 94402
(415) 358-0271
Phyllis Schneider, Director
Fax # (415) 358-9450
Provides services in San Mateo County and Silicon Valley.

Solano County Small Business Development Center
320 Campus Lane
Suisun, CA 94585
(707) 864-3382
Ed Schlenker, Director
Fax # (707) 864-3386
Provides services in Solano County.

Southwest Los Angeles County Small Business Development Center
21221 Western Avenue, Suite 110
Torrance, CA 90501
(310) 782-3861
Bart Hoffman, Director
Fax # (310) 782-8607
Provides services in Southwest Los Angeles County.

Southwestern College Small Business Development and International Trade Center
900 Otay Lakes Road, Bldg. 1600
Chula Vista, CA 91910
(619) 482-6393
Mary Wylie, Director
Fax # (619) 482-6402
Provides services in southern San Diego County.

Valley Sierra Small Business Development Center
1012 Eleventh Street, Suite 300
Modesto, CA 95354
(209) 521-6177
Kelly Bearden, Director
Fax # (209) 521-9373
Provides services in Merced, Mariposa, Stanislaus and Tuolumne Counties.

Valley Sierra Small Business Development Center
1632 "N" Street
Merced, CA 95340
(209) 385-7312
Joan Sullivan, Director
Fax # (209) 383-4959

Weill Institute Small Business Development Center
1330 22nd St. Suite B
Bakersfield, CA 93301
(805) 322-5881

Jeffrey Johnson, Director
Fax # (805) 395-4134
Provides services in Kern, Inyo, and Mono Counties.

For further information contact:

California Small Business Development Center Program
Office of Small Business
Agency of Trade and Commerce
801 K Street, Suite 1700
Sacramento, CA 95814
(916) 324-5068
Fax (916) 322-5084

Know the SCORE

A third source of government supported free advice is SCORE, the Service Corps of Retired Executives. This is a U.S. Small Business Administration assisted program that puts small business people in touch with volunteers, retired or active. Again, their advice to you is free for the asking. Most SCORE counseling sessions last an hour or so, but some clients get around ten hours of free consultation. In addition to the free one-to-one advising, many SCORE chapters run free or very low-cost Small Business Seminars. Check into it! You may find a seminar on "Marketing Your Small Business" or "How to Start a Small Business" or "Cash Flow Problems of the Small Business." Many of these workshops are held evenings or Saturdays so people who want to keep their current job while scoping out a new business can attend.

Check the following list for a SCORE contact in your area. Or, contact the nearest office of the U.S. Small Business Administration if the numbers listed here do not work for you. Or, look at your Pacific Bell Yellow Pages. Immediately before the yellow pages begin, there is a green-page section. On the last green page in most California phone books there is a section that describes SCORE and lists SCORE regional offices throughout the state. One way or another, do it! These are good people.

SCORE Counseling Locations

All sessions are by appointment only.

ARROYO GRANDE
Chamber of Commerce
150 E. Branch Street
(805) 489-1488

ATASCADERO
Chamber of Commerce
6550 El Camino Real
(805) 466-2044

BAKERSFIELD
Chamber of Commerce
1033 Truxtun Avenue
(805) 327-4421

CALIFORNIA CITY
Chamber of Commerce
Box 8048
(619) 373-8676

CAMBRIA
Chamber of Commerce
518 Canterbury Lane
(805) 927-1366

CAPITOLA
Chamber of Commerce
621B Capitola Avenue
(408) 475-6522

CHICO
500 Main Street
P.O. Box 3038
(916) 891-5556

FRESNO
SBA District Office
2719 N. Air Fresno Dr., Suite 107
(209) 487-5605 ext. 726

GLENDALE
330 North Brand Boulevard, Suite 190
(213) 894-3016

GROVER CITY
Chamber of Commerce
177 So. 8th St.
(805) 489-9091

HANFORD
Chamber of Commerce
213 W. 7th Street
(209) 582-0483

HEMET
1700 E. Florida Avenue
(909) 652-4390

HOLLISTER
San Benito County EDC
321 San Felipe Road
(408) 636-1882

KERNVILLE/LAKE ISABELLA AREA
Kernville Chamber
Community Bldg., Kernville
(619) 376-2629

MARIPOSA
Mariposa County EDC
5320 Hwy. 49 North, Suite 2
(209) 966-5042

MERCED
Merced County SBDC
1632 N Street
(209) 385-7312

MODESTO
Stanislaus County EDC
1012 11th Street, Suite 201
(209) 521-9333

MONTEREY
P.O. Box 1770
(408) 649-1770

MONTEREY PENINSULA
Chamber of Commerce
380 Alvarado Street
(408) 648-5350

MORRO BAY
Chamber of Commerce
895 Napa, #A-1
(805) 772-4467

OAKLAND
2201 Broadway #701
(510) 273-6611

PALM SPRINGS
555 South Palm Canyon, Room A206
(619) 320-6682

PALMDALE
c/o Paul Heindel, Chair
2150 West Avenue 08
(805) 948-4518

PASO ROBLES
Chamber of Commerce
1118 Spring
(805) 238-0506

POMONA
c/o Chamber of Commerce
363 S. Park Avenue
(714) 622-1256

REDDING
747 Auditorium Drive
(916) 225-4433

REDLANDS
1251 E. Lugonia Avenue, #15
(714) 793-6656

RIDGECREST
Chamber of Commerce
301-A China Kale Blvd.
(619) 376-8331

SACRAMENTO
660 J Street, Suite 215
(916) 551-1446

SALINAS
Chamber of Commerce
119 E. Alisal Street
(408) 424-7611

SAN DIEGO
c/o SBA, 880 Front Street, Room 4237
(619) 557-7250

SAN FRANCISCO
211 Main Street, 4th Floor
(415) 744-6827

SAN JOSE
96 North 3rd Street, Suite 260
(408) 288-8479

SAN JUAN BAUTISTA
Chamber of Commerce
201 Third Street
(408) 623-2454

SAN LUIS OBISPO
Chamber of Commerce
1039 Chorro Street
(805) 543-1329

SANTA ANA
901 W. Civic Center Drive, Suite 160
(714) 836-2709

SANTA BARBARA
3227 State
(805) 563-0084

SANTA CRUZ
Chamber of Commerce
1543 Pacific Ave.
(408) 423-1111

SANTA MARIA
1650 East Clark Avenue, #252
(805) 934-2620

SANTA ROSA
La Plaza West/Suite B177
2300 County Center Drive
(707) 524-7171

SCOTTS VALLEY
Chamber of Commerce
10 Camp Evers
(408) 438-1010

SONORA
Chamber of Commerce
55 W. Stockton Road
(209) 532-4212

STOCKTON
401 N. San Joaquin Street, Room 215
(209) 946-6293

TAFT
Chamber of Commerce
314 4th Street
(805) 765-2165

TEHACHAPI
Chamber of Commerce
209 E. Tehachapi Blvd.
(805) 822-4180

VENTURA
c/o SBA, Suite 10, Bldg. C-1
8477 Telephone Road
(805) 642-1866

VISALIA
Tulare County EDC
2380 W. Whitendale
(209) 627-0766

WATSONVILLE
Chamber of Commerce
801 Freedom Blvd.
(408) 724-3849

Get a Telephone

Also worth mentioning is the California Small Business Advocate's telephone hotline. Just punch in (916) 327-HELP on your touchtone phone and be ready to listen to a tape-recorded message on anything from fictitious names to foreign trade. The topics covered by tapes include:

- Starting a business
- Financing resources
- State-sponsored financing
- Management and technical assistance
- State and local programs
- Federal small business programs
- Regulatory and tax considerations
- Information on toxics
- Settling disputes with state and federal agencies
- Current small business conferences and seminars and more . . .

If the recorded message isn't enough, you can punch in 3# and leave a message. If you give the machine your name and number, you'll get a call back as soon as a staff member can get to it.

Another useful telephone hotline is the SBA's toll-free "Answer Desk." Just dial 1-800-U-ASK-SBA, and a recording allows you to select useful information for small businesses in many areas including where to get financial assistance, opportunities for minorities and women, and where to get counseling and training. The hotline is open 24 hours a day, and if you call during the day you will get personal assistance.

Get a Modem

For those of you with access to a computer and modem, you can take advantage of the SBA's new on-line electronic bulletin board. "SBA On-Line" provides immediate, toll-free, 24-hour access to information including training programs, seminars, loan programs, and countless other SBA programs. Individuals with 2,400-baud modems can dial 1-800-859-INFO, and those with 9,600-baud modems can dial 1-800-697-INFO.

Special Help for Special Folks

Let's face it, in spite of the word "mom" in "mom-and-pop stores," most businesses large and small have traditionally been run by men. Take a closer look and you'll see that most businesses have been run by males who also happen to be white. California has nothing against white males, and indeed encourages plenty more white males to start and operate businesses. You may have noticed, all the free help sources discussed and listed above will serve anybody, without regard to race, color, gender, veteran status, etc. All are encouraged to "Go For It."

However this is not the end of the story. Because of several factors, today we have a lopsided white male world. There has been discrimination, and in the past not many women or minorities were encouraged to think about small businesses. There is still no such thing as a free lunch, but there are a few tips and suggestions to help make business ownership more accessible to those previously left out, from women to minorities to the disabled to veterans. This brief book will not go into detail on these rapidly changing programs, but be advised: if you are in a group with special needs, special help may be available. Of course you will want to follow all the advice given in this entire book. After all, in the final analysis, your business will be made or broken on your own.

Assuming that you have followed all the ideas given so far, now take time to ask around. Are there special groups or programs that could be of help to you? For example, NEDA has several offices around the state that offer special assistance to minority-owned businesses. How can you find out who might be available in your area to cater to groups with your special needs? Check the SBIs and SBDCs and the local SCORE chapter. Ask if there are programs with special advice or assistance that you should know about. In addition, consider checking the following:

Minority Business Development Centers (MBDC)

Anaheim MBDC (Serves Orange County)
Anaheim MBDC
Mirando, Strabala & Assoc.
856 N. Rosa Street, Suite 200
Santa Ana, CA 92701

Bakersfield MBDC (Serves Kern County)
NEDA—San Joaquin Valley, Inc.
218 So. H Street, Suite 103
Bakersfield, CA 93304
(805) 837-0291
Fax # (805) 837-0295

Fresno MBDC (Serves Fresno County)
NEDA—San Joaquin, Inc.
2010 N. Fine, Suite 103
Fresno, CA 93727
(209) 266-2766
Fax # (209) 266-8542

Los Angeles MBDC (Serves Los Angeles County)
1000 Wilshire Blvd., Suite 700
Los Angeles, CA 90017
(213) 627-1717

Los Angeles Minority Business Development Center
601 South Figueroa St., Suite 1370
Los Angeles, CA 90017
(213) 488-4949

Oxnard MBDC (Serves Ventura County)
Fountaine, Quintanilla & Associates
451 W. 5th Street
Oxnard, CA 93030
(805) 483-1123

Riverside MBDC (Serves Riverside/San Bernardino counties)
290 North "D" St., Suite 303
Riverside, CA 92401
(714) 386-5266

Sacramento MBDC (Serves Sacramento, Placer, Yolo counties)
NEDA San Joaquin Valley, Inc.
1779 Tribute Rd., Suite J
Sacramento, CA 95815
(916) 649-2551

Salinas MBDC (Serves Monterey County)
Salinas Minority Business Development Center
14 Maple St., Suite D
Salinas, CA 93901
(408) 422-8825

San Diego MBDC (Serves San Diego County)
San Diego State University Foundation
7777 Alvarado Court, Suite 310
La Mesa, CA 91941
(619) 668-6232

San Francisco MBDC—San Francisco Office (Serves San Francisco, Alameda, Contra Costa, Marin, San Mateo counties)
Grant Thornton
One California St., Suite 2100
San Francisco, CA 1941
(414) 989-2920

San Francsisco MBDC—Oakland Office (Serves San Francisco, Alameda, Contra Costa, Marin, San Mateo counties)
Grant Thornton
1000 Broadway, Suite 270
Oakland, CA 94607
(415) 465-6756

San Jose MBDC (Serves Santa Clara County)
150 Almaden Blvd., Suite 600
San Jose, CA 95150
(408) 275-9000

Santa Barbara MBDC (Serves Santa Barbara County)
Fontaine, Quintanilla & Associates
331 N. Milpas St., Suite G
Santa Barbara, CA 93103
(805) 965-2611

Stockton MBDC
NEDA
305 N. El Dorado St., Suite 200
Stockton, CA 95202
(209) 467-4774

Minority Business Development Agency, U.S. Department of Commerce

Northern California Office (Includes Regional Office)
221 Main Street, Room 1280
San Francisco, CA 94105
(415) 744-3001

Southern California Office
9660 Flair Drive, Suite 455
El Monte, CA 91731
(818) 453-8636

Transportation, California Department of (CalTrans) Office of Civil Rights/Disadvantaged/Women-Owned Certification

1120 N Street, Room 2545
Sacramento, CA 95814
(916) 654-4576

You could also check your local library for the following directories:

National Directory of Minority and Women Owned Business Firms, published by Business Research Services, Inc., 2021 Midwest Road, Suite 300, Oakbroak, Illinois 60521, (312) 953-8616.

Regional Directory of Minority and Women Owned Business Firms, published by Gale Research, Book Tower, Department 77748, Detroit, Michigan 48277, (800) 223-GALE.

Get a Library Card

Although you can get four or five books on "How to Write a Business Plan" in any large bookstore, you can also find out how to write your business plan by doing a little research in your nearby library. A business plan can be whatever you want it to be, from a two-page set of ideas to a full 30-page document with marketing plans and financial projections. In any case, you should have some kind of written plan, and the library is a good place to start looking. Of course, the helpful folks listed above may advise you on your plan too. A word of caution: don't hire a consultant to write your plan so you can get a nice big loan. First, you probably won't get the loan anyhow. Second, *you* should write your own plan. That way, *you* know what you need to do. It's usually great to ask for help. It's even okay to pay for help. But writing the business plan for *your* business? You need to be deeply involved, *yourself.*

One useful publication you might find at the library is William Alarid's and Gustav Berle's *Free Help From Uncle Sam to Start Your Own Business* (Puma Publishing Co., 1992). This book provides many sources for small businesses similar to the alternatives we provide.

Contact the Government

Many small business owners see the government as a sort of natural enemy (sometimes with good reason). On the other hand, the government may have just the information you need. The following list is merely suggestive. Much more is available for those who dig around. *Bottom line:* If someone else has already solved the problem you face now, no sense reinventing the wheel!

First, check into the *Small Business Resource Directory* published by the California State Department of Commerce, Office of Small Business. Write to them at 1121 L Street, Suite 600, Sacramento, California 95814. Or, call (916) 445-6545 or (916) 324-5068. Ask where you can look at a current copy. This guide has about 50 pages of names and phone numbers, so it can't be sent to everybody in the state, but the office will at the minimum tell you where you can look at the latest edition.

You can also ask for a copy of *A to Z,* a pamphlet designed to give you a quick overview of the governmental resources available to California small businesses. Contact the same office and ask for your own copy.

Last but not least, consider all the inexpensive publications available from the U.S. Small Business Administration. The following list may not include all the available publications and videotapes by the time you want to get information for your business. But at minimum, look over this list. There is sure to be at least ONE item that applied directly to you and your plans.

Videotapes ($30.00 Each)

"Marketing: Winning Customers With a Workable Plan" (VT1)

This program, developed by two of the country's leading small business marketing experts, offers a step-by-step approach on how to write the best possible marketing plan for your business. You'll also learn the best methods for determining customer needs, how to identify and develop a working profile for potential customers and much more.

"The Business Plan: Your Roadmap To Success" (VT2)

This videotape teaches you the essentials of developing a business plan that will help lead you to capital, growth, and profitability. It tells you what to include, what to omit, and how to get free help from qualified consultants.

"Promotion: Solving the Puzzle" (VT3)

Advertising, public relations, direct mail, and trade shows are the parts of the promotion puzzle. Each piece is important to the whole and each piece works to reinforce the others. This videotape and workbook package shows you how to put the pieces together to present a sound promotional plan aimed at targeting new customers, increasing sales and getting the most for your promotional dollar.

Publications ($.50–$2.00)

PRODUCTS/IDEAS/INVENTIONS

Ideas Into Dollars (P12)
Avoiding Patent, Trademark and Copyright Problems (PI2)
Trademarks and Business Goodwill (PI3)

FINANCIAL MANAGEMENT

ABC's of Borrowing (FM1)
Profit Costing and Pricing for Manufacturers (FM2)
Basic Budgets For Profit Planning (FM3)
Understanding Cash Flow (FM4)
A Venture Capital Primer for Small Business (FM5)
Accounting Services for Small Service Firms (FM6)
Analyze Your Records to Reduce Costs (FM7)
Budgeting In a Small Service Firm (FM8)
Sound Cash Management and Borrowing (FM9)
Record Keeping in a Small Business (FM10)
Simple Break-Even Analysis for Small Stores (FM11)
A Pricing Checklist for Small Retailers (FM12)
Pricing Your Products and Services Profitably (FM13)

MANAGEMENT AND PLANNING

Effective Business Communications (MP1)
Locating or Relocating Your Business (MP2)
Problems In Managing a Family-Owned Business (MP3)
Business Plan for Small Manufacturers (MP4)
Business Plan for Small Construction Firms (MP5)
Planning and Goal Setting for Small Business (MP6)
Should You Lease or Buy Equipment (MP7)
Business Plan for Retailers (MP9)
Choosing a Retail Location (MP10)
Business Plan for Small Service Firms (MP11)
Checklist for Going Into Business (MP12)
How to Get Started with a Small Business Computer (MP13)
The Business Plan for Home-Based Business (MP15)
How to Buy or Sell a Business (MP16)
Purchasing for Owners of Small Plants (MP17)
Buying for Retail Stores (MP18)
Small Business Decision Making (MP19)
Business Continuation Planning (MP20)
Developing a Strategic Business Plan (MP21)
Inventory Management (MP22)
Techniques for Problem Solving (MP23)
Techniques for Productivity Improvement (MP24)
Selecting the Legal Structure for Your Business (MP25)
Evaluating Franchise Opportunities (MP26)
Small Business Risk Management Guide (MP28)
Quality Child Care Makes Good Business Sense (MP29)

MARKETING

Creative Selling: The Competitive Edge (MT1)
Marketing for Small Business: An Overview (MT2)
Is the Independent Sales Agent for You? (MT3)

Marketing Checklist for Small Retailers (MT4)
Researching Your Market (MT8)
Selling by Mail Order (MT9)
Market Overseas with U.S. Government Help (MT10)
Advertising (MT11)

CRIME PREVENTION

Curtailing Crime—Inside and Out (CP2)
A Small Business Guide to Computer Security (CP3)

PERSONNEL MANAGEMENT

Checklist for Developing a Training Program (PM1)
Employees: How to Find and Pay Them (PM2)
Managing Employee Benefits (PM3)

The final word: the future belongs to those who work hard and work smart. Since you worked your way this far through this book, you are sure to be among those who work smart. Now, it's up to you to work hard. Go for it!

Index